UNDERSTANDING PHILOSOPHY

for A2 Level

AQA

UNDERSTANDING PHILOSOPHY
for A2 Level
AQA

Roy Jackson, Sue Johnson, Keith Maslin, Mel Thompson and Rupert Woodfin

™ Nelson Thornes
a Wolters Kluwer business

Text © Roy Jackson, Sue Johnson, Keith Maslin, Mel Thompson
and Rupert Woodfin 2005
Original illustrations © Nelson Thornes Ltd 2005

Published in 2005 by:
Nelson Thornes Ltd
Delta Place
27 Bath Road
CHELTENHAM
GL53 7TH
United Kingdom

06 07 08 09 / 10 9 8 7 6 5 4 3 2

A catalogue record for this book is available from the British Library

ISBN 0 7487 9253 8

Page make-up by Acorn Bookwork

Printed and bound in Slovenia by DELO tiskarna
by arrangement with Korotan-Ljubljana

contents

illustrations   vii

acknowledgements   ix

about the authors   x

preface   xi

PART 1 : topics   **1**

philosophy of mind   1

I – Dualism   3
II – The Mind/Brain Identity Theory   16
III – Analytical Behaviourism   28
IV – Functionalism   39
V – Property-dualism   48
VI – The Problem of Other Minds   59
VII – Personal Identity   69

political philosophy   85

I – Political Ideologies   86
II – Freedom   108
III – Law   113
IV – Authority   124
V – The State   128

philosophy of science   131

I – Foundations of Science   132
II – The Progress of Science   158
III – The Social Sciences   187

PART 2 : texts   201

Aristotle: *Nicomachean Ethics*   202
David Hume: *An Enquiry Concerning Human Understanding*   236
John Stuart Mill: *On Liberty*   290
Nietzsche: *Beyond Good and Evil*   316
Russell: *The Problems of Philosophy*   346
A. J. Ayer: *Language, Truth and Logic*   391

bibliography   425
index   430

illustrations

Sir Winston Churchill (1874–1965)   4
The functional specification of pain   40
The internal state of the machine   43
Mental event/physical event   56
The Scales of Justice   87
Plato (c.428 BC–348 BC)   87
Jeremy Bentham (1748–1832)   100
Martin Luther King Jr. (1929–68)   117
Mahatma Gandhi (1869–1948)   118
Aristotle (384 BC–322 BC)   135
A rational understanding of the world   137
Roger Bacon (1214–94)   141
Francis Bacon (1561–1626)   143
A scatter graph   154
Karl Popper (1902–94)   159
Thomas Kuhn (1922–96)   165
Is the world understandable?   179
Aristotle (384 BC–322 BC)   202
David Hume (1711–76)   237
The contents of the mind   245
The copy principle   247
John Stuart Mill (1806–73)   292
The preserved body of Jeremy Bentham, founder of utilitarianism   292
Friedrich Nietzsche (1844–1900)   317
Bertrand Russell (1872–1970)   348
Different types of statement   376
Knowledge of things/knowledge of truths   383
A.J. Ayer (1910–89)   392

acknowledgements

Photo credits:
Classic Image/Alamy pp. 100, 207; Corbis V94 (NT) p. 87; Corel 642 (NT) p. 135; Geogphotos/Alamy p. 292; The Graphic/Mary Evans Picture Library p. 292; Illustrated London News V1 (NT) p. 4; Illustrated London News V2 (NT) p. 118; Keystone/Hulton/Getty p. 159; Bill Pierce/Time Life/Getty p. 165; Popperfoto/Alamy pp. 87, 117, 141, 143, 202, 317, 348, 392.

about the authors

Dr. Roy Jackson is a full-time lecturer in Philosophy at Esher College, Surrey, having previously lectured at the Universities of Durham, Kent, and King's College London. He has many years experience as an examiner and is the author of *Nietzsche: A Beginner's Guide* and *Plato: A Beginner's Guide* for Hodder and *The God of Philosophy* for TPM. Roy has also made many contributions to journals and magazines including *Think*, *Dialogue* and *The Philosophers Magazine*.

Sue Johnson was one of the first teachers to offer Philosophy in school when it became available as a post-16 qualification. She has been Reviser for the A level for most of the life of the examination. She has contributed to *Philosophy Now* and is resident crossword compiler for *The Philosophers' Magazine*. Having taught for 22 years, she now works as an adviser, consultant and freelance writer in the fields of philosophy, educational employment law, religious studies and related issues.

Dr Keith Maslin is a graduate of the universities of Keele, Oxford, and London. He has worked in universities and further education, both in the UK and abroad, and is currently Head of Philosophy at Esher College in Surrey. Previous publications include *An Introduction to the Philosophy of Mind* (Polity Press, 2001). His main philosophical interests are Philosophy of Mind, Hume, and Wittgenstein.

Mel Thompson, formerly a teacher and A level examiner, now works as a freelance writer, specialising in Philosophy and Ethics. His many titles include philosophy titles in the *Teach Yourself* series, A level textbooks for Religious Studies, a large-format, illustrated handbook of philosophy entitled *World Philosophy* and, most recently, a study of *Philosophers Behaving Badly*. His website (www.mel-thompson.co.uk) provides information on all his books and forthcoming lectures, as well as a range of additional notes on topics suitable for A level students.

Rupert Woodfin (1949–2004) graduated with a BA Hon in Sociology and and MSc in Sociology from Salford. His teaching career began with three years in London comprehensives in the early 1970s. However, from 1976 he taught Sociology in FE colleges working at Boston FE college until 1981 and subsequently at Exeter College in Devon. He and a colleague introduced A level Philosophy to the college in 1990 and it became a very popular subject with several groups a year studying the subject. Rupert was also chair of examiners for AQA for about ten years and helped draft the new specifications for AS/A2. Other publications include *Introducing Aristotle* and *Introducing Marxism*. Although not technically qualified as a Philosopher, as his career showed, he had a deep love for the subject.

preface

This book provides thorough and detailed coverage of the entire AQA A2 Philosophy specification. Although it is aimed primarily at A level students, it will also be of value to undergraduates, particularly in the early years of a degree, as well as others taking an interest in Philosophy for the first time. The book is concerned not merely to provide information about individual thinkers and philosophical themes, but to enable readers to develop their own capacity for philosophical reflection upon, and engagement with, the various topics treated in the text.

The book is divided into two halves, the first dealing with themes, and the second with the contributions of particular philosophers in the specified texts. Theories are clearly and sympathetically explained, together with the reasons given in support of them, and there is an ensuing critical discussion and evaluation of both the theories and the supporting reasons. In this way students are enabled to become familiar with the content and style of philosophical debate and reflection, thereby helping them to enter, and ultimately to contribute to, the debates for themselves. To this end review activities are provided throughout the text to enable and check understanding. Students should try to do these activities for themselves, either individually or in small groups, but teachers can also set them for both class and homework assignments.

The importance of trying to explain philosophical ideas in writing cannot be stressed enough: it is usually only through attempting to articulate ideas precisely in writing that a sound understanding can be achieved and misunderstandings of issues can be uncovered. In the course of doing the necessary reading for the review activities, readers should not be surprised if they have to read passages more than once. This is entirely natural in Philosophy owing to the complexities of the concepts and the arguments it contains, but with persistence most difficulties will yield. It goes without saying that, in the case of the texts, the book should be read alongside them.

To aid understanding, each chapter begins with a glossary of important terms to be found in that chapter, and in addition brief paragraph summaries are provided to the left of the text throughout the work. Extended writing practice is supplied at the end of each section, by questions, either modelled upon, or directly drawn from, past examination questions. Recommended reading can be found at the end of chapters and there is an extensive bibliography at the end of the book.

K.T. Maslin

PART 1
topics

philosophy of mind

I	Dualism	3
II	The Mind/Brain Identity Theory	16
III	Analytical Behaviourism	28
IV	Functionalism	39
V	Property-dualism	48
VI	The Problem of Other Minds	59
VII	Personal Identity	69

Introduction

There is a cluster of problems that help to define the philosophy of mind and to set its agenda. First and foremost among these questions is the issue of the nature of the mind; what, to put the question another way, is its mode of being or existence? Should the mind be conceived of as a non-physical entity, a soul, or, flying to the opposite extreme, is the mind simply one and the same thing as the living material brain? Or are both these answers equally and oppositely wrong? Should the mind be thought of as consisting in actual and potential outward behaviour, as analytical behaviourism maintains, or is it better conceived of as like a computer program run on the hardware of the brain?

Secondly, a related question concerns the relation of the mental to the physical. Could mental events and states turn out to be merely a subset of physical events and states, or are they non-reducible in this way? And if they are not so reducible, how do the mental and the physical mutually affect each other if they are so different in nature from each other, as they appear to be – the mental apparently possessing a radical privacy lacked by purely physical events?

Thirdly, there are questions concerning the epistemology of the mental. Can we know of the existence of minds other than our own, and if so, how, given that all we witness of other people is their outward behaviour? How can we be sure that what we take to be other people are not in fact zombies, their outward behaviour concealing a bleak mental emptiness?

Lastly, what is the nature of the subject of experiences, as opposed to the experiences themselves? Should the subject of experiences be thought of as existing over and above the experiences themselves or rather as somehow constructed out of the experiences, as Hume's bundle theory of the self maintained? What does the identity of a person over time consist in? Is it the physical continuity of the body, or the brain? Or are both these answers mistaken, personal identity being better understood as psychological continuity of character traits, and especially memory?

It is to these sorts of issue, and the others that grow out of them, to which we shall be turning in the chapters that follow.

1

Dualism

important terms

Dualism: dualism takes two forms: substance-dualism and property-dualism. According to substance-dualism the mind is a non-physical entity capable of existing in its own right independently of the body. Property-dualism allows only physical substances but claims these possess two different kinds of property: non-physical mental properties such as consciousness, and physical properties.

Leibniz's Law: due to Gottfried Leibniz (1646-1716) this is also known as the Identity of Indiscernibles. It states that if an object A is one and same as an object B, then all the properties of A will be the same as those of B, and vice versa. It is a useful tool for evaluating identity claims such as the claim that mental states are one and the same as brain states, because if just one property can be found that belongs to one half of the alleged identity but is absent in the other half, then the identity claim is false.

Substance: a substance is a thing that can exist in its own right, in logical independence of anything else, unlike properties, which have to exist as the properties of some thing or other.

Key topics in this chapter

- Substance- and property-dualism
- Mind/body interaction
- The concept of the soul

Introduction

The ancient Greek philosopher, Plato (c.427 BC–347 BC), espoused dualism, but its most famous exponent in modern philosophy was René Descartes (1596–1650) and it is his version of the theory – Cartesian dualism, as it is now known – that we shall concentrate upon here.

Dualism maintains that human beings are composed of two quite disparate components: the non-physical mind or soul, and the physical body, linked together during life, but separating at death. The person, the subject of experience and states of mind generally, is identical to the soul, not the body. The soul is a substance, hence Cartesian dualism exemplifies what is known as *substance-dualism*. It is vitally important to be clear how the term 'substance' is being used in this context. Most emphatically it does not correspond to the everyday usage in which a substance is a kind of stuff, as illustrated by the remark: 'What kind of stuff is your ballpoint pen made of?' (Answer: plastic.) Rather, in accordance with a long tradition in philosophy, a substance is a thing, an entity, that can exist in its own right, without dependence on anything else. If this sense of substance is not distinguished from the use of the term to denote some kind of stuff, it would be easy to embrace the view that minds or souls are made of something, perhaps the attenuated matter, the ghostly ectoplasm, of spiritualists. Not even some modern-day thinkers appear to have been as clear about how the notion of a substance is to be understood as they might have been. Hence we find Paul Churchland writing: 'The distinguishing claim of this view [substance-dualism] is that each mind is a distinct non-physical thing, an individual "package" of non-physical substance ... an individual unit of mind-stuff quite distinct from your material body' (Churchland 1988: 8). But, as we have been at pains to emphasise, minds or souls are not made of anything; the point of calling them substances is to signal that they are being thought of as things that can exist independently of anything else.

Logical substances contrasted with properties

Substances may be contrasted with features or properties which must be the features or properties of things. For example, a car or a rose can be red, but it is not possible to have redness floating about loose and separate on its own. In a similar way, the conditions or states of things cannot exist independently of the things whose states of conditions they are. A person may have a

3

heavy build, but it would make no sense to suppose that their build could exist separately from them. Similarly, in *Alice in Wonderland*, the Cheshire Cat might or might not wear a grin on its face, but the idea that the cat might disappear and leave the grin behind was a deliberate philosophical joke on Carroll's part.

In addition, a substance is a *continuant* that persists throughout the changes to the features or properties it possesses. Unlike an event, it does not have temporal stages that can be traced from the beginning of the event until it is over and done with. So, for example, you and I are continuants: we have changed a lot since we were born, but we have persisted throughout the very considerable alterations in ourselves. On the other hand, the event of our birth has not persisted. In each of our cases, it started presumably with contractions on our mother's part, continued with her going into labour, and eventuated in our gradual emergence into this world. As well as being a continuant, not only is a substance a particular that may have properties predicated of it, but in addition, as Aristotle stressed, it cannot be predicated of anything else. It can be predicated of Winston Churchill that he was a cigar smoker, that he was a politician, and that he was a human being, but Winston Churchill himself cannot be attributed as a feature to something else, i.e. he cannot be predicated as a property of some other thing.

Winston Churchill (1874–1965)

review
activity

1. Explain briefly what is meant by describing the soul as a substance.

2. How do properties differ from substances?

Essential and non-essential properties

Descartes draws on the medieval tradition of distinguishing between essential and accidental properties. An essential property, an essence, is the property that makes the thing in question the kind of thing it is and which it cannot survive without. By contrast, an accidental property is one that is not integral to the identity of the thing in question and which it may lose whilst still continuing to exist. Thus, Winston Churchill might have conceivably become less heavy than he was, but he could not have ceased to be human and yet retain his identity.

For Descartes, there are fundamentally only two kinds of substance comprising the world: physical matter, which is incapable of thought, and whose essence is extension in space; and minds or souls, which lack extension, but whose essence is thinking or consciousness: 'By the noun *"thought"* I mean everything that takes place in us so that we are conscious of it, in so far as it is an object of consciousness' (Descartes 1986: 167). Descartes deliberately extended the French verb *penser* – 'to think' – to cover all mental states, not merely cognitive activities, so even being in pain, or feeling jealous, would count as thinking.

Consciousness or thinking as the essential feature of the soul

In making consciousness the essence of the soul, Descartes was committing himself to the view that there cannot be minds or souls that are not thinking. Do we then cease to exist during a dreamless sleep or a coma, and if we did, what would the relation of the person who went to sleep be to the person who woke up in the morning? Their numerical identity as a single mind is ruled out: the mind that is annihilated by sleep cannot be one and the same as the mind that the morning gives birth to, on the principle that a thing cannot have two beginnings. To avoid embarrassments of this kind, Descartes had to accept that even in the most profound slumber, we are, nevertheless, still conscious; and indeed, in a letter to an unknown correspondent (Geach and Anscombe 1970: 266), he insisted that the human soul is always conscious, even in the mother's womb.

Privacy of mental states and the problem of other minds

The soul, completely lacking extension, is in principle indivisible, and this has been used as a reason for maintaining its immortality. Ordinary physical things decay and cease to exist because they fall to bits, but the soul possesses no parts into which it could fall. Although dualism is not nowadays a popular theory among philosophers, it is embraced by many people, especially those who follow a religion, and a clear reason for its appeal is that it provides for survival in a non-physical form after death.

Souls, by their very nature as non-physical mental substances, are not detectable by the senses. This has the effect of making a person's mental states radically private in the sense that they are accessible only to the individual whose states of mind they are. This privileged access is not available to other people; they can have no acquaintance with mental states other than their own. Dualism thus poses a major epistemological difficulty: from our own individual perspective, can we ever really know that other minds exist or what they are like?

By contrast with the soul, the human body is not a substance, strictly speaking, but only a portion of the material world, which, taken as a whole, is a substance. Arrangements of matter, however complex, are incapable of thought and consciousness, thus the notion of a conscious robot would be dismissed out of hand by Descartes. Animals, or the brutes, as Descartes refers to them, lack souls. They are therefore effectively nothing more than intricate machines, devoid of mentality.

review
activity

Draw a table with two columns headed 'soul' and 'body' respectively, and complete it to contrast the properties of the soul with the properties of the body.

There is a weaker variant of dualism that will need examination in due course, namely *property-dualism*. Property-dualism rejects non-physical soul substances, maintaining instead that subjects of experience possess two different kinds of property, non-physical mental features, as well as physical properties. For reasons concerning the order of exposition, property-dualism will be discussed in a subsequent chapter.

Descartes' arguments for substance-dualism

We will consider three of Descartes' arguments for substance-dualism:

1. the argument from imaginability
2. the argument from doubt
3. the argument from clear and distinct perception.

1. The argument from imaginability

Argument from imaginability

This argument is very closely related to the argument from doubt, as we shall witness, but makes use of the notion of what can be imagined or pretended to be the case and therefore needs a separate treatment. In the *Discourse on Method and Meditations* it runs:

> *Then, attentively examining what I was, and seeing that I could pretend that I had no body and that there was no world or place that I was in, but that I could not, for all that, pretend that I did not exist, and that, on the contrary, from the very fact of doubting the truth of other things, it followed very evidently and very certainly that I existed; while, on the other hand, if I had only ceased to think, although all the rest of what I had imagined had been true, I would have had no reason to believe that I existed; I thereby concluded that I was a substance, of which the whole essence or nature consists in thinking, and which, in order to exist, needs no place and depends on no material thing; so that this 'I', that is to say, the mind, by which I am what I am, is entirely distinct from the body, and even that it is easier to know than the body, and, moreover, that even if the body were not, it would not cease to be all that it is.*
>
> (Descartes 1968: 54)

The strategy this argument depends upon is this: you are to try to think, or imagine away, those features that are not essential for your continuing existence. When these features have been identified and eliminated, whatever features are left will be those you cannot exist without and which are truly inseparable from you, thereby constituting what is essential for your existence. Now it does seem possible to imagine what it would be like to become disembodied, whilst continuing to have experiences. In fact, reports of out-of-body experiences often take this form. People have reported that whilst being operated upon, it seemed to them that they left their bodies and, from a spectator's point of view, could look down upon themselves on the operating table. Now, whilst we need not deny that people really do have such experiences and are not making them up, there is clearly a question mark over whether what the experiences represent as happening really does occur. We shall not endeavour to settle this issue here. The point of the example in the present context is that whether or not people really do leave their bodies, we do not, at least, seem to have any difficulty in understanding what is being claimed. This provides some ground for thinking that disembodied existence is both conceivable and possible.

However, by contrast, if you try to imagine or conceive that you are not thinking or conscious, then this thought must be false, because in order to have it you plainly must be thinking. So, whilst you can imagine away the existence of your body, you cannot imagine away your thinking. As this feature alone cannot be eliminated, you must be entirely non-bodily in nature, your essential and sole property consisting in thought or consciousness. However, as we shall see, this argument cannot establish its conclusion.

Over-reliance of Descartes' argument on first-person present tense usages

Firstly, it may be granted that, at the moment Descartes is thinking, he cannot intelligibly conceive, or imagine, he is not thinking. If he tries to think that he is not thinking, then obviously he must be thinking to have this thought. But this does not mean that he cannot conceive of himself as not thinking at some later time. There are all sorts of first-person present tense statements about oneself that must be false if they succeed in getting made, but this does not mean that there are no circumstances in which they could be true. I cannot assert now, truly, that I am asleep, or dead. But, quite clearly, being awake, or alive, are not features that are inseparable from me. It is perfectly conceivable that at some other time I might be asleep, or dead, even though I myself, at that time, would not be in a position to describe myself in these ways.

Imaginability is no guide to possibility

Secondly, imaginability is not necessarily any guide to possibility: what seems to be imaginable may not really be possible. For example, I appear to be able to imagine time travel. I get into the time machine in 2004, and emerge into the totally changed world of 1969. But could this really happen? A common objection is that if it could, I might go back in time and kill my grandfather. But then I would never have been born, and thus not in a position to go back in time in the first place! The appearance of this contradiction bodes ill for the genuine possibility of time travel. Similarly, although it seems possible for me to imagine having experiences in disembodied form, it might be that in order to be able to think and be conscious, certain complex physical processes have to go on inside me, and, therefore, that being embodied is integral to my continuing existence as a conscious agent. If that is so then disembodied existence would turn out to be not a genuine possibility after all. A contemporary of Descartes, Thomas Hobbes, saw the essential point when he wrote: 'It may be that the thing that is conscious is the subject of a mind, reason, or intellect, and so it may be something corporeal; the contrary is assumed, not proved' (Geach and Anscombe 1970: 28).

review activity

Explain and evaluate Descartes' argument from imaginability.

2. The argument from doubt

This argument employs the epistemic notion of doubt. To understand it we need to recall that, in the *Meditations*, Descartes employs what is known as methodological scepticism as a device for attaining knowledge. He vows to reject not only what is false, but also anything that can be called into doubt. Only that which is beyond the reach of doubt will qualify as knowledge. This will lead to an unduly restrictive account of what we know: whole swathes of things we would ordinarily say we know will have to be rejected if Descartes is right.

When applying his method, Descartes firstly turns his attention to knowledge claims based on sense-experience. The senses have often deceived us regarding distant and minute objects: towers that seem round when viewed from far away turn out to be square on a closer approach; blood that looks red to the naked eye presents an entirely different appearance under the microscope. But although he might be mistaken about these sorts of things, Descartes himself points out that surely he cannot be in error about sitting in his chair in his dressing gown and holding a piece of paper in his hands? However, he immediately reminds himself that he has often dreamt he was sitting by the fire when in fact he was asleep in bed, so how can he be sure that he is not dreaming now? Moreover, even though it is true that a square has four sides, and two plus three makes five, whether Descartes is awake or sleeping, God could have deceived him, if he had so wished, about even these simple things. In fact, is it not possible

> *that there is, not a true God, who is the sovereign source of truth, but some evil demon, no less cunning and deceiving than powerful, who has used all his artifice to deceive me. I will suppose that the heavens, the air, the earth, colours, shapes, sounds, and all external things that we see, are only illusions and deceptions which he uses to take me in. I will consider myself as having no hands, eyes, flesh, blood or senses, but as believing wrongly that I have all these things.*
>
> (Descartes 1968: 100)

However, there is one thing Descartes maintains that the demon cannot deceive him about, and that is, whilst he is thinking, he exists. Doubting counts as a kind of thinking, so if Descartes attempts to doubt that he is doubting, it must follow that he is thinking, and if he is thinking he must exist to be doing so. Descartes appears to have arrived at the one thing that cannot be doubted and hence can qualify as knowledge: '*Cogito ergo sum*' – 'I think therefore I am'. With this argument Descartes believes he has established that he is a thing whose sole essence is thinking or consciousness, a substance that has no extension or any other physical attributes.

The argument relies on what is known as known as Leibniz's Law, which may be stated thus: if A is numerically identical with B (one and the same as B), then every property that A possesses is possessed by B, and vice versa. It follows that if there is at least one property possessed by A but which is not possessed by B, and vice versa, then A cannot be one and the same as B. This principle is applied in the following argument which summarises Descartes' remarks above:

1. I can doubt that my body exists.
2. I cannot doubt that I exist.
3. Therefore, by Leibniz's Law, I am not identical with my body or any part of it.

However, by constructing a parallel case, we can begin to appreciate why this mode of argument cannot establish its conclusion. Consider the argument:

1. I can doubt that Charles Dodgson wrote *Alice in Wonderland*.
2. I cannot doubt that Lewis Carroll wrote *Alice in Wonderland*.
3. Therefore, Charles Dodgson is not one and the same as Lewis Carroll.

The conclusion, quite clearly, is false. What has gone wrong here? Suppose the reason I can doubt that Dodgson, but not Carroll, wrote the book in question, is that I do not know that Carroll was Dodgson's pseudonym. But the fact that I do not realise that the reference of Dodgson is to one and the same person as the reference of Carroll, does not mean that it cannot be. Similarly, from the fact that a person might be described in two completely different ways, only one of which is known to me, it does not follow that both descriptions cannot apply to him or her. To everyone, the hideous Mr Hyde looked entirely different from the familiar respectable Dr Jekyll, but they were one and the same person nevertheless. Cases like these, where psychological verbs such as 'know', 'believe', 'doubt', 'imagine' 'dream', 'wonder', and so forth are involved, constitute exceptions to Leibniz's Law. These verbs name what are known as *intentional* states, and are consequently known as intentional verbs. The objects or states of affairs that these verbs concern comprise a representational mental content that may have no reality corresponding to it in the physical world. So Gaby may be wondering about the fountain of youth, even if no such thing exists. She may also dream about the fountain of youth, but the mental stance, the attitude she takes towards it has then altered. She first wondered about the fountain of youth, now she is dreaming about it. The mental states denoted by the verbs above (and it is obviously possible to think of many more verbs of this type) represent the subjects they concern under *aspects*, or under different descriptions, and one and the same person or state of affairs can be presented under different aspects or descriptions which a person may not connect with each other. If I dreamt that Mr Hyde attacked me in the street, then, not knowing the identity of Hyde with Jekyll, it does not follow that I dreamt that Dr Jekyll attacked me. In fact, nothing could have been further from my mind than to be assaulted by the innocuous and gentlemanly physician. By contrast, where a non-psychological, non-intentional verb is involved, if I were actually attacked by Mr Hyde, then it follows that I was attacked by Dr Jekyll, even though I did not know the true identity of my assailant.

review
activity

1. How does Descartes try to use doubt to establish that he is a substance whose nature consists entirely in thinking or consciousness?

2. Why does the argument fail?

3. The argument from clear and distinct perception

The argument runs as follows:

[B]ecause I know that all the things I conceive clearly and distinctly can be produced by God precisely as I conceive them, it is sufficient for me to be able to be able to conceive clearly and distinctly one thing without another, to be certain that the one is distinct or different from the other, because they can be placed in existence separately, at least by the omnipotence of God … And … from the mere fact that I know with certainty that I exist, and that I do not

observe any other thing belongs necessarily to my nature or essence except that I am a thinking thing, I rightly conclude that my essence consists in this alone, that I am a thinking thing, or substance whose whole nature or essence consists in thinking.

(Descartes 1968: 156)

However, the fact that I do not observe that anything belongs to my nature except consciousness does not mean that nothing else does so belong. The following two statements are easily confused with each other:

1. I do not notice anything belongs to my nature or essence except consciousness.
2. I notice that nothing else does belong to my nature or essence except consciousness.

However, a moment's inspection reveals that (1) is not equivalent to (2), neither does (2) follow from (1), yet it is (2), not merely (1) that Descartes hopes to establish. There is also an ambiguity in the wording of the first part of this passage.

Descartes might be claiming either:

1. I can distinctly conceive of my mind and body *separately* from each other.
2. I can distinctly conceive of my mind and body as *being separate* from each other.

(1) can be taken to mean that I can think about my mind without thinking at the same time about my body, and vice versa. This is surely possible, just as I can think about the shape of something without thinking about its extension, or about its extension but not its shape. But the fact that these *thoughts* can occur independently of each other, does not mean that the same is true of what the thoughts are *about*. Although shape and extension can be considered independently of each other, the one cannot exist apart from the other. Anything that has a shape must possess extension, and what is extended must possess some shape or other. Thus, by parity of reasoning, thinking about my mental features separately from my physical ones, and vice versa, is no guarantee that the two really can exist independently of each other, contrary to what Descartes wishes to maintain.

review
activity

Explain and evaluate Descartes' argument from clear and distinct perception for substance-dualism.

Problems for dualism

The arguments for dualism that we have examined do not appear to establish it. Still, there may be other arguments that there is no room to consider here which might be more successful, and indeed, in the absence of any arguments for it, dualism could still be the correct account of the nature of the mind.

However, there are two major difficulties with the theory, which we shall now discuss.

1. The mind/body relation

Mind/body interaction

We commonly accept that the mind affects the body and the body affects the mind. For example, the words you are reading were produced because I typed the original manuscript, and I did this because I wanted to write a useful book for A-level students. In other words, part of the cause of the words you are reading was my desire to produce them: my desire, a mental state, had a physical effect in the world, via my actions. Equally, when I respond to a spoken question about what I have written, this can only be because the sounds comprising the words uttered have affected my eardrums and as a result nerve impulses have been transmitted along the auditory nerves to the brain. The mind or soul, according to dualism, is then affected by the physical events in the brain, causing it to hear the words spoken.

The seat of the soul: the pineal gland

Descartes conjectured that the place in the brain where it connects with the soul was the pineal gland, a pea-sized gland in the middle of the limbic system in the middle of the brain. He thought, for instance, that images from each of the eyes are conveyed up the optic nerves to the pineal gland. These images are then fused to form a single image, and it is this image that the mind or soul contemplates when we perceive. (The same is supposed to be true in the case of imagination, except that the image on the gland is generated internally without any input from the senses.) A major reason for locating the seat of the soul in the pineal gland, for Descartes, was that it is apparently very mobile. Moving very easily one way and the other, it is very sensitive to the light touch of the soul and is easily affected, thus making it a suitably receptive and sensitive instrument.

The problem of interaction

However, as Descartes himself realised, there is a very serious objection to this account, which no amount of neurophysiological inventiveness can get round. The problem is this: how can the incorporeal soul, lacking extension, affect, and in turn be affected by, the extended physical body? The objection was well stated by Princess Elisabeth of Bohemia, who wrote to Descartes in 1643:

> *I beg of you to tell me how the human body can determine the movement of the animal spirits* [a kind of rarefied blood, in vaporous form, believed, according to theories of the time, to be contained within the pineal gland and nerves in general] *in the body so as to perform voluntary acts – being as it is merely conscious ... substance. For the determination of a movement seems always to come about from the moving body's being propelled – to depend on the kind of impulse it gets from what sets it in motion, or again, on the nature and shape of this latter thing's surface. Now the first two contact, and the third involves that the impelling thing has extension; but you utterly exclude extension from your notion of the soul, and contact seems to me incompatible with a thing's being immaterial.*   (Geach and Anscombe 1970: 112)

Descartes acknowledged the difficulty, but several exchanges of letters later confessed, in effect, that he was not able to solve it.

However, in *Meditation V*, Descartes made another attempt to explain how mind and body interact with each other. Descartes noticed that when we feel pain, we do not perceive the pain from a distance in the way we perceive damage to the wing of our car. When our foot is hurt, for example, we spontaneously point to the place where we feel the pain, and perhaps rub the spot with our hand. By contrast, we do not feel anything in the place where the wing is bumped and dented. Moreover, when a painful stimulus is applied to our foot, nerve impulses are caused to go to the brain, but we do not feel the pain in our brain – we feel it in the foot. Again, this is unlike a warning mechanism in a car, where a sensor connected from the radiator to the dashboard causes a warning light to flash to show that the water level is low. By contrast, when we need a drink, or some food, we feel thirsty or suffer hunger pangs. We do not discover our need for food or drink in the detached manner of the driver observing a gauge in the instrument panel of his or her car.

In order to account for these observations, Descartes suggests that the mind is not merely linked to the body, via the pineal gland, but 'united to, and as it were, mixed up with, the body' (Geach and Anscombe 1970: 117). Mind and body are not just connected, but fused to form an amalgam, a 'substantial union' as Descartes calls it, which is essential to our human nature:

> *Human beings are made up of body and soul, not by the mere presence or proximity of one to another, but by a true substantial union … If a human being is considered in itself, as a whole, it is an essential union, because the union which joins a human body and a soul is not accidental to a human being but essential, since a human being without it is not a human being.*

(Cottingham 1993: 75)

Descartes' second attempt to explain mind/body interaction: soul and body are intermingled

By contrast, if an angel, an incorporeal spirit that had never been embodied, acquired a body, there would be no substantial union between the angel and the body but merely a causal connection, in which case the angel would not feel sensations of pain, but merely perceive the physical disturbance intellectually. In claiming that body and soul are intermingled, Descartes would appear to have given up dualism, at least regarding sensations, which should now be regarded as forming a hybrid class, midway between the pure non-physical acts of intellection of the soul, and physical bodily happenings. Sensations are not purely physical, nor purely non-physical and mental, but genuine psycho-physical unities. It is significant that, in this regard, Tim Crane has suggested (see Crane 2003: 248) that Descartes' position is very close to that of the contemporary philosopher Sir Peter Strawson, who put forward the view that the concept of a person should be regarded as logically primitive. By this he means that a person is a single entity to which both physical and mental properties attach. We should not think of a person as an embodied soul, or as an ensouled body, because that amounts to a refusal to acknowledge the mental/physical unity that a person exemplifies.

Problems for the intermingling theory

There is, however, a serious difficulty with Descartes' proposal that the mind is mixed up with the body, namely how can a soul, lacking all dimensions, be intermingled with an extended body? Gin can be intermingled with vermouth in a dry Martini, because the molecules of gin, which are extended, can mingle with the extended vermouth molecules. But where one side of the supposed intermingling relation lacks all extension, the very possibility of mixing or intermingling is excluded. Descartes' explanation of the substantial union of mind and body has to be reckoned a failure, although it remains suggestive and thought-provoking.

review
activity

1. Outline Descartes' two attempts to account for mind/body interaction.

2. What reasons are there for thinking these cannot succeed?

2. The problem of counting souls

David Hume (1711–76) maintains that we can have no genuine concept of a soul, and that the term is, in effect, meaningless. This conclusion is the result of his empiricist account of how concepts are acquired. According to Hume, we receive vivid and strong impressions from the senses. These impressions give rise to fainter copies of them, and these images comprise concepts, or, as Hume calls them, 'ideas'. If we are not clear about a given idea, Hume recommends that we trace it back to its origins in sense-experience: 'Produce the impressions or original sentiments from which the ideas are copied. These impressions are all strong and sensible. They admit not of ambiguity. They are not only placed in a full light themselves, but may throw light on their correspondent ideas, which lie in obscurity' (Hume 1975: 62).

All meaningful concepts must be applicable to a possible experience

However, we will never, in principle, be able to find an impression of the soul because it is incorporeal and lacks extension. We cannot, therefore, have any idea or concept of the soul, and the term has to be dismissed as lacking a meaning. Hume offers a genetic thesis regarding the conditions for concepts to be possible; for a concept to be genuine we have to be able trace it back to its origins in sense-experience. Kant (1724–1804), if anything, saw even more clearly the essential point that Hume was trying to make, namely that for a concept to be meaningful it must be *applicable* to a possible experience: the *origins* of the concept, strictly speaking, are neither here nor there. The point has been well made by P.F. Strawson (1919–) in his critique of Kant, *The Bounds of Sense*:

> [T]here can be no legitimate, or even meaningful, employment of ideas or concepts which does not relate them to their empirical or experiential conditions of their application. If we wish to use a concept in a certain way, but are unable to specify the kind of experience-situation to which the concept, used in that way, would apply, then we are not really envisaging any legitimate use of that concept at all. In so using it, we shall not merely be saying what we do not know; we shall not really know what we are saying. (Strawson 1966: 16).

The problem of individuating and re-identifying souls

Let us now assess Cartesian dualism in the light of this principle. Descartes maintains that one, and only one, soul is connected with a particular living human organism throughout life. But suppose it is conjectured that many such souls, a thousand say, all thinking the same thought, speak through a person's mouth at a given time. Or suppose that, over a given period of time, a whole succession of soul-substances are associated with one living body, each soul transmitting its thoughts and feelings to the soul that succeeds it, just as momentum is transferred from one ball to another in a series of elastic balls by striking the first member of the series. The point Kant is making is that if we are to speak intelligibly of the soul, we must be able to give some account of what counts as one soul, as opposed to many. We need a criterion of individuation by means of which one soul can be told apart from another, at a given instant, as well as a way of differentiating between the situation in which we encounter one and same soul again, and the situation in which we encounter a resembling, but numerically different, soul.

Let us apply this requirement to persons thought of as living flesh and blood. Take, for example, the identical twins, Felipe and Pedro, whom I once taught. Even after two years it was extremely difficult to tell them apart. Nevertheless, one fundamental difference between them persisted, namely that they could not occupy the same space at the same time, nor could the routes they traced through space and time exactly coincide. Thus, however much alike Pedro and Felipe were in all other respects, their spatial locations at any given time, or at successive times, were unique to each of them. Thus, a firm anchor of identity and individuation was always in principle available, and the same is true of physical things generally.

But this criterion of identity cannot apply to souls because they are not space-occupying things. We thus have no way, in principle, of distinguishing between a situation in which one soul speaks through a person's mouth, and many such souls do so. It then becomes questionable whether ultimately we have any clear concept of the soul at all. If we cannot specify what counts as one, we cannot specify what counts as many, as many souls are merely one multiplied several times. It might be argued in reply that at least in my own case, from a first-person viewpoint, I know there is only a single non-physical subject of experience associated with my body. But Kant anticipates this objection, writing: 'The identity of the consciousness of myself at different times is ... only a formal condition of my thoughts and their coherence, and in no way proves the numerical identity of myself as a subject' (Kant 1963: 342).

Incoherence of the concept of the soul: impossibility of individuating and identifying non-physical substances

It is indeed true that, for any thought to be counted as mine, it must be one and the same self or 'I' that is conscious of that thought, but that alone does not establish that I am an unextended incorporeal substance. To prove that conclusion, I would have to say what features of my experience entitle me to conclude that I am a single non-physical thing, but there is nothing merely in having a succession of thoughts and experiences that supports that conception of myself. It is true that when I ascribe a thought to myself I do not use any criterion of identity as I do when I ascribe a thought to someone else, an attribution I could plainly be mistaken in, ascribing the thought to the wrong person. In my own case, the question 'I am having this experience but is it mine?' makes no sense. But although I do not employ a criterion of identity when I ascribe experiences to myself, such criteria are available to third persons, because I am an embodied being that can be individuated and re-identified; and thus the notion of a single subject of experience never ultimately lacks a foundation. This is what lies behind Kant's remark that:

> I may further assume that the substance which in relation to our outer senses possesses extension is in itself the possessor of thoughts, and that these thoughts can by means of its own inner sense be consciously represented. In this way, what in one relation is entitled incorporeal would in another relation be at the same time a thinking being, whose thoughts we cannot intuit, though we can indeed intuit their signs in the field of appearance. Accordingly, the thesis that

souls (as particular kinds of substances) think, would have to be given up; and we should have to fall back upon the common expression that men think, that is, the very same being which, as outer appearance, is extended, is (in itself) internally a subject, and is not composite, but is simple and thinks.

(Kant 1963: 340)

review
activity

For what reasons do Hume and Kant dismiss the notion of the incorporeal Cartesian soul as meaningless?

The Mind/Brain Identity Theory

important terms

Intentionality: Intentionality is the feature of those mental states that possess a representational content, picturing the world as being a certain way, whether or not it actually turns out to be as it is pictured. For example, beliefs qualify as Intentional states, as do desires, hopes and fears.

Intrinsic and derived Intentionality: the Intentionality of the mental states of persons is said to be intrinsic and not derived from other Intentional systems. Computer programs, by contrast, are not intrinsically about other states of affairs. Their semantic content ultimately derives from us, because we are there to interpret them. Hence their Intentionality is derived.

Monism: monism is the view that only one type of thing exists. Materialistic monism maintains that everything is physical in nature. Immaterialistic monism maintains that everything is non-physical or spiritual in nature.

Naturalism: the view that everything that exists is part of the natural world and explicable purely in terms drawn from the natural sciences.

Ontological reduction: an ontological reduction contrasts with an analytical reduction. An analytical reduction maintains that talk about one sort of thing can be rendered into different terms without loss of meaning. For example, talk about the mind can be rendered into talk about behaviour. An ontological reduction maintains that one phenomenon is one and the same as another phenomenon but that talk about the two apparently different

Key topics in this chapter

- Reductionism
- Mental states
- Intentionality

Introduction

The mind/brain identity theory stands in stark contrast to dualism. Firstly, it denies a dualism of material and immaterial substances; the only substances that exist are physical extended things. The theory thus exemplifies monism, materialistic monism to be precise, because it is also possible to be an immaterialistic monist like Berkeley (1685–1753), who held that the only substances are non-physical spirits or souls. Materialist theories of mind had been espoused widely before the twentieth century by writers like Henri LeRoy, Thomas Hobbes, Baron d'Holbach, and de la Mettrie (who wrote *L'Homme Machine* and *L'Homme plante* [Man a Machine and Man a Plant]), but the identity theory was given its most explicit and technical characterisation in the twentieth century by writers such as the Australians U.T. Place, J.J.C. Smart, and David Armstrong.

The identity theory and reductionism

A basic statement of the theory is soon provided: mental states are identical with brain states. The theory is *reductionist*: mental states are nothing over and above brain states. In this way the mental is reduced to the physical; mental phenomena do not enjoy an existence and a nature separate from, and independently of, physical phenomena. Ultimately they turn out to be a class of those phenomena. This is what philosophers refer to as an *ontological* reduction: the existence of mental phenomena, contrary to what dualism affirms, turns out to be just the existence of physical phenomena, states of the brain in this case.

It is important to distinguish this position from an *analytical* reduction. A good example of an analytical reduction is the claim that all talk about trilaterals can be rendered without loss of meaning into talk about three-sided figures. Plainly, the two kinds of statements are identical in meaning, that is why to say a trilateral is a three-sided figure is to state an analytic truth. A more ambitious phenomena is not equivalent in meaning. For example, heat does not mean kinetic energy of molecules, but heat is in fact kinetic energy of molecules. The reduction of heat to kinetic energy of molecules is thought of as giving the true nature of heat.

Qualia: qualia comprise the phenomenological contents of experience and are supposed to be private and subjective to the individual person, existing over and above public, physical events in the brain.

Analytical contrasted with ontological reduction

The type-type identity theory

example of an analytical reduction is provided by phenomenalism, which claims that all statements about physical objects can be rendered, without loss of meaning, into actual and possible sense-experiences. It seems highly doubtful that this reductive programme can be successfully carried out, however. Analytical behaviourism, which forms the topic of the next chapter, claims in a similar vein that all talk about mental states can be rendered without loss of meaning into talk about actual and possible behaviour.

The identity theorists, by contrast, never wanted to claim that the meaning of talk about mental states was equivalent in meaning to talk about brain states. Thus, if I were to assert that I was thinking certain thoughts but that nothing was going on in my brain at the same time, or even that I did not have a brain, but a head full of sawdust, I might be mistaken, but I would not have contradicted myself, because talk about brain events is quite different in meaning to talk about thoughts. An example that was used by the identity theorists to make what they were claiming clear is provided by this statement: *the morning star* is identical to *the evening star*.

Clearly this is not asserting that the phrase 'the morning star' is equivalent in meaning to the phrase 'the evening star' because the one plainly means the star that appears in the morning and the other means the star that appears in the evening, and 'morning' and 'evening' are not synonymous terms. Nevertheless, in talking about the morning star we are talking about the evening star, even if we did not realise this, because the reference of the two objects is in fact to one and the same celestial body, namely the planet Venus, which makes its appearances at two different times of the day. This example is essentially no different from the Dr Jekyll and Mr Hyde example provided in Chapter I. The descriptions of Jekyll and Hyde are quite different from each other, but this does not prevent Hyde from being one and the same man as Jekyll. The fact that it is opaque to me that the reference of the name 'Hyde' is to one and the same man as the reference of the name 'Jekyll', cannot rule out the numerical identity of what prima facie appear to be two different men In a similar fashion, it was claimed that just because I fail to realise that the reference of expressions describing my thoughts is the same as the reference of expressions describing my brain processes, this cannot mean that we are not in fact talking about one and the same set of events.

The type-type identity theory

In support of their claim that mental states are in fact identical with brain-states, identity theorists paraded a number of successful reductions drawn from the sciences. Centre stage was the kinetic theory of heat. At one time heat was conjectured to be some mysterious kind of calorific fluid that flowed from hot bodies into colder bodies, thereby raising their temperatures. Now we know that the temperature of a body consists in the vibration of its molecules and that the temperature of a gas is the average kinetic energy of its molecules. Similarly, lightning is a pattern of electrical discharges, not thunderbolts hurled by the gods, water is H_2O, and genes are encoded sequences on DNA molecules. None of these identity statements is analytically true, and each of them can be denied without logical contradiction. They cannot be known *a priori* and demonstrated in the manner of the true statements of mathematics and geometry. It took empirical research to uncover these identities, hence they are known *a posteriori*. Unlike the identity of the morning star with the evening star, which concerned only a single individual, the scientific identities above all concern classes or types of phenomena. The identity theorists suggested that the same would turn out to be true with respect to the different types of mental states, and that pains, for example, would be discovered to be identical with certain types of neural processes, say C-fibres firing. We thus arrive at what is known as the *type-type* identity theory, which claims that a given type of mental state will be found to be identical with a given type of brain-state. The theory claims that, like the identity of water with H_2O, or lightning with electric charges, the identity of pains with C-fibres firing is universal and invariant. Wherever there is water, there is H_2O, and wherever there is H_2O, there is water. Similarly, whenever C-fibres fire there is pain, and whenever there is pain, C-fibres will be found to be firing. The precise details of the identities of pains with neural events can be discovered only by patient empirical research. The advent of modern scanning technology, positron emission tomography and functional magnetic resonance imaging, whereby activities in the living brain could be portrayed on a screen, gave hope that different types of mental events would be found to be invariantly correlated with different types of brain-event, and that the best and most obvious explanation of these correlations was the identity of the mental and physical events in question. Even before scanners were invented, it was known that there was a close correspondence between a person's mental life and what went on in his or her brain. More than 100

Broca's area

years ago a doctor, Broca, discovered, when carrying out an autopsy on a patient who had suffered from speech recognition difficulties, that damage had occurred to a specific area in the left hemisphere of the patient's brain – Broca's area, as it is now known in his honour. More extensive research using imaging has shown the exercise of different mental capacities is correlated with activities in different parts of the brain, enabling mental functions to be mapped onto it.

review
activity

1. What does the type-type mind/brain identity theory claim? How does this differ from an analytical reduction?

2. What are the advantages of the type-type mind/brain identity theory as a theory of the mind?

The token-token identity theory

Token-token identity

There is a weaker version of the type-type theory: the *token-token* theory. A token is a particular instance of a type, so for example, a puddle of water would be a token of the type water. The type-type theory entails that every token of one type will be identical with a token of the second type: for example, every token of the type water will be identical with a token of the type H_2O, and vice versa. However, there can be cases where a token of one type could be identical with tokens of different types. For example, consider the type *timepiece*, various tokens of which can be found on people's wrists and on innumerable mantelpieces. Now every token of the type *timepiece* will be identical with some arrangement of physical parts designed to tell the time, but clearly these types of arrangement can be indefinitely various in their construction. In other words, although there is no single type of arrangement, a token of the type *timepiece* will be identical to one of the tokens of the various types of arrangement available. So my watch could be digital and housed in stainless steel, whereas your watch could be analogue and protected by a plastic case: two tokens of the type watch, but two different tokens of the types *digital and stainless*, and *analogue and plastic*.

Which version of the identity theory, the type-type or the token-token, is the most plausible? We certainly accept that the type-type theory applies in the case of the scientific identities: water is always H_2O, and lightning is always constituted by electric charges. But it seems unduly restrictive with regard to mental states, because it implies that mentality must be confined to human biological systems. Moreover, if the type-type version is true, then pain must always be identical with C-fibres firing and the same would apply in the case of the identities of all other types of mental state.

Multiple realisability of mental states

There are, however, good reasons to believe the token-token theory is more plausible in the case of the mind. Firstly, why shouldn't creatures with totally different biologies from ours have minds, or even conceivably non-biological systems? Why should mentality be restricted to human brains? Naturally, it could be true that only carbon-based organisms have the capacity to have minds, but this is not something on which we can pronounce *a priori*. Only experience can reveal to us what sorts of arrangement will permit mentality to occur. Secondly, we know that in the case of stroke victims a mental function lost through damage to a particular area of the brain is sometimes reinstated when a different part of the brain takes over. This is what philosophers refer to as the multiple realisability of mental states: in theory the same type of mental state could be realised, or incarnated in, different types of physical setup, just as the same information can be stored on hard or floppy discs, in document form, on a screen, and so forth. This line of thinking, as we shall see, led to another theory of the mind, functionalism, which forms the subject of Chapter IV.

review
activity

1. How does the token-token identity theory differ from the type-type theory?

2. What strengths does the token-token theory identity theory have over the type-type theory as an account of what the mind is?

Strengths of the identity theory

Strengths of the identity theory

The identity theory has a number of important strengths. Firstly, simplicity is reckoned to be a virtue of theories and the identity theory is parsimonious. It allows only one kind of substance, material substance, and it advocates that what we take to be mental properties are ultimately physical in character. Secondly, by comparison with dualism, it renders the mind comparatively unmysterious. The origins and natures of spiritual soul-substances are obscure to say the least, and beyond the scope of empirical enquiry. By contrast, we have traced the origins and development of the brain from its inception in simple creatures up through the evolutionary scale to human beings. Whilst there remains much about the structure and functioning of the brain that we do not understand, steady progress is being made and the nature of the mind is gradually being revealed to us. Thirdly, the problem of how mind and body interact with each other, which Descartes could not solve, disappears, because there is simply the physical brain and its states, controlling the body through the central nervous system in ways which are well understood. Lastly, we can immediately understand why changes to the brain due to disease, injury and drugs, lead to alterations in our mental lives. Strictly speaking, those physical changes are identical with mental alterations, if the identity theory is correct. It also comes as no surprise to learn that as the brain grows in size and complexity as we ascend the evolutionary scale, mental functioning correspondingly becomes more sophisticated.

Problems for the identity theory

Leibniz's Law as a test of identity

The first objection to the identity theory which we shall consider turns on the application of Leibniz's Law (see p. 8):

1. Brain states and processes have a spatial location.
2. Mental states and processes do not have a spatial location.
3. Therefore mental states and processes cannot be brain-states and processes.

The spatiality objection

At first glance this argument seems unassailable, but closer inspection reveals a confusion that robs it of its force. There is no problem with premise 1. The brain is a composite entity, a logical substance that can exist in its own right (see p. 3), and it therefore has a literal location in space, as do the processes that take place within it. But according to premise 2, it makes no sense to attribute spatial locations to mental states and processes such as beliefs, intentions, emotions, thoughts and sensations. Whilst a brain process might be taking place three inches behind my left eye, it makes no sense to locate my jealous feeling in that location, or to claim that a belief can be found just above my right ear. Even a sensation does not have a literal location in space. If I feel a pain in my toe there will doubtless be neural events taking place in the nerves in the toe, but there is not a thing, the pain, inside the toe. Hence it seems impossible, according to this line of reasoning, that mental states and brain-states should be identical.

The problem with premise 2, however, is that it embodies the error of tacitly assuming that mental states are logical substances. The characterisation of mental states using noun-like expressions leads us into this error. It then seems, in common with other logical substances, that mental states must have a literal location in space, yet when we try to specify it, we produce only nonsense, so the identity theory has to be dismissed from the very start. However, it is possible to circumvent this objection by reformulating the identity theory. We need firstly to remember that beliefs, intentions, sensations and emotions are not logical substances.

Nagel's attack on the spatiality objection

When a person has a pain, for instance, this does not denote a relationship between two things: the person on the one hand, and the pain on the other. Instead the pain is a condition, or a property, of a single thing, and as such it will exist wherever the person happens to be. The point was well made by the philosopher Thomas Nagel (1937–). If the identity claim is adjusted so that it is to hold not between a brain process and the occurrence of a pain but instead between 'my having a certain sensation or thought, and my body's being in a certain physical state, then they will both be going on in the same place – namely, wherever I (and my body) happen to be ... even if a pain is located in my right shin, I am having that pain in my office at the university' (Nagel 1970: 218). However, if we then insist on demanding precisely where in the person the pain is located, we merely reprise the error of treating a pain as if it were a logical substance. Instead we need to remember that sensations and mental states generally, as the states and conditions of a person, cannot be given a more specific location than where the person happens to be.

review activity

Explain why the objection to the identity theory described above, namely that physical states are locatable in space, whereas mental states are not, does *not* succeed as an objection to the theory.

What is it like to be a bat? Nagel's objection to the identity theory

A more robust objection to the identity theory is supplied by the fact that whereas brain processes are public, mental states would appear to be private to the person whose states they are. Brain states can only be known from a third-person objective perspective: a person is in no better position than anyone else regarding what is taking place in his or her brain. I find out what is going on in my brain in essentially the same way that I discover what is taking place in yours, either by direct observation of the brain, or by means of a scanner. By contrast, a person would seem to have a privileged access to his or her own states of mind denied to outside observers. In order to say how they feel, people do not have to go through any process of observation or inference. A person's mental states enjoy an inviolable privacy and are known from a first-person subjective point of view that cannot be eliminated. This is essentially the stance taken by Thomas Nagel in his well-known article 'What is it Like to be a Bat?' (Nagel 1974: 435–50). The lives and experiences of bats are very different from ours. For example, they find their way around using echolocation, a faculty that we lack, and they habitually sleep upside down. We can only speculate what it must be like to be a bat. We cannot know because we cannot attain to the bat's subjective viewpoint, nor can a bat know what it is like to be us, because our first-person human viewpoint is not accessible to it. Given these differences in the nature of our knowledge of our own mental states on the one hand, and our brain-states on the other, it is difficult to see how the two could be identical.

The non-identifiability of mental with physical properties

In response, it might be argued that brain states can be accessed in two different ways, from the *inside* by the person who brain states they are, and from the *outside* by other people. From the external perspective, brain states will appear to be physical processes, whereas from the internal perspective they will be experienced by the person as states of mind. This way of regarding the matter does perhaps have the advantage of enabling us to avoid a duality of events and substances. Unlike dualists, we do not have to postulate a stream of physical occurrences in the brain and a separate stream of mental events in the mind. Instead, a single series of physical events in the brain can suffice, which can be experienced from two perspectives. However, it seems that whilst we can avoid a duality of substances, we cannot avoid a duality of properties. If it is postulated that my toothache is identical with neural processes taking place inside a decayed tooth, there must be some features by means of which the items on the left and right sides of the identity sign can be identified independently of each other, otherwise both halves of the identity cannot be pinned down. But what I am aware of when I feel the agonising throb in my tooth, and what I am aware of when I see a scan of the processes in my tooth, are very different features that appear to be completely distinct from each other. Concentration on the throb reveals nothing of the physical nature of the processes going on in the tooth, and conversely, scrutiny of the physical processes in the tooth reveals nothing of the nature of the throb. It seems impossible then to avoid a dualism of properties, mental and physical, even if it is accepted that there are only physical brain events. The phenomenal features of my experience when I have a toothache, the qualia – as they have been dubbed by philosophers – constituting how it feels to me, appear strongly resistant to identification with, and reduction to, physical features of the central nervous system.

How can mental states be physical states?

Against this conclusion, Thomas Nagel once expressed the hope that in the future a scientist might observe a process in his brain and remark that, neurologically, that is what Nagel's enjoying the taste of his cigar looks like. But Nagel went on to add that at present we haven't the faintest glimmering of how a taste subjectively experienced by someone could simultaneously be a public physical process accessible in principle to everyone.

review
activity

1. How does the subjectivity of mental states constitute an objection to the identity theory?
2. Does it succeed?

Intentional mental states

The final difficulty for the identity theory that we shall discuss here is posed by the existence of *Intentional* mental states, or the *propositional attitudes* as they are also known. An Intentional mental state is one that is about, or directed upon, a representative mental content. The term 'Intentional' is derived from the Latin *intendere*, 'to aim at' in the sense of aiming an arrow with a bow – *intendere ad arcum*. The technical word, 'Intentionality', is now standardly used to refer to mental states that possess a representational content. It is important not to confuse Intentionality with doing something intentionally, or with a further intention, although the notion of a focus upon an object is a common feature of these terms.

The Intentionality of many mental states is best illustrated by an example. I cannot just believe, full stop. If I believe, then I must believe that something or other is the case. So, for example, I might believe that the Royal Festival Hall is on the South Bank. In this case my belief is true. My belief represents the Royal Festival Hall as being on the South Bank, and as a matter of fact it is, so my belief turns out to be true. But obviously I can have false beliefs. Suppose I believed instead, wrongly, that the Albert Hall was on the South Bank. In that case the content of my belief misrepresents what is the case.

Intentional mental states

A belief exemplifies what Bertrand Russell (1872–1970) called a *propositional attitude* and comprises two components. Firstly, there is the representative content of the belief, specified by a propositional 'that' clause – 'that the Festival Hall is on the South Bank', 'that the Albert Hall is on the South Bank'. Secondly, there is the cognitive attitude or stance that is taken towards the content; in this case the content is *believed* to be true of the world. However, there are many different possible attitudes that could be taken towards the content of a propositional attitude. For example, I could *hope* that the Albert Hall is on the South Bank, *regret* that it is, *wish* it were not, *imagine* that it is, *doubt* that it is, and so on and so forth. A moment's thought reveals that the bulk of our mental states exhibit Intentionality, though perhaps reports of sensations such as pains and itches should be omitted from the list – what state of affairs does my pain represent, for example? This is controversial, however, and has been the subject of much debate.

Franz Brentano (1838–1917), who revived discussion of Intentionality, the topic having fallen into neglect after the Middle Ages, asserted that all mental phenomena exhibit Intentionality, and that it constitutes in effect the hall mark of the mental that distinguishes it from material phenomena. There are issues concerning how the various attitudinal components, for example, the nature of belief, desires, intentions, wondering, and so forth, of the propositional attitudes are to be analysed and understood, but this is a topic that cannot be taken further here. For the present, the focus will be on the representational content. The problem posed for the identity theory can be stated in the form of an argument thus:

1. Intentional mental states represent, or are about, states of affairs external to themselves, including states of affairs that do not, and perhaps never did, exist. For example, beliefs, dreams, desires, intentions, emotions, and thoughts, possess a representational content.
2. No purely material brain states can possess a representational content.
3. Therefore, Intentional mental states cannot be identical with brain states.

Naturalism regarding Intentional mental states

As the argument is valid and (1) is undeniably true, a materialist must find a way of rejecting (2). The problem, however, is that it is very difficult to understand how physical arrangements of particles in the brain can represent other states of affairs, including non-existent ones. What is required is an explanation couched purely in terms of the entities, properties, and concepts recognised by physics, biology and chemistry, a naturalistic explanation, as it is called. The explanation will take the form of a specification of necessary and sufficient conditions, only these will not be the logically necessary and sufficient conditions employed in defining a concept such as art, for example, but naturalistic necessary and sufficient conditions drawing upon true scientific theories.

review
activity

1. What is Intentionality as a feature of many mental states?

2. How does it represent a difficulty for the mind/brain identity theory?

In this spirit the American philosopher Jerry Fodor writes:

I suppose sooner or later the physicists will finish the catalogue they've been compiling of the ultimate and irreducible properties of things. When they do, spin, charm, and charge [microphysical properties] will appear on their list. But aboutness surely won't: Intentionality simply doesn't go that deep.

(Fodor 1987: 97).

Fodor and the language of thought: Mentalese

In other words, the dedicated materialist cannot accept that Intentionality is a basic, irreducible, non-physical feature of the brain, which cannot be analysed in other terms. In order to make the mind fully part of the natural physical world, there must, he maintains, be a way of explaining how the states of a physical system like the brain can represent or be about other states of affairs. Fodor believes that the brain has its own language, *Mentalese*, and that the symbols of this language comprise computational states of the brain which are realised in the processes taking place in the neurons and synapses. But even if we grant for the sake of argument that there are such states, combined in ways analogous to the words and phrases which make up natural languages so as to yield sentences of Mentalese, how these states can be about, or represent, states of affairs other than themselves still cries out for explanation.

Naturalising Intentionality: resemblance

Two types of naturalistic theory have been proposed, the first employing the notion of resemblance, and the second utilising causation. According to the first theory, a representation R, represents a state of affairs S, if, and only if, R resembles S. However, this theory falls at the first hurdle. Felipe resembles his identical twin Pedro, but Felipe is not thereby a representation of Pedro, so resemblance is not sufficient for representation. It is not necessary either. The name 'Felipe' looks nothing like Felipe himself, but nevertheless may be used to represent him. Moreover, resemblance is a symmetrical notion, whereas representation is not. If Felipe resembles Pedro, then Pedro resembles Felipe, but a picture or representation of Felipe is not itself represented by Felipe.

*Naturalising
Intentionality: causality*

The second analysis aims to explain aboutness in terms of causality. Very roughly, if certain types of brain state, B, are caused in a regular and reliable manner by certain sorts of external stimuli, A, then those brain states may be said to be about, or to represent, those external factors. The relation between the brain states and the stimuli exhibits causal co-variation: the brain-states vary systematically as a result of the stimuli. A good example of causal co-variation which occurs naturally is provided by tree rings. The kind of ring a tree lays down depends upon the kind of weather obtaining in the year the ring is formed. We can discover correlations between types of ring and types of weather, and use this information to extrapolate what the weather must have been like in past years when no weather records were made or kept. There is thus a sense in which the rings represent, or are about, the weather in the years in which they were laid down. Thermostats also provide an example of how Intentionality is to be analysed in purely physical, mechanical terms. Thermostats are designed so that their states vary systematically as a result of changes in the ambient temperature. When the temperature is too high, the thermostat passes into an internal state which leads to the heating being shut off. When the temperature is too low, the internal state of the thermostat turns the heating back on. There are many ways in which a thermostat might carry out the functions described above, but commonly thermostats contain a bimetallic strip which bends and makes an electrical contact which turns the heating on when it is too cold, and then bends the other way, breaking the contact when it is too hot. The internal states of the thermostat are thus caused to vary in a systematic and reliable manner by the ambient temperature, and may thus, according to the causal analysis, be said to represent that temperature. A typical expression of this doctrine is provided by Marvin Minsky, a cognitive scientist and researcher into artificial intelligence at Michigan Institute of Technology, who has said, quite seriously, that his thermostat has three beliefs: it's too hot in here; it's too cold in here; and it's just right in here.

*Objections to
naturalistic accounts of
Intentionality*

We need not, however, follow Minsky in crediting thermostats, or tree rings for that matter, literally with beliefs about the environment. A principal objection is that to the tree itself the rings can mean or represent nothing because trees lack consciousness. A representation is only a representation insofar as it represents a state of affairs to a conscious agent. The rings represent what the weather was like to us, but not the tree, because we interpret the meaning of the rings in the manner described. Similarly, lacking awareness, a thermostat cannot literally hold true or false beliefs about the ambient temperature. A purely naturalistic account of Intentionality is instantly vitiated by the requirement that the meaning of the rings needs interpretation by a conscious agent if they are to function genuinely as representations, unless of course consciousness is itself capable of being accounted for naturalistically. The point made earlier (see p. 22) concerning the irreducibility of the phenomenal features comprising our experience, the qualia, to physical features of the brain, strongly suggests that no such account will be forthcoming.

Reliable indication

*Reliable indication as a
naturalistic account of Intentionality*

The physical causal regularities described above are known standardly as instances of reliable indication: tree rings reliably indicate what the weather must have been like; smoke reliably indicates fire; black clouds reliably indicate thunderstorms. For the materialist, a mental state, that is a brain state, B, represents another state of affairs, A, if, and only if, B reliably indicates A. The expression 'if and only if', which we have encountered before, states the *causally* necessary and sufficient conditions for B to represent A. In other words, the proposed reduction of Intentionality or aboutness is not an analytical one. The reductive materialist is not claiming that talk about representation and aboutness is semantically equivalent to reliable indication. To deny that Intentionality is ultimately nothing over and above reliable indication is not self-contradictory, anymore than is the denial that water is H_2O. It is merely that if Intentionality is in fact nothing over and above reliable indication, as water is in fact nothing over and above H_2O, then to deny these equivalencies is to say something false.

In detail, what the proposed analysis is claiming is that:

A *necessary* condition for B, (a mental state/brain state) to represent A, is that B is reliably caused by A. Therefore, if B is not caused by A, or not reliably caused by A, then B cannot be said to represent A.

Reliable indication is not a necessary condition of Intentionality

A problem, however, is that we are able to think about things which do not exist and hence cannot have caused our thoughts about them. I can think about a golden mountain, or the bogeyman, and believe that there are fairies at the bottom of my garden, even though none of these things exists. I can contemplate what I am going to do tomorrow and envisage what might happen in various future situations, and clearly events which have not happened and situations which have not yet arisen, cannot be the causes of my speculations about them. I can thus represent things to myself in the absence of reliable indication. In other words, it is not necessary, contrary to what the reliable indication theory claims, that my representations should have been causally produced by what they represent.

An extension of this point is that it is also possible for me to *misrepresent* things to myself. For example, I may believe wrongly that the Elgin Marbles have been returned to Greece, when in fact they are still in the British Museum. But it is difficult to see how I could have this mistaken belief about the location of the Marbles in the absence of the situation consisting in the Marbles actually being in Greece.

Reliable indication not a necessary condition of Intentionality

The analysis also claims that a *sufficient* condition for B to represent A is that it is reliably caused by A. But now imagine the following possibility. I have a scanner attached to this computer, which, having scanned an original document, causes a copy to be produced. Unfortunately the copier has acquired a systematic fault. For some reason it cannot scan the word 'not' and regularly leaves this word out of the copies it produces. In other words, the operation of the scanner is such that it can be relied upon always to leave out the word 'not'. Hence every time I copy the Ten Commandments I end up with a list of injunctions to steal, to murder, to commit adultery, and so forth. But it is quite clear that my copies do not represent the Ten Commandments. Plainly they seriously *misrepresent* them. But if reliable indication is *sufficient* for representation to take place, and my machine operates reliably to produce documents with the word 'not' omitted, then we would be forced to say that my copies of the Ten Commandments *do* represent the Commandments. As they do not, it seems that it cannot be a sufficient condition for B to represent A, that B should be reliably indicated or caused by A. It may be objected: your copies of the Ten Commandments fail to represent them because the scanner systematically malfunctions. If the copies were produced in the right way, then they would represent the original. But how are we to specify what is the right way? We will trap ourselves in circularity if we say that the right way is the way which leads to an accurate representation being produced.

There are three final objections to the causal analysis which we shall consider. The first focuses on the fact that co-variation is a *transitive* notion. B, a mental state co-varies with A, the external stimulus which gives rise to it. Changes in A give rise to corresponding changes in B. But suppose, as is usually the case, the causal chain running from A to B has more than one link in it. In the case of perception there will be a number of causal links involving the nervous system linking the stimulus A with the perception B. Suppose for simplicity's sake there are just two links, C and D, between A and B. Then every time B co-varies with A, it will co-vary with C and D equally, yet the perception is of A, not of C or D.

The second objection concentrates on *co-extensiveness*. The meaning of the term 'triangle' is different from the meaning of 'trilateral', yet every item which falls under the concept of a triangle necessarily falls under the concept of a trilateral. Thus, every triangle I encounter will also be a trilateral, and vice versa. How, then, is the belief that I see a triangle before me, rather than a trilateral, to be accounted for, given that triangles and trilaterals are necessarily coextensive?

Lastly, there is the related problem of *co-instantiation*, which can be illustrated by Quine's famous example of a native speaker of a language not known to us who utters 'Gavagai' as a rabbit goes past. Does he mean 'There goes a rabbit' or 'There goes an undetached rabbit part?' Rabbits, and their undetached parts, are not coextensive, but wherever there is a rabbit there will necessarily be an undetached rabbit part. If a rabbit is instantiated, so necessarily will an undetached rabbit part, and both give rise to a belief. But which belief – the belief there goes a rabbit, or the belief there goes an undetached rabbit part – as both features are co-instantiated? As in the case of co-extensiveness it is difficult to understand how the causal theory can explain the difference between the two beliefs.

review
activity

'What weaknesses does reliable indication as a naturalistic theory of Intentionality possess?

III

Analytical Behaviourism

important terms

Analytical behaviourism: analytical behaviourism maintains that all talk about the mind can be reduced, without loss of meaning, to talk about actual and possible outward behaviour.

Cartesianism: Descartes embraced the view that the mind and body are two radically different entities or substances. The mind or soul lacks extension in space and its essence consists in consciousness or thinking. The body is incapable of thought and awareness and its essence is extension in space.

Disposition: a dispositional property of a thing states how that thing would behave were certain conditions to be fulfilled. Thus, solubility is a dispositional property of salt, that is to say, that were it to be immersed in water, it would dissolve. A person of an irritable disposition need not actually be fuming, but would be prone to do so in certain circumstances.

Verificationism: verificationism is a central doctrine of logical positivism which claims that unless a statement can be verified empirically, at least in theory, the statement is devoid of meaning.

Key topics in this chapter

- 'Hard' and 'soft' behaviourism
- The nature of the mind
- The verification principle
- The Turing test

Introduction

Although dualism and the mind/brain identity theory conceive of the mind in very different ways, they share the common assumption that the mind is a substance. Analytical, or logical behaviourism as it is also called, rejects this assumption, and proposes instead that the mind is better thought of as a pattern of actual and possible publicly observable behaviour. More precisely, the claim is that statements about mental states and events can be reduced, without remainder, to statements which describe actual and potential behaviour. In other words, what is being proposed is an analytical reduction of the mental to behaviour, (see pp. 16–17) hence the title of the theory.

A great advantage of analytical behaviourism is that it eliminates the problem of other minds, the problem of whether, and how, we can know of the existence of minds other than our own. Descartes bequeathed the idea that the history of a human being is really the history of two streams of collateral events, one stream comprising events involving the public material body, and the other consisting of purely private occurrences in the theatre of the mind, accessible in principle only to the person whose mind it is, and known infallibly by them. But if this Cartesian picture is correct, it seems that we are forever prevented from knowing that there are minds other than our own, so that, strictly speaking we cannot know that there are other people. For all we can tell, what we take to be other people resembling ourselves, might really only be mindless zombies.

This picture of the mind has been felt to have even more alarming consequences. The problem is not merely that we cannot know of the existence of other minds, but that all talk of mind, even in our own case, threatens to become meaningless. According to Ludwig Wittgenstein (1889–1951), words must acquire their meanings in a public social context. It must be possible to distinguish between correct and incorrect usages of words: a word that could

Impossibility of a logically private language to describe one's own mental states

be used any way one wanted could not be a word. There must be rules governing the uses of words, and this implies a check must be possible in order to determine whether a rule is being followed or broken. If the words of a language are supposed to acquire their meanings by naming states of minds which are logically private to the individual, it will be impossible to determine whether the words are being used correctly or not. It might be thought that at least the individual concerned will know, but Wittgenstein points out that an independent and objective public criterion of correctness is required, and this is not available to the individual confined to their private Cartesian theatre: 'Whatever is going to seem to be right will be right, which only means that we cannot speak about right here.'

Behaviour, by contrast with private inner mental states, can provide the public criterion against which ascriptions of mental states, whether to oneself or others, can be assessed for correctness. This topic will be revisited in more detail in Chapter VI, when the problem of other minds is discussed further.

review
activity

1. Briefly explain what analytical behaviourism claims about the nature of the mind.

2. Outline the advantages of analytical behaviourism as a theory of the mind.

'Hard' and 'soft' behaviourism

There are several different varieties of behaviourism, but we shall concentrate on 'hard' and 'soft' behaviourism. A preliminary characterisation of these two different approaches will be supplied before we move on to a more detailed account.

Hempel's 'hard' behaviourism

Carl Hempel (1905–97) is representative of the hard behaviourist approach and Gilbert Ryle (1900–76) of the soft. The motivations of these two philosophers for adopting behaviourism were quite different, and consequently this had a major effect on the way in which they thought behaviourism should be formulated. Hempel was a logical positivist and member of the Vienna Circle. He was concerned with turning psychology into a science, and as such, he intended it to employ only the concepts, explanations, and methodology of a 'hard' science, like physics. Consequently, the public behavioural descriptions which are to replace our standard attributions of states of mind to people using statements that contain mental terms are to be rigorously replaced by statements employing only a non-mentalistic vocabulary.

By contrast, Ryle's aim was the demolition of the Cartesian conception of the mind, which he characterised with 'deliberate abusiveness', as 'the Dogma of the Ghost in the Machine'. He repudiated not only the idea of the mind as a non-physical substance, but in particular the notion of a person's mental life as consisting in a series of happenings on a private mental stage. Moreover, Ryle was not overimpressed by the methods of science, and consequently did not share Hempel's vision of a scientific psychology purged of all mental idioms. He eschewed a radical reductionism of the type Hempel was proposing, writing that 'The hallowed contrast between mind and matter will be dissipated, but dissipated not by either of the equally hallowed absorptions of Mind by Matter or of Matter by Mind, but in a quite different way' (Ryle 1973: 23). Consequently, we find no attempt in Ryle to replace our mental vocabulary with terms employing exclusively physical concepts. Beginning with Hempel, let us now examine hard and soft behaviourism in detail.

Hempel's 'hard' behaviourism

The verification principle and its application to the problem of other minds

As a logical positivist Hempel subscribed to the verificationist principle of meaning. Setting to one side the analytic truths of mathematics and geometry, the theory maintained that for a synthetic statement to be meaningful it had to be verifiable empirically. This did not mean that in practice it had to be verified, but only in theory. The meaningfulness of a statement was guaranteed as long as it was conceivable that it could be verified by some set of observations or experiments, even if these were not actually carried out. But if the mental states of other people are private to them in the manner Cartesian dualism maintains, then the existence and character of such states is not even verifiable in principle. Hence, according to the verification principle, statements about the minds of other people must be devoid of significance. In response it might be argued that even if that is so, at least we can verify statements about our own minds. However, this would probably be ruled out by subscribers to the verification principle on the grounds that such supposed verification could not be objectively evaluated by third persons and so could not count. But if talk about others' mental states is really equivalent to talk about their actual and possible behaviour, meaning is restored to such talk, as the behaviour of other people is plainly observable and verifiable.

review activity

Briefly explain what the verification principle is and how it can lead to analytical behaviourism.

Intentionalistic characterisations of actions

This brings us, however, to the question mentioned earlier of how such behaviour is to be described. Two kinds of behavioural description are possible, those employing the concepts of the sciences, and those using mental or Intentional terms. 'Angela raised her arm' would be an example of the second mode of description as it imports an action to Angela, something that she did, either intentionally or unintentionally. Where human agency is concerned, the request for the agent's reasons for the performance of the action in question is always in place, reasons which specify what the agent wanted to achieve and why he believed that end would be served by the particular action. Even if the action is unintended, at least the agent can report that she did not intend to do what she did, or did not know what she was doing. The point is that where actions are concerned, mentality is being explicitly or implicitly attributed to the person in question.

Non-Intentional characterisations of actions and the avoidance of circularity in the behavioural analysis

But Angela's action could also be described in terms which give no clue as to whether or not it was an action. Such a description might look like this: 'A human appendage was observed over an interval of time to change its position from such and such spatial coordinates to so and so spatial coordinates.' This is what the psychologist C.L. Hull referred to as a description couched in the language of 'colourless bodily movements' *and* it represents the kind of language to which Hempel must confine himself, not only because it accords with his ideal of reducing psychology to physics but also because it avoids importing circularity into the proposed behavioural analysis of mental expressions. When providing a reductive analysis of any phenomenon, the analysis must not mention the phenomenon itself; otherwise the analysis will merely repeat itself. It would be like giving a definition of a word and using that very word in the definition.

Problems for Hempel's 'hard' behaviourism

In the light of this requirement let us examine Hempel's analysis of 'Paul has toothache'. The proposed analysis goes as follows:

1. Paul weeps and makes gestures of such-and-such kinds.
2. At the question 'What is the matter?' Paul utters the words 'I have a toothache.'
3. Closer examination reveals a decayed tooth with exposed pulp.
4. Paul's blood pressure, digestive processes and the speed of his reaction, show such-and-such changes.
5. Such-and-such processes occur in Paul's nervous system.

Circularity in the Hempelian analysis

Conditions (3), (4) and (5) should be immediately eliminated. The causes of toothache and its physiological accompaniments are surely not part of what it *means* to have toothache. It would not be self-contradictory to assert that one had toothache, yet nothing that was usually physiologically associated with toothache was occurring (compare p. 22). (1) and (2) are also unsatisfactory, but for a different reason, namely that they effectively attribute states of mind to Paul, and hence render the analysis circular. 'Weeping' and 'making gestures' are things that agents *do*, as indeed is the utterance of words, and so mentality is implied. Moreover, Paul could not respond to the question 'What is the matter?' unless he *understood* it, and similarly he must *understand* the words comprising the sentence 'I have a toothache'. In addition, in uttering this sentence Paul presumably wants to tell the truth so that something may be done about his suffering, but clearly 'wanting' is a psychological term of which the analysis must dispose on pain of circularity.

The requirements of a non-circular analysis mean that Hempel has to find some way of specifying those patterns of behaviour, described purely as bodily movements, involved in Paul's suffering from toothache – something, as we have seen, he barely attempts to provide. This is not at all surprising, as it constitutes a very tall order. A major barrier to the successful completion of the analysis is to be found in the fact that there is no one-to-one correspondence between types of action and types of bodily movement. Different types of action may be performed by the same type of bodily movement: a finger raised in the air may constitute pointing upwards, indicating a batsman is out, insulting someone, signalling for procedures to be paused, and so forth. Conversely, the same type of action may be executed by means of different types of bodily movement: saving a goal may be done by kicking the ball, punching it, grasping it, blocking it with one's body, and so on.

The analysis has to proceed in two stages. Firstly, it has to specify those behaviours, and only those behaviours, described in ordinary everyday terms that are involved in having toothache. Then, in order to avoid circularity, each item of behaviour has to be analysed into colourless bodily movements. The first requirement alone appears impossible to achieve. What sorts of things might Paul plausibly be thought to engage in when he has toothache? He might shout, cry, moan, curse, thump the wall, grimace, jump up and down, and so on. An analysis would have to take the form of an elaborate list of all the alternative things he might do, so it might begin:

Paul has toothache = either Paul is shouting, or he is crying, or he is moaning, or ... or ... (This list of alternatives using the word 'or' is called a *disjunction*, and hence the analysis is known as a disjunctive analysis.)

The problem of completing the analysis of 'Paul has a toothache' in purely physical terms

The problem, however, is that it begins to look as if the analysis could never be completed, as there is an indefinite variety of things Paul might do as a result of having toothache. The difficulty is magnified even more by the fact that each possible type of action comprising the disjunction can also be constituted by an indefinite variety of types of bodily movement characterised without reference to states of mind. In this way the analysis could ramify indefinitely, thus defying its completion.

The problem of identifying which behaviours are to figure in the analysis without circularity

There is, moreover, an additional objection to the second half of the analysis, namely the problem of how we are to identify the sorts of bodily movements it is to include. Described merely as colourless movements, there are no obvious patterns or groupings into which these behaviours fall which enable us to identity those which should, and those which should not, be included in the analysis of a particular type of action. Naturally, if we specify a type of action, it is not difficult to think of the sorts of bodily movement that might be involved in it – licking a stamp, for example. But there is a prohibition on proceeding in this manner, because the identification of the bodily movements is dependent on the identification of the action. It is the description of the action that gives the bodily movements their unity and their appropriateness for inclusion in the analysis, and it is only the identification of the action that renders the grouping intelligible and identifiable. But once again, this imports circularity into the analysis, as it crucially depends upon a reference to what is essentially a mentalistic description.

The problem of eliminating all mental terms from the analysis

A different kind of circularity is given rise to by the fact that actions do not occur because of single mental states but from combinations of them. A desire/belief pair helps to illustrate the point. How might we analyse in behavioural terms the statement 'Ollie wants a beer'? Supposing there is a fridge nearby with a beer in it, we cannot simply say that Ollie will go and get the beer. He will only do this if he also believes that there is a beer in the fridge, that he hasn't given up drinking, that there isn't something he wants to do more, and so forth. Leaving to one side these additional factors which may prevent Ollie from acting, the point is that the analysis of the desire in terms of behaviour also involves a reference to a belief which has not been analysed in behavioural terms. This cannot be permitted and some way of spelling out in behavioural terms what having the belief that there is a beer in the fridge amounts to will have to be found. The solution cannot be found by saying that Ollie believes there is a beer in the fridge means that he will go and get it, because this is true only if he wants a beer. But now a reference to a desire has appeared as an unanalysed item in the analysis. It begins to look as if belief-possession cannot be spelt out in behavioural terms without reference to a desire as an unanalysed mental state, and equally, possession of a desire cannot be specified without reference to a belief as an unanalysed mental state. It might be suggested that Ollie believes there is a beer in the fridge can be captured behaviourally in the following manner: if asked 'Do you believe there is a beer in the fridge?' Ollie would answer in the affirmative. But naturally, he will only reply if he *wants* to answer the question. Moreover, his *understanding* of the question and the words involved in answering it is presupposed. No behavioural analysis may be allowed to contain unanalysed mental terms, but it strongly appears that however far our analysis in behavioural terms proceeds, it will be forced at some stage to have recourse to unanalysed mental terms.

review activity

Explain in your own words the problems faced by Hempel's 'hard' behaviourism.

Ryle's 'soft' behaviourism

Mental states can be seen in outward behaviour

Let us now examine Ryle's behaviourism in contrast to Hempel's. Unlike Hempel, Ryle did not sign up to the verification principle, so he had no motive to discard as meaningless statements that could not be verified in a scientific manner. Neither did he possess the related ambition to reduce psychology to physics, so the problem of analysing states of mind in terms of colourless bodily movements did not arise for him. He was quite happy to allow unanalysed mental terms into his analysis, remarking once that he was never anything more than 'only one arm and one leg a behaviourist'. He maintained, for example, that: 'Overt intelligent performances are not clues to the workings of minds; they *are* those workings. Boswell described Johnson's mind when he described how he wrote, talked, ate, fidgeted and fumed' (Ryle 1973: 57) [emphasis added]. Johnson's mind is not hidden behind his behaviour, but reflected in it. We do not merely see colourless bodily movements when we observe Johnson behaving in various ways, but full-blooded actions that embody and manifest his mental processes.

The notion that mental states are hidden and private is a category mistake

In maintaining that overt intelligent performances are the workings of minds, Ryle was repudiating the Cartesian view that people live through two collateral histories, one consisting in public physical occurrences, and the other in accompanying ghostly happenings on a private stage. To suppose otherwise, Ryle maintains, is to commit a category mistake, illustrating it with the now well-known story of the visitor who asks to see the University of Oxford. Having seen various colleges, the Bodleian Library, the Radcliffe Camera, and so forth, he then complains that he has still not seen the university. His mistake is obvious: he is thinking of the university as another building he has not yet been shown, whereas it is clear that the university is just the totality of the colleges and other institutions making it up. We make the same mistake, according to Ryle, when, having seen human beings going about their everyday lives and interacting in the way they do, we complain that we have witnessed merely their outward public behaviour, and not the activities of the mind lying behind such behaviour and informing it. It comes as no surprise that Ryle was subsequently stigmatised as a behaviourist. If minds are manifest in behaviour and not hidden away behind it, then mental and physical occurrences it would seem are not, in Hume's words, 'distinct existences'. It seems we are left not with mental states lying behind a person's behaviour and serving as the cause and explanation of it, but only the behaviour itself.

review
activity

Explain in your own words how Ryle's 'soft' behaviourism differs from Hempel's 'hard' behaviourism.

Of course, the story is more complicated than this, as it is not difficult to think of mental states that do not manifest themselves in behaviour. A toothache comes on during a concert but I do not moan or wince or fidget around. Out of consideration for others I suppress this behaviour, and no one suspects that I am in agony. But if the agony abides, yet the behaviour expressing it is nowhere in evidence, is Ryle not forced to concede that a hidden mental life can exist separately from behaviour?

To overcome this difficulty, Ryle has recourse to the notion of a disposition. When the toothache comes on, I do not actually have to groan, wince, etc. Instead, it is sufficient that I am disposed to do these things. In other words, there are circumstances in which I *would* do these things, when the concert is over, for example. Similarly, to describe a windowpane as brittle it does not actually have to be shattering, but merely that it would shatter if struck hard enough. According to Ryle, if something has a disposition, then this amounts to nothing more than for a number of hypothetical 'if ... then ...' statements to be true. In this way Ryle hopes to avoid having to posit non-behavioural mental states. He writes: 'To possess a dispositional property is not to be in a particular state, or to undergo a particular change; it is to be bound or liable to be bound to be in a particular state, or to undergo a particular change when a particular condition is realised' (Ryle 1973: 43).

Mental states are not merely occurrent, but dispositional

But surely there is more to a disposition than this. Glass will shatter when struck and the reason for this disposition lies in its microstructure which, if altered by annealing, say, would render the glass immune to shattering. In the same way, a belief is a non-behavioural state of mind which in combination with an appropriate desire gives rise to outward behaviour. To have a belief is not merely for a whole lot of 'iffy' statements to be true – that is, statements which describe what a person would do *if* certain conditions were fulfilled.

activity

Why does Ryle have recourse to the notion of a disposition in providing a behavioural analysis of mental states, and how may it be criticised?

Problems for Ryle's 'soft' behaviourism

Behaviour cannot be explained in terms of behaviour: the analysis is circular

This brings us to an especially important point. We commonly explain people's behaviour by reference to their mental states. A desire for a beer, together with a belief that there is one in the fridge, leads me to go to the fridge. A sudden stab of pain makes me cry out. The thought that I had a near miss with another car makes me tremble. These explanations appear to be causal in character, even to the extent of entailing counterfactual conditionals which some have thought are the hallmark of causality. If I hadn't wanted a beer (or had not believed there was one in the fridge), I would not have gone to it. If the stab of pain, or the thought of a near miss, had not occurred, I would not have cried out, or trembled. But if the pain, the desire, and the thought are all to be rendered in purely behavioural terms, how can they be used to explain my behaviour, because I shall then be attempting to explain behaviour in terms of itself? The explanation of a piece of behaviour cannot lie, so to speak, on the same level with it. Instead it has to be conceived of as an underlying cause, different and distinct from the behaviour it explains. As Hilary Putnam has commented, in trying to render all talk of the mental in behavioural terms the key error lies in construing causes as logical constructions out of their effects.

activity

How does behaviourism render explanations of a person's behaviour in terms of his or her mental states impossible?

The Turing test amounts to behaviourism: evidence for mental states = what constitutes mental states

Essentially the same mistake infects the Turing test, which aims to provide a way of telling whether something has a mind or not. The test maintains, very reasonably, that if two things closely resemble each other in their behaviour and it is granted that one of them has a mind, the same must be granted of the other. Where there is no significant difference in the behaviour between the two things, it would be unreasonable to attribute a mind to one but not the other. There has to be some reason, some genuine difference, for withholding the attribution. The test works like this: there are two screens, and hidden behind one is a human being and behind the other a machine – a digital computer, say. Questions are then put to whatever is hidden behind the screens and a dialogue we shall suppose ensues. Now, if the person carrying out the test cannot tell the difference between the responses received from the human being behind the screen and the responses received from the machine, if a mind is granted in the first place, it must, out of consistency, be granted in the second. As described, the test is extremely limited because only a small segment of behaviour, real or apparent linguistic behaviour, is available. But now, to make it more realistic, suppose an android has been constructed out of inorganic matter, something like Data from the series *Star Trek*, has been so refined that someone unacquainted with him could not tell him apart from a human being in both his appearance and manner of behaving. Well, according to the Turing test we should then have constructed a conscious machine with a mental life even if we could not explain how that life arose. We seem to be forced to admit, on pain of inconsistency, that Data, despite his origins and construction, is a conscious and feeling being, a person pretty much like us. We should be guilty of racism against robots, a prejudice rooted in our belief that something made of such different materials could not, at the end of the day, be fundamentally like us in possessing a sophisticated mental life.

This conclusion, however, is resistible. Data *behaves* like us, but it does not follow he actually *is* like us. The mistake lies in treating the *evidence* for states of mind as *constitutive* of those states of mind. In other words, behaviour is regarded not merely as evidence of mentality, but as actually comprising it. States of mind have been reduced, effectively, to what counts as signs of their existence. By a different route we would appear to have arrived back at behaviourism, but behaviourism as we have begun to see, is not an adequate theory. It would be perfectly possible for something to behave like a human being yet be totally devoid of consciousness, the starting point for the problem of other minds, it will be recalled (see p. 28).

review
activity

What is the Turing test, and what fundamental error does it commit?

Intuitively, perhaps the strongest objection to behaviourism is represented by the response that if we were to adopt it, we should all have to feign anaesthesia. There is something it feels like to have toothache, or to have pins and needles in one's foot. Sensations possess a phenomenal experiential content that is omitted if they are reduced to patterns of actual and potential behaviour. I do not visit the dentist merely to have my behaviour changed, but to get rid of the pain that is troubling me. Accounting for sensations constitutes an especially intractable obstacle, as does the experience of visualising something in the mind's eye; something that it seems intuitively obvious need not show itself in outward behaviour. Ryle tries to deal with this case in the following way:

> *A person picturing his nursery is, in a certain way, like that person seeing his nursery, but the similarity does not consist in his really looking at a real likeness of his nursery, but in his seeming to see his nursery itself, when he is not really seeing it. He is not being a spectator of a resemblance of his nursery, but he is resembling a spectator of his nursery.*
> (Ryle 1973: 234)

Can behaviourism account for the inner, phenomenological features of mental states?

The first sentence of this passage does not appear to add anything to the description of the person as seeing something in his mind's eye, but merely restates what is going on. Ryle must deny that the person is a spectator of a mental resemblance of his nursery, an Intentional content (see p. 23), otherwise his behaviourism will be wrecked, and this forces him into the convolution of the last sentence. In what way, behaviourally, do I resemble a spectator of my nursery when 1 imagine it? There are all sorts of circumstances in which I might be imagining my nursery, including lying inert in the darkness in bed. In the latter case particularly, how then could I plausibly be described as behaving like a fully clothed, upright spectator of my nursery, looking at it in full daylight? It is not, however, surprising that Ryle has no very illuminating account to give of seeing in the mind's eye, or sensations for that matter, for it does just appear to be a fact that these phenomena consist in private episodes of consciousness that resist capture in outward public behaviour.

Knowledge of mental states from a first-person perspective is based on neither observation nor inference

There is another feature of sensations, as well as some other mental states, which poses a problem for the behaviourist, namely that I am able to report, without observation or inference, what sensations I am experiencing or how I am feeling. You, on the other hand, have to rely on what I do and say. Behaviourism gets this the other way round. If just my sensations and feelings are my behaviour, or a tendency to behave in a certain way, and nothing more, then it would appear that I have to observe myself in a mirror to determine my state of mind, or to wait until my disposition to behave is realised in action before I can report what it is. The point has been neatly captured in the old joke: One behaviourist meets another on the street and says: 'You feel fine. How do I feel?'

review
activity

In what ways do mental states such as sensations and seeing in the mind's eye pose a problem for the behaviourist?

Failure of the possibility of pretence as an argument against behaviourism

It might be thought that the possibility of pretence gives the lie to behaviourism. Just as someone could suppress their pain behaviour, so they could pretend to be in pain. In that case, we would have pain behaviour but not pain, so how could one be identical with the other? The example aims to show that it is possible to have behaviour without a corresponding mental state, so that mental states must be more than merely behaviour. There are good reasons for thinking this to be true as we have seen, but this example cannot establish this conclusion and for the following reason. If people pretend to be in pain, then they are doing this intentionally, and doubtless with a further intention, to avoid going to school perhaps. But this mental state, more complex than merely being in pain, the behaviourist can argue, can be analysed into the play-acting behaviour that comprises the pretence. Even if being in pain cannot be behaviourally analysed, for there is no pain, the mental state constituting pretending to be in pain can be. So the argument from pretence does not establish what it was designed to prove, namely that there can be behaviour without mental states, and so the latter cannot be reduced to the former.

The possibility of zombies as an argument against behaviourism

The possibility of zombies, however (see p. 28), would establish the falsity of behaviourism. It will be recalled that zombies are outwardly just like us. They seem to behave in the same sorts of ways in which we do and yet they lack consciousness and a mental life generally. This does appear to be an intelligible possibility, unmarred by contradiction, and in turn raises the question, if behaviour is not logically sufficient for mental states to be present, is it logically necessary? Is it possible, for example, to be in pain yet never express it? Hilary Putnam's fantasy of super-Spartans or super-Stoics attempts to demonstrate this possibility. In this community the adults have the ability to suppress all involuntary pain behaviour. Even whilst experiencing the agonies of the damned they do not wince, groan, or scream, but report that they are in pain in quiet calm voices. They have important ideological reasons for this practice and they are happy to admit it takes a great effort of will and years of training to practise it successfully. It might be pointed out that the children in this community will not be conditioned in the way the adults are, and it is the pain behaviour they involuntarily exhibit that enables the term 'pain' to be used in the community. Putnam responds by supposing that after several million years the super-Spartans start to have children who are born fully enculturated who already share the beliefs of their society, in particular the belief that one must acknowledge that one is in pain only in a calm and unagitated manner. Despite the fact that there is no unconditioned natural pain behaviour in the community, it cannot be concluded that the super-Spartans lack the capacity for experiencing pain. Putnam takes his fantasy to extreme lengths, imagining that eventually super-super-Spartans, X-worlders, are produced, who not only do not exhibit natural pain behaviour but will not even talk about pain. X-worlders pretend not to know what it is to be in pain, nor even to know the meaning of the word 'pain', even though they know perfectly well what 'pain' means and that they do sometimes suffer from pain. Putnam comments:

> If this last fantasy is not, in some disguised way, self-contradictory, then logical behaviourism is simply a mistake. Not only is the second thesis of logical behaviourism – the existence of a near-translation of pain into behaviour talk – false, but so even if the first thesis the existence of 'analytic entailments'. Pains are responsible for certain kinds of behaviour – but only in the context of our beliefs, desires, ideological attitudes, and so forth. From the statement 'X has a pain' by itself no behavioural statement follows – not even a behavioural statement with a 'normally' or a 'probably' in it.   (Putnam 1975: 330)

Disembodied existence as an argument against behaviourism

The possibility of disembodied existence (discussed briefly on p. 6) would also mean that behaviourism is false. It might seem to people that they could see things, or that they could feel pains in their bodies, even though in their disembodied state they had neither eyes nor bodies. Descartes' argument from clear and distinct perception also perhaps shows that even if there are no disembodied states in this world, there is a possible world in which the mental and the physical do come apart from each other, and this alone would establish the falsity of analytical behaviourism.

IV

Functionalism

important terms

Functionalism: functionalism conceives of the mind as a programme run on the hardware of the brain, whereby sensory inputs are converted into behavioural outputs. Metaphysical functionalism provides a formal philosophical analysis of the inputs and outputs, whilst psycho-functionalism investigates what actual neural mechanisms enable the function to be discharged.

Materialism/physicalism: materialism maintains that all that exists are physical objects and physical properties.

Metaphysics: metaphysics concerns questions about the nature of existence which fall outside the purview of the sciences. Typical questions in metaphysics are: what is the nature of causation? What is the mind and how does it differ from the body? What is the difference between things and their properties?

Semantics and syntax: semantics is the study of the meaning of words and statements and how it is possible. Syntax is the study of the language structures by means of which statements get made.

Key topics in this chapter

- Metaphysical and psycho-functionalism
- The Turing machine
- Consciousness and subjectivity

Introduction

Functionalism, like analytical behaviourism, rejects the notion of the mind as a thing, a logical substance, and conceives of it instead as a *function*. The function of a thing is essentially what job it does and it is easy to think of a myriad of examples of functions, as we shall see shortly. Typically a function involves taking a certain input and converting it into an output. So, to take a very simple example, think of a corkscrew. The input is a bottle with a cork in it, and the output is the bottle minus the cork. The function of the corkscrew is to remove the cork, but as everyone knows, corkscrews come in all different shapes and sizes, from a simple pull corkscrew to the waiter's friend, which employs leverage against the rim of the bottle neck to facilitate the removal of the cork, to the highly elaborate devices now appearing in shops where the bottle neck is clamped, the screw inserted in one go, and the cork then levered out in one easy movement. How corkscrews are designed does not matter very much as long as they do the job efficiently and are reasonably durable. Clearly, there are limits to what corkscrews can be made of if they are to perform their functions: a chocolate corkscrew would be, as they say, as daft as a chocolate teapot. Summarising, we can see that a distinction can be drawn between:

- The function of a thing – the job it performs and the nature of the input it converts to an output.
- The actual set of arrangements that enable the function to be executed, what is sometimes described as the occupant of the causal role that enables the function to be discharged.

Functions neither physical nor non-physical but abstract

It is not only artefacts, of course, that discharge functions. The various organs of the human body – the heart, kidneys, lungs, and so forth – perform various jobs, as do human beings in the roles they adopt – think of the monarchy, the legislature and the judiciary, for example. A prime example of a complex device that executes a function is a computer which takes an input and by means of an algorithm, a set of simple steps, converts it to an output. Indeed, it was the advent of the digital computer which had a major influence on the formulation of functionalism as a theory of the mind. The distinction between the function of a thing and the actual set of arrangements that make the discharge of the function possible leads us to the realisation that functions, by their very nature, are multiply realisable. If a person suffers heart disease, the function of the heart could be taken over by a mechanical heart, and if the Queen dies, the monarchy does not cease to function as Prince Charles can step into her Majesty's shoes. What this is leading up to is the point that a function can be specified abstractly, and in complete independence of the arrangements that may embody it and make its execution possible. This means that strictly speaking the function itself should be thought of as neither physical nor mental, but as neutral between the two. This fits in with what certain functionalists have maintained, that in theory mental functions could be equally discharged by processes in an immaterial soul, as by the physical arrangements comprising the brain and central nervous system. However, despite recognising the need to make this concession, in practice functionalists are materialists, or at least inclined to materialism of some stripe, maintaining that the causal occupant of the functional role is in fact the brain in the case of human beings and the higher animals.

Metaphysical functionalism

What does the functional specification of a mental state, say, pain, look like? It may be represented thus:

The functional specification of pain

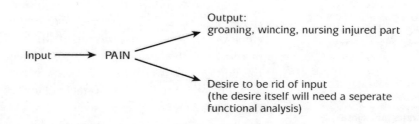

Input ⟶ PAIN

Output:
groaning, wincing, nursing injured part

Desire to be rid of input
(the desire itself will need a seperate functional analysis)

Metaphysical functionalism is the formal specification of a mental state in terms of inputs and outputs

In other words, what typically happens when someone receives an injury to his or her body is that there is an input in the form of tissue damage and an output in the form of pain-behaviour. Once this specification of the function has been provided, an exhaustive description of it has resulted according to functionalism. The mental state is nothing more than the system of relations characterised in terms of inputs, outputs, and other mental states which will also require a functional analysis. This purely formal specification of a mental state is known as *metaphysical functionalism*, (sometimes it is simply called functionalism) and it derives from our commonsense understanding of what mental states are. It is supposedly a conceptual truth, something that could not be otherwise.

Psycho-functionalism

Functions are multiply realisable

The formal specification of a mental state in functionalist terms proceeded purely conceptually and was based on our everyday understanding of what mental states are in terms of typical causes and effects, but it says nothing about what set of arrangements actually enable the function to be discharged. This is something that we cannot know merely by sitting in our armchairs and philosophising, but demands empirical research. From the standpoint of meta-physical functionalism, the mind is a black box whose internal arrangements and processes are not open to view, and can only be brought to light by empirical research. It is thus, in theory, possible, as we said earlier, that mental functions could be discharged by processes in a ghostly soul, as there is nothing in the formal abstract specification of the mental function that rules this out. However, functionalists maintain that in the case of human beings we know perfectly well what enables mental functions to be discharged: it is, as a matter of fact, the human brain. Notice at this point the difference between psycho-functionalism and the identity theory. The identity theory wanted to identify various types of mental state with various types of brain state: a given type of mental state was literally one and the same as a given type of brain state. Psycho-functionalism, by contrast, maintains that, at least for human beings, it is the brain that does the job, but it recognises that a mental function can never be identified with the material arrangements that enable its discharge. Thus, psycho-functionalism leaves open the possibility, as we have partially seen, that some other set of arrangements could equally discharge the function. In this way, mentality need not be rigidly tied to human brains. Remember, if mental states are brain states in the manner in which water is H_2O, then wherever and whenever there is water there will be H_2O, and vice versa. Moreover, there cannot be water unless H_2O is present, or H_2O present unless there is water. Functionalism has the advantage over the mind/brain identity theory in that it is willing to allow that mentality may be associated with entirely different physical systems. So, if there are Martians with green slime in their heads, but these Martians can apparently act, talk and think just as we do, then we will have to conclude that it is the slime which supports the mental function. Going further, it cannot be ruled out *a priori* that one day we will be able to build a thinking machine, an android, something like Data in *Star Trek*. Naturally, this may turn out to be impossible. It might be that only living carbon-based organisms of a certain construction can be minded, and that inorganic constructions will never have minds. But that is a matter of fact upon which philosophers have no right to pronounce in advance of patient investigation of the facts.

review activity

Explain the difference between metaphysical and psycho-functionalism.

Computational or Turing machine functionalism

The Turing machine

As we remarked earlier, the functionalist theory of mind was inspired to a large extent by the advent of digital computers. (Analogue computers in the form of neural nets will be left to one side here, for reasons of space.) The whole purpose of computers is to compute functions, that is, to take a certain input and to transform it by a set of discrete steps, each requiring no intelligence or special insight, into an output. The set of instructions by means of which a computer does this is called an *algorithm,* and Alan Turing (1912–54) explicated how algorithms can be computed using the notion of what is called a Turing machine. A Turing machine is not an actual machine, but a notional one, and specifically a way of showing how algorithms may be computed. The machine consists of a tape divided into squares, and a tape-head that can write a symbol, a 1 or 0, on the tape, or overwrite an existing symbol, one symbol per square only. The tape-head can also read the symbols on the tape. The tape can be moved from left to right, and right to left, one square at a time. The machine is also capable of being in two types of internal state, S1 and S2. What the machine does in operation is specified by what is called a machine table, a list of instructions that tells the machine what to do. The general form of the instructions will be that if the machine is in state S1, and reading a particular symbol, X, then it will either write or erase a symbol, stay in S1 or change to S2, and move the tape either left or right. In this way various arithmetical computations can be carried out. The precise details of this process need not concern us at the moment, but the interested reader is recommended to see Tim Crane's excellent *The Mechanical Mind* (Crane 1995) for a more detailed account.

There are functions, however, other than mathematical ones that Turing machines can carry out, and a neat illustration that helps to make the process clearer is provided by that of a cola machine, devised by Ned Block, and which frequently occurs in the literature surrounding functionalism. What we want from the cola machine is a device that will do four things:

1. Deliver a bottle of cola if a £1 coin or two 50p pieces are put in the slot.
2. Do nothing if only one 50p piece is inserted.
3. Deliver a cola if another 50p piece is then inserted.
4. Deliver a cola and a 50p piece if £1.50 is put in the machine by accident.

The representation of the machine table opposite tells the machine what to do in the light of these requirements.

There are four possible ways, (A), (B), (C) and (D), in which the machine can behave depending upon what a customer does.

(A) The machine is in state S1. A customer inserts 50p. Nothing comes out of the machine, but internally it goes into state S2.

(B) The machine is in S2, 50p having been inserted. The customer then inserts another 50p. The machine delivers a cola and then goes back into S1 to await another customer.

The internal state of the machine

Input

Internal state of machine	50p	£1
S1	• Don't deliver a cola • Change to S2 (A)	• Deliver a cola • Stay in S1 (B)
S2	• Deliver a cola • Change to S1 (C)	• Deliver a cola and 50p • Change to S1 (D)

(C) The machine is in state S1. The machine delivers a cola and stays in S1 to await another customer.

(D) The machine is in S2 because 50p has just been inserted. A £1 coin is then inserted by mistake. The machine delivers a cola and 50p, and then goes back into S1 to await another customer.

The functional state of the machine is defined, and exhausted, by the description of inputs, outputs, and changes in internal states. Naturally, the machine needs an actual embodiment if it is to execute its function, but this can be indefinitely various. In other words, the function is multiply realisable, something the type-type mind/brain identity theory could not cater for.

The human mind as a Turing machine table

It should now perhaps be becoming clearer how all this is supposed to relate to a theory of the mind. Put basically, the suggestion is that we conceive of the human mind as a highly complex machine table that takes inputs in the form of sensory and perceptual information, outputs them in the form of behaviour, as the initial characterisation of a metaphysical functionalist theory of the mind demonstrates. Doubtless, in the case of human beings, the machine table that specifies how inputs are to be converted into outputs would be enormously complicated, and would be arranged hierarchically into subsystems. Computational functionalism provides us with an information processing model of the mind which can explain our abilities, and offers us our best chance of explaining why human beings are the beings they are, together with their capacities and abilities. Dualism, by contrast, merely provides us with a blank cheque that cannot be cashed.

review
activity

How did the invention of computers help to inspire functionalism?

Strengths of functionalism

Functionalism undoubtedly has a number of strengths:

1. It avoids behaviourism's error of identifying mental states with actual and possible behaviour, but it also avoids having to posit mysterious non-physical souls. Moreover, because functions, by their very nature, can be multiply realised, functionalism is not committed to the narrow chauvinistic thesis that insists that mental states can exist only as the states of human (and animal) brains.

2. Thinking of mental states in terms of their typical causes and effects fits in well with our common-sense view of the mind.

3. The problem of mind/body causation disappears. We cannot say, for example, that pain thought of as an entity or a state existing independently of pain-behaviour, brings that behaviour about. Pain, or perhaps more accurately, being in pain, is the whole functional state described in terms of inputs, outputs, and relations to other mental states, equally to be defined functionally. Behaviour is not caused by pain; rather, it is a constitutive part of the whole functional state which comprises being in pain.

Nevertheless, despite these advantages, functionalism has to face up to serious weaknesses.

Problems for functionalism

There are essentially two major difficulties functionalism has to face, in line with the objections that can be levelled at other materialist, or at least, materialistically oriented theories. Firstly, can functionalism accommodate Intentionality? Secondly, and relatedly, can it make room for subjectivity, that is, consciousness and the qualia that comprise experience? It would appear that the theory fails on both counts for the following reasons.

The Chinese room argument

The Chinese room argument is due to John Searle, and has become something of a minor classic in the literature on functionalism. It is aimed at showing that a digital computer, merely by virtue of instantiating a programme like the machine table illustrated by the functioning of the cola machine, cannot possess genuine thought and understanding. A genuine thought, or a belief, possesses a meaning, a semantic content, but the operations carried out by the cola machine do not mean anything to it and do not have a content for it. The words I am typing now do mean something to me, because I am conscious of them and are aware of what they mean, but they mean nothing to the word processor on which I am typing them as it lacks consciousness.

Computer programmes lack a semantics

To demonstrate this conclusion, Searle asks us to imagine that he is in a room which he cannot leave. He has never learnt Chinese and has no understanding of it. A card with Chinese characters is posted through a slot on the left-hand side of the room, and Searle's task is to match these characters with others listed in a rule book and post these out through a slot on the other side of the room. So, suppose Searle receives a card with a squiggle-squiggle on it and finds it is paired in the rule book with a squoggle-squoggle. Accordingly he picks up a card with a squoggle-squoggle on it and posts it out of the room. Given that he has no understanding of Chinese, there is no way in which he can find out what the Chinese characters mean. To Chinese speakers outside the room, the characters do have a meaning. Let us suppose that the incoming characters are questions in Chinese, and the outgoing characters answers to these questions, but Searle in the room cannot possibly know this. In other words, computer programmes lack a semantics as far as the computer, or the symbol manipulator in the Chinese room is concerned. The point of Searle's analogy is that Searle-in-the-room is imitating what goes on in the CPU of a computer and this kind of symbol manipulation cannot lead to any kind of understanding of the symbols being manipulated. Notice that in putting forward the Chinese room argument, Searle is not denying that purely material systems could possess Intentionality. He has not foreclosed that possibility merely by denying that semantics is intrinsic to a computer programme, although it is true, from various things he says elsewhere, that Searle is not convinced that attempts to reduce Intentionality to causality, to naturalise it, will be successful.

Rejection of the systems reply

An objection which has been levelled at Searle's thought-experiment is the so-called systems reply. This agrees that Searle-in-the-room would not understand Chinese merely by pairing Chinese characters, but claims instead that the whole system, the room, the rule book, the windows, the programme and so forth understands Chinese. However, as Searle points out, if he has no way of getting from the syntax to the semantics whilst he is in the room, nor does the whole room as it has no resources for endowing symbols with meaning that Searle does not possess.

review
activity

How is the 'Chinese room' argument an attack on functionalism, and how successful is it?

The problem of subjectivity

We have seen that neither the mind/brain identity theory nor analytical behaviourism, in their different ways, could accommodate the fact of the subjectivity and privacy of conscious experience; or, as Thomas Nagel put it, the fact that there is something it is like to be us, just as there is something it is like to be a bat, or any other sentient creature.

Several thought-experiments have been devised to support this conclusion, of which I shall briefly describe just two. The first of these is the 'Chinese mind', argument of Ned Block. The strategy behind the argument is this: think of a system whereby functions are executed, where inputs are transformed into outputs, but where it is grossly implausible to attribute mental or subjective features to the system. Here the requirements of a functional analysis of mental states are formally present and yet consciousness and subjectivity are not catered for, so there must be important aspects of mentality that functionalism leaves out. Block asks us to imagine a human body outwardly like our own but internally very different. Its sense organs are connected to a bank of lights in the head, and further connections are made to motor output neurons via a set of buttons. Inside the head is a group of little men called G-men because they execute operations on a G-square, which is just one square of the complex machine table that describes you. A card is posted on a bulletin board in the head with a G on it, this telling the G-men to get ready. An input light, I1, goes on, and this makes a little man press an output button O1, and change the card on which G is written to an M. G and M correspond to the internal states of the machine which we characterised before as S1 and S2 when considering the example of the cola machine. In other words, the little men implement the machine table that functionally characterises you, just as a group of people might stand inside the cola machine and implement its machine table by taking in money and giving out a cola and, where appropriate, change.

Functionalist analyses cannot accommodate consciousness and subjectivity

Would this group of little men, considered not as individuals but as a group, enjoy subjective awareness? It seems strongly counter-intuitive to suppose that they would. It might be objected that each of the little men enjoys awareness, so subjective experience is present after all. But this misses the point of the example. What is internal to each of the little men is irrelevant; the point is that do the little men, merely by virtue of executing the function of changing G-squares to M-squares, and acting as the causal occupants that discharge the functional role, thereby enjoy subjective experience? If anything, it seems even clearer that they do not. Block drives home the point he is making with an even more extravagant example. We are to suppose that the Chinese government has been converted to functionalism and that the entire population of China has been equipped with two-way radios that connect them with other people and with the artificial body described in the previous example. The bulletin board in the head is replaced by satellites which can be seen from all over China. The entire system of the population of China communicating with each other by radio, together with the satellites, can be seen as comprising a huge artificial external 'brain'. The system could be functionally equivalent to you or me, but it would not thereby have any kind of awareness or subjectivity in the way in which we do. In other words, there is nothing it is like to be the Chinese mind, considered as a whole, which is why, ultimately, it cannot count as a mind at all, and functionalism fails as an account of mentality.

A second argument, due to Frank Jackson, is also aimed at showing that functionalism cannot make room for subjective awareness. We are to imagine the case of Mary, a distinguished scientist who specialises in investigating the brain mechanisms that deal with vision. When a person sees a ripe tomato, for example, Mary can provide a full neurophysiological description of what takes place in that person's visual system. However, Mary has spent her entire life in a black-and-white environment and has never experienced the redness of a tomato. One day, however, she is released from her monochromatic world and experiences the redness of the tomato for the first time. Does Mary learn anything new when she has this experience? If we conclude that she does, then it appears that she comes to know something over and above the purely physical details of colour perception with which she was formerly acquainted, namely the experience of seeing red. In other words, a purely physicalist account of colour perception leaves something important out, namely the subjective experience of colour. Set out formally Jackson's argument runs:

1. Before her release, Mary knows everything physical there is to know about other people.
2. But she does not know all there is to know about other people because she learns something new about them on her release.
3. Therefore, there are truths about other people, and herself, which go beyond the physicalist story.

Physicalism cannot make room for consciousness and qualia

In response, Paul Churchland points out that Jackson's argument equivocates on the word 'know'. What Mary knows before her release is tantamount to Russell's 'knowledge by description', whereas the knowledge she acquires of colour after her release is 'knowledge by acquaintance'. But this does not amount to new knowledge, to knowledge of something different from the physical. Rather, Mary comes to know the same physical fact in a new way, acquiring a new representative or imaginative ability. What are we to make of this counterclaim? Well, we may agree that Mary, on her release, is able to exercise her capacity to see red for the first time, a capacity she was prevented from exercising before. But is the exercise of this capacity all she gains, or does she acquire something more, namely the knowledge of what it is like to see red, an item of phenomenological awareness that was lacking before, and which is, therefore, over and above the purely physicalist story of colour perception, which she knew in detail whilst still in her black and white world? It seems to me that this is the right conclusion to draw, and that, therefore, physicalism does indeed leave something important out. As Searle remarks in a very recent book:

> The point of the argument is not to appeal to ignorance of the bat specialist or Mary. The point of the argument is that there exist real phenomena that are necessarily left out of the scope of their knowledge, as long as their knowledge is only of objective, third-person, physical facts. The real phenomena are colour experiences, and the bat's feelings, respectively; and these are subjective, first-person, conscious phenomena. The problem in Mary's case is not just that she lacks information about some other phenomenon; rather, there is a certain type of experience that she has not yet had. And that experience, a first-person subjective phenomenon, cannot be identical with the third-person, objective neuronal and functional correlates. The point about the epistemology, the information, is just a way of getting at the underlying ontological difference.

(Searle 2004: 97)

activity

For what reasons is functionalism thought to be unable to account for consciousness and subjectivity?

V Property-dualism

important terms

Biological naturalism: this is a term coined by the American philosopher John Searle. Mental phenomena are a class of biological phenomena and do not exist outside the order of nature in a supernatural or non-natural world. Searle speaks of them as caused by, and realised in, the structure of the brain, but at the same time, with seeming paradox, repudiates strict materialism.

Epiphenomenalism: according to epiphenomenalism, the brain produces mental features, but these are powerless to act back upon, and affect the physical world.

Supervenience: a supervenient phenomenon arises from, and depends upon, its subvenient base. There can be no changes in the supervenient phenomenon unless there are changes in the subvenient base, but the converse does not apply, owing to the possibility of the multiple realisability of the supervenient phenomenon by a variety of subvenient bases.

Key topics in this chapter

- Micro- and macro-level behaviour
- The concept of supervenience
- Epiphenomenalism

Introduction

Substance-dualism as we have seen (p. 3) maintains that there are two fundamentally different sorts of things: non-physical minds and material bodies. Persons, the subjects of experience and consciousness in general, are to be identified with non-physical minds or souls. Two kinds of property may also be distinguished: non-physical mental properties, and physical properties. Mental properties attach to non-physical minds or souls, and physical properties to material bodies. Thus, for the substance-dualist, persons have no physical features, whilst their bodies possess no mental features.

Property-dualism

Property-dualism, by contrast, is prepared to accept a dualism of properties of the sort just sketched, but rejects a dualism of substances, maintaining instead that substances comprise a single type, namely material substances. It is willing to allow, however, that material substances may possess both types of property, both non-physical mental features as well as material properties. Unlike the mind/brain identity theory, which maintains that mental properties are nothing over and above physical brain-properties, property-dualism is non-reductive: mental properties are not identical with physical properties, nor reducible to them. In denying a dualism of substances, property-dualism could also be classified as a form of monism. However, because it combines monism with regard to substances, but dualism with regard to properties, property-dualism can also be called non-reductive monism.

review activity

Construct a diagram that brings out the differences between substance-dualism and property-dualism.

Searle's biological naturalism

What are the material entities that property-dualists have in mind when they speak of these things possessing both mental and physical features? A survey of the literature surrounding this area soon reveals that it is the brain to which both mental and physical properties are ascribed. John Searle is typical of a philosopher who takes this view. According to Searle, the solution to the mind/body problem is simple and has been around for years.

Biological naturalism

Here is Searle's proposal, made in his 1984 Reith Lecture series *Minds, Brains, and Science*: brains *cause* minds, and minds themselves are features of the brain, *realised* in its physical processes. Searle calls his position *biological naturalism*, *biological*, for the obvious reason that it invokes the biological processes of living organisms; and *naturalism* because it aims to explain the existence and nature of minds by invoking purely physical processes: 'Mental events and processes are as much part of our biological natural history as digestion, mitosis, meiosis, or enzyme secretion.'

To make clearer what he means by asserting that mental features are realised in the brain, Searle uses an analogy. Consider the behaviour of water at the ordinary macro-level of everyday objects. We know the way it slops around in a container that is agitated, the fact that it takes up the shape of the vessel it is in, and that it can be poured from one container to another. But why does water behave the way it does? The answer, Searle suggests, is to be found at the micro-level, in the fact that water is composed of millions of individual water molecules. The macro-features, Searle claims, are caused by the micro-features, and in just the same way the behaviour of the micro-elements of the brain, the nerve cells and their connections, give rise to consciousness and our mental lives in general.

Levels of description cannot be logically related to each other

The analogy requires some comment. Firstly, it is true that there are two levels of description of the behaviour of water, our ordinary everyday ways of talking about water before we understand the true nature of water, and the scientific description cast in terms of the behaviour of molecules. But we cannot speak of one level of description causing another because descriptions are not non-linguistic events or states of affairs. It is events, which are non-linguistic in character, which enter into causal relations with each other, and as such, events themselves cannot be logically related to each other, although descriptions of events can. Descriptions, as part of language, can be logically related to each other, and these logical relations can be discerned by reason alone, as when we assert that if someone is an only child, then it follows that they have no brothers and sisters. But cause and effect are related contingently as a matter of fact and, as Hume emphasised, can only be discovered on the basis of experience.

Behaviour at the micro-level constitutes behaviour at the macro-level

Secondly, as Hume pointed out, causal relations can only hold between distinct phenomena, but the behaviour of water at the micro-level and its behaviour at the macro-level are not distinct. It would be more accurate to describe the macro-behaviour as *constituted* by the micro-behaviour. The micro-behaviour of the water is just the macro-behaviour viewed very close up. We could view water sloshing in a tank, and then imagine viewing the same water through a microscope. If the magnification could be increased without limit, in theory we could eventually see collections of individual molecules swimming around in the tank. In this sense the liquidity of the water is realised in the behaviour of its micro-elements. It is not *caused* by their behaviour, however, but, as we have seen, *constituted* by it.

review
activity

Explain and critically evaluate the analogy Searle makes between consciousness and the brain, and the micro- and macro-behaviour of water.

If consciousness is constituted in the same manner by the behaviour of the micro-elements of the brain, then it is indeed, in the sense explained, realised in the structure and behaviour of the brain. But now consciousness has been reduced to a physical phenomenon and Searle has effectively embraced a version of the mind/brain identity theory. This interpretation is borne out by other things Searle said at the time. For example, in *Intentionality* (1983), he says that thirst is localised in the hypothalamus, and that visual experiences are right there in the brain where the firing of a vast number of neurons has brought them about.

However, by the time *Searle and His Critics* was published in 1991, we see Searle drawing back from the brink of radical materialism and disavowing it. To appreciate Searle's new stance it will be necessary to say something about the notion of supervenience, and this will be approached through the work of Donald Davidson.

The token-token identity theory and supervenience

Holism of Intentional states as an objection to the type-type identity theory

Davidson rejected the wholesale reduction of the mental to the physical that the type-type identity theory implied, because he thought Intentional states are subject to the constraints of rationality and normativity. This is because such states can be logically related to each other and can sometimes conflict. Intentional states, in other words, are holistic. For example, we may be guilty of holding contradictory beliefs because we do not spot the inconsistency. Once we do discern it, however, we give up one or both beliefs, because we demand rationality of ourselves. Similarly, when we interpret the behaviour of another we do so by trying to ensure the Intentional states we ascribe to that person into a coherent whole. Whilst people can occasionally be irrational, this is only because most of the time there is a background of rationality. Davidson claims that if we try to imagine a totally irrational animal, this is equivalent to imagining an animal without thoughts. The need to attribute a pattern of consistent and coherent Intentional states is what Davidson refers to as '*the constitutive ideal of rationality*', and it has no application with regard to purely physical states such as brain-states, because brain-states do not, and cannot, stand in logical relations to each other. Because the domains of the mental and the physical are different in this key respect, Davidson can see no way in which strict psycho-physical laws connecting events under their mental descriptions with their physical descriptions are possible, so the smooth reduction of the mental to the physical which was possible in the case of the reduction of temperature to mean molecular kinetic energy is ruled out.

review
activity

For what reasons does Davidson reject the type-type mind/brain identity theory?

Davidson therefore adopted a token-token identity theory (see p. 18). Davidson thinks of mental events as concrete, non-repeatable particulars, similar to logical substances. His rejection of substance-dualism meant that there were no non-physical mental events, but only physical ones. But these events not only had the physical properties by reason of which they were physical events, but also irreducibly mental properties as well. Davidson was unwilling to allow that an event might have mental and physical properties that coexisted as a matter of brute fact, but which were merely accidentally related, so to speak, and bore no relation to each other, as an object might be round and red without these features having any connection with each other. He therefore proposed that mental features *supervene* on physical properties. A literal translation of 'supervene', and the noun 'supervenience' that we derive from it, is '*to arrive on top of*'. The idea is that the supervenient phenomenon arrives on top of a basal subvenient phenomenon. Davidson characterises supervenience in the following way:

> *Although the position I describe denies there are psycho-physical laws, it is consistent with the view that mental features are in some sense dependent on, or supervenient, on physical characteristics. Such supervenience might be taken to mean that there cannot be two events alike in all physical respects, but differing in some mental respects, or that an object cannot alter in some mental respect without altering in some physical respect.* (Davidson 1980: 214)

Mind-body supervenience

There has been an enormous proliferation of discussions regarding the nature of supervenience, but Davidson's remark captures an essential aspect of the notion. There would seem to be three elements of supervenience regarding which there is widespread agreement.

1. Irreducibility

Supervenient phenomena are not reducible, analytically, or ontologically, to subvenient phenomena. In the context of the philosophy of mind, the mental is not ontologically reducible to the physical.

2. Co-variation

Supervenient phenomena are determined by, and co-vary with, changes in the underlying subvenient base. In particular, there can be no mental alteration without a corresponding physical alteration.

3. Dependence

Supervenient phenomena emerge from, and are dependent for their existence and character upon, their subvenient base. With regard to mental phenomena, it is the underlying physical phenomena that are primary, and this is why Davidson's position amounts to a weak form of physicalism, non-reductive monism, tantamount to property-dualism.

Consciousness as a non-reducible emergent property

We are now in a position to discern the similarity of Searle's position in his later writings to that of Davidson. Attacking the philosopher David Armstrong who advocates a strong physicalism, Searle writes:

> For Armstrong, solidity, consciousness, and Intentionality are all in the same boat as heat: there is nothing there in addition to the behaviour of the micro-elements. Now that is emphatically not my view and I believe it is mistaken. Supervenience, however strict, does not entail reductionism. From the fact that a property is supervenient on the behaviour of lower-level elements it simply does not follow that there is nothing there except the behaviour of the lower-level elements. In the case, for example, of consciousness, we have a supervenient, but nonetheless non-reducible property. That, indeed, is the difference between, for example, heat and consciousness. Consciousness is a separate and non-reducible property and in that sense it is, I guess, emergent
>
> (Searle 1991: 182)

review activity

What is the token-token mind/brain identity theory, and how does it make use of the concept of supervenience?

The problem of consciousness

The objection has been raised by writers such as Colin McGinn and David Chalmers that it is hard to understand how physical brain events could cause so different a phenomenon as consciousness. As McGinn graphically puts it, how can the *water* of the brain give rise to the *wine* of consciousness – the emergence of consciousness from physical processes has something of the air of a miracle about it. In the same vein, Searle writes:

> We don't have anything like a clear idea of how brain-processes, which are publicly observable, objective phenomena, could cause anything as peculiar as inner, qualitative states of awareness or sentience, states which are in some sense 'private' to the possessor of the state ... how could these private, subjective qualitative phenomena be caused by ordinary physical processes such as electro-chemical neuron firings at the synapses of neurons.
>
> (Searle 1997: 194–5)

Perhaps, however, the puzzlement of these writers is misplaced. Hume pointed out that, prior to experience, anything could be the cause of anything, and there is no reason why causes and effects must resemble each other. A falling pebble, for aught we can tell, might extinguish the sun, and a man, by a simple wish, control the planets in their orbits. In relation to the question of how brain-processes could conceivably give rise to consciousness, Hume writes:

> *If you pretend ... to prove that ... a position of bodies can never cause thought; because, turn it which way you will, 'tis nothing but a position of bodies; you must by the same course of reasoning conclude, that it can never produce motion; since there is no more apparent connection in the one case than the other.* (Hume 1978: 247)

No reason a priori to rule out brain-events as the cause of consciousness

If physical to mental causation seems unaccountable, then equally so must physical to physical causality. We cannot complain that we have some privileged understanding of how one physical event causes another physical event which we lack in the case of how one physical event causes consciousness, because all we ever observe, even in the case of physical to physical causality, is a certain type of event regularly following another type of event and exemplifying a counterfactual dependence upon it. And equally, we all know from our own experience that physical to mental causality occurs, as when being stuck with a pin causes us to feel pain, or the sight of terrible suffering shocks and horrifies us.

review activity

How may Hume's analysis of causation be used to demystify the mind/body relation?

Problems for property-dualism

Property-dualism has the virtue of allowing for the reality of consciousness, instead of trying to reduce it to physical processes in the manner of the strong materialism of the type-type identity theory. It also avoids having to postulate immaterial Cartesian souls, and the problems attendant on this conception of the mind. Nevertheless, there are a number of problems it has to face.

What is the supervenience relation?

What precisely is the nature of the relation between the subvenient base and the supervenient phenomenon? One suggestion is that it is rather like the way in which a picture 'emerges' from a collection of pixels. Changing the pixels will change the nature of the picture and two pictures that have exactly the same arrangement of pixels will resemble each other exactly. Here it would appear that the collection of pixels is constitutive of the picture in a way which parallels the constitution of the macro-features of water by its micro-elements.

How could consciousness be identical with brain-processes?

Applied to consciousness, however, it is difficult to see how the physical behaviour of thousands of nerve cells could literally comprise awareness. How possibly could a myriad of physical events amount to a person's awareness and experience of the world? If there is a theory that could explain this, we currently have no conception of what it would look like. By contrast, it is easy to understand how Tony Blair could be one and the same person as the Prime Minster of Great Britain, and it is only marginally slightly more difficult to appreciate the identity of the morning star with the evening star: one and the same planet appears in different regions of the sky at different times of the day. Even in the cases of water and of heat, it is relatively simple to understand the identity of the phenomenon as it is described at the macro-level with the phenomenon as it is characterised at the micro-level. In the first case, water is composed of H_2O, and in the second, energy in the form of heat put into a gas in a closed container is converted into the increased kinetic energy of the molecules comprising the gas, leading to a rise in pressure. But we would appear to have no theoretical framework at present that can be utilised to explain how micro-physical events could comprise consciousness.

Supervenience of the mental on the physical across all possible worlds

A second suggestion is that there is some relation of non-analytic, metaphysical necessity linking the subvenient to the supervenient. David Papineau is a proponent of this approach. Papineau argues that the only way in which we can secure the ontological inseparability of the mental from the physical is 'to establish supervenience of the mental across all metaphysically possible worlds' (Papineau 2002: 37). This would mean that physical duplicates would necessarily possess identical types of mental state and the possibility of zombies, creatures that are physically just like you and me, down to the smallest detail, but lacking minds, would be ruled out. The inseparability of the mental from the physical could be secured, of course, by *identifying* the mental with the physical. If the mental just is the physical, then the supposition that it could exist separately from the physical would amount to the incoherent demand that a phenomenon should be separable from itself. However, for reasons given earlier the identification of the mental with the physical seems to be an impossibly strong requirement.

Tim Crane, in his recent *Elements of Mind* (2001), takes a diametrically opposite approach to Papineau. Crane thinks zombies are possible, and philosophical accounts of the supervenience relation must make room for them. He therefore suggests that the relation between consciousness and the brain is not a conceptual or metaphysical necessity but a contingent, natural, nomological (lawlike), connection. This means that the mental is distinct from the physical and both halves of the mental/physical relation could in theory exist apart from each other, thus allowing for the possibility of zombies on the one hand, and disembodied subjects of experience on the other.

Searle's account of the supervenience relation has affinities with Crane's because Searle thinks that 'from everything we know about the brain that macro-mental phenomena are all caused by lower-level micro-phenomena,' and given this is so, we need no longer employ the terminology of supervenience: 'once you recognise the existence of bottom-up, micro to macro forms of causation, the notion of supervenience no longer does any work in philosophy. The formal features of the relation are already present in the causal sufficiency of the micro-macro forms of causation' (Searle 1992: 126).

Supervenience as a contingent causal relation

This is sufficient to satisfy Crane's requirement that the supervenience relation is contingent, and not necessary, as causal relations are contingent and not necessary. But, as we have seen, Searle's example of micro- to macro-causation, the motion of molecules at the micro-level giving rise to the behaviour of the water at the macro-level is, flawed because the macro-behaviour just is the micro-behaviour viewed from a different perspective.

The fact that there is no general agreement as to how supervenience is to be understood weakens any theory that employs it, and insofar as property-dualism incorporates the notion, there must be some doubt regarding its adequacy. However, to formulate a variety of property-dualism that dispenses with supervenience suffers from the defect of failing to explain how the mental and physical features of neural events are related to each other.

Does supervenience lead to epiphenomenalism?

A major problem for property-dualism is that it appears to make the mental causally impotent. Mental phenomena are reduced to mere epiphenomena which are caused by physical phenomena but which are powerless to influence them. The direction of causation is one way, from the physical to the mental, bottom-up, but not from the mental to the physical, top down. However, this is a deeply repugnant conclusion. Surely the human mind – our plans, desires, beliefs, and intentions – has brought about changes in the world and made a difference to it. Mental states do not dangle impotently on the coat-tails of physical occurrences, like spectators who are merely along for the ride.

Supervenience and epiphenomenalism

How is supervenience supposed to lead to epiphenomenalism? There are two strands to the argument. Firstly, the idea of the impotency of the mental appears to be deeply implicated in the notion of supervenience. Recall the characterisation of supervenience as no mental change without a corresponding physical change. This means that the mental cannot vary independently of the physical, which is put firmly in the driving seat. But if the mental cannot vary independently of the physical, this means that ultimately it is the physical which is responsible for the existence and character of mental states. Sometimes this is put by saying that new causal powers do not emerge at the level of the mental. How could they, if it is the physical that determines the nature of the mental? If new causal powers did emerge, mental states would become capable of acting independently of the physical states that had given rise to them.

Indeed, it might be argued the supervenience doctrine should be modified, and effectively abandoned, by keeping bottom-up physical to mental causation, but also by allowing the mental to have causal powers of its own, top-down mental to physical causation. This is not only in conformity with our experience – after all it is asking too much to believe that our desires acting in combination with our beliefs have no effect on the world, and that it would be just the way it is without any mental causation – but it is also in line with Hume's insight that, to judge the matter *a priori*, anything could be the cause of anything.

review
activity

How is supervenience supposed to lead to epiphenomenalism?

The completeness of physics doctrine

However, we are not out of the woods yet, owing to the operation of a commonly accepted principle the *completeness of physics* or the *causal closure of the physical world*. This runs as follows:

Every physical event has a physical cause that is *sufficient* to bring it about, given the laws of physics.

If this principle is allowed, we can begin to appreciate how the mental might still be deprived of a causal role, even if supervenience has been jettisoned. Consider the diagram below:

Mental event/physical event

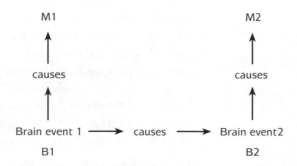

Causal overdetermination

A physical event, B1, causes a mental event, M1, and a physical event, B2, causes a mental event, M2. B1 is causally sufficient to bring about B2, and so there would appear to be no room for M1 to play any part in causing B2, nor does it cause M2, all the work of causation being done by B1 and B2. However, it might be suggested that although B1 is sufficient on its own to bring about B2, why shouldn't M1 also play a causal role in bringing about B1 and in this way avoid relegation to the status of a mere epiphenomenon? However, to suggest that although B1 alone is sufficient to cause B2, M1 also causes it, is to propose that effects can be *overdetermined* by their effects. Overdetermination claims that an effect can have more than one cause and each cause operating on its own, without the other, would have brought about the effect. The firing squad is the usual example used to illustrate the point. A soldier on the left shoots the prisoner, and at the same time a soldier on the right does the same thing. Hence, even though the shot from either soldier acting alone would have sufficed to kill the prisoner, the prisoner is killed by both soldiers.

Philosophers, however, have been very wary of overdetermination for the following reason. Causal statements entail true counterfactual conditions which state that if the event which is the cause had not occurred, then nor would the effect. So if the soldier on the left caused the prisoner's death, then this entails that if the soldier had not fired at the prisoner, the prisoner would not have died. But this is false, because the prisoner would have died anyway owing to the action of the soldier on the right. This pattern of argument may be repeated for the soldier on the right. This leads to the curious result that neither soldier can be said to have caused the prisoner's death, because in both cases the counterfactuals entailed by the causal statements are false. Given that the prisoner did die, we must conclude that either the soldier on the left killed him, or that the soldier on the right did. These alternatives are mutually exclusive: both soldiers cannot have simultaneously killed the prisoner. (Of course, it is possible he was killed by neither soldier, but by some hidden third party, but this is not a possibility we are considering.)

Problems for causal overdetermination

In the face of these difficulties, what should our strategy be? How can mental events be given a causal role in explaining behaviour? One possibility would be to reduce mental events to brain events. There is then no possibility of over-determination of brain-events by separate mental and physical causes. Brain events are simply caused by other brain-events, and we have merely a species of physical-to-physical causation. But for the reasons given earlier, the adoption of an identity theory does not seem plausible. Another possibility would be to reject the counterfactual analysis of causality. Unfortunately the analysis is well entrenched and is used to distinguish those causal generalisations which constitute the laws of nature from mere accidental generalisations that do not comprise lawlike necessities. Thirdly, we might abandon property-dualism altogether and resurrect substance-dualism. But again, for the reasons provided earlier, this is a deeply unattractive option.

Mental events possess their own causal powers

Lastly, we could reject the principle of the causal closure of the physical world. There are some physical occurrences, such as human actions, that are not brought about by purely physical causes. Such actions require physical causes in the form of neurological events together with events involving the muscles, but these are not sufficient to produce the actions alone. It would indeed be strange if they could. That would be like supposing that my taking a marriage vow by uttering the words 'I do', could occur without the contribution of any conscious intention on my part, purely as a result of physical events happening in my brain and body. A better proposal is that we should allow that mental events, although given rise to by brain processes, do acquire their own causal powers, and these mental events, in conjunction with physical events, lead to our actions. This is not overdetermination but simply the recognition of the fact that any event is the product not of a single occurrence but a conjunction of many factors. Merely striking a match, for example, will not cause it to light unless other conditions are fulfilled, such as that the match is not damp and oxygen is present.

review
activity

1. How does the principle of the causal closure of the physical world lead to epiphenomenalism?

2. How might it be possible to avoid epiphenomenalism?

Final comments

There is another difficulty property-dualism has to face which comes from an entirely different direction. Inspired by Wittgenstein, and supported by the work of writers such as Gilbert Ryle, P.F. Strawson, Peter Hacker, and more recently E.J. Lowe, the complaint is that property-dualism locates mental properties in the wrong place. In asserting that mental properties are dependent upon the physical properties of the brain it can appear that the brain itself is being credited with the possession of mental states. Indeed, in claiming that mental properties are features of the brain and realised in it, Searle subscribes to this doctrine. Exactly the same tendency is exhibited by the language of thought hypothesis, which claims that the brain has its own language and that it contains representations of other states of affairs. But it is not brains that feel pain, make promises, intend to go on holiday, think about philosophy, and write books, but flesh-and-blood people, acting and talking in a public world.

Persons, not brains, as the possessors of mental states

Thus Wittgenstein writes: 'Only of a living human being and what resembles (behaves like) a living human being can one say: it has sensations; it sees; is blind; hears; is deaf; is conscious or unconscious' (Wittgenstein 1986: para. 281). In attributing mental states to the brain one is attributing what properly belongs to the whole person to a part of that person, albeit an admittedly vitally important part. The error can be illuminated perhaps by an analogy. My car has the capacity to accelerate quickly, and to reach a top speed of 100 miles an hour because of its engine. But it is not engines that accelerate and speed along the road, but cars. On its own an engine is capable of very little. It is immobile and cannot go anywhere, let alone accelerate up the road. A particularly good analogy, suggested by Peter Hacker in a recent conversation, points out that whilst clocks can only tell the time because of their internal mechanisms, it is senseless to attribute telling the time to the gears and leavers that move the hands. Similarly, brains, on their own, can do nothing. They cannot speak, fall in love, betray people, save lives, express gratitude, or any of the myriad things that people do in everyday life. As parts of people, however, they *ground* the capacities for speech and action which take place in a public world. The brain, to use some useful terminology derived from Aristotle, is the *vehicle* of the capacities for thought, language, and action possessed by people. But it makes no sense to attribute those capacities to the brain itself, much less the exercises of those capacities.

review activity

In the light of the discussion above, explain why it would make no sense to attribute a mental life to a brain in a vat.

VI

The Problem of Other Minds

Key topics in this chapter

- The existence of other minds
- Wittgenstein's approach
- Strawson's approach

Introduction

So far we have been concerned with questions concerning the nature of the mind. We now turn from this metaphysical issue to the epistemology of the mind, and specifically to the question of how the existence of minds other than our own can be known. In Chapter 2, the attempt to identify the mind with the brain was rejected. Equally, in Chapter 3, the reduction of the mind to patterns of actual and potential behaviour was reckoned a failure. A key reason for dismissing both of these theories was that they could not account for the radical privacy of the mental. Dualism at least had the virtue of accommodating the privacy of the mental, albeit at the price of conceiving of the mind as an incorporeal soul, but, in any case, we do not have to be dualists to retain the doctrine of the privacy of the mental as Nagel powerfully argued in his 'What is it Like to be a Bat?' (see p. 21).

The privacy of the mental as the source of the problem of other minds

But if mental states possess the radical privacy sketched earlier, how can we know of the existence of states of mind other than our own? There seems to be no room for the question to arise in our own case. I do not need to observe my behaviour in a mirror to know what I am thinking and feeling. It is not necessary for me to go through any procedure of making observations, and drawing inferences on their bases, to be able to report my state of mind to other people. In other words, I appear to have a direct and privileged access to my own mental states which is lacking with regard to the mental states of others. I cannot directly observe the mental states of others: the most I can witness is their behaviour in the form of what they say and do; and it is on this basis that I reach conclusions about the existence and nature of their states of mind.

The problem of other minds

The problem of knowledge of other minds can therefore be stated thus: mental states are not reducible, either analytically or ontologically, to physical states, such as brain states. Neither do they consist in actual or potential publicly observable behaviour. How, then, may we move from knowledge of brain states, or behaviour, to knowledge of the mental states of others?

The mental states of others cannot be deduced from their behaviour

Only two kinds of inference are available to us, deductive inference and inductive inference. It would appear that deductive inference is excluded from the very start. Talk about mental states is not analytically equivalent to talk about behaviour; therefore, deductive inference is impossible, as statements about mental states are different in meaning from talk about public behaviour. Pains, for example, as Hilary Putnam has remarked, thought of as the causes of pain behaviour, cannot be constructed out of, and reduced to, their effects. To attempt to infer mental states from behaviour would amount, in effect, to putting more into the conclusion than is contained in the premises, hence inference by deduction cannot possibly succeed.

review
activity

Explain why it is impossible to deduce statements describing mental states from statements describing behaviour.

The argument from analogy for the existence of other minds

We are left, therefore, with induction. In induction, the inference is ampliative, and the information contained in the conclusion goes beyond what is contained in the premises. A famous attempt to use induction to explain how knowledge of other minds is possible is supplied by the argument from analogy that was stated by John Stuart Mill in the nineteenth century:

> *I conclude that other human beings have feelings like me, because, first, they have bodies like me, which I know in my own case, to be the antecedent condition of feelings; and because, secondly, they exhibit the acts and other outward signs, which in my own case I know by experience to be caused by feelings.*
>
> (Mill 1889: 243)

The argument from analogy for the existence of other minds

Put more briefly, Mill may be represented as saying, in effect, I know that when I feel sad, I cry. Therefore, when I observe you, a person similar to me, in relevantly similar circumstances, crying, I may infer, inductively, that you feel sad. It is a bit like walking down a street and seeing shadows on the blinds of other people's houses of people apparently sitting down to their dinner. I cannot enter their houses to check directly whether this is so, but when I come to the blinds of my own house and see what looks like the shadow of my wife on the blinds preparing dinner, I can then enter and confirm that this is what is taking place. If the inference can be confirmed directly in my own case, then by analogy it seems reasonable to conclude that what goes for my own case goes for others, although in this case I have no way of directly confirming it.

Problems with the argument from analogy: Wittgenstein's criticisms

However, it might have occurred to you that the inference is rather precarious. How can I generalise from just *one* case, my own, to *all* others, especially when I lack any means of directly confirming the correctness of the inference? This objection, considered alone, seems very powerful.

review activity

What is the argument from analogy for the existence of other minds and what weaknesses does it suffer from?

Wittgenstein's rejection of a logically private language

However, there is another criticism due to Wittgenstein, which, if correct, is even more damning and far-reaching. The essence of Wittgenstein's attack is that the argument from analogy presupposes that I can go from my own case to that of others. The argument from analogy claims, in effect, that I know what I mean by the words I use to describe my own mental states because I have direct acquaintance with those states in the radical privacy of my own mind, and the question then becomes how this knowledge of my own mental states can be extended to the mental states of others. But this is not a possible starting point according to Wittgenstein. I cannot acquire a mental vocabulary purely by acquaintance with the private items that comprise my experience and then try to extend it to the mental states of other people. Rather, mental terms, even in my own case, must acquire their meaning and application in a public social context. In other words, mental terms acquire their meanings from essentially a third-person public perspective, and this perspective makes possible and governs the meaningfulness of first-person ascriptions of mental states, not involving observation or inference, by individual people to themselves. Such, in broad outline, is Wittgenstein's approach to the question of how a mental vocabulary is possible in the first place.

review activity

Why is the argument from analogy not a possible starting point for justifying belief in the existence of other minds according to Wittgenstein?

Wittgenstein's rejection of private ostensive definition and private rule-following

The formulation of the Cartesian doubt presupposes that we inhabit a public world

Let us now look at the details of Wittgenstein's approach. Firstly, we need to recall that Cartesianism assumes that solipsism – the view that, as far as I can tell, only I and my mental states exist (see p. 8) – is a possible state of affairs. There may be no world outside my mind. But, so the Cartesian doubt maintains, I can still use language to think and to formulate the sceptical question 'Surely it is possible that I am the only person that exists and there is nothing beyond the world of my own private experiences?' If this is a genuine possibility, then my words, including the words I employ to ascribe various states of mind to myself, could acquire their meanings and use in one way only, namely by referring to the radically private states of my own mind. But it is this assumption that Wittgenstein rejects: words can only acquire their meanings in a public social context. If he is right, this pulls Cartesianism inside out: the very possibility of formulating the sceptical doubt about the existence of an external world and the mental states of others presupposes there must be such a world for the doubt to be formulated in the first place. This means, in turn, that mental terms must have an application in a public realm whether to oneself or others, and the implication is clear, namely that as we may meaningfully ascribe mental states to others as well as ourselves, knowledge of other minds is possible. In summary, Cartesianism, and the private internalist theory of meaning it entails, is not a possible position from where to begin, and the falsity of this perspective is presupposed by its formulation from the very outset.

How does Wittgenstein arrive at his conclusions? Firstly, he rejects the notion of a private ostensive definition in which a person supposedly points a mental finger, as it were, at his own private mental states, in order to name them and thus endow the names with meaning. Secondly, he then attempts to show that language is a rule-governed activity that is not possible if its vocabulary is supposed to refer to logically private states with which only the individual person may be acquainted.

To explain why private ostensive definition is not possible Wittgenstein asks us to imagine a person who holds up a pencil and says 'This is tove,' chosen because it is not an English word. Someone asks 'What do you mean? Do you mean the *shape*, or the *colour,* or that *type* of thing, or just *that one?*' In order to do this, the person must already have the vocabulary of shape, colour, type, and so forth. But how is this acquired? It is tempting to think that the private linguist concentrates his or her attention on the shape rather than, say, the colour, and by a mysterious act of the mind somehow means the shape. But Wittgenstein again presses the question: how is *that* done? The point he is leading up to is that it is only through multifarious activities which take place in a public setting that ostensive definition is possible. Thus someone may come to acquire the concept of the colour blue in the following manner:

> *Suppose someone points to a vase and says 'Look at that marvellous blue – the shape isn't the point.' – Or: 'Look at the marvellous shape – the colour doesn't matter.' Without doubt you will do something different when you act upon these two invitations. But do you always do the same thing when you direct your attention to the colour? Imagine various different cases. To indicate a few:*

> *'Is this blue the same as the blue over there? Do you see any difference?' – You are mixing paint and you say 'It's hard to get the blue of this sky.'*
> *'It's turning fine, you can already see the blue sky again.'*
> *'Look what different effects these two blues have.'*
> *'Do you see the blue book over there? Bring it here.'*

'This blue signal-light means...'
'What's this blue called? Is it "indigo"?   (Wittgenstein 1986: para. 33)

Rejection of private
ostensive definition

By contrast, none of these activities would be available to the Cartesian self locked in its private world in solitary confinement. The point Wittgenstein is making is that the acquisition of concepts and language requires a background of customs and activities. To appreciate the point fully, suppose someone has never heard of board games before, much less played one. One day this person overhears two people talking about a chess king, and asks what is meant. Let us assume he manages to understand, in the first instance, that the words 'chess king', refer to a piece of carved ivory that one of the two people is holding. It is clear that he still will have no inkling of what a chess king is. The ground for his understanding has not yet been paved and would involve knowing such things as what board games are, how and why they are played, the nature of board games, the kind of moves chess pieces can make, how check-mate is achieved, and what this means, and so forth. The person in question would also have had to try playing chess, to have a few try-outs and dry runs at the game before the concept of a chess king had been fully grasped. But again, locked into a private world, none of these resources will be available. The mere acquaintance with an object that falls under a concept cannot guarantee possession of the concept. Thus Wittgenstein aptly remarks: 'Do not believe you have the concept of colour within you because you look at a coloured object – however you look. (Any more than you possess the concept of a negative number by having debts.)' (Wittgenstein 1986: para. 33).

review
activity

What is private ostensive definition, and what problems with it does Wittgenstein identify?

The impossibility of
private rule-following

Wittgenstein's second attack on the notion of a language, a logically private language whose words supposedly acquire their meanings by reference to a realm of private objects with which only the user of the language can, in principle, be acquainted, focuses on the impossibility of private rule-following. Suppose, for the sake of argument, a person could, contrary to Wittgenstein's first argument, give himself a private ostensive definition of a word. He has, say, had a particular sensation, and baptised it 'S'. In this way he supposedly begins to create a dictionary in the privacy of his own imagination. The next time the person feels the sensation he can consult this dictionary and mentally look up what he called it when he originally gave himself the private ostensive definition. Hence he is enabled to judge that he is feeling 'S' again. But for this to work the person must remember correctly what 'S' stands for, otherwise 'S' will be used wrongly. But how is the person to know whether he is using 'S' correctly and genuinely following a rule for its application, and when he is using 'S' incorrectly and not following the rule? The problem is that whatever is going to seem to me to be right will be right, but that means we cannot speak about right here. It must be possible to distinguish between genuinely following a rule for the use of a word, and only thinking, mistakenly, that a rule is being followed. But this presupposes an independent check is possible, something that cannot be catered for in the world of the private linguist. It is, Wittgenstein remarks, as if someone should buy several copies of the same morning paper in order to confirm the correctness of a story in one of them.

activity

What is a logically private language and why is it impossible according to Wittgenstein?

Wittgenstein's positive account of how mental terms acquire a meaning and a use

So, if mental terms cannot acquire their meanings by naming logically private states of mind, what is Wittgenstein's positive account? The answer is that they acquire their meanings in a third-person public social context. Wittgenstein offers two accounts here. According to the first, behaviour serves as the criterion against which the use of mental terms is to be assessed for its correctness or incorrectness. So when ascribing mental states to others, the ascriptions will have to fit in with the rest of their observable behaviour in the right sort of way. And even in the case of a person ascribing mental states to herself without observation or inference, criterionless self-ascription as it is called, the words she uses to characterise her state of mind must cohere with the rest of her non-linguistic behaviour. So, for example, if someone is tickled and giggles and laughs and then says she is in pain, she can be corrected for using an inappropriate term. Even in my own case, when I report my state of mind without recourse to observation of my behaviour, criterionless self-ascription as it is known, my words must fit in with the rest of my behaviour if they are to be used correctly.

The replacement of natural pain behaviour by the use of mental terms

Mental terms come to replace natural pain behaviour

Wittgenstein's other suggestion is that the use of mental terms, 'pain', for example, gradually come to replace natural expressions of mental states. A moan or the exclamation 'Ouch!' do not describe the pain that gives rise to it. Rather, it is a natural manifestation or *expression of the pain*, and this gradually comes to be replaced with sentences such as 'I am in pain', 'It's hurting a lot', 'I'm in agony', and so forth.

An immediate problem with this suggestion is that the statements expressed by the use of sentences have different properties from natural expressions of pain. Statements have truth-values, can stand in logical relations to each other, can be negated, and can serve as the components of conditional statements, none of which is possible for natural expressions of mental states. A second problem is that interpreting the claim that moans and groans are unlearned manifestations of pain, it is natural to interpret this as claiming that a non-behavioural inner state causes an outward behavioural one. The situation is rather like one in which a disease, measles say, gives rise to spots. But there is a significant disanalogy. It is possible to check up empirically that the measles virus is present in the body, but it is not possible to check up in this manner that the appropriate type of mental state is causing the behaviour in question. However it appears that the possibility cannot be ruled out that there is no underlying mental cause of the behaviour and that what we take to be a normal minded person like ourselves is in fact a zombie devoid of any mental life.

review
activity

What positive account does Wittgenstein offer of how talk about the mental states of others, and oneself, is possible?

The criterial approach to the problem of other minds

Behaviour as the criterion that governs the applicability of mental terms

As we have seen, mental terms are only supposed to be possible because they are used in accordance with a rule, and following a rule is only possible where it can be determined whether or not the rule is being adhered to. There thus has to be a test for the correctness or incorrectness for the use of the mental term, and this is supplied by public behaviour. But it may be wondered if this really amounts to the reassertion of analytical behaviourism, that the meaning of mental terms consists entirely in descriptions of actual and possible behaviour. Wittgenstein himself resisted this interpretation when he rejected the charge that he was really a 'behaviourist in disguise', and some Wittgensteinians appear to want to maintain the position that whilst a behavioural criterion constitutes an essential part of the meaning of a mental term, its meaning is not totally exhausted by the behavioural description. Whilst there is not a deductive entailment between the behavioural criterion and the ascription of a mental state, the behavioural criterion does not indicate a merely contingent connection between it and the ascription of the mental state in the manner presupposed by the argument from induction. Instead, it is suggested that the criterion is non-inductive evidence for the presence of the mental state in question, but this does not amount to a deductive entailment between behaviour and mental states. It appears then, that we are being offered a middle way between a mere contingent link between behaviour and mental states, on the one hand, and a deductive entailment, on the other. Thus, Peter Hacker writes: 'the criteria for being in pain do not entail that the person is in pain. They are logically good evidence, which is, in certain circumstances, defeasible [can be defeated]. But if not defeated, the criteria confer certainty' (Hacker 1997: 38). In this way, it is submitted, the proponent of the criterial approach wants to borrow from the best features of deduction and induction, but to discard what is likely to obstruct an account of how knowledge of other minds is possible.

Problems with the criterial approach

Does the criterial approach lead straight to behaviourism?

There are, however, some residual worries regarding the criterial approach. Firstly, is a middle way between deduction and induction genuinely possible? Do not these modes of inference exhaustively divide up the field between them, leaving no room for another mode of inference to be fitted in? Secondly, as Galen Strawson has claimed, there is the worry that once an appeal to criteria is allowed, the account can rapidly slide down into anti-realism, and thus into a behaviourist account of the meaning of mental terms. Anti-realism claims that the meaning of a statement is constituted by its assertibility conditions, those conditions which, if fulfilled, would license the application of the statement to the circumstances in question. In the present case, the assertibility conditions whose fulfilment legitimates the ascription of mental states to others from a third-person perspective, or even to oneself from a first-person perspective, comprise outward public behaviour. But now mental states appear to have been reduced to actual and possible behaviour. A three-step movement is involved according to Strawson. The '*epistemic*' level, how it can be *told* that a person is in pain, determines the '*semantic*' level, what it *means* to assert that the person is in pain, which in turn determines the '*ontological*' level, what it *is* to be in pain, what the *nature* of pain ultimately is. From the surrounding discussion it should be apparent that Wittgenstein's positive account of how mental terms acquire their meanings, and precisely what constitutes those meanings, is controversial. The discussion cannot be continued further here, however, and the reader is encouraged to make his or her own foray into the area.

review

activity

What is the criterial approach to the problem of other minds, and what problems does it encounter?

Strawson's approach to the other minds problem

Behaviour constitutes the criterion for the ascription of mental states, from both a third-person and first-person perspective

The last treatment of the other minds problem that we shall examine is due to P.F. Strawson, and its debt to Wittgenstein will be obvious. In *Individuals*, Strawson states the central plank of his thesis: 'It is a necessary condition of one's ascribing states of consciousness, experiences, to oneself, in the way that one does, that one should also ascribe them, or be prepared to ascribe them, to others who are not oneself' (Strawson 1959: 99). To put this another way, self-ascription is possible if, and only if, other-ascription is possible. This would seem to settle the issue of the existence of other minds at one go. I cannot start purely from my own case as the argument from analogy presupposed, that is, by attributing mental states to myself and then by wondering whether, and how, they could be ascribed to others. It is only if they are ascribable to others that I can ascribe them to myself. Hence there must be other minds. Now I can only ascribe mental states to others if I can identify others, and distinguish one subject of experience apart from another. But this is only possible if other persons are thought of as embodied, as having physical characteristics, because only then will there be possible experience situations whose fulfilment will license the application of the concept of another subject of experience. If persons are thought of as non-physical souls, *pace* Descartes, then it will be impossible to apply criteria of individuation and identity over time to them as we saw on pp. 13–15. In other words, to use Strawson's terminology, persons must have M-predicates, material object predicates, as well as P-predicates, predicates that attribute, or imply, the ascription of conscious states. But there must also be some grounds available upon which P-predicates are justifiably ascribable, even in my own case, although these are not explicitly invoked when I ascribe mental states to myself. It is clear what these grounds must consist in as we cannot directly observe the mental states of others. They must consist in outward actual and possible public behaviour. In line with Wittgenstein's stance, this is what Strawson calls a logically adequate criterion, and in this way we arrive at the position discerned earlier, namely that third-person ascriptions make possible first-person criterionless ascriptions.

Problems for Strawson's account

How successful is Strawson's account? Firstly, as we witnessed earlier, there is the danger that we will finish up with a slide down into analytical behaviourism: talk about mental states becomes equivalent to talk about actual and possible behaviour. Secondly, and perhaps more radically, it has been objected that Strawson's account begs the question, that is, it assumes in advance, that mental states may be attributed to what are ostensibly other people. But that, of course, is the very point at issue.

A very clear statement of the objection was provided by A.J. Ayer in *The Concept of a Person* (1963). Ayer imagines a fantasy of a human being brought up from his earliest years by automata, zombies in effect, who resemble and behave like human beings. A voice over a loudspeaker stresses the similarities between the automata and the child, and instructs the child in the use of words that describe his own mental states. Eventually he learns how to apply the same words to the automata on the basis of regularities in their behaviour. In other words, the child satisfies Strawson's criterion that he must be able, and willing, to apply mental terms to others as well as to himself. Nevertheless, all the attributions of mental states he makes to the automata are false, as they are merely mindless machines. As Ayer himself puts it:

> *The example shows not only that one might be able to ascribe experiences to oneself whilst being invariably mistaken in ascribing them to others, but also that the criteria which are taken to be logically adequate for ascribing experiences to others may determine no more than that some locution is correct, that in such and such conditions this is the proper thing to say; it does not follow what is said is true.*
> (Ayer 1963: 108)

If Ayer is correct, then Strawson does not provide a satisfactory solution to the problem of other minds, and the additional difficulties with Wittgenstein's approach remain. The problem of other minds has the look of one of the central and perennial problems in the philosophy of mind, one that will run and run, and we commend it to you.

review activity

How does P.F. Strawson attempt to solve the problem of other minds, and what problems does his account encounter?

VII Personal Identity

Key topics in this chapter

- Numerical and qualitative identities
- The split-brain thought-experiment
- The Lockean approach to personal identity
- Personal identity and physical continuity

Introduction

Before discussing the issue of personal identity it is important to distinguish between qualitative and numerical identity. Without a firm grasp of this distinction it is fatally easy to become muddled where questions of identity are concerned.

The distinction between numerical and qualitative identity

A good example of qualitative identity is provided by Tweedledum and Tweedledee, who are identical twins. Because they are exactly similar in their features or qualities, philosophers describe them as being *qualitatively* identical, and clearly there are two people here, not one. By contrast, consider the case of Jekyll and Hyde mentioned earlier (see p. 9). Hyde looks quite different from Jekyll, but nevertheless is one and same man. In other words, Hyde is *numerically* identical with Jekyll, although *qualitatively* he looks very different. In discussing personal identity our concern is with numerical, not qualitative identity, hence the question concerning the nature of personal identity may be posed as follows: what makes you now one and the same person as you were when you were a baby a number of years ago?

review activity

Explain the difference between numerical and qualitative identity using your own examples.

Obviously you have altered a lot qualitatively over the intervening period, but the person you are now is numerically identical with the baby you used to be. But in what does this numerical identity consist? What is it about you that makes you one and the same now as you were then? Notice that this question is not merely asking how I might *tell* that a person at a later time is one and the same as a person at an earlier time. Normally, I recognise that the person now in front of me is one and the same as the person I taught last week by his physical appearance, and perhaps to some extent even by the clothes he usually wears, or the style and colour of his hair, but clearly these cannot be essential to the person's numerical identity over time. A person could change

69

his clothes, or alter his hairstyle, but he would remain one and the same person throughout. He might even undergo extensive plastic surgery, even down to altering his fingerprints, but this would not affect his identity.

What constitutes a person's identity over time?

What then, by contrast, is essential to a person's numerical identity over time? This is a *metaphysical* question, not merely the *epistemological* one of how we can tell that we are re-encountering one and the same person. In answering it we will need to have recourse to the concept of logically necessary and sufficient conditions.

The requirement is that we should be able to complete the formula:
A person P at time t1 is numerically identical with a person P at an earlier time t0 if, and only if . . .

It should be apparent that this is a *reductive* account of personal identity which aims to spell out what constitutes personal identity in terms which do not, to avoid circularity, mention or imply personal identity itself. However, it is possible that the concept cannot be reduced. It might turn out to be logically primitive and not construable in other terms. This is a topic to which we shall return towards the end of this chapter. We shall examine four theories of personal identity in the next few sections. These maintain respectively that personal identity consists in:

1. numerical identity of the soul
2. numerical identity of the body
3. numerical identity of the brain
4. psychological continuity.

Numerical identity of the soul

Numerical identity of the body is neither necessary nor sufficient for personal identity

As we saw in Chapter I, Cartesian dualism maintains that the person is identical with the incorporeal soul, not the material body. It follows then, on this view, that the identity of the body plays no role in determining the identity of the person. The fact that people currently have one and the same body as they did when they were a baby is irrelevant to their identity. The soul could, in theory, leave the body it currently inhabits and take up residence in a new one. In other words, a person could have a body swap. Numerical identity of the body is therefore not logically *necessary* for a person's identity to be preserved. Just as you can change your clothes without your identity thereby being disturbed, so you could change your body. Neither is numerical identity of the body logically *sufficient* to guarantee the identity of the person, as after the original occupant of the body has departed, a new soul, and there-fore a different person, might enter in. There are two possibilities: same person, different body; and different person, same body. The notion of transferring from one body to another after physical death, the transmigration of souls or metempsychosis as the Greeks called it, or reincarnation as it is more commonly known, is a central feature of several religions, Hinduism and Buddhism being among them.

The impossibility of identifying and re-identifying souls

However, as we have already seen in Chapter I, there are major difficulties in conceiving of a person as a soul. Firstly, it is doubtful whether there are cogent reasons for believing that souls exist. Secondly, and even more importantly, because criteria of individuation and identity for souls are necessarily not available, the notion is of dubious coherence. If there is nothing in our experience that can enable us to tell souls apart from each other at a given moment, or to re-identify them over time, then it appears we are forced to conclude ultimately the notion of the soul is devoid of meaning.

It has to be said, however, that not all philosophers would agree with this conclusion. For example, Richard Swinburne makes the point that how we *tell* one soul apart from another, and what *constitutes* one soul's being numerically different from another soul, do not necessarily amount to the same thing. To say that the notion of the soul is meaningless unless we have some means, in theory, of telling that one soul is numerically different from another, smacks too much of verificationism, the doctrine that unless statements can in principle be empirically verified, those statements are devoid of significance. We can make sense of states of affairs being true, Swinburne points out, of which we can have no evidence – and therefore no way of telling – that they are true. To suppose otherwise is to maintain that the constitution of reality, and the way we know it, must always coincide. This seems unpardonably arrogant as it disallows that how things are, and how we understand them to be, can diverge. Perhaps then, souls may be allowed after all, contrary to their rejection by Kant and Hume, but this difficult issue will be left to readers to decide for themselves.

review activity

What reasons are there for not providing an account of personal identity in terms of numerical sameness of soul?

Numerical identity of the body

Continuity of the body of one and the same organism as a criterion of personal identity

Given the philosophical difficulties into which dualism plunges us, let us seek an alternative account of personal identity. One such alternative is supplied by physical continuity – a person P1 at time t1 is numerically identical with a person P0 at an earlier time t0 if, and only if, P1 is physically continuous with P0. The simplest version of this theory maintains that a present person is numerically identical with a past person if, and only if, they have one and the same body now that they had in the past. The body must meet the same criterion for identity over time as other physical objects, namely spatio-temporal continuity. It must trace a continuous track through space and time, a track that will necessarily be unique as no two physical objects can occupy the same space at the same time, or the same spaces at successive times. This requirement is not upset by the fact that a person's body is continuously changing, shedding molecules of skin but building up new tissue at the same time. Even though all the molecules in our body supposedly change over a period of years, so that qualitatively our adult body is very different from our childhood one, it is nevertheless still numerically the same body, because the old matter is lost very slowly, and the new matter absorbed, is gradually integrated with the existing structure which is thereby continuously preserved.

If, however, the organisational and functional structure of the body is dissolved and physical continuity is lost, then so is the identity of the person. In the past this posed a stumbling block for attempts to provide for life after death by appealing to resurrection by God. Religious believers in the Anglican tradition accepted that dualism was false, and that human beings were genuine psycho-physical unities, single entities possessing both mental and physical properties. At death people totally cease to exist, but God, by an act of sheer divine omnipotence, ensures their ultimate survival by resurrecting them. There is some uncertainty as to precisely how God is to achieve this, but let us suppose for the moment that he literally gathers up all the appropriate molecules that once helped to constitute the deceased's body and out of them creates a functioning structure. The resultant person resembles the person who died, exhibits the same personality traits, and above all, makes memory claims that exactly match what the dead person is known to have experienced and done. Should we conclude that the original person has been resurrected? Tempting though this conclusion is, it must be resisted. The original person ceased to exist when he or she died and his or her body underwent dissolution. One thing cannot have two beginnings; therefore the apparently resurrected person would have to be regarded instead as merely a brilliant replica. But this is of no comfort to those who hanker for personal survival. As Anthony Flew has graphically remarked, the news that a replica of me will appear after my death is of about as much interest as the news that my appendix will be preserved eternally in a bottle. An alternative account of how resurrection might be possible, anchored in functionalism, will be given later in this chapter.

review activity

What problem does the physical continuity of the body pose for attempts to account for personal survival of death by resurrection by God?

Numerical identity of the brain

Even if physical continuity should turn out to be essential for personal identity, it cannot consist in the numerical identity of a person's body because of the possibility of a brain transplant. This was envisaged by Sidney Shoemaker. Two people, Brown and Robinson, have operations that involve removing their brains. Unfortunately, Brown's brain is put back by mistake into Robinson's body, and Robinson's brain is put into Brown's body, this person subsequently dying, leaving Robinson's body with Brown's brain. Following Shoemaker, let us call this person Brownson.

Let us suppose that when Brownson wakes up and looks in the mirror he receives a shock. Instead of seeing Brown's face looking back at him, as he is expecting, he sees Robinson's face. Moreover, Brownson not only has a personality similar to Brown, and not Robinson, but his memory-claims regarding his past actions and experiences fit Brown's and not Robinson's life. In such a case, it would be difficult to avoid the conclusion that Brownson was indeed Brown and not Robinson. It might be felt perhaps that this way of arguing is merely assuming the conclusion in advance. However, the claim is powerfully supported by materialist theories of mind. If the mind just is the brain, or if a person's mental life is distinct from brain-activity but dependent for its existence upon it, as property-dualists maintain, then the conclusion that Brownson is Brown seems well-nigh irresistible. As Brown continues to exist as Brownson, with a numerically different body from the one he first possessed, the continuity of the body theory of personal identity cannot be correct. Clearly, however, it does not rule out the possibility that personal identity requires the continuity of some crucial part of a person's body, namely the brain. Yet, as we shall see, in time even that conclusion was rejected by some philosophers.

review
activity

What reason is there for thinking that the numerical identity of the body cannot ultimately serve as a criterion of personal identity?

The fantasy of brain transplants led to further thought-experiments inspired by the work of David Wiggins and Derek Parfit (1942–). Suppose Allison's brain was divided in two by severing the central commissure that holds the two hemispheres of the brain together and allows them to communicate with each other, the left hemisphere being placed in one body, and the right in another, the brains of these two other people having first been removed from their skulls. When the person who has received the left hemisphere, Lallison, as we shall call her, wakes up, she exhibits similar personality traits to Allison and makes memory-claims that fit Allison's life in close detail. However, precisely the same occurs when the person who received the right hemisphere, Rallison, wakes up. Which of these two new people, Lallison or Rallison, is identical with Allison? There is no reason for privileging one over the other. Could it be, therefore, that both Lallison and Rallison are numerically identical with Allison? Plainly not, as the following argument demonstrates:

(Let '−' mean 'is numerically identical with'.)
1. Allison = Lallison
2. Allison = Rallison
3. Therefore, Lallison = Rallison

This is a contradictory result. One numerically different individual uniquely occupying a particular space is asserted to be one and the same as another numerically different individual uniquely occupying another particular space. From the moment the fission occurs, the two resulting individuals can begin to move around the world, carving out their own unique tracks through time and space. The contradiction arises because identity is a transitive relation. If A is numerically identical with B, and B with C, then logically A is numerically identical with C.

What then has happened to Allison as she cannot be one and the same as both Lallison and Rallison, nor are there any grounds for identifying her with just one of these individuals? Should we conclude that Allison has ceased to exist? The problem, however, is that there seems to be a sense in which Allison is still around, for both Lallison and Rallison make memory claims that fit Allison's life. If we suppose, moreover, that each has been kept in the dark about the existence of the other, then, apart from having acquired a new body, it will seem to them that there is no interruption in their mental life. Each will take it that they have had a straightforward brain transplant involving no division of the brain. As Parfit remarks, in a case like this how can a double success amount to a failure?

Fission as a challenge to the view that personal identity is all-or-nothing

The difficulty was subsequently eased by abandoning the assumption that personal survival presupposes identity. In the past when the issue of personal survival was debated in the context of the resurrection of the body, the question was whether the post-mortem persons would or would not be numerically identical with the pre-mortem persons. As numerical identity is all-or-nothing, and as death destroyed the continuity of the body, it was concluded that the resurrectees could not be identical with the persons who had died, but were merely replicas. In the present case it was argued that survival could be a matter of degree. Allison's brain is not destroyed: each hemisphere continues to exist, albeit separately from the other. Assuming each hemisphere individually contains enough of Allison's personality traits and personal memories, then the continuation of the hemispheres means the survival of Allison, albeit as two numerically different people. The situation can be compared to a tulip bulb that divides. If I pulp the bulb, then it ceases to exist. But if the bulb naturally divides, then it survives as both halves, even though neither half could be said to be numerically identical with the original bulb. Naturally, a tulip bulb, unlike Allison, does not have a mental life, but if, as we have supposed, the mind depends for its existence upon what takes place in the brain, then the fission of the brain ensures both physical and psychological continuity, and hence Allison's survival.

review activity

Describe the split-brain thought-experiment and explain how it is supposed to show that personal survival without identity is possible.

Psychological continuity

Physical continuity of the brain was considered to be important only insofar as it ensured the psychological continuity of the person's mental life. We can see this if we suppose to the contrary that every time someone had a brain transplant, or their brain was divided, this had the effect of completely scrambling their mental life, changing their personality, and, most importantly, wiping out all memories. It is strongly arguable that a person who suffered philosophical amnesia of this extreme sort would have ceased to exist. If, later, after the memory wipe, a core of new memories was laid down, these would effectively constitute a numerically different person from the original who suffered the trauma. The emphasis on psychological continuity as crucial for personal survival, and not merely the physical continuity of the brain, or some part of it, was anticipated by John Locke, and has affinities with functionalism. In the twentieth century, in the hands of Derek Parfit, it has led to the development of a psychological continuity theory of personal identity that builds on the insights of Locke. Locke's view is best given in his own words:

> For, it being the same consciousness that makes a man be himself to himself, personal identity depends on that only, whether it be annexed only to one individual substance, or can be continued in a succession of several substances. For as far as any intelligent being can repeat the idea of any past action with the same consciousness it had of it at first, and with the same consciousness it has of any present action, so far it is the same personal self. For it is by the consciousness it has of its present actions that it is self to itself now, and so will be the same self as far as the same consciousness can extend to actions past or to come, and would be by distance of time no more two persons than a man be two men by wearing other clothes today than he did yesterday – with a long or short sleep in between: the same consciousness uniting those distant actions into the same person, whatever substances contributed to their production.
>
> (Locke 1961: chap. XXVIII, section 10)

The Lockean approach: the importance of psychological continuity

What Locke is essentially saying is that personal identity does not consist in the persistence of a thing, a substance, whether it be a material substance like the body or brain, or an immaterial substance like a Cartesian soul. Instead, it comprises continuity and connectedness between a series of experiences. The substances in which these experiences are instantiated are irrelevant to personal identity. What matters is that as long as there is a connected series of experiences there is the identity of a person comprised of those experiences, even if this chain is transferred from one substance to another, whether it is material or immaterial. It should be apparent that this conception of mental states as instantiated in substances but not reducible to them is reminiscent of functionalism.

There is, however, a difficulty with what Locke is claiming. Locke is saying that a present person is one and the same as a past person if, and only if, the present person can remember, from a first-person perspective, what the past person underwent and did. But this is surely too strong a condition. Even if I totally forget what I did last week, this does not mean that I cannot be one and the same as the person who performed that action. Memory cannot therefore be a necessary condition of personal identity. Thomas Reid (1710–96) developed the objection further with his example of a brave ensign. When the ensign was a boy he stole some apples and was flogged as a consequence. Later, when he was a soldier he captured a standard in battle, and later still he became a famous general. Now suppose the following to be true:

1. The ensign can remember stealing the apples, so he is one and the same as the schoolboy.
2. The general can remember taking the standard, so he is one and the same as ensign.
3. But the general cannot remember stealing the apples, so he is not one and the same as the schoolboy.

Reid's objection to Locke's account

However, if the general is the ensign, by (2), and the ensign is the schoolboy by (1), then, by the transitivity of identity, the general is the schoolboy. (If x = y, and y = z, then x = z.) But according to (3), the general is not one and the same as the schoolboy. Hence we get the contradiction that the general both is, and is not, numerically identical with the schoolboy. As making memory a necessary condition of personal identity has led to this result, it would seem that this requirement has to be rejected.

review activity

In your own words, explain Reid's objection to Locke's account of personal identity in terms of memory.

Parfit's response to Reid's objection

Overlapping memory chains

Derek Parfit has proposed a way to get round Reid's objection. A present person, P1, can be one and the same as a past person, P0, providing there is enough of what he calls continuity and connectedness – C&C – between memories as well other psychological features. If P1 can remember, from a first-person perspective, from the 'inside', what P0 experienced, then P1 is numerically identical with P0. In a case like this there is a direct connection between the memory and the experience remembered. But even where direct connections are lacking, there can still be identity providing there are overlapping memory-chains. The idea is that today, Sunday, I can remember what I did on Saturday, but not what I did on Friday. But never mind, on Saturday, I can remember what I did on Friday, but not on Thursday. On Friday, however, I can remember what I did on Thursday, but not Wednesday, and so on and so forth backwards. The overlapping memory-chains supply continuity, even if there is no direct connection between a memory and the experience remembered in every case. As long as there is enough connectedness of the sort described, then P1 can be said to be one and the same as P0. But how much connectedness is enough? Parfit draws a distinction between strong and weak connectedness, because connectedness is a matter of degree, and maintains that strong connectedness must obtain for the identity of the person to be preserved. He defines strong connectedness as follows: P1 is numerically identical with P0 if the number of connections that hold on any day is as at least half the number of connections that hold over every day in the lives of every actual person. Parfit suggests the following definition of personal identity:

(1) There is psychological continuity if, and only if, there are overlapping chains of strong connectedness. P1 today is one and the same as P0 at some past time if and only if (2) P1 is psychologically continuous with P0, (3) this continuity has the right kind of cause, and (4) it has not taken a branching form. Personal identity over time consists in conditions (2) to (4) obtaining.

Parfit's analysis of personal identity as psychological continuity

Conditions (3) and (4) need some explanatory comment, and we will deal with (4) first. (4) deals with a possibility mentioned earlier, namely that if the hemispheres of a person's brain were separated and placed in separate bodies, the resulting persons could remember, from the inside, what the original person experienced: Rallison and Lallison could remember what Allison did and underwent from a first-person, not merely a third-person spectator's viewpoint. Thus, both Rallison and Lallison are psychologically continuous with Allison, and in this sense Allison survives as both, but they cannot both be numerically identical with Allison on pain of contradiction as we saw earlier. That is why Parfit's analysis, as he rightly sees, has to rule out branching cases of the sort described if his account is to amount to an acceptable definition of personal identity. Condition (3) is included to rule out the possibility of what are known as wayward causal chains. A memory, if it is to be a genuine memory, not only has to be caused by the experience remembered, but in the right way. Essentially the memory-chain should run internally through the person in question and not take a route outside of that person, passing through a third person, for example. I might remember an experience and recount it to another person. Years later, when I have totally forgotten the original experience, that person may remind me of what I told him, and this may have the effect of making me believe that I am genuinely remembering the original experience, when in fact I am not. Nevertheless, the false memory impression was caused, ultimately, by the original experience, such that had it not caused me to tell someone else about it, they would not have been in a position to remind me of it, and thus the false memory impression would not have arisen.

There is, however, a problem with ruling out wayward causal chains in the manner described. Remember: the analysis proffered by Parfit is supposed to be providing a reductive analysis of personal identity. It cannot, therefore, without circularity employ the very notion it is supposed to be analysing, namely that of one and the same person. Yet it appears it is this very notion that is being appealed to when it is stipulated that for an apparent memory to be the genuine memory the analysis requires, the causal chain must run through one and the same person, and not through a numerically different third party.

review activity

What problem is faced by Parfit's attempt to rule out wayward causal chains when accounting for personal identity?

Butler: memory presupposes personal identity and cannot constitute it

There is a problem generally with the use of memory as an essential component of an analysis of personal identity, namely, as Bishop Joseph Butler (1692–1752) pointed out, memory presupposes personal identity and cannot therefore constitute it. It is true that if P1 can remember, in the right way, what P0 did or underwent, then P1 is one and the same as P0. If I can remember teaching Mark last week, then I must be one and the same person who taught Mark last week. This is because 'I taught Mark last week' is a shorter version of 'I remember that I taught Mark last week'. But for this sentence to make sense, the reference of the two occurrences of 'I' must be to one and the same person throughout. In other words, in both its occurrences, 'I' must refer to numerically the same person throughout. In the first of its occurrences, it refers to a person in the present, as in 'I remember' (now); and, in the second of its occurrences, it refers to one and the same person in the past, as in 'I taught' (then).

Personal identity and continuity without physical continuity

As we saw earlier, Locke proposed that personal identity could be understood purely in terms of the relations holding between mental states, in particular memory, and Parfit developed this into the Continuity and Connectedness theory (C&C) with the proviso that neither branching nor wayward causal chains occur. It should be fairly obvious that this analysis is purely formal in the sense that it does not specify what actual arrangements have to be in place for the conditions specified to be fulfilled. In the actual world these arrangements are constituted by the brain and the physical processes that take place within it. However, as functionalists saw, the same function could theoretically be executed by different sets of arrangements. What really matters is *that* the function is discharged, not *how* it is carried out. Locke anticipated this insight when he argued that the substances in which the function is instantiated are irrelevant to personal identity, and Parfit builds upon the same point with his fantasy of a brain-state transfer device.

The brain-state transfer device

You enter a cubicle and the device scans the relative positions of all the molecules in your body, which is then vaporised, the information gleaned by the device being transmitted to a distant planet where it is used to create a molecular duplicate of you from the molecules on the planet's surface. The duplicate looks like you, behaves like you, and seems to be able to remember, from a first-person perspective, what you experienced. Is this duplicate really you, or only a brilliant replica? Parfit claims it would be you. It is granted that you do not have the same body and brain that you had on earth, but this is irrelevant, because what matters is the preservation of your psychology, including, most importantly, your memories. Normally it would be the brain that does all this, whereas in this case a machine has done it. But does this really matter as long as the continuity of your mental life was preserved? Notice this fits the Lockean account of personal identity precisely: 'For, it being the same consciousness that makes a man be himself to himself, personal identity depends on that only, whether it be annexed to one individual substance, *or can be continued in a succession of several substances*' (Parfit 1984) [emphasis added].

The branch-line case

This analysis can also cope easily with branch-line cases. Suppose the machine malfunctions and does not vaporise your body, but the duplicate appears as usual on Mars. Then two versions of you exist, and the situation is similar to the brain-fission case, as the psychological continuity of each these persons with the original person is preserved, in the one case by your brain, which was not destroyed, and in the other by the scanning machine. Once again we have continuity and hence survival, but not identity. If one of these duplicates subsequently dies, say the one on Earth, then the survivor on Mars will be you, as there is no other competition for the title which that person wins by default.

The Locke/Parfit approach is rather like treating the person as a function or programme run on the hardware of the brain, the material embodiment being irrelevant to the person's identity over time. In the same way that information can be transferred from one floppy disc to another, so the person likewise could go from body and brain to body and brain. This account of personal identity enables us to solve the problem posed earlier, namely how precisely is resurrection of the body supposed to be possible. It will be remembered that this posed two problems for theologians: firstly, which molecules are to be gathered up from the various sets of molecules that have constituted a person's body and brain at different stages of his life; and, secondly, what happens if, on the Final Day, there are not enough molecules to go round?

Personal identity and functionalism

The functional analysis enables us neatly to sidestep these problems. Anything a brain-state transfer device can do, God can do at least as well. When you die your body and brain are destroyed, but God preserves the program, the psychological connectedness and continuity that constitute your mental life, and thus your continuing personal existence. There can be no objection from functionalists to this proposal as they were willing to agree that programs are abstract in nature, and nothing in principle debars them from being instantiated in non-physical, as well as physical, arrangements. God actually can do a lot better than brain-state transfer devices because he can clean up defective programmes, acting in effect as a moral physician, and thus perfecting us for heaven.

review activity

How does Parfit propose to cater for personal identity without physical continuity?

Physical continuity reaffirmed

Is the brain-state transfer device genuinely person-preserving, or is it in effect an execution chamber, which ensures merely that a duplicate of the person who enters it, but not the person herself, appears on Mars? Peter Unger, in his book *Identity, Consciousness, and Value* (1990), takes the latter option. Unger thinks that describing the scanning device as a brain-state transfer device merely begs the question in favour of the view that the person is transported with their psychological continuity intact. It is easy to go along with such a theory because, in line with science fiction writing, it appeals to our imaginations: the idea that we might travel, at the speed of light, to distant planets by means of such a device is immensely appealing.

The importance of physical continuity

But Unger believes that the scanning device should be described, much more soberly, as a taping device that merely records the information regarding the position of your molecules. The identity of a person is grounded in the physical continuity of the brain which continuously preserves a person's psychological capacities. Unger points out that there is no logical or conceptual necessity about this: there may be possible worlds where personal identity does not have a physical basis, but these worlds are not our world. In our world, the importance of the physical continuity of the brain for the preservation of a person's psychological capacities is the theory best supported by the facts as we know them. Unger is fairly liberal regarding what can happen to a person's brain without the preservation of its psychological capacities being lost. The brain could be freeze-dried and later thawed out. It could be frozen, halved, and quartered, then reassembled and thawed out, perhaps without detriment to its preservation of a person's psychological capacities. However, vaporising a person's brain and dispersing its elements into thousands of nerve cells, or bits of nerve cells, means that in such a case we cannot continue meaningfully to speak of the preservation of the psychological capacities of the person whose brain it was. At that point the person has permanently disappeared. Even if, by some miracle, it were possible to reassemble the scattered particles into a functioning brain, the resulting individual would not be one and the same as the original person. As we remarked earlier, one thing cannot have two beginnings. If this is what the resurrection of the body demands, then not even God can achieve it, as it is logically impossible; and to demand of God that he should do the logically possible is ultimately making a confused and contradictory demand that amounts to no demand at all.

review activity

Explain Unger's objection to Parfit's psychological continuity theory of personal identity.

Personal identity without reduction

Non-reductive conceptions of personal identity

There are philosophers who would reject equally attempts to explain personal identity in terms of either psychological or physical continuity. To explain a concept in terms other than the concept itself is a form of reductionism, and this is rejected by some thinkers today. For such thinkers, personal identity is what it is and does not consist in something else; it is a conceptually primitive notion, comprised by neither the physical continuity of the brain nor the causal relations between psychological states, particularly memory. Accordingly, a non-reductionist account of personal identity can envisage a case where the person suffers complete and total amnesia in which all past experiences and features are lost and yet remains one and the same person nevertheless. Thus, Richard Swinburne has averred that even if we do not agree with stories of persons passing through the river of Lethe and then acquiring a new body, we can make sense of them as they do not appear to be vitiated by contradiction. The theory that regards personal identity as primitive, and thus not analysable into more basic concepts, naturally also affirms that the identity of the person has nothing to do with the identity of their body, or any part of it, such as the brain. The non-reductive theory would thus appear to amount to a commitment to substance-dualism. The person, the unitary subject of experiences, that persists and remains one and the same despite even radical changes to its mental life, and whose identity has nothing to with the body, has to be thought of as a simple, logically indivisible, Cartesian substance. In other words, it is a soul.

If this theory is true, it has important consequences for the split-brain thought experiment discussed earlier. As the person cannot divide and cannot therefore be conceived of as surviving as two separate people, there are only two possibilities regarding what can happen. Firstly, the person goes to neither hemisphere, so that the human beings that result from the brain transplant are in effect zombies, as no person or soul is associated with either of them. Secondly, the person goes either to the right hemisphere, or to the left hemisphere, but, Swinburne maintains, there is no philosophical principle, or natural laws, that can be applied to tell us where the soul will go. That, he believes, is either down to God, or to chance. A virtue of this view of the person is that it provides a determinate answer to a thought-experiment devised by Bernard Williams.

Non-reductionism and the split-brain thought-experiment

Suppose you are the person on whom the split-brain transplant is to be performed. The surgeon tells you that this will not amount to death, because you will survive as two new people who can each remember, from the inside, what the original you did and underwent. Suppose now, however, the surgeon is insane and announces that one of the resulting people will be horribly tortured, whilst the other will receive a million pounds. What should you think of such a prospect? What you want to know is whether you will be unlucky and be tortured, or whether you will be lucky and get the million pounds. But on the view that survival without identity is possible, there is no clear determinate answer regarding what will happen to you. It seems that we are forced to say that as one of the people you will suffer, and as the other you will be rewarded. But this seems unsatisfactory: what you want to know is what will happen to *you*, the original person who has a single viewpoint on the world. The issue that underlies this perplexity is this: how can what appears to be essentially a single viewpoint from which the world is experienced, your perspective, become two?

The dualist theory at least avoids this perplexity. Leaving aside the possibility that the soul goes to neither hemisphere, at least you can understand that one of the resulting human beings will be tortured and the other will not, and you can only hope that you will go to the hemisphere of the person who receives a million pounds.

Physical and psychological continuity essential for personal identity

Finally, which theory of personal identity is to be preferred? It seems to me that residual doubts about the intelligibility of the notion of the soul remain, and hence Swinburne's account is ultimately unattractive. Attempts to reduce mental states to physical states also seem to be unsuccessful and implausible. In line then with J.L. Mackie's remark that 'a materialist view of the thinker is less controversial than a materialist view of thoughts' (Mackie 1976: 202), it seems best to regard the identities of persons in this world as dependent upon those material structures that underpin and preserve the continuity of a person's psychological capacities, especially memory.

some questions
to think about

1 What features of mind and body have led some philosophers to suppose that the two are separate and distinct? Evaluate whether this view is justified.

2 Does behaviourism offer a satisfactory solution to the mind/body problem?

3 Can any version of dualism successfully account for mind to body causation?

4 Mind and brain: two or one?

5 What is the problem of other minds and can any solution be found to it?

6 Can materialist theories of the mind account for consciousness and Intentionality?

7 Discuss whether only human beings can be persons.

8 To what extent can analogies with computers enable us to understand the relationship between mind and body?

9 In what ways can the mental and the physical be distinguished?

10 How adequate is the Turing test as a way of deciding whether some machines, such as robots and computers, have minds?

11 What is solipsism and is it possible?

12 Evaluate the claim that personal identity depends upon psychological continuity through time.

13 Evaluate the argument from analogy as an argument for the existence of other minds.

14 What evidence is there to suggest that our mental lives depend upon the activities of our brains, and can it establish that no mental states can exist without a functioning brain?

15 Evaluate substance-dualism as a theory of the mind/body relationship.

16 If mental states were brain-states, would the problem of other minds be identical to the problem of other brains?

17 Describe and critically assess functionalism as a theory of the mind and body.

18 If my mind and body are different substances, or have different properties, how do mental events cause physical events?

19 There are no logical objections to the claim that the mind is identical to the brain. What are criteriological accounts of our knowledge of other minds, and are they successful?

further reading

▶ Churchland 1988 is clear and brief and provides useful discussions of the major issues.

▶ Crane 1995 is an excellent introduction to functionalist conceptions of the mind.

▶ Guttenplan (ed.) 1984 is an excellent introduction and reference book.

▶ Heil 1998 is pitched at a more sophisticated level than the previous book, but students should find it stimulating and challenging.

▶ Kim 1998 is especially valuable for gaining an overview of the subject and for addressing the question of whether materialist theories of the mind can succeed.

▶ McGinn 1982 is outstandingly good, but tough. It is worth persevering with.

▶ Searle 1989 is very accessible, stimulating and challenging. All students should read this book.

▶ Smith and Jones 1986 is very clear and accessible with a useful discussion of dualism.

political philosophy

I   Political Ideologies   86

II   Freedom   108

III   Law   113

IV   Authority   124

V   The State   128

Political Ideologies

Autonomy: self-government. The ability to make one's own decisions and act upon them. It can apply to states, groups and individuals.

Consequentialism: the view that an action is right if its consequences are beneficial.

Democracy: government of the people by the people. Direct democracy is government whereby all electors vote on all governmental issues; representative democracy involves electors choosing who will represent their interests in Parliament.

Eudaimon: the good life. According to Aristotle, this is virtuous living according to reason, which forms the basis of happiness.

Ideology: a body of political ideas that forms the basis of policy.

Meritocracy: government by those who have proved themselves worthy or fit for the responsibility.

Natural law: the ethical theory that whatever is natural is right; that morality should be found in the mind of the people rather than in regulation or revelation.

Oligarchy: government by a small exclusive class.

Social contract: the theory that the people and the government mutually agree on a reciprocal system of rights and duties.

Theocracy: rule by God.

Timarchy: government by a small group of free men over a large slave class.

Tyranny: government by one unelected individual who imposes his will upon the population.

Key topics in this chapter

- Conservatism
- Liberalism
- Socialism
- Anarchism

Introduction

Political philosophy consists of analysing how societies are, in fact, governed and organised, and of evaluating social organisation and government from an ethical standpoint. It is also concerned with the proper interrelationships between the various institutions and authorities within the state. Historically, the most important issue here has tended to be the relationship between political and religious institutions and authorities. Having faded somewhat as a question in recent times, this issue is once again coming to the fore in many parts of the world. Before the activities of political philosophy can get under way, it is necessary to define a large number of terms and concepts. Perhaps the most basic of these is the question: 'What is society?' Some of the most important ethical concepts needing definition are autonomy, justice, democracy, rights and obligations.

Political philosophers attempt to show how it is possible to achieve social goods. This raises questions about whether or not ends justify means (for example, is it OK to go to war in Iraq even though the weapons of mass destruction which were the declared reason did not exist, if the result is an improvement in the political situation in the Middle East?). Another issue is how to ensure that government can function efficiently whilst guarding against abuse of power.

The major practical concerns debated within political philosophy have varied over time, according to the events of the day. At present, serious issues facing Western governments include discrimination of various sorts, population growth (or the lack of it), environmental concerns such as global warming and the holes in the ozone layer, the inequality of resources between richer and poorer countries and how to address the resultant problems and immigration policies. A political philosopher may try to identify the ethical response to these and other issues, and the means by which governments can put these responses into practice.

It is obvious, therefore, that political philosophy overlaps with many other areas of study, within philosophy and in other fields. Ethics, law, psychology and sociology are only some of these.

The figure representing Justice stands with a set of scales, which symbolise the weighing up of the evidence for and against the accused. The decision of guilt or innocence is decided upon the weight of the evidence. The figure is some-times blindfolded to show that nothing but the evidence counts: wealth, gender, race, social status, reputation cannot affect the outcome of a fair trial.

The Scales of Justice

Walk past any primary school playground and there's a good chance you'll hear someone shouting 'That's not fair!' The concept of fairness, or justice, seems to be acquired very early. As adults, we all continue to want fair treatment (as we see it), although whether we wish to extend such treatment to others might vary from person to person!

The efficient running of society and the flourishing of the individual

The organisation of society

Justice and right treatment are of vast importance in our individual and social lives. For Plato, (c.428 BC–374 BC), justice was the key concept when he considered the fundamental question of political and ethical philosophy: how should we organise society so that it functions well as a whole and enables its individual members to flourish? For Plato, it was crucial that political life should be based upon the ethical principles of the just community.

A brief overview of Plato's ideal republic

Plato believed in an elitist, though meritocratic, state as the ideal. For the individual, Plato wrote, justice is a good in itself. In the just individual, reason rules. The 'spirited' aspect of the psyche, responding to reason, helps to control the appetites. Plato believed that the people within a state fell into three categories, just as the psyche can be divided into three parts. The rulers, or philosopher-kings, correspond to reason. They are the thinkers and strategists. Having encountered the Form of the Good, they can see what is right for society. The Guardians, or auxiliaries, are analogous to the 'spirited part' of the psyche. They are active and carry out the necessary functions, as instructed by the philosopher-kings. Most ordinary people – the hoi polloi – are equivalent to the appetites. They should obey orders for their own good. A just society, organised according to Plato's theories, would, he believed, be a flourishing community. However, autonomy could only realistically be aimed at, let alone achieved, by the ruling elite. The welfare of the state as a whole was

Plato (c.428 BC –348 BC)

87

far more important than the welfare of any particular individual. Attempts to define the proper relationships between the individual and the state, and between freedom, law and authority, have led to a wide spectrum of political ideologies in modern times. Plato, in the *Republic*, was probably the first to try to address these issues systematically. He defined four types of government from his own observation.

Types of government in the classical period

Timarchy

Timarchy applied only to Sparta and Crete in Plato's time and exists nowhere today. It will therefore not be discussed at length here. Put briefly, timarchy consisted of a small and disciplined ruling class that controlled a larger slave class. Plato believed that this would inevitably collapse in time. The other three types, however – oligarchy, democracy and tyranny – were and are common. An oligarchy is a society ruled by a wealthy minority. Plato disapproved of oligarchies on several grounds. He distrusted the profit motive and thought that greed was immoral. He believed that the poor would be exploited by the rich and that this could eventually lead to revolution.

Democracy

Government by the people

Democracy literally means government by the people. 'The people' in this context has rarely if ever meant all of the inhabitants of a state. In Plato's Athens, the electorate comprised of free adult male citizens: actually a minority of the population. About 250 000–300 000 people lived in Athens at the time: of these, about 45 000–50 000 were entitled to vote. However, it was the Assembly of electors, and not their elected representatives, who held the power. All major decisions were made by a referendum of the entire electorate. This is direct democracy, which differs from the representative democracy with which we are familiar today. As nation states became more populous, it became impossible to gather the entire electorate together to debate upon and vote on every suggested measure. In the modern world, therefore, democracies generally vote for representatives who will debate and vote on behalf of their constituents. There is usually also a second chamber of government (such as the House of Lords in the UK), which tries to ensure that a powerful lower chamber does not act unreasonably. The legal system may also determine that a government measure is in fact unlawful.

Plato disapproved of democracy, as, in the words of Thucidydes, it meant 'committing the conduct of state affairs to the whims of the multitude' (Book II p. 65). In Plato's view, the majority of the people lacked the insight required to make right decisions. Most people vote for what they want, rather than what they need. This leads politicians, he argued, to pander to the wishes of the electorate rather than to rule according to the principles of a just society. The freedoms of democracy are also criticised. A growing dislike of authority leads to the fragmentation of society and, ultimately, class war between rich and poor. His Simile of the Ship (in the *Republic*) is his most famous criticism of democracy in action.

Tyranny

The collapse of democracy

Tyranny might grow out of the collapse of democracy. The tyrant is essentially an individual. His rule (it usually is a he) is the exercise of personal preferences. Ultimately, like all the other systems that Plato considers, tyranny is seen as self-destructive. Able contemporaries will need to be destroyed before they become rivals for power. Therefore, there can be no long-term succession. The tyrant is under constant strain to maintain his position. He is also, by definition, of criminal tendencies and probably mentally unbalanced. His rule will end, sooner or later, with mental collapse or death, followed by chaos.

Plato's prescription

The philosopher-kings

Plato's preferred alternative was rule by the philosopher-kings, an academic elite who would be selected on the grounds of their ability and then given suitable training for their future role. The Guardian auxiliaries would combine the functions of the modern-day civil service, police and armed forces. Everyone else (the vast majority) would be in the third and lowest class. Whilst it would be perfectly possible, and, indeed, encouraged, that a child of any parents be 'promoted' or 'demoted' to another class, depending upon the level of his or her ability, one's role in life would be determined by one's measured ability.

It is worth noting, in passing, that this was the rationale behind the grammar, technical and secondary modern school selective system which used to be the norm in England and Wales. Introduced in 1944, this placed children at age 11 in schools suited to their ability as measured by intelligence tests. The technical schools no longer exist, but 161 grammar schools still select the top 25 per cent of the ability range in their areas. The other 75 per cent in these areas go to high schools (formerly secondary modern schools) or to the few comprehensive schools, often Church-run, in the relevant area. Grammar schools were intended to provide an academic education for future leaders. Technical schools were supposed to provide functionaries with the necessary skills and secondary modern schools were to provide a basic education for the rest.

In Plato's *Republic,* life for the rulers and guardians would be austere. They would own no private property. Family life, as we understand it, would not exist. State nurseries would be responsible for the upbringing of children. Sexual intercourse and conception would be organised with a view to optimal genetic advantage. Plato would almost certainly have approved of Aldous Huxley's *Brave New World*, where foetuses are grown in bottles and genetically, chemically and psychologically prepared for their future careers, and might well have welcomed the controversial concept of 'designer babies' that is currently exercising the minds of both amateur and professional philosophers.

The philosopher-kings would actually have no desire to rule – in Plato's view, a wish for political office is proof of unfitness to hold it. They would far rather study philosophy. However, recognising their duty to put their talents and state-provided education at the service of society, they would benevolently set out to give the people what they needed, rather than what they wanted. Plato seems to have held a touching belief that natural ability plus training in mathematics and philosophy would lead to moral goodness. In the *Republic*, he sets out the qualities which he argues are possessed by a philosopher: 'good memory, readiness to learn, breadth of vision and versatility of mind, and [to be] a friend of truth, justice, courage and discipline [with] education and maturity to round them off (Plato's *Republic*: Book VI)'. He seems not to have thought of the modern cliché that 'All power corrupts, and absolute power corrupts absolutely'.

Individual liberty and autonomy are modern concepts

Eudaimon

Plato's pupil, Aristotle (384 BC–322 BC), believed that the role of the state was to train people to be virtuous. He believed that the *eudaimon* was the goal of all people, though not everyone could achieve it. Therefore the state, through education, had a major role to play in providing the appropriate training. He famously commented that 'Man is a political animal', (Aristotle: Politics) meaning that people can only function within the context of society. Therefore, friendship and other-directed virtues such as courage, generosity and justice were of great importance. Consequently, like Plato, he saw the state as more important than the individual people within it. An eccentric or maverick individual had the potential to cause harm. Unlike Plato, however, Aristotle believed that, on balance, democracy was a good system as it is more stable than oligarchy and a larger group of individuals is likely to possess more wisdom than a small group. He disagreed with Plato's recommended system of government on the grounds that friendship and private property are 'the greatest safeguard against revolution' (Aristotle: Politics). He also believed that, in any case, Plato's system was unworkable.

Individualism, as understood today, is actually a fairly modern concept. In times past, most people understood their identity to lie within their family, tribe, class, religious group or nation. Nothing in classical philosophy relates to the political divisions which we see today. Left- or right-wing, centrist, liberal, anarchist would have been unknown terms and concepts to Plato and Aristotle. Whilst Plato's recipe for the ideal republic has been criticised as a 'dictatorship of the virtuous Right' (Crossman, Plato Today: 1937), it could just as easily form the basis for a dictatorship of the virtuous Left, as noted by Bertrand Russell (*Practice and Theory of Bolshevism* p. 30). Whilst oligarchies tend to be right wing, many right-leaning people would regard oligarchy as a morally unacceptable system. Democracies produce governments of all types, and tyrannies are by definition individualistic.

Theocracy was an issue in the past and may be in the future

Religious authority and the power of the state

Modern political divisions did not really appear in recognisable form before the seventeenth century. Between Aristotle and the Enlightenment, most political philosophers were concerned with the proper relationship between religious authority and the power of the state. Also, between the period of the Early Church (approximately to 320) until around the seventeenth century, the idea that any individual could understand God's will was unacceptable. The Church told the people what God's will was on any given issue. Augustine (354–430), believed that one should accept the authority of the state unless and until this conflicted with one's duty to God. That which God commanded was right, therefore any consequentialist theories in ethics or philosophy were mistaken at best. Aquinas (c.1224–74), who commented upon Aristotle and was a supporter of natural law theory, believed that the responsibility of government was to provide the right conditions for people to attain religious goals. Like Augustine, he acknowledged governmental authority but believed that if God's will was otherwise, governmental decree should be resisted. For both Augustine and Aquinas, therefore, the individual was of importance because each person has a soul to be saved. The way to receive salvation is to please God, which, effectively, meant to accept the authority of the Church. Governments should be obeyed unless they contradicted the Church. So although the individual was regarded as important, he or she had to accept some ultimate political authority, whether that be the authority of the Government or the authority of God as explained by the Church. Given the current rise, in many parts of the world, of evangelical involvement with national politics, these sorts of considerations might well become live issues in the future. Theocracy is allegedly operative in some states today. A number of Islamic nations, for example, live under sharia law. A growing number of people from many religions would like to see, if not theocracy, then at least more notice to be taken of 'Divine Will' in government. An example of this in practice is George W. Bush's decision to withdraw monetary aid from family-planning charities which, among other services, give women access to medical abortions. The problem, of course, is that God's will (if it makes sense to talk of such a thing at all) has to be interpreted and enacted by fallible human beings. Turning to the modern age of politics as generally practised and taught, we now have to establish an overview of political ideologies, and how each of them tries to argue that their particular way of organising society would lead to an efficient state of flourishing individuals.

review activity

Explain the relationship between the state and people according to the major political philosophies.

Government

Monarchy from the mediaeval period to the present – a brief overview

The divine right Throughout most of the world, most states were, historically, monarchies. The king (or, very occasionally, the queen) had absolute power. Subjects could only own land or possess power so long as the monarch was happy for them to do so.

Monarchs were believed to hold power by 'divine right' – in other words, it pleased God to have that person in that position. If a monarch was deposed, this was seen as an indication that God was no longer pleased for him or her to reign.

Social position was largely fixed. If your parents were serfs – possessions of the overlord – then you, also, were a serf. If the lord to whom you belonged realised that you were an intelligent serf, you might be educated in order to serve him in a clerical capacity if he foresaw a need for a clerk or a scribe. If you were very fortunate, you might be granted your freedom, but unless you performed some major service, such as saving your lord's life, you probably would not. Wealth and power were inherited, and social status depended upon them.

The monarch was expected to keep order – in other words, to maintain the status quo. Foreign invaders should be repulsed, and crime should be punished. In this way, people could go about their daily lives in safety.

The origins of social contract theory

The monarch's authority

Here we have the beginning of the concept of social contract. Gradually, the idea became current that the monarch's authority was to be obeyed, not necessarily because God so willed, but because he or she provided security in return for loyalty. The analogy is to the father of a family. The father provides protection – from hunger, by his earnings, and from danger, by his willingness to defend the family – and in return, the family accepts his authority. An obvious criticism springs to mind. A brutal father can inflict more damage within the home than may be posed by external threats. In the same way, a tyrannous monarch may be more harmful than beneficial to the country. Social contract theory would say that in such a case, it would be permissible for the people to overthrow the monarch and set someone else in his or her place. The difficulty here is to see who would have the authority to make such a challenge, and how it would be known in advance that the successor would keep to the social contract once in power.

The development of varying types of government

In practice, some monarchies (such as in France) were overthrown by revolutionary force. In some cases, a form of democratic government succeeded. In others, the incoming ruler(s) proved to be as bad as the previous regime. Many such unpopular systems have in their turn been overthrown. Other monarchies, as in Britain, gradually accepted checks and balances upon their authority, so that a democratic government is responsible for legislation, with the monarch having a largely advisory and ceremonial function. In most of the developed world today, some form of social contract arguably subsists between the government and the people. The government retains power so long as the people continue to support it through the ballot box. Between elections, the government retains power so long as a majority of elected representatives (for example, in Britain, the Members of Parliament) continue to support it in parliamentary votes.

Formal social contract theories: background

The covenant with God

Formal social contract theory began in the seventeenth century and grew out of renewed interest, among Protestants, in the Hebrew Bible (Old Testament). According to Hebrew teaching, the relationship between humanity and God is that of a covenant, or contract. All humans are under the covenant made with Noah, to refrain from specified evils and to worship God. In return, there will be no future worldwide destruction. The Jews are parties to the covenants with Abraham and Moses whereby, if they obey the 613 laws, the Almighty will ensure their continued survival as a race and their habitation of the Promised Land. Seventeenth-century scholars and philosophers addressed such questions as whether the covenant was between the society and God, or between each individual and God, or between individuals mutually to obey God's laws. The concept of contract or covenant was then applied to secular society. Who is bound by the contract? What is he or she bound to do? How can we tell when a contract has been broken? How can it be enforced? Who has the authority to decide and take appropriate action? As a result of such discussions, a number of theories were devised to explore how a group of individuals without government or any other cohesive force might have formed a society, worked out their mutual obligations and decided upon a leader who would enforce those obligations. The key concept here is consent – the consent that a rational individual would give were he or she to be starting from a state of nature. Inevitably, individual philosophers' views of what human life would be if there had never yet been a government or overarching authority (i.e. if living in a 'state of nature') affected their views of how a social contract would have been formed. Each formal social contract theory is, therefore, grounded in the beliefs of an individual philosopher about how society would have come about originally, given the philosopher's basic perception of the dominant aspects of human nature. For each social contract theory there is a myth, or story, of how societies came to be.

Formal social contract theories: Hobbes

A sole monarch

Thomas Hobbes' (1588–1679) political philosophy, expounded in *Leviathan*, shows a very pessimistic view of human nature. He believed that all people are fundamentally self-centred. Consequently, he says, left to themselves, everybody will compete and fight with everybody else. Such a situation will lead to continual fear. As no one can be sure that his crops will not be stolen, or that he will be paid for his labour, no one will work. Life will be 'nasty, brutish and short'. The solution, for Hobbes, is for everyone to agree to refrain from robbery, rape, murder, etc., in return for everybody else doing the same. All should then make a free gift of their right to act according to nature to a sole monarch, on the grounds that a division of power would lead to social breakdown and a return to selfish competition. Only a sole ruler would have the power to enforce the law. Anyone who overthrew the monarch would, by definition, then have the same power. To this extent, might, in Hobbes' view, was right. The sovereign, having been gifted the rights of all members of society, thus has absolute power. Hobbes thought that a sovereign monarch would enforce moral rules, as the interests of the monarch and the people would coincide. The sovereign would also be under the natural law forbidding ingratitude. Given Hobbes' view of human nature, there seems to be a contradiction here. Why should a monarch do anything other than exploit the people for his or her own benefit? Nonetheless, Hobbes maintained that, once in place, the monarch should be obeyed unless one was breaking the law in order to protect one's own life, or until the monarch was no longer able to enforce his or her own laws. Otherwise, the suffering of individuals (if it occurred) was the necessary side effect of social stability. 'The safety of the people is the supreme law.' Hobbes seems to be saying that obedience to law is the overriding duty of all, regardless of any moral issues. A sovereign monarch who ordered the ethnic cleansing of a minority should be obeyed by all but the victims, who have the right to try to save their own lives, but no means by which to do so.

Hobbes' view of human nature is controversial. His opinion that we are inherently self-centred is, interestingly, in line with much religious teaching. Christianity, for example, teaches that selfish disobedience (as illustrated in the myth of Adam and Eve) is the reason for the presence of evil in the world. Buddhism teaches that 'Life is suffering. Suffering is caused by selfish desire. Suffering will stop if selfish desire is crushed.' All the major religions teach that the right way to live is to turn away from selfishness (one's natural state) and become other-directed – towards God, or ultimate reality. Religious teaching about behaving well towards others states that it is one's moral duty to do so, because God, or the religious code, declares that this is ultimately right. Humanism, which is an atheistic philosophy, also teaches that one should direct one's efforts towards others, or humanity in general, rather than just pursuing one's own interests. Many humanists would also say that this is a moral duty because the well-being of all overrides individual interests. The good of humanity as a whole, and the equal rights of all, are regarded as the overwhelming priorities. Most humanists would also agree that individuals have a tendency to selfishness which should be overcome.

The basic rules of morality

Hobbes was himself concerned to show that both Scripture and reason supported his moral and political views. This was at least partly because he thought that most people, given the choice between obeying God or obeying the monarch, would choose to obey God, which is likely to be as true of believers now as it was then. The proportion of believers in any given population may, however, have changed. Hobbes' belief that power is what counts is also open to question. Having power does not, in the eyes of most people, give one the right to exercise it to the disadvantage of others, even if this does lead to social stability. The rights of the individual are generally held to have importance, and if these are overriding, then some social unrest may be thought a necessary price to pay in the interests of morality. There can, arguably, be an agreed set of basic rules to ensure that we do not revert to barbarism, without the disadvantages of an absolute monarch wielding unfettered authority.

Formal social contract theories: Locke

John Locke (1632–1704) argued in his *Second Treatise of Government* that, in a state of nature, people lived in loose groups and had a duty to God to refrain from murder, theft and so on. This duty also gave people the right to defend themselves and their property against such wrongs. However, some people did not act according to their duty. Others were unable to exercise their right to self-defence, whilst some might, on the other hand, go too far. He envisaged that the rational response to these dangers would be the appointment of a judge, who would enforce social obligations, and who would remain in post by the will and consent of the people. (Interestingly, there was a period of effective rule by judges in early Hebrew society, although Locke's critics did not seem to be conscious of this.) Objections to Locke's views included the charge that there was no record of the actual creation of political authority – the freely given consent of the people leading to a political system – but that, in practice, everyone seems to have been born into a particular, existent society. Locke replied that, by remaining in a society, one is giving tacit (unspoken) consent. People were, he argued, able to join other societies, or even to found new ones. Whether this is, or ever has been, feasible for even a minority of people is open to question. Alternatively, if the authorities were generally unpopular within a society, said Locke, it was legitimate for them to be overthrown, as they no longer commanded the consent of the people. The mechanisms by which the consent of the people can be determined and judges stripped of their authority are not clearly explained.

Those with property have power

Another contentious aspect of Locke's views is his assertion that natural rights include the right to property. Locke bases this upon a number of arguments. Possession of property is necessary, he contends, for survival. It is certainly true that, in the animal kingdom, control of territory is basic. The creature that holds the territory has access to its food, water and shelter. As a consequence, and only because of, this, the male animal will be able to attract a mate and propagate his genes. Biologists tell us that the instinct for territory is fundamental for precisely these reasons. Locke further argues that property is the reward for labour. Through work, we add value to our environment. Additionally, Locke believed that God intended the industrious to inherit the earth. This last point exemplifies the Protestant work ethic. It is the duty of each person to support himself or herself through honest labour. In return, we receive material comfort and wellbeing in the form of food, shelter and other comforts. This is, in Locke's view, morally correct. Honest work should lead to personal benefits. Others would argue that the possession of private property increases inequalities and, perhaps more perniciously, perpetuates inequality through succeeding generations. The entrepreneur, who, through his or her own efforts, amasses a fortune, can leave his or her children so much money that they have no need to work at all. The state, it can be argued, should intervene so as to ensure that no one can possess huge riches. This can be achieved through, for example, high levels of taxation upon personal income. (In the late 1970s, under a Labour government, the top rate of tax on income derived from investments was 97.5 per cent in Britain.) Alternatively, or additionally, capital gains tax could be levied at a high rate on inherited wealth. The resulting income to the treasury could be used to benefit the worse-off in society, giving them access to freedom of choice and social justice. Attractive as these things may be, there are some practical issues to be addressed. When taxes rise, the well-off tend to emigrate to countries where rates are lower. It is not clear, either, that the amount of capital in a given state is fixed – in other words, that if I receive more income, someone else will receive less. It is possible that the overall amount of capital within an economy can increase because of greater productivity, or for other reasons. The freedom for individuals to amass capital might well only mean that relative, rather than absolute, poverty increases. Many would also agree with Locke's thesis that greater effort deserves greater reward, in the interest of justice. Some would wish to argue that greater ability, or possession of a skill that is in short supply, is also deserving of financial recognition.

Formal social contract theories: Rousseau

The social contract and fellow feeling

Jean-Jacques Rousseau (1712–78) also believed that the key to any successful social contract was consent. In *Social Contract* he questioned Hobbes' analysis of human nature, arguing that a creature so described would not be able to live in a society, let alone come to agreement about how society should be organised. Traits such as sympathy and pity would be regarded as perverted, were we really to be as innately selfish as Hobbes believed. Rousseau thought that sympathy, conscience and reason are as natural to us as is self-preservation. It is society that corrupts our naturally good nature. 'Man is born free; and everywhere he is in chains': human depravity is not innate, but learned behaviour. He argued that 'the general will' should be sovereign. The general will tends to promote liberty, equality and fraternity. Indeed, it also arises from fraternity – the fellow feeling we have for others. The nature of the assembly or other seat of authority that enacts the general will is not of the first importance. Critics point out that the problem is identifying the general will. According to Rousseau, this involves putting all purely personal desires to one side, and each person desiring the common good. The outcome of this exercise is the discovery of the general will – an abstraction of the will of the people for the good of society. One has to question whether such a thing is possible. Firstly, even if one does not share his views about the intrinsic goodness of some aspects of human nature, it is debatable whether anyone can be purely objective. Secondly, how can we know the way to achieve the common good? Rousseau admits that this latter could be difficult, so says that we should desire what we perceive to be the common good. This still leaves us with the likelihood that there will be many differing perceptions, with no obvious way to discern which of them is correct.

Formal social contract theories: Rawls

The difference principle

John Rawls, (1921–) in *A Theory of Justice*, concentrates upon the concept of justice as fairness. No social institution, he argues, should benefit any individual or group at the expense of others. This means that sexual, racial and religious discrimination are wrong. Rawls goes further than this, however, in arguing that people of unequal ability should only be differently rewarded for their work if the different rewards are for the benefit of society, particularly the worse-off members of it. This is called 'the difference principle'. It might, therefore, be valid to pay more as an incentive to those whose work fuels productivity, but other than for good reason, differential rewards would be unjust. Rawls arrived at his theory by imagining that we all start from an original position in which we have no idea of our race, social status, religion, or any other distinguishing factor. How would we choose to run our society? Being under a veil of ignorance as to our own position, we would have to be equally concerned as to the wellbeing of all individuals. We would therefore want equal liberty for all – the only constraints that we would choose to impose upon any individual would be those that protected the liberty of others. We would want equality of opportunity, so that those of equal ability and motivation had equal chances of success. We would want equal rewards unless differential rewards were to the benefit of all, and would approve of a concern for the worse-off, as we might be among them. Rawls argues that these principles are right, and that utilitarian principles (which are designed to promote the common good) are not the best basis upon which to organise society. That which is right, says Rawls, overrides that which is good. Under utilitarianism, the maximum total good might unfairly disadvantage minorities such as unskilled workers. As with all social contract theories, there is the problem that we do not start from an original position under a veil of ignorance. We start from where we are, and possess whatever advantages or disadvantages our birth and upbringing may give us. Whilst we may all have a (real or hypothetical) sympathy with the worse-off, it is not clear that the advantaged within society would freely make the sacrifices implied by Rawls' system. Nor is it clear that the disadvantaged are in a position to bring about the changes which Rawls advocates. In response to Rawls, Robert Nozick (1938–2002) argued for classical liberalism. The imposition of a system of justice such as Rawls describes would, he maintained, jeopardise individual liberty, including, for example, the right to deal in property. In the view of classical liberalism, individual freedom overrides all other rights.

Political ideologies

A political ideology might, at its lowest, be defined as 'a coherent structure of ideas, agreed by a number of people, relating to the proper organisation of society'. Most political ideologies have four aspects: a view of human nature; a view of history; a view of the importance of the individual or group; a view of the role of the state. Depending upon the views held about each of these aspects, differing ideologies will vary in their prescriptions for social organisation and government. Human nature may be seen as fundamentally selfish or fundamentally philanthropic. People may be viewed as basically rational or basically emotional beings. Differing lessons will be adduced from history. Whether or not all people are of equal value may be disputed. To what extent the state should try to provide for its citizens' needs will be an issue, as will whether law should be coercive (forcing people to adopt approved lifestyles) or prohibitory (simply concerned with forbidding actual wrongs). All political ideologies have to address such issues. Probably the most fundamental of these is the relative importance of the state (made up of those official bodies which wield power, and those that carry out its functions), society (consisting of the people as a whole) and the individual.

Liberals and anarchists

Liberals and anarchists will tend to favour the individual, whilst acknowledging the claims of society as a whole in certain areas of life. Anarchists reject the legitimacy of the state, whilst for liberals the function of the state is to protect individuals. Conservatives will acknowledge the claims of the individual, but will also place emphasis upon the importance of the role of the state in providing the security and continuity within which individuals can most effectively operate. Socialists, as their name implies, will argue for the primary importance of society as a whole. Hence there will be varying answers to the question of who has legitimate authority, and who should wield power over whom. Should authority reside within the autonomous individual, who possesses rights and can exercise freedom? Alternatively, should society – the will of the people (or the majority of those who vote) – be paramount? Or should we cede authority to the state, in which reposes the wisdom of the ages garnered from the lessons of the past?

Another issue concerns obligation. To what extent do individuals, society and the state owe duties one to another? How can we weigh up the competing claims for individual self-determination, the welfare of all individuals, the common good of society and the security of the state?

This leads us to ask what, if anything, we should be forced to do or to refrain from doing, and on what principles? For example, should we insist that children be taught, even against their wills? If so, why? For their own good, as education is a benefit (arguably) for its own sake, and/or because educated people gain economic advantage? Or for the good of society, as we need an educated workforce to ensure mutual wellbeing? Or because a common educational heritage helps maintain the security and continuity of the state?

Finally, in this context, we have to consider what constitutes justice. How does justice relate to law? Who should punish whom, and for which offences? And what do we want punishment to achieve? Is it the betterment of the individual for his or her own sake, the protection of society, or the security of the state?

How do major political philosophies define the common good?

Democracy

This section concerns itself with representative, rather than direct, democracy. Democracy literally means 'government by the people'. In fact, virtually every regime in the world claims to be democratic. In the former Soviet Union, where only members of the Communist Party were permitted to stand for election, it was claimed that there was democracy, as every citizen was not only entitled, but required, to vote. They had the choice between voting 'yes' or voting 'no' for the official Communist Party candidate. As dissidence was likely to make life difficult, it is perhaps unsurprising that the 'yes' vote was regularly well above 90 per cent. In no country is there a 'one person, one vote' system. All democracies give the vote only to adults. The age at which one becomes an adult varies from one state to another. In Britain, it changed from 21 to 18 years of age during the 1970s. There is now some debate as to whether 16- and 17-year-olds should be given the vote. Women only gained voting rights in most countries during the twentieth century, and in some places they still may not vote. Other excluded groups include, in various places, those who are certified insane, convicted criminals or current prisoners. In Britain, members of the House of Lords may not vote in general elections, as they already have a voice in Parliament. The rules about who may stand for election are also extremely variable. In practice, running an election campaign is so expensive that only those with the support of a political party (and, therefore, access to funding) or the very rich can attempt it, except in very unusual local circumstances. There is also the problem of which voting system to use.

First past the post   Under 'first past the post' (the system widely used in Britain) the person with the most votes wins the seat, even if he or she has gained only a minority of the votes cast. In other words, if Adams receives 10 000 votes, whilst Brown and Cook receive 9999 votes each, then Adams will be the duly elected member. Under transferable voting (used, for example, in Eire), second and other preferences will be taken into account. There are advantages and disadvantages to both systems. 'First past the post' systems tend to lead to a clear majority for one party, and hence to a stable government which can enact its policies. On the other hand, it can be the case that the party with more votes wins fewer seats, as happened to the Conservative Party under Ted Heath in 1974. Transferable voting might more accurately reflect the spectrum of political opinion in the country, but frequently leads to no party having an overall majority. This means that coalition governments have to be negotiated, and there is less stability, coherence and continuity of policy and legislation.

Should voting be compulsory? Under any system, if only one person bothers to vote, his or her choice will be the elected candidate – although there may be hundreds of thousands of others in the constituency who would have preferred someone else but didn't take the opportunity to say so. For this reason, many countries, including, for example, Australia, do have a compulsory system. (Those who feel disinclined to support any candidate can spoil their ballot papers.) There is a moral question here: in a democracy, is it one's duty to vote? Does the possession of rights necessarily imply corresponding obligations? (If so, then 'animal rights' is clearly a contradiction in terms. It is also difficult to see how a newborn baby can have any duties or obligations, although most of us would probably argue that he or she had rights.) There are other fundamental questions, too: is it really democratic that once elected, MPs can bring about laws and other measures of which their constituents disapprove? Had there been referenda on, for example, the invasion of Iraq in 2003, or the question of university funding in 2004, would the outcomes have been different? Further to this, are all people sufficiently wise to make an informed judgement? As we have already seen, Plato did not think so.

In other walks of life, after all, we rely upon experts. For medical matters, we consult people with medical qualifications; only a recognised art historian can verify that the painting we found in granny's attic is really a long-lost Turner, and so on. Would it not be sensible to leave the choosing and/or the running of Government to those with training in political matters? If we believe that the universal franchise is the best way to produce a government, then should political theory and practice be taught to all? If so, can we trust teachers to be impartial between competing theories? (Whether religious studies teachers manage to be fair to all faith systems might be relevant here, or, indeed, whether English teachers are fair to all writers, or historians to all historical analyses.)

Utilitarianism

Jeremy Bentham studied law and became disillusioned with the way in which it was practised in England. He set out to analyse what the law should be. His philosophy of utilitarianism, which states that we should aim for 'the greatest happiness for the greatest number', has been enormously influential in all areas of society. Bentham's embalmed body is kept in a glass box at University College, London, and is sometimes brought out to sit at meetings and dinners.

'Good' equals happiness

The basic principle of utilitarianism is 'the greatest good for the greatest number', where 'good' equates to happiness or pleasure. Jeremy Bentham (1748–1832) rejected social contract theories because each of them was derived from a theory of early society for which there is no proof. Truth cannot be founded upon fiction. Real contracts derive from real laws. Human nature, said Bentham, naturally tends to search out pleasure and avoid pain. Therefore, laws should be formulated so as to maximise pleasure and minimise pain. As everyone has these same desires, Bentham eventually concluded that democracy was the most effective system of government, and campaigned for the extension of the franchise. He was successful, in that more people got the vote, but did not achieve his desired end of one person, one vote, and a secret ballot. Bentham famously rejected the idea of natural rights as 'nonsense on stilts'. Real rights, he maintained, as with real contracts, are derived from real laws. Rights necessarily imply duties; failure of duty justifies punishment to the extent that the pain inflicted by the punishment is proportionate to the pain saved to others as a result of it. Communities are composed of the individuals within them: government actions are right insofar as they promote the happiness of the individuals governed. (This view that community is a convenient shorthand fiction was rather eerily reflected in Conservative Prime Minister Margaret Thatcher's famous declaration, in the 1980s, that 'there is no such thing as society'.)

A right system of law and government will, therefore, promote those things that will lead to utility, namely subsistence, abundance, security and equality. These necessarily include the freedom to buy and sell property. The free market is the best means of producing and distributing goods, and this maximises happiness. Other utilitarians have argued that we must temper the market by the provision of a welfare state to protect the more vulnerable people within the community.

All utilitarians agree that we must continue to discuss how subsistence, abundance, security and equality can best be achieved, as things change over time. We must look to the future consequences of laws in order to decide upon their utility, not to the events of the past. John Stuart Mill (1806–73) developed and explained Benthamite arguments. He held that a government elected by a majority should be obeyed as it has the right to enact the views of the majority. It should be noted that J.S. Mill believed that all sane adults should be entitled to vote, and was an active campaigner for women to have the franchise. However, under democracy, there is always the danger that the rights of minorities might be overlooked or ignored. Therefore, government should concern itself only with legislation that affects the public sphere. Whatever one does in private, affecting no one else, is no concern of the state. Other philosophers have held that secure government, even if some of its legislation is not in accord with the principle of utility, is better than anarchy and should therefore be supported. Only if resistance to a bad government would lead to good government can it be justified. The calculation (and, some would argue, the prescience) required to decide whether resistance would in fact be beneficial overall is generally acknowledged to be fraught with difficulty.

Further, there is the question of whether a law that does not promote utility in a particular case should be obeyed. As an example, in general, laws against trespass and criminal damage tend to promote happiness. If I break into your house and vandalise your furniture, pouring paint stripper over your car as I leave, I will no doubt be causing unhappiness overall. But what of those who destroy trial fields of genetically modified crops? If, as they may claim, they are preventing potentially harmful – and uncontrollable – organisms from reaching the human food chain and damaging the health of us all, their actions may be utilitarian. Exceptional cases need exceptional responses. However, identifying truly exceptional cases is no easy task. It is also true that people may conscientiously object to the methods by which utilitarian ends are achieved. Ridding a country of a dictator might, overall, increase happiness, but principled objection to war or assassination would lead to the rejection of such methods of bringing about an otherwise desirable result.

Conservatism

Laws based on lessons learnt from the past

Generally speaking, the conservative view of human nature is somewhat similar to that of Hobbes. People tend to be basically self-centred, and it is necessary for authority to enforce civilised behaviour. The law should promote order, social cohesion and moral standards. Rightful authorities are hallowed by tradition. To throw away the wisdom of the past is foolish and can only lead to social unrest and individual misery. Society is organic – it grows and evolves throughout history. Change is, therefore, slow and only comes about when necessary. Whilst reform is frequently beneficial, as planners may have been wrong in their forecasting of the future, revolution is an error, replacing tradition, monarchy, aristocracy and the Church (or their equivalents in other societies) with power for those who have the greatest physical strength or other advantages. Authoritarian and hierarchical societies, it is argued, work better. When people know their duties, and are brought up to fulfil them, society functions well. Provided they do perform their duties, however, they should have freedom of thought, expression and action in their lives within the limits of morality. 'The grosser forms of vice' are destructive to the individual and therefore detrimental both to one's own character and to others in society. People sometimes need to be protected, for their own good, from their baser instincts. Unrestricted freedom threatens political stability, social order and cohesion. Whether the imposition of a public morality is necessary or even desirable is a subject of debate. Is there, in, fact, such a thing as a generally agreed definition of public morality? This is a particularly pertinent question in a society such as Britain where many different religions are practised, and where a majority rarely attend worship but would almost inevitably claim to possess moral standards derived from one source or another. If there is no consensus as to right behaviour, is it proper for the time-hallowed values of previous generations to be imposed upon society as a whole? Could this be interpreted as tyranny, and if so, by a majority (made up of whom?) or a minority (consisting of which group or groups?). It is also worth making the point that moral standards and beliefs change over time. Unmarried cohabiting couples were strongly disapproved until at least the 1960s. Now, churches which run marriage preparation classes expect that the couple will be living together in advance of the ceremony. This could, of course, be seen as an example of the conservative contention that evolution is the way in which changes in societal values take place.

Paternalism Government, according to conservatives, should be limited to ensuring the security of the realm and providing a framework of law that promotes social order and cohesion. Centralisation of, for example, welfare policies, industries, etc., tends to lead to inefficiency. Rational and informed people should be left to judge what is in their own best interests, which will include looking after themselves and their families and ensuring, through charity or otherwise, that no one is so badly off that he or she is unable to use his or her talents to the full, or feels in need of turning to crime to support himself or herself. The irrational and uninformed should either be educated, or, if this is impossible, protected from themselves. Some redistribution of wealth and other goods is therefore part of conservative ideology. Paternalism, as practised by many successful businessmen in times past, is often, though not exclusively, a conservative characteristic. Many examples of paternalism can be found in the nineteenth-century industries of Britain, where manufacturers built housing for their workers, provided medical care for them and their dependents, and schooling, up to and including university fees where appropriate, for their children. Thus, conservatives can argue that to interfere with the individual freedom of others, in the interests of those others, will, in the long run, be to their benefit and give them more freedom of choice. For example, the state or the parents who insist upon education for children are enabling those children to gain access to a range of career options that are not available to the uneducated. Just as children, left to themselves, might opt for a diet consisting entirely of burgers and ice cream, to the detriment of their health and longevity, so some adults who are inclined to follow their emotions and desires for short-term gratification will tend to cut themselves off from opportunities. .Helping the deserving poor is regarded as a duty, whilst providing state benefits for all (whether deserving or not) may be seen as encouraging sloth, giving those who work justified feelings of resentment, sapping initiative and entrepreneurial activity, and encouraging bureaucratic bossiness and interference. Concern for the deserving poor, such as the elderly and the disabled, is, however, a conservative characteristic. Social cohesion derives from instinctive feelings of love and loyalty, and a shared history, code of ethics and cultural norms. As David Goodhart has pointed out, (*Prospect* magazine January 2004), people on the whole feel happier in the company of others who share the same cultural norms and who feel they all contribute to the same communal good. Every successful society therefore has secure roots which enable it to flourish and develop. To give primacy to individual theoretical reasoning is to encourage the fragmentation of society. By contrast, acceptance of the practical reason of historical experience guarantees continuity. Each society, therefore, develops its own system of rights throughout its own history. It is relevant to note here that Edmund Burke (1729–97), a founding father of conservatism, was active in his efforts to encourage the emancipation of the American colonies and Ireland from English rule, and that of India from the mismanagement of the East India Company. In the view of conservatism, the concept of universal rights is an error. Universal equality cannot exist in practice: there are real differences between people and between nation states and no amount of social engineering can alter this.

A philosophical conservative would not, however, advocate the perpetuation of a stable society if its basic principles were opposed to conservative principles. An example of this would be Eastern Europe during the Cold War. Conservatism accepts that free market capitalism is the most efficient way to ensure the success of the economy – history, after all, would seem to bear this out. Nor is conservatism opposed to immigration. Those who wish to relocate and are prepared to accept the basic norms of the society into which they move, whilst contributing to that society by their economic endeavours, are doing no wrong. Indeed, they can be a positive asset to their adopted community.

Critics of conservatism would point out that members of social hierarchies will tend to act in the interests of those hierarchies – that the 'working class' will continue to 'know their place'. Whether revolutions have in fact remedied social inequality and increased freedom is a moot point. Perhaps a better founded criticism is that scepticism as to the accuracy of individual human reason and planning does not encourage exploration in the scientific or other fields. Conservatism carried to extreme would discourage any progress at all, as was arguably the case in Japan prior to the Second World War and in China for many centuries until the advent of the barbarians.

In practice, conservative and other governments tend to differ in their actions only by degree. There may be more or less taxation, greater or lesser spending on public services, but, although emphases will differ, the basic institutions of state will continue. The arguments tend to be about the best means to provide goods – does a comprehensive or selective system provide the best education? Is privatisation or public ownership the most efficient way to provide services such as healthcare and public transport?

Liberalism

The harm principle The fundamental principle of liberalism is a distinction between the public and private spheres. Insofar as it is possible, the liberal maintains that everyone should have personal freedom. The only valid reason for restricting the freedom of the individual is to protect others from harm. This 'harm principle' is central to all varieties of liberal thought. Beyond this, liberalism does not seek to lay down moral standards for individuals in their private lives. Ironically, it could be argued that freedom, within the limits of the harm principle, is itself a moral standard upon which liberals insist, and which is just as authoritarian as any other. As the old joke has it, 'liberals are tolerant of everything except intolerance'. Some people would argue that there are various less than wise life-style choices of which we should be intolerant, such as smoking or promiscuous sexual behaviour. The roots of liberalism lie in the sixteenth century. Following the wars of religion, it may well have been the case that a growing realisation of the impossibility of agreement in matters of faith led to an understanding that people simply had to agree to differ, if they wanted peace. Whether peace – let alone peace at any price – is an overriding good is another question. From an acceptance of freedom of religion grew a further acceptance of freedom of conscience, speech, association and occupation. Freedom of sexual orientation and expression is a more recent addition to the list. The role of government is simply to ensure that those with differing beliefs and lifestyles should be able to coexist without causing one another harm. Liberalism may also be described as 'laissez-faire' (letting things go on), or, as we used to say in the 1960s, 'do your own thing'.

Modern and welfare liberals

Critics argue that in giving pre-eminence to the individual, liberalism simply justifies the free market and self-interest. Instead of seeing him or herself as part of a community – be that a nation, a religion, or whatever – the liberal pursues his or her own ends regardless. Modern liberals certainly divide into classical liberals, or libertarians, who support the free market (this is a mainly European movement, exemplified in the work of, for example, J.S. Mill, Friedrich August von Hayek (1899–1992) and Nozick), and welfare liberals, or liberal egalitarians, who argue for equality of opportunity, or, more radically yet, for equality of resources. These latter are more likely to be encountered in North America, and include Rawls and Ronald Dworkin (1931–). Hayek and Nozick both argue that individual liberty is the fundamental right, and that any other consideration is secondary.

A further problem with liberalism is that it seems to say that no particular belief system or lifestyle is better than any other. If all are of equal value, or, at the least, are equally tolerated, what is the point of choosing? At the extreme, it would seem that there is no such thing as objective truth, only a multiplicity of varying preferences. Liberals would usually reply that they do, in fact, accept that some beliefs and lifestyles are preferable to others, but that anyone has the right to choose, even if he or she makes incorrect or unwise choices. Moreover, plurality of opinion forces all of us to consider the validity of our own choices in the light of opposing arguments. Utilitarian liberals in particular would uphold this view. Kantian liberals argue that individual reasoning is the highest of human qualities, and is therefore of value in itself. *Modus vivendi* liberals argue that state coercion in matters of belief would lead to civil strife, which is best avoided.

Another view is that people are unable to make informed choices unless they have the necessary education to enable them to do so. They also, arguably, need to observe a diversity of lifestyles from which they can choose. It is possible that a truly liberal society might be so fragmented that people only lived within their own small groups, so that variety of enacted opinion was not available to be witnessed. What, after all, holds a liberal society together? If there are no shared values except the need to refrain from harming others, which requires self-discipline, then how can such a society survive in the long term? Conservatives and others would argue that values such as obligation, duty, virtue and justice are prerequisites for a cohesive community. Welfare liberals would respond that they do indeed value community, reason and fairness and that they have therefore met this criticism whilst avoiding the pitfalls of other ideologies. Anarchists reject liberalism because, in their view, it does not go far enough in stressing the primacy of freedom. Whether there can be any truly private sphere is also an issue. It may be argued that choosing to commit suicide is a purely personal act – but the family and friends of the suicide might well disagree. Even if there are no family or friends, various people in authority (pathologist, police, coroner) will be involved in the aftermath, and the expense of the inquest will fall upon taxpayers. John Donne (1573–1631) famously wrote that 'no man is an island ... any man's death diminishes me'. Other situations where the reality of a clear distinction between the public and private spheres is questionable include, for example, drug use and pornography. Driving or working whilst under the influence of drugs (including legal substances, such as alcohol) fall clearly into the public sphere. However, even those who only indulge recreationally in their own time may be burdening the health service and/or the criminal justice system. Buying and looking at pornography may be a private act, but purchasers create a market, satisfaction of which might involve the exploitation of vulnerable people. Additionally, if it is the case that viewing pornography tends to corrupt or deprave, there are further implications for other members of society.

In practice, most modern democracies are largely liberal in outlook, if not in name. Other political systems have either adapted themselves to liberal values of rights, liberty and equality of opportunity, or have survived only by brute force, and then have usually been overthrown. The almost universal acceptance of liberal values is, in fact; one of the major problems in the study of political philosophy today: 'Liberalism is hegemonic' (David Rawlinson, in conversation: 2003). Almost all students of the subject approach their studies with the underlying assumption that liberalism is self-evidently right. Anyone who could attain Nagel's 'view from nowhere' in this regard (were that to be possible) might achieve some interesting insights.

Socialism

Marx' outlook

Socialism in its various forms arose in response to, and as an argument against, capitalism. For Karl Marx (1818–83), capitalism was a system whereby the workers were exploited by the capitalists. The workers sold their labour to the owners of property (the capitalists), who benefited from that labour. The capitalists owned the means of production. Ownership of capital and the means of production bestow power. There is no way, in Marx' view, that anyone who owns property and the power which flows from it will willingly give them up. Only when the workers (proletariat) realise that they are being exploited will they rise up and take power for themselves. This will lead to the proletarian dictatorship, which will be followed by the communist revolution. After the revolution, people will be free to be themselves. There will be an equal society and 'the state will wither away'. Marx regarded this process as the inevitable consequence of history. An obvious point to make is that history does not seem to bear out his thesis. Marx expected that Britain, as the first industrialised state, would be the first to experience the revolution and the resultant communism. In fact, Britain has continued to be a (more or less) capitalist state for the 150 years or so since Marx outlined his theory. Marx also failed to foresee that capitalism would lead, as it has done, to an enormous growth in the middle classes. Those countries that allegedly did adopt communism (notably Russia and China) moved straight from feudalism (pre-industrial society) to a proletarian dictatorship. In the former Soviet Union what has succeeded the proletarian dictatorship is capitalism. In China, further developments are still awaited. Marx can also be criticised for having a rather rosy view of the working classes. What evidence is there that, once in charge, people will continue to work for the benefit of society as a whole? In the Soviet Union, equal pay and status for all were rapidly abandoned when it was found that many workers did as little as possible until given incentives to do more. In terms of economic success, and the individual and societal benefits which it brings, capitalism seems more effective than unmitigated socialism.

Other socialist theories try to adopt a less optimistic view of human nature whilst addressing social injustices. Inequalities between individuals and groups, competitiveness and individual self-interest are seen as wrong. All these things lead to the exploitation of the weakest in society, whom socialism tries to protect. In general, socialists believe that either the equitable redistribution of property, or the total abolition of private property, would be a necessary step in eradicating inequality. Socialists in general tend to concentrate upon the economic system as an engine of change. An economic system run upon socialist principles features state ownership of the means of production and investment, as equal a distribution as possible of income and wealth, and the democratic election of a government that deals with these economic issues. Those socialists who also advocate state control of all aspects of the economy are known as 'central planning socialists'. However, central planning socialism has not usually been possible in a truly successful democracy.

The distribution of income and wealth

The state ownership of the means of production and wealth is, arguably, less efficient than free market capitalism. Employed bureaucrats do not have the same personal interest in the success of an enterprise as do private owners or shareholders. On the other hand, private firms may be tempted to save money at the risk of imperilling safety or the wellbeing of their employees. Equal distribution of income and wealth is interpreted in various ways. Some argue for actual equality – the same income to each individual. Others maintain that greater effort should yield greater reward. Others again insist that everyone should receive what he or she needs. All of these interpretations raise problems. If all individuals receive the same income, surely some will spend it all, whilst others save and thus accrue wealth? How can effort realistically be measured? Two people doing identical jobs might well need to put in differing amounts of effort because of their differing abilities. How can need be assessed? It may be that I need to read detective stories in order to have the necessary escape mechanism to preserve my sanity, whilst someone else might need to regularly attend Covent Garden Opera for the same reason. I may need to eat more or less food, and of different types, from someone else, in order to remain healthy. Democratic government, to be meaningful, implies a choice between ideologies. Socialist claims that the people, once they understand the issues, will choose socialism, do not appear to be justified by the facts. In most democracies, where there is a choice between ideologies, there has been some level of alternation between the political parties over time. Central planning, as has already been noted, does not tend to coexist with democratic government, and seems to be very much less efficient than the free market in providing a robust economy.

The role of individual freedom within a socialist society should be considered. In general, it would be argued that social justice necessarily requires restrictions upon individual liberty, and that these restrictions must be accepted for the benefit of society as a whole, particularly its weaker members. This thesis would be called into question by both liberals and conservatives.

Anarchism

Freedom is paramount

Anarchists tend to believe that people are capable of living together in peace and goodwill without the need for authority. Leo Tolstoy (1828–1910) used the doctrine of peace and love expounded in the Christian gospels to support this view, although it has to be recognised that his was not the view of most anarchists. Almost by definition, anarchists vary quite widely in their views of how society should be organised. All agree, though, upon the primary importance of freedom. This not only means the abolition of the state, but the rejection of all authority – that of exploitative capitalists, rule-bound bureaucrats, bossy teachers, and domineering parents. Law, and its agents, such as the police, are rejected, as are armies which are seen as government-run bodies whose purpose is to oppress. Some anarchists assert that justice, equality, wellbeing and similar values are as important as, or run alongside, freedom. Other anarchists, such as Max Stirner (1806–56), probably one of the more extreme anarchists, rejected all values except freedom. He maintained that ethics, love, private property, religion, the family, the state, government and all other limiting factors upon individuality should be rejected.

Some anarchists, such as Michael Bakunin (1814–76) argue for violent revolution and the overthrow of all authority, whilst in the twentieth century others such as Ivan Illich (1926–2002) see the way forward as education, leading gradually to a wholesale rejection of institutionalised authority. Most anarchists hope for a future where people will freely band together as equals. Whilst they might choose some from among their number to be administrators, these people will not have power over their fellow humans but will simply be carrying out necessary tasks for the benefit of the community. Many hold that private property should not exist in such communities – people will 'hold all things in common' as was said to be the case in the Early Church (Acts 2: 64). The major criticism of anarchism is that it seems to have an over-optimistic view of people's ability to cooperate. Whilst there have been occasional anarchist communities established (and possibly the communes of the 1960s and 1970s could be interpreted as such), none has been of any great size, and none has lasted for long. The importance of anarchism is that it reminds us of the need to question the concept of institutionalised authority, and to ask whether established power is either necessary or desirable.

Freedom

important terms

Utilitarianism: the principle that we should aim at 'the greatest happiness for the greatest number'.

Key topics in this chapter

- Positive and negative freedoms
- Rights

Types of freedom

Negative and positive freedoms

Freedoms are traditionally divided into two types: negative freedom (freedom from constraint and interference by others) and positive freedom (freedom to act and achieve). Negative freedoms include freedom from hunger, thirst, imprisonment, slavery, and other ills. Positive freedoms include freedom to hold and express opinions, travel, marry, and obtain other goods, and freedom for self-realisation. Positive freedom may need to be developed in individuals. Parents, teachers and other authorities enable people to have positive freedoms by encouraging them to identify their individual goals and equipping them with the tools to pursue them. Negative freedom is most concerned with mapping out a private sphere within which one is sovereign, thus limiting the role of the state. Positive freedom may justify interference on the grounds that it is better to encourage and develop one's 'higher' ambitions only. State interference is justified by some on the grounds that it encourages personal development and individual participation in public life. It has to be asked how far such interference should go. There is always the danger that governments will be accused of bringing about a 'nanny state'. Government campaigns to increase the consumption of fruit and vegetables have occasioned some debate. Concern about increasing obesity is leading to further advice – or, as some would say, nagging – from the Department of Health. Anti-smoking legislation is increasing all the time. Does it increase our positive freedoms to be hectored into a healthy lifestyle? It may be true that non-smoking, slim people live longer and are more active, but some would contend that the freedom to indulge in pleasure, even if the chosen pleasures cause damage to oneself, is also of value.

Negative freedoms logically underpin positive freedoms. There is no point having the freedom to choose anything you want to eat unless the place where you happen to be has freedom from famine. Similarly, there is no point having the freedom to buy anything you choose in the supermarket unless you are free from poverty. If it is the case, however, that basic needs are met, one must consider the relative importance of different types of freedom. Conservatives would argue that it is important that the law should promote order, moral standards and social cohesion, as these things lead to positive freedoms. It could also be held, by social democrats among others, that social justice is another crucial value that the law should uphold.

Hegel's view Utilitarians and liberals traditionally concentrate upon negative freedoms – freedom from state interference in your private life. Others, however, such as Georg Hegel (1770–1831), rejected this view of freedom. Freedom from constraint is the freedom to act upon whim, he argued, and this is not true freedom. We have to ask why people make the choices they do, and realise that we are in fact moulded by external forces to desire those things that we want. The perceived need for more and more comfort, he said, is 'suggested to you by those who wish to make a profit'. Therefore, when we act as consumers in the market place, we are not acting freely – we are being controlled by external influences that tell us what we should want and do. In modern society, these influences would include advertising and peer pressure. Only if we realise the effect of such things and take control of these forces can we be truly free. The way to control these forces is by the use of reason. As all humans are capable of rational thought, it should be possible for all members of society to rationally decide what they want, rather than being swayed by the vagaries of fashion and commercialism. The whole of society will desire the same things, which will be the things they actually need, or those things which they desire for good reason. The enacted will of society will then be identical with the desires of all members of it, and people will be truly free – free from irrational longing. Freedom, therefore, can only be found within a cohesive society predicated upon rational thought. It could be argued, however, that people do not in fact usually, or even often, act rationally. Emotion seems to be a much more compelling driving force than is reason. Some psychologists would go so far as to suggest that we make emotional decisions, and only then do we try to find rational justification for them. It is interesting to note that increased economic wellbeing, measured as gross per capita income, does not lead to a perceived increase in happiness. In material terms, Britons are, on average, much better off than were their parents and grandparents, but surveys do not show a corresponding increase in how happy people feel. The phrases 'cash rich, time poor', 'downsizing' and 'wishing to spend more time with the family' suggest that the wellbeing of individuals and of society as a whole is less dependent upon economic factors and the distribution of wealth, and more dependent upon non-material values, than has sometimes been supposed by some political philosophers – and this concept is even further removed from the beliefs and perceptions of many active politicians.

Other philosophers have argued that the desire for privacy, separateness and individuality are the sign of a dysfunctional personality. We are who we are because of our relationships with others and our social roles. To desire aloneness is to be maladjusted. In a truly mature society, the values of one will inevitably be the values of all.

It is certainly true that the concept of individual freedom is a relatively recent development. For the ancient Greeks, freedom meant the ability to participate in government. Provided they could do so, the government, which they had chosen, had the right to regulate all areas of life. The concept that there is a private sphere with which the state should not concern itself in fact only came into being around the sixteenth century, and was most clearly explained by Henri Benjamin Constant de Rebecque (1767–1830).

Freedom and the state

The role of the state in providing freedom is usually interpreted today in negative terms. The armed services and the police force provide freedom from fear (of enemy occupation and of crime). Welfare systems provide freedom from poverty, homelessness and untreated disease or injury, and so on. There are laws to prohibit slavery and other constraints. Should the state try to enforce positive freedoms? For example, freedom to enjoy life to the full might mean prohibiting alcoholics access to liquor, or prohibiting the obese from eating more than they need and/or forcing them to take more exercise. Unwise choices, which will lead to misery, and which, therefore, would not be freely chosen by anyone in possession of the facts, and who was free from commercial interests and peer pressure, might be prohibited – such as the freedoms which currently exist to indulge in adulterous affairs or to smoke cigarettes. Would it be possible, or desirable, to live under a regime where everything not specifically permitted by law was forbidden?

In any case, some would argue, we can never be entirely free to choose. We are all limited by physical and environmental factors over which we have no control. A seven-stone adult does not, realistically, have lumberjacking as an available career choice. Neither is it practical for someone with limited mathematical understanding to aim for accountancy.

Rights

Constitutional rights

The fundamental question is whether or not we possess rights simply by virtue of being existent human beings, or whether rights are conferred upon us within a social context. Modern political thinking seems to hold the former view: there is a United Nations Declaration of Universal Human Rights. The American constitution holds it to be self-evidently true that all people have the right to 'life, liberty and the pursuit of happiness'. This could be expressed in more philosophical terms as being the rights to freedom and to wellbeing. Freedom involves the capacity to untrammelled action, within the limits of the harm principle, and wellbeing involves life, health, opportunities for education, making a livelihood and pursuing pleasurable action, again, within the limits of the harm principle. It is also generally accepted that the possession of rights involves corresponding duties or responsibilities: at the least, the recognition that others have the same rights; further, that one should actively promote the rights of others. Thus, for example, it may be claimed that someone who receives a reasonable income (however that is defined), should pay taxes in order that others might have the benefits of restored health, or of education.

In some societies, people actually receive none of these supposedly universal rights. This does not mean that the rights do not exist – simply that they are currently unenforceable. I have a right to freedom of movement (arguably), but if I am kidnapped, my rights are being denied – it is not that I no longer possess that right, simply that I am not in a position to exercise it. There are usually limits upon the category of rights-holders: children, the mentally less able and the mentally ill are generally held to possess the right to life, but their right to exercise liberty and the pursuit of perceived happiness is curtailed, allegedly for their own good and that of others, and because they are not in a position to make informed choices. We curtail the right to liberty of some criminals in order to preserve the rights of other members of society.

God-given rights

In previous times, and, indeed, for believers today, rights are conferred by God. The prohibitions, universal in all religions, against murder, theft, etc., protect the rights of others to life and property. Honouring one's father and mother preserves the right of the elderly to be free from poverty. Prohibitions against adultery protect the right of children to know their roots, and to legitimacy. Prohibitions against 'false witness against thy neighbour' protect one's right to reputation. The Hebrew laws about Shabbat (the weekly day of rest) even protect the rights of animals against overwork and exploitation. Rights endowed by religion are not so much self-evident in the light of reason, but duties to other humans, other creatures and the environment enjoined by the Creator. Any human who refuses to acknowledge these rights is failing in duty and is morally wrong.

Legal rights

There are those, by contrast, who hold that we possess rights only insofar as the law permits us to do so. That which is permitted, is our right: that which is not, is not. Rights are 'children of the law'. Laws should protect utilitarian interests. For example, in Singapore, until recently, the sale and use of chewing gum was forbidden. No one had the right to put whatever they wanted into their mouth – the law held that chewing gum was, among other things, a pollutant (it tends to be discarded in the street and is not biodegradable), and for this and other reasons it was not allowed. We therefore have to consider whether rights derive from the way things are (i.e. are natural and innate) or whether they are a social construct. If the former, then we all must logically possess the same rights, and laws which deprive us of these rights are bad laws. If the latter, then rights can properly vary between different societies, or even different groups within societies, and the final word belongs to the law.

Given the lessons of recent history, the idea of universal human rights is attractive. Adolf Hitler was very careful to pass laws that made his persecution and mass murder of Jews and other groups lawful. The Nuremberg trials, however, held unequivocally that such actions were wrong, and breached the right to life, as well as other rights. It remains to be asked, though, how far we can take the concept of universal rights. If education is a universal right, then are countries that do not provide free schooling wrongfully depriving the next generation? Does a government that charges tuition fees for university courses breach the rights of its poorer citizens? Indeed, do universities which select students on academic merit deny a right to education held by all, including the less academically able?

To take another example: do women have the right to bear children? In some central European countries under the Soviet regime, women were encouraged, and in some cases may have been forced, to have abortions because there was concern about the dangers of overpopulation. In China, for example, the law prohibits all but rural farmers from producing more than one child. In most countries, these practices are seen as being in contravention of the basic human right to reproduce. But, even if we accept that such a right exists, does this mean that infertile individuals and couples should have unlimited access to treatments without charge? Should society bear the expense of these procedures? Further, should such medical provision be made for those who are single, or in homosexual relationships, or who are beyond the usual age of childbearing? If the right to reproduce exists, does it conflict with utilitarian principles in, for example, an overpopulated state, or if the cost of enabling conception places a burden upon the exchequer? If there is a clash between utility and rights, which of them should take priority?

Other situations where social utility and natural rights might be in conflict include the right to freedom of worship and association versus the utility of social control and cohesion, or the right to own property versus the utility of a new road or other facility which is intended to be of benefit to the community as a whole.

Conflicting interests

A recurring theme in this section has been the conflicts that might arise between individuals, the good of society and the demands of justice. An individual may have to refrain from acting as he or she would wish because doing so would damage society. One who damages society is usually held to be liable to punishment, in the interests of justice. Punishment usually involves deprivation of a right: probation and community service restrict freedom of movement; a fine deprives one of private property; prison deprives one of liberty. Holding the varying demands of individuals, society and justice together is not easy. In order to do so, it is necessary to establish whether, why and from whence people have rights; the relative importance of the individual and society; and what justice entails.

review
activity

Differentiate between the various concepts of freedom.

Law

Key topics in this chapter

- Principles of law
- Justice
- Morality
- Disobedience
- Punishment

Basic functions of law

Origins

Originally, all codes of law were religious. They all bore a remarkable similarity to one another, with some local variation. This has led some scholars to hold that these laws were, in fact, the product of human reason (perhaps the reason of a particularly wise individual or group within each society), with differences attributable to local conditions. Others would argue that the similarities show that they were all, indeed, from God or some Supreme Authority, and the differences can be explained by human fallibility and misunderstanding.

Even as societies became, on the whole, more secular, laws continued to be based upon religious codes. For example, until the 1960s in Britain, male homosexuality (which is forbidden in the biblical book of Exodus) was a criminal act. Adultery (also forbidden in the Judaeo-Christian code) was punishable in the courts. Suicide (which was regarded as murder of oneself, and as usurping the function of the Almighty, or 'playing God') was a crime although, in the nature of things, only unsuccessful attempted suicides could be prosecuted. Entering into a suicide pact is currently illegal.

A time of change

The secularisation of society led in many places, including Britain, to a large number of these laws being repealed or changed. It is noticeable that utilitarian and liberal principles informed the changes. Homosexual activity became lawful between consenting adults in private – note the emphasis upon the private sphere and the freewill of others. Adultery, whilst still grounds for divorce, became a moral rather than a criminal issue – what goes on in one's private life is not the concern of the criminal courts. Abortion, formerly (though, in view of some biblical teaching, perhaps controversially) seen as a breach of the prohibition of murder, became lawful under certain (ironically, arguably more biblically based) conditions. (In the Hebrew Scriptures (or Old Testament) the law laid down that where a woman was assaulted, she should be paid damages according to the severity of her injuries. If, at the time of the assault, she was pregnant, and suffered a miscarriage, she should be paid

113

damages for the loss of the baby only after 'quickening' (the time she first felt the baby's movements) – which occurs around the 20th week of pregnancy. Prior to that, the loss of the baby was not regarded as the loss of a separate life that warranted compensation. It can therefore be argued that an abortion prior to around 20 weeks of pregnancy is not, biblically, regarded as the loss of a separate life. Currently abortion is permitted generally up to the 24th week of pregnancy, although in exceptional circumstances it may take place later.) The rationale for the legalisation of abortion was, however, entirely utilitarian and liberal – the right of a woman to avoid the pain of an unwanted child and to have sovereignty over her own body.

In other parts of the world, governments passed, and still pass, laws designed to ensure the survival or security of society, or of the incumbent regime. Here, the emphasis is on the wellbeing of the whole, or of the ruling faction, even at the expense of the suffering of some individuals or groups. Thus, for example, women may not drive in Saudi Arabia, as it is held that the consequences of such freedom would lead to social unrest and the breakdown of family life. In some countries, mainly in the Middle East, religious codes are still the only basis for the legal system.

In order to decide what laws we should have, therefore, it is necessary to see what the underlying principles of society are, or what we believe they should be. Do we wish to please God? If so, various religious codes exist. Do we wish to maximise individual liberty? If so, we must look to utilitarian or similar principles. Do we want an ordered society, with shared values and ideology? If so, which values and ideology? The nature of the law we believe we should have will, logically, flow from the answer to these questions. It is important to realise that laws do not only restrict action. Many are, indeed, of the form (in spirit if not in fact) 'thou shalt not . . .', but without employment law we could not meaningfully enter into contracts, without matrimonial law we could not obtain the benefits of recognised marriage, and without consumer protection law we could not insist upon redress for faulty goods and services.

Law, justice and morality

Can all laws be fair?

Most people involved with the law, and also many laypersons with relevant experience, would argue that it is possible for something to be legal but unjust. In fact, many lawyers and others involved with the legal system will tell you that 'justice and the law are not synonymous'. In the civil courts, quite apart from the problems of proving your case – even if it is right – it is surprising to many that some disapproved actions are not unlawful.

Take the case of an employee who is bullied by his or her line manager. Bullying, where this simply means being unpleasant and finding fault, is not an offence. If remarks are made or actions performed which are racist, sexist, or offend against the Disability Discrimination Act, then they may be unlawful, but if they simply consist of snide remarks, they probably are not. There is no such offence as bullying. If the employee is stressed by the line manager's behaviour, it may well be that nothing unlawful has occurred. Stress is not, in law, damage. If the employee becomes clinically depressed or suffers some other recognised mental illness, then and only then might he or she have a case against the line manager, but only if it can be shown that the line manager's behaviour was the only possible cause, and that it was foreseeable that the behaviour would cause the damage, and that the employee has suffered detriment (usually financial loss) as a result. So three months' sick leave on full pay would not count as detriment; any other stressful situation in the employee's life, such as bereavement, would impede proof of causality; and in any case, if the line manager was equally nasty to others who did not break down, such an outcome might not have been foreseeable.

History gives many more examples of arguably more obvious and extreme unjust actions which did not breach the law. Reference has already been made to Nazi Germany under Adolf Hitler: one can add the treatment of Ugandan Asians and others under Idi Amin; apartheid in pre-1994 South Africa; the laws discriminating against non-whites in the USA until the 1960s – the list seems endless.

The relationship between law and morality is even less close. Adultery, as has already been mentioned, is legal (in the sense that it is not punishable) but generally regarded as immoral. Eating meat is legal, but plenty of vegetarians would question its morality. In most countries, drinking alcohol is legal for adults, but many people, on religious or other grounds, would condemn it. The question that must be asked in this context is: which is primary, law or morality? Should the law reflect absolute moral standards, or define those moral standards which are applicable in any given society at a particular stage in its history? We therefore have to define law, justice and morality.

Justice and morality Law is prescribed by the state, and varies between states and over time. Justice is what is fair, and different views are held as to that. Morality is what is right – once again, there is no agreed definition. Liberals would argue that the law both can and should enforce moral principles insofar as these principles are utilitarian in their effect. Laws should guarantee individual liberty, within the limits of the harm principle. Thus, people are protected from exploitation (a moral principle) whilst society can benefit from new thoughts and ideas. This leads to progression for both individuals and the community as a whole. Conservatives might argue that some moral principles are basic and the law should reflect these. There are natural rights within each society, and these should be enshrined in legislation. Others might say that law is concerned with preventing damage to the state, or to the community as a whole. Morality goes further than this. Immoral acts that do not threaten the entire society are dealt with in other ways. People may choose not to associate with those who indulge in immoral behaviour. Those in public life whose adulterous affairs are reported in the press often feel forced to resign from office. At a more mundane level, it is perfectly acceptable for me to mow my lawn on a Sunday afternoon in Britain. In many parts of Germany and Switzerland, however, neighbours will inform anyone who does likewise that it is the accepted norm that Sunday afternoons should be for peaceful enjoyment, undisturbed by auditory interference from lawnmowers, loud music, or any other source. I would not necessarily be breaking a law, but I would certainly feel the force and suffer the effects of moral disapproval. Others again would argue that the law simply defines one's rights and duties within a particular state. Morality is not fixed: people decide which standards to adopt for themselves and act accordingly. A more extreme view yet is that both law and morality are social constructs and neither has any absolute force. It is more convenient, in general, to obey the law, but that is as far as it goes. Morality varies according to time and to place. Once again, it may well be easier to accept the force of the prevailing view and to behave accordingly, but one does not have to accept that the prevailing view is right in any absolute sense.

The practical issue, therefore, is how one can or should respond when the law contradicts one's perceptions or beliefs about justice and morality. In other words, if the law says one thing and your conscience says otherwise, what should you do? Socrates saw no contradiction with this. He was condemned to death on entirely trumped-up charges of perverting the youth of Athens and failing to obey the dictates of the official religion. Whilst in his cell awaiting execution by poisoning, he had plenty of opportunity to escape, and was indeed expected, by the authorities and by his friends, to do so. Instead of which, he maintained that having enjoyed the benefits of the Athenian legal system throughout his life, it would be wrong for him to refuse to accept its judgement now. Whether this is an issue of morality, justice, or both, is perhaps difficult to determine. He therefore remained in his cell, drank the hemlock, and died. St Paul was faced with a somewhat similar situation, and also refused to escape, but for different reasons. When imprisoned for completely spurious reasons in Macedonia, he was given the opportunity to escape by an earthquake (allegedly miraculous) which shook the foundations of the prison and broke all the locks. The guard, assuming that the prisoners had all taken advantage of this and gone, was about to kill himself, as he would have been executed for dereliction of duty had there been a mass breakout. Paul hastened to reassure him that no one had left. When the order from the magistrate to release him subsequently arrived, Paul insisted that he would not leave until he had received an apology for his earlier ill-treatment. It would seem that compassion for the guard's situation (a moral issue) stopped him from leaving in the first place, and a desire for right treatment (a matter of justice) led to his refusal to go quietly later on. (The desired apology was made in the end.)

Resistance to the law   Others have decided differently. Rosa Parkes refused to give up her seat, as the law required, to a white passenger on a bus, and thus initiated political action that led to equal rights under the law for all racial groups in the USA. Mahatma Gandhi's campaign of civil disobedience and passive resistance led, ultimately, to Indian self-government. As I write, there are old-age pensioners refusing to pay the increases in their council tax bills because they believe that the amount demanded is unjust. Respectable citizens who suffer from arthritis and other debilitating diseases are illegally buying and using cannabis to relieve their pain and other symptoms. Indeed, the British Medical Association is on record as saying that doctors should be able to prescribe cannabis in appropriate cases, just as they always have been able to administer heroin, morphine and other drugs when no other treatment is as effective. Here, a moral duty upon doctors to relieve suffering is impeded by a legal ban preventing access to a suitable drug.

Just and unjust laws and possible responses

What is a fair law?

A just law is one which is fair. An unjust law is unfair. In order to decide if a law is fair, we need to see whether its effect on some people or groups is to their unreasonable disadvantage. There may be good reasons for treating some people differently from others. Those practising as doctors must possess recognised qualifications and be registered with their professional body. We do not, generally, think of this as unfair treatment of those without qualifications – we see this as protection for patients. A law, however, which said that, for example, red-haired people were forbidden to study medicine, would generally be regarded as unjust. Some will argue that those laws which do not accord with natural moral law, or with human rights, or the dictates of reason, are unjust. Those who adhere to social contract theory will stress the necessity of the consent of those under the law. The power of the state is in the gift of the people, they would say, and it should not be abused. Marxists would hold that consent is not actual, but is manufactured by those in possession of power. If all else fails, force will be used to compel obedience. Thus, in a divided (non-communist) society, there can be no such thing as legitimate authority according to Marxist doctrine. Our obedience to law is in fact a symptom of our powerlessness. Legal positivists hold that law is morally neutral. Moral rights and obligations have no objective existence, but we are in fact obliged to obey the law and entitled to such rights as it may bestow. If we believe that that which is lawful is not necessarily right, what, if anything, should we do in response?

Reference has already been made to racial segregation and persecution in various times and places. It is now widely agreed that the laws that permitted, or enforced, such discrimination, were morally wrong and deprived some individual people, or groups of people, of justice. The treatment of women in times past; the lack of franchise, educational opportunity and so on is now, in most places, condemned.

In the various campaigns for equal rights, there have tended to be two schools of reaction: peaceful demonstration and violent disturbance. Martin Luther King, the leader of the Black Civil Rights Movement in the United States, modelled his tactics upon those of Mahatma Gandhi. Passive resistance

Revd Martin Luther King Jr. was a black Baptist minister who became leader of the American Civil Rights Movement. His insistence upon non-violence was inspired by the example of Mahatma Gandhi. King's efforts helped African Americans to gain equal rights under the law with the passing of the Civil Rights Act, 1964, and the Voting Rights Act, 1965. He was assassinated in 1968, aged 39.

Mahatma Gandhi trained as a lawyer, but gave up his practice to live in South Africa from 1893 to 1914, where he opposed racially discriminative laws against Indian residents. Returning to India, he became leader of the Home Rule movement, and led campaigns of civil disobedience in order to try to gain independence for the country. Frequently imprisoned, he renewed his efforts every time he was released. In 1947, India and Pakistan became independent states. Gandhi was assassinated in 1948.

involved ignoring the segregation laws, and offering neither resistance nor cooperation when the police or the armed forces arrived. Consequently, peaceful demonstrators had to be carried away from the scene by police officers or soldiers. Other forms of peaceful protest included a boycott of buses, in the USA, because the company discriminated against black passengers. This led to a damaging loss of revenue for the bus company. Other protestors for various causes have adopted more violent methods, ranging from damage to property to bombing campaigns causing loss of life and personal injury. Are any of these responses justified?

Peaceful protest   One argument is that if one lives in a society, one should obey the rules. This is part of the social contract. If we don't like the rules, we can legitimately leave and join a society that is more to our taste. Alternatively, we can employ lawful means of persuasion. In a free democracy, we can lobby MPs, publish articles, make speeches, write to the newspapers, etc. in an attempt to influence public opinion and persuade Parliament to change the law. A second approach is to refuse to obey the law in question, but without infringing anyone else's rights. Thus, one could refuse, on grounds of conscience, to pay council tax, and accept the resulting prison sentence. The third option is the use of violence, possibly including damage to property and persons, in order to make one's point. This may be difficult to justify to others, but is usually defended on the grounds that the alleged wrong which one is suffering is so great that it outweighs any suffering caused to others. It may also be claimed that the tactics would not be used if peaceful means could succeed, so that those at fault are the intransigent authorities, who won't listen, rather than the protestors, who can only bring their case to notice in this way. Whether any means of protest is morally justified, and in what circumstances, is a matter for continuing debate, as is the status of many laws. Should legislation aimed at protecting animals from suffering prevent some religious communities from using traditional (and ritually prescribed) methods of slaughter? Should the state deny people the right to wear religious symbols (such as the Islamic veil, the Sikh turban and the Christian crucifix) as has happened in France? Should smoking be banned in public places (such as pubs in Ireland) or does this infringe people's human rights to enjoy a legal substance? After all, arguably, alcohol causes more damage to society in general than does tobacco. At another level, are the inhabitants of an occupied country, whose government has signed a truce with the invading force, entitled to try to overthrow the occupying power? Were those who tried to assassinate Hitler during the Second World War morally wrong?

A few animal rights and anti-abortion campaigners consider that it is morally acceptable to kill those who experiment upon animals, or who perform legal abortions. They argue that their actions are justified as they are trying to prevent a greater evil.

Punishment

All states punish offenders. The reasons for punishment include retribution (making the criminal pay in some way for the crime); deterrence (making people unwilling to commit crime because if they do they will be punished, and making those who have been punished once unwilling to experience it again); protection (removing criminals from society so they are not at liberty to reoffend and endanger others); rehabilitation (providing training, treatment, and so on to enable the person to live a normal life in society); and reform (to turn the offender into a better person by means of inflicting punishment).

Beyond reasonable doubt

The effectiveness of all of these aims is open to question. In order for any of them to succeed, the criminal first has to be convicted. Only a minority of crimes leads to a conviction. Many offenders are not caught and many prosecutions end in acquittal. Whilst it seems self-evidently correct, on both moral and practical grounds, that the innocent should walk free, the requirement in Britain for a case to be proved 'beyond reasonable doubt' inevitably entails that some guilty people do so too, as was clearly stated by the judge at the trial, for murder, of Dr John Bodkin Adams in 1957 at the Old Bailey. Adams was accused of murdering one of his patients, Mrs Edith Alice Morrell, who was 81 years old. She had been seriously ill for about two years, following a stroke. On her death, Dr Adams inherited some silver, and was also given Mrs Morrell's Rolls Royce, thanks to the generosity of her son. Six years after her death, Dr Adams was accused of murdering her by large doses of heroin and morphine. There is no doubt that huge quantities had been prescribed, and, had they been administered, they would almost certainly have proved fatal. However, the nursing notebooks produced at the trial did not record the use of anything like the quantities on the prescriptions. The prosecution maintained that the doctor administered the drugs whilst the nurses were not present. The judge ruled that, in law, only the doses recorded in the books constituted evidence. There was the possibility that the drugs unaccounted for were being 'illicitly trafficked'. (Dr Adams was, later that year, prosecuted and fined for forging prescriptions.) In his directions to the jury, the judge told them: 'We pride ourselves ... that a man who is convicted by a jury is undoubtedly guilty. The price of making sure that the innocent are not convicted must be that the guilty sometimes go free.'

Dr Adams was acquitted after 44 minutes of deliberation by the jury. The Attorney-General then announced that a further charge, for the murder of Gertrude Hullett, had also been made against Dr Adams, but that this would not be pursued. Some people at the time believed that he was in fact guilty of eight or nine murders. Dr Adams was struck off the medical register in 1957 but reinstated in 1961. He returned to his practice until he retired. He died, aged 84, in 1983. Several accounts of the trial have been written, including *The Best We Can Do* (Sybille Bedford, 1958).

Retribution

The guilty mind and the guilty action

The concept of retribution has moral force because of its insistence that only the guilty should be punished. It is generally agreed that guilt is made up of two factors. One is the intention to do wrong, or the 'guilty mind'. The other is the performance of the offence, or the 'guilty action'. Thus, anyone who had no intention of causing damage will either be acquitted or, if mentally ill, treated for his or her condition. Only those who knowingly break the law will be punished as a result. There have been successful defences to charges of serious crimes on these grounds. Those who are, in legal terms, insane, can always plead not guilty by virtue of insanity. Drivers with excess alcohol in the bloodstream have been exonerated because they have shown that their drinks were 'spiked' unbeknown to them. (However, those who added the alcohol to their drinks have been punished instead!) A man is on record as having been acquitted of murder because the jury accepted that he was sleep-walking at the time, and, in his dream, believed that he was defending himself against a violent intruder, rather than attacking the friend who was staying overnight. In other cases, punishment has been less severe where there was an intention to commit a lesser crime, but not to cause the eventual degree of damage which in fact occurred. Hence the relatively lenient sentences for some robbers who have killed members of the public in the execution of the crime, rather than temporarily disabling them, as was the intention.

Deterrence

It is a fact that most convicted criminals who are imprisoned and then released return to the cells following a subsequent crime. Reoffending rates do not suggest that prison is usually a deterrent to further crime. In some cases, it is difficult to see how the prospect of punishment could deter. Crimes of passion, for example, are usually unpremeditated and carried out in circumstances where rational consideration of possible future consequences is not likely to take place. Those who are committed to some cause will not be deterred by threatened punishment, and such people might even welcome the opportunity for 'martyrdom'. There are also some recidivists (repeat offenders) who are unable to function when released into society and who deliberately commit further offences in order to be reincarcerated. Only when they are within an ordered institution, where their choices are limited, can they cope. Whether this is the cause or the effect of frequent imprisonment is a matter for psychiatrists and criminologists to determine. Nonetheless, supporters of the theory of deterrence point out that their concern is for the benefit of society both now and in the future. Even if the experience of prison does not necessarily put existing criminals off committing further offences, it is possible that the threat of incarceration might well deter the currently law-abiding from joining the criminal fraternity.

The protection of society

When considering whether punishment of criminals protects society, it is obviously true that anyone who is locked up cannot harm society at large for the duration of his or her prison sentence, but sooner or later the vast majority of prisoners have to be released. Therefore, unless it is clear that prison deters, rehabilitates or reforms such people, it is difficult to see how society gains protection in the long term. Unless we are to pursue a policy of mass executions or lifelong incarcerations it is not clear that protection provides a sole justification for punishment. Those who are punished other than by imprisonment, for example by being placed on probation, fined or given community service orders, are thereby not prevented from reoffending should they choose to do so.

Rehabilitation

Rehabilitation does seem to achieve success in some cases. The focus of rehabilitation is to provide appropriate education or treatment in order to change behaviour. Certainly, convicted persons who successfully undertake educational courses whilst in prison are less likely to reoffend than those who do not. Anger management courses, which some offenders on probation are ordered to do and which are offered to some prisoners, also seem to have some good results (although whether Edward Grundy in Radio 4's *The Archers* gains long-term benefit remains to be seen!). Some sexual offenders can be taught, in intensive group and/or one-to-one counselling sessions, to control their actions even though they cannot control their desires. Behaviour management techniques can be learnt so that one can 'be tempted, yet do no sin'. However, the provision of such courses is time consuming and expensive, and their efficacy is often doubted by the wider public.

Reform

It is not obvious that many prisoners are reformed simply by their experience of imprisonment. Unlike rehabilitation, which attempts to prevent offending behaviour through treatment, reform is predicated upon the principle that offending intention is eliminated through punishment. It seems, however, that a decreasing tendency to wish to commit crimes is a function of maturity, rather than the experience of sanctions. It is argued that, for some, the company of other offenders simply teaches them more effective ways of committing crimes and avoiding capture in the future.

Crime prevention

Who commits crime and why?

Many would argue that, logically, we should be aiming to prevent crime rather than to catch and punish the criminals after the act. In this case, it would make good sense to try to analyse and understand what causes people to commit crimes in the first place. Perhaps hearteningly, the social group most likely to be convicted (males aged between 17 and 24) seems on the whole to grow out of the tendency to offend and go on to lead relatively blameless lives after a period of adolescent lawlessness. Even for those most ardently in favour of crime prevention, it is admitted to be unrealistic to expect that any political system could or should prevent the birth of males, or their passing through the ages of 17 to 24s, once born. Moral and other objections would doubtless be made about suggestions for a female-only society, or one in which males were put down at age 16, or even one where males were imprisoned for the most dangerous seven years of their lives! There are other indications, however, of a propensity to commit crime which might properly be considered governmental responsibilities. The poorest in society are the most likely both to commit crime and to be victims of crime. Alleviating poverty, whether by means of a welfare system or otherwise, it has been argued, would reduce the rate of crime. People who can lawfully obtain what they want will not be tempted to steal it from others. Most crime is committed by those of low educational attainment. It would seem to be logical, therefore, to posit that raising educational standards might lower the crime rate. An educational system which enabled people to utilise their full potential would help them to understand the arguments against criminality, and provide them with a means of escaping poverty through gainful employment.

Children from single-parent families (except the offspring of widows and widowers) are also disproportionately represented among those convicted of crimes. This has led some, especially among those of conservative tendencies, to argue that it would be beneficial both to individual children and to society as a whole if stable marriages were to be encouraged or rewarded in some way. This could be done, for example, by increasing tax benefits for married couples. It has been suggested that couples who remain together should be financially rewarded, by the state, on significant wedding anniversaries. Some have suggested that single parenthood should be actively discouraged, for example, by no longer giving unmarried mothers priority in the allocation of rented accommodation. Against these suggestions there are arguments that equity requires everyone, whatever their lifestyle, to be treated in the same way. There are those who hold that divorce should become less quickly and easily obtainable. Plans to require separating couples to undergo a period of counselling before they could obtain a divorce were drawn up, but later abandoned, under a Labour government in the 1980s.

Marxists would argue that crime is a social construct, and that the fundamental problem is the alienation within society. Under communism, there would be peaceful coexistence. Conservatives would lay an emphasis upon the importance of instilling a sense of duty and respect in people. Liberals would argue that mutual tolerance and a respect for privacy would obviate many problems. Anarchists would question the legitimacy of any state and the laws which it imposed, holding that people, if left to themselves, will tend to coexist peacefully.

The problem faced by any political system, in practice, is to find what works. Crucially, too, in a democracy, the price must be one which the public is prepared to pay. If punishing the innocent was a deterrence to others, most of us would probably reject it, either on moral grounds or out of fear that we might be one of the unlucky victims. This is true despite Voltaire's observation in *Candide* that '*Dans ce pays-ci il est bon de tuer de temps en temps un amiral pour encourager les autres*'. ('In this country [England] it is thought well to kill an admiral from time to time in order to encourage the others.') Efforts to deter terrorism have led to miscarriages of justice and the conviction of the innocent, such as the Birmingham Six and the Guildford Four. The indefinite detention, without charge or trial, of suspected terrorists is currently causing much concern and political debate.

If alleviating poverty would be the most effective crime-cutting measure, this would almost inevitably involve increased taxes. A different education system perhaps with smaller classes, or regular one-to-one counselling for those most at risk, would face the same political difficulty. Educational programmes within prison are expensive, and often raise objections along the lines that 'law-abiding people have to pay for evening classes, but criminals get them laid on for free'. It is unlikely that any democratic government would even attempt to regulate the sexual activities, divorce rate and other personal relationships of the community – the outcry about the right to private life would be too great. Here, perhaps, is one of the greatest weaknesses of democracy – indeed, an exemplification of Plato's objection. Survey after survey indicates that most people believe that criminals deserve retribution. A majority of people in Britain favour the death penalty for murder. Those who work in the criminal justice system, and especially those who study it, are almost unanimous in saying that rehabilitation is what we should be aiming for. But rehabilitative programmes cost money, time and effort and this is a price that popular opinion seems to say the public is unwilling to pay.

The general perception that those who carry out criminal acts are freely choosing to do so can also be challenged. Some would argue that social circumstances, inherited tendencies, or environmental factors are the causes of crime. If punishment is to be justified, it is generally agreed that this can only be justified on the grounds that the person carrying out the crime deliberately and consciously chose that course of action from a number of real options. If this is disputed, systems of justice, law and punishment may need to be rethought.

review
activity

How may legal punishment be justified?

IV

Authority

important terms

De facto: that which exists in fact, whether or not it is right.

De jure: that which is rightful.

Deontology: the belief that ethics should be based upon duties, not upon the consequences of actions.

Key topics in this chapter

- Duty to the state
- Resistance to authority

Authority, power and legitimacy

Authority is the ability to say what is the case, or to order that something should be done and be obeyed. A teacher will be an authority on his or her subject: if the head of geography says that the arc of a great circle is the shortest distance between two points on the face of the earth, his or her expertise should mean that this statement is believed. As well as being an authority (on his or her subject), a teacher is also in authority. He or she has the right to tell his or her students what to do, within limits. In other words, he or she may set work, insist upon appropriate behaviour according to school policies, and so on. In the first case, the authority derives from knowledge – a quality which the teacher has as a person. Others, such as art historians, lawyers and other skilled persons are also authorities within their own fields. In the second case, the authority is delegated: the law says that all young people should receive an appropriate education; local education authorities and other bodies set up schools; governors and senior managers decide how to run the schools; teachers ensure that education takes place by enforcing discipline and imparting knowledge, etc. Those who govern states may derive their authority in a number of ways. It may be by conquest (I've won the war and you will therefore do as I say or else); by force (do as I tell you or you will suffer); by heredity (I am the legitimate heir of the previous Head of State, therefore I am now Head of State and, consequently, have the right to tell you what to do); by consent (you voted for me, so I am entitled to make decisions in the name of the people). There are other claims to authority apart from governmental: the Pope has authority over the Roman Catholic Church, as he is believed by its members to have been chosen by God as their spiritual leader; individual clergy of any religion or denomination have the authority to teach and guide their congregation, as they are seen as being called by God, trained in doctrine and endorsed by their institution; parents have authority over their children; all employees are under the authority of their line managers, and so on. All of these are, at least in part, authorities by virtue of their office or position.

Authority may also be derived from tradition. It is, or has been, customary to show deference to certain persons or groups and to some institutions. The professional classes, the landed gentry and the nobility have all traditionally been shown respect. The Church and other institutions are also traditionally authorities, and indeed are still so regarded by many in times of crisis or difficulty.

Some individuals possess charismatic authority. Their personal traits, such as a capacity for inspirational oratory, or their captivating charm, result in their emerging as natural leaders or social stars. Some evangelists, military personnel, politicians and people in the world of popular culture would fall into this category.

Power and legitimacy

In the political field, authority, to be effective, must be allied to power. A government that cannot enforce the laws it passes might as well not bother enacting them. Power is usually exercised through the executive: the civil service, which ensures that taxes are collected etc.; the police and the courts, who enforce the criminal law and the highway code; civil courts, which deal with such things as contract and employment law; and the armed forces, who protect against external enemies and provide support if necessary for the other executive arms. In other fields, authority may be powerless. A teacher who tells 30 unruly teenagers to sit down does not actually possess the physical force to make them do so. Nor can he or she necessarily threaten them with a punishment so unpleasant that they will obey. Religious leaders, similarly, are not usually in a position to ensure that their teachings are followed. The third element to be considered is legitimacy. A government might have the power to enforce its edicts, but still be illegitimate. If there has been electoral fraud, so that a minority party has nonetheless been declared to be in government, that party's government is illegitimate in a democracy. An invading army that deposed the local government would also be seen as having usurped power illegitimately. A legitimate ruler, therefore, might lack power but still have right on his or her side. This is the claimed position of various royal heirs whose reigning ancestors were overthrown by force. Less controversially, perhaps, it could also be seen as the position of various elected persons in the world today who have been forcibly prevented by the incumbent party from taking up the political role which the voters wish them to have. A current example of this, as I write, is the case of Myanmar (Burma), where the democratically elected leader, San Suu Kyi, has been held in internal exile by the military regime for most of the time since she won the general election in 1990. Power is *de facto* – it exists. Authority is *de jure* – it derives from legitimacy, and is related to rightness rather than fact. It is not, however, always easy to distinguish the two. It is also hard to see how personal charisma, for example, can be shown to have legitimacy. Should it therefore be regarded as imparting power, derived from a compelling personality, rather than as bestowing authority?

Obedience to the state

The democratic process

In a theocracy, where all share the same religious belief, the state is the executive arm of the Almighty. Obedience to the state is therefore required of all, unless and until the state's edicts deviate from official doctrine. Most states, however, do not run along these lines. Generally speaking, the more democratic the state, the more dissent, or disagreement, is tolerated. In Britain, there is, theoretically at least, no limit upon the number of candidates permitted to stand for election. Provided an individual meets the requirements of citizenship, is not a member of one of the (fairly small number) of prohibited categories of person, is over 21 years of age, has the necessary number of seconders, and can pay the deposit, he or she may stand. Martin Bell became an independent MP in 1997, albeit in very unusual circumstances. A local GP won a parliamentary seat in 2001, purely upon the platform of saving his local hospital from closure. A Monster Raving Loony Party candidate has been elected unopposed to his local council. Both the Communist Party and the British National Party have won council seats in opposed elections. It is permitted to speak against the government, and against particular governmental actions. Speaker's Corner in Hyde Park is specifically recognised as a platform for the free expression of any views. It is permitted to go into print to oppose authority. It is even permitted to peacefully protest by way of marches and demonstrations, as happened, to name one recent example, in 2003 when the Prime Minister, Tony Blair, took Britain into the war against Iraq. Actual disobedience to the law is, however, punishable. Mass disobedience has, nonetheless, led to some changes in the law. Repeated cases of people being prosecuted for possession of cannabis have eventually led to a position where owning a small amount of the drug for personal use no longer leads to automatic trial. Demonstrations against the poll tax, some of which shaded into criminal damage, led to changes in the means by which raising local revenue is undertaken.

One of the fundamental questions which have to be considered is where one's duty lies. Is it to God, or a moral code, or the truth? If so, there may well be reasons to oppose the state on occasion. It is no coincidence that active religious believers and academics are usually, so to speak, 'the first to be up against the wall when the revolution comes'. These are precisely the people who insist that there is a higher authority than the state, and they owe an overriding allegiance to this higher authority. Those who follow a deontological (duty-based) ethic are always likely to be dissident in certain matters.

Even if we accept that we have a duty to the state, upon what is it grounded? If the basis of duty is contract or covenant, then, logically, the state may be disobeyed if it fails to fulfil its side of the bargain. If one of the roles of the state is the protection of individual liberties, including the right to privacy, and if the compulsory ownership of ID cards will tend to curtail individual liberties, then the deliberate destruction of, or refusal to carry, such cards would, arguably, be justified. If a duty to the state is based upon consent, then there is an even wider field for disobedience. 'Not in my name' was a slogan used by anti-war protestors in 2003, but could be applied in other areas. Should those who voted for another party be expected to conform to the edicts of the elected government? Suppose congestion charging (making motorists pay to enter town centres) became national policy, against the wishes of the majority – would it then be right to refuse to pay the fee? On the other hand, if we are obliged to obey the state through coercion ('do this or else you'll be punished,' as 'might is right') then there is little if any scope for active, practical dissent.

Resistance to authority

It can be argued that authority should not be resisted. On utilitarian grounds, a stable society might be better than anarchy. On other moral grounds, living within a society and enjoying its benefits might oblige one to accept the corresponding disadvantages. It is questionable whether the views of one individual, who may be uneducated, mentally unstable, morally unsound, or unaware of the complexities of a situation, should count against the considered judgement of the incumbent leaders of society. It may even be questioned whether the mass of the population is able to make wise decisions. In opinion polls, there is always a majority vote in favour of capital punishment for murder – but Parliament, on a free vote, has rejected this course of action on several occasions during the last few decades. Early in 2004, Radio 4's *Today* programme, highly regarded for intelligent reporting of news and current affairs, invited listeners to formulate a new law. A backbench MP had already agreed to introduce the resulting suggestion as a Private Member's Bill, if he had the opportunity. He was appalled when a majority of listeners who expressed an opinion wanted to legalise the defence of one's own property, even at the cost of killing an intruder. (This may well have been because of a case in 1999 when Tony Martin, a farmer, shot and killed a teenager who broke into his home. Mr Martin had often been burgled before, and claimed that experience led him to believe the police would not arrive for some time should he call them. Mr Martin was found guilty of murder, which was reduced to manslaughter on appeal, and he was imprisoned. It was held that he had gone beyond the use of 'reasonable force' which the law currently allows.)

Various comments from politicians and journalists following Radio 4's initiative were to the effect that people obviously did not understand the laws that already exist permitting self-defence and the protection of property. Others, mainly in the popular press, maintained that people did understand, but believed the law did not go far enough in enabling people to protect themselves and their belongings. Resistance to authority may have a number of results. It may lead to changes that tend to increase autonomy. It may, however, cause a tightening up of authority – if drivers persistently exceed the speed limits, then maximum permitted speeds may be lowered in response. In some cases, those in authority might be displaced by resistance – but it is not always possible to predict who or what will replace them.

The State

Key topics in this chapter

● The role of the state

According to *The Oxford Companion to Philosophy*, the state is 'the political organisation of a body of people for the maintenance of order within its territory by coercion.' (Dr Stefan Gosepath, Hochschule der Kunste, Berlin).

It is first necessary to note, therefore, that some societies may be stateless. This was the position of the Jews during the Diaspora, which lasted from AD 70 until after the Second World War. Whilst unquestionably constituting a society, with agreed norms and behaviours, the Jewish people had no state or homeland within its control. This was one of the reasons why it was possible for Jews to be persecuted in Nazi-occupied territory – even before borders were closed Jews had no country of their own to which they could emigrate. If stripped of their citizenship, they became stateless persons, only able to move to other countries with the permission of the governments of those countries, not by right. This same fate has befallen others, albeit on a much smaller scale, both before and since. The United Nations Declaration of Human Rights does state that there is a basic right to citizenship, but this is not implemented in all countries or for all individuals.

The exercise of power by the state

States claim that they are the only legitimate holders of power. Those who exercise power within the state do so on the orders of, or with the permission of, that state. The armed forces, the police and the civil service carry out the commands of the state. Teachers may only impose such sanctions as the state permits. Corporal punishment is now forbidden within British schools, although it was permitted into the early 1980s. Physical force may only be used by teachers for the protection of people and property, for example, restraining a student who is attacking another. Similarly, parents may only discipline their children within the scope of the law. In Britain, physical chastisement is permitted 'within reason'. In many parts of Europe, smacking one's own child is unlawful.

Anarchists reject the need for, and the legitimacy of, any state. Others generally acknowledge that the state has both the right and the duty to defend its territory against external threats and dangers. Under Hobbesian social contract theory, all states are in permanent competition, if not at war. This would only cease to be true if there were to be an international government, either bringing about or deriving from a world state. The fate of dissident individuals, were such a situation to come into being, is an interesting subject of contemplation.

The extent of the state's power

There is much dispute about the role of the state within its own boundaries. Minimalist views hold that the state has the role of ensuring that public actions (those which affect others) are regulated, in order to maintain security within the realm. This could entail, as Sir Thomas More (1478–1535) pointed out, 'a conspiracy of the rich who call their intrigues laws' – in other words, the exercise of power by the few over the many, for the advantage of the few. Social contract theories would hold that state action is legitimate provided that the people have consented. Democrats would include the proviso that the few should have been elected by a majority of the many. Marxists would maintain that, under capitalist systems, the state manufactures consent but does not in fact act in the interests of the many.

Whether the state should go beyond the securing of its borders and the public safety of its citizens is another area of debate. If the state attempts to redistribute wealth, conservatives might oppose such action on the grounds that taxation for such purposes is, in effect, theft. Other conservatives might argue that the eradication of poverty tends to eliminate civil strife, and is, therefore, a legitimate means of protecting the liberties of citizens. Socialists would argue which the state should aim to provide the good life for all citizens, and might well defend even more radical policies than to 'squeeze the rich until the pips squeak' (Denis Healey, Budget Day, May 1978). There are other theories that do not start with the claims and desires of the individual, which are then enacted by the state. Rather, it can be argued that only within the state can the individual make any meaningful choices at all. It is the state which is the foundation of all values.

Communitarians would argue that our identity only has reality within a framework of social relationships. They hold that human life consists, in fact, of 'embodied and embedded' individuals who operate and function within a social network. They also argue that human life is better and more fulfilled when it is constructed with primary regard to communitarian, public and collective values. Rampant individualism is both unnatural to us and counterproductive. Communitarians do, however, respect the reality and importance of individuals. It is in this that they differ from some forms of Marxism.

Fascists go further than communitarians and insist that the state is the only arbiter of values and morality. The individual must conform. Refusal or inability to do so will lead to coercion, punishment or elimination. Fascism believes in the national will, enforced by a national leader. The events of the twentieth century have largely destroyed the credibility of fascism as a philosophical doctrine. However, there are worrying signs that some elements of society are once again turning to rampant nationalism, perhaps because they want to find scapegoats for their own relative disadvantage. As migration becomes an increasingly common phenomenon, this movement may once again become a force with which we shall have to reckon.

review activity

1. Define 'duty', 'covenant', 'contract', 'coercion' and 'consent' in your own words.

2. Define 'left wing' and 'right wing' in your own words. Give examples from existent political parties.

Summary

- Political philosophy analyses social organisation and governments, and tries to decide how society should properly be run.
- Political ideologies are based upon beliefs about human nature, history, the importance of the individual and of the state.
- Anther important factor are beliefs about which goods have most value.
- The questions surrounding the issues of rights and obligations are also crucial.
- The dominant political philosophy of the state in which we live determines how we are treated and the actions required of us.

some questions to think about

1   To what extent does the individual have duties to the state?

2   Are there such things as natural human rights?

3   Is the state justified in interfering with family life? If not, why not? If so, on what grounds and in what circumstances?

4   When, if ever, might it be morally justifiable to break the law?

5   On what grounds can we decide that someone is responsible for his or her own actions and wellbeing?

6   Is democracy the best way of organising society?

7   Should the state aim for the flourishing of the individual or the wellbeing of the masses?

further reading

▶   Probably the most influential work of recent time is Rawls 1999 (revised edition).

▶   MacIntyre 1981 is also well worth reading.

▶   For a more in-depth look at the subject, Sabine 1996 (3rd edition) is a worthwhile read.

philosophy
of science

I   Foundations of Science   132

II   The Progress of Science   158

III   The Social Sciences   187

Foundations of Science

important terms

A priori/posteriori: *a priori* is the term used for knowledge that is gained by reason, prior to experience; *a posteriori* refers to knowledge gained through experience.

Constant conjunction: Hume's alternative to causation. We see two events always in close proximity to each other in time and space and assume that the first 'causes' the second, but without any adequate justification.

Deduction: the logical process of drawing inferences from abstract propositions.

Deductive-nomological method: the method of explaining aspects of the world with reference to universal laws.

Hypothetico-deductive method: the method of testing a hypothesis by deducing from it a number of predictions, and then devising experiments to test those predictions.

Induction: a scientific methodology which involves drawing up generalisations and theories on the basis of repeated observations of the phenomena under investigation.

Materialism: the view that the world consists of nothing but physically existing material.

Reductionism: the view that complex entities can be reduced to, and explained in terms of, their constituent parts.

Relativism: the view that we cannot give a universal or objective account of reality, and that all attempts to do so are limited by the point of view of an observer.

Key topics in this chapter

- The origins of natural philosophy in ancient Greece
- Aristotle
- Induction: reasoning from evidence
- Falsification
- The instrumentalist view of science

Introduction

What does it mean to say that a theory is 'scientific' or that a person is working as a 'scientist'? In general, saying that people are 'scientists' refers less to what they are studying as to the methods that they use, the kind of theories they produce and the degree of detachment or objectivity they bring to their study. In the most general terms, it depends on 'scientific method'. A scientist will be expected to:

- Gather evidence.
- Devise a hypothesis to explain it.
- Test out that hypothesis by means of experiments.
- Discard the hypothesis, or refine it, if it does not correctly predict the results of those experiments.
- Be objective in trying to find the best available explanation for the phenomenon being examined.

Science gives information, but also solves problems and leads to the development of technology. We say that knowledge is scientific if it is gained using a method broadly as outlined above. It is not the same thing as knowledge gained through intuition or imagination (which is not, of course, to say that scientists may not sometimes need to use intuition and imagination in their work). Although a scientific theory may be described as beautiful, it is not artistic, or subjective, or a one-off. To be scientific it needs to be universal and able to be tested out.

Modern science has existed for about 400 years, starting with the discoveries and theories of the seventeenth century. But before that there were thinkers who considered the reason why things in the world are as they are. They asked the same questions that a modern scientist might ask. What they were doing was generally termed 'natural philosophy'. 'Philosophy of science' itself was a term first found in the nineteenth century, in the writings of William Whewell. Basically, it is the rational examination of the way in which science works. (Just as 'ethics' is the rational examination of moral choices or political philosophy looks at the theories used in political debate.)

Hence the 'philosophy of science' will examine the method used in science, the nature of scientific theories, the way in which science makes progress, and the aims of science. There are various ways in which we may evaluate a scientific theory:

- Is it true?
- Is it the simplest explanation for what is being examined?
- Does it fit in with other theories that we believe to be true?
- Does it help to explain things that we otherwise cannot understand?
- Is it productive? In other words, does it form a useful platform from which we can move on to examine other things?

What will soon become clear, as we look at the way in which science works and has developed, is that it is not enough to ask if a theory is true. A theory may be useful, even if it is thought to be inadequate. It can be 'true', if by that we mean 'the best explanation we have at the moment' but it may not be true in any absolute sense.

So there are broad questions that link back to questions of epistemology:

- What is truth?
- Is it absolute or relative?
- Is our knowledge always partial and capable of being revised?

Consequently, the focus for the student needs to be on the *methodology* of science, rather than the content. The question is about the extent to which the methods that science has used and is using are able to provide some kind of knowledge that is not relativistic, not rooted in the attitudes, values and culture of the individual scientist. In many ways the arguments that characterise the philosophy of science are familiar ones. What counts as knowledge? Do we only experience appearances or can we get through to reality?

Early Greek thinkers

The pre-Socratics
In the West, the earliest thinkers to engage in what we would not think of as science are known as the pre-Socratics, as their work pre-dated that of Socrates. They started asking scientific questions and were providing answers that were, although usually wrong, recognisably scientific in nature. Before that time, people generally believed that the forces that controlled everyday events were taken to be spiritual or religious. If one asked why a tragedy or a triumph had happened, the conventional answer would be that someone or some community was cursed or favoured by the gods, or that someone or something was possessed by an evil spirit, say, the spirit of a river in which someone had drowned. The only way to control or try to control these forces was to make sacrifices or to intercede in some other way with the god or spirit.

Explaining the world

The pre-Socratics are remarkable because they began to provide answers to the problems or questions which faced ordinary people that did not make reference to spiritual or religious forces, but instead tried to explain one event in the natural world by reference to other natural events, so that tragedies and misfortunes could be explained in ways that seemed reasonable to ordinary people. For example, Thales (sixth century BC) is famous for predicting an eclipse of the sun. We can imagine how terrifying such an event would be if completely unexplained. From a religious or spiritual point of view it really would have seemed as if the gods had withdrawn their favour – they had taken away the life-giving sun. Thales, however, was able to show that it was simply due to the relative motions in the sky of the sun and the moon. He also asked a question which was utterly remarkable for that time: is there one basic substance out of which all the different things that we see are made? He thought that basic substance was water. His conclusion may have been wrong (today, scientists would say that the most basic element in the universe, from which all else has developed, is hydrogen), but his question started the whole process of analysis – fundamental to science.

Atomism

Democritus (fifth century BC) is famous for developing the concept of the atom, that which is indivisible. This is the precursor to modern materialism (the belief that everything in the cosmos comprises of, and can be explained by reference to, physical matter and energy). According to the Greek atomists, everything is made of atoms. They are all identical and cannot be cut or have their shape changed or compressed. The differences between the things that we see are accounted for by the different ways that the atoms are arranged, and the fact that they come in different sizes. Even the thoughts that we have are ultimately atomic; things in the world emit smaller, ghost-like atoms which pass through our sense organs and thus to our minds. So, Democritus not only had a materialist view of the world, but also a materialist theory of perception.

Reductionism

Analysing things into their constitutive atoms led to another approach that has been regularly used within scientific thinking ever since: reductionism. Reductionism is a theory that insists that explanations of things or states of affairs in the world could only be explained by *reducing* them to their smallest constituent parts; for Democritus, the atoms. By understanding the nature of the parts, we will be able to understand the nature of the whole. For contemporary reductionists, *everything* can or will be explained through knowledge of the most basic laws of physics.

It does not matter that the ideas of the pre-Socratics were wrong; most scientists over history have been shown to be wrong in one way or another. The important thing is that they were thinking in a new and radical way that would allow humans to understand the world in a way that was not dependent on the irrational, the mystical or the religious. However, they all existed at a time when the majority of people did live in a world of mystical irrationality, and so it is not surprising that their theories pushed the limits beyond what could be logically proved. Pythagoras and his followers believed that the world was essentially mathematical, that if the appearances of things were stripped away what would be found would be pure number. This sounds like modern physics in some ways, but Pythagoras also believed that the mathematical secrets that he was discovering were applicable to music and medicine. We tune a musical instrument to make it harmonious, and medicine requires us to tune the human body in the same way.

The key feature to recognise in all this is that these philosophers were looking for an overall explanation. In considering that health constituted a mathematical balance in the body, Pythagoras was moving in the direction of seeing that fundamental understanding of the nature of the world could lead to practical benefits for humankind. Understand what balance is about and you will live well – in other words, he was examining human nature as part of an overall rational universe.

review
activity

1. Explain, in your own words, why the explanations of the natural world provided by the pre-Socratics were different to those of their predecessors.

2. Explain the Materialism of Democritus.

There are two great philosophers in early Greece who have dominated all later thinking: Plato and Aristotle. From a broad philosophical standpoint, Plato introduced all the big questions that have occupied the thoughts of later generations. But it is Aristotle who examined nature in a way that led to the development of science.

Aristotle (384 BC–322 BC)

Aristotle's contribution

Aristotle (384 BC–322 BC)

Aristotle, one of the greatest thinkers of all time, is particularly associated with the development of science. Both he and Plato were deeply disturbed by *scepticism*, the view, popular at that time, that true knowledge of the world around us is impossible, and that, in effect, any one view is therefore as good as any other. Both Plato and Aristotle were horrified by this view because they saw that it could lead people into *solipsism* (that the only thing knowable is individual human awareness) and that it played into the hands of *sophists*, who were more concerned to win arguments through skilful rhetoric than to find the truth. Another consequence of scepticism, for Plato and Aristotle, was that it would undermine any moral system. Because there were no morals that lay beyond the day-to-day perceptions of the individual person, no moral rules or principles could apply to all equally. Right and wrong would come to depend on who was stronger. They both believed that some form of knowledge, outside the personal perception of the individual, was necessary.

Note: the debate was between the relative importance of *physis* (nature) and *nomos* (law). The key question: is it possible to have a moral system and laws that are rooted in nature? And, if they are not so rooted, do I need to obey them? Are they merely cultural products and essentially unnatural? This, of course, has been a fundamental theme in ethics, touching on issues of absolutism, relativism and natural law.

Both Plato and Aristotle worked, in their own way, towards a systematic theory of knowledge. Plato's road was ultimately unscientific; he came to depend on the idea of the 'Forms' that were simultaneously real but not physical. His ideas were a triumph of human intellect and have left a lasting impression on humanity, but they have little to tell us about science.

Aristotle, unlike Plato, was an empiricist; that is, he believed that all knowledge started with sense experience. He considered that knowledge of the world was possible for humans if they had the right training and experience, and that it could be gained directly from examination of the physical things that the world contained – trees, animals, mountains, and so on. His approach was practical, pragmatic and observational.

This was very different from the 'reductionist' approach, which assumed that the whole was no more than the sum of its parts, and could be explained entirely on that basis. Aristotle believed that it was possible to study complex things in themselves, that they had an essence, an *ousia*, which was a genuine object of study in itself. In this, his work moved beyond that of the atomists.

review
activity

1. What was Aristotle's basic approach to the question of how we should explain the world?

2. In what way did Aristotle's approach differ from that of reductionism?

Of course, the terminology he used was unlike that which we would use today. He would not call himself an empiricist, for example, but his emphasis on knowledge of what he called particulars (the actual, existing things in the world) showed him to be a precursor of empiricism as a tradition.

Contemplation and deliberation

Aristotle divides the mind up into two parts: the rational and the irrational. The latter is concerned with feelings, emotions and desires, but the former is intimately tied up with science, as we would expect. Rational knowledge is also divided up into two categories. There are some things and parts of the world, he thought, that we cannot have a hope of changing or influencing. This includes the domain of the stars and the 'wanderers' (the planets), but also such things as motion and mass, the way that plants and animals grow, the occurrence of floods or droughts and the saltiness of the sea. There are also things that we can influence and change. This includes the things that are in our own lives and over which we can exercise choice: how to make a bridle for a horse, what to sow as a crop in a particular field, how to organise the constitution of a state. These things we deliberate about and then make choices. However, those things that cannot be transformed, which are eternal and fundamentally unchanging, we cannot deliberate about because we cannot make choices concerning them. We cannot choose for it not to rain, or for the stars to move relative to each other, or to live forever; all we can do is contemplate and understand these things.

This can be expressed by way of a diagram:

A rational understanding
of the world

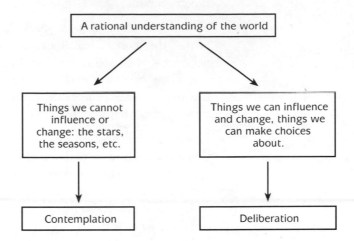

For Aristotle the search in science is for underlying principles, which are eternal and unchanging. But Aristotle's general principles do not exist in a separate realm (as did Plato's) but rather are based on, and abstracted from, the individual things that can be studied. We generalise only in order to understand what individual things have in common. However, we could also use induction, moving from individual observations about things and events upwards towards higher and higher levels of generalisation or theory. These two, induction and deduction, were to be used in tandem to achieve knowledge.

Aristotle considered that, in order to describe something, one should use four different causes:

1. The *material* cause was the matter out of which that thing was made.
2. The *formal* cause was the shape, nature or essence of the thing.
3. The *efficient* cause was the thing that had brought something about – the most usual sense in which we use the term 'cause'.
4. The *final* cause was the purpose or place that something occupies within the whole scheme of things.

For Aristotle, it was not sufficient to describe something simply in terms of what it was made of (which would lead to materialism or reductionism) or what had brought it about. A full description required us to take into account its form or essence and its purpose or place in the overall scheme of things.

Form and matter   Any 'thing' in the world therefore consisted of two parts: the 'matter' which was just undifferentiated 'stuff', and the 'form' from which it derived its own particular character. Matter has the potential to be many things, and becomes something in particular only when it is actualised by the form. This makes sense if we look at it from the point of view of the ancients. They would see a tree growing from the earth and would understand that the matter of earth and water was being given the form of the tree. Modern science tells us that the form is physical and is in the microscopic DNA in the seed. Similarly, the ancients would watch a carpenter making a cabinet and would understand

137

that the craftsman was putting a form or purpose into the raw material of the wood. We would understand that the purpose is entirely in the mind of the craftsman.

Notice that when Aristotle speaks of 'form' here, it is not the same as Plato's idea of the 'Forms', which are eternal realities. Aristotle does not accept the need for this eternal realm. The 'form' is that which makes a thing what it is. The 'form' of a table is not the material (wood) out of which it is made, nor is it the carpenter who made it, but it consists of an understanding of what a table is, and what it is there to do – its essential nature and purpose.

However much Aristotle may have anticipated modern science in his examination and classification of the natural world, there is one important thing missing – experiments. He was purely observational, and drew conclusions from the neutral observations that he made. Consequently, his ideas were untested and many very odd ideas of his came to be accepted for centuries. For example, he said that a body moves through the air at a rate proportionate to its weight and the air resistance. He was right about the air resistance, but it was not until Galileo that anyone tested the issue of weight and found it to be quite wrong. It was not until Roger Bacon, more than a thousand years later, that the importance of experimentation for science was recognised.

review
activity

1. Outline the differences between deliberation and contemplation.

2. What are the two differences between Aristotle's methods and those of modern science?

Particulars and universals

Aristotle did, however, make another contribution to the foundations of science that is still at the heart of modern debates on truth, validity and appearance, despite the fact that it has been argued over for 2500 years. This concerns the discussion over the nature and status of particulars and universals. A particular is an actual and specific thing or object that we can experience, such as this tree or that dog or that table. A universal is a class of objects, such as 'trees' or 'dogs' or 'tables'. The problem lies in the nature of the relationship between the two. As we have seen, Aristotle makes the assumption that objects exist, and that they consist of both form and matter. The problem lies in the fact that if only objects existed, then it would be very hard to see how we could have any knowledge of them beyond fleeting and partial experiences; we would live in a kaleidoscope of temporary and unrelated events, rather like the way we assume it must be to be a goldfish. Aristotle saw that to have knowledge, and certainly scientific knowledge, we have to be able to know about the forms or essences of things, because it is these that link the various members of classes together.

For example, what do a log thrown over a stream and the Golden Gate Bridge have in common? The material of which they are made is quite different, but they share the common function of getting us across water, they are both bridges. We humans have the ability both to see the appearance of an object and to understand its form or essence – what makes it a bridge rather than something else.

There has also been a debate among philosophers as to whether general terms, or 'universals', which are used for a whole class of things, refer to something that is actual, or only to something in the mind. Are they simply a convenient way of describing a number of similar objects? I use the universal 'dog' to embrace a wide variety of animals on the basis of their shared characteristics. Plato took the view that only the universals (Forms) were real, and the particulars were mere shadows. Aristotle challenged this. For him, the particular thing was real, and spoke instead of the 'form' or 'essence' being what made a thing what it is. Hence, for Aristotle, the form of a thing does not just exist in the mind, but is a valid way of describing it (i.e. its 'formal' cause – what causes something to be a dog as opposed to a cat, for example). The 'final' cause is one that science generally has not been required to consider. Within biology, and also in an anthropic approach to cosmology, there is a consideration of the aim or purpose of things, but generally science has left all such matters to philosophy or religion to consider. It has concentrated on what the world is like and how it works, rather than asking why it exists or what purpose it serves.

Overall, however, we can see that it was Aristotle who, by his careful examination of things, his classification of them into different types, and his conviction that the experiences world was real and worth examining (as opposed to Plato's negative evaluation of it) that established a basis for natural philosophy and science.

review
activity

1. Explain the distinction Aristotle makes between matter and form in his description of a thing.

2. Why do you think science has paid little attention to Aristotle's idea of a 'final' cause?

Science and scientific method

Induction and deduction

Aristotle's assumption was that there were essentially two methods of reasoning towards scientific knowledge: induction and deduction. The former entailed reasoning 'upwards' from observations in the world as experienced, whilst the latter involved reasoning 'downwards' from abstractions and generalisations towards the explanation of particular observations. These methods implied an acknowledgment of two key ideas. Firstly, no science could be done without observation; scientific work required workers to experience directly in the natural world the objects of their interest. But secondly, necessarily implicit in any scientific endeavour was reason; no one could do science without using rational thought – observation was not enough in itself. Hence it was Aristotle who introduced two basic features of the scientific method – induction (the building up of a theory on the basis on evidence) and deduction (the prediction of results from the application of a theory).

There were, of course, other kinds of knowledge that were not amenable to induction and deduction. In many arts, imagination and creativity enhance what is seen. In religion, a person may believe something on the basis of faith, rather than evidence. In emotional or moral situations, people may have convictions of which they feel certain, but which cannot be justified on the basis of evidence of any sort. It is possible to claim that none of these forms of knowledge is valid (a view known as 'scientism'), and sometimes there are clashes between scientific and non-scientific forms of knowledge, as happens, for example, in some debates between religion and science, generally when people are not clear about the bases upon which they are arguing, and may try to give a religious belief the status of a scientific theory, or vice versa.

Nevertheless, it is Aristotle who initially set out the different scientific disciplines, and considered the basics of scientific method. For many centuries, secular philosophy was banned by the Christian Church, but from the thirteenth century, promoted particularly by Aquinas, Aristotle's work was translated and made available in universities in the West, and became so hugely influential. For the development of science, however, it was important that Aristotle's methods should be understood, without necessarily accepting all his conclusions, and at times his work was in danger of becoming an obstacle to scientific development simply because he was regarded as an authority who could not be questioned or challenged.

review
activity

What alternatives are there to induction and deduction as sources of knowledge?

Induction

Induction is a deceptively simple concept. We make a number of observations of some aspect of the world and all these observations seem to tell us the same thing. On the basis of this, we assume that every other example of this aspect of the world, including all those that we have not yet observed, is going to tell us the same. The classic example involves swans. Someone might say that every swan they have ever seen is white, therefore, all swans are white. The basic flaw of induction is obvious here; some swans are not white, the person simply has not seen any of them. Of course we all use induction in our everyday lives: when the kettle whistles we assume the water is boiling; when we turn on the television we assume a picture will appear. This process of making assumptions based on experience seems to be a basic feature of human life. However, the key question for us here is whether it is the correct method of conducting science. The debate has a long history, but we can take it up in the Middle Ages.

Two Bacons

Roger Bacon

Confusingly, there are two Bacons, both of whom saw what we now call induction as vital for the scientific enterprise. The first is Roger Bacon (1214–94); the second is Francis Bacon (1561–1626).

Born in Ilchester, Somerset in 1214, **Roger Bacon** seems to have come from a reasonably well-off background, but the family lost much of their property in the chaos of Henry III's reign. A number went into exile, but Roger was able to attend university at Oxford, studying geometry, arithmetic, music and astronomy. He became friends with Adam de Marisco and Robert Grosseteste, Bishop of Lincoln. He probably took clerical orders in 1233 and soon after this travelled to Paris, the contemporary centre of intellectual life. At that time academic and clerical life (which amounted to much the same thing) centred around two powerful monastic orders. These were the Franciscans, whose intellectual inspiration was Alexander of Hales, and the Dominicans, led intellectually by Albertus Magnus and Thomas Aquinas. Bacon found, because of his scientific training, that there were many defects in the body of learning that confronted him in Paris. Some of Aristotle's writings were known, but only in very poor translations into Latin. Nevertheless, the scholars Bacon met refused to learn Greek. Natural philosophy (as science was called), insofar as it was studied at all, was generally based on translations of Aristotle, whose work was seen as authoritative, and whose premises were accepted without challenge. Bacon took the bold step of rejecting the narrowness of this approach. He left Paris and returned to England in 1247. The evidence that we have suggests that, working with Robert Grosseteste or at least under his influence, he continued with some distinctively scientific work involving lenses, magnification and mirrors; he seems to have wanted to apply geometry to optics.

In 1257 he finally left Oxford, maybe because of ill health, and entered the Order of Friars Minor. However, his interest in science continued, and in 1266 he wrote to the Pope suggesting that he could produce a kind of compendium of all scientific knowledge. The Pope, unfamiliar with such requests, asked for it straight away. Bacon quickly produced three works (The *Opus Maius*, the *Opus Minus* and the *Opus Tertium*), but had to do so in secret, as his superiors regarded his work as more or less heresy. He wanted to convince the Pope that secular science was valid, useful and did not contradict the word of God. In this, his task was similar to that of Thomas Aquinas, who was working at that time in Italy, trying to show that Aristotle's philosophy could give rational support to Christian beliefs.

Roger Bacon was a very religious man (as were all scholars at that time in a world heavily influenced by religion). He nevertheless recognised the importance of reason and observation, and his writings reveal a man born out of his own time in the way that he was preoccupied by issues of what later generations would call natural science. He was interested in experimental science, certainly, but he also considered optics, mathematics and moral philosophy as vital for every priest. This did not make him popular in the church. He foresaw the invention of steam engines, microscopes and telescopes, wrote about the reflections of light, mirages and the use of concave mirrors to start fires, discussed gunpowder, the diameter of celestial bodies and their distance from one another and speculated on the tides. He demonstrated that the Julian calendar, in use at the time, was wrong. David Dee said of him, speaking in 1582 about the reform of the calendar:

None hath done it more earnestly, neither with better reason and skill, than hath a subject of this British Sceptre Royal, done, . . . called Roger Bacon: who at large wrote thereof divers treatises and discourses to Pope Clement the Fifth about the year of the Lord, 1267. To whom he wrote and sent also great volumes exquisitely compiled of all sciences and singularities, philosophical and mathematical, as they might be available to the state of Christ his Catholic Church.

Bacon said, in *On Experimental Science*, 1268:

There are two ways of acquiring knowledge, one through reason, the other by experiment. Argument reaches a conclusion and compels us to admit it, but it neither makes us certain nor so annihilates doubt that the mind rests calm in the intuition of truth, unless it finds this certitude by way of experience. Thus many have arguments toward attainable facts, but because they have not experienced them, they overlook them and neither avoid a harmful nor follow a beneficial course. Even if a man that has never seen fire, proves by good reasoning that fire burns, and devours and destroys things, nevertheless the mind of one hearing his arguments would never be convinced, nor would he avoid fire until he puts his hand or some combustible thing into it in order to prove by experiment what the argument taught. But after the fact of combustion is experienced, the mind is satisfied and lies calm in the certainty of truth. Hence argument is not enough, but experience is.

This is evident even in mathematics, where demonstration is the surest. The mind of a man that receives that clearest of demonstrations concerning the equilateral triangle without experiment will never stick to the conclusion nor act upon it till confirmed by experiment by means of the intersection of two circles from either section of which two lines are drawn to the ends of a given line. Then one receives the conclusion without doubt. What Aristotle says of the demonstration by the syllogism being able to give knowledge, can be understood if it is accompanied by experience, but not of the bare demonstration. What he says in the first book of the Metaphysics, that those knowing the reason and cause are wiser than the experienced, he speaks concerning the experienced who know the bare fact only without the cause. But I speak here of the experienced that know the reason and cause through their experience. And such are perfect in their knowledge, as Aristotle wishes to be in the sixth book of the Ethics, whose simple statements are to be believed as if they carried demonstration, as he says in that very place. (Thatcher 1901: 369–76)

By the term 'demonstration', Bacon means *logical* demonstration, what we would refer to as deduction. He is politely pointing out that the great Aristotle contradicts himself. In the *Metaphysics* he says that deduction is superior to experience and observation, but in book six of the *Ethics* he says that they are of equal weight.

Bacon is not clear here on the distinction between experiment and experience; as we shall see, 'experiment' has acquired a range of quite specific meanings. However, his insistence on an empirical basis for knowledge – the hand in the fire to experience the heat – is, in the end, an insistence on induction, the view that the origins of sound knowledge lie in learning from repeated experience. Theory, reason and argument alone are never adequate.

review
activity

In what way did Roger Bacon improve on the epistemological methods of his time?

Sir Francis Bacon, who later became Lord Verulam, the Viscount St Albans and Lord Chancellor of England, was born of a prosperous and very well connected family in London in 1561. His father, Nicholas, was Lord Keeper of the Seal, and his mother Anne was very well educated in her own right, speaking not only Latin and Greek but also French and Italian. She was sister-in-law to Sir William Cecil, later Lord Burghley, Elizabeth I's chief counsellor, perhaps the most powerful man in England.

At the age of 12 Francis entered Trinity College, Cambridge. At that time the Cambridge curriculum consisted of tedious and pointless scholasticism (which essentially took the view that Aristotle had discovered all the knowledge there was to know, and that the job of scholars was to work out the implications, often in infinite detail). This experience gave Francis a lifelong dislike and indeed contempt for Aristotelianism, although he retained a respect for the works of Aristotle himself. In 1576 he began to study law. Three years later his father died but, because he was the youngest of many heirs, he found himself almost without any income. Nevertheless, he completed his studies in the early 1580s. He then embarked on a career in politics which was to consume most of his time for the rest of his life. He made little progress during the reign of Elizabeth I, because she resented his opposition to her taxation policies. However, with the accession of James I in 1603 his fortunes changed and he made rapid progress, and in 1618, after holding many senior roles, he was made Lord Chancellor, a position of enormous power and influence. However, it was not to last, and in 1621 he was charged with accepting bribes. He pleaded guilty, received a heavy fine and was sentenced to the Tower of London. In fact, the fine was later waived and he spent only a few days in the Tower; nevertheless, his political career was finished. He lived a further five years, and dedicated this time to completing as far as he could his life's work of reforming learning and the development of the scientific method for the 'use and benefit of men'. His disgrace must have been hard for him to accept, but for us the result was a body of writing that gave a powerful impetus to the development of science.

He was a complex and difficult man; a giant intellect, but, in his own words, a 'most dishonest man'. He was also seen by many as an arrogant, calculating man who often treated others contemptuously.

Francis Bacon

Another key figure for understanding the development of scientific method is Francis Bacon (1561–1626). He sought to promote a dynamic system of thought based on inductive and empirical systems, the purpose of which was to create and promote new inventions to the betterment of humanity. His radical vision was to see human destiny as progressive and improving, rather than static or cyclical.

Distempers of learning

Before we look at Bacon's views on induction, it is worth noting what he saw as the main faults of the scholasticism of his time. He called these the 'distempers' (diseases) of learning. He first identifies them in his 1605 work *The Proficience and Advancement of Learning*:

1. The first he called 'fantastical learning' (also called by him 'vain imaginations'). This is pseudo-science. It has no empirical basis and consists mostly of wishful thinking. He would include magic, astrology and alchemy. Today, we might be inclined to include the ideas that people can be healed by various crystals or other minerals, acupuncture and homeopathy. The point is not that these ideas are wrong but that there is no reliable empirical evidence for them.

2. The second distemper he called 'contentious learning' or 'vain alterca-

tions'. This he saw as debate for its own sake. Here there is no desire for new knowledge but only for the opportunity to score points off an opponent. This is what he would refer to as 'Aristotelianism', involving endless hairsplitting and pedantry.

3. The third distemper was 'delicate learning' or 'vain affectations'. This is perhaps the hardest of the distempers for us to understand today. He means a preoccupation with prose style itself rather than with the meaning or content. An elegant turn of phrase is more important than what it actually says. The words are more important than what they tell us: the writing is divorced from reality.

Pointless theorising   The point about all of these distempers is that they represent a waste of time and ability. Those who fall prey to them could be spending their time doing something useful and progressive. Instead the writers seek only to enhance their own reputations, maintain ancient and redundant forms of knowledge and theorise pointlessly. Bacon believed that all the energy put into them needed to be redirected into activities that would lead to genuine progress, and this would need to be based on real empirical work.

These distempers are essentially problems for scholars. Bacon also believed that all humans were prone to problems or difficulties of thinking that prevented them from seeing the world as it actually is. These are the famous 'idols'. This is an odd word to us, but he takes it from the Greek term *eidolon* which means 'image' or 'phantom'. In his book the *New Organon* (or, *True Directions Concerning the Interpretation of Nature*), he identifies four idols:

1. *The Idols of the Tribe*. These are simple human failings, common to us all and impossible to eradicate. All that we can do is recognise them and take precautions. He means things like the imperfections of our senses, our tendency to find order and structure in things where no such order exists, our inclination to believe to be true what we wish to be true, and our tendency to jump to conclusions without adequate evidence.

2. *The Idols of the Cave*. These are not innate, as the idols of the tribe are. They are cultural. We are all brought up within particular systems of belief, which vary from person to person and culture to culture. They distort our thinking and make us prone to prejudice. They lead us to accept some authorities and reject others without good reason.

3. *The Idols of the Market Place*. The problem here is with language itself and the way in which it can be misleading. Clear and accurate thinking is impossible if the language we use is faulty. He calls them the idols of the market place because he sees the main culprit in the propagation of faulty language in the interaction of people with each other and the way in which misunderstandings can be propagated simply in conversation. Words are invented for things that do not in fact exist, and words acquire a vagueness and ambiguity which makes them impossible to apply with accuracy. A contemporary example might be the term 'democracy'. This happens in ordinary everyday speech, but more importantly, it happens in the specialised discussions of the various academic communities.

4. *The Idols of the Theatre.* Here Bacon is pointing to the way in which people can become preoccupied, indeed obsessed, with some all-encompassing scheme of thought. These can be religious, political or philosophical. All are equally dangerous as they prevent us from appreciating, or indeed seeing, contrary evidence. Today we might identify Marxism, Fascism, existentialism, creationism or feminism as such idols. For Bacon, the problem with them all is that they are founded on much too narrow an empirical base.

Bacon considered the distempers and idols to be hindrances in the pursuit of real knowledge. We should either avoid them, or, if they cannot be avoided, we should at least be aware of them and take them into account in our thinking. However, even if we know to avoid the problems, this does not tell us what method we should actually adopt in the pursuit of knowledge. Bacon's answer is outlined in the *Magna Instauratio* and in the *New Organon*. It is his method of 'true and perfect induction'.

True and perfect induction

He saw his new system as significantly different from the pointless deductions of the scholastics and an improvement on the Aristotelian model of induction. This latter system begins with individual observations and other experiences and then generalises upwards to high level theories and principles. Having arrived at 'the most general propositions', it is then possible to work back downwards by a process of deduction to various intermediary propositions. For example, by observing a few dogs it should be possible to conclude, by induction, that all dogs bark. This is the general proposition. Then, by a process of deduction, one could conclude that as a red setter is a dog, it too will bark. The problem with this, as Bacon rightly points out, is that if the general proposition is wrong, which it could easily be as it is based on only a few observations, then the propositions deduced from it may well be false as well.

Bacon's alternative is more labour-intensive but, he thought, more reliable. He advocated that we move 'regularly and gradually from one axiom to another, so that the most general are not reached till the last'. This means that we don't jump to conclusions on the basis of only a few observations or experiences. Instead we move gradually, step by step, examining each generalisation on what he called 'the ladder of intellect' in great detail, both by simple observation but also by experimentation. In the dog example, Bacon would require us to examine every breed of dog in all circumstances, presumably experimenting on them by irritating them in some way, to see if they bark. Furthermore, because of the inadequacies of our senses (the idols of the tribe) we should use scientific instruments wherever we can. Each generalisation (or 'axiom') can then be relied upon and used as a stepping stone to the next level upwards. Even a falsification (a piece of evidence that goes against the expected generalisation) is useful because it stops the scientist from going down the wrong path and wasting time.

When do you stop?

However, there are significant questions to be asked of Bacon's method. When does one stop collecting facts and observations and say that one has achieved a satisfactory generalisation? When is one allowed to move from particular observations to an abstract proposition? How many observations need to be made, how many experiments need to be conducted? A thousand? A million? There seems to be no answer to these questions in Bacon's system. One can imagine scientists using the Baconian method spending their entire career in the collection of facts. William Harvey, who discovered the circulation of blood, suggested that Bacon's view of science was 'like a Lord Chancellor'. He meant that Bacon saw science as would a politician responsible for the country's finances – always adding up the evidence and making calculations.

The alternative is to recognise that, whilst based on a body of empirical research, almost all important scientific discoveries or advances have involved intuition and imagination. Scientists make intuitive guesses. Many, perhaps most, will prove to be wrong, but progress has come from the guesses that were right. Gathering evidence is not enough in itself; there needs to be a creative input from the scientist.

review activity

1. Explain briefly what Francis Bacon saw as 'distempers' and 'idols'.

2. Describe Bacon's interpretation of induction.

3. What criticism can be made of this?

Hume's problem of induction

Probably the most important and powerful criticism of induction was made by David Hume (1711–76). He recognised that induction makes two related assumptions:

1. That an entire class of events or objects are the same, that is, they all have the same properties. For example, pure water always freezes at 0° centigrade.
2. That the future will always be like the past. For example, water always has in the past frozen at 0° centigrade; therefore it always will freeze at that temperature.

He denied that either of these can be accepted without qualification. The fundamental problem is that of circularity; he says that there is no non-circular way of establishing either general (theoretical) knowledge or particular knowledge about things that we have not actually observed. Essential to both of the above assumptions is the third, more profound, assumption:

3. That, because induction itself has worked in the past, it will continue to work in the future.

The uniformity premise   The problem with this, as Hume pointed out, is that here we are using an inductive argument to confirm the validity of inductive arguments. We are 'begging the question' and assuming the truth of that which we are attempting to explain. The only way around this is to adopt what is known as the 'uniformity premise', which holds that the unobserved resembles the observed.

The argument about water freezing would then become:

1. All water observed in the past has frozen at 0° centigrade.

2.   The unobserved resembles the observed.
3.   Therefore, water will always freeze at 0° centigrade.

Can we accept the uniformity premise? Well, our experience has shown us that the world does seem to be quite uniform. However, that experience of uniformity is based only on our own limited experiences of the world. Therefore, the uniformity premise is based on induction, and we are back where we started. As Bertrand Russell was later to point out, even if our experience has demonstrated to us that past futures resemble past pasts, we can only assume that future futures will resemble future pasts if we also already assume that the future resembles the past. We cannot escape the circularity. (Russell's own view was that induction is simply an unexplainable and unjustifiable but universal feature of human cognition.)

We cannot even appeal to more fundamental laws of chemistry or physics. If we try to justify our claim that water freezes at 0° centigrade not only on the basis of observation but also on the basis of our understanding of the chemical and physical structure of water molecules, we will, in the end, be forced to admit that our knowledge of chemistry and physics is also based on observations and therefore inductive.

Hume on causation   Hume's criticism of induction is related to his understanding of the common idea that one thing can be said to cause another. He pointed out that we proportion our belief that something is the case to the evidence we have for it. If we have a large number of experiments that give consistent results, and just the odd one that gives a different result, we tend to assume it is the majority that are correct and that the isolated one is defective in some way, or subject to some unrecognised extra factor. If we see that A happens before B, and never find that B happens without A having previously happened, we conclude that A is the cause of B. However, all we have actually observed is the 'constant conjunction' of A and B – and from this we have assumed that A causes B. But this reduces our idea of causality to an 'association of ideas', a psychological habit, not something that we can prove to exist in the world as we observe it.

On the other hand, Hume does not dismiss induction entirely, because he recognises that it is an indelible feature of human thinking and that it is 'essential to the subsistence of human creatures'. He also says that causation can have a kind of certainty. This seems to be contradictory, but it is not if we remember that, for Hume, reasoning consists only of the comparison of ideas and the establishing of relationships between them. It does not consist of establishing relationships between ideas and the real world. So, causation has its own kind of certainty when it is 'satisfactory' to the mind; the mistake is to see the causal relationship as something that can be proved to be external to the mind.

In conclusion, we can say that what Hume wants us to learn from his criticism of induction and from his other doubts is that our beliefs about the world are not simply based on reason, but on the non-rational psychological principle of custom – in other words, seeing one thing as causing another is a habit we get into. Our knowledge and understanding of the world is limited. To understand the limits of what we can know, we must develop a science of human nature, which can explore the nature and limits of principles such as that of custom. It will be inevitable that some (or many) of our beliefs will be non-rational in nature and we must accept this, using what mental abilities we can to match our beliefs to whatever evidence is available. There will always be room for scepticism and ambiguity, but we can do no more.

review
activity

1. Explain why Hume considered induction to be problematic as a scientific method.
2. What is the 'uniformity premise'?
3. How did Hume view causation?

John Stuart Mill's response

Mill (1806–73) more or less ignored Hume's problem. He saw induction as having an inevitable role in science and saw his main task in this field as improving on its reliability. His core belief was that if the mind was a part of the natural world, which he thought it was, then there can be no knowledge of nature that is *a priori* (that is, known prior to experience). Either there can be no knowledge at all, or knowledge must be based in raw experience, in other words, *a posteriori*. Thus, like Hume, Mill is a radical empiricist.

Apparent inferences or real inferences?

He makes an important distinction between inferences that are 'merely apparent' and inferences that are 'real'. The former only *seem* to be reasonable and rational, whereas the latter, despite their empirical and therefore inductive roots, have genuine cognitive content, i.e. they are rational and accurate. He illustrates his point by claiming that mathematics and logic contain real propositions and inferences, but, because no real proposition or inference is *a priori*, we must learn geometry, mathematics and logic by experience, not by reason. We mistakenly take them to be *a priori* because their negation seems inconceivable to us, but this is only because they are so strongly supported by induction. In theory we may still find a four-sided triangle.

In his *Systems of Logic* (1843), he outlined his five principles of induction: the method of agreement; the method of difference; the joint method of agreement and difference; the method of residues; and the method of concomitant variations. We need not go into the details of these, but their common feature, and the real basis for scientific progress, is a matter of elimination, or of difference. Suppose two events differ slightly. We try to find something that was present in the former but not in the latter. If such a thing can be found, then it can be identified as the cause (or a key part of the cause) of the difference and all other factors can be eliminated. Mill believed that causation was universal; that is, nothing ever happens without a cause. Furthermore, he thought that a cause could only operate locally, that is, it must be physically linked in some way with its effect; it cannot operate at a distance. Mill therefore argued that the elimination of those factors that are clearly not causal, provided a new method of science (or 'natural philosophy', as he would probably call it) – the method of 'eliminative induction'.

Eliminative induction   We begin with a simple process of enumerative induction, where, on any number of occasions, we observe some event in ordinary life and note that it is always preceded by some other event. We see the preceding event as the cause and therefore believe we have explained the event. The truth of this as a valid source of knowledge is acknowledged by all reasonable people. This is Mill's sole justification for the basis of induction. He simply does not take seriously Hume's problem of the circularity of induction. However, he does not seek to claim that simple enumerative induction is foolproof, he says that 'though a valid process, it is a fallible one, and fallible in very different degrees: if therefore we can substitute for the more fallible forms of the process, an operation grounded in the same process in a less fallible form, we shall have effected a very material improvement. And this is what scientific induction does' (Mill 1843).

How then is this improvement to be achieved? His answer is quite simple: the unscientific inductions of ordinary people accumulate, they begin to relate to each other, they hint at wider generalisations, they are repeatedly confirmed by further experiences. Eventually they give rise to second-order inductions which themselves suggest that all events are subject to some uniformity of causation, that is, all events have causes. This assumption is the basis for eliminative induction. A belief in the validity of the latter method allows scientists to search for the causes of events or phenomena by a process of *eliminating all those factors which are clearly not causes*. To do this they will use either observation or experimentation. The fact that eliminative induction provides us with generalisations and theories that are valid, coherent and repeatedly confirmed, further justifies us in our belief that everything has a cause. That in turn justifies our confidence in the countless enumerative inductions that are the basis for the whole system. For example, people have seen water freeze countless times and have come to see the cause as temperature. The scientist wonders why this happens to water and to other liquids. By a process of elimination he or she excludes a range of possible causes, and thus arrives at a valid cause – that the molecules of certain liquids align themselves into a crystalline structure at certain temperatures. This is eliminative induction.

Suppose we have a range of phenomena and we want to know what has caused them. Following Mill's method of agreement and difference, we would need to ask two questions:

1. What factor is *always* present when this phenomenon occurs?
2. What factor is *never* present when this phenomenon fails to occur?

Mill also pointed out that the traditional method of logical deduction gives us no new knowledge; everything we conclude from a deduction such as a syllogism is actually already known in the major premise (e.g. if we know that all men are mortal, we also know that Socrates is mortal; we don't need to prove it). He says of this example: 'The inference is finished when we have asserted that all men are mortal. What remains to be performed afterwards is merely deciphering our own notes.' It is a mistake to believe that deciphering your own notes is the discovery of new knowledge.

review
activity

1. Mill believed that geometry, mathematics and logic were empirical. Why was that? Do you agree with him?

2. Distinguish between enumerative and eliminative induction.

Criticisms of Mill on induction

How convincing is Mill's eliminative induction? Quite apart from the fact that he does not deal with Hume's profound objections, he does not seem to have recognised the damage that radical scepticism did to established and traditional beliefs. He seemed to have regarded Hume as giving a 'psychological explanation' of the uniformity of nature (in terms of the habits of mind that we develop) without recognising that Hume also offers very real logical objections to the claim that we can have certain knowledge of causality. Hence Mill's whole use of induction remains vulnerable to Hume's criticisms.

He may have pushed his claim that *all* knowledge comes through experience too far. In particular, his claim that we know about geometry, mathematics and logic only through simple enumerative induction seems quite crude and unlikely. After all, what would a four-sided triangle be like? It seems impossible to say. Surely such a thing is either logically or linguistically unachievable.

A further significant point, which we will explore in more detail later, is known as the 'theory-dependence of observation'. Mill largely assumes that the evidence people contribute to an inductive argument is in some way neutral; that is, it is untainted and uninfluenced by their past experiences or by their particular culture or upbringing. Most philosophers of science today would agree that this is impossible; that we always experience things in a way that is deeply influenced by our past experiences and our present culture. To put it another way, we tend to see what we expect to see.

We can ask a further question of 'eliminative induction': how can we know that we have eliminated all irrelevant (i.e. non-causal) factors in seeking a cause? Like enumerative induction, it is a process that is always capable of being extended and refined, and therefore never able to provide an absolutely definitive answer. Just as Hume was aware that one should always be prepared for new and conflicting evidence, so one can never be sure that there is not another factor that has not been eliminated, because one is not yet aware of it, and that unknown factor might actually be the cause of the phenomenon we are examining.

review
activity

What criticisms can be made of Mill's approach? Are they justified?

The hypothetico-deductive method

During his lifetime, Mill conducted a protracted argument with William Whewell. Although both men were concerned with scientific method, they came to it from very different philosophical backgrounds. Whewell was influenced by Kant, who had argued that our experience of the world is shaped by the way our mind works, and that causality is something that the mind imposes upon experience. By contrast, Mill was solidly in the empiricist tradition, and considered all knowledge to be based on sense-experience.

Whewell believed that scientists needed to intuitively look for hypotheses to explain the phenomena they were examining. A good hypothesis was one that explained all the observed events and facts; a bad hypothesis was one that failed to explain all the events and facts. A distinction had to be made between the facts the scientist studies and the theories or hypotheses that the scientist uses in order to organise and explain them. Mill believed that the problem with this method was that it was perfectly possible for more than one hypothesis to account for the observed events. His contention was that a hypothesis had to be based on the evidence, not imposed on it. How otherwise would one choose between hypotheses? This was to become an important issue for twentieth-century physics: how, for example, was it possible simultaneously to hold two very different theories of light, seeing it either as a wave or a stream of particles? Today, scientists recognise that different theories can complement one another and are judged on criteria of usefulness.

Colligation   Whewell believed that the facts alone were not enough; they had to be strung together like pearls on a string in order for them to make sense. He used the term 'colligation' for the process of bringing facts together, and distinguished colligations from inductions. He considered that it was essential to have mentally produced concepts or theories in order to bind facts together and make sense of them.

> *When anyone has seen an oak-tree blown down by a strong gust of wind, he does not think of the occurrence any otherwise than as a Fact of which he is assured by his senses. Yet by what sense does he perceive the Force which he thus supposes the wind to exert? By what sense does he distinguish the Oak-tree from all other trees? It is clear upon reflexion, that in such a case, his own mind supplies the conception of extraneous impulse and pressure, by which he thus interprets the motions observed, and the distinction of different kinds of trees .... The Idea of Force, and the idea of definite Resemblances and Differences, are thus combined with the impressions on our senses and form an indistinguished portion of that which we consider as the Fact.*   (Butts 1989)

Whewell and Mill both agree that we move from particular observed facts to generalisations or theories to explain them. The disagreement stems from where such generalisations come from: for Mill they come through the process of induction itself, for Whewell they arise within the mind of the scientist, as a means of making sense of the evidence, and there are no facts that are independent of the human process of knowing them.

Following Whewell, many philosophers of science have come to emphasise the role of the hypothesis, which they see as a speculation, conjecture or even a guess designed to solve some scientific problem. They have also returned to the method of deduction as part of the process of confirming or denying the hypothesis. In a nutshell the hypothetico-deductive method, which this represents, holds that a scientific theory is a general statement (a 'hypothesis') from which particular inferences or conclusions can be deduced. Those conclusions are then tested out. If they prove correct, they give support to (or 'corroborate') the hypothesis; if not they falsify it. Take the hypothesis that all animals require oxygen in order to live. From this we predict that, as they are animals, rats will require oxygen. An experiment is performed and the resulting oxygenless dead rats confirm the original hypothesis.

review
activity

1. Explain the term 'hypothesis'.
2. What is the important distinction between Whewell's and Mill's positions?

The Raven paradox

Actually, as with induction, there is a logical problem over what, precisely, the term 'corroboration' means. It is usually taken to mean some kind of evidence that supports another idea. However, it falls foul of the so-called Raven paradox. The hypothesis that all ravens are black (whether in induction or in the hypothetico-deductive method) is usually taken to be corroborated only by observations of black ravens. However, the logical equivalent of 'all ravens are black' is 'all non-black things are not ravens'. An observation of a red tomato is an example of a non-black thing that is not a raven and so can be taken to be a corroboration of 'all non-black things are not ravens'. It follows logically from this that the statement 'this is a red tomato' is corroboration for the hypothesis that all ravens are black. This seems to be valid, but also seems to be absurd. The problem is largely ignored by those interested in the methodology of science. If anything, the paradox should be more evidence for the theory dependence of observation, for the fact that we cannot divorce one observation from all our previous ideas and experiences. Any observation is embedded in a matrix of pre-existing theories and hypotheses that most of us tend to categorise as 'common sense'.

As we shall see later, the dispute between Whewell and Mill continues to be relevant. In the last century, both Kuhn and Feyerabend argued persuasively that scientific truth is simply what the scientific community agrees it to be; that it is contingent and relative to the group of scientists and their community. The importance of the hypothetic-deductive method is that it avoids this conclusion and maintains a *realist* perspective, holding that science can give us an accurate or at least partially accurate picture of how the world really is. An hypothesis is shaped by the scientist to explain some aspect of the world. From the hypothesis a prediction is deduced. The prediction is tested by experiment or observation.

The hypothetico-deductive method depends crucially on the actual measurements, the quantifications that are taken as a result of the experiment (or observation where an experiment is not possible, such as in astronomy). If they do indeed corroborate the hypothesis and do not falsify it, then we gain increased confidence in that hypothesis. However, no matter how many experiments we carry out that corroborate the hypothesis, the latter can never be taken to be proved with certainty. Falsifying evidence may turn up in the future.

review activity

1. Explain the Raven paradox.
2. What is the hypothetico-deductive method?

How scientists respond to falsification

In practice, it is understandable that scientists should initially try to defend their hypothesis in the face of falsifying evidence. The first thing they will seek to do is to establish that their instrumentation and equipment is working properly. If all is well with the equipment, they will go on to establish with confidence that all the conditions that fit with the hypothesis were fulfilled in the experiment. For example, was it conducted within the correct parameters of temperature? Were the samples used of sufficient purity? Was a biological sample contaminated by some rogue fungal growth (a big problem in biology, apparently)? Thirdly, the scientists may go on to recheck any auxiliary assumptions that they have made as part of the design of the experiment. These assumptions might include establishing that a particular piece of equipment will provide them with the kind of information they expect it to, or that a particular compound or biological sample is actually made up in the way that the textbooks say it is. Finally, when all these other issues have been resolved and no problems can be found, the logical conclusion to reach is that the hypothesis is wrong and must be abandoned. This process of trying to defend an initially falsified hypothesis does make sense. It is perfectly possible that a good hypothesis might be thrown out by mistake and the scientist needs to take precautions against this.

review activity

What steps might a scientist take before accepting the falsification of an hypothesis?

Poincaré's contribution

Jules Henri Poincaré (1854–1912) came from a powerful and influential family; his cousin Raymond was both the president and the prime minister of France. He himself was an extraordinary scholar, with interests in mechanics, mathematical physics, probability theory and astronomy, as well as an enduring interest in the philosophy of science. Like Whewell, he rejected an entirely empiricist account of the methodology of science. He held that experience alone could neither confirm nor deny the validity of a theory. Nevertheless, it has an important role in science if, and only if, it is taken together with hypotheses. These latter are actually 'metaphors', to use his own term, and it is only by using these that we are capable of generating new facts and predictions. If we did not employ such metaphors, science would consist only of a gigantic list or inventory of observations.

However, as Mill pointed out, one problem with this approach is that it is often the case that more that one hypothesis will explain a given set of observations, and so how do we choose between them. Poincaré's answer is that we should always choose the simplest. The simplicity of an hypothesis is second only in importance to its ability to generate predictions. This is a version of 'Ockham's razor'. William of Ockham was a fourteenth-century scholar who advocated that, given a choice of explanations, the simplest and most straightforward was probably the best.

Poincaré used the term 'metaphor' to describe theories or hypotheses because he did not believe that they were real. Hypotheses cannot be directly observed. We cannot go out and observe Newton's laws of thermodynamics; we can only observe their effects. Consequently Poincaré believed that it made no sense to claim that they were real entities, *they were simply instruments by which we could make predictions and explain the facts as we observe them.* This means that scientists may entertain more than one hypothesis at a time and could revive old, discredited hypotheses if new evidence warranted it.

His was an exceptionally flexible attitude to scientific theorising. Imagine a graph on which are plotted a series of points. The points represent a series of specific observations, say, the observations of a particular species of bird in varying kinds of natural environment, such as those with differing temperatures.

A scatter graph

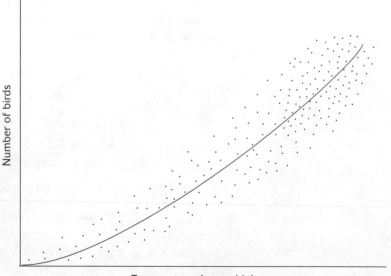

Number of birds

Temperature: low to high

The points may be fairly scattered, perhaps because of difficulties in making observations or other random factors. However, the scientist will want to draw a curve on the graph, which represents the relationship between the distribution of the birds and the environment in a more systematic way. This curve will be the hypothesis, and it is entirely the product of the human mind. Furthermore, there may be more than one curve that fits with the dots.

What Newton did

A real example may help to make the point. It has long been accepted that the measuring techniques and instruments available to Isaac Newton were just too crude and basic for them to have allowed him to 'find' his theories on thermodynamics and gravity by inductive means. He had to couple his basic observations with a gigantic leap of imagination to establish his new view of how the physical world works. Poincaré believed that we should go with the curve that gives the best predictions and is the simplest. Nevertheless, we will be free to choose whichever interpretation is most useful to us and which is in accordance both with observations we have made and the predictions we make as a result. For this reason, Poincaré characterised some hypotheses and theories as 'conventions' as well as metaphors, because a successful hypothesis became the conventional way of understanding the world.

In some ways, Poincaré (like Whewell) follows Kant, who also believed that the totality of our knowledge was ordered by mental categories into which all sensory experiences were fitted. All humans had to see the world in the same way because all use the same mental categories. For example, we see the world in terms of Euclidean geometry because our minds are organised in such a way that they must see it like this. However, Poincaré lived in a world that had discovered many alternatives to Euclid's geometry. He recognised that we use Euclid in ordinary everyday life because it is the most useful at making predictions about how things will be. In other circumstances, such as when we study astronomy, we need to use other geometries. The difference, then, between Poincaré and Kant is that the latter saw our mental categories as fixed and permanent, rather like spectacles that you can never remove, whilst the former thought that we could change the categories whenever we liked as long as they accorded with experience. We can put on whatever spectacles we choose.

> *The geometrical axioms are therefore neither synthetic* a priori *intuitions nor experimental facts. They are conventions. Our choice among all possible conventions is guided by experimental facts; but it remains free ... In other words, the axioms of geometry ... are only definitions in disguise.* (Poincaré 1902)

And when should we abandon a conventional hypothesis?

> *Simply when it ceases to be useful to us – i.e., when we can no longer use it to predict correctly new phenomena. We shall be certain in such a case that the relation affirmed is no longer real, for otherwise it would be fruitful.*
>
> (Poincaré 1902)

Instrumentalism

Poincaré's work can be seen as an early example of 'instrumentalism', which is the general view that we should not see scientific theories as 'real' in the sense that they represent the natural world as it really is, but as instruments which help us to make sense of our experiences. This remains a very controversial concept, as we shall see. Nevertheless, some of Poincaré's ideas have had a lasting effect and are widely accepted:

- An explanation cannot be described as scientific unless testable predictions can be made from it.
- The testing of a theory can never give us certainty.
- A theory may enable us to assess, clarify or correct our experiences.
- Even falsified theories are valuable, because they can point us in new directions and stop us from wasting time.

review
activity

1. In what sense did Poincaré see hypotheses as metaphors?

2. What difference is there between Poincaré's position and that of Kant?

3. What is 'instrumentalism'?

The deductive-nomological method of explanation

An alternative to Poincaré's instrumentalist view of science which, nevertheless, still worked within the same deductive tradition, is the rather intimidatingly named deductive-nomological method, also known as the 'covering law' model of explanation. This was developed and refined by Carl Gustav Hempel (1905–97). Hempel was strongly influenced by 'logical positivism'. This was the view that the meaning of a statement can be given in terms of the method by which it can be verified and that, if verification through sense-experience was not possible, then the statement is meaningless. It made Hempel a realist rather than an instrumentalist. He believed (at least for most of his career) that explanations were to be deduced from laws (the word 'nomological' means 'requiring law') that were both universal and true; universal in the sense that they applied at all times and in all places, and true in the sense that they were genuine statements that described the world as it really was – they were not just tools for making predictions. In fact, Hempel believed that explanation and prediction were the same things. We begin with a law that is true and some sort of observable situation; we then deduce from these two things an explanation or prediction of the fact that is of interest to us.

In evaluating this way of arguing, it is important to keep in mind that scientific explanations should be asymmetrical. In other words, if you use X to explain Y, you cannot then use Y to explain X. This is a danger with the covering law model. For example, the existence of oxygen may explain why life is present (in that oxygen is needed in order for there to be life), but it makes no sense then to say that the existence of life explains why oxygen is present. Causes do not work backwards!

In recent years, the philosophy of science has tended to focus more on the description of how scientists work rather than the logical structure of their pronouncements, and Hempel has fallen out of favour because his model is so rigid and prescriptive. As with the hypothetico-deductive in general, the emphasis falls far too heavily on the relationships between the theories and the statements that follow from them. As a result, the method encourages a lack of interest in the relationship between the theories and what the scientists actually do in terms of experimenting and providing evidence. The testing of any theory is considerably more complex than the hypothetico-deductive method implies.

review
activity

In what sense is the deductive-nomological method realist rather than instrumentalist?

11

The Progress of Science

important terms

Anti-realism: general term for the view that we are not justified in accepting the existence of anything that cannot be observed directly, but that all theoretical entities used in science are conceptual, problem-solving tools (instrumentalism), liable to replacement if a better theory is found.

Falsificationism: the approach to testing hypotheses based on the attempt to find results that are contrary to predictions and therefore render the hypotheses false.

Heuristic: an informal (i.e. non-logical) method or device for learning, explaining or problem solving.

Incommensurability: two areas of thought that cannot be compared with one another because they do not share units or methods of measurement.

Instrumentalism: the view that scientific theories are essentially tools for solving problems, and should be judged on their ability to do so.

Paradigm: a set of interconnected background theories and assumptions that determine the way people understand the world.

Realism: the view that scientific claims provide a picture of the universe as it really is (rather than seeing them as socially determined or reflecting the workings of the human mind).

Key topics in this chapter

- Falsificationism and its implications
- The theory dependence of observations
- Paradigms and scientific revolutions
- Realism and instrumentalism

Falsificationism

Probably the best known exponent of the hypothetico-deductive method was Karl Popper. His method has come to be known as falsificationism. The broad thesis of Popper's falsificationism is quite straightforward. Like Poincaré, he believed that scientific theories were tentative speculations whose purpose was to explain features of the world and to solve the problems experienced by previous theories. Any new theory is tested by observations and experiment. However, because of the problem of induction, tests that confirm the theory are not taken as indicating its truth. Instead, the falsification of a theory through testing is seen as the important step. No theory can be proved logically to be true through testing, but a theory can be proved logically to be false. Falsified theories are abandoned or may be modified. Theories that are not falsified are retained but they are not taken to be 'true', because they may well be falsified in the future. However, as this processes goes on in all parts of science, we can have increasing confidence in the theories that resist falsification. In this way, whilst we may never get to the truth about the nature of the world, we can get closer and closer to it. This makes Popper a realist, albeit a rather sophisticated one.

Avoiding erosion

Whilst the main principle of falsificationism is fairly straightforward, a number of implications need to be explored. The first is the way that falsificationism avoids a key problem of induction. Inductive arguments can be eroded. The simple inductivist position – 'I've seen a lot of white swans, therefore all swans are white' – is unsustainable, as we have seen. The alternative within the inductive position includes probability: 'I've seen a lot of white swans, so probably all swans are white'. Counter examples weaken the position

Karl Popper was probably the most important philosopher and methodologist of science in the twentieth century. His work has had an enduring impact in the realist tradition of philosophy of science and many who are prominent in the field today were taught by him whilst he was at the London School of Economics. His work was inspirational to a whole generation of scientists and philosophers who thought that the growing power of scepticism in the twentieth century was a direct attack on science itself. For example, he has a web site dedicated to him, called 'the Karl Popper Web' (http://www.eeng.dcu.ie/%7Etkpw/) whose aims are to:

1. Promote, explore and defend the heroic and critical ethos of science through philosophical debate.
2. Promote the sense of wonder that forms the motivation for science and philosophy.
3. Critically explore and apply the work of Sir Karl Popper, a key figure in the defence of science.
4. Make this accessible to new audiences and participants: beginners to science and philosophy, the newly opened societies of Russia, eastern and central Europe, less developed countries, the young and the disabled.

Not many philosophers get such attention. One important reason for this was that he saw scepticism and relativism in general as direct threats to humanity. This was because if we deny the existence of any objective truth or reality, then we lose the ability to make ethical choices; we find ourselves in a position where we cannot defend any moral judgements. This opens the door to totalitarianism, whether it be communism, fascism or, indeed, that of Plato's Guardians. All his life he was a strong defender of truth in science and the 'open society' – a liberal democratic society where assumptions and conventions could and should be challenged rigorously.

He was born in 1902 in Vienna, which, at that time, could be seen as the intellectual and cultural centre of the world. Both his parents were intellectuals and inspired in him a love of learning and music, and an interest in social and political issues. He was not happy at school and began to attend the University of Vienna in 1918. Here, still as a young man, he had a brief but intense flirtation with Marxism and left-wing politics in general. However, he rapidly came to be disillusioned by what he saw as the dogmatism of Marxism and the doctrinaire character of socialist thought. He also took an interest in psychoanalysis and the work of Freud and Adler in particular. An important moment in his intellectual development came when he listened to a lecture by the physicist Albert Einstein. He saw in Einstein a willingness to criticise and to challenge ideas in a way that seemed to be completely absent in Marx, Freud and Adler. The theories of the latter three seemed to have been designed in such a way that they could not be challenged; only confirmed. In the work of Einstein, however, there were opportunities to test the theories and to demonstrate that they were wrong (if they were wrong).

He gained a Ph.D. in philosophy in 1928 and, inevitably, came into contact with the dominant philosophical group in Vienna at the time. This was the famous 'Vienna Circle' that gave rise to the philosophical movement of 'logical positivism'. The main intent of the circle was to demonstrate that science as a whole had only one method, and that method was the verification of theoretical claims by some kind of empirical experience. Anything that failed to meet this criterion was meaningless. Thus, most forms of metaphysics including religion, which cannot be verified in this way, were dismissed as nonsense. Popper shared the Circle's high regard for science but was never a member because he was highly critical of key elements of their programme. In particular, he rejected the key idea that the meaning of a statement about the world was determined by the way in which it could be verified. In 1934 he published *The Logic of Scientific Discovery* in which he laid out his criticisms of positivism and his own, falsificationist, view of how science progresses. This book made his reputation and his career flourished. However, as a Jew watching the growth of Nazism in Germany, he knew that he had to leave Austria. In 1937 he moved to New

Zealand to teach at the University of Canterbury and remained there for the duration of the war. He moved to England in 1946 and taught at the London School of Economics, becoming Professor of Logic and Scientific Method in 1949. He was knighted in 1965 and retired in 1969, but continued to write, lecture and broadcast until his death in 1994.

We should not leave a biography of Popper without mentioning the incident of 'Wittgenstein's Poker'. In 1946 Popper attended a meeting of the Cambridge Moral Sciences Club. At that time the club was dominated by one man, said by many to be the most important philosopher of the twentieth century. The man was Ludwig Wittgenstein, born also in Vienna like Popper but two decades previously. Both men were proud, bad-tempered and had little time for those who disagreed with them. Wittgenstein was responsible for two major philosophies in his lifetime. The first, published in *Tractatus Logico-Philosophicus*, inspired the Vienna Circle in their development of logical positivism. But by 1946 he had come to reject his old ideas and had adopted a very different position. This was, briefly, that meanings and our understanding of the world depend on the conventions of language use. As language changes, so does our understanding of the world. This was exactly the kind of position that Popper hated, and the discussion at the Moral Sciences Club became very heated. What happened next is the subject of much dispute, but it seems that Wittgenstein waved a poker at Popper in what most saw as a threatening manner. The whole story is given in more detail in the excellent book *Wittgenstein's Poker* by David Edmonds and John Eidinow (2001). The book also contains clear and readable accounts of the philosophical positions of the two men.

further: 'I've seen a lot of white swans and only a few black ones, so probably most swans are white.' The erosion of the position eventually makes the claim worthless, with the added difficulty of never knowing *when* the claim is worthless.

There is also another problem with induction, based on probability, which falsification avoids. Mathematically, induction produces a conclusion based on a limited number of observations which applies to a much larger number of possible observations. The number of possible observations may even be infinite. The problem arises from the fact that the larger the number of possible observations in relation to the actual observations, the lower the probability that any claim made on the basis of the actual observations is true. The probability of a coin turning up heads is one in two, but the possibility of a die turning up six is one in six, because there are six possibilities. If the number of possibilities is *infinite*, then the probability of any statement based on a limited number of observations is zero. If I see 1000 white swans, there is still the logical possibility of an infinite number of other, unobserved swans, and so the probability of the statement 'all swans are white' being true is zero. In falsificationism, if a statement or claim is deduced logically from some hypothesis or theory, then, if the statement is shown by observation to be false, it follows that the hypothesis or theory is also false. Put simply, one counter-example disproves the theory. An absence of counter-examples, even when they are sought, allows us to continue working with the theory. Falsificationist theories cannot be eroded in the way that inductivist theories are. They are either not yet shown to be wrong, or wrong.

review
activity

Make notes, in your own words, on the way in which falsificationism overcomes these limitations of induction.

Risk in science

For a theory to be scientific, it must be possible to show that it is false. A theory only tells us something useful if it is *risky*, that is, if it offers opportunities to show that it is false. A theory that claims to give an explanation for whatever evidence is produced is of dubious value. Popper was particularly concerned with the 'demarcation problem', his term for the decision about what constitutes valid science and what is actually only pseudo-science, purporting to give scientific results, not failing to follow accepted scientific methodology in reaching them. In particular, Popper took hostile views on psychoanalysis and Marxism.

His complaint was that in psychoanalysis, as propounded by Freud and Adler, there seem to be absolutely no practical ways of showing the theories to be false. Because the unconscious mind is by definition not open to observation, anything that is explained by reference to the unconscious mind cannot be independently examined and the conclusions challenged. This complaint, in itself, cannot invalidate the process of interpretation of dreams and the examination of the unconscious that Freud initiated, but it does illustrate the way in which certain claims are not open to the sort of scrutiny that Popper regarded as the norm for science.

Popper had similar criticisms to make of Marxist theory. He was of the view that Marx's research was initially scientific, in that he proposed a theory that made predictions. However, when these predictions were not borne out, the theory was not taken to be falsified, but was saved by the addition of many bolt-on chunks of new theory which explained away the failure of the prediction. Any scientist can find *ad hoc* hypotheses in this way to protect their theory and make it compatible with observations, but by doing so they render the theory unscientific. The theory becomes pseudo-science, and that, thought Popper, was exactly what had happened to both psychoanalysis and Marxism.

On the other hand, Popper did not regard all non-falsifiable theories as worthless. For example, a theory might not be testable now, but it could become testable in the future, with advances in technology. We cannot at the moment make direct observations to test theories about the behaviour of the centre of the earth, but we may be able to do so in the future. The effects of climatic change as a result of global warming have been difficult to test because of the enormous complexity of the subject matter but, gradually, a scientific consensus was being reached.

activity

1. Why, according to Popper, is it a good thing for a theory to make risky predictions and explanations?

2. What did he think was wrong with Marxism and Freudian psychoanalysis?

The importance of opportunities to falsify theories

Science seeks the maximum amount of information. Consequently, the more opportunities there are to falsify a theory, the better the theory. This is because the more a theory attempts to explain, the more wide-ranging it is, the more opportunities there will be to test it. Theories that make small claims that are not falsified may be confirmed but are not really significant. Every time I drop my pencil on to the desk is another failure to falsify gravity, but it would be silly to claim it as such. Theories that make grand claims that are not falsified despite intensive testing, such as Darwin's theory of evolution or Einstein's theory of relativity, are of enormous value because they explain so much. However, just because these two theories have not yet been conclusively falsified does not mean that they may not be falsified in the future.

To say that Mars moves around the sun in an ellipse is not as valuable as saying that *all* planets move around the sun in ellipses, because the latter is more wide-ranging and offers more opportunities for testing and falsification. Popper himself said:

> *I can therefore gladly admit that falsificationists like myself much prefer an attempt to solve an interesting problem by bold conjecture, even (and especially) if it soon turns out to be false, to any recital of a sequence of irrelevant truisms. We prefer this because we believe that this is the way in which we can learn from our mistakes; and that in finding that our conjecture was false we shall have learnt much about the truth, and shall have got nearer to the truth.*
>
> (Popper 1969)

activity

How, for Popper, is progress in science achieved?

Criticisms of falsificationism

One key objection to Popper's method is that it focuses attention on only one theory at a time, and implies that one falsification of a theory must lead to its abandonment. There are three problems associated with this:

1. As we have seen, rejection of a theory may be a mistake. There may be problems with the experimental equipment, or a mistake in calculation or calibration. More research may go on to confirm or support the

theory. Popper was aware of this as a problem but many claim that his solutions do not go far enough.

2.   Practising scientists tend not to work in a way that is focused on only one theory at a time. They tend to work in 'research programmes', bodies of interconnected theories in one general area, supported by a set of fundamental assumptions. As we shall see later, Lakatos deals with this problem in his own work on scientific methodology.

3.   However, the most important criticism of falsificationism (and also of induction) is known as the 'theory-dependence of observation'. This criticism challenges two assumptions of those theories: firstly, that science starts from observation; secondly, that observation provides an assured basis for scientific theorising.

Now, these criticisms do not challenge the fundamental claim that a theory can be shown to be false if it makes predictions that are shown to be wrong. What they do is seek to modify the application of such an approach. The scientific community needs to remain open to the possibility that it is the experimental data which appears to falsify a theory that is itself the cause of the trouble. Then there is the possibility that a theory may continue to be of value, even if it may be challenged. And thirdly, there is a shift in the assessment of all data that are gathered through experiment and observation – an assessment that takes into account the perspective of the person gathering the data (see below). These criticisms do not so much dismiss Popper's views as set them in a broader context, thus preventing an over-simplistic approach to dismissing theories when contrary data is found.

Theory-laden observations?

To begin with, a visual image such as that of an oak tree does not strike the retina whole and fully formed, to be transported by the optic nerve to the brain as a visual image. The psychology and philosophy of perception is still contentious, but it is generally agreed that what strikes the retina are fleeting, fragmentary and unconnected sensory stimuli of some kind. The information is transmitted to the brain, where the visual image is constructed. The act of seeing does not start and end at the eyeball.

Optical illusions offer an easy demonstration of this, for example, the famous 'duck-rabbit' drawing, which can be 'seen' as a duck or as a rabbit but not as both at the same time. The brain is capable of creating either image from the stimuli, and most people can switch from one to the other. A simple experiment can demonstrate this process at its most basic level. Looking at a screen, a person is shown, very briefly, a black dot and then, within half a second, another black dot at another, randomly chosen part of the screen. The observer will actually 'see' the black dot move from one position to the other. A little thought shows us that this must be a construction of an image by the brain because the subject did not know where the second dot was going to appear. In a movement of this kind, any part of the movement that precedes the final position must come before it in time. So, either the subject can predict the future of the image, or the apparent movement is made up after the appearance of the second dot.

Polyani argues here that we must learn how to create and understand images:

> *Think of a medical student attending a course in the X-ray diagnosis of pulmonary diseases. He watches, in a darkened room, shadowy traces on a fluorescent screen placed against a patient's chest, and hears the radiologists commenting to his assistants, in technical language, on the significant features of these shadows. At first, the student is completely puzzled. For he can see in the X-ray picture of a chest only the shadows of the heart and ribs, with a few spidery blotches between them. The experts seem to be romancing about figments of their imagination; he can see nothing that they are talking about. Then, as he goes on listening for a few weeks, looking at ever-new pictures of different cases, a tentative understanding will dawn upon him; he will gradually forget about the ribs and begin to see the lungs. And eventually, if he perseveres intelligently, a rich panorama of significant details will be revealed to him: of physiological variations and pathological changes, of scars, of chronic infections and signs of acute disease. he has entered a new world. He still sees only a fraction of what the experts can see, but the pictures are definitely making sense now and so do most of the comments made on them.*　　　　　　　　　(Polyani 1969)

The perception of colour provides another example. One might take the naive view that a colour is a colour, and is recognised as such by everyone. However, the spectrum of colours familiar to us – red, orange, yellow, green, blue, indigo, violet – was invented by Isaac Newton, following his experiments with prisms. Initially he could see six colours, but wanted the spectrum to resemble the harmonic scale in music, so he convinced himself that he could see a seventh colour, indigo. Other cultures do not classify and therefore do not see colours in the same way. When visiting a tribal group in Amazonia, an anthropologist watched a group of men painting the side of a long hut. The first half they had painted black but then had run out of paint. For the second half they got hold of some blue clothes dye. The result was, to the anthropologist, quite obviously a two-colour wall. However, the men of the tribe simply did not see this; to them, blue and black were the same colour.

The public language of perception

The second point to make is that whilst the actual experiences of perception are private and confined to the person doing the perceiving, any statements that are made on the basis of this experience are public. As such, they must be made in the form of public, shared language. Such a language must be made up of theories of one kind or another, be they common everyday theories or theories in science with a high degree of sophistication. We have theories about what counts as a 'tree' or 'dog' or 'cat'. We may not recognise these as theories in everyday life, but they are still informal theoretical categorisations and it is difficult or impossible to see how we could talk to each other without them. Consequently, theory must precede any public observation statement; otherwise we could not make the statement. The precision of an observation statement will be determined by the precision of the theoretical framework within which it is made.

In science, clear and precise theories, with clear methods and techniques of measurement, will be necessary for clear and precise observation statements to be made. Consequently, the theory must come first. If the theory is wrong, then the observation statements will also be wrong. Aristotle had a theory that things moved through space at a speed determined by air resistance and the weight of the object, consequently he 'saw' heavier objects falling faster than light ones. This was believed until Galileo demonstrated it to be false.

As a result of this, we have to conclude that the observations that underpin induction and falsification are not neutral or objective for the following reasons:

1. We cannot make individual private observations without some pre-existing theoretical framework that we have adopted from our past experiences right back to childhood, and which 'conditions' the observations.
2. We cannot say anything about these observations to other people without, at the same time, employing some sort of theoretical basis in the language that we use.

Popper was aware of this problem. His solution was to conduct observations with the utmost rigour and to ensure that the statements were as public as possible within the community of scientists. This is valuable advice, but does not solve the problem, because the community of scientists will mostly be using the same theoretical framework.

As we shall see, Popper's colleague at the London School of Economics, Imre Lakatos (1922–74), developed a perspective on the methodology of science which tried to take this point into account.

review activity

Explain why the theory-dependence of observation causes problems for the assumptions that (a) science starts from observation, and, (b) observation provides an assured basis for scientific theorising.

Kuhn: paradigms and scientific revolutions

In the early 1960s there appeared a major challenge to the hypothetico-deductive model, to falsificationism and to all previous models of scientific methodology. It came from the work of Thomas S. Kuhn (1922-96), especially in his seminal book *The Structure of Scientific Revolutions*.

Thomas Kuhn was born in Cincinnati in the United States in 1922. He taught at Harvard University from 1949, moving to the University of California at Berkeley in 1956 where he became professor of history of science five years later. In 1964 he became the M. Taylor Pyne Professor of Philosophy and History of Science at Princeton. In 1979 he moved again, this time to the Massachusetts Institute of Technology and eventually became the Laurence S. Rockefeller Professor of Philosophy. He became a Guggenheim Fellow in 1954.

He received a number of honorary degrees and was awarded the George Sarton Medal in the History of Science. He wrote *The Structure of Scientific Revolutions* (1962) whilst a young graduate student studying theoretical physics. It was controversial because it attacked the conventional view of the nature of science and its progress, and it tried to answer philosophical questions in a historical way. Nevertheless, the book has secured its place in history, selling over a million copies in 16 languages.

Paradigms

Kuhn argued that science is not characterised by the steady, cumulative growth of a corpus (or body) of knowledge, it is not an accumulation of information. Instead it is characterised by peaceful periods when nothing much happens, punctuated by dramatic and extraordinary changes. Following each of these changes, scientists, and eventually ordinary people, come to see the world in radically different ways. The key term, which has become very well known, is that of 'paradigm'. As many have pointed out, Kuhn is not precise in the way that he uses the term. However, he takes it to mean, broadly, a set or collection of interconnected ideas and beliefs held by all or almost all scientists about how the world is to be understood. He said that paradigms were necessary for science because (using the term 'natural history' to mean the natural world – the subject matter of science) 'no natural history can be interpreted in the absence of at least some implicit body of intertwined theoretical and methodo-logical belief that permits selection, evaluation and criticism'. Paradigms not only tell the scientists what is important and what is not, what they should do and what they should ignore, they are also crucial in delineating particular subjects such as biology or physics. Each has its own paradigm. A paradigm shift heralds a scientific revolution: 'a scientist's world is qualitatively trans-formed [and] quantitatively enriched by fundamental novelties of either fact or theory.'

The quotations that follow (taken from *The Structure of Scientific Revolutions*) give a flavour of how radical Kuhn's ideas were in the context of the traditional views of the scientific method. In the first he points out that history tells us that it is the young newcomer to a scientific field who typically makes the important steps forward:

> [*Individuals who break through by inventing a new paradigm are*] *almost always ... either very young or very new to the field whose paradigm they change ... These are the men who, being little committed by prior practice to the traditional rules of normal science, are particularly likely to see that those rules no longer define a playable game and to conceive another set that can replace them.*
>
> (Kuhn 1962)

He points out that the conventional view so restricts the meaning of a theory that it cannot be accepted if it conflicts with any later theory that makes predic-tions about the same phenomena. He illustrates this by explaining why Einstein's relativity does not show Newton's physics to be wrong – directly contradicting the falsificationist position:

> *The best-known and the strongest case for this restricted conception of a scientific theory emerges in discussions of the relation between contemporary Einsteinian dynamics and the older dynamical equations that descend from Newton's* Principia. *From the viewpoint of this essay these two theories are fundamentally incompatible in the sense illustrated by the relation of Copernican to Ptolemaic astronomy: Einstein's theory can be accepted only with the recognition that Newton's was wrong. Today this remains a minority view. We must therefore examine the most prevalent objections to it.*

> *The gist of these objections can be developed as follows. Relativistic dynamics cannot have shown Newtonian dynamics to be wrong, for Newtonian dynamics is still used with great success by most engineers and, in selected applications, by*

many physicists. Furthermore, the propriety of this use of the older theory can be proved from the very theory that has, in other applications, replaced it. Einstein's theory can be used to show that predictions from Newton's equations will be as good as our measuring instruments in all applications that satisfy a small number of restrictive conditions. For example, if Newtonian theory is to provide a good approximate solution, the relative velocities of the bodies considered must be small compared with the velocity of light. Subject to this condition and a few others, Newtonian theory seems to be derivable from Einsteinian, of which it is therefore a special case. (Kuhn 1962)

He therefore makes the point that Newton's theory was correct, but within the limited range of conditions that were testable at that time. Simply because, at very high velocities, that theory breaks down, does not mean that it needs to be discarded. Kuhn therefore dismisses the principles of falsificationism, for if, as the falsificationist suggests, all anomalies and puzzles were taken to falsify a theory, then more or less all scientific theories would need to be abandoned. Kuhn is therefore able to develop a more sophisticated view of how science develops, one in which revolutionary paradigm shifts punctuate periods of 'normal' science. Controversially, Kuhn claimed that during periods of 'normal' science – the periods between revolutions – scientists were not at all objective, critical or rigorous. He describes them as 'solving puzzles', the puzzles being thrown up within the paradigm in which they worked. The solution of the puzzle was not to change the paradigm, or to produce new knowledge; it was to protect the paradigm by explaining any existing anomalies. The scientists actually know what results they want from their researches and set up experiments in such a way that they produce these results. Their job is to reconcile the facts as they present themselves in research with the currently accepted theories and paradigm. Results and observations that contradict existing wisdom tend to be ignored, set aside for 'future consideration' when techniques and instrumentation might be better suited to explaining them (away). The Aristotelian and Ptolemaic versions of physics and cosmology were believed for more than a thousand years in the face of much contradictory evidence. Cesare Cremonini (1550–1631), an Aristotelian scholar from Padua, refused to look through Galileo's telescope in case he saw things that might undermine the Aristotelian world view. Kuhn says: 'Novelty emerges only with difficulty, manifested by resistance, against a background provided by expectation.' As we have seen, more often than not it is the young scientist, or the scientist new to the field, who precipitates the crisis and the revolution, because they are not steeped in the traditions of the existing paradigm.

Incommensurability

When a new paradigm arises to challenge the old, the two are both incompatible and incommensurable. This latter word is important. 'Incommensurable' is an adjective that describes a situation where two or more things cannot be compared in any way, such as size or value, because they have no common means of measurement. Think of it as something like asking the question 'which is greater, 10 litres of water or 10 metres of rope?' The question is impossible to answer because there is no common measuring system. What Kuhn is saying is that you cannot make a judgement about a new paradigm from within the old, and vice versa, because the means for making the judgement have changed from the old to the new. A Newtonian physicist cannot make a judgement about Einsteinian physics because Einstein changed the means of measurement and comparison. As we shall see, the concept of incommensurability is also important for Paul Feyerabend, who takes it even further than Kuhn.

Most controversially, Kuhn argues that we need to abandon the quest for ultimate truths in science. He says 'we may have to relinquish the notion, explicit or implicit, that changes of paradigm carry scientists and those who learn from them closer and closer to the truth. The progress of science is really more like the process of evolution according to Darwin. Evolution is not progressing "towards" anything in particular, it is just happening.'

The 'crown of creation'   Paradigms change as a result of a range of factors, many social and economic as well as technological and theoretical. They may become more detailed, but there is no discernible way that it can be claimed that there is an 'ultimate' paradigm. Those Victorians who grudgingly came to accept Darwin's theory often did so in the belief that humankind was the ultimate species, the 'crown of creation'. There was, and is, no reason to believe this, and there is no reason to believe that in science there can be a final 'theory of everything'.

review
activity

1. What is a 'paradigm'? What happens in scientific revolutions?
2. What is meant by 'incommensurability'?
3. Why may Kuhn be described as a relativist?

Kuhn and the social sciences

Sociologists, psychologists, economists, and so on have engaged in a debate for many decades among themselves and with others over whether or not their disciplines should be considered to be sciences. We shall be exploring this issue in more detail in the next chapter. However, it is relevant here because the implications of Kuhn's work are that those who work in these disciplines cannot be scientists because they do not have a paradigm. This makes them significantly different from established sciences such as physics or chemistry, where more or less all those working in the fields agree on the basics.

Those who have taken even a cursory look at sociology and psychology will have found that they are characterised by a number of fundamentally different theories that compete with one another. For example, 'structural' theories compete with 'agency' theories to explain how humans behave. A *structural theory* assumes that individual people do what they do because of constraints and controls that are imposed on them by society or the political or economic order. I do what I do because of my class background, or the legal and political environment in which I live. Thus, my actions are largely determined by factors that are outside me, and over which I have little control. Those external factors may include the values that I have been taught as a child, and have now (perhaps unconsciously) adopted as my own. An *agency-based theory* assumes that, in order to understand why people act as they do, we need to understand how they see the world and on what basis they consciously make decisions. Thus it is based on the free choices of individuals, rather than the structures of the society within which they find themselves. Which of these approaches is the more fundamental? Unless there is a single overall 'paradigm', how do scientists in that field set about their normal work within that paradigm?

Kuhn's general complaint, therefore, is that the so-called social sciences lack an agreed paradigm. Or rather, they have either not yet reached the stage when they can develop a paradigm, or they have too many paradigms. In either case, Kuhn would say that this renders them unscientific.

The characteristics of a good theory

Kuhn held that, collectively, the scientific community generally came to a conclusion about which theories were valuable and which were not, although there might be a great deal of debate in order to achieve that conclusion. However, such debate need not focus on the personal preferences of particular scientists, but on the inherent qualities of the theories under consideration. In *The Essential Tension* (1977) he set out the five qualities by which he considered a scientific theory should be judged. They are:

1. accuracy
2. consistency
3. scope
4. simplicity
5. fruitfulness.

Clearly, it is important for a theory to be accurate, but an accurate theory may not tell us very much, may not link to other theories, or lead on to help us develop further theories. Hence the scope and fruitfulness of a theory needs to be taken into account. A theory that is very useful need not be immediately rejected, even if questions about its accuracy are raised.

Criticisms of Kuhn

Kuhn is accused of idealism, relativism and irrationalism. However, before we look at each of these charges specifically, we should look at the wider background of his controversial ideas. Kuhn trained as a scientist, but much of his work is in the history of science. Therefore, it could be claimed that he was by profession an historian rather than a philosopher. Indeed, when *The Structure of Scientific Revolutions* was first published it was seen as an attack on the philosophy of science in general and the response from philosophers was generally hostile. He was often accused by philosophers of producing not just a history of science but a sociology of science, and, in either case, of avoiding the key questions. To a certain extent, this remained true. In the period 1976–83, *The Structure of Scientific Revolutions* was the most cited book in arts and humanities in the United States (a citation is a reference to a book in an academic article), yet in the *Oxford Companion to Philosophy* Kuhn is dismissed in a few lines – about the same number as many quite minor philosophers. Kuhn was not happy with this; he really wanted to be seen as a philosopher. John Zammito said in a lecture:

Kuhn, in his heart of hearts, wished most of all to be taken as a philosopher of science and his entire enterprise in the wake of The Structure of Scientific Revolutions *was to win acceptance among philosophers of science, however much he was taken to have been the great overthrower of the tradition that they represented.*

(Zammito 1998)

Kuhn himself was attempting a paradigm shift in the philosophy of science, and the philosophers didn't like it. They saw straight away that Kuhn's new picture of science left no way open for judging rationally between competing theories. Zammito goes on to say that this was 'utterly threatening to the two most important concepts they associated with natural science, namely rationality and progress.' They accused Kuhn of surrendering science to 'mob psychology' and said that his account of normal science was insulting to practising scientists.

The end of logic

We can conclude, then, that the debate about Kuhn's work is also a debate about professional rivalries and jealousies. Traditionalists in the philosophy of science felt that Kuhn was simply providing what the liberal arts and humanities had always wanted – a reason for knocking science from its pedestal as the only proper form of knowledge. At worst, the arts and the sciences were fundamentally the same, at best, the arts were superior to science. This is a prejudice that had been around for several hundred years. However, the accusation goes deeper. Kuhn could also be seen as reviving the scholastic hostility that provided Galileo with so many difficulties, or even the epistemological and ethical relativism of the sophists in ancient Greece. Up until now, the philosophy of science concentrated on the logical relationships between evidence and theories and the differences between science and pseudo-science. Kuhn's great crime was to render logic irrelevant and put history and sociology in its place.

A further point is that Kuhn is very selective in the *kinds* of science that he discusses. Physics has a very high profile, so does astronomy and cosmology, and it is in these fields that Kuhn finds most of his examples and illustrations. However, there are a number of more modest scientific areas (such as aeronautics, oceanography or pharmacology) that don't seem to experience dramatic paradigm shifts but demonstrate a gradual accumulation of settled results with few, if any, anomalies. They are often practical and limited in their scope but are nevertheless important to us.

review
activity

1. Explain the criticism of Kuhn that he surrenders to 'mob psychology'.
2. Do Kuhn's views render logic irrelevant, as critics might claim?

In formal terms Kuhn is accused of being an idealist, a relativist and an irrationalist. We need to look at each of these in turn.

Idealism

Idealism has a number of different definitions, but what these definitions have in common is that they say that what is *real* is essentially *mental*. Idealists include George Berkeley, who considered that 'to be' was 'to be perceived', and Kant, who believed that all knowledge is limited to sense perceptions and that we cannot know things as they are in themselves. For idealists it makes no sense to talk about a reality existing separately from our minds, because, even if it is there, we can never have any access to it. Also, all the mind can do is to reveal to us its own contents. Consequently, when we think we are examining the world, we are really examining the contents of our own minds.

Kuhn is seen as an idealist because the paradigms within which we are ensnared are mental; they are products of human minds. In *The Structure of Scientific Revolutions* Kuhn is ambivalent about this. At some points he seems to be saying that scientists before and after a paradigm shift do not see the same thing, which would be an idealist position. At other points he seems to be saying that whatever it is that the scientists are looking at has not itself changed over paradigm shifts, which would make him a realist. In later writing he is much less subjective, much less of an idealist. He says that there really are objects and relationships in the world and that they remain unchanged. What changes is our way of classifying them. What happens during a paradigm shift is that we see different kinds of similarities and different kinds of differences, or we come to see some similarities and differences as more important than others. In the past, whales used to be regarded as fish because, like other fish, they lived in water – that was the important similarity. Latterly we have come to see whales as mammals because we now regard their similarities with other mammals as being more important than their similarities with fish, especially the facts that they are warm-blooded, they bear their young alive and they breathe with lungs. Whales themselves have not changed. Overall, therefore, although he can at times sound like an idealist, Kuhn is not consistently idealist in his views, and his argument about the influence of paradigms in the development of science does not require an idealist viewpoint.

Relativism　It is difficult to argue that Kuhn is not a relativist. 'Relativism' is one of those catch-all words that can mean many things. Generally, it can be taken to mean the view that individuals and groups see and understand the world in different ways and there is no way of making judgements about which is the correct one. It is summed up in the famous quotation from Socrates' opponent, Protagoras, 'Man is the measure of all things, of that which is, that it is, and of that which is not, that it is not.' Kuhn is quite explicit. One cannot find a position outside those of the paradigms from which an evaluation of worth, value or accuracy can be made which relates to the paradigms. There is no position that we can take from which we can decide which paradigm is right and which is wrong. We can ask that they be as simple as possible, that they should refer to as much of the world as possible and should match up with observations as much as possible. But this is not enough, because there may well be disagreements over what counts as simplicity and generality in a particular area of scientific interest. Furthermore, the theory-dependence of observation remains a problem for any attempts to verify or falsify a paradigm. We may also find that the desire for simplicity and the desire for generality conflict with each other. Although it is an attractive idea, there is no logical reason why the simplest paradigm should at the same time be the most general (applying to as many things as possible).

Irrationalism

Irrationalism in philosophy is not a matter of making the occasional mistake in reasoning. It is a principled stand which claims that certain kinds of knowledge are impossible to attain through reason, but can be achieved through faith or intuition. The issues that this kind of knowledge concerns itself with are of the utmost importance; questions such as the purpose of human life or the metaphysical basis for the existence of the universe can only be known through faith or intuition and the source of the knowledge must in some way be transcendental, as it cannot come directly through what we experience. Because they deal with such important questions and can provide answers, then faith and intuition must be superior to reason. Irrationalism of this kind is commoner outside philosophy than within it. For example, it is the basis for much 'new age' thinking.

Given this definition, it seems unfair to accuse Kuhn of irrationalism. The basis for that claim is that he argues that there is no good *reason* for switching from one paradigm to another; the change is not reasoned therefore it is not rational. However, Kuhn does not write in the way that we would normally associate with irrationalism. Scientists working in different paradigms do talk to each other and so provide each other with *reasons* why their own paradigm is correct. Scientists working in the same paradigm, doing 'normal' science use reason all the time and would condemn any knowledge-claims based on faith or intuition – or, at least, they would demand that the faith or intuition be supported by reason and evidence. Indeed, it is the failures in prediction, assessed rationally, that may lead to the recognition that a paradigm is inadequate. Nevertheless, for Kuhn the final arbiter of the paradigm shift is the scientific community itself, which suggests that the choice is sociological rather than strictly rational.

review activity

Explain why Kuhn has been criticised as being:

1. an idealist

2. a relativist

3. irrational.

Say whether you consider such criticism to be justified.

Lakatos and sophisticated falsificationism

It is a convincing criticism of Popper that he focussed far too closely on individual theories or explanations. Ultimately, the falsification of a theory rests on the dependence of any observation on some sort of theoretical context, and this context does not seem to be liable to the kind of falsification that Popper had in mind, despite his claims. His colleague Imre Lakatos, whilst maintaining what was essentially a realist stance, provided a more sophisticated falsificationism, which was almost sociological in its emphasis. He was also working in response to Kuhn's 'revolutionary' ideas, and it is possible to see evidence of these in his work. The key to Lakatos' picture of science was not the individual theory but instead the 'research programme'. Science for Lakatos was an activity undertaken by scientists all over the world, and in some sense coordinated, if only by the need to agree on what is significant, what is interesting and what is redundant (this would not rule out disagreements and rivalries between scientists). He agreed that there cannot be knowledge in the sense of a corpus of information that accurately and completely mirrors the world. Science cannot be a torch lightening a darkened room which, once it has highlighted everything, has done its work. But he did believe that there can be a growth of knowledge, which the unique character of the scientific endeavour can move forwards so that new and reliable explanations of the world emerge from the combined activities of the community of scientists. The process of adopting, abandoning, changing and replacing theories is itself rational. A good research programme is one that accounts for all the old findings and makes new predictions. A bad one is a programme that is static, one that slots new observations into pre-existing theoretical categories. Consequently, a progressive, interesting programme is one in which there are many anomalies, many observations that cannot be accounted for. This is why the Aristotelian programme as it was in the Middle Ages was a bad programme and the Copernican programme was good. The Aristotelians simply denied that there could be any anomalies – to the extent of refusing to look through telescopes – whilst the Copernicans highlighted them, and were therefore able to make progress.

> The time-honoured empirical criterion for a satisfactory theory was agreement with the observed facts. Our empirical criterion for a series of theories is that it should produce new facts. The idea of growth and the concept of empirical character are soldered into one. (Lakatos 1970)

Negative and positive heuristics

Lakatos introduces two key concepts that are liable to misunderstanding. These are the 'negative heuristic' and the 'positive heuristic'. A heuristic is a device for, or style or method of, learning or enquiring.

The basic core of a scientific programme contains the essential theories upon which the whole programme rests and which are assumed to be accurate by the participants in the research programme. Their confidence is such that the core is protected by a *negative heuristic*, in other words, the core is not open to testing or prediction. The method of enquiry (the heuristic) is one that does not lead to that care being falsified. In the Newtonian paradigm, no scientists sat about in laboratories throwing pencils up in the air to see if they defied gravity; they simply accepted the paradigm.

A *positive heuristic*, on the other hand, is applied to the 'protective belt' of supporting theories that surround the core. It contains many distinctive parts of the research programme which may be relatively unrelated, linked only through their adherence to the key ideas of the basic core. In the positive heuristic there will be many anomalies, unexplained or contradictory observations, and many predictions, some of which will be shown to be false and some borne out. It is here in the positive heuristic that progress is made, which makes it a 'progressive' research programme. A failing or 'degenerating' research programme is one in which there is no positive heuristic. Such a programme has only a negative heuristic applied to the unchallengeable core; unchallenged by contradiction and new evidence, it goes nowhere.

Using this distinction between the positive and negative heuristic, between the 'hard core' of a programme that defines it and the 'protective belt' that can be tested, experimented on and changed, Lakatos believed that he could accomplish two things. Firstly, he would be able to address a serious problem in the falsificationist position, which is the fact that theories can always be modified in the face of contradictory evidence by adding new assumptions and concepts that explain away the contradiction. It was this problem that caused Popper such disquiet with Marxism and Freudian psychoanalysis and led him to put such emphasis on the need for good theory to make bold, startling predictions. Secondly, Lakatos hoped to respond to Kuhn's paradigmatic model of science by showing that the changes that took place in research programmes were rational and necessary.

Copernicus and Kepler

For example, Copernicus (1473–1543) suggested that the sun was at the centre of the universe, and that all of the six planets known at that time revolved around the sun in circles. He assumed that the planets moved in circular orbits, because circular motion was considered to be perfect, and therefore appropriate for heavenly bodies. However, this did not match observations. He therefore argued that the planets moved through *epicycles* (an epicycle is the path traced out by a point on the circumference of one circle as that circle moves round the circumference of another). To account for the observed motions of all of these planets and of the moon, he needed about sixty such epicycles. However, Kepler (1571–1630) showed by his astronomical observations that they did not move in circles but instead in ellipses, with the sun at one focus, each of them sweeping through arcs of equal area in equal times. From a Popperian point of view, this would mean that the Copernican theory was falsified. Copernicus had boldly conjectured, for example, that the moon revolved around the Earth in a circle whilst the Earth itself revolved around the sun in a circle. Kepler showed this to be false. However, in practice we do not see this as a refutation at all. We regard Kepler as having been an advance on Copernicus' work and a justification of Copernicus' claim that the planets revolved around the sun. Whether they revolve in a circle or an ellipse is much less important than the central assertion.

Newton and Kepler

In a similar way, Newton (1642–1727) developed Kepler's work and introduced significant changes. Newton's gravitational force meant that the sun itself was not stationary as Kepler had thought, but moved under the gravitational influence of the planets. However, because it was so massive, its motion, compared to that of the planets, was minor. Popper might well take this to be a falsification of Kepler, but this seems unreasonable. We would probably say that both Kepler and Newton were working within the Copernican paradigm. They both accepted the core aspects of Copernicus' work, but rejected some auxiliary parts. And Newton did the same for Kepler. This process inclines us to see this period of science in Kuhnian terms. There was a paradigm which was very different from that of Ptolemy or Aristotle. Within that paradigm, Kepler and Newton were solving problems or puzzles, and not challenging the central core, what Lakatos would call the 'negative heuristic'.

At the same time, Lakatos is aware of the danger highlighted by Popper that it is always possible to help out an ailing theory by adding new auxiliary concepts and ideas, which prevent it from being falsified and abandoned. It could be argued that both Kepler and Newton had added their new assumptions to Copernicus' original ideas, to 'explain away' discrepancies that they had discovered through their astronomical observations. Therefore, Copernicus should be rejected. This seems perverse to us today, and no doubt also was at the time, for intelligent natural scientists. Kuhn's picture of science seems to fit much better. The 'bold conjectures' required by Popper (instead of *ad hoç* assumptions) are not possible within a paradigm, because the paradigm itself determines the kind of observations that can be made.

Therefore, Lakatos wanted to develop a methodology for science that recognised the development and problem solving of a research programme, or paradigm, but at the same time he had to find a place from which he could rule out bolt-on, *ad hoc* assumptions put in place simply to save a theory. This he does with his distinction between a 'hard core' which describes a set of fundamental assumptions about how things are and a methodology for approaching them, and a protective belt of associated theories which can be experimented with and changed. Paired with these are the negative heuristic, which provides rules forbidding the alteration of the hard core, and the positive heuristic, which provides rules that determine how and in what circumstances parts of the protective belt can be altered or eliminated.

Thus, in astronomy, the Copernican assumption that the Earth revolves around the sun, and that other heavenly bodies do the same is the hard core, protected by rules that say that rejecting this assumption is not possible within this research programme. Kepler's and Newton's modifications are auxiliary theories within the protective belt, and the positive heuristic provides rules that say that these auxiliary theories can be altered as a result of observation and testing. The modifications proposed by Kepler and Newton are successful because they both account for all the previous observations and lead to some new predictions that are born out by new observations.

Newton's theory of gravity is a good example of this. His core theory was that there are three laws of motion and a law of gravity. His auxiliary theory was that the fundamental force that kept the Earth revolving around the sun, and the moon revolving around the Earth, was gravity. This accounted for all that had been observed before. However, Newton was also able to explain (and predict) the movement of the tides as a result of the gravitational force of the moon. This was new. It meant that the research programme was making progress.

Progress in science Lakatos saw this picture of science as beneficial in two ways. Firstly, the theory itself made progress, because it was a fuller and more complete version of what went before. Secondly, and this is what makes Lakatos a realist, each new auxiliary theory, if borne out, reveals new parts of the universe of which we were not previously aware. The fog clears and we begin to see how things actually are.

But prediction is risky for the scientist. A forecast may turn out to be false, in which case the whole auxiliary theory, which the scientist might have been working on for years, will have to be abandoned. However, without this personal risk, we can never be sure that the auxiliary theory is not simply propping up an outdated theoretical core.

Degenerating and progressing research programmes

A research programme is described as 'degenerating' if its predictions are not borne out, and when other scientists fail to replicate its findings. It is 'progressing' if it produces predictions that are confirmed. Geomancy (sometimes known as *feng shui*) is an old science based on the core theory that lines of force radiate out across the whole earth, and that an understanding and detection of these lines will lead to success for humans, in some way or another. However, it has not made any new predictions that have been borne out; it has simply adjusted its auxiliary theories in order to protect itself, or rather the proponents of geomancy have. The same can be said of astrology. They are both degenerating programmes.

Nevertheless, a programme that is failing to produce good predictions, or any predictions at all, cannot be abandoned until there is a better research programme to replace it. This is because we can never be sure that the predictions will not one day be made that solve its problems – we can never be sure that the problem is with the core. This can be illustrated by looking at the discovery, early in the nineteenth century, that the orbit of the planet Uranus (at that time thought to be the furthest planet from the sun) failed to match the predictions for it derived from Newton's theory of gravity. Scientists tried to make adjustments to the theory, but none was successful in matching prediction to the actual motion of the planet. This could have led to the abandonment of the Newtonian core, which consisted of his three laws of motion and the law of gravity. However, the core theory had been very successful for a century and few were willing to contemplate discarding it, especially as there appeared to be no alternatives. Eventually it was suggested that the problem would be solved if there were to be another planet, further from the sun than Uranus, which was affecting the latter's orbit. The position of the new planet was predicted according to Newton's laws. Observations shortly revealed, in the right place, the planet Neptune. A risky auxiliary theory, the existence of another planet, was corroborated, and the Newtonian core theory was saved. The research programme was progressing.

On the other hand, a similar situation can lead to the abandonment of a research programme. The planet Mercury was discovered in the latter part of the nineteenth century, and, again, was found to move in a way that failed to fit with Newtonian predictions. This time no auxiliary theories helped. Another planet, to be called Vulcan at the time, was proposed but was not found. Eventually the entire Newtonian core was abandoned because a better research programme, based on Einstein's theory, was available. This explained everything that Newtonian theory did in a very different way, but explained the motion of Mercury as well. Lakatos' point is that if Einstein's theory had not been available we would not have abandoned Newton, because we could never be sure that the problem could not be solved by another, future, auxiliary theory that no one had thought of yet. Thus Lakatos disagrees with Popper's view that falsification of a programme quickly leads to rejection. His position, therefore, moves towards that of Kuhn. For Popper, a theory can be tested and rejected on the basis of experimental data; for Kuhn and Lakatos, testing involves the comparison of two competing theories to account for that experimental data.

Lakatos describes a scientific methodology in which knowledge grows in two ways:

1. Growth resulting from the emergence of brand new research programmes with core theories is very different from anything that went before.
2. Growth resulting from the constant modification and improvement of the protective belt of auxiliary theories.

The former, involving a dramatic and revolutionary leap in thinking, establishes the ground rules. It sets, for the auxiliary theories, the kind of phenomena that can be investigated, the methods by which they can be investigated and the criteria for success in investigation.

review activity

1. Distinguish between a progressive research programme and a degenerating research programme.

2. Carefully explain the differences between the application of the positive and negative heuristics within a research programme.

3. Did Lakatos believe that science could produce an accurate and true picture of the world?

Realism and instrumentalism

Realism

In the philosophy of science there is a broad division of opinion between those who believe that, albeit with great difficulty, science can establish an accurate picture of the world as it really is (or at least a close approximation to it) and those who do not believe that this is possible. The former group can be described as *realists*, the latter as anti-realists or instrumentalists. Realism entails not only that the things we sense directly, such as mountains, trees and animals, are really there in the outside world, but also those things that we cannot sense directly, the theoretical entities that are used in science, such as atoms or electrons, can be shown to be real.

Instrumentalism

For those who cannot accept this, because of the many criticisms of induction and falsification, the only alternative may be the sceptical position of claiming that knowledge of the world is impossible, and that what we take to be knowledge is all illusion – the shadows on the walls of Plato's cave. However, there is an alternative that has become increasingly popular: *instrumentalism*. According to this view we should abandon the argument over whether theories are true or not, in the sense that they give an absolutely accurate picture of reality, and instead see them as *instruments* by which we explain and, crucially, predict the phenomena that we experience. *Consequently, a theory is not judged on its truth or falsity but on its usefulness or effectiveness.* The instrument (the theory) is seen as a tool for achieving our goals and solving our practical problems. The idea is not entirely recent. Copernicus said of his heliocentric universe (with the sun at the centre) that it should not be taken to be a real picture of how the universe is, but simply as an aid to astronomical calculation. He may have done this for political and religious reasons (it was dangerous to suggest something that appeared to contradict scripture), and his theory did not actually simplify the calculations that much, but in doing so he, perhaps accidentally, established the idea of a theory as an instrument, to be judged on the basis of its usefulness.

Pragmatism

However, the main impetus for instrumentalism came from the American philosophy known as pragmatism, and in particular from the work of John Dewey – the other founders of pragmatism being William James and, above all, C.S. Pierce. Pragmatism is generally seen as an epistemological theory of truth; in other words, it asks *how* we come to know what is true. It is usually contrasted with the *correspondence theory of truth*, that is, the view that there is a direct link between the statement that is claimed to be true and the external reality to which it refers. Hence it is particularly relevant to issues in the philosophy of science. Dewey believed that there was no essential difference between ordinary everyday thinking and scientific thinking. The only differences were minor, in things like the rigour of measurements and the explicitness of hypotheses. Therefore scientific thinking was to be judged by the same criteria as ordinary thinking. Does it do the job? Does it solve the problem? Is it effective in getting what I want? Dewey described instru-mentalism as 'an attempt to constitute a precise logical theory of concepts, judgments and inferences in their various forms, by primarily considering how thought functions in the experimental determinations of future consequences'.

Central to pragmatism and instrumentalism is a rejection of the notion that there are absolutes in knowledge – chunks of knowledge that are irreducible, that cannot be broken down and explained by other ideas, and which are metaphysically 'fixed' in place in that they cannot change or be shown to be wrong. Instead, for the pragmatist, all knowledge should be considered as provisional, as temporary, as a working hypothesis always ready to be replaced by something more effective.

Instrumentalism versus realism

We could sum up the argument between instrumentalists (or anti-realists) and realists in the following way. We begin with the basic question 'is the world (the universe) understandable?' The realist answer is 'yes', and science is the means by which we achieve this, using the hypothetico-deductive method, a lot of care and a lot of rigour. The instrumentalist answer is 'no' or at least not in the usual sense of the word 'understand' as 'seeing things as they really are'. There may be two reasons for our inability to do this:

1. We humans are just not clever enough. The universe defeats us with its complexity and it always will.
2. The universe is by its own nature impossible to understand; it is a brute fact (a fact that does not have an explanation) that the fundamental rules that govern the universe are unknowable.

For both reasons, our only alternative is to make up explanations that serve our purposes as humans and that work for us in achieving what we want. This is instrumentalism.

Is the world understandable?

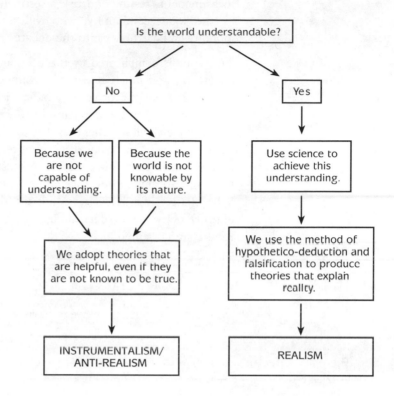

Beneficial to whom?

Pierce saw this as a true scientific method, as a means of reaching objective standards. The scientific process was to be one where the procedures and values of the scientists ensured that it was self-correcting. He thought that the meaning of some statement or claim in science was to be determined by the consequences, and by this he meant the observational consequences in the experimental process. If these consequences were beneficial in scientific, terms then the statement was true, if not, the statement was not true. Dewey and James did not agree, and advocated a more 'social' version of pragmatism in which the community as a whole was involved, not just the scientists. James saw the decision about whether the consequences were beneficial was essentially subjective and personal. It was an individual decision. Dewey, probably more realistically, thought that the decision was made by all people, including scientists and that the criteria used for the decision were also moral and aesthetic, as well as scientific.

This illustrates a division of opinion within pragmatism and therefore within instrumentalism generally. Is science an objective, impersonal enterprise from which the personal preferences and values of the scientists are excluded? Or is science about meeting the needs and fulfilling the wishes of particular individuals or groups, as James and Dewey would suggest? Pierce thought that the latter approach undermined what pragmatism was about and could lead to an idiosyncratic and ever changing scepticism.

This might seem like pointless hair splitting but it is not. If we take modern debates such as those over genetically modified crops or human cloning we are forced to confront the question of who should make the decisions. Should it be the scientists, as Pierce would say, using the standard scientific criteria of measurement, testing and risk assessment? Or should the decision be made by the wider community, who will certainly want to introduce issues of morality and aesthetics into the debate?

This issue is complicated by the economics of scientific research. Science is expensive, and much research is commercially funded. Such funding raises questions about the objectivity of science. If a department receives a grant from a pharmaceutical company to research into certain drugs, for example, that company will in general expect to see results that are relevant and beneficial to its own operations. If nothing relevant is generated, then the funding is likely to cease. Hence, to an increasing extent, the sources of research funding determine the range of scientific research that is undertaken. In light of this, it is relevant to ask whether science can ever be said to be entirely objective in determining what is studied and the way in which results are presented.

review activity

1. Outline, in your own words, the distinction between realism and instrumentalism.

2. Why is instrumentalism often seen as a version of pragmatism?

3. There are different views on what it means to say that a theory 'solves a problem' or 'is useful'. What are these views and why is the debate important?

Against Method and *Farewell to Reason*

These are the titles of two books by Paul Feyerabend. They neatly sum up his position on the philosophy of science. He thought that there was no particular methodology that science should adopt and neither did he see reason as an important part of science. His was a very radical position. In one way it could be said that he took Kuhn's position and pushed it to its extreme. He also took instrumentalism and expanded the idea of 'usefulness' as a criterion for success in science to cover whatever anyone wanted. His catchphrase was 'anything goes'. He himself said that he had developed an 'anarchistic' theory of knowledge. This put him at odds with almost the entire establishment of the philosophy of science.

Feyerabend summarises his own ideas most effectively in the 'Analytical Index' of *Against Method*, from which the brief quotations in the section that follow are taken.

Feyerabend sees science as essentially an anarchistic enterprise, and he argues that this is more likely to encourage progress than is more 'law-and-order', in particular he argues that 'we may use hypotheses that contradict well-confirmed theories and/or well-established experimental results. We may advance science by proceeding counter-inductively' (Feyerabend 1975). He contrasts this with

Paul Feyerabend was born in Vienna in 1924. His father was a civil servant and his mother a seamstress. He fought in the Second World War, was promoted to lieutenant and was awarded the Iron Cross (a medal for bravery). After the war he returned to Vienna to study history and sociology but rapidly switched to physics in which he took up a positivist position. During these years he was strongly influenced by the ideas of the Vienna Circle and became a leading member of the so-called Kraft Circle, which was a student club formed around Viktor Kraft, who had actually been a member of the Vienna Circle before the war. He met Karl Popper at about this time. Possibly one of the most influential events was a talk given to the Kraft Circle by Ludwig Wittgenstein.

In 1951 he was awarded his doctorate and came to England. He originally wanted to study under Wittgenstein at Cambridge but Wittgenstein died before he arrived. Instead he went to the London School of Economics to work under Karl Popper and spent a great deal of time studying quantum theory and Wittgenstein's very difficult *Philosophical Investigations*. It is interesting to wonder how this went down with Popper, whose ideas conflicted with those of Wittgenstein (see the incident of the poker in Popper's biography on p. 160). In 1953 he returned to Vienna and translated Popper's *The Open Society and its Enemies* into German. In 1955 he returned to England and took up a teaching post at the University of Bristol, but three years later he moved to the University of California (Berkeley) first as a visiting lecturer and then, a year later, he took up a permanent position there and became a naturalised US citizen.

It was here that he began to develop his distinctive position, arguing in a paper that there was no particular problem with scientific theories that was not a problem with all theories in all areas of study and in everyday thinking; all theories are hypotheses. By 1968 he was arguing that scientists should try to maximise the number of different theories in order to maximise the number that were falsified. He was moving away from the ideas of his mentor, Popper.

By 1969 he abandoned empiricism, arguing that we don't need theory *at all* in the development and the testing of scientific theories, and by 1970 had written an essay called *Against Method: Outline of an Anarchistic Theory of Knowledge*. This was later to be expanded into what became his most famous book.

In 1974 Imre Lakatos died. He had been a friend of Feyerabend's since their days at the London School of Economics and they had been planning to write a book together called *For and Against Method*. By this time Feyerabend had developed the view that successful scientists used any methods they could to get results, even if, in the process, they broke the empiricist rules. He was becoming a relativist in the tradition, as he saw it, of Protagoras. Science was an art. Ideas change, but progress is an illusion. In 1987 he published *Farewell to Reason*, a set of articles and papers that reinforced his position on relativism.

In 1989 Feyerabend left Berkeley for Italy and Switzerland, resigning the following year. He continued to publish until 1993 when it was found that he had an inoperable brain tumour. He died the following year, at home in Zurich.

the more cautious approach, which considers only those hypotheses that tend to endorse established theories:

> *The consistency condition which demands that new hypotheses agree with accepted theories is unreasonable because it preserves the older theory, and not the better theory. Hypotheses contradicting well-confirmed theories give us evidence that cannot be obtained in any other way. Proliferation of theories is beneficial for science, whilst uniformity impairs its critical power.*

(Feyerabend 1975)

In a sense, this develops Popper's view that the task of science is to probe and try to falsify established theories, in order to test them out. However, Feyerabend wants to go one step further, by insisting that all theories, even if widely rejected, have a part to play in that process:

> *There is no idea, however ancient and absurd, that is not capable of improving our knowledge. The whole history of thought is absorbed into science and is used for improving every single theory. Nor is political interference rejected. It may be needed to overcome the chauvinism of science that resists alternatives to the status quo.*   (Feyerabend 1975)

Feyerabend also points out that the reason why one particular theory gains approval rather than another may well depend on factors other than the evidence that supports them. Take the example of Galileo, who, aided by the use of a telescope, argued for a Copernican view of the solar system. However, he offered no *theoretical* reasons why the telescope should be expected to give a true picture of the sky. He points out that:

> *The first telescopic observations of the sky are indistinct, indeterminate, contradictory and in conflict with what everyone can see with his unaided eyes.*
>   (Feyerabend 1975)

But that:

> *Galileo introduces these [telescopic] phenomena as independent evidence for Copernicus whilst the situation is rather that one refuted view – Copernicanism – has a certain similarity with phenomena emerging from another refuted view – the idea that telescopic phenomena are faithful images of the sky. Galileo prevails because of his style and his clever techniques of persuasion, because he writes in Italian rather than in Latin, and because he appeals to people who are temperamentally opposed to the old ideas and the standards of learning connected with them.*   (Feyerabend 1975)

He looks at the earlier debate between science and myth, and suggests that it has ceased without either side having definitively won. He is even critical of Lakatos' attempt to establish criteria for the valid development of science:

> *Even the ingenious attempt of Lakatos to construct a methodology that (a) does not issue orders and yet (b) puts restrictions upon our knowledge-increasing activities, does not escape this conclusion. For Lakatos' philosophy appears liberal only because it is an anarchism in disguise. And his standards which are abstracted from modern science cannot be regarded as neutral arbiters in the issue between modern science and Aristotelian science, myth, magic, religion, etc.*   (Feyerabend 1975)

Thus is it impossible from within the accepted norms of science to set down criteria to determine what should be within the accepted norms of science! Indeed, he goes so far as likening science to a religion:

> *Thus science is much closer to myth than a scientific philosophy is prepared to admit. It is one of the many forms of thought that have been developed by man, and not necessarily the best. It is conspicuous, noisy, and impudent, but it is inherently superior only for those who have already decided in favour of a certain ideology, or who have accepted it without having ever examined its*

advantages and its limits. And as the accepting and rejecting of ideologies should be left to the individual it follows that the separation of state and church must be supplemented by the separation of state and science, that most recent, most aggressive, and most dogmatic religious institution. Such a separation may be our only chance to achieve a humanity we are capable of, but have never fully realised.

(Feyerabend 1975)

Anything goes

Feyerabend believes that there really is no way available to make judgements about one domain of thought and ideas from within another. This is true for all domains, not just science. Scientific theories may be incommensurable (i.e. they cannot be compared, because they do not share common terms), but so are science and religion. They are different language systems, employing their own rules and concepts, and justifying themselves to themselves rather than with reference to some external, objective yardstick, which does not exist. In other words, *the support, verification and validation of science come from within science itself*.

The same is true for religion. If we take the example of faith-based knowledge, we can see that within religion this has a vital role. Empirical claims to religious knowledge do exist, such as the view that the universe is so complex and detailed that a designer must exist, or the view that religious revelations and visions give evidence of God. However, many religious people would insist that such empirical evidence is not necessary. The search for evidence for the existence for God shows a lack of faith. Belief in God should come from an inner conviction and, for Catholics, that conviction should include a belief that the Church itself – embodied particularly in the person of the Pope – can pass on the word of God. On the other hand, when it comes to science, the concept of faith is missing, and therefore faith has, according to standard methodology, no role to play whatsoever.

This debate is usually conducted between science and religion, but the implications of Feyerabend's view is that any domain of ideas and concepts is incommensurable with any other. Consequently, astrology, spiritualism, Marxism, fascism, liberal economics and 'deep-green' ecology are all self-contained, self-justifying and isolated from each other.

review activity

Explain in your own words the justification that Feyerabend gives for his view that 'anything goes'.

Criticisms of Feyerabend's views

Relativism and irrationalism

Feyerabend is open to the full range of criticisms that are normally levelled at sceptics. The problem is that he would happily agree with most of the criticisms. The standard accusations that are made are that he is a relativist and an irrationalist:

- He agrees with the charge of relativism and writes extensively in justification of the relativist position. He simply does not believe that there is an objective position available to us from which judgements can be made on the 'truth' or otherwise of ideas.

- He also agrees that he is irrational. Rationalism as a stance or attitude is just another way in which ideas can justify themselves. What is rational within one domain is irrational within another, and vice versa. Within deep green ecology it is rational to believe that the natural world is sentient, in conventional science this view is seen as irrational.

We have already examined issues concerning relativism, and have noted the way in which the views of Kuhn and others have been called relativist. However, in the case of Feyerabend, the relativism is more thoroughgoing. It is not merely that the simultaneous existence of different theories is inevitable, or that there are no common terms by which they could be compared. For Feyerabend, variety is welcomed, with the conviction that all theories, however counter-intuitive or apparently discredited, have a part to play. It is this that many mainstream scientists would find it difficult to accept, as in testing out theories (in what Lakatos would term the 'protective belt') they work on the assumption that the adequacy of a theory, and whether it is fit for the purpose to which it is put, is something that can be assessed rationally on the basis of its predictions. To let go of the requirement that a theory should satisfy some form of rational assessment, or that it should be employed (if it is fruitful) in spite of its limitations, until a better can be found, is to go against a very long and hugely successful tradition of scientific methodology.

Might is right? However, there is a moral criticism of Feyerabend that is more powerful. It is neatly summarised in John Krige's response to Feyerabend's famous phrase: if 'anything goes', according to Feyerabend, then 'everything stays' according to Krige. What he means by this is that if Feyerabend is right and we cannot make judgements between competing theories in science, or between science and religion, then nor can we make judgements between competing moral and political positions. We are, in effect, back with Thrasymachus the sophist in saying 'might is right'. The moral or political position held by the strongest individuals, groups or nations will be the one to prevail, and, as generally the strongest in a society are the rulers, then there is little reason why their views should not prevail. History seems to tell us that underlying changes in regimes and in morality are a result of rational and intellectual critiques, which lead to something better. Feyerabend tells us that we cannot make the judgement that something is 'better'. An example could be the politics of the enlightenment, when philosophers such as John Locke provided the intellectual justification for opposition to the divine right of kings – the idea that kings were anointed by God to rule in his stead, and were therefore infallible. The result, in the end, was parliamentary democracy, and most today would want to say that this latter system is 'better' than the autocratic rule of a king. Presumably, Feyerabend would disagree; at least to the extent of saying that we have no valid criteria for claiming that it is 'better'.

Freedom of choice? The same goes for morality and the autonomy of the individual. Both moral and political life is based on both the ultimate assumption of the free will of the individual adult, and the assumption that they act on the basis of a moral choice. People choose to act freely and they act in a way that they think they 'ought' to act. Furthermore, we hold people responsible if they act in a way that contravenes the accepted codes of morality in a particular society. We don't normally say of a thief, and less so of a paedophile, that their actions are their own choice and that they have a right to make such a choice and to hold the views that underlie it, but this is what seems to be implied by Feyerabend's position. A relativity in knowledge leads to a relativity in all fields including that of morality and politics.

Sometimes we are inclined to accept this degree of freedom, as in the case of art and aesthetics. We may say that people have a right to choose what style of art they prefer (although, of course, this was not the case in totalitarian regimes such as Nazi Germany or Soviet Russia). But we let people exercise this choice because it does not matter very much. No one is actually hurt by these choices, and it leads to a charming variety. This is not the case with serious political and moral choices. When Hitler decided on the basis of strongly held feelings that the Jews of Europe should be killed it did matter, it led to appalling actions. Yet for the thoroughgoing relativist it is not possible to use the term 'appalling'. They would have to say that Hitler was entitled to his opinions and entitled to act on them.

Feyerabend the hippy?   This is not to say that Feyerabend himself held views that would endorse such things. Rather, it is an exploration of the implications of his anarchistic relativism in other aspects of human life. Feyerabend's answer might well be to say that, as an anarchist, he would expect the fundamentally good nature of humans to show through, allowing them to tolerate the views of other individuals and groups. Some have suggested that one reason for his taking this view is that whilst at the University of California campus at Berkeley he was exposed to the prevailing atmosphere of liberation, anti-authoritarianism, anti-capitalism and new-age thinking that we associate with the hippy movement of the late 1960s and early 1970s. Presumably the argument would be that authoritarian, totalitarian and capitalist regimes of the past have obscured and distorted real human nature and prevented a manifestation of this tolerance. This is an attractive position, but only from a democratic, liberal point of view.

Human nature   The evidence of history seems to show that humans are not very tolerant and will generally try to impose their own ideas on others, often by force, and the great leaders of history are rarely known for their reserve and self-effacement. Yet a particular idea of human nature lies at the core of all great systems of social, political and moral theory. Each has its own picture of what it is to be human. But if Feyerabend is right, then all such pictures are incommensurable. There is no reason to believe that his picture of humans is any more accurate than any other picture of humans.

At the heart of Aristotle's thinking was an idea that humans had purposes or functions, and that these purposes constituted human nature. To fulfil them was to live well, not to fulfil them was to live badly. John Locke's picture of a human mind at birth was that of a *tabula rasa*, a blank slate, waiting for experience to fill it with ideas. Marx's picture of human nature was of plasticity; humans could be moulded in a variety of different ways. Fascists saw human nature as noble and aggressive, at least if you fitted their racial stereotype. Sartre argued that people could create their own nature by their actions. Yet, according to Feyerabend's approach, all these human natures can be viewed as incommensurable, justified in their own terms and just as right (or as wrong) as his own optimistic view.

review
activity

1. Explain why Feyerabend's views may be described as relativist and irrational.

2. What does Feyerabend mean by 'anything goes'? If this view is applied to scientific theory, should it equally be applied to moral or political positions?

3. What does incommensurability mean? Explain why it is an important concept for Feyerabend.

In this last section, we have deliberately moved on from theoretical questions about progress within the physical sciences, to look at the implications of such thinking for morality and politics. Human society and human behaviour are phenomena like any others, and it is perfectly natural that scientific methods should extend to the study of humankind. But can the social sciences, as they are called, follow the norms that are applied to the physical sciences? Indeed, should psychology and sociology be considered sciences? It is to these questions that we must now turn.

The Social Sciences

Key topics in this chapter

- What are the social sciences?
- Social facts
- Methodological objections to social science
- Social reality
- Behaviour and action

important terms

Anomie: normlessness; a situation in which normal moral and social codes have broken down or become inapplicable.

Ideal types: the identification of the key features and relationships of a social phenomenon, such as capitalism, and their assembly into a model. It is associated with Max Weber.

Participant observation: a social scientific method involving joining the group of people being studied, in order to better understand their definitions of the situation and motivations.

Positivism: the rejection of metaphysics and the insistence that what counts for science (and knowledge in general) is that which can be observed and measured.

Replicability: the ability to repeat an experiment or observation with the same results.

Teleological explanations: explanations of things and processes in terms of some kind of purpose or function.

Value freedom: research results that are free from the influence of one's own attitudes and values.

The social sciences, as formal academic subjects with departments in universities, are of relatively recent origin, although the topics with which those subjects have been concerned have been significant features of philosophy as the ancient Greeks. Indeed, Aristotle would have included what we now label 'social sciences' in what he called ethics and politics. Today, the subjects covered within the general term 'social science' are generally taken to be:

- sociology
- psychology
- anthropology
- politics
- economics.

In addition to these, some topics studied in geography could also be included. Ever since their establishment in the nineteenth century there have been arguments over whether the social sciences are *really* sciences. Sociology in particular has been criticised for not conforming to the accepted norms of science. The others have better reputations. Geography benefits from having been established for a long time, as does politics. Anthropology has long been of interest, especially to the middle classes and the aristocracy, because of curiosity about how others in the world live. Economics can become very technical and mathematical, and has established itself as an essential discipline in the management of national finances. Psychology is enormously popular with students at all levels, and presents the trappings of science in the form of experimental data and statistics, even if these are sometimes challenged.

Sociology therefore stands out from among these disciplines as the one that is most easily challenged in terms of its methodology and scientific claims. In considering the arguments about whether the social sciences can claim to be genuinely scientific (i.e. conforming to those principles about what counts as valid science, in terms of its methodology and so on) it is therefore convenient to focus mainly on sociology.

However, this discussion rather begs a number of important questions. First of all, is it right that the natural sciences should be allowed to define the norms of science? It is true that the natural sciences, using the sorts of methods we have outlined in the earlier sections of this book, have made great progress, but does that imply that their methods are the *only* valid way to understand the world? Is it possible that the social sciences can make equally valid claims, and be judged on criteria that are different from those that would apply to the natural sciences?

The origins of sociology

Many of the key features of sociology were established in the latter half of the nineteenth century. Karl Marx (1818–83) was hugely influential for both sociology and politics. His research into the phenomena of social and political change provided him with facts upon which to base his theories of class conflict, and he attempted to show that change was rooted in the material basis of human life, the supply of commodities and so on. Although developing the philosophy of Hegel in order to provide the basis of his 'dialectical materialism', he certainly presented his work as scientific, in that it was a theory based on the observed and recorded 'facts' of society. The same was true of Emile Durkheim (1858–1917), who established the basis of sociology, and Max Weber (1864–1920). Durkheim considered that collective tendencies – the trends that become apparent when social statistics are examined – were forces as real as those in the world of physics. So, like Marx, he considered that, gathering information about social behaviour, he was getting data, as would any scientist, to be used as a basis for framing and testing out theories.

Positivism

They wrote, broadly, within the positivist tradition. This is close to the common-sense view of science held by ordinary people. Positivism in science is seen as anti-metaphysical. It does not look for the underlying, fundamental conditions for existence, but simply tries to describe the phenomena as we experience them. Science, for the positivist, is the study of what can be observed and measured; anything that cannot be measured is irrelevant, and knowledge of it is impossible. Positivism is clearly within the empiricist tradition. However, positivists tended to make one further assumption. This was that the universe was deterministic, that it ran according to strict rules of cause and effect. If we understood these rules, then we would be able to predict, exactly, what would happen in the future.

Durkheim is perhaps the most well-known advocate of sociology as a science, especially in his books *The Rules of the Sociological Method* and *Suicide*. Commenting on Durkheim, Robert Alun Jones says:

> *The reader of* The Division of Labor in Society *would have understood that 'sociology' is a science which, like biology, studies the phenomena of the natural world and, like psychology, studies human actions, thoughts, and feelings. What he might not have understood was that Durkheim conceived of sociology as the scientific study of a reality* sui generis, *a clearly defined group of phenomena different from those studied by all other sciences, biology and psychology included. It was for these phenomena that Durkheim reserved the term social facts, i.e., 'a category of facts which present very special characteristics: they consist of manners of acting, thinking, and feeling external to the individual, which are invested with a coercive power by virtue of which they exercise*

control over him.' Since these facts consisted of actions, thoughts, and feelings, they could not be confused with biological phenomena; but neither were they the province of psychology, for they existed outside the individual conscience. It was to define the proper method for their study that Durkheim wrote The Rules of Sociological Method *(1895).*

(Jones 1986: 60–81)

Social facts

The crucial point for Durkheim was his postulated 'social facts'. These were not physical things, which would make them the subject of the physical sciences, but nor were they psychological entities, which belong only to individuals. Social facts existed in a different domain, and sociology was the discipline that studied them scientifically. He demonstrated his method in his best known book, *Suicide*. In this he showed, firstly, that suicide rates varied considerably from society to society and from time to time. Secondly, he demonstrated that the reasons for these variations could only be explained in the realm of social facts. Neither psychological nor physical factors could explain them. For example, suicide rates are considerably higher in Protestant cultures than in Catholic cultures. One reason for this, said Durkheim, was that Catholic countries had a higher level of social integration than Protestant countries. A Catholic country, with its close-knit families and communities, formed a kind of mutual aid society, supporting individuals in difficulties. The nature of the religious beliefs was also significant. He argued that Catholicism had a complex structure of supernatural entities (God, the Virgin Mary, saints, and so forth) to provide spiritual nourishment for the individual; whereas Protestantism emphasised only God and the individual. These explanations were in terms of 'social facts'.

Suicide also increases at a time of rapid social and economic change or disruption. Durkheim explained this by using the concept of *anomie*. Anomie, literally, is a state of formlessness, a state in which the normal, expected modes of behaviour and ways of relating to each other no longer apply. People don't know what they are supposed to do or how to act. The old ways no longer apply because of the rapid social change, and new ways have yet to be established. Suicide rates increase. When stability returns, suicide rates drop. Again, the explanation is at the level of the social, not the psychological or the physical.

review activity

1. Explain 'social facts'.
2. What is positivism?

Objections to social science

We need to be clear on the different kinds of objection that can be raised against the idea of a social science. They are the *methodological* and the *ontological*. Methodological objections are concerned with the extent to which social sciences can match up to the rigorous standards of the scientific process. Ontological objections are about what it is that the social sciences study, and in particular they raise the question of whether there is anything there to study at all.

Methodological objections

The first point to make is that, having examined all the criticisms that have been made of conventional scientific methodology, there is a real question mark over whether science itself is a science. It would be pointless for the social sciences to try to emulate the methodology of the natural sciences if the latter's claims to provide a special, superior kind of knowledge prove to be hollow. However, the debate does not take place in these terms, but on those defined by the natural sciences, so we need to examine how the social sciences measure up to conventional scientific methodology.

Observation   Natural science uses observation, experimentation, testing and measurement, and replicability. It is also value-free. All of these are difficult to some extent for the social sciences to copy, and sometimes it is impossible to do so. Observation must mean, in the social sciences, the observation of people, and this is often not possible without influencing the behaviour of those being observed. Psychology uses laboratories extensively for its work, and it is argued powerfully that this is not a 'natural' environment and that it therefore distorts the behaviour being observed. Behaviourist psychology is the archetypal social science in that behaviourists take a hard positivist line: that which cannot be observed should be ignored. The mind is a 'black box' that is inherently impossible to study, as we cannot see into each others' minds. Therefore, the mind is not an appropriate subject for scientific study. However, almost all of their work takes place in the 'unnatural' surroundings of the laboratory, and the observations that they do make are liable to be distorted. Another point that is sometimes made is that the subjects observed in these circumstances are of a similar type – often undergraduate students. Hence the evidence obtained in these circumstances is influenced by the methods used in gathering it.

Some social scientists, especially sociologists, use interviews and questionnaires. However, there are similar doubts about these. People, when interviewed, have a tendency to provide answers that they think the researcher *wants* to hear rather than what they really think. Political scientists always find that, in interviews, voters will say that they want more spending on health, education and social services, but in the same interview they will also say that they want lower taxes. These are not compatible, and it is likely that they say they want more spending on the welfare state because that is what they think they ought to say. Sociologists are keen on 'participant observation' as a means of overcoming this. The researcher actively participates in the group or culture that they are studying, learning about them from the inside. Adolescent gangs and football supporters, for example, have been studied in this way. The problem here is that the researcher may not be able to maintain their value-freedom and objectivity. They may, to some extent at least, adopt the perspective of the group that they join.

Experimentation   Experimentation is largely impossible for the social sciences. It is not ethical to experiment on people in a way that may have damaging consequences for them. Twin studies are a case in point. It would be very useful for a range of psychological and sociological researchers if large numbers of identical twins were separated at birth and brought up in very different circumstances. This would tell us a lot about the relative importance of inheritance and environment in human development. However, for moral reasons, this cannot be done, as it would clearly not be in the best interests of the twin babies to be separated. Researchers must therefore rely on the relatively few instances where such separations have already taken place.

Similarly, sociologists and psychologists have a range of different ideas about what constitutes the most effective kinds of schooling and education. A very useful experiment would be to set up different systems, enrol similar groups of children into the different systems and see how they got on. Again, this is not possible for ethical reasons. We must educate children in what is currently thought to be the best method, but without the evidence to show that it *is* the best method.

The post-war tripartite system of grammar schools, technical high schools and secondary modern schools was established at least in part on the basis of the pre-war work of a psychologist, Cyril Burt. He had carried out extensive work on twins, and concluded that intelligence was largely inherited and could not be influenced by the environment. Hence, if their levels of intelligence were already fixed, it seemed sensible to separate children at the age of 11 into different schooling systems, each aimed at their appropriate level. However, in the 1960s, it was found that much of Burt's research was fraudulent; that he had made it up. Hence the idea of separating out children into different types of school on the basis of fixed, inherited levels of intelligence was challenged, and more attention was paid to the development of intelligence through creating an appropriate educational environment in which each child could develop at his or her own pace.

Obeying orders?

Psychologists can perform some experiments in their laboratories, but these are subject to ethical constraints, which mean that the experiments concern relatively unimportant issues. Exceptions to this were the famous Milgram experiments, conducted in the early 1960s. They were set up in order to understand why it was that apparently normal people could, when given orders, carry out acts of brutality, as in the Holocaust. Volunteers for these experiments were paired up, but, unknown to the actual volunteer, his or her partner was actually an actor. The volunteer was asked to read out questions to the partner who was separated off in another room. The volunteer was given a device which appeared to be capable of delivering electric shocks to their partner, starting with a mild shock, up to 450 volts, which was labelled as dangerous. They were told to deliver an increasing level of shock every time their partner got an answer wrong. When they protested, volunteers were told that the experimenter took full responsibility and that they should continue, in spite of the cries of their actor 'partner'. sixty-five per cent of the volunteers, in those circumstances, went on to deliver what appeared to be the full 450 volts, none stopped below 300 volts. The experiments were branded unethical, but they clearly illustrated the fact that, when given orders and told that they would not be responsible for the results, most people appeared to be ready to deliver lethal shocks to someone whom they believed to be another innocent volunteer.

Testing and measurement

Testing and measurement are equally problematic. The hypothetico-deductive method suggests that we develop a theory and then deduce a consequence from it. We then make predictions and test to see if the predictions are accurate. This almost always involves, in the natural sciences, experimentation (although not in every case; astronomy would be an exception here). For the reasons outlined above, experimentation of this kind is not acceptable in the social sciences. This means that for testing, the social scientist must find occasions in society where the circumstances that they want to test have come about naturally and spontaneously. They might, for example, suggest that deviant and criminal behaviour is caused by a certain kind of upbringing. They would then have to establish whether and to what extent convicted criminals had this kind of upbringing. This is difficult.

In a natural science laboratory, great efforts can be taken to exclude any other factors that may interfere with the test. This cannot be done in open society. For example, the researchers above may well find that convicted criminals do have this kind of upbringing. But how do they know that the upbringing in question does not cause the people who have received it to be *caught* rather than to commit the criminal act.

Measurement in the social sciences is a problem for similar reasons. In a lab, measurements of the most astonishing precision can be made. In open society, measurements, usually in the form of statistics, are inaccurate and ambiguous. This applies to all the social sciences. The reason for this inaccuracy and ambiguity is that the production of the statistics is itself a social process and a variety of factors will come into play as a result. Criminal statistics are a notorious case in point. Police forces may well have different policies that determine who they prosecute and who they simply warn. Particular local circumstances (such as concerns over ethnicity in crime or awareness of sexual assaults) may cause police in one city to act differently from police in another city. Courts may use their powers in different ways. The conclusion from this is that criminal statistics are unreliable – compared with what would be required as evidence for a theory in the natural sciences – as a basis for a sociological theory.

Replicability

Replicability is a notoriously difficult issue in the social sciences. This is the stipulation that scientific experiments and tests, if they are valid, should be capable of being repeated with the same results. It might be possible to organise this in psychology laboratories, but even here it is not easy because of the way that certain circumstantial factors may change. In any case, as we have seen, psychology experiments cannot tell us a great deal because of the ethical constraints on what can be done to human subjects. Elsewhere in the social sciences, replicability is impossible because it is impossible to find identical circumstances. Two studies of the relationship between husbands and wives (a common topic in sociology) cannot be said to be replications because attitudes and values change geographically and over time. To be precise, the wording of a questionnaire may not be understood in the same way by two groups of people separated geographically, culturally or over time – so one can never get a fair comparison between different sets of data.

Value-freedom

Finally, value-freedom is seen by conventional scientific methodologists as an essential; the scientist must be indifferent to their results and must be objective.

They must never allow their own personal feelings to intrude on and influence their research. Actually, as we have seen, scientists may well not act in a strictly impartial way, because they may have a vested interest in the survival of their own pet theories. However, it is presumably fairly easy to avoid being emotionally or morally involved in the activities of some chemicals or subatomic particles. It is less easy and maybe impossible to remain indifferent to, and emotionally uninvolved with, issues that touch the researcher personally – issues involving ethnicity, gender and class, for example. Most social scientists do have strong feelings about their research programmes, and in many cases this is why they chose them. It is hard to believe that they can successfully exclude these feelings from their work. Nevertheless, it is precisely this that many social scientists claim they do. If they cannot, then, from the perspective of the methodology that applies to the natural sciences, social science fails to be properly scientific.

In conclusion, the methodological analysis maintains that, if the social sciences are to be considered science, three requirements need to be met:

1. The practical methods of the social sciences match those of the natural sciences.
2. Social science has a universal validity; whilst allowing for cultural variations, it is capable of being applied to all humans in all situations.
3. It is value-free and not distorted by the social scientist's own values or perceptions.

A social science must match up to all three if it is to establish its claim to be scientific in a way that matches that of the natural sciences. It seems evident that each social science has different levels of success when measured against the criteria. For example, psychology might claim to use scientific methods, but is less strong in its claim to be value-free and universal. Economics can claim to be rigorous in its systematic nature and in the quality of its measurements and highly developed models, but cannot be said to be universal, in that humans are not always solely motivated by economic issues.

review activity

What are the key methodological objections to the claim that the social sciences are genuinely scientific?

Ontological objections

Ontological objections concern the problems arising from *what it is* that social scientists are studying, rather than *how* they are studying it. The issue is that natural scientists study things, whilst social scientists study people. This is an oversimplification, and ignores the question of whether animals are things. However, animals are sufficiently unlike humans in key respects to make the question irrelevant in this context. Moral philosophers may take a different view in their own area.

The difference between studying humans and studying things gives rise to a horrible confusion between *causal explanations* and *teleological explanations* (those that concern intention or purpose). The fact that this confusion is unvoiced makes the situation worse. If we set aside for now Hume's denial of causal connections, we can see that conventional science sees causation as real. Experiments are usually designed to manipulate factors that can vary so that a key factor in causation can be identified, allowing the claim to be made that 'A causes B'. The causal factor invariably proceeds in time whatever it is that it causes. Teleological explanations, on the other hand, make assumptions about the function, intention or purpose of the subjects of study. Causation in the natural sciences deals with physical entities such as mass and energy. At one time it was assumed that causation 'acted locally' in the sense that a cause had to have some kind of physical link with its effect, and that it could not act 'at a distance'. This was then made more problematic with the introduction of fields of force, where, as with gravity, one object affects another, although they appear to by completely separated physically. This was an important factor that distinguished Newtonian physics from the earlier physics of Descartes, who insisted that causes could only act locally.

Teleological explanations in social science (and elsewhere) deal with intended consequences, but it is not clear who or what is having these intentions, the scientists or the people being studied. The person filling in the lottery card is nowhere near the Caribbean island they intend to buy if they win, but the island – or rather the idea of the island in the mind of the person concerned – is one of the many causes of their action in buying the ticket.

There are two important problems here:

Problem one

Social sciences often find themselves studying things that are intangible, such as 'society', 'the economy', 'culture', 'political ideology'. Do these things actually exist in the sense that the rocks for the geologist, the plants for the botanist, the chemicals for the chemist can be said to exist? Clearly, they do not.

'Social structure'   Let us take the concept of 'society', as it is used in sociology. Durkheim, in his writings, sometimes seemed to be suggesting that above every community of people there hovered a 'collective consciousness' that was the repository of the norms and values of the community as a whole. This is a metaphysical nonsense, but Durkheim was forced into this position by his need to demonstrate that 'societies' exist, that they are social facts. In terms of the natural sciences, there is no such thing as society; there are just human beings, houses, factories, parks, schools, roads and so on. These exist physically. Society, on the other hand, has no physical existence. It is a metaphor. The same is true of 'social structure'. It is true that people behave in regular, predictable ways. People do jobs, marry, have children, go to school. It's also true that when individual humans disrupt the settled patterns of behaviour, by stealing or violence or disruption in their work, then others behave towards them in a way designed to constrain their behaviour, they are locked up etc. But none of this indicates the existence of a *separate* thing called a society, distinct from the individual humans that make it up. The sociologist assumes that all these pieces of regular, predictable behaviour in aggregate make up a thing called a 'society.' However, we should not be led to think that non-physical entities are limited to the social sciences. A human being is no less 'real' for being

comprised of millions of separate cells and atoms; nor is a painting any less 'real' than the tiny spots of pigment that make it up. *All* the sciences have to deal with the issue of complex entities, and to pretend that 'society' somehow does not exist is to take a crude, *reductionist* view that is no longer viable.

Functional prerequisites　Having made the assumption that the aggregation is 'real', and is an entity in its own right and not just the sum of its parts, the sociologist is able to study it in its own right in a scientific manner; in other words, sociology is a science. They are able, for example, to compare societies and to decide on what parts are essential for their existence – the so-called functional prerequisites. These could be, for example:

- to keep the members of the society alive
- to regulate and promote the reproduction of new members
- to socialize new members into effective adults
- to produce and distribute goods and services
- to maintain order within the group, and to protect it from external threats
- to promote and maintain a set of norms and values that both motivates and controls group members.

Ideal types　These prerequisites are very sensible and are surely necessary for the smooth running of people's lives. The problem does not lie with them; people do and have always lived in communal groups, just like many other animals. The problem is with the assumption that a 'society' is something separate from its individual members and the consequent claim that the study of that society is a science. There are ways round this. From the point of view of pragmatism and instrumentalism, all scientific theories are useful instruments that allow us to predict and control the world. They are not to be seen as attempts to picture the reality. The theory of society is no different; it is a useful instrument that helps us humans to achieve what we want, in this case, presumably, the efficient running of our communities. The eminent sociologist Max Weber, one of the founding fathers of sociology, moved some way towards this with 'ideal types'. He (unlike Marx) did not believe that it would be possible to find in sociology the kind of universal natural laws that characterise the natural sciences. He replaced them with ideal types, which were imaginary in the sense that they did not claim to represent reality directly but which provided a model of how some feature of society worked, excluding everything that was irrelevant and focusing on, and even exaggerating, the key features that were to do with causation. Examples would be his ideal types of capitalism and of bureaucracy.

Problem two

It used to be said, a few decades ago, that animals behave and people act. What was meant by this was that, having little or no self-awareness, animals simply reacted to stimuli from the basis of an inherited pattern of behaviour. They either behave in a particular way because they have been conditioned to do so by reward or punishment, or because they have inherited that particular form of behaviour. My cat comes running because it has been conditioned by the sound of a fork in its food dish to do so. This is learned behaviour. A rabbit will cower, quite still and silent, if it sees a cross above it because it has inherited that behaviour. It is a defence response to a predatory bird, and is not something the rabbit can learn, because if it moved it would probably be dead.

Behaviour and action

Most people would agree that humans behave, but they also *act*, in the sense that they are also capable of reflecting and choosing what to do; it is the ability to act rationally that, from the time of Aristotle, was considered a distinctive feature of the human condition. They therefore have an understanding of the situation they are in (which may differ from the understandings of others) and they act with a purpose – they *intend* something. That is not to deny that many actions are instinctive, perhaps inherited as a disposition, or the result of early training, but that is not the whole story. So when we talk about our own lives and those of others we do so in terms of purpose and intention, we talk teleologically. If we want to understand someone else, we need to know how they define the situation they face, and what their intentions are.

Materialism

Consequently, we have three ways of understanding what humans do and why they do it. We can study their behaviour, as we would any other animal, making as many observations and measurements as we wish, but ignoring the subjective intentions and purposes. Or we can study their actions by talking to them and asking how they see the situation and what their purpose is. Finally, we could combine the two. In the social sciences, all three of these methods have been used. In psychology, there is an important tradition of behaviourism that ignores the mental, regarding it as fundamentally unscientific because it cannot be observed. The underlying philosophical position here is one of materialism – all talk of the mind and of consciousness is somehow mistaken; what we take to be an entity, the mind, is actually a process. In sociology there is an equally important tradition, going under a variety of names including 'interactionism' and 'ethno-methodology', which stresses the significance of purpose and understanding. The first approach, behaviourism, is able to make claims to be scientific, mainly because it avoids any talk of unobservables. The second approach, concentrating on conscious action and intention, finds it much harder to make the claim to be scientific. On the other hand, proponents of this approach rarely care whether it is scientific or not, because they claim that their methods produce much better and richer data than the behaviourists. Mixing the two methods, the third alternative, has produced much good, solid, social scientific research.

Max Weber, a century ago, advocated the use of the third method. He firmly believed that a sympathetic understanding of the people being studied was a massive advantage. He called his method *Verstehen*. You can't ask an animal what it is doing, still less a piece of metal or some chemicals. But you can ask a human, and they will probably answer. You can also observe them, count them and measure them, which may or may not confirm your sympathetic understanding. These two together form the fullest and most rounded picture of social reality. Here are two extracts in which he makes his point:

> *Sociology (in the sense in which this highly ambiguous word is used here) is a science which attempts the interpretive understanding of social action in order thereby to arrive at a causal explanation of its course and effects. In 'action' is included all human behaviour when and insofar as the acting individual attaches a subjective meaning to it.*   (Heydebrand 1994)

In other words, sociology is not concerned about instinctive or physical actions – the sort of actions that humans share with other species – but with action to which the individual ascribes meaning and significance.

> *Understanding may be of two kinds: the first is the direct observational understanding of the subjective meaning of a given act as such, including verbal utterances. We thus understand by direct observation, in this sense, the meaning of the proposition 2 × 2 = 4 when we hear or read it. This is a case of the direct rational understanding of ideas. We also understand an outbreak of anger as manifested by facial expression, exclamations or irrational movements. This is direct observational understanding of irrational emotional reactions. We can understand in a similar observational way the action of a woodcutter or of somebody who reaches for the knob to shut a door or who aims a gun at an animal. This is rational observational understanding of actions.*

> *Understanding may, however, be of another sort, namely explanatory understanding. Thus we understand in terms of motive the meaning an actor attaches to the proposition twice two equals four, when he states it or writes it down, in that we understand what makes him do this at precisely this moment and in these circumstances. Understanding in this sense is attained if we know that he is engaged in balancing a ledger or in making a scientific demonstration, or is engaged in some other task of which this particular act would be an appropriate part. This is rational understanding of motivation, which consists in placing the act in an intelligible and more inclusive context of meaning. Thus we understand the chopping of wood or aiming of a gun in terms of motive in addition to direct observation if we know that the wood-chopper is working for a wage, or is chopping a supply of firewood for his own use, or possibly is doing it for recreation. But he might also be 'working off' a fit of rage, an irrational case. Similarly we understand the motive of a person aiming a gun if we know that he has been commanded to shoot as a member of a firing squad, that he is fighting against an enemy, or that he is doing it for revenge.* (Heydebrand 1994)

This position has gained greater strength during the twentieth century because of the later philosophy of Wittgenstein. He was concerned to explore the way in which human understanding and action was related to language. In particular he considered that it was important to examine language in a radically different way. Previously, and in his earlier philosophy, language could be said to correspond to reality, so that it was accurate when each statement could be mapped against a corresponding state of affairs in the world. This fitted a conventional view of science, and the logical positivists, who so enthusiastically developed the early work of Wittgenstein, wanted language to have the precision of science, with words mirroring things that exist in the world, and dismissing as meaningless any form of language that could not be verified with reference to sense-experience.

Language and science   However, in his later account of language, Wittgenstein gives a very different picture of language. He describes our use of language using the analogy of a game. Just as games are distinguished from one another because each is played using a set of rules, so we use language in a variety of different ways, each way having its own rules a set of language games. The meaning of a word depends on the meaning of the sentence it is within; but equally, the meaning of a sentence depends upon the meaning of the words that make it up. The meanings of both sentences and words are determined entirely by the community of language users and can, and will, change. Therefore, any study of individuals or societies must consist entirely of an understanding of the rules of these language games. These rules don't exist outside language. Therefore, the study of humans is fundamentally different from the conventionally viewed natural sciences, where the rules of methodology are outside of, and separate from, the subjects of study. Therefore, the study of the social sciences can never be conventionally scientific. Peter Winch develops the implications of Wittgenstein's ideas in his book *The Idea of a Social Science and its Relation to Philosophy*. Wittgenstein himself would see even conventional science as being another form of language game.

As we have seen, there are real questions now over whether conventional science is itself scientific. If the social sciences produce interesting, useful data, does it matter whether or not we consider them to be conventional science? There are strong arguments for abandoning the whole debate as outdated and pointless.

review activity

1. Social scientists say that they study 'society'. Is there such a thing?
2. What is the significance of the fact that social scientists sometimes use teleological explanations?

Afterword

On the edges of contemporary physics there are odd things happening, and they have a significance for the philosophy of science. Classical physics is reductionist. The assumption is the same as that held by Democritus in ancient Greece. To understand an object or a process you need to break it down into its smallest constituent parts. The properties of these parts will, when added together, explain the properties of the whole. The latter is not greater than the sum of its parts. This view is itself based on a further assumption, that of separability – the idea that the smallest of all entities are separate from each other and can be seen as constituting themselves and only themselves. At the moment the best candidates seem to be infinitesimally small vibrating strings or loops of energy. The problem is that they don't seem to be separate. In quantum physics there is clear evidence to indicate the non-separability of individual entities. In particular, it seems that if a change is induced in one quantum system, then the change will also take place in another system physically remote from the first. This clearly contradicts a fundamental tenet of causation: that which forbids action at a distance.

One conclusion that can be drawn from this is that the state of a system is *not* determined by the states of its constituent parts, but that at some point there appear emergent properties. Systems at a quantum level are *entangled* with each other in some way that goes beyond our normally experienced three dimensions. Maybe when things are as small as this, other dimensions that we are not aware of in our everyday lives are important. The whole *is* greater than the sum of its parts.

Whatever the future for physics, or any of the other sciences, it is important to recognise the process and methodology by which science goes about its work, both in order to appreciate the nature of its claims, and also to distinguish clearly between genuine science and views that may claim to be scientific but lack the objectivity and careful weighing of evidence that characterise genuine scientific research. For this reason alone, the philosophy of science has a continuing and valuable role.

some questions
to think about

1   Was Hume right to question whether we can ever know that one thing causes another?

2   Are you a realist or an anti-realist when it comes to the status of theoretical entities such as electrons?

3   Feyerabend took the view that, when it comes to scientific theories, 'anything goes'. Do you agree with him?

4   Can a scientist ever be wholly objective in his or her view of reality?

5   Is a reductionist approach, seeing reality in the smallest constituent parts, adequate to describe a complex entity, such as a human being?

6   Should sociologists and psychologists call themselves 'scientists'? Should astrologers? If not, why not?

7   Is a single piece of conflicting evidence enough to falsify a theory?

8   Paradigms don't shift very often. Why not?

9   Are there any aspects of human life that are not suitable as objects of scientific examination?

10 Are there limits to what science should be allowed to do?

further
reading

▶ Newton-Smith (ed.) 2000 includes a wide range of contributions on all aspects of the philosophy of science, valuable for in-depth information for students and teachers on both individual thinkers and particular topics.

▶ Thompson 2003 gives a concise outline of the subject, written particularly for students at A level.

▶ For an anthology covering many of the key topics, see Curd and Cover 1998.

▶ For the most able student at this level, Papineau (ed.) 1996 is very informative and readable, although densely packed.

PART 2
texts

I   Aristotle: *Nicomachean Ethics*   202

II   David Hume: *An Enquiry Concerning Human Understanding*   236

III   John Stuart Mill: *On Liberty*   290

IV   Nietzsche: *Beyond Good and Evil*   316

V   Russell: *The Problems of Philosophy*   346

VI   A. J. Ayer: *Language, Truth and Logic*   391

Aristotle: Nicomachean Ethics

Aristotle (384 BC–322 BC)

Aristotle's life and works

Following in the footsteps of the great philosophers Socrates and Plato, Aristotle is at least their equal in terms of the contribution he has made to the history of thought more generally and philosophy more specifically. He was born in the far north of Greece in Stagira in 384 BC, the son of a court physician to the King of Macedon. He was sent to Athens for his education and, at the age of 18, enrolled in the Academy (the philosophical school founded by Plato) in Athens where he remained for 20 years. Initially, he was a pupil of Plato but became himself a popular and esteemed teacher at the Academy. With the death of Plato in 347 BC, Aristotle – perhaps due to disagreements with Plato's successor – left Athens and spent the next 12 years in political exile, eventually ending up in Macedonia as personal tutor to the boy who was to become Alexander the Great. He returned to Athens in 334 BC after Alexander had become king of Macedonia, and he established a rival institution to the Academy called the Lyceum, also known as the Peripatetic School due to Aristotle's habit of 'walking around' (in Greek, *peripatein*) the gardens whilst teaching. In 321 BC. Aristotle, essentially a resident alien, considered it wise to leave Athens due to the anti-Macedonian feeling at that time and he withdrew to Chalcis where he died a year later at the age of 62.

Very little reliable information exists as to Aristotle's character and personality. Allegedly he was something of a dandy who liked to keep up with the fashions and had a penchant for jewellery. His lectures were popular as he was a good speaker, and he gave evening lectures on less difficult subjects for a wider audience. He was persuasive in conversation and witty but also has been accused of arrogance. In terms of his writings, only about one-fifth of these survive, although what remains covers a vast range of subjects on logic, language, psychology, physiology, the arts, ethics, law, politics, zoology, botany, biology, astronomy, mathematics, chemistry, and so on. What obviously comes across from his writings is that Aristotle believed that the true philosopher was a 'lover of wisdom', whatever branch of knowledge that may involve. In this pursuit of knowledge, he did not believe this involved being cloistered away, but in engaging in conversation and, if need be, controversy with one's fellow man.

In terms of his writings in philosophy, like the works of Plato, it is not possible to separate his metaphysics from his logic, or his theory of knowledge from his ethics, or his politics from his work on psychology. Aristotle was a part of the wider movement at systematisation and unification of Greek philosophy and this is reflected in his doctrines, which sought to create a synthesis, with varying degrees of success. It is also difficult, if not counterproductive, to attempt to determine a progressive development in his thought, as some have done; for example, to see his earlier writings as essentially Platonic, whilst his later, more mature work, as more 'empirical' and anti-metaphysical. However, whilst he was to become a critic of Plato's Theory of the Forms, it is inaccurate to portray Aristotle – rather like the image of him in the famous painting by Raphael, *The School of Athens* – as someone who rejected metaphysics altogether. In fact, in agreement with Plato, he believed that ethics and politics must be underlined by the more general deliberations of metaphysics and epistemology. Also, Plato himself modified his own Theory of the Forms in later life and it would not be going too far to say that there is some overlap between Aristotle and Plato regarding Ideals. Where Aristotle distinctly differs from his great teacher is in having less concern for abstract disciplines such as mathematics as the answer to the ultimate explanation of things and, instead, looking to studies in biology in an attempt to detect patterns of behaviour and the *phusis* or nature of things; hence his work *Physics*, which was followed by his *Metaphysics* (*meta* meaning 'after'). The former is concerned with the nature of the things whilst the latter considers the more general underlying truths.

A look at some of the titles of his works, of which there are over 150, gives some indication of the variety of topics, for example, *On Justice*, *On the Poets*, *Lectures on Political Theory*, *On Animals*, *On Astronomy*, *On Plants*, *The Art of Rhetoric*, *On Magnets*, *On the River Nile*, to name but a few. His two most famous works in our age, however, are the *Metaphysics* and the *Nicomachean Ethics*. It should also be stressed that most of these works were not intended for publication, but were little more than Aristotle's own lecture notes. In this sense, his writings differ from that of Plato's which, on the whole, have a target audience in mind and are constructed on that basis. Aristotle's works have undergone a degree of 'editorial input' in an attempt to make them readable, hence the work we will be looking at is known as the *Nicomachean Ethics* named after his son Nichomachus, who probably put it together, with mixed results. There is also a lesser known work called *Eudemian Ethics* which is generally (although not exclusively, for example see Kenny 1978) considered to be an earlier, less mature work. However, here we will be considering only the *Nicomachean Ethics* and it is this that will from now on be referred to simply as *Ethics*.

Nicomachean Ethics Books I, II, III 1109b to 1115a4, VI and X: the context

Aristotle did write works for publication, especially during the time he taught at the Academy, but alas only fragments of these remain. As the works that do survive were mostly compiled from his notes, the results often require dedicated reading. The *Ethics* is no exception to this. The notes for this work were most likely compiled whilst Aristotle was teaching at the Lyceum and no doubt his lectures would have been far more balanced than what has been put together as a book here. In parts the content is very condensed, whilst in other parts sparse, there are inconsistencies, topics jump from one thing to another without warning, and the topics themselves are not evenly divided according to the books and chapters. The reader must keep this in mind and see it as a work in progress, and we should at least be thankful that it survived at all.

Some Greek terms   Before we can launch into the book itself it is helpful to come to grips with certain Greek terms and their not-always-helpful English translations. Firstly, we need to be clear what Aristotle's primary intention is in this work. Essentially he is asking the question: what do we aim for in life? What makes a human life worthwhile? Simple enough questions, but ones that do not necessarily have simple answers. Aristotle is similar to Plato in adopting the now common philosophical strategy of challenging people's assumptions by addressing the 'common-sense' view of what makes a worthwhile life (in Greek this principle is known as *eudoxa*, the 'received opinions' of most people) and then subject them to philosophical analysis. The *eudoxa* of the average ancient Greek would not differ from what the 'average Joe' in any street today would retort if asked the question, 'What do you aim for in life'? 'Happiness!' However, Aristotle rightly does not treat the received opinion as meaning simply an emotional state of euphoria for, again, most people when pushed would seek to define what they mean by happiness and it would soon become evident that it is a rich and varied thing. Hence the word 'happiness' may not be the most appropriate word, although it is the most widely used translation. The Greek word is *eudaimonia*, which more recent scholars often prefer to translate as 'fulfilment' or 'human flourishing', thereby avoiding the overtones of physical pleasure or joy that may be associated with happiness. Also, when Aristotle uses the term 'virtue' this should not be understood in the strictly moral sense in the way it contrasts with vice. The Greek word is *arete*, which may be better translated as 'excellence'. So, for example, if I were to say that the footballer's virtue lies in his being a strong defender, then I am highlighting his excellence or his particular skill. *Arete* is, however, also used in its moral sense in the text when Aristotle talks of moral character.

Nicomachean Ethics Book I

Political science and the study of the Good

The first three chapters of Book I are largely introductory, considering the nature of ethics (that is, the best way to live) as well as methods employed in studying ethics. Before even addressing the question 'What is the best way to live?' Aristotle considers the more general question, 'Why do anything at all?' He notes that sometimes we spend our time *making* things (a statue or a chair), and other times we simply *do* things (go for a walk, socialise, and so on). In terms of the things that we do, some we do simply for their own sake, such as listening to music or reading a novel, but sometimes we do things (and make things) for some other aim: we read a novel because it is on the A level syllabus or we go for a walk to get healthier. In addition, most of the things that we do require knowledge of how to do them. We cannot read a novel unless we have knowledge of the language and nor can we walk unless we have knowledge of how to walk! So we not only have a reason for many of the things we do, but we also acquire practical knowledge so that we can do them. Aristotle then asks if there is some particular practical knowledge over and above all the others. If there is, then to understand it would mean we could understand how our knowledge of things relates to each other and why we end up doing anything at all. It may surprise some readers that Aristotle's candidate for the highest science is politics.

The Good

It is typical of the ancient Greek view that the individual and the state are inseparable, and so any understanding of what ethics is must be seen in the context of the relation the individual has to the state. Whilst the good of the individual was important, the good of the community, which consisted of many individuals, was paramount. Aristotle did not see ethics as universal and unchangeable. He believed that ethics was subordinate to political science (which is essentially applied ethics) and was an inexact science at that. The best that one could do was to look to the citizens and observe what, at that time, was considered the good thing, and to extrapolate from that a set of principles. The 'Good', then, is not some Platonic concept associated with Truth, but more of *an empirical account of how men behave in society*. Aristotle states at the very beginning of Chapter 1 that all human actions and choices aim at some good. This 'Good' is therefore defined as the ultimate end of the actions and choices that are made. There are, of course, many different ends as there are many different kinds of activity: the end for medical science is health, the end for economic science is wealth. The Good, however, is the *supreme* Good; that which is desirable for its own sake and is the ultimate determinant for all our other actions and choices. Aristotle points out that knowledge of this Good would have great value for us in conducting our lives in an ethical manner.

Aristotle's logic proceeds as follows: With all As (A being activities) we strive for Bs (B being that particular aim for that activity) and so B is superior to A. However, as B is not the 'ultimate end', then B is also for the sake of C (C being the next aim), which is for the sake of D, and so on. Aristotle's argument that this process, if it were to go on ad infinitum, effectively constitutes an unsatisfied desire, which one could hardly equate with 'Good' in the ultimate sense. Therefore, there has to be a Good that is desired *for its own sake* and not for some other end. Adopting this view, if an individual sets out with the goal of attaining a university degree, for example, the attainment of the degree would not satisfy his or her desire because the desire would then be for something else, such as to make money to pay off the university fees. Consequently, there must be some ultimate Good at the end of this, otherwise we are faced with an infinite regress of desires until, at any rate, we die.

In Chapter 2, Aristotle emphasises the importance of politics. Man is a political animal and politics, for Aristotle, was the most complete of the practical sciences. The purpose of the state was to create a society that was the best possible for its people to lead good lives, and this can only be achieved if the state knows what Good is so that it can aim for it. In this respect, Aristotle was in complete agreement with Plato.

The limitations of ethics and politics

In Chapter 3, Aristotle considers the limitations of the enterprise he is about to undertake. He rightly notes that when dealing with people there are always going to be a variety of opinions as to the nature of the Good. Ethics is not a science like geometry and, as such, there cannot be such a great degree of precision. However, despite Aristotle urging caution at this point in supposing that the study of ethics or politics can provide us with any definitive conclusions in the same way science does, readers should be aware that Aristotle, as he writes on, does not necessarily endorse that point. Aristotle goes on to warn that the study of this subject requires a certain degree of maturity coupled with the use of reason.

review
activity

1. For Aristotle, what is the relationship between politics and ethics?
2. What, for Aristotle, is the purpose of studying ethics?

An examination of happiness (*eudaimonia*)

What, then, is the ultimate Good that we all strive for? Aristotle, at the beginning of Chapter 4, replies that it is 'happiness' or, as we have already stated, *eudaimonia*, which does not mean happiness as in the sense of euphoria, but rather a state of well-being, although even the latter term is too general to do it justice. As will become clearer as you read through *Ethics*, by *eudaimonia* Aristotle is referring to an *activity* rather than a particular state of mind (although it is expected that the latter will follow from the former). This activity is that which Aristotle identifies as unique to humanity: *the activity of the soul in accordance with reason.*

Aristotle is only too aware that people differ greatly over what they mean when they say they strive for happiness; for some it is synonymous with wealth, for others it is status. Also, a person's views can change. Those who fall terribly ill may alter their view of happiness from the possession of wealth to the possession of health. Likewise, younger people's views of happiness are frequently more self-centred until they marry and have a family. Philosophers, too, differ as to the concept. As we have already noted, those of a Platonic bent would see happiness as an absolute, abstract Good.

Two kinds of knowledge

Importantly, Aristotle remarks that there are two kinds of knowledge: that known to us and that known absolutely. This idea that knowledge can be divided into two kinds has remained a tenet of philosophy to the present day and, in more modern, post-Kant, terminology, the former, 'knowledge known to us', is synthetic *a posteriori*, whilst the latter, 'known absolutely', is analytic *a priori*. For Aristotle, ethics, which is a branch of political science, constitutes synthetic *a posteriori* knowledge and, therefore we must adopt an inductive approach to the study of what is happiness.

Higher and lower pleasures

In Chapter 5, Aristotle states that how a person understands happiness is dependent upon the kind of life that person leads. He outlines three kinds of life. Firstly, there are those who lead a 'bovine' existence in which happiness is equated with sensual pleasure. These people, Aristotle believed, consisted of the majority. Secondly, there are those men of state affairs for which happiness is associated with honour, although Aristotle notes that honour itself seems a superficial goal and it is rather that people seek to be honoured because of their virtue. Finally, there is the contemplative type for whom happiness is synonymous with the true Good, *eudaimonia*. Aristotle also remarks upon the businessman who seeks wealth, but this cannot be seen as an end in itself for wealth is attained as a means to something else; what wealth can purchase. Here Aristotle is subscribing to the notion that there are such things as 'higher' and 'lower' pleasures, which was a distinction later famously outlined by the English utilitarian philosopher John Stuart Mill (1806–73). Aristotle, of course, belonged to a rather elite set and so it would have been reasonably clear to him what would be regarded as higher pleasures. He would, no doubt, shun the gambling halls in favour of the theatre. The modern-day equivalent would perhaps be the distinction between drinking 15 pints of lager at a nightclub in Newcastle, or a night at the opera. However, such distinctions can be very blurred; for example, the trend for the middle classes to go to football matches. Aristotle's point may not be that there are higher and lower pleasures in the 'pleasure-seeking' sense, but rather in what *accompanies* the pleasure. For example, studying philosophy may well be regarded as a pleasure (or an excruciating pain) but in addition to this there is a *worthwhile* element in that it is a quest for knowledge. A fulfilled life will be an enjoyable one, but also a worthwhile one. The problem still remains, however, that such terms as 'worthwhile' and 'fulfilled' are incredibly vague and seemingly diverse.

Criticism of Plato's Form of the Good

Before Aristotle moves on to a more detailed account of exactly what he means by *eudaimonia*, in Chapter 6, he launches into a critique of Plato's concept of universal Good or the Form of the Good. It is certainly understandable that Aristotle needs to address this issue, despite the fact that Plato was a friend of his, because it was a popular conception of the Good at that time. Whereas Plato argued that there must be one universal form of that Good that applies to all things, Aristotle states that there surely cannot be one universal ideal of the Good, or an 'essence' of Good, as the term is used relative to particular individuals, places, circumstances and times. How, then, can one single ideal encompass both the absolute and the relative given that it does not have one particular meaning? For example, what an individual understands as a good diet in one culture or time could differ greatly to that of another culture or time. Likewise, a slice of chocolate cake would be 'good' if it was your first slice, but perhaps not if it is your tenth in succession!

Further, the idea of good is used in numerous categories. There are different standards of good in different fields and walks of life. For example, 'good' could be a reference to moral goodness, but also to a good (as in 'useful' or effective) work tool or a good (as in relaxing, peaceful, or whatever your preference) place to go on a holiday. In addition, Aristotle uses an example of 'whiteness' to show that Good itself can be no different from particular good things in the same way a whiteness itself can be no different from particular white things. Even if such a Good were attainable, which Aristotle doubts, he fails to see what possible use it could be given that we live in the world of particulars.

Definitions of the Good and happiness

The next six chapters are devoted to Aristotle's examination of what he means by happiness. In Chapter 7, Aristotle repeats that what is understood by the Good varies in different arts and other activities; however, it does share the characteristic that in all cases it is the *end* for which everything else is done.

However, as there are many different ends they cannot, by definition, all be the ultimate end; i.e. that which is pursued as an end in itself. What can be determined as an unqualified end in itself is happiness. Such things as honour, pleasure and intelligence are all chosen only partly for themselves because it is expected such things will also lead to the 'greater good' of happiness. Conversely, no one chooses happiness for the sake of something else, such as honour, virtue, and so on.

Not only must the Good possess the highest degree of finality, but it must also be *self-sufficient*. That is to say, it is something which by itself makes life worthwhile. Here Aristotle is again pointing out that man is not a solitary animal; he defines his happiness in terms of his relationships with others, that is, his family, friends and fellow countrymen. Consequently, the one thing that is both sought for its own sake and is self-sufficient is happiness. If it is self-sufficient, then nothing can be added to it, and so you would be self-fulfilled only when *nothing* else, whether it is winning the lottery, falling in love with the person of your dreams, immortality, and so on, would make you *more* fulfilled, for there is no 'more' that can be added. A fulfilled life cannot be improved upon. Aristotle wants to say that we all want to be happy, as in fulfilled, and that we all have different ideas of what it means to be happy, which is reasonable, but is it then correct to say that we all want the *same* happiness? Whilst there is certainly something in this analysis of what it means to be 'satisfied' or 'happy', the assumption that there must be an ultimate Good, as opposed to a series of never-ending but various goods, is open to scrutiny. This problem is accentuated when we consider the fact that presumably *all* activities must be aiming towards the same end. Suppose you have three people in a room, person A likes to eat grapefruit every morning, person B paints pictures of wheelbarrows, and person C cannot walk past a mirror or window without looking into it. Now to ask these people why they engage in such activities would result in a series of responses, and it would seem a little odd if ultimately they conclude that it is to live a fulfilled life yet, Aristotle would argue, it is also satisfactory to settle for person A saying 'because I like the taste of grapefruit', person B saying 'because I can only draw wheelbarrows' and person C saying 'because I'm incredibly vain'. But could all three ever come up with the same ultimate purpose for their actions?

However, there has also been some debate in recent scholarship as to whether or not Aristotle was actually proposing *one* Good or, more accurately, when Aristotle talks of the Good, or *eudaimonia*, this should be seen as a 'package' of activities (the so-called inclusive view) rather than one single thing (the so-called dominant view). For the former view, J.L. Ackrill argues that *eudaimonia* must consist of a package of worthwhile things that are desired for their own sake, although also part of the all-inclusive package of *eudaimonia*. Whereas, the latter view has been proposed by, amongst others, Richard Kraut, who criticises Ackrill for seemingly suggesting that Aristotle would have adhered to the view that *eudaimonia* is some sort of pick-and-mix collection of activities lacking an overall coherence and rationale. The jury, it has to be said, remains out on this one and the reader will have to make up his or her own mind.

review
activity

1. Describe the reasons Aristotle presents for rejecting the Form of the Good.
2. What do you understand Aristotle to mean by 'happiness' or 'fulfilment'?

The function (*ergon*) argument

However, to say simply that happiness is the highest Good is, Aristotle readily admits, something of a cliché. In order to provide a clearer account he relates it to what he understands as the proper function (*ergon*) of a human being. The relation of *eudaimonia* to function is an important one. For example, if the function of a car is to get you from A to B, then to ask the question 'Is that car good?' is to ask 'Does it perform its function well?' Similarly, if we want to say that a human being is good it is the same as saying, 'Does he perform his function well?'

Aristotle does raise the point that some might question the idea that a human being has a function as such, but argues that, in the same way that parts of the body – the eyes, ears, and so on – have particular functions, it makes sense to talk of the body as a whole having a function. Similarly, people of a certain trade, be they shoemakers or sculptors, also have a function, which is to perform their profession as best they can. But what is the unique function we possess as human beings?

Reason as the proper function

To resolve what the function is we need to look for what distinguishes human beings from other creatures. This cannot be mere biological survival and growth because this is something shared with other life forms, so nor can it be a life of sensations because other animals possess this too. Rather, what is distinctive is the possession of reason and so, Aristotle concludes, this must then be the proper function of the human being.

Does it make sense, at least for the modern reader, to talk of human beings as having a function? Using analogies with shoemakers and sculptors does not quite work, for those who have a particular trade inevitably have a function attached to this: a sculptor's function, by definition, is to sculpt. Yet the 'role' of a human being is not so clearly defined; it is not a skill, a trade, or a socially defined role as such. Likewise, the analogy of parts of the human body with the whole body is no more effective, for the parts of the human body relate to a greater whole which is the human organism, whereas the body is not part of a greater organism that we are aware of. Whilst humans may have a role as defined by society, which may therefore be seen as a 'greater organism' in this sense, we are not entirely defined by it, but at least to some degree are the definers.

The whole concept of human beings having a function, or an 'essence' of some kind, was well challenged by the French existentialist philosopher Jean-Paul Sartre (1905–80) in his work *Existentialism and Humanism* (1992) (an AS text, incidentally) when he compared human beings with the function of arte-facts and, specifically, the paperknife:

> *If one considers an article of manufacture as, for example, a book or a paperknife – one sees that it has been made by an artisan who had a conception of it ... Thus the paperknife is at the same time an article producible in a certain manner and one which, on the other hand, serves a definite purpose, for one cannot suppose that a man would produce a paperknife without knowing what it was for.* (Sartre 1992)

Whereas a paperknife has essence before existence, a human being has 'existence before essence'; that is, a human is not designed for a specific purpose (in Aristotle's terms, *telos*) by a divine artisan. Without God, the human creates his or her own essence; he or she is free to define his or her own purpose. The scholastic Christian theologian, St Thomas Aquinas (1225–74), himself an avid reader of Aristotle, redefined the concept of function in religious terms by arguing that human beings do indeed have purpose because they have a divine artisan that is God. Aquinas developed the idea of human function to argue for an objective (God-given) morality referred to as the principle of natural law. Nature, being 'God's signature', provides us with guidance as to how to fulfil our purpose (humans also being an integral part of nature). The natural law approach still dominates Catholic moral thinking and has been considered a valuable approach to dealing with moral issues that do not have a biblical precedent. For example, the most discussed application of the natural law argument within the Catholic Church relates to sexuality and, Aquinas argues, through a process of a rational determining of God's purpose in nature we are able to conclude that the final cause of the sexual act is the procreation of children and, therefore, any action taken to frustrate this final cause, such as contraception, homosexuality or masturbation, is morally wrong. The obvious weaknesses of such an approach include the fact that, despite our reasoning skills, it is difficult to determine what is 'natural'. For example, in a state of nature, one human may kill another for the sake of preservation, which seems to go against the Christian virtue of 'turn the other cheek'.

The is-ought fallacy In addition, the Scottish empiricist David Hume (1711–76) made this important observation:

> *In every system of morality which I have hitherto met with, I have always remarked, that the author proceeds for some time in the ordinary way of reasoning, and establishes the being of a God, or makes observations concerning human affairs; when of a sudden I am surprised to find, that instead of the usual copulations of propositions, is, and is not, I meet with no proposition that is not connected with an ought, or an ought not. For as this ought, or ought not, expresses some new relation or affirmation, it is necessary that it should be observed and explained; and at the same time that a reason should be given, for what seems altogether inconceivable, how this new relation can be deduced from others, which are entirely different from it.* (Hume 1978: 469)

Here Hume is stating the 'is-ought' fallacy. For example, it is a fact that slavery still exists in some form or other in a number of countries: that is an 'is'. However, the fact itself is morally neutral; it is only when we suggest that we 'ought' to rid the world of slavery that we are making a moral judgement.

The fallacy rests in asserting that the 'ought' statement logically follows from the 'is', but there is no reason for this to be the case. In the same way, even if it can be argued that it *is* a fact that humans naturally possess reason and this is what distinguishes them from other animals, it does not logically follow that we *ought* to exercise our reason to live a fulfilled life.

It has been suggested that translating *ergon* as 'function' is unsatisfactory and that a better translation would be something like 'human characteristic'. Whilst this may make the analogies with artefacts, human organs and so on less appropriate this does not alter Aristotle's primary aim here in saying that human beings have something distinctive and unique about them, that this is associated with a fulfilled life, and this should therefore be the basis for ethics. As Professor Richard Norman has noted:

> It is distinctive of us as human beings that we are the only species capable of destroying all life on this planet, by means of a nuclear war, but that is no reason why we should do it. Why, then, from the fact that rational activity is distinctively human, should it follow that we ought to live according to reason?
>
> (Norman 1998: 46)

There are, in fact, many other things that are distinctive of human beings that other creatures do not possess, such as gambling, giving money to worthwhile causes, writing poetry, lying, getting drunk, and so on, yet it is one thing to say these are unique to humans and another to say that we should do them. Aristotle may respond to this argument by admitting that humans engage in these activities but, in some cases (lying for example), humans are not using their reason well, which begs the question how can we know we are using our reason well? Would not the elusive jewel thief be exercising his reason well in always being one step ahead of the police? In addition, Aristotle argues that the unique characteristic that humans possess is applicable to *all* humans. There is no differentiation between scholars and sportsmen, soldiers and artists, etc. Nor, for that matter, between men and women, yet Aristotle argues, in Chapter 5 of Book I, that women – and slaves for that matter – though possessing reason, have it to a lesser degree than men. Rather, the proper function of women is to obey men, and for slaves to obey their masters. Evidently Aristotle believes that only free men possess reason to a sufficient degree, but even here account has not been taken of the differing temperaments and natural abilities that might suggest one individual would consider what amounts to a fulfilling life to be very different from another. Whilst it is difficult to determine from the text, it seems that Aristotle did not mean to say that other human activities, such as eating, sleeping, exercise, sex, and so on, are unimportant, but rather they do not in themselves constitute a fulfilled life. Rather, it is the *intelligent* actions that matter most, which is reminiscent of the utilitarian philosopher J.S. Mill's concept of higher and lower pleasures that we mentioned earlier.

At the end of Chapter 7, there follows a somewhat confused series of assumptions that needs clarification. It progresses thus:

1. The proper function of the human being is the activity of his or her soul in accordance with reason.
2. Aristotle gives the example of the harp player to demonstrate that there is a distinction between simply functioning and functioning *well*. A harp

player's function is simply to play the harp, whereas a *good* harp player's function is to play the harp well.

3. In the same way, the function of a good man (that is, a virtuous man) is to perform his function well.

4. A function is performed well when performed in accordance with the virtue or excellence (*arete*) attached to it.

Therefore, what is good for men (i.e. what is 'happiness') is an activity of the soul in accordance with excellence or virtue, and this is something that should be the preoccupation of a lifetime and should not be measured in moments.

Here Aristotle has introduced the concept of *arete* in relation to happiness. This is most often translated as 'virtue' or 'excellence'. It is not, therefore, sufficient to look back at one's life and say that one has had a 'happy' life, unless happiness is related to virtue or excellence in the context of having performed one's function. Hence the connection between virtue and happiness and why the term *eudaimonia* is better translated as 'well-being' or something along those lines.

Aristotle on the soul   Aristotle makes regular reference to the soul and it is important to understand what he means by this. Again, translating the Greek *psyche* as 'soul' can be misleading, as Jonathan Barnes has noted: 'But "soul" is a misleading translation. It is a truism that all living things – prawns and pansies no less than men and gods – possess a psyche; but it would be odd to suggest that a prawn has a soul, and odder still to ascribe souls to pansies' (Barnes 2000: 105).

A fact about the world we live in is that some things – chairs, tables, etc. – are inanimate, whilst other things – tree, animals, people, and so on – are alive. The latter are what Aristotle says contain *psyche*; they are *animate*. This is what he means by 'soul'. This concept of the soul is a topic he elaborated upon in his influential work *De Anima* (*On the Soul*). Usually known by its Latin title, this was probably written later than *Ethics*. According to Aristotle, living things are a 'substance'; the body of a human, therefore, is the matter of a living thing, whilst its soul is its 'form', that is its characteristics, which cover every function including sensation, movement and reproduction. Aristotle gives various examples in *De Anima* to illustrate his point. One is the example of the axe: if it were a living thing, then the matter from which it is made (its 'body') is the wood and metal, whilst its form or soul would be what makes it an axe, that is, its capacity to chop. The soul and the body are not, as Plato would state, two distinct entities, but are different parts or features of the same thing.

Aristotle divides the soul into a rational and an irrational element. The irrational part of the soul is concerned with nutrition, growth and sensation, which are qualities that it shares with vegetative life and animals, and in themselves are not distinctive. The life particular to human beings is the rational element. The rational part of a person can be either active or passive. It can be passive in that it obeys the dictates of reason, whereas it can be active in that it exercises the ability to engage in thought. What, then, is distinctive of human beings is the ability to engage in activities that follow the principles of reason. In other words, it is not enough merely to *possess* reason and remain passive as a result, but rather one must actually *engage* in life with reason as the guide.

Our soul is a part of our nature, and so when we talk of what it means to be fulfilled we are talking about what it means to live according to our nature; synonymous with living according to our soul, or *psyche*. In this sense we seem to be predetermined.

In Chapter 8, Aristotle adopts the philosophical approach of testing his logic against the available evidence. By 'evidence' here he goes on to consider generally held opinions regarding happiness to see if his definition is in harmony. Firstly, when considering the word 'good' and how it is applied to things, he divides it into worldly goods, goods of the body, and goods of the soul. The latter he considers to be the higher good because the former two, whilst needed for complete happiness, are not able to provide happiness alone. And so, as Aristotle has already noted, happiness is an activity of the soul. Secondly, he notes that the happy person leads a good life, and so this also fits with Aristotle's definition of happiness as well-being. Thirdly, the features that people look for in happiness, such as virtue, practical wisdom, theoretical wisdom, and prosperity, are also included in Aristotle's definition of happiness. Finally, Aristotle's definition also conforms with those who define happiness as virtue or as a particular virtue as he has stated that happiness is in accordance with the activity of virtue. That is, to be virtuous in one's actions is to be happy.

Note that Aristotle adds that happiness also requires the possession of some external goods such as a healthy and attractive family, good friends, wealth, political influence, and so on. This is an interesting caveat, as it supposes the ability to be happy and virtuous is something that only some can afford! Similarly, there is some degree of good luck involved, such as being born to a good family and being blessed with good health. In Chapter 9, Aristotle states that happiness is most likely attained through being virtuous in association with study and training. However, although it is a necessary condition, it is not a sufficient condition that one is virtuous in order to be happy. For example, a person who is virtuous may encounter misfortune such as financial problems or ill health. Despite behaving as a rational agent in being successful in this respect, there may still be factors beyond the person's control that act as barriers to happiness.

Aristotle concludes his definition of the good person in Chapter 10. Happiness is a quality that must be measured over a whole life, and so it is not something that can be determined in relation to a specific action, but nor is it something that can be determined after one has died! It is better to lead a happy life than just a virtuous life, but, at the same time, one cannot be happy and not virtuous. Virtue, for Aristotle, is the best course of action to take, although the greatest happiness can be achieved by being virtuous without adverse conditions; that is, as part of a life that is healthy, wealthy and successful.

The following three chapters act rather like addendums to lectures. In Chapter 11, Aristotle addresses the question as to whether the dead are affected by the fortunes of their descendents or friends. Here, Aristotle promptly concludes that, if the dead are affected at all, it is slight and of little significance. In Chapter 12, he asks the question whether happiness is something to be praised or something to be honoured and valued. However, Aristotle reiterates that happiness is an absolute good, whereas praise is conferred in regard to the quality of that thing and its relation to other things. So, happiness is something that cannot be compared to other goods because it is an absolute Good and belongs more in the realms of the divine. We do not praise or value happiness in the way that we do pleasure or justice, because happiness itself is the standard that is used to measure the value of other goods. Happiness is perfect and, therefore, beyond praise.

Finally in Book I, Chapter 13 addresses the issue of what is the nature of virtue or excellence that the soul is required to be in conformity with in order for happiness to be achieved. Recall that, for Aristotle, ethics was an enterprise of political science and, he notes, the statesman has a vested interest in making the citizens of his state good people. Aristotle astutely notes that the statesmen should have a familiarity with psychology, which is what he means when he refers to the workings of the soul. Aristotle recalls that the soul consists of two elements, one rational and the other irrational, and it is pointed out that whether this separation of the two parts is to be treated literally or metaphorically is largely irrelevant. Further, the irrational element is itself divided into two parts: the vegetative and the emotional; the latter can be made to be obedient to the dictates of reason.

Having established this, Aristotle concludes the first book by stating that the distinctions of the soul are analogous to the classifications of the virtues. Some virtues are intellectual (for example, wisdom, understanding, prudence) and are the virtues of the rational soul, whereas the moral virtues (generosity or self-control) belong to the irrational element. This important distinction will be expanded upon in Book II.

review activity

1. What does Aristotle mean by 'function' and how does this relate to virtue?

2. What is the relationship between the soul and virtue?

Nicomachean Ethics Book II: the moral virtues

The role of habit

In Chapter 1, Aristotle reiterates that there are two kinds of virtue: the intellectual and the moral. In Book II he is concerned with the moral virtues, or 'character' (the intellectual virtues are left until Book VI). Whereas intellectual virtue is acquired through the process of study, the moral virtues – being of an irrational nature – are acquired through habit and practice. For Aristotle, unlike Plato, we are not born with morals, they are not an innate thing, but rather we are morally neutral creatures who become either good or bad as a result of our upbringing. Whilst we are not born with innate moral virtues we do possess the *capacity* to be virtuous, whilst the virtues themselves are cultivated through habit and practice. We have rather an habitual *disposition* (what Aristotle calls *hexis*) as part of our nature, but acquiring the habit of being virtuous is not an automatic disposition such as growing, digesting food, having sensations, and so on, are. Aristotle compares the moral virtues (*aretai*) to the acquisition of skills (*technai*). For example, a man will become a good builder provided he practises and acquires the habit of building well; if he does not, then he will be a bad builder. Likewise, a person can become a just person only by habitually acting justly, and a temperate person can only become temperate by exercising self-control. It is through performing virtuous acts that we become virtuous. In the same way we can train a person to become a good builder, we can train someone to be virtuous. The concern, then, is with forming the right habits so as to make a good character; it is a matter of our actions and our relations with others that mould us. Consequently the importance of an early education, and the role of the state in this respect, is emphasised. Having outlined the importance of the moral virtues, Aristotle, in Chapters 2-4, details his methodology.

The acquisition of virtue

Aristotle's concern, at the beginning, is not so much with what virtue *is*, but rather how to *become* virtuous. He rightly notes that moral philosophy is not a science and so any approach to methodology in this field will lack scientific accuracy. Aristotle's intention is to consider, through observation, what good behaviour consists of. He notes that, just as too much or too little food or exercise is bad for the body, so moral qualities can also be destroyed through immoderacy. For example, someone who is afraid of everything becomes a coward, whilst someone who fears nothing becomes reckless. In order to acquire the virtue of courage, in this case, the person is required to establish a *mean* in the same way someone should not eat or exercise too much or too little in order to be healthy. Here, then, in a preliminary manner, Aristotle introduces his famous doctrine of the mean that he goes on to develop in Chapters 6–9.

If moral virtues are not innate, how are we to know whether we are being virtuous or not? In Chapter 3, Aristotle states that the standard to go by is the degree of pleasure or pain that accompanies it. The quest for pleasure encourages us to act badly, whereas the concern over pain prevents us from behaving well. In Chapter 4, Aristotle anticipates an objection that may be raised at this point: how can a person perform just actions if he is not already just, for surely, if he was unjust, he would not be performing just actions? If we use the builder analogy again, a builder cannot be a good builder merely by being a good builder! However, this is not a reasonable criticism, for the point is not in the process but in the end product; a builder will *become* good through good practice because he has the faculty to become so. It is what is produced that matters. Virtuous acts, however, are not to be acquired merely by a matter of chance but must proceed from knowledge within the agent. Aristotle gives the analogy of the grammarian when he says that it is quite possible to find someone who speaks according to the rules of grammar without actually having any knowledge of those rules, but it would be wrong to describe the person as literate or well versed in grammar. Likewise, there is a difference in simply being virtuous by chance or blind imitation and being virtuous as a result of a certain state of mind and attitude. There are three conditions required in order to be truly virtuous:

1. The agent must have full knowledge of what he or she is doing.
2. The agent must deliberately choose or will his or her act.
3. The act must proceed from a fixed moral character.

In the example of the builder, or any artist or craftsman for that matter, aside from the first requirement, the other two conditions are not a necessity. So being virtuous requires much more than simply acquiring good habits or imitating in some kind of automaton way. Similarly, even if one has knowledge of morality – for example, one is a student of ethics – this does not make that person 'moral'; what is of greater concern is conduct and motive.

Defining virtue　　Having outlined, however briefly, how a person is to become virtuous, Aristotle now sets out by giving a formal definition of virtue. He begins in Chapter 5 by determining its genus (that is, the class to which virtue belongs) and, in Chapter 6, its species (what distinguishes it from other members of its class). This method of defining virtue may seem curious to the modern reader, but it must be remembered that Aristotle, amongst his many talents, was a zoologist and biologist and he believed that all things could thus be defined.

Virtue, Aristotle argued, must be an aspect of the soul and the contents of the soul can be listed accordingly: passions (feelings), dispositions (that which enables us to have passions), and habits (our states of character and how we bear our passions). He dismisses the possibility of virtue being synonymous with the passions, for we do not praise the passions, such as anger, fear, envy, pity and so on, as such. It depends when we have the passions and why. Virtue requires a degree of choice, whereas passions do not involve choice, for we do not choose to experience anger or fear. Aristotle utilises similar considerations in ruling out dispositions as synonymous with virtue, for someone is not praised or blamed for having the *ability* to feel anger, pain and so on. Therefore, virtue must equate with how we bear our feelings, for example, if we become too angry over a small affair then we have a bad disposition towards anger. Whilst we receive our capacities from nature, we do not become virtuous as a result of nature and so virtue must belong to the genus of habits or states of character.

Having determined that virtue belongs to the class of dispositions, Aristotle now, in Chapter 6, moves on to explain what *kind* of disposition, bearing in mind that there are many. In answer to this, Aristotle states that whatever disposition, or characteristic, makes him a good man and causes him to perform his function well is therefore a virtue. This might seem somewhat ambiguous, and he attempts to explain what he means by providing the example of an eye: whatever it is that makes an eye 'good' (i.e. good sight) and allows it to perform its function (to see) well is therefore the virtue of an eye. An eye, of course, is much simpler to explain in terms of function and utility than a person is, hence Aristotle's present reluctance – until he elaborates on his doctrine of the mean – to be tied down specifically. Whilst such a tactic may strike the reader as frustrating, it is also an acknowledgement on Aristotle's part of the complexity of human nature compared with other things to be found in nature. Also, Aristotle does not wish to be accused of coming up with static definitions of virtue and thus be charged with the same criticisms he uses against Plato's Theory of the Forms.

activity

Critically discuss Aristotle's definition of virtue in terms of habit.

The doctrine of the mean

Objective and relative means

It is at this point that Aristotle elaborates upon his famous doctrine of the mean. Any continuous activity, which includes feelings and actions, can be divided into parts. These can be unevenly divided so that one part is larger than another, or they can be divided in half, which can be defined as the mean between too much and too little. There are objective means (the 'mean in the relation to the thing'), for example, the mean of ten is five. However, human beings, as already noted, do not so readily refer to objective means (again, bear in mind the contrast with Plato here and the reference to the objective Forms as a guide to life). In the feeling and actions of people the mean must be relative simply because people are different: four eggs for breakfast may be too much for a person who usually suffices with a piece of fruit, whereas it is too little for a weightlifter. There cannot be the right number of eggs for breakfast that can be applied to everyone!

Aside from human beings, other things that aim for a relative mean (the 'mean in relation to us') are the arts and crafts. For example, a beautiful table is not only relative to the beholder, of course, but for the craftsman a beautiful table cannot be produced following objective standards of beauty. Moral virtue, likewise, is a disposition to choose the mean relative to oneself. *The mark of virtue is to experience an emotion at the right time, towards the right objects or people, for the right reason, and in the right manner.* This is evidenced from experience in that we criticise excess and deficiency but praise the mean. The mean can always be determined by the rational mind by reference to the two vices of excess and deficiency, but should not be understood as a universal mid-point or counsel for moderation in all circumstances.

A balance between feelings and reason

The danger for such a doctrine is that it may appear somewhat vacuous. To say that someone should act in the right way at the right time towards the right people, and so on, hardly seems to give us much in the way of concrete advice. What is important here is to understand that the mean is to be determined by *reason* (in Greek, *logos*) and so it is required that the person making the judgement as to what is 'moderate' or not be a rational person; that is, someone of practical wisdom and well educated in what it means to be virtuous. Aristotle, like Plato, expresses a concern over the seeming contrast between feelings and reason, and then attempts to establish some kind of balance between them. In the case of Plato it seems (for his argument here is ambiguous) that the emotions need to be 'reigned in' by reason, whereas Aristotle adopts a more subtle approach in that the passions are regulated by 'practical wisdom' (*phronesis*).

Situation ethics

As already noted, Aristotle has previously emphasised the difference between practical and theoretical knowledge and it is obvious that Aristotle's rational principle levels great importance on practical wisdom. Practical wisdom is concerned with particulars, rather than universals; with what you should do at a particular time, in a particular place. The 'vacuity' of the argument is that it lacks general rules and principles to follow, yet its very appeal is that Aristotle acknowledges that general rules cannot apply to particular situations. His theory forms the basis of what has been called 'situation ethics'. In response to the question, 'how do we know what to do if there are no specific rules to guide us?' we can say that we know because we have acquired the knowledge through habit and training. Aristotle has been criticised on the basis that there seems to be a conflict here with what he says about people having a 'function' or 'purpose', but, as already stated, Aristotle's concept of function in relation to humans is that we have the *disposition* to be virtuous, not that we innately know what virtue is.

However, the problem remains that ethics becomes somewhat subjective. The individual uses his rational judgement to determine when an emotional response is appropriate (and therefore, virtuous) or not, yet such judgements are based upon what the individual has been habituated by. The source of our rational standards, then, seems to derive from whichever particular culture one is habituated by. In Chapter 7, Aristotle uses a chart on which the moral virtues and vices are diagrammed and these examples, such as courage, temperance, fairness, truthfulness, generosity, and friendship, are taken from the morality of Athenians, and so the assumption is made that his audience would share the same values. It raises the question of whether the use of a doctrine of the mean would work with a different set of values, or whether Aristotle is arguing that any person of practical wisdom would arrive at the same set of values that are regarded by ordinary Athenians: if it is the latter, then he is arguing for objective moral values derived from reason. Aristotle's remarks earlier that ethics is not an exact science suggests that we should not take his formula too literally and that he is not attempting to argue for uniformity of moral laws. Nonetheless, concerns may still be expressed about why the ordinary Athenian should accept Aristotle's list of virtues merely because they happen to be the standard of that culture. Aside from the fact that any culture attempts to inculcate to some degree its own set of moral values and would not be morally neutral, Gerard Hughes points out:

> [I]f the moral code in which the young are educated includes teaching the distinction between what is basic and what is less obvious in ethics, and includes the outlines of a method of assessing moral beliefs, one can justifiably claim that no alternative training can be shown to be less indoctrinatory. Aristotle might justifiably claim that in stressing the role of time and experience and balance, he has made it quite clear that in the complexities of ethics one cannot leap to conclusions. (Hughes 2001: 80–1)

In Chapter 8, Aristotle elaborates upon his formula: there are three kinds of dispositions. Two are vicious (one characterised by excess, and the other by deficiency) and one is virtuous (that is, the mean). Excess and deficiency are opposed to each other and to the mean, whilst the mean, though opposed to both extremes, may be considered excessive to someone who has a deficiency, whilst deficient to someone who lies in the excess category. For example, a coward may regard a brave man as reckless whilst a reckless man would regard mere bravery as cowardly! This raises the problem of how a person is to determine a mean if, say, for the reckless person bravery would be a deficiency. Here Aristotle seems unconvincing in concluding, in Chapter 9, that the decision ultimately rests with 'perception' and we must choose the lesser of two evils. Aristotle makes reference to praise and blame here as a guiding force, for we are blamed when we deviate from the mean and praised when we do not. Again, however, this suggests a need for peer pressure and uniformity as to what constitutes virtue.

review
activity

1. Is the doctrine of the mean an adequate account of moral virtue?
2. Does it make sense to connect virtue with function?

Nicomachean Ethics Book III 1109b to 1115a4: Moral responsibility

At the start of Book II, Aristotle stated his concern with moral action. More specifically, the concern here at the beginning of Book III is with moral responsibility. Beginning with the assumption that only voluntary (Greek *hekon*) actions are virtuous he now sets out to develop his concern with the nature of voluntary action and choice. In Chapter 1, Aristotle states that a person should only be praised or blamed for what he or she does voluntarily, and so he needs to clearly define what is meant by 'voluntariness'. Aristotle begins by considering actions that are usually (that is, in an Athenian court of law) regarded as involuntary and therefore not subject to praise or blame. There are two ways of denying that something was done voluntarily:

1. By showing that what was done was under compulsion.
2. By showing that what was done was as a result of ignorance.

Compulsion

In the case of compulsion Aristotle seems to provide a definition: something is compelled if its origin comes from outside the agent who contributes nothing. The examples he uses are of a sea captain who is forced to change course by a storm or by mutineers, and of someone being overpowered and forced to go somewhere. Aristotle needs to be careful here when using the word compulsion because of his awareness that people have often used as a defence that they were compelled to do something by, for example, the goddess of love, and so they would claim not to be responsible for their actions. However, Aristotle would say that as they are the agent of the action then they are responsible. Aristotle admits that not all cases are so clear cut. For example, what if someone were forced to rob a bank in order to save the lives of his family who were being held captive? In this case, the robber is acting 'voluntarily' in that he can choose not to act at all (presumably in the earlier example of the sea captain the mutineers had taken over control of the ship) and he does contribute to the act, but he should nonetheless be exonerated because there is an element at least of involuntary action. However, there are obvious grey areas here as to what can and cannot be exonerated; a point Aristotle does elaborate upon when discussing madness in Book VII. In such cases when someone acts out of some psychological compulsion can we then say they are responsible? In such cases, Aristotle pleads for exoneration and, indeed, pity and forgiveness.

Acting because of *ignorance*

When someone acts in ignorance it may be because he is not aware of all the facts of a particular situation. Aristotle provides a number of examples such as passing on knowledge that one did not know was given in confidence, mistaking a sharpened spear for a practice (blunted) spear, giving someone medicine with fatal consequences, and showing someone a loaded catapult which goes off and injures someone! In the case of these actions they are not performed *voluntarily* and, provided the person subsequently regrets his actions, they are also not *non-voluntary* acts. Why aren't these actions performed voluntarily? If we take one of his examples, say, revealing the secret, Aristotle defines an action in terms of the agent's desires and thoughts at the time of the act. In this case, the agent did not desire, and did not think, that he was revealing a secret so, for him, revealing the secret was not, in fact, the act, for he did not perceive it that way. Once the agent has discovered that he has, in fact, revealed a secret, it can then be said he was an unwilling agent provided he regrets his action.

Acting in *ignorance*

The examples above that Aristotle provided are cases of things done *because of* ignorance, but he also refers to actions done *in* ignorance. Aristotle gives the examples of someone who is drunk or in a rage as cases of acting in ignorance: that is, it is a result of something else such as drunkenness or anger. Someone, it is argued, does not sing loudly in the street at midnight *because* he is ignorant, but rather he is *in* a drunken state. To put it another way, it is *because* someone is drunk that he acts *in* ignorance. Those acts done because of ignorance are categorised as *universal* ignorance. For example, an evil person commits evil acts which he does not regret (and so, therefore, are non-voluntary) but, because he is ignorant of what is right and wrong in this case, it may be argued that he is not culpable. However, ignorance of what is right and wrong is a universal ignorance and so the evil man in this case is liable to censure. A person is not to blame if he acts in ignorance and regrets his act because this is related to ignorance of *particular circumstances*. In this case the act is involuntary. In defining what exactly a voluntary act is, then, and therefore to consider the agent of that act responsible, Aristotle argues that when the origin of the act lies with the agent (i.e. he is not forced by some external thing) and when he is fully cognisant with the particular circumstances, he is therefore morally responsible. Someone who acts as a result of rage is, therefore, responsible because it is not a result of ignorance and this is then a non-voluntary act. Likewise the example of someone who is drunk, as this person was in a state of ignorance because of drunkenness. Whilst the cause may rest with the alcohol to some extent, the agent is still responsible for imbibing in the first place. However, a full understanding of moral responsibility also has to be seen within the context of what Aristotle says about choice and deliberation.

Choice

Aristotle, in Chapter 2, then moves on to discuss choice or decision making (neither being entirely suitable translations of the Greek *prohairesis*) which is closely related to virtue. Whilst choice is the result of one's initiative it is not the same thing as a voluntary act. For example, an animal may do something voluntarily, but this may not be a result of choice or decision making. The same is the case when we do things spontaneously. The reason Aristotle wants to make such a distinction is that such voluntary acts not related to choice do not fall under the sphere of moral responsibility. For example, an infant may spontaneously eat all its dinner but it is still too young to do so out of choice. The parent may well praise the infant for eating its food, but, Aristotle believed, this is not a *moral* appraisal. This is an important point, for to merely state that someone is morally responsible as a result of anger would mean that an angry child is behaving immorally or, to give another example, an overexcited animal tearing up a piece of furniture is to be blamed in a moral sense. Aristotle, however, would argue that infants and animals do not enter the moral sphere because they are not engaged in the process of decision making when they act voluntarily or willingly.

Deliberation In Chapter 3, Aristotle states that choice involves deliberation, which is concerned with what is in our power and can be done. Deliberation is concerned with means and not ends, and so when we deliberate we are concerned with which is the best of all the means available for achieving an end. This form of reasoning relates to what Aristotle said about ends and means in Book I. In terms, then, of what is the object of our deliberation, it is not the end because we deliberate about what is to be done and then we act for the sake of something else. It does not make sense, therefore, to say we deliberate over the end because then that would be acted upon for the sake of something else. The ends are, he says, *wished* for and the means *chosen*. The objects of choice and deliberation are the same, although the object of choice is determined on the basis of deliberation. And so there seems to be a process going on here: you *wish* for something and so you *deliberate* upon it, then *choose*, then *act*. The essential problem here is in what sense are acts that are *not* deliberated upon moral? Presumably, in the same way that animals and children are not part of the moral sphere because they do not deliberate upon their actions, any adult that also does not deliberate would also not be morally responsible for those actions, but this seems somewhat incongruous. As an example, if a child is about to run into a busy road, you reach out and grab the child, presumably without having the time to deliberate upon this act. Yet surely this is a praiseworthy action, unless it could be argued that your act is not entirely instinctual but is the result of past deliberations (that is, past experience of what is right and wrong, and so on) and so is not exactly the same thing as reflective instinct in the same way that moving your hand away from a fire is (Hughes 2001: 132).

Wish Chapter 4 is concerned with the topic of 'wish' or 'wanting' (*boulesis*). Whereas choice, as determined by deliberation, is concerned with means to an end, wish is concerned with the end itself. However, a person deliberates about how to achieve what one wishes, so 'wish' in this sense is not the same thing as desire – as in I desire some chocolate – and, in fact, you might wish for something that you do not particularly *desire* to do, such as wishing to give up smoking. A wish, then, involves some element of reasoning. Plato would argue that we would always wish for the Good in the absolute sense of the term, whilst the Sophists, for example, argue that we wish for what seems good *to us*. For Aristotle, this relates to his doctrine of the mean in that the good relates to the virtuous individual in given circumstances. For example, the person of virtuous character who is sick would wish for a particular diet to make him well. To attain his wish (regardless of whether or not the diet is 'pleasant') he would deliberate upon what actions are required. However, such a diet depends upon the form of sickness and would be inappropriate for another individual with a different kind of illness. There cannot be, then, a 'universal' wish applicable to all; likewise, it is still possible to achieve general principles when considering particular situations and so it is not entirely a subjective matter either. If it were, in the Sophist sense, then it would not matter what diet you adopted.

And so the object of wish is an end, whilst the objects of deliberation and choice are the means to that end. As actions are concerned with means, then actions are based on choice and, therefore, must be voluntary. Aristotle's conception of moral responsibility is that every person is personally responsible for his own acts as it is in his power to act or to refrain from acting provided he is not ignorant of the situation and is not the cause of his own ignorance (such as drunkenness for example). Here, Aristotle is echoing the principle of Athenian law at the time. The law penalised evildoers provided they had not acted involuntarily as a result of compulsion or ignorance. Socrates had maintained that whilst a person would willingly do good, no person could willingly do evil. That is, viciousness is not a state anyone would willingly wish to be in. Aristotle, however, argues that even if we can willingly be virtuous, we can also willingly choose to be evil. It could be argued that the view that all virtues and vices are voluntary, and that every man is fully responsible for his actions, seems incredibly harsh. First of all, a 'defence' may be that not everyone has, or has been given the opportunity, to be brought up to be habitually virtuous. They are, therefore, a product of their environment. Secondly, as he has already stated in Chapter 2, those who display a 'universal ignorance' of what is right and wrong, for whatever reason, may also have some defence. In both cases, should not the agent be pitied rather than condemned?

Praise and blame   Aristotle simply rejects this on the basis that we praise people based on the view that they act willingly, whilst we blame people for the same reason and they are therefore being negligent. However, many law courts of today would take account of development psychology when delivering guilt. Whilst Aristotle admits that people are sometimes incapable of doing better than they do, he would still argue that at some time in the past they did have the opportunity to choose to be different and are therefore responsible for not choosing rightly. Those who turn out to be wicked are still, then, responsible for the way they turned out, at least to some degree, merely by being human (as aside from animals and, for that matter, children who are not yet 'human' in the sense of morally responsible) and having the capacity of independent, rational thought. However, to make use of the analogy of someone acquiring a skill, as Aristotle himself does, can the craftsman be held responsible if he is bad at his craft if he has only been taught that way? Aristotle is concerned that if we cannot blame adults for the acts they do, then we cannot praise them either, but it seems curious that, as rational beings, we cannot take account of other circumstances and conditions, such as psychological development, to be able to assert that in certain cases the agent acts *because of* ignorance.

Aristotle then goes on to detail the individual virtues, but this is not required reading for the syllabus.

review

activity

1. How does Aristotle define moral responsibility?
2. What is his distinction between voluntary and involuntary action?
3. Is Aristotle wrong to ignore psychological or metaphysical considerations when assigning praise or blame?

Nicomachean Ethics Book VI: the intellectual virtues

Recall that there are two kinds of virtue: the intellectual and the moral. In Book II, Aristotle began his elaboration of the moral virtues (or 'character'), which are acquired through habit and practice. He now considers the intellectual virtues, which are acquired through the process of study. In Chapter 1, Aristotle reminds the reader of what has been discussed already. Recall that the person of virtue has been defined as someone who acts according to the doctrine of the mean to achieve a mean state between excess and deficiency. Recall also that true happiness (*eudaimonia*) has been defined as an activity of the soul in accordance with virtue, and virtue exists in the intellectual as well as the moral sphere.

Necessary and contingent things

As explained in Book I, the soul has two parts; the rational and the irrational. The rational faculty, which processes information and devises rules, is itself divided into two parts. One part Aristotle refers to as the scientific faculty and the other part is the calculative faculty. The former is concerned with non-contingent (fundamentals or first principles that are not subject to variation) things such as the changes in the heavens, the nature of God, medical science, or the principles of metaphysics. The concern here, however, is with the latter faculty, which is concerned with contingent (subject to variation and change) things and its concern is to deliberate upon how we can change things (keeping in mind its targets are things that can be changed) and why we act in one way rather than another. It is important to use 'right reason' (*orthos logos*) in order to be good at practical wisdom, although Aristotle has yet to determine what he means by 'right reason'.

The three elements of the soul

In Chapter 2, the soul is divided into three elements that control action (*praxis*). These are sense perception (or sensation), reason (or intelligence), and desire (or appetite). Sense perception is not relevant here as it is a quality shared with other animals and does not play a part in initiating action. However, reason and desire are important. Moral virtue relates to choice and choice is deliberate desire. Whereas the object or reasoning in the scientific faculty is absolute, necessary truth, the object of the practical faculty is truth in harmony with right desire. Put briefly, virtuous action is determined by a combination of reason and desire, with reason the more dominant partner. Aristotle moves on to make a distinction between actions and what is produced (*poiesis*) as a result of the actions. Whilst the ultimate aim is to produce (I say 'produce' but fulfilment, for Aristotle, is not a 'product' of actions as such, but rather what makes up a person's life when he or she acts according to the mean) fulfilment, or *eudaimonia*, the agent must be aware of the *actions* to produce *eudaimonia*, for it is these that must be virtuous and lie within the mean. Whilst making analogies between practical wisdom and practical skills has its limitations – limitations Aristotle himself acknowledges – it may help to some extent. As an example that Aristotle himself provides, whilst the aim of the doctor is to produce health, he or she must have full understanding of the medicines required and in what quantities. What Aristotle does not seem to be saying is that we should act morally *in order to* achieve fulfilment and, besides which, as Aristotle has previously stated, the moral sciences are not as exact as the medical sciences, for example, there are no necessary truths, and so we cannot have an exact idea of what *eudaimonia* actually *is*. Rather, we should live our lives according to our actions which must accord to the doctrine of the mean and, as a result, we have *eudaimonia*. We are fulfilled.

The five faculties of the soul

In Chapter, 3 Aristotle states that there are five faculties or 'modes' which the soul uses in order to arrive at truth. Two of these belong to the calculative faculty: the arts (*techne* or applied science) and prudence (*phronesis* or practical wisdom). The other three belong to the scientific faculty: pure science (*episteme*), theoretical wisdom (*sophia*), and intuitive wisdom (*nous*). Conviction and opinion have been omitted because they can result in false conclusions, whereas, Aristotle believes, these five states are infallible. Aristotle then goes on to detail the five modes of thought, starting with pure science which, he states, is concerned with things that are necessary and eternal such as the laws of physics. Pure science can be taught by induction or deduction.

In Chapters 4–7, Aristotle elaborates on the other modes of thought. The arts are subordinate to practical wisdom, which acts as the guide for using things produced by art. Those things that are produced by art are contingent (that is, not a part of natural law) and, in this case, products of humans. 'Art' can include 'the arts' as we understand them – painting, poetry, and so on – but also utilitarian things such as tools, machines, etc. Practical wisdom is the power of right deliberation about things that are good for oneself. It is also contingent and, unlike scientific dispositions, it can be influenced by pleasure or pain. Examples of disciplines in which practical wisdom is the dominant element include political science and economics. Intuitive wisdom is how we grasp the ultimate premises from the first principles of science. By the process of induction the mind is able to grasp universal truths. For example, the definitions of things, such as eclipses, animal species, and so on, are arrived at by looking at many instances and grasping what is essential to all of them. Rather than deduce it logically, you are able to simply 'grasp' it intuitively. Theoretical wisdom Aristotle considers the highest form of wisdom and is a form of union between intuitive wisdom and pure science. The person with theoretical wisdom has exact knowledge of all the disciplines (philosophy, mathematics, physics and so on) and has an intellect that grasps the truth of fundamental principles and can contemplate upon ultimate universals. It is the faculties of practical wisdom (*phronesis*) and theoretical wisdom (*sophia*) that Aristotle places particular emphasis on in determining what he means by happiness.

The importance of practical wisdom

Aristotle ends Chapter 7 by reflecting upon the crucial role of practical wisdom and its relation to particulars and universals. This is an interesting passage and it is worthwhile considering what Aristotle means by 'universals' and 'particulars', keeping in mind Plato's definitions. By 'universal' Aristotle means when we talk about types of things rather than particular things. For example, to say 'vegetables are good for a person' is universal in the sense that it is not concerned with any particular vegetable or any particular person. Aristotle states that *practical wisdom is concerned not only with universals, but with particulars* because actions are concerned with particulars. For example, whilst one might know that vegetables are good for health, it is also vitally important to know *which* vegetables contribute to *which* aspects of one's health. Moving away from the vegetable and health analogy to Aristotle's concern with the virtuous life there are some difficulties here which he elaborates upon in Chapter 8. He says here that the young lack practical wisdom (prudence) because, although they may well be good at geometry and mathematics, they lack experience with particulars; that is, the many individual situations that come only with age. He points out that practical wisdom is not like scientific knowledge, for the latter is concerned with universal principles. In terms of moral action, whilst a universal moral principle may be 'honesty is a virtue', the agent may act immorally, or incorrectly (in the sense of unwisely) without being able to grasp the particular. For example, applying the universal 'honesty is a virtue' to telling someone they look fat in that dress might be unwise and not particularly praised as a virtuous act. And so practical wisdom requires someone to not only understand what honesty is but also to be able to discern when to apply the virtue correctly. This can only be achieved by drawing upon past experience and hence, though the young student may be able to understand the term 'honesty', he or she has yet to possess practical wisdom.

In Chapter 9, Aristotle states that practical wisdom, then, is the first principle of good deliberation, for it allows us to evaluate a situation in terms of its universal characteristics and to decide the right way and time to act. In deliberating what means have to be employed, the agent clarifies his or her understanding of the end for which he or she should be aiming. It seems, then, that practical wisdom requires a combination of understanding both the means and the ultimate end: one cannot be appreciated without the other. Whilst it may be correct to say that the ultimate end is *eudaimonia* (and this in itself is not something to be deliberated upon for it is something implanted in us by nature) we nonetheless need to deliberate upon what *eudaimonia* consists of if we are to consider the actions required to achieve it.

In Chapter 10, Aristotle outlines the relationship between practical wisdom and understanding (*sunesis*). Although these are different things, they function on the same plane: practical wisdom issues commands whilst understanding passes judgement on these commands. Chapter 11 then looks at the relationship between practical wisdom and judgement (*gnome*, sometimes translated as 'good sense'). Whereas practical wisdom is something we acquire after lengthy experience, judgement is innate. We say a person exercises good judgement when, for example, he or she is able to forgive someone. That is, he or she is sympathetic and appreciates what is fair. Judgement, understanding, practical wisdom, and intuitive wisdom are nearly always found in the same persons and they all tend toward the same goal.

A balance between reason and the emotions

In Chapter 12, Aristotle raises an interesting question: what is the *use* of the intellectual virtues? More specifically, what useful purpose do practical wisdom and theoretical wisdom serve? For example, Aristotle states, we do not have to learn to be doctors in order to look after our health, for it is sufficient to simply follow the advice of a doctor. Further, having knowledge of what is good will not make us good and so is it not enough to obey our moral virtues and to live according to spontaneous virtuous inclinations acquired though habit? However, Aristotle believes that is not enough to simply possess an inclination to be virtuous, for you also have to have an appreciation and understanding of how one's inclinations fit according to particular situations. The agent may feel inclined to be honest towards someone but this inclination is not brought into clearer light unless the agent understands what action is required at that moment in time and place in order to be an honest act. Aristotle is adopting a holistic vision of human nature by taking account of both our emotional response to other people and situations and also our understanding and judgement as rational people that provide coherency to our actions. Our emotional responses to situations, governed by our moral virtues, act as a springboard for action, but our intellectual virtues provide the necessary rationale behind the action.

Emotivism

Such a holistic vision can expose Aristotle to criticisms from, on the one hand, and perhaps best epitomised by the Scottish philosopher David Hume, those who might argue that the emotions should play a much larger role than the intellect, and, on other hand, those, such as Immanuel Kant and, indeed Plato, who argue that the emotions should play little, if any, role and reason should rule. What view one takes here is dependent upon whether the reader thinks that reason and emotion are essentially compatible or not, and it is worthwhile considering each of these diverse approaches to ethics. Emotivism has already been referred to earlier and it takes relativism to an extreme individualistic position. David Hume believed that *sentiment* was the source of right and wrong. That is, if you choose to help someone in need, you do so as a result of your feelings rather than based on reason. We all have a capacity for compassion towards our fellow human being which impels us to act. The theory itself was developed by the British philosopher A.J. Ayer (see the chapter on Ayer in this book for more) who argued that ethical statements and moral judgements are emotive responses such as expressions of preference, attitudes or feeling. This theory is sometimes known as the 'hurrah/boo' theory. To say that killing is wrong is to say 'boo to killing' and to say that generosity is right is to say 'hurrah to generosity!' As he states himself in *Language, Truth and Logic* (2001):

> *For in saying that a certain type of action is right or wrong, I am not making any factual statement, not even a statement about my own state of mind. I am merely expressing certain moral sentiments. And the man who is ostensibly*

contradicting me is merely expressing his moral sentiments. So there is plainly no sense in asking which of us is in the right. For neither of us is asserting a genuine position. (Ayer 2001: 107–8)

One suspects that Aristotle would be horrified by such a position. For Aristotle, how one responds to a given situation is not merely an emotional response but is carefully *trained,* for we have to be able to judge an appropriate response. In addition, when we make moral judgments – though motivated by our emotions – they often go against our emotional inclinations, which suggests that there is something more in play than a basic emotional reaction. The inevitable conclusion of Ayer's emotivism is that ethical statements are meaningless, for they do not really assert any views at all, simply expressions of feeling. Understandably, emotivism has its critics, notably James Rachels in his book *The Elements of Moral Philosophy* (1993) who argues that there is much more to moral statements than simply an expression of feeling because moral judgements do appeal to reason, just as any judgement appeals to reason. The statement 'I like cheese' needs no reason, whereas the statement 'I like killing' does, for it is not an arbitrary reaction.

Ayer's form of emotivism has also been termed as *ethical non-naturalism* simply because of its opposition to naturalism. The concept of 'the Good' is not something that is a natural, and therefore universal, component that human beings have (in Aristotle's terms, a function) but an emotional response to a given situation. G.E. Moore in his *Principia Ethica* (1903) argued that 'good' could not be defined and attempts to do so commit the *naturalistic fallacy.* Goodness, Moore argued, is not a natural property at all unlike, say, 'yellowness', which is a natural property of, say, buttercups. As he says, 'If I am asked "What is good?" my answer is that good is good, and that is the end of the matter. Or if I am asked "How is good to be defined?" my answer is that it cannot be defined, and that is all I have to say about it' (Moore 1903: 3). It is somewhat puzzling to determine how, if good is not a property and, he states, cannot be detected by the senses in the same way that yellow can, we are to detect when something is good? Moore argues that we cannot give any reasons *why* something is good, rather it is *intuitively self-evident* that something is either good or bad, true or false in the same way we know intuitively that two plus two is four is true (hence the fact that the theory is also related to what is known as *intuitionism*). However, Moore is not asserting that 'good' is a metaphysical entity either, although we are left with an inconclusive understanding here of exactly where our intuitive notion of good does come from. To say good derives from our intuition begs the question, 'Where do our intuitions come from?' for which Moore seems to have no satisfactory reply.

Reason and duty

Those who place greater emphasis on reason as the source of our moral judgements would argue that Aristotle does not go far enough in asserting the role of reason. Immanuel Kant argued that there is an objective moral law and that we know this through reason, they are a priori synthetic. In his work, *Groundwork for the Metaphysics of Morals* (1785), Kant argues that the highest form of good is *good will*, and to have a good will is to do one's duty. Importantly, we should act out of duty and not emotion. A human action is not morally good because we feel that it is good, but rather because it is rationally right. You may intuitively wish to give money to a beggar, but it is not a right action unless you are doing this act out of duty based upon rationally derived moral principles. This is a *deontic* view of morality by which action-guiding principles are its essence. Universal rules are established which require persons to perform or omit certain actions, irrespective of whether or not the person *possesses* those virtues, whereas, for Aristotle, a person must *be* virtuous in order to act virtuously. Whereas the deontic view allows for independent criterion for actions, the Aristotelian view – or, in more modern terms, the *aretaic* view (deriving from *arete*) – refuses to do so. No argument or proof is presented as to why an action is right or wrong and so there is no standard test that can be applied to a given act. Rather, the emphasis is on the person of virtue who, by the fact that he or she is a virtuous person, simply 'sees' what is right or wrong in a given situation. This, at first, seems to smack of intuitionism and opens Aristotle up to the same epistemological criticisms such as how do we know who a virtuous person is and what is the right thing to do? In the words of William Frankena, 'Virtues without principles are blind'. The same goes for the concern with the relativism of such values and the fact that what counts as virtue changes according to time and place:

> *Whereas Aristotle valued pride as a special virtue, Christians see it as a master vice. An ancient caveman facing a herd of mastodons with a spear would be thought by his community to have 'excessive' fear if he abandoned his fellow tribesman and fled whereas contemporary society would make no such judgement. Capitalists view acquisitiveness as a virtue, whereas Marxists see it as a vice.* (Pojman 2001: 170)

However, again, it is important to emphasise the holistic element of Aristotle's ethics. It is, he would argue, simply impractical to apply universal standards to specific circumstances. Further, one cannot expect someone to know what is right in a specific circumstance unless suitably trained. It is not sufficient to be concerned with what to do, but rather to place emphasis on the agent and how he or she feels about things. The emphasis is more on *character* than some seemingly divorced set of moral laws that must be obeyed. Whilst duty-based ethical theories do not deny the role of character (Geoffrey Warnock, for example, argues that the moral agent should be encouraged to acquire what he calls 'good dispositions'), it is here that Aristotle's 'virtue theory' comes into its own and has more modern proponents.

Virtue theory   Virtue ethics seeks to produce excellent persons who act out of spontaneous goodness and act as moral exemplars for others to follow. Instead of concentrating on what is the right thing to do, the focus is on how we can be better people. It has re-emerged as a major ethical theory since the mid 1950s with such supporters as Elizabeth Anscombe, Philippa Foot, Alasdair MacIntyre, and Richard Taylor. Aristotle is not so concerned with principles, but rather emphasises the importance of a good upbringing, of good habits and self-control so that the good person cannot help but do good. Modern virtue theory has been accused of engaging in a degree of romantic nostalgia for ancient times when there was a clear set of virtues (Annas 1992: 136), as opposed to the seemingly nihilistic conception of morality as 'meaningless'. This concern with the state of morality comes across in, for example, MacIntyre when he says, 'we have – very largely, if not entirely – lost our comprehension, both the theoretical and practical, of morality' (Macintyre 1981: 2). The concern seems to be more with criticising what is regarded as the present moral crisis and perceiving the ethics of the ancient Greeks through rose-tinted spectacles. Whilst Aristotle might make little mention of moral principles, they are often implied in what he says.

Intellectual virtues and moral virtues combined

Aristotle also stresses in this chapter that practical wisdom is not merely a matter of being 'clever', although it might be interpreted this way if it were not for the fact that practical wisdom works hand in hand with moral virtue. For example, there is no doubt that a doctor can be very good at being a doctor through cultivation of the intellectual virtues, and practical wisdom in particular, but a doctor could use wisdom for evil ends if he or she so chose. This is what Aristotle means when he talks of 'cleverness' being ignoble. Noble cleverness, however, is the practical wisdom gained in study of medicine coupled with the habit of being morally virtuous. Therefore, the inclination to do well has to correspond with an understanding of means and ends.

In the final chapter of Book VI, Aristotle states that it is quite common for someone to have acquired one natural virtue and not another, for example, a person can be naturally good at singing and bad at running. Yet Aristotle believes this is not the same with the moral virtues. That is, it is not correct to say that someone can possess the virtue of courage and not possess honesty, for example. Aristotle wants to assert that a person of good character is a good character in *every* respect, not just in certain respects. This is consistent with his views on appreciating the mean according to particular circumstances. As an example, imagine you have a friend who is particularly sensitive to criticism and also believes she writes good poetry. One day she produces one of her poems and asks your opinion. You happen to consider it to be incredibly awful but, as you are a virtuous person in the Aristotelian sense, you dampen your honesty with other virtues that you recognise as appropriate in this case, such as kindness, friendliness, and so on. Rather than simply state that the poetry is rubbish, you offer some constructive criticisms in a diplomatic manner. Obviously, practical wisdom has an important part to play here.

review
activity

1. Discuss Aristotle's division of the virtues into moral and intellectual.

2. What are the problems associated with virtue theory?

Nicomachean Ethics Book X: pleasure (*hedone*) and its relation to goodness

In what way is pleasure connected with *eudaimonia*? It has already been noted that the translation of *eudaimonia* as 'happiness' is perhaps not the best, and something like 'fulfilment' seems more in tune with Aristotle's meaning. Given this understanding of *eudaimonia* the relation to pleasure seems less clear-cut. Undoubtedly, being fulfilled would presumably be a *satisfying* experience, not just something to be done out of onerous duty. Also, presumably, one who has achieved fulfilment would find life to be an enjoyable experience. So it does seem to make sense to talk of a connection between pleasure and *eudaimonia* to some extent.

The topic of pleasure has already been discussed in Book VII and it may seem a little puzzling as to why Aristotle brings up the subject again here. However, the reader is reminded once more that the *Ethics* is an edited work as opposed to a complete work and it seems most likely that Book VII and Book X were originally written at different times for different purposes before being collected together by the editor or editors. Books V, VI and VII of the *Nicomachean Ethics* also appear in his lesser known *Eudemian Ethics*. The most widely held view is that Book VII (as well as Books V, and VI) were the earlier works, whilst Book X is a more mature work, although not all scholars would accept this and some would state the opposite (for example, Gosling and Taylor 1982, Chapters 11 and 15). Having previously examined the role of desires in relation to moral failure, the discussion of pleasure in Book VII, sensibly enough, concentrates on what pleasure is and why it should lead people to act against their better judgement. At the beginning of Book X Aristotle reiterates the connection between pleasure and the moral virtues and then leads on to a discussion of *eudaimonia*. So, whereas, in Book VII, Aristotle considers whether some pleasures may actually be of benefit in leading a fulfilled life, the concern of Book X is whether pleasure *is* the good life. Those who have been following the text closely should probably know that his answer is in the negative, but, more specifically, the question is about whether the life of happiness is the *pleasantest*. That is, would someone who has attained *eudaimonia* actually also be having more fun than someone who has not?

The importance of pleasure and pain

In Chapter 1, Aristotle rightly points out that pleasure and pain are extremely important for any person and can have a decisive influence on whether or not he or she achieves happiness. He briefly refers to two schools of thought with regard to pleasure: those that hold it is the supreme good and those that hold that it is absolutely bad. Aristotle sets out to show that neither view is the correct one, and, in Chapter 2, presents the views of Eudoxus, who thought that pleasure is *the* good.

Eudoxus' argument

Eudoxus was a philosopher who attended Plato's Academy at around the same time as Aristotle. He argues that pleasure is the supreme good because all people, and animals, desire it as an end in itself. This might seem a convincing argument, for observation shows that all things do seem to aim for pleasure. Further, pain is universally avoided and so surely its contrary would be pursued. In addition, whist there may be many things that are no doubt good, what makes those goods *better* is when pleasure is added to them. Aristotle reflects upon what is actually meant by 'pleasure' with awareness that defining the term, in Greek *hedone*, is not a straightforward matter. Aristotle's audience would have been aware of his references to other philosophers of his time on this matter, although the debate is to some degree lost to a modern audience. Aside from that of Eudoxus, at points he considers what may be the view held by Speusippus, who, perhaps to the chagrin of Aristotle, took over the running of the Academy after Plato's death. Some of the views, however, are clearly a reference to Plato's own discussion of the matter in, most notably, *Philebus*.

Because of the word *hedone* and its associations with the hedonist movement, pleasure, even in Aristotle's time, could have negative connotations, but there was nonetheless a recognition that this need not be the case at all, depending upon what one understands by the term. For example, to drink when one is thirsty or eat when hungry are hardly negative pleasures but, in fact, a matter of physiological necessity. Nonetheless there seems to be this apparent conflict between the pursuit of one's moral duty and engaging in pleasure per se. Whilst there is a general acknowledgement that pain is a bad thing, the question Aristotle seeks to address early on here is whether pleasure is its opposite, that is, a good thing. He seems to be referring to Speusippus (I say *seems* to be because it is not altogether obvious that he is referring to Speusippus here) who apparently held the view that pleasure was not a good thing at all or, perhaps more accurately, a neutral thing, as opposed to Eudoxus who states that it is *the* good. The main criticism of Eudoxus' view, however, is that, whilst his argument can demonstrate that pleasure is *a* good, it does not show that it is *the* Good. For example, it is undoubtedly true that one good is health and so you should eat your vegetables, but if it is also a pleasure to eat vegetables then you simply have two goods, and two goods are better than one. In fact, pleasure cannot therefore be *the* Good because pleasure plus health, in this case, is better and one cannot have something better than the Good! Further, as Aristotle points out in Chapter 3, if pleasure is *the* Good, then how would it be possible to distinguish between good and bad pleasures?

Pleasure is not a process

The reference to Plato is interesting here, for, in his *Philebus*, he quotes the view of those who say that pleasures are instances of becoming rather than being; in other words a process rather than a state. For example, you experience pleasure as you are becoming healthy, but not when you are in a state of health. If such a view of pleasure is correct, it makes a mockery of the view that pleasure is good because what is considered as good are the goals that we aim for rather than the processes. It follows that those who pursue pleasure, then, are constantly in a state of becoming rather than being. Interestingly, this Platonic view (for Plato seems to generally accept this concept of pleasure) would fit comfortably with Buddhism. Aristotle, however, is not prepared to define pleasure in this way. In Book VII (Chapter 12) he states that they are not processes but final states of actualisation and he is consistent in repeating this view in Chapter 4 of Book X. Aristotle's views on pleasure are related to his teachings on potentiality and actuality. For example, in the writing of this chapter the actuality is the completed chapter, whilst the process is in the writing of it. It has the potential to be a chapter but will not be so until it is actualised. The process, then, is a transitional movement which takes a period of time and strives towards an end. Pleasure, Aristotle argues, is a complete state at any given moment of its existence. This may seem a strange argument to uphold. For example, in satisfying a desire for food I proceed to eat, but is not the pleasure coming from the process of eating the food? Aristotle says not, for although the final end is to satisfy the desire for food and gain pleasure from this, each stage, such as the effects each mouthful has on my taste buds, is an achieved state in itself. By another illustration, Aristotle refers to the act of sight: I see a tree; I do not *come* to see a

231

tree. Likewise, I experience pleasure; I do not *come* to experience pleasure. Like sense perception and thought, it is a perfect, indivisible and self-contained act.

It is still, however, rather unclear as to what, for Aristotle, pleasure actually is in terms of a definition. The analogy he uses in Chapter 4 with the faculty of perception (hearing or sight for example) is not entirely straightforward. What he seems to be stating is that the complete exercise of, say, the faculty of hearing, is when you can hear the best thing that can be heard. What is meant by the 'best thing' is open to debate; presumably a wonderful piece of music perhaps. When the person is engaged in the activity of hearing a beautiful piece of music, then he or she is engaged in the most perfect and pleasant activity possible. Provided your faculty, in this case hearing, is in perfect working order and what you are experiencing is the 'best' of its kind, say a fine symphony, then nothing can be added to make this experience more pleasurable than it is. This applies to other activities, whether it is reading a book, or being in company with good friends; the activity and the pleasure it engenders are one and the same thing. Pleasure is a distinguishable but nonetheless inseparable aspect of activity. Without activity there can be no pleasure. Human beings are not able to engage in continuous activity, and so continuous pleasure is not possible. However, pleasure, by perfecting all human activity, can be regarded as perfection of human life.

As concluded in Chapter 5, pleasure is not the highest Good because it does not exist independently from action. Nonetheless it is an essential element of the Good because the Good can only be attained by action and perfect action must be accompanied by pleasure. To support this view, Aristotle once more refers to his function argument. Pleasure consists of not one kind of experience, but a variety according to the activities. Further, each species of animal has its own corresponding pleasures according to its function. And so, what is specific to human *eudaimonia* is the good performance of those activities which are specific to humans and, as already stated, the good performance is accompanied by the finest pleasure. Of course, the problem here is with the function argument overall: human beings seem to be far more complex when determining their 'function' and what constitutes a pleasurable activity differs from one person to the next. However, Aristotle is determined to reject the notion that 'man is the measure of all things' and pleasure is whatever the individual finds pleasurable. For Aristotle, what is pleasurable is what is determined by the virtuous person. If we go back to the analogy of the faculty of hearing, if someone has faulty hearing, then he or she is not capable of full enjoyment of a fine symphony in the way someone with perfect hearing is. Likewise, someone who is faulty in a moral sense, a depraved or vicious person, can also not appreciate what true enjoyment is. Consequently, there are higher and lower pleasures. As Aristotle points out in Chapter 6, it is wrong to confuse happiness with various kinds of amusements that involve pleasures of the body, for these are neither virtuous nor ends in themselves but relaxing diversions. The pleasures of a depraved person are not the same as the pleasures of a good person: *identifying* the good person, the role model, so to speak, remains the problem of course.

review activity

Contemplation (*theoria*) and fulfilment (*eudaimonia*)

At long last, from Chapter 7, Aristotle is ready to determine what human fulfilment, *eudaimonia*, actually consists in. Fulfilment is activity in conformity with the highest virtue, and this virtue Aristotle identifies as contemplation (*theoria*) upon theoretical knowledge (*sophia*). This is a person's highest human capacity and is an activity that is characteristic of the gods. At this point Aristotle drifts into Platonic territory as he describes *theoria* as the intellectual grasp of the highest objects; those that are perfect and changeless. Is this, then, contemplation of the Forms? It is not clear what Aristotle would include as the highest objects, although his earlier reference to theoretical wisdom would include knowledge of such seemingly non-contingent things as scientific knowledge, mathematics and physics. The contemplative life reflects upon the unchangeable and eternal truths that govern the universe, and from this contemplation the soul derives a feeling of purity and stability. This kind of contemplation is not in any way contingent upon the existence of other people or matters of the world. The relation between the soul and body is mostly elaborated in *De Anima*, and has been detailed to some extent when we looked at the function argument earlier. To add here, Aristotle does not have a conception of the soul similar to Plato, for he does not see it as something entirely distinct from the body. However, Aristotle does become somewhat 'mystical' when he refers to one particular faculty of the soul; that of pure thought which, he states, does live on after the death of the body and is united with divine thought. This concept of the soul, in line with Aristotle's view of God, lacks any individual personality however.

Contemplation as divine

What distinguishes human beings from other animals is that we have a mind and *eudaimonia* consists in making the best use of our minds. Our rational faculties allow us to engage in practical wisdom, and it is this that Aristotle has so far laid great emphasis upon, so it comes as something of a surprise for him to now state that theoretical wisdom is the highest Good, bearing in mind his own views on the variation of people and situations and his antagonism towards Platonic pure reason as a guide to life. Aristotle himself states in this chapter that nothing is actually gained from *theoria* except the act of contemplation itself, which seems to imply that it is highly impractical, if not useless. He then goes on to say that a life of contemplation is actually unobtainable for humans because it is a luxury that is reserved for the gods and so to live a life of contemplation is to live a divine life rather than a human life. The best we can hope to achieve is something *akin* to the gods.

In Chapter 8, Aristotle elaborates what he understands by the divine life, and these views are reflected in his *Metaphysics*. When Aristotle talks of the gods in the plural sense he seems to mean the more anthropomorphic characters that colour Greek myth. However, when he refers to God in the singular he means something very different. This God exists necessarily; he does not depend on anything else for his existence. He never changes or has any potential to change and he has no beginning or end. This eternal being is also immaterial, for if he were to be made up of any kind of matter he could not then be immutable. As God is immutable, he cannot engage in any kind of physical, bodily action for there is no 'body' or movement. What, then, does God do? God is pure intellect; his activity is *theoria*. What, then, does God contemplate upon? God could not think about anything which could cause him to change or be affected in any way, so this leaves out the material world. Aristotle states in his *Metaphysics* that God only contemplates upon himself, God is 'thought of thought'. God knows only himself and is not affected by the material world in any way. According to this view of God, human beings cannot possibly attain such a divine level of *theoria* for, to begin with, we are not immaterial. We have bodies that need feeding and looking after, which are inevitable distractions from the business of contemplation. Yet Aristotle seems to insist that this is what we should strive for if we are to attain *eudaimonia*, which seems a curious conclusion given what Aristotle has previously said, not to mention his empirical insights into the people of Athens at the time who, with a very few exceptions, could not accommodate the luxury of pure contemplation. Aside from the limited possibilities of achieving this conception of *eudaimonia* – except for the elite – it is highly debatable that this would really constitute an ideal existence.

The importance of practical wisdom for achieving happiness

A *potential* way out here is that Aristotle is actually presenting two separate possibilities for achieving *eudaimonia*. One is the life of *theoria* the other is the life of *phronesis* (practical wisdom or prudence), for in the first sentence of Chapter 8 he states that the life of practical wisdom is more in accordance with human activity. Again, the problem lies in interpreting the Greek, for most translations state this activity is 'secondary' or 'second-class' to that of the life of *theoria*, whereas it has been suggested that one possible interpretation is that Aristotle merely means that it is a *second option* (Hughes 2001: 47). However, I do not think this view is really sustainable as Aristotle presents a hierarchical structure of happiness, with the lower animals at one end, which in fact are entirely incapable of any kind of *eudaimonia*, and the gods, or God, at the other. Humans, for their part, walk a tightrope between the two. The more a person can afford the luxury of contemplation, then the more he or she will be fulfilled, but, realistically, as being human is a basic fact, then practical wisdom will have to suffice. Perhaps the most generous interpretation of what Aristotle is aiming at is the best form of *eudaimonia* that humans can achieve – a synthesis of practical and theoretical wisdom. For example, a practical understanding of the moral life is incomplete without 'metaethics', and a good politician not only needs to appreciate the day-to-day workings of political life, but also to have a clear grasp of political theory. I say this is a generous interpretation, because unfortunately – and especially if the reader were to take Book X in isolation (which of course he or she should *not* do) – then the reader would surely struggle to drag this interpretation out from the text.

Having now provided us with a definition of what *eudaimonia* is, Chapter 9 concludes by considering who or what is to be responsible for the nurturing of virtuous people. The development of these ideas is left to his *Politics*.

However, in summary, Aristotle states that the upbringing of the good citizen requires laws and this, in turn, requires the involvement of the state. Aristotle, like Plato before him, recognises the important role of the state in providing education, if only because of its power to do so upon often unwilling participants. In this sense, ethics and politics are inevitably linked and may, in fact, be regarded as branches of the same discipline, for a good state is one governed by sound ethical principles devised and administered by moral statesmen who have in their turn been educated to be virtuous, as opposed to sophists who make claims to virtue that they do not really possess.

review activity

1. What is the role of practical wisdom (*phroncsis*)?

2. What, according to Aristotle, is the supreme human activity? What arguments does he give for this position?

some questions to think about

1   Would Aristotle's 'good' person be a morally good person?

2   Evaluate the claim that there is such a thing as the Good for humankind.

3   In what ways does the Greek concept of *eudaimonia* differ from, say, a Christian concept?

4   How, according to Aristotle, do we acquire virtue?

5   Is the doctrine of the mean an effective guide to morality?

further reading

▶ Barnes 2000 provides a good, and short, overview of Aristotle and his philosophy generally.

▶ The best commentary on his *Ethics* available at present is undoubtedly Hughes 2001.

▶ Norman 1998 provides an accessible presentation of Aristotle's doctrine of the mean and the function argument especially.

▶ More detailed, and more difficult, commentaries on specific themes include a collection of critical essays by Moravcsik (ed.) 1967, a series of essays written by Ross 1964, and another series by Rorty (ed.) 1980.

David Hume: An Enquiry Concerning Human Understanding

Compatibilism: the belief that although all our actions are caused or determined, they can be done freely, just as long as they are not compelled or constrained. The true opposite of free will is constraint, not causality, according to Hume.

Determinism: the claim that all events are caused and rendered inevitable by earlier events.

Empiricism: the theory that all concepts and knowledge ultimately derive from sense-experience. The philosophies of Locke, Berkeley and Hume exemplify empiricism.

Habit: habit, or custom, as Hume calls it, operates when we are so accustomed to experiencing one type of thing B, following another A, that the next time A occurs we cannot help expecting or inferring B. Hume thinks it is a non-rational process, related to instinct.

Ideas: concepts, conceived of as faint copies of more vivid sense-impressions. We use concepts when we think, remember, and imagine.

Impressions: sense-experiences which are strong and vivid.

Indeterminism: the theory that some events do not have causes which determine them to occur.

Induction: an inductive argument is one in which the premises do not logically entail the conclusion because the conclusion contains information beyond what is found in the premises. Such inferences are said to be ampliative. The typical form of an inductive argument is: All the Xs observed so far have been Ys, so all the Xs there are, are Ys. The problem of whether induction can be rationally justified, to which Hume first alerted us, remains a much-debated issue to this day.

Liberty: Hume's term for free will.

Matters of fact: Hume's term for

Hume's life and works

David Hume was born on 26 April 1711 in Edinburgh. In 1723 he went to Edinburgh University but left without taking a degree, which was normal at the time. He returned to the family estate, Ninewells, in Berwickshire, to study law, but found he could not settle to anything except philosophy. After a brief spell with sugar merchants in Bristol in 1734, Hume migrated to France where it was cheaper to live, and worked on *A Treatise of Human Nature*, which was published in 1739. It met with a poor reception, falling, in Hume's own words, 'dead-born from the press'. His *Essays, Moral and Political*, published in 1741, was much better received, however.

In 1745 Hume applied for the Professorship of Ethics and Pneumatical Philosophy at Edinburgh University but was turned down, almost certainly due to religious intolerance. In fact, Hume was never to hold an academic position in his life, though he did serve the British Government as a diplomat in Vienna and Turin, and subsequently Paris, where he was much beloved of the French *philosophes*, who called him *Le Bon David*. In 1748 he published *An Enquiry Concerning Human Understanding*, and in 1751 the second *Enquiry concerning the Principles of Morals*. In 1752 he was once again prevented by opponents from entering academic life, failing to secure the University Chair in Logic at Glasgow. Undaunted, he began work on *Dialogues Concerning Natural Religion*, but this was not published until 1779, three years after his death. In 1754 the *History of England* began to appear as well as *Four Dissertations*; *The Natural History of Religion*; *Of the Passions*; *Of Tragedy*; and *Of the Standard of Taste*. Hume thought of adding *Of Suicide* and *Of the Immortality of the Soul*, but was dissuaded by the publisher for fear of giving offence to the religious authorities. Having returned home to Edinburgh in 1769, Hume was struck with a disorder of the bowels, probably cancer, in 1775. He died serenely on 25 August 1776.

A note on the text

An Enquiry Concerning Human Understanding represents a much shorter and pared down version of *A Treatise of Human Nature*. There is no discussion of space and time, and the topic of identity, including Hume's important contribution to the topic of personal identity, is entirely omitted. The discussion of synthetic statements which are made true or false by how the world is.

Naturalism: naturalistic explanations are essentially scientific explanations, where these can include the concepts and theories to be found in psychological and social sciences. They exclude supernaturalistic explanations of events, that is, explanations that appeal to agents existing outside of the order of nature, such as a God, and they limit themselves to explaining in descriptive terms why a phenomenon occurs, rather than attempting to provide a philosophical justification or rationale for it.

Necessary connection: the alleged necessary link between a cause and an effect. Hume denies that experience of cause and effect supplies any impression of necessary connection, and hence no corresponding idea or concept.

Probability: the likelihood an event will occur in given circumstances based on the frequency of its occurrence in the past.

Rationalism: the theory that knowledge and understanding of the world can be derived from reason alone without any need for sense-experience. The philosophies of Plato, Descartes, Spinoza and Leibniz represent different manifestations of rationalism.

Relations of ideas. Hume's term for analytic statements which exemplify relations between concepts and can be known to be necessarily true or false purely by virtue of the meanings of the terms they contain.

David Hume (1711–76)

the reasons why we believe in the existence of external physical bodies is much shortened, Hume making no mention of the importance of constancy and coherence of our sense-experiences for this belief. However, the *Enquiry* does contain two novelties, Section XI: 'Of a Particular Providence and a Future State'; and the justly famous Section X: 'Of Miracles', which Hume had written at the time of the *Treatise* but withheld from publication in that book.

There are several editions of the *Enquiry* available, but the one used here is the L.A. Selby-Bigge, third edition, with the text revised and notes by P.H. Nidditch, Clarendon Press, Oxford, 1975. It is the page numbers of this edition that are referred to throughout the text. The edition has the advantage of numbered sections, which make it easy to refer to, especially when teaching. It also contains the second *Enquiry concerning the Principles of Morals*. We shall also be referring to *A Treatise of Human Nature*, L.A. Selby-Bigge, second edition, with the text revised and notes by P.H. Nidditch, Clarendon Press, Oxford, 1978.

Introduction: Hume on human nature

The titles of David Hume's *A Treatise of Human Nature* and *An Enquiry Concerning Human Understanding* make clearly manifest that above all Hume was a philosopher of human nature. He shared the ambition of a number of other thinkers around the time he lived of founding a science of man. Hume had been deeply impressed by the achievement of Newton who, through his theory of universal gravitation and the laws of motion attendant upon it, had provided a systematic and thorough account of the motions of celestial and terrestrial bodies. Hume sought to emulate Newton's achievement in the sphere of what was known then as moral science. In this context 'moral' does not simply mean having to do with ethical issues, questions about right and wrong conduct and duties and obligations. Its purpose rather was to signal that moral science was to be directed upon what were then known as moral subjects, living, thinking, feeling and acting human beings, as opposed to the objects and phenomena comprising inanimate nature which, by contrast, were the province of the natural philosopher or scientist.

Hume wanted to explicate the nature of the human mind and the principles that govern its functioning. His account was to embrace answers to questions such as: how does the mind acquire its contents, the materials upon which it operates when it thinks and feels, and what is the nature of those contents? What fundamental propensities govern the functioning of the mind, causing us to think, feel and act in the particular ways that we do? What are the limits to human reasoning and discovery? How, on the basis of fleeting and discontinuous experience do we arrive at a conception of the world as a realm of objects and events that exist independently of us and with what warrant? These are not merely questions about human psychology, though answering them does involve Hume in psychological theorising, but philosophical questions in their own right. It soon becomes apparent when reading Hume that it is impossible to understand the solutions he proposes to the philosophical issues he confronts without discerning how his views are embedded in, and animated by, his theory of mental activity and his account of human nature generally.

Hume's naturalism

The invocation of psychological mechanisms to explain how we arrive at our conceptions and beliefs is an expression of Hume's naturalism. When confronted with a philosophical problem, Hume typically supplies a causal account of why we believe as we do. Thus, with regard to such issues as why we believe that there is an external world, that there is a single continuing self that has experiences but is not reducible to them, that causes necessitate their effects, and that the future will resemble the past, Hume abjures from attempting to provide a rational justification of these philosophical beliefs, resting content with a description and explanation of the psychological mechanisms that operate to lead us to these beliefs.

Hume was distinctive in how he proposed to discover the workings of the mind. His account was to have a single basis: experience. It is this, together with his theory of knowledge in general, that makes Hume an empiricist. Unlike some previous attempts to explicate human, nature which were founded on speculation and what Hume referred to dismissively as 'hypothesis', the attempt to engage in *a priori* theorising uninformed by observation and experiment, Hume's aim was to discover the facts and only then attempt to frame a theory to explain them. In this vein he writes:

> *I found that the moral philosophy transmitted to us by Antiquity, labor'd under the same Inconvenience that has been found in their natural Philosophy, of being entirely Hypothetical, & depending more upon Invention than Experience. Every one consulted his Fancy in erecting Schemes of Virtue & Happiness without regarding human Nature, upon which every moral Conclusion must depend.*
> (Klibansky and Mossner 1969: 16)

Knowledge of the workings of the mind to be based upon experience

Hume's alternative approach is reflected in the subtitle of the *Treatise: An Attempt to Introduce the Experimental Method of Reasoning into Moral Subjects*. This can make it sound as if he is proposing to initiate a research programme in empirical psychology, but Hume had no proper conception of what this would involve, and in fact this endeavour was not to come to fruition until the advent of modern psychology and its methods more than a hundred years later. In gathering the facts of mental structure and function, Hume was restricted firstly, to the introspection of his own mind, and secondly, to observations of the behaviour of people in contemporary common life and in historical accounts. In regard to the second method for discovering the workings of the mind he writes: 'We must ... glean up our experiments in this science from a cautious observation of human life, and take them as they appear in the common course of the world, by men's behaviour and company, in affairs and in their pleasures' (Hume 1978: xix).

With regard to the use of introspection, Hume was aware of one aspect of its limitations:

> *When I am at a loss to know the effects of one body upon another in any situation, I need only put them in that situation, and observe what results from it. But should I endeavour to clear up after the same manner any doubt in moral philosophy, by placing myself in the same case with that which I consider, 'tis evident this reflection and premeditation would so disturb the operation of my natural principles, as must render it impossible to form any just conclusion from the phenomenon.*
> (Hume 1978: xix)

Hume acknowledges that there is a limit to how far we can penetrate into the fabric and operations of the mind. In accordance with his empiricism, that limit is set by experience, and if we try to transcend this limit, the result will only be nonsense. In the introduction to the *Treatise* he writes:

> *For to me it seems evident, that the essence of the mind being equally unknown to us with external bodies, it must be equally impossible to form any notion of its powers and qualities otherwise than from careful and exact experiments, and the observation of those particular effects, which result from its different circumstances and situations. And tho' we must endeavour to render all our principles as universal as possible, by tracing up our experiments to the utmost, and explaining all effects from the simplest and fewest causes, 'tis still certain we cannot go beyond experience; and any hypothesis, that pretends to discover the ultimate original qualities of human nature, ought at first to be rejected as presumptuous and chimerical.*
>
> (Hume 1978: xvii)

In this respect Hume was at one with Newton who, when asked what gravitation was, replied that he did not make hypotheses, that is, he did not try to enquire into what was beyond the scope of human experience and comprehension, resting content with describing what gravity *does*, rather than trying to say what gravity *was*. In the next few sections a more thorough account will be provided of the historical background to Hume's empiricism and his place within this tradition.

review activity

How did Hume envisage a science of human nature would be possible?

Intellectual background: Hume and the empiricist tradition

Hume may be viewed as representing the culmination of empiricism, begun in Britain by his predecessor John Locke (1632–1704) in *An Essay Concerning Human Understanding* (1690), and continued by George Berkeley in *A Treatise Concerning the Principles of Human Knowledge* published in 1710, one year before Hume's birth. These three philosophers are consequently commonly referred to as the British Empiricists. Hume initially formulated his empiricism in *A Treatise of Human Nature* (1740) but this massive work of over 600 pages at first met with a poor reception. It was to be some years before Hume's genius was properly recognized, and, in the meantime, to make his ideas more accessible, Hume wrote *An Enquiry Concerning Human Understanding* (1751), which represents a greatly reduced version of the *Treatise* and freed from what Hume termed 'scotticisms', Scottish idioms.

The nature of empiricism

Rejection of innate ideas

What essentially is empiricism? The doctrine has a number of strands and may also be expressed in different ways. To begin with, it is the claim that all the *materials* of knowledge and understanding ultimately derive from a single source: *experience*. Hume had taken over this thesis from Locke who had attacked and repudiated a doctrine held by a number of thinkers at the time, namely that innate knowledge and concepts exist in minds prior to all experience. Descartes (1596–1650), for example, had maintained that God had placed the idea of himself in the human mind prior to all experience, to be, as it were, the mark of the craftsman stamped upon the work. Others, like John Edwards, had written in *A Free Discourse Concerning Truth and Error*, (Edwards 1701), that there are 'Natural impressions and Inbred notices of True and False,' such as that 'we ought to venerate, love, serve and worship the Supreme Being'.

Locke maintained, on the contrary, that from its inception, the mind is *tabula rasa*, like a blank sheet of paper upon which nothing has yet been written. It is experience, through the medium of the senses, which furnishes it with what Locke called 'ideas':

All the materials of reason derive from experience alone

Let us suppose the mind to be, as we say, white paper void of all characters, without any ideas. How comes it to be furnished? ... Whence has it all the materials of reason and knowledge? To this I answer in one word, from experience; in that all our knowledge is founded, and from that it ultimately derives itself. Secondly, the other fountain from which experience furnisheth the understanding with ideas is the perception of the operation of our own minds within us, as it is employed about the ideas it has got ... I call this REFLECTION, the ideas it affords being such only as the mind gets by reflecting on its own operations within itself. (Locke 1961: 77–8)

review
activity

What was Locke rejecting when he repudiated the existence of 'innate' ideas, and what did he propose was the source of all our ideas?

Locke is often notoriously unclear as to what he means by 'idea', but in Book II, viii, 8, he writes: 'Whatsoever the mind perceives in itself, or is the immediate object of perception, thought, or understanding, that I call idea'(Locke 1961: 104).

Ideas as the immediate objects of perception and understanding

The important point to grasp is that Locke does not think of the immediate objects of perception as public physical objects – tables, trees, clouds and the rest – but rather as a series of mental contents which exist privately in the mind of the perceiver and whose existence, like pains, depends upon their being perceived. Ideas also, moreover, may figure as the contents of thoughts with which the faculty of the understanding operates. This 'Way of Ideas' as Locke called it, is common to all the empiricists under consideration: neither Berkeley nor Hume called it into question, but adopted it uncritically from Locke. As we shall see, it leads to radical scepticism concerning whether we can ever know that there is an independently existing reality, an external world outside our minds, as well as to an impoverished and inaccurate account of what it means to possess concepts.

review
activity

Describe two ways in which ideas are said to differ from physical objects.

All meaningful concepts must be applicable to a possible experience

A second and crucially important feature of empiricism is its insistence that all meaningful concepts or ideas must either derive from, or be applicable to, sense-experience. Strictly speaking these are two distinct points, not merely two different ways of saying the same thing. The first point concerns the *origins* of concepts or ideas and was made by Hume in the following way. Concepts are to be thought of as faint copies of more vivid sense-impressions. This has two consequences: firstly, if a concept is unclear, trace it back to the sense-impression from which it was copied. This will help to make the concept clearer. Hume will recommend this method when trying to make the notion of a causal link between events more perspicuous. Secondly, and vitally, if a concept cannot be traced back to a corresponding sense-impression, it is to be discounted as void of sense. So, for example, the Cartesian view of the mind as a non-physical soul lacking all dimensions would be rejected as empty by Hume because it is impossible, in principle, to have sense-experience of a soul. However, the point that Hume was striving for, despite his talk about the origins of concepts, was that any meaningful concept must be applicable to a possible sense-experience. The point was seen more clearly by Immanuel Kant (1724–1804) and is well summed up by P.F. Strawson (1919–) in his book on Kant, *The Bounds of Sense*:

> [T]here can be no legitimate, or even meaningful, employment of ideas or concepts which does not relate them to their empirical or experiential conditions of their application. If we wish to use a concept in a certain way, but are unable to specify the kind of experience-situation to which the concept, used in that way, would apply, then we are not really envisaging any legitimate use of that concept at all. In so using it, we shall not merely be saying what we do not know; we shall not really know what we are saying. (Strawson 1966: 16)

So, for example, if someone claims to have a concept of a snark, to know what the word 'snark' means, but then is completely unable to describe or identify snarks, then plainly he or she has no genuine concept of a snark after all. The need for concepts to be applicable to sense-experience, if they are to be concepts at all, has the alarming consequence that the problem of whether there is an external world beyond the veil of our private sense-impressions that gives rise to them is strictly a question that cannot even be posed, for such a world is supposed to lie, in principle, beyond all conceivable experience, and hence any attempt to refer to it must result in unintelligible gibberish. It is to Hume's great credit that he discerned this difficulty, writing in the *Treatise*:

> Now since nothing is ever present to the mind but perceptions, and since all ideas are deriv'd from something antecedently present to the mind; it follows, that 'tis impossible for us so much as to conceive or form an idea of anything specifically different from ideas and impressions. *Let us fix our attention of ourselves as much as possible: Let us chace our imagination to the*

heavens, or to the utmost limit of the universe; we never really advance a step beyond ourselves, nor can conceive of any kind of existence, but those perceptions which have appear'd in that narrow compass. This is the universe of the imagination, nor have we any idea but what is there produc'd.

(Hume 1978: 67–8, emphasis added)

The meaningfulness of talk about the external world can be restored providing it is made to refer solely to a series of actual and possible sense-experiences. This is the thesis of phenomenalism, which can be found in the philosophy of John Stuart Mill and was developed further in the writings of twentieth-century philosophy. Hume never adopted phenomenalism, preferring to give a psychological, rather than a philosophical, account of why we believe there is an external world. Berkeley's solution to the problem of the existence of the external world was to reduce it to sets of impressions which are placed in individual minds by God. Even if we are not perceiving the sets of impressions that comprise physical objects, God always is, so they do not go in and out of existence when we are not around.

Hume's reflection of Berkeley's Idealism

Berkeley's theory would be rejected by Hume for two major reasons. Firstly, as God is conceived of as an incorporeal spirit, this conception would be condemned as nonsense by Hume's criterion of significance as in principle we can have no experience, and therefore no impression, of such a being. Secondly, as we shall see later in the context of Hume's discussion of cause and effect, all knowledge of cause and effect must be founded upon experience. This means that to be able to pronounce on the cause of a phenomenon, we must be able to observe that cause at work. But in maintaining that God is the cause of our impressions that is precisely what, in principle, we cannot do. Exactly the same stricture would apply if we were to maintain that our impressions are caused by, in principle, unobservable physical objects, which is why Hume says that impressions arise in the soul from causes unknown.

Concepts must be applicable to a possible experience to be meaningful

Incidentally, Hume does later suggest how we can arrive at an intelligible concept of God: we think of a human mind or person, eliminate all weaknesses and vices, and then magnify the positive virtues left without limit. As this concept derives from something within our own experience – we have all had experience of human minds in action through what people say and do – it meets the empiricist criterion of significance explained above.

review
activity

Explain in your own words the importance of the distinction between the origins of our ideas or concepts and their applicability to a possible experience.

Knowledge of the world is founded ultimately entirely upon experience

A third important strand of empiricism is that it maintains that all knowledge and understanding of the world, the nature of reality, are ultimately founded entirely upon experience. Logic and reasoning aid our understanding of the nature of things, indeed are essential to it, but the raw materials to which they are applied derive from the senses.

The rejection of rationalism

Rationalism and its rejection

The three strands of empiticism explained in the preceeding pages amount to the rejection of rationalism, exemplified in the works of Plato (c.429–347 BC), Descartes (1596–1650), Spinoza (1632–77), and Leibniz (1646–1716). Plato utterly rejected sense-experience as a source of knowledge and true understanding: acquaintance with the world of everyday objects by means of the senses amounts merely to opinion and belief. Ultimately only the reasoning involved in doing mathematics, geometry, and philosophy can supply knowledge.

Descartes' rationalism

Descartes, whilst not rejecting and despising empirical investigation – he carried out extensive anatomical investigations and work in optics, for example – had a strong tendency to elevate reason above experience. Starting from his famous '*Cogito ergo sum*', ('I think therefore I am') and a principle closely connected with it – the clear and distinct rule – Descartes attempted to demonstrate that the world could be neatly divided into two distinct realms: the kingdom of non-physical souls or minds, and the realm of matter which, by its very nature, he believed, was incapable of consciousness and thought. Descartes also sought to prove, solely on the basis of logic by means of the ontological argument: that God must exist, and as God is perfect and hence no deceiver, our belief that there is a world existing independently of us must be true. God would not suffer his creatures to be systematically deceived and mocked with falsehood. Descartes insisted that only statements like analytic truths, which could not conceivably turn out to be false, could count as knowledge, and this led him, like Plato, towards the propositions of mathematics and geometry as the paradigms of what can be truly known.

Spinoza's rationalism

In the same vein, Spinoza's *Ethics* is set out like a geometrical system. Beginning with self-evident axioms, postulates, and definitions, Spinoza attempted, purely by logical deduction, to demonstrate that there can only be one infinite substance that does not depend for its existence upon anything else. This substance may be called either God or Nature and it possesses infinite attributes. (An attribute is, in effect, a property or feature.) We have knowledge of just two of these attributes, namely extension and thought. Mind and body are not distinct things, substances that could exist independently of each other, but a single reality conceived under two aspects, the mental and the physical. Mind and body move completely in step with each other and this is unsurprising because they are, in a sense, one and the same phenomenon seen from two different angles. Hume rejected Spinoza's philosophy, characterising it as a 'hideous hypothesis' because it is 'almost the same with that of the immateriality of the soul'.

Our final rationalist, Leibniz, employed what he called two 'Great Principles' to serve as the foundations of all his reasoning. The first of these is the Principle of Contradiction, by means of which 'we judge to be false what contains a contradiction and to be true what is opposed to or contradicts the false'. An example of this principle in action is not merely when we inform someone that they should not believe both a proposition and its opposite, on pain of contradicting themselves and thereby effectively saying nothing, but when we demonstrate to someone, much as Socrates does in his famous dialogues with various individuals who purport to know the truth about some philosophical matter, that they have unwittingly contradicted themselves.

Leibniz' rationalism

The second great principle is the Principle of Sufficient Reason, according to which 'we consider that no fact can hold or be real, and no proposition can be true but there be a sufficient reason why it is so and not otherwise, even though for the most part these reasons cannot be known by us' (Savile 2000: 32). By the steady application of these principles Leibniz claimed to have demonstrated that God exists and that the universe he created represents the best of all possible universes, containing the maximum amount of variety possible in accordance with the greatest degree of order possible. This leads Leibniz to a vision of the universe as composed of what he called 'monads'. Monads have no extension and thus are not composed of parts. They cannot cease to exist, therefore, by falling apart, and are eternal, unless God, himself an infinite and perfect monad, chooses to annihilate them. Each monad mirrors the entire universe from its own point of view, sometimes very confusedly, sometimes more clearly. Only God mirrors the entire universe perfectly and translucently. Monads are not in space; rather space exists in them, but only as what Leibniz called 'a well-founded appearance'. Monads are windowless; nothing comes into them or goes out of them; in other words monads do not affect each other. Each monad's actions and history unfolds according to an internal principle, rather like the spring of a watch unfolding.

Hume would have rejected Leibniz' theory of monads for essentially the same reason that he dismissed Spinoza's rationalism. Hume's avowed and ultimate aim in the *Enquiry* is to set limits to what can intelligibly be asserted and thought, to curb the pretensions of those who seek to transcend all possible experience, making claims that literally make no sense and, therefore, necessarily lack any rational foundation.

review activity

What do you understand by rationalism and how does it differ from empiricism?

Section II: 'Of the Origin of Ideas'

The contents of the mind

Perceptions and their qualities

This section contains a detailed account of Hume's empiricism. To comprehend it we first need to understand how Hume views the contents of the mind. Hume broadly classifies all mental states into *perceptions*. Following Descartes, Hume maintains that it is of the essence of perceptions that we are aware of them. The notion of a perception of which we were never conscious, and never could be conscious, is a contradiction in terms. In this way, perceptions are just like pains and other sensations: it makes no sense to talk of an unfelt pain or an unexperienced itch. Moreover, perceptions appear as they are, and are as they appear. It is, as Hume puts it, impossible that consciousness should ever deceive; the knowledge we have of our perceptions is incorrigible, a view we find in Hume's predecessor, René Descartes. In the case of perceptions, what you see is what you get: perceptions cannot appear to lack qualities they possess, or, conversely, appear to possess qualities they lack.

Perceptions are logically private to the individual: that is to say, only the person whose perception it is has access to it, privileged access, as it has come to be known. In other words, in principle, by the very nature of the case, only I can have direct access to my perceptions, and only you can have direct access to yours. In short, the entire contents of the mind possess a privacy that is logically inviolable. Lastly, perceptions are what Hume calls distinct existences and can exist loose and separate from each other, no perception depending for its existence on any other. This means in turn that the existence of any perception does not imply the existence, or indeed the non-existence, of any other perception. Hence Hume's conception of experience has been called atomistic in character, individual atoms of perceptions constituting the basic elements out of which it is composed.

review activity

What does Hume mean by 'impressions'? In what way do impressions differ from how we usually think of physical objects?

Impressions and ideas

Perceptions in turn can be categorized into *impressions* and *ideas*, as the diagram below illustrates:

The contents of the mind

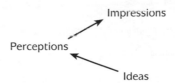

Impressions comprise sensory experiences, such as seeing, hearing, touching, tasting and smelling, but also inner experiences such as emotional states and desires that are introspectible. In the *Enquiry*, impressions of the first kind are called 'outward sentiments' or 'outward sensations', whereas in the *Treatise* they are called 'impressions of sensation'. Inner experiences are called 'inward sentiments' or 'inner sensations' in the *Enquiry*, but 'impressions of reflection' in the *Treatise* where this expression is intended to convey that we become aware of them by reflection on our own states of mind.

In addition to impressions there are also ideas. An idea, for Hume, is frequently equivalent to a concept, used in thinking and reasoning. Construed as concepts, ideas constitute the meanings of general words, just as they did for Hume's predecessors, Descartes and Locke. However, not all ideas function as concepts in Hume's philosophy: sometimes ideas are just data and contribute nothing towards meaning and, therefore, thought. Examples of ideas as mere data are the images that float into the mind when one daydreams as well as the mental images that sometimes occur when one remembers or imagines. Hume distinguishes between the ideas of memory and imagination in two ways. Firstly, he thinks the ideas of memory are stronger and livelier than those of the imagination. Secondly, memory preserves the original order of the ideas recollected, whereas the imagination has the liberty to transpose and change the order of its ideas.

Ideas are faint copies of impressions

There is a marked qualitative difference between impressions and ideas according to Hume. Impressions are lively, vivid and forcible by contrast with ideas, which are faint and dull: 'The most lively thought is still inferior to the dullest sensation' (Hume 1975: 17), although Hume is willing to allow that the ideas of memory sometimes are intermediate between an impression and an idea. However, Hume is not entirely consistent in the manner in which he demarcates impressions from ideas as he is willing to allow that if the mind is disordered by disease or madness, ideas may reach the 'same pitch of vivacity' as impressions and in this respect be indistinguishable from them. It is clear that some other principle is being employed to distinguish ideas from impressions in this kind of case and it is not difficult to discern that it can only be an appeal to objectivity: impressions are perceptions in some sense of an objective reality (Bennett 1971: 223–4), whereas the hallucinations of the insane are purely subjective, and therefore never qualify as impressions, however vivid. What counts as experience of an objective reality involves a complicated story for Hume, invoking the notion of the constancy and coherence of impressions. It certainly does not, and cannot, make an appeal to experiences of independently existing physical objects, as by Hume's own theory of the contents of the mind, we can have no acquaintance with physical objects.

activity

How does Hume distinguish between ideas and impressions?

Returning to the main discussion, however, impressions and ideas can also be divided into the simple and the complex: a simple impression or idea is one that cannot be discerned to have smaller components, whereas complex impressions and ideas are built up out of the simpler most basic elements. As an instance of a complex impression Hume gives the example of an apple: the colour, taste and smell are all united in it but they can readily be perceived not to be the same as each other and can be distinguished. By implication, the colour of the apple, according to Hume, is a simple impression, admitting of no further distinctions. In other words, it does not appear, at least at first glance, to be composed of simpler parts. However, this conclusion seems to be mistaken because the hues and intensities of colours may be distinguished from each other. Hume does not go into further details concerning the criterion for the simplicity of impressions and ideas, and ultimately the notion of simplicity is left rather vague.

The origins of ideas

Hume proceeds to explain how ideas originate and are formed, and this constitutes a key plank of his empiricism which has important and far-reaching consequences for his philosophy. Hume maintains that impressions of sense, which are strong and vivid, give rise to ideas which are fainter copies of them. In fact, Hume wants to argue for the stronger conclusion that all simple ideas, without exception, must have been preceded by, and result from, simple impressions. This conclusion, could it be established, would be sufficient to rule out innate ideas, ideas that are in the mind prior to all experience. The thesis that all simple ideas ultimately derive from simple impressions has become known in the literature as The copy principle and is illustrated in the diagram below:

The copy principle

Impressions

(Strong, vivid, which make up the contents of sense experience)

Ideas

(Faint copies used in thinking and reasoning)

Every simple idea constitutes a copy of the simple impression from which it originates; for example, an idea of blue derives from, and resembles, a sense impression of a particular shade of blue. However, whilst there can be complex ideas copied from complex impressions, there can also be complex ideas that have no corresponding impressions. This is because once the mind has a number of simple ideas available to it, these can be combined into complex ideas that have no correspondence with complex impressions.

Ideas can be combined to form complex ideas which have no corresponding impressions

Hume's well-known example is of a golden mountain. None of us has seen such a mountain in reality, but we have seen mountains and we have seen gold. As a result we can combine the ideas derived from these impressions to form a new complex idea. Hume observes that the imagination has full scope to assert itself and can combine the most incongruous ideas to form monsters and scenes the like of which were never seen or heard of, transporting us in an instant by thought to the most distant regions of the universe. Even the idea of God, an infinitely wise, intelligent and good being, arises in this way, and is the result of reflecting on human qualities and magnifying without limit those we consider desirable such as goodness and wisdom. In providing this account of the origin of the idea of God, Hume helps to render redundant Descartes' trademark argument which claims that only God can serve as the origin of the idea of Himself, placing it within us to serve as the mark of the maker upon his work.

Although all our ideas are caused by impressions, this should not be thought to have the consequence that ideas should be viewed as entirely passive, lacking any powers of their own. It happens sometimes, Hume remarks, that an idea can act back upon the mind to give rise to a new impression, and this impression can, in its turn, give rise to a new idea. Clearly, this process, could, in theory, run on forever. The impressions given rise to by ideas form an important subclass of the impressions of reflection mentioned earlier, and we shall have recourse to this topic later in the context of Hume's discussion of causation, where it assumes considerable importance. Before leaving this topic, an illustration of an idea giving rise to an impression of reflection is provided by Hume's claim that it sometimes happens that an idea of pleasure or pain 'returns upon the soul' producing new impressions of desire and aversion, hope and fear.

Hume's principle of empiricism

Hume recommends that if an idea or concept is unclear, we should trace it back to its origins in sense, where its features may be discerned more clearly.

However, this method has an important corollary, namely that if no sense impression corresponding to the concept in question can be found, it will have to be concluded that the concept is not genuine after all, and any assertion employing it is devoid of meaning. This criterion for the meaningfulness of assertions has been dubbed by some commentators Hume's *principle of empiricism* and it will be apparent that it has deep implications for what we can think and reason about, much less know. Although at first sight it may appear that we have limitless scope in what we imagine or conceive, our thought is really much more confined because it can only operate on the ideas we possess and these, without exception, must ultimately have derived from sense-experience. In this way Hume sets limits to what can be thought and conceived because all the materials of thinking and imagining can be derived only from outward and inward sentiments which comprise our experience.

Hume's genetic thesis regarding the origins of ideas

It needs to be made explicit that Hume's empiricism, as characterized so far, is a *genetic* thesis which focuses on the origins of our ideas. At first glance it appears to be making the *a posteriori* claim that, as a matter of fact, all ideas are copies of impressions. Hence it ought, in theory, to be empirically falsifiable, by producing an idea that has not been derived from a precedent impression. Hume offers two defences of his thesis. Firstly, it is incumbent upon anyone who claims that there are ideas not copied from impressions to produce those ideas, but it seems reasonably clear that he does not seriously think any such person will be forthcoming. Secondly, Hume gives the example of a person born blind. Such a person could form no idea of colours because he lacks the necessary experience of them. Likewise, a person born deaf could form no conception of sounds. Whilst these are reasonable suppositions – we never do find, as Hume remarks, congenitally blind and deaf people who know what sounds and colours are – Hume does not strictly prove his case because, conceived of as an empirical hypothesis that admits of no exceptions purely as a matter of fact, Hume cannot rule out the possibility that in the past, or at some time in the future, there will be cases where it is discovered that some people are found to have ideas that did not derive from correspondent impressions. Admittedly, it would be extremely surprising to find a congenitally deaf person who had composed a symphony, or a person blind from birth who had painted a portrait, but these are genuine possibilities nonetheless. Commentators have pointed out, however, that although Hume writes as if his empiricist thesis about the origins of ideas was *a posteriori* in character, in actual fact he treats it as an unfalsifiable *a priori* analytic principle, not seriously expecting counter-examples to it. As we shall see, with a slight adjustment, Hume's genetic principle which is strictly *a posteriori* and synthetic can be modified to yield a corresponding *a priori* analytic principle.

The missing shade of blue as a counter-example to the genetic thesis

We will come to this topic shortly. For the moment it is important to notice that having put forward his genetic principle Hume immediately produces a counter-example to it, which, if acceptable, would overturn his whole thesis in an instant. Hume asks us to imagine a person who has been acquainted with all colours and shades except just one particular shade of blue. Would such a person be able to conjure up from their imagination the idea of that shade? The case is not like thinking of a golden mountain, never seen before, because that is a complex idea composed of simple ideas that have been derived from corresponding impressions, and there would be no difficulty in someone putting the idea of gold and the idea of a mountain in their imagination. By contrast, the idea of the shade of blue is a non-composite simple idea not made up of more basic elements, so it is difficult to understand where this idea could come from, if not from a corresponding impression. Nevertheless, Hume thinks it is possible that someone could generate such an idea from his imagination, concluding 'that the simple ideas are not always, in every instance, derived from the correspondent impressions' (Hume 1975: 21). By this admission Hume falls into inconsistency and wrecks his genetic hypothesis regarding the origins of ideas; after all, it only takes one counter-example to falsify an empirical generalization. But he brushes this objection aside as so singular that it does not provide a ground for the abandonment of his genetic thesis.

However, there is a much better way of dealing with the 'missing shade of blue' example that avoids the inconsistency of which Hume is guilty. Hume's genetic thesis can be seen as the ancestor of the theory of meaning adopted by contemporary empiricists. Hume offers a psychological account of how ideas are acquired. The account is backward looking and the focus of the question Hume poses about the missing shade is whether some particular person or other who had not first seen that shade could know what it would look like. The theory of meaning that Hume bequeathed to contemporary empiricism, by contrast, is not concerned about how concepts are learnt, or whether they could be learnt under certain conditions, but what it *means* for an idea or concept to be meaningful. Whether various people could or could not acquire the concept of the missing shade without having seen it first is neither here nor there. Instead, what needs to be spelt out is what is required for concepts, the meanings of general terms, to be possible.

Hume's meaning empiricism

The requirement is soon stated: any meaningful concept must be applicable to a possible experience. In other words, there must be a set of conditions that could constitute the content of a possible experience and whose fulfilment would licence the application of the concept in question to those conditions. This is the *a priori* principle of meaning, now known as *meaning-empiricism*, towards which Hume was feeling his way.

To witness its application, suppose that by the very nature of the case there was in principle no conceivable experience-situation whose fulfilment would justify the application of an allegedly meaningful concept or idea. In that kind of case the alleged concept would not be genuine after all, and hence devoid of significance. Hume's insight into this matter was paramount and cannot be overestimated. The principle of significance embodied by the meaning-empiricism he helped to formulate puts a powerful weapon in our hands, enabling us to demarcate sense from nonsense, and thus avoid much fruitless labour debating issues that are ultimately unintelligible. The employment of this principle is a recurrent theme in Hume, intertwined throughout his entire philosophy, and it will be instructive to provide a concrete illustration of it in action.

review
activity

Explain the importance of the distinction between the *origins* of concepts and their *applicability* to possible experiences for empiricism.

The term 'substance' has had a long and complex history in philosophy. To prevent misunderstanding arising, *substance* does not refer to any kind of stuff of which things might be made, contrary to the popular usage of the term. Rather, in one central usage, a substance is a thing that can exist in its own right, independently of other substances. In this sense of the term, substances are continuants that persist throughout changes to them, and they have properties or features. Properties need substances: it is not possible to have properties floating around loose and unattached: they can occur only as the properties of substances or things. Equally, substances need properties, the notion of a substance lacking all qualities, a bare particular, appears to make no sense.

However, somewhat confusingly, there has been another concept of substance extant that came to prominence in the seventeenth and eighteenth centuries, and this is the idea of a substance as some sort of underlying substratum or support for the sensible qualities of objects. An analogy that helps to illustrate the point at issue is that of a pincushion with pins sticking in it. The pins correspond to the qualities of the object, and the pincushion to the object itself, which possesses the qualities, and unifies them as a cluster of features. It seems hard to avoid thinking of substances and their qualities in this sort of way. After all, we draw a distinction between the thing that possesses the qualities and the qualities possessed: we do not say, for example, that the object is nothing but its qualities, nothing over and above them. But we should not allow ourselves to think of a substance in this kind of way, as a bare featureless substratum, different in kind from the qualities it possesses. This conception of a substance, as Leibniz saw, is illusory. In his *New Essays Concerning Human Understanding*, devoted to an examination of John Locke's *An Essay Concerning Human Understanding*, he commented:

> *If you distinguish two things in a substance – the attributes or predicates, and their common subject – it is no wonder that you cannot conceive anything special in this subject. That is inevitable, because you have already set aside all the attributes through which the details could be conceived.* (Leibniz 1982: 218)

By contrast, applying his principle of empiricism, Hume mounts a different kind of attack on the notion of a hidden unknowable substratum, focusing not on material things, though the same considerations would be equally applicable, but on the claim that there must be a mental substratum in which our perceptions inhere:

> *I desire those philosophers, who pretend that we have an idea of the substance of our minds, to point out the impression that produces it, and tell distinctly after what manner that impression operates, and from what object it is deriv'd. Is it an impression of sensation or reflection? Is it pleasant, painful, or indifferent? Does it attend at all times, or does it only return at intervals? If at*

intervals, at what times does it principally return, and by what causes is it produc'd? (Hume 1978: 233)

Hume's attack is continued in the passage below, which shortly follows it:

We have no perfect idea of anything but of a perception. A substance is entirely different from a perception. We have, therefore, no idea of a substance. Inhesion is suppos'd to be requisite to support the existence of our perceptions. Nothing appears requisite to support the existence of a perception. We have, therefore, no idea of inhesion. What possibility then of answering that question, Whether perceptions inhere in a material or immaterial substance, *when we do not so much as understand the meaning of the question?*

(Hume 1978: 234)

review activity

How may Hume's account of the necessary conditions for concepts to be meaningful be used to attack the notion of an unperceivable material substratum as a support for properties?

Critical evaluation of Hume's account of concepts

Although the importance of Hume's insight that all genuine concepts must be applicable to possible experiences cannot be overestimated, his account of what it is to possess an idea or a concept is radically flawed. A criticism of Kant's, directed at Locke and Leibniz originally, is pertinent here: 'Locke sensualised all concepts of the understanding, as Leibniz intellectualised all appearances' (Kant 1963: 283).

Assimilation of the sensory to the intellectual

According to Kant (1724–1804), we should distinguish between the *sensibility* – in the eighteenth-century language of faculties or departments of the mind, that which provides sensory input – and the *understanding*, from which arise concepts. The trouble with Locke and Hume, however, is that they construe concept possession as if it were like having a particular sensory experience: a concept comes to be thought of as like a sense-perception, a mental image, only fainter. But this assimilation of the sensory to the intellectual fails to recognise the completely general character of concepts, hence Kant's observation that Locke – and the same applies to Hume – *sensualised* all concepts of the understanding. To think of a concept as a mental image is to confuse it with, to seek to reduce it to, the very things that may fall under the concept, the particular things revealed by sense-experience which comprise the instantiations of the concept.

Another objection is provided by Wittgenstein (1889–1951). What, Wittgenstein asks, would show that someone grasped, or possessed, a certain concept? The answer is not that they have a mental image, but rather that they have the capacity, the ability, to apply the concept in question to items given in actual or possible experience. Thus, if someone claimed to know what a King Charles spaniel was but, when asked to pick out all the King Charles spaniels at a dog show, failed to identify correctly a single one, we could safely conclude that he or she lacked the concept of that particular breed of dog. The argument against identifying concepts with mental images, or even particular mental states, may be stated formally as follows:

Possession of a concept is the possession of an ability

1. Concept-possession involves possession of an ability (the ability to apply the concept to things that fall under it).
2. Possession of a mental image does not involve possession of an ability.
3. Therefore, concept possession is not equivalent to the possession of an image.

Mere acquaintance with a thing does not guarantee possession of the concept of that sort of thing

A third objection, also hailing from Wittgenstein, is that mere acquaintance with a thing that falls under the concept, contrary to what is implicit in Hume's account, does not amount to, or guarantee, possession of the concept. Acquaintance with a particular chess king, for example, will not, by itself, guarantee that someone will understand what a chess king is. To acquire the concept one must be an agent actively involved in a public world and its practices, that is to say, in this case one must have familiarity with games in general, and board games in particular, and have tried chess out. The mere passive registration of images will not amount to the possession and mastery of the correlative concepts.

Mental images not necessary for concept-possession

Wittgenstein also points out that having a mental image is not *necessary* for possession of the corresponding concept. The point is well made by Colin McGinn:

> [A] *great variety of images, feelings, etc., may accompany understanding a particular word, either for the same person on different occasions or for different people; no one of these experiences seems to be essential for understanding a word in a particular way. And even if there were a de facto uniformity, possibly as a result of some psychological law, we could still conceive of cases of the same understanding in which a different conscious content is present. The failure to appreciate this point stems from concentrating upon the most common or typical kinds of accompaniment and erecting this correlation into a necessity – an error that arises from assuming that understanding must consist in a distinctive type of experience. And Wittgenstein's point is that introspection just does not bear out this theoretical assumption.*
>
> (McGinn 1984: 6)

Mental images are not sufficient for concept-possession

Neither is it *sufficient* for a sign to have meaning, to stand for a concept, that some item comes before the mind. When using the word 'cube', for example, it is not sufficient that an image of a cube should come into one's mind, because the picture does not determine how the sign is to be used: a plethora of meanings can be invented – in itself, the mental image is semantically inert. Thus the image could be interpreted variously as: 'Here is a cube; If there is a cube, then . . .; There is no cube here; Bring me a cube,' and so forth. The image of a cube could even be used as a sign for another shape. The point is that there is nothing in an image, whether mental or physical, which determines its application. In fact, to get rid of the temptation to invest the mental image of a cube with an occult character, which is supposed, magically and mysteriously, to endow it with meaning, Wittgenstein urges us to replace the mental image of, say, a colour, with a painted physical sign. Now if the painted sign is dead and cannot determine meaning, then neither is there reason to think the mental image can determine meaning.

Understanding is dispositional, not occurrent

Lastly, understanding a concept is dispositional and non-occurrent by comparison with mental states like having a mental image or experiencing a certain feeling. We may imagine an image for a few minutes, and we can conceive our reverie being interrupted and then resuming again. But understanding a concept is not clockable in this way, nor intermittent in the way in which contemplating a mental image could be.

review
activity

Explain in your own words any *two* of what you regard as the most important criticisms of Hume's account of the nature of ideas or concepts.

Section III: 'Of the Association of Ideas'

In Section II, Hume provides an account of the *contents* of the mind, together with an explanation of how those contents are acquired. In Section III he turns his attention to the question of how the mind *operates* upon those contents, specifically ideas and impressions, to combine them into more complex ones. Although Hume grants that the imagination is free to connect what ideas it pleases, he nevertheless believes that there is some constraint upon it and that some universal principles of association must be operating to explain regularities in our patterns and trains of thought. Our ideas do not just occur at random, 'but introduce each other with a certain degree of method and regularity ... Were the loosest and freest conversation to be transcribed, there would immediately be observed something which connected it in all its transitions' (Hume 1975: 23). We have all had experience of this phenomenon. In the course of a conversation we suddenly find ourselves talking about a completely different topic from which we started, and wonder how we got onto it. With effort, however, it is usually possible to trace the associations between the various thoughts which led us off track from the original topic under discussion. Hume also claims that the principles of association explain why 'languages so nearly correspond to each other' (Hume 1978: 10). We may interpret this last remark of Hume's as asserting that for mutual understanding between speakers of different languages to be possible, a certain commonality of structure and function must be presupposed. As, however, the surface appearances of languages are very different to each other it must be the deeper aspects of structure to which Hume is referring. Corresponding to this structure, and informing it, there must be common patterns of thought, otherwise no one would be able to understand another, and to make himself understood.

Hume believes that the principles of association are the equivalent in the science of humankind to gravitation in the natural world. Just as the elements of planetary systems are held together by gravity, so 'a gentle force ... commonly prevails' (Hume 1978: 10) to combine ideas in certain common patterns: 'Here is a kind of *attraction*, which in the mental world will be found to have as extraordinary effects as in the natural' (Hume 1978:

10–11, emphasis added). Like Newton, who himself did not attempt to speculate about what gravity was but restricted himself to describing its effects, Hume similarly restrains himself from trying to explicate why the principles of association obtain:

> [A]s to its causes, they are mostly unknown, and must be resolv'd into original qualities of human nature, which I pretend not to explain. Nothing is more requisite in a philosopher, than to restrain the intemperate desire of searching into causes, and having establish'd any doctrine upon a sufficient number of experiments, rest contented with that, when he sees a farther examination would lead him into obscure and uncertain speculations.   (Hume 1978: 13)

Principles of the association of ideas

Hume identifies three principles of association: *resemblance*, *contiguity* (proximity of one to thing to another in time or space), and *cause and effect*, explaining them respectively in the *Enquiry* as follows: 'A picture naturally leads our thoughts to the original: the mention of one apartment in a building naturally introduces an enquiry or discourse concerning the others: and if we think of a wound, we can scarcely forbear reflecting on the pain which follows it' (Hume 1975: 24).

Problems with the association of ideas

There are specific problems with each of these principles, as well as with Hume's account generally. Firstly, the analogy with gravity suggests that, just as bodies in the natural world attract each other gravitationally by virtue of their masses, so ideas actively associate themselves with each other. It is not clear, however, whether it makes any sense to attribute any powers to ideas considered in themselves. Moreover, in attributing powers to ideas, this gives the mind itself no work to do; it merely becomes the 'container' of the ideas. Terence Penelhum usefully expands upon this criticism:

> [I]f the course of my mental history is determined by the associative attraction of my perceptions, so that they cause one another to arise, there seems no place, perhaps even no clear sense, to the suggestion that I, the mind or soul that has them, can exert any influence over their course. All the mind does is include them.   (Penelhum 1993: 122)

Applying this insight to Hume's first principle of resemblance we are led to the conclusion that it is not that one idea produces another idea merely because it resembles it, but rather that *we* notice the resemblance and as a result form an association between the two ideas in our mind. If we fail to notice the resemblance, then the association will not be formed: the point is that it seems to make no sense to speak of the association being formed independently of our mental agency. In fact, going further, it might be questioned whether it is meaningful to speak of resemblance holding, except from the point of view of a conscious being. In other words, resemblance is an observer-relative notion. In this connection Harold Noonan comments:

> [I]t is very much in the spirit of Hume's philosophy to say that resemblance is not something that is in the world independently of observers. It is a fact that human beings are so constituted that they perceive certain things as resembling or similar, and perceive other things as dissimilar. This fact determines the concepts available to us and explains how the training in language we are exposed to results in our possession of the concepts we, in fact, have. But other creatures, without in any way being in error, could perceive quite different sets

of things as resembling, and in consequence naturally acquire on the basis of their linguistic training a quite different set of concepts. Thus from a god's eye view there are no similarities in the world, or there are as many as there are possible conceptual schemes by which the world can be organised. There are, however, no 'joints' in nature such that one conceptual scheme, based on one way of perceiving similarities and dissimilarities, might cut nature at the joints and another not. (Noonan 1999: 156)

There are also problems with the remaining two principles, as Calvin Pinchin points out in his *Issues in Philosophy* (1999). Having noted the problem with resemblance just discussed, Pinchin turns to contiguity in time and place. Ideas can be temporally related, but what sense attaches to the notion of the spatial relation of ideas? 'We can have an idea of a book being on a table, but this is not the case of our *idea* of the book being *on* our *idea* of a table' (Pinchin 1999: 23). Hume should restrict himself to talking about ideas only, but he talks as if he were describing physical objects. The same confusion infects Hume's third principle:

There can be no doubt that when, for example, our thought of a gun calls up the thought of a dead man, there is some principle of association involved and one in which a grasp of causal relationships plays a part. The causal relationship, however, is not a natural relationship between ideas considered as mental images. It is not that our mental image of a gun is causally related to our mental image of a dead man. It is not even clear that mental images can enter into causal relations with each other. It seems, therefore, that of Hume's three principles, only half of the second one (contiguity in time) is even a possibility. (Pinchin 1999: 23)

Apart from the specific difficulties with the principles of association just discussed, it is difficult to believe that only these three principles underlie and explain all the workings of the mind. Indeed, there is strong reason to believe that Hume did not accept this position himself. Firstly, despite the remark directed at himself in the *abstract* that 'if anything can intitle the author to so glorious a name as inventor, 'tis the use he makes of the principle of the association of ideas' (Hume 1978: 661), Hume grew dissatisfied with this simple attempt to explain our mental functioning, and this manifests itself in the fact that whilst the statement of the principles occupied 15 pages in the first edition of the *Treatise*, in the *Enquiry* it is reduced to just three paragraphs spanning two pages. Moreover, as Stroud aptly observes:

Despite the suggestions in the more programmatic parts of Hume's writings that the association of ideas, on the analogy of the principle of gravitation, can account for everything that goes on in the mind, when he actually gets down to the detailed business of explaining the origins of some of our most pervasive forms of thinking, feeling, and acting, he does not force everything into a rigid associative mould. (Stroud: 1977: 37)

review
activity

What criticisms can be made of Hume's principle of the association if ideas?

The formation of abstract or general ideas

We shall draw attention to these alternative accounts in later chapters. Let us bring this chapter to a close, however, with a discussion of Hume's account of the formation of abstract or general ideas. This topic is omitted from the *Enquiry*, but it is important because it provides an immediate and striking example in support of Stroud's claim that the association of ideas does not by any means pervade all aspects of Hume's theory of mental activity.

Hume's copy principle commits him to the belief that the meaning of a word, the concept or idea it expresses, is an image. But an image, by its very nature, is determinate and particular. If I think of a man, for example, the image that comes to mind must be of a particular man of some definite size, shape, colour, and other qualities. How then, can I think, not of a particular man, but of men in general? How can a particular image become general in its application and represent all different sizes, shapes and colours of men, but not any man in particular? Locke's answer was to invoke abstraction: we are to leave out what is peculiar to each different particular man, retaining only the element that is common to them all. But what could this element possibly be, and how could it find its embodiment in an image? How, to turn to Locke's other example, could we compose the image of a triangle which must be 'neither Oblique, nor Rectangle, neither Equilateral, Equicrural, nor Scalenon: but all and none of these at once' (Locke 1961: vii, 9). This is clearly an impossibility, and for that reason was attacked by Berkeley in a famous passage in Section X of the introduction to *The Principles of Human Knowledge*:

> *Whether others have this wonderful faculty of abstracting their ideas, they best can tell: for my self I find indeed I have a faculty of imagining or representing to my self the ideas of those particular things I have perceived and of variously compounding and dividing them. I can imagine a man with two heads or the upper part of a man joined to the body of a horse. I can consider the hand, the eye, the nose, each by it self abstracted from the rest of the body. But then whatever hand or eye I imagine, it must have some particular shape and colour. Likewise the idea of a man that I form to my self, must be of a white, or a black, or a tawny, or a straight, or a crooked, a tall or a low, or a middle sized man. I cannot by any effort of thought conceive the abstract idea above described [that is, one retaining only what is common to all men].*
>
> (Berkeley 1910: Section 10)

What this amounts to is the rejection of ideas conceived of as indeterminate in character:

> '[T]is a principle generally receiv'd in philosophy, that every thing in nature is individual, and that 'tis utterly absurd to suppose a triangle really existent, which has no precise proportion of sides and angles. If this therefore be absurd in fact and reality, it must also be absurd in idea; since nothing of which we can form a clear and distinct idea is absurd and impossible ... Now as 'tis impossible to form an idea of an object, that is possest of quantity and quality, and yet is possest of no precise degree of either; it follows, that there is an equal impossibility of forming an idea, that is not limited and confin'd in both these particulars. Abstract ideas are therefore in themselves individual, however they may become general in their representation. The image in the mind is only that of a particular object, tho' the application of it in our reasoning be the same, as if it were universal.*
>
> (Hume 1978: 20)

In the latter part of this passage Hume can be seen to be endorsing Berkeley's view, which he has referred to earlier, namely that 'all general ideas are nothing but particular ones annexed to a certain term, which gives them a more extensive signification, and makes them recall upon occasion other individuals which are similar to them' (Hume 1978: 17).

In other words, we have experience of a number of particular things which resemble each other and we come to apply a general term to all of them. So a connection is established between the term and the particular sorts of things. When the name comes to mind, or is mentioned, it draws into the mind a particular idea of one those things because a custom linking the term to a number of those things has been established. On other occasions, according to our needs, other particular ideas may be drawn into the mind:

> [We] keep ourselves in readiness to survey any of them, as we may be prompted by a present design or necessity. The word raises up an individual idea, along with a certain custom; and that custom produces any other individual one, for which we may have occasion. (Hume 1978: 20–1)

How the customary connection is formed, Hume does not pretend to explain:

> The only difficulty, that can remain on this subject, must be with regard to that custom, which so readily recalls every particular idea for which we may have occasion, and is excited by any word or sound, to which we commonly annex it. The most proper method, in my opinion, of giving a satisfactory explication of this act of the mind, is by producing other instances, which are analogous to it, and other principles which facilitate its operation. To explain the ultimate causes of our mental actions is impossible. 'Tis sufficient if we can give any satisfactory account of them from experience and analogy. (Hume 1978: 22)

Section IV: 'Sceptical Doubts concerning the Operations of the Understanding' Part I

Relations of ideas and matters of fact

Relations of ideas

Hume divides all propositions or statements into two classes, namely relations of ideas and matters of fact. This division has come to be known as *Hume's Fork*. Relations of ideas correspond to what would now be called analytic statements, statements which are necessarily true or false and whose truth value depends upon the meanings of the terms they contain. Such statements, as Hume points out, do not describe states of affairs in the world and are true or false quite independently of the way things are. They are neither confirmable, nor confutable, by observation and experiment, and, when true, comprise non-empirical knowledge. They are discovered to be true by reason alone, 'by the mere operation of thought'. Such statements comprise the truths of geometry, mathematics, algebra and, we may add, logic. The negation of an analytic truth, for example, the denial that the square of the hypotenuse is equal to the sum of the squares of the other two sides, is a contradiction in terms; in Hume's terms, it is inconceivable. Only analytic truths, i.e. true relations of ideas are demonstrable by reasoning; synthetic statements, statements comprising matters of fact, are knowable only through experience.

Matters of fact   By contrast with relations of ideas there are matters of fact, statements which describe how the world, as a matter of contingent fact, happens to be. Such statements can be denied without contradiction. Hume's own example is the statement that the sun will rise tomorrow. It is not self-contradictory to deny this statement, to maintain that the sun will not rise tomorrow. If the sun did not rise tomorrow, then the statement would, as a matter of fact, be true: what would make it true would be reality turning out to be as the statement characterises it as being. In other words, in the case of factual statements, the possibility of their being true or false is an integral feature of them, as their truth or falsity depends entirely on whether or not things in the world are as the statement describes them as being. Their truth or falsity cannot be determined by pure reasoning, by the operation of thought alone, as in mathematics and geometry, but is discoverable purely by experience. Unlike the negation of an analytic truth, the negation of a true synthetic statement is entirely conceivable.

review
activity

Complete the table below to bring out the differences between relations of ideas and matters of fact.

Relations of ideas	Matters of fact
• Can be known by reason alone • Are necessarily true or false • • • • • •	• Can only be known on the basis of observation and/or experiment • Are . . . • • • •

Knowledge of states of affairs beyond current sense-experience and memory

But what can we know about the existence of states of affairs other than those whose existence and nature we are now currently perceiving, or which we remember to be the case? Hume's answer is that all reasoning about matters of fact is founded on the relation of cause and effect: 'By means of that relation alone we can go beyond the evidence of our memory and senses' (Hume 1975: 26).

What this means becomes clearer with the use of an example. Suppose, Hume says, a man were to find a watch on a desert island. (This recalls the eponymous hero of Defoe's *Robinson Crusoe* finding a footprint in the sand in Defoe's novel, which had not long been published when Hume was composing his earlier book, the *Treatise*.) From the existence of the watch he would then be able to infer that there had once been people on that island, even though he had never seen them. How would that be possible? Solely from past experience, which has shown that watches are the result of human invention and contrivance and are commonly carried around by people and sometimes lost. As Hume says, 'here it is constantly supposed that there is a connection between a present fact [finding the watch] and that which is inferred from it' [the existence of someone who made or owned the watch] (Hume 1975: 27).

All inferences regarding states of affairs of which we have had no direct experience is founded on knowledge of cause and effect

Similarly, if I hear a voice intelligently discussing some issue or other, but I cannot see anyone because it is dark, I may legitimately infer that someone is present because past experience has established a connection between hearing a voice and then discovering the owner of that voice. Knowledge of the connection of one phenomenon with another arises purely from experience: it cannot, as Hume puts it, be known *a priori*, before and independently of all experience. To use another example, suppose that on one day very few students come to the class on time in the morning. I therefore conclude there must be something wrong with the trains or buses. How can I make this inference? Because in the past I have established, on the basis of experience, that when there are problems with transport and the roads, students invariably come in late. But before all experience I could not know this.

review activity

In what way, according to Hume, can we acquire empirical knowledge beyond the evidence of our senses and memory?

Knowledge of cause and effect

How do we acquire knowledge of cause and effect? Let us suppose that Adam sprang into being with all his faculties fully formed and intact. But even then, prior to further experience, he could not know purely from the knowledge that water is fluid and transparent, and could be drunk and bathed in, that it possessed the power to drown and suffocate him – that would have to be revealed by experience and experience alone.

> *No object ever discovers, by the qualities which appear to the senses, either the causes which produced it, or the effects which will arise from it; nor can our reason, unassisted by experience, ever draw any inference concerning real existence and matter of fact.*
> (Hume 1975: 27)

Causes and effects are events which are completely distinct from one another. In the event which is the supposed cause, nothing can be discerned of its possible effect, nor from a supposed effect alone can we know anything of its cause. What effects an event does actually have, or what the cause was of a particular event, can be established only by observation of both sets of events. Observation of one event alone will not tell you what effects it has, nor of what caused it. 'In vain ... should we pretend to determine any single event, or infer any cause or effect, without the assistance of observation and experience' (Hume 1975: 30).

All knowledge of cause and effect is founded upon experience

If someone were presented with two smooth pieces of marble for the first time, he or she would never be able to tell in advance that the flat surfaces would adhere to each other and need great force to be separated in a direct line, whilst making little resistance to lateral pressure. Occurrences like this can never be discovered purely by *a priori* reasoning. *A priori*, anything could be the cause of anything, and what the actual causes of a phenomenon are can never be read off from the effect, as the effect is entirely distinct from its cause. This flies in the face of the scholastic causal adequacy principle, beloved of Descartes, when he attempted to argue that if we have an idea of God, an infinite being, this idea can only have been caused by God himself, as there must be at least as much reality in the cause as in the effect, and we are merely finite creatures.

With these reflections in mind, Hume assigns a very modest role to human reason. We can discover the causes of things to a certain extent, but the discovery of the ultimate causes of things is something which will ever elude us:

> [U]*ltimate springs and principles are totally shut up from human curiosity and enquiry. Elasticity, gravity, cohesion of parts, communication of motion by impulse; these are probably the ultimate causes and principles which we shall ever discover in nature; and we may esteem ourselves happy, if, by accurate enquiry and reasoning, we can trace up the particular phenomena to, or near to, these principles. The most perfect philosophy of the natural kind* [Hume means by this natural science] *only staves off our ignorance a little longer ... the observation of human blindness or weakness is the result of all philosophy, and meets us at every turn, in spite of our endeavours to elude or avoid it.*
>
> (Hume 1975: 30–1)

This should not be taken as a despairing conclusion, but rather as a timely reminder that we can speak intelligibly only of what lies within possible experience. Hume wants to curb our pretensions to pronounce upon those things of which we have, and can have, no experience and knowledge. Reason must be kept within its proper bounds. Thus, whilst geometry can assist us in the application of the law of motion that the moment or force of any body is in the compound ratio or proportion of its solid contents and velocity, and, that a result, a small force can move a heavy weight, yet that law, like all natural laws, can only be established to be true on the basis of experience:

> *Geometry assists us in the application of this law, by giving the just dimensions of all the parts and figures which can enter into any species of machine; but still the discovery of the law itself is owing merely to experience, and all the abstract reasonings in the world could never lead us one step towards the knowledge of it.*
>
> (Hume 1975: 31)

review activity

Explain in your own words, and using your own examples, how we come to acquire knowledge of cause and effect.

Part II

How have we been able to draw a conclusion about an absent matter of fact from a state of affairs which we presently perceive? From knowledge of a causal relation between the present and the absent facts, has been Hume's answer. And how has such knowledge of cause and effect been established? Again, Hume has his reply ready: on the basis of experience.

But now Hume wants to press the question further. 'What,' he asks 'is the foundation of all conclusions from experience?' What Hume is getting at is this: we take experience as our guide to how the future will be, and also as to how the past was, as the example of the man finding a watch on a desert island shows. But with what justification do we do this? If, for the sake of a clear exposition of the argument Hume is giving, we restrict ourselves to the question of whether we can have knowledge of the future based on past experience, suppose I notice, to use Hume's own example, that past experience has established that bread nourishes me and I conclude that in the future it will go on doing so. But with what justification? It may be replied that before when I made predictions about the future on the basis of past experience, those predictions were later borne out in the course of time when what was predicted came about. In the same way, I have every reason to think that what I predict now, say, the sun's rising tomorrow, will come about, based on past experience. It always did rise, without exception, and this affords an overwhelming reason for thinking it will continue doing so tomorrow and the day after that.

But Hume's point is that this claim itself relies upon the belief that the future will be conformable to the past:

> We have said that all arguments concerning existence are founded on the relation of cause and effect; that our knowledge of that relation is derived entirely from experience; and that all our experimental conclusions proceed upon the supposition that the future will be conformable to the past. To endeavour, therefore, the proof of this last supposition by probable arguments, or arguments regarding existence, must evidently be going in a circle, and taking that for granted, which is the very point in question. (Hume 1975: 35–6)

Russell made the same point, perhaps more graphically, when he wrote:

> It has been argued that we have reason to know that the future will resemble the past, because what was the future has constantly become the past, and has always been found to resemble the past, so that really we have experience of the future, namely of times which were formerly future, which we may call past futures. But such an argument really begs the very question at issue. We have experience of past futures, but not of future futures, and the question is: Will future futures resemble past futures? This question is not to be answered by an argument which starts from past futures alone. We have therefore to seek for some principle which shall enable us to know that the future will follow the same laws as the past. (Russell 1967: 36–7)

An attempt may be made to argue that the conclusion that the future will resemble the past is the result of a chain of reasoning, a case of logical deduction such as we find between the premises and conclusions in a deductive argument. But, Hume says, point out what that deductive step, that chain of demonstrative reasoning, consists in:

> These two propositions are far from being the same, I have found that such an object has always been attended with such an effect, and I foresee, that other objects, which are in appearance similar, will be attended with similar effects. I

shall allow, if you please, that the one proposition may justly be inferred from the other: I know, in fact, that it always is inferred. But if you insist that the inference is made by a chain of reasoning, I desire you to produce that reasoning.

(Hume 1975: 34)

Can induction be justified?

In the case of deductive reasoning it is not possible to get more out of the conclusion than is contained in the premises: what indeed is happening in a deductive proof is that information that is contained implicitly in the premises is being made explicit in the conclusion. But in the case of the two propositions Hume cites above, the meaning of the first proposition is quite different from the meaning of the second. The first refers exclusively to what has happened in the *past*, the second to what will happen in the *future*. But given this difference of meaning, it is impossible that the second could be deduced from the first alone. This kind of reasoning is called *inductive reasoning* and its hallmark is that the premises never logically entail the conclusion, so that the premises may be asserted, and the conclusion denied without a logical contradiction resulting. The question of how, and whether, induction can be rationally justified has been troubling philosophers ever since Hume first drew attention to it.

The point Hume is making is brought out well by Anthony Flew in a detemporalised version of the argument: universal conclusions about matters of fact cannot be validly deduced from less than universal premises of the same sort. That is, from 'All so far observed or otherwise known Xs are or have been θ,' it cannot be deduced that 'All Xs have been, are and will be θ' (Flew 1986: 53–5). In other words, just because all so far observed or known Xs have been θ, this can plainly be no logical guarantee that all the Xs there are, including all those not observed or known, have been, or will be, θ.

As Hume puts it himself:

You say that one proposition is an inference from the other. But you must confess the inference is not intuitive; neither is it demonstrative: Of what nature is it, then? To say it is experimental, is begging the question. For all inferences from experience suppose, as their foundation, that the future will resemble the past, and that similar powers will be conjoined with similar sensible qualities. If there be any suspicion that the course of nature may change, and that the past may be nor rule for the future, all experience becomes useless, and can give rise to no inference or conclusion. It is impossible, therefore, that any arguments from experience can prove this resemblance of the past to the future; since all these arguments are founded upon the supposition of that resemblance.

(Hume 1975: 37–8)

review
activity

Hume writes that, 'When a man says "I have found, in all past instances, such sensible qualities conjoined with sensible powers," [and when he says], "similar sensible qualities will always be conjoined with similar secret powers," he is not guilty of a tautology, nor are these propositions in any respect the same.'

In what way can this passage be seen to be denying that we can logically deduce conclusions about the future from present and past experiences?

It will not do, Hume says, to turn round in objection to this and say, in effect, but in the course of your everyday life you certainly do continue to act in the full belief that the future will be like the past: you do not, for example, put your hand on a hot stove having learned from experience that in the past this has caused painful burns. But although Hume is happy to accept that this is a common practice in which he himself, like everyone else, shares, nevertheless, this does not supply a philosophical foundation or justification of the practice:

> As an agent, I am quite satisfied in the point; but as a philosopher, who has some share of curiosity, I will not say scepticism, I want to learn the foundation of this inference. No reading, no enquiry has yet been able to remove my difficulty, or give me satisfaction in a matter of such importance.
>
> (Hume 1975: 38)

Hume's answer to this problem, which is given in Section V, Part I, is hinted at in the closing pages of Section IV: 'it is not reasoning which engages us to suppose the past resembling the future, and to expect similar effects from causes which are, to appearance, similar' (Hume 1975: 39). We shall be examining this response in more detail in the next section.

review activity

Hume writes that:

For all inferences from experience suppose, as their foundation, that the future will resemble that past, and that similar powers will be conjoined with similar sensible qualities. If there be any suspicion that the course of nature may change, and that the past may be no rule for the future, all experience becomes useless, and can give rise to no inference or conclusion. It is impossible, therefore, that any arguments from experience can prove this resemblance of the past to the future; since all arguments are founded on the supposition of that resemblance. (Hume 1975: 37–8)

Explain in your own words the point that Hume is making here.

Section V: 'Sceptical Solution of these Doubts' Part I

Can induction be justified?

Custom and habit

In this section Hume takes up the question that he left himself at the end of Section IV: if it is not by reasoning that we proceed to draw conclusions about the unknown and unobserved from past experience, on what basis is this done? Hume's answer is *custom* or *habit*:

> [W]herever the repetition of any particular act or operation produces a propensity to renew the same act or operation, without being impelled by any reasoning or process of the understanding, we always say, that this propensity is the effect of Custom ... All inferences from experience, therefore, are effects of custom, not of reasoning.
>
> (Hume 1975: 43)

Is Hume setting the standard for the justification of induction self-contradictorily high?

It is worthwhile at this point to weigh the implications of what Hume is saying. To reach conclusions about the future on the basis of past experience is not, he maintains, something that involves either the understanding or reason. We can explain why, in terms of habit or custom, we are irresistibly inclined to conclude that unknown and unobserved instances of a certain type will resemble known and observed instances of that type. But that is to give the non-rational causes of why we make these inferences. It is not in any way to justify or support any such inference in the sense of giving rational reasons or good evidence for it. What Hume would seem to be doing here, though it needs to be made explicit, is taking deductive inference, inference in which the conclusion in a valid proof is logically entailed by the premises, as in mathematical, geometrical and logical proofs, as the standard or paradigmatic case of providing a rational justification or support for a conclusion. But, judged by this criterion, an argument from experience hopelessly fails to measure up, as the essential characteristic of such an argument is that it is precisely the kind of justification in which the conclusion contains information which is beyond that contained in the premises of the argument and hence cannot be entailed by them. Were such a conclusion logically entailed, it would not then be an argument from experience, but a mathematical or logical demonstration. It would seem, then, that Hume is setting the standards of rational justification self-contradictorily high, by acknowledging on the one hand the fact that in an argument from experience the conclusion cannot be logically entailed by the premises, yet on the other implicitly operating with demonstrative proof in which premises do entail conclusions in valid arguments as the sole standard of justification and reason-giving.

However, there is no easy answer to the request that induction should be justified, and certainly no space here to enter into an examination of the large and complex literature that surrounds the topic.

Part II

The nature of belief: vividness

Part II deals with the topic of what it is to hold a belief. 'Wherein,' Hume asks, '… consists the difference between … a fiction and a belief?' We can invent stories in the most minute detail through the use of our imaginations, but we do not thereby automatically find ourselves believing that those stories are true. The difference, Hume says, cannot lie in the joining of an idea to a work of the imagination which has the capacity of rendering it true: we can join the head of a man to the body of a horse but we have not the power of turning this fiction into a true belief. Beliefs, as the philosopher Bernard Williams has pointed out, aim at truth. If we believe a statement, then we believe it is true. But what makes a belief true is some state of affairs existing independently of us, and by merely imagining a man's head joined to a horse's body, we at the same time recognise that this is not enough to bring about a state of affairs which would make it true that there really is to be found a man's head joined to a horse's body.

Hume goes on to argue that the difference between fiction and belief lies in 'some sentiment or feeling, which is annexed to the latter, not to the former, and which depends not on the will, nor can be commanded at pleasure'. Hume thinks it is very difficult to define what this sentiment is, and in default offers a description. He offers in effect two criteria. Firstly, 'I say that belief is nothing but a more vivid, lively, forcible, firm, steady conception of an object, than what the imagination alone is able to attain' (Hume 1975: 49).

Vividness of ideas as a criterion of belief

In other words, when entertaining a proposition that for Hume consists in having ideas which are copies of impressions in one's mind, those ideas which make up belief are more vivid and strong than those which are involved in the reveries of the imagination. But, as we saw before, it is easy to level objections against this. Vividness of ideas cannot be sufficient to make something a belief, because we can conceive of someone, or ourselves, with a strong and vivid imagination. A story may strike us with more force, even though we know it is only a story, than a true life account of things. Neither is vividness of ideas necessary to belief. A pallid, lacklustre account of a disaster may still for all that be true, and be recognised and believed to be true.

Beliefs as the governing principles of our actions

Hume's second suggestion, which he does not develop, is contained in remarks that in belief as opposed to the imagination, our conceptions are caused to 'weigh more in the thought' and are given 'a superior influence on the passions and imagination'. This is going in the right direction, as we shall shortly see, but even then it is not quite right, because we can easily conceive that some imaginations can exercise a very powerful influence on people's thoughts and passions, as with Macbeth's 'present fears are less than horrible imaginings'.

Beliefs are maps by which we steer

Where Hume is more nearly correct is in his brief remark that in belief ideas are rendered 'the governing principle of our actions' (Hume 1975: 50). Thus, for example, if I really do believe that the house is on fire as opposed merely to imagining that it is, I shall not hesitate to flee it. Hume's suggestion prefigures an illuminating remark of the Cambridge philosopher, F.P. Ramsey (1903–30): 'Beliefs are maps by which we steer.' Beliefs have practical consequences for our lives, which are lived, not locked up in the recesses of the private realm of the mind, but in a world of public objects that we have effects upon, and which in turn affect us. Hume was slow to come to see that beliefs cannot consist merely in vivid mental images because he had not perfectly emancipated himself from the very thin Cartesian conception of experience as 'the passing show', *a* kind of internal mental theatre.

The dispositionality of belief

Beliefs are dispositional, not occurrent

There are other reasons for thinking that belief cannot consist merely in having images. Firstly, when I am asleep at night, I still retain my beliefs, but I am not currently aware of them, or of any images. What this brings out is that beliefs are dispositional, not occurrent. I do not have to be perpetually aware of my beliefs, which would be an impossible task: it is sufficient that I can bring them to mind, and act upon them, as and when necessary. Secondly, there are many beliefs which it is impossible to conceive of as consisting in images because of their abstractness. If I have the belief that having images is neither logically necessary nor sufficient for having a belief, what imagery could conceivably embody this complex philosophical belief? Lastly, finding out what beliefs other people have, or other people finding out what beliefs I have, does not consist in trying to discover what mental imagery may or may not be passing through their minds. Rather, it is through their conduct, and mine, including what we say, that our beliefs will be revealed.

Section VI: 'Of Probability'

Tensions in Hume's account of probability

Psychological account of how beliefs in probabilities are acquired

Hume's account of probability, in this very short chapter, anticipates what he will say later in his discussion of miracles. However, it is possible to find tensions within it from its very inception. One strand finds its expression through Hume's account of belief. Why do we believe that the more frequently an event has occurred in the past, in given circumstances, the greater the probability of its occurring in the future? Why, for example, do we believe it is more likely that the weather in Britain will be better in July than in January? Hume's initial answer, drawing on his account of belief, is that repetitions of events print themselves more firmly on our imagination, giving it more force and vigour than it receives from events which occur less frequently. But this naturalistic account, which appeals entirely to an alleged psychological mechanism, offers no reason for thinking that it is more reasonable, or more justified, to believe that it is likely that the weather will better in July than in January in Britain.

Experience provides rational warrant for our beliefs about probability

The other strand in Hume's thinking about this topic may be discerned in a footnote at the start of Section IV. Contrary to what Locke suggested, arguments should not be divided merely into demonstrative and probable: that is, into logical and mathematical proofs on the one hand, where, in valid arguments the conclusions follow with complete certainty from the premises that logically entail them, and on the other, into inductive arguments based on experience, where there is a lack of logical entailment between the premises and the conclusion. If we make this simple division, we shall be led to say that it is only probable that all men will die, or that the sun will rise tomorrow. Yet surely this is too hesitant, too cautious: rather, we have the right to assert that we know these things will occur, without the shadow of a doubt, exceptionless past experience of the occurrence of the events in question fully warranting us in concluding that they will occur in the future. In Hume's words, in addition to demonstrations and probabilities, there can be proofs, 'meaning such arguments from experience as leave no room for doubt or opposition' (Hume 1975: 56).

Internal and external justifications of induction

Of course, this is built on the assumption that the future will continue to resemble the past, and there would seem to be no non-circular way of establishing its truth, as Hume's discussion of induction revealed. But within the *framework* or *practice* of induction there is no doubt that we do calculate the likelihood of the occurrence of a certain type of event on the basis of its frequency in the past and regard this process as rationally warranted. We have, as Strawson recommends in *An Introduction to Logical Theory*, to draw a distinction between asking whether a *particular* belief is justified in terms of good or bad evidence for it, and here we appeal to, and apply, inductive standards. But this is different from asking whether the *practice* of appealing to, and applying, inductive standards *in general* is justified. 'If we cannot answer,' Strawson remarks, 'then no sense has been given to the question' (Strawson 1952: 257). It is a bit like, Strawson goes on to point out, asking whether or not a particular enactment of a law is legal. That is to be judged against the background of established legal or constitutional rules and standards, the law of the land. But we cannot ask whether the legal system as a whole is legal or not, for there are no extraneous, independent legal standards to which we could conceivably appeal.

Although he makes it nowhere explicit in his writings, Hume effectively adopts the kind of response suggested by Strawson, leaving the question of how induction as a practice is to be justified behind, and focusing on how we justify particular beliefs. That is why Hume can write, without inconsistency, that a wise man proportions his belief to the evidence, that it is, in other words, eminently reasonable to grant that past experience can, and should be, our only guide to belief about matters of fact and the likelihood of future occurrences.

review activity

What is the importance of the difference between attempting to justify particular beliefs by the inductive standards, and justifying inductive standards as a whole?

Section VII: 'Of the Idea of Necessary Connection'

This section contains Hume's analysis of cause and effect, which is arguably the single most important and far-reaching contribution he made to metaphysics and epistemology. The originality of Hume's discussion of causality, together with the radical break he made with previous views of the nature of causation, cannot be overestimated. It will be instructive, therefore, before supplying the details of his positive account, to outline briefly the conceptions of causality he was rejecting, and why.

Aristotle had drawn a distinction between four different kinds of cause: material, formal, efficient, and final. The material cause is 'the constituent from which something comes to be'. So, for example, the bronze of a statue is the cause of the statue in that it is the material that comprises the statue and endows it with its particular characteristics. There is some obscurity in the notion of a formal cause, 'the form and pattern', as Aristotle refers to it, but Jonathan Barnes explains it in this way:

> *Consider the following example: 'what it is and why it is are the same. What is an eclipse? – Privation of light from the moon by the earth's screening. Why is*

there an eclipse? or: Why is the moon eclipsed – Because the light leaves it when the earth screens it.' The moon is eclipsed because the moon is deprived of light by being screened and things deprived of light by being screened are eclipsed. Here the middle term, 'deprived of light by being screened' explains why the eclipse occurs; and it states the form or essence of an eclipse – it says what an eclipse actually is. (Barnes 1982: 54)

Aristotle's conception of causality

The third kind of cause, the efficient, corresponds closely to our familiar everyday notion that one event brings about another event, that the administration of poison, for example, brings about sickness and death. By a final cause Aristotle is thinking of the purpose or goal served by some action, for example, taking exercise in order to remain healthy. This concept of cause is far removed from the notion of an efficient cause as the maintenance of health comes *after* the exercise and not before.

Hume cuts through this fourfold distinction of causes by eliminating it at one stroke. In the *Treatise* he writes: 'all causes are of the same kind, and ... there is no foundation for that distinction, which we sometimes make betwixt efficient causes ... and formal, material, and exemplary, and final causes' (Hume 1978: 171). The elimination of Aristotle's distinction helps to simplify the analysis of what will turn out to be a complex enough issue in its own right.

A second target for dismissal is the rationalist conception of causality according to which the effect must be contained in the cause. This models causality on conception and birth: only if the effect is already present in the cause as a child is pre-contained in the womb, can the cause ultimately give birth to it. The reasoning that lies behind this way of thinking argues that the effect will have certain features, but as these cannot have come from nowhere, they can only have been inherited from the cause. Lovejoy sums up this way of conceiving causality well when he writes:

That 'there cannot be more in the effect than there is in the cause' is one of the propositions that men have been readiest to accept as axiomatic; a cause, it has been supposed, does not 'account' for its effect, unless the effect is a thing which the eye of reason could somehow discern in the cause, upon a sufficiently thorough analysis. (Lovejoy 1962: 286)

This principle, subsequently known as the causal adequacy principle, was employed by Descartes in an attempt to prove God's existence.

Now it is manifest by the natural light that there must be at least as much reality in the efficient and total cause as in its effect: for whence can the effect draw its reality if not from the cause? And how could this cause communicate its reality to its effect, if it did not have it in itself? (Descartes 1968: 119)

Trademark argument for God's existence

Applied to the issue of God's existence, Descartes' reasoning runs as follows: I find the idea of God within me, an idea of an infinitely powerful and perfect being. But this idea of infinite perfection could not have originated purely from within myself, because I am a finite and imperfect being. As the cause must contain at least as much reality as the effect, and the effect embodies the idea of infinite perfection, there is only one possible source of this idea, namely God himself. So God placed the idea of himself in me, and therefore God must exist.

Causes cannot be known a priori

Hume totally rejects the causal adequacy principle. Firstly, prior to all experience, anything can be the cause of anything, and there is no reason to suppose that the features of the effect must have been present in the cause. Observation of the effect, however closely it is scrutinised, will never reveal the nature of the cause: we cannot read off causes merely from their effects. Hume writes:

> *The mind can never possibly find the effect in the supposed cause, by the most accurate scrutiny and examination. For the effect is totally different from the cause, and consequently cannot be discovered within it ... A stone or piece of metal raised into the air and left without any support, immediately falls: but to consider the matter a priori, is there anything we can discover in this situation which can beget the idea of a downward , rather than an upward, or any other motion, in the stone or metal? ... In a word, then, every effect is a distinct event from its cause. It could not, therefore, be discovered in the cause, and the first invention or conception of it,* a priori, *must be entirely arbitrary.*

(Hume 1975: 29–30)

Causality is not an instance of logical deduction

Lastly, Hume rejects the assimilation of causality to logical deduction. From the premises 'All A are B' and 'All B are C', we can tell, purely on the basis of reason, that it follows that 'All A are C'. This conclusion can easily be seen to be implicitly contained in the premises. But as effects are entirely distinct from their causes, an effect cannot be told merely from its cause, or a cause purely from its effect. In other words, purely by the use of reason alone, we can never logically deduce the effect from knowledge of the cause alone.

review
activity

What is the causal adequacy principle and on what grounds does Hume dismiss it?

Knowledge of causes and effects founded entirely upon experience

Upon what, then, is knowledge of cause and effect founded? Hume answers once again with the single word: experience, and, we may add, experience of a particular character. It is only because of the repeated conjunction of one type of event A with another type B that we form the belief that A is the cause of B. Experience of the repeated conjunction of A and B gives rise to the expectation that when A occurs, B will follow. In other words, a customary association of A with B is formed in the mind of the observer. All knowledge of cause and effect is ultimately based on this kind of experience according to Hume, and only experience, and never reason, can reveal which events are related to each other as cause and effect. Such, in extremely brief outline, is Hume's positive account of causation. But how was he led to formulate it and to what ultimately does it amount? It is this topic to which we turn in the next section.

Hume says that there are 'no ideas ... more obscure and uncertain than those of power, force, energy or necessary connection' and that his first task is to make these terms clearer. It soon becomes apparent that his aim, more precisely stated, is to explain what is meant by 'necessary connection'. To make Hume's purpose clearer, think of a case where you go out of your house and slam the front door. An instant later a car backfires. Did the closing of the door cause the car to backfire? Our first reaction would be to say no: the conjunction of the two events was a mere coincidence, an impression that is strengthened when we slam the door again and no subsequent backfire is heard.

By contrast, in other cases, those in which we say that one event is the cause of another, we believe there is some kind of connection between the events, and that the pairing is neither accidental, as in the first case, nor the result of a single underlying cause. I hit a golf ball, and it veers off the fairway and into a neighbouring garden, where it smashes a householder's kitchen window. Or I ingest deadly nightshade berries and as a result am violently sick. It is not merely a coincidence, or a statistical freak, that the first of the events described in these two cases was followed by second. The golf ball's striking the window, and the window's subsequently shattering, are events that are somehow linked together in a strong sense, such that were a second or third golf ball struck against a windowpane with the same degree of force, the pane would again break. Likewise, anyone of a similar constitution swallowing a similar amount of deadly nightshade berries could also be expected to fall ill in the same sort of manner that I did.

Is there a necessary connection between cause and effect?

But of what nature is this link, this connection, between events? We commonly speak of the event we describe as the cause, making, or necessitating, the event we describe as the effect to occur. If a window is struck with the appropriate amount of force by a hard object like a golf ball, we feel not merely that it *will* break, but that it *must* break: this is an unavoidable, an inevitable, outcome. Causes are not merely followed by their effects, they are somehow necessitated by them; there is a peculiarly intimate connection between the events such that the one produces, or brings into existence, the second. Causes and effects are bound to each other in some way; they are not merely sequential. That, as I envisage it, is more or less the everyday view of what causation amounts to. The causal relation, the connection between the events, is stronger than constant conjunction. It is, or at least is commonly taken to be, some sort of necessitating relation, in Hume's words, a *necessary connection*. But is there really any such relation, as characterised, after all, and if there is, precisely what is its nature and how do we discover it?

In order to examine this idea of necessary connection and to discern its nature, Hume begins by reminding us of a doctrine he outlined in Section II, namely that all our ideas or concepts are fainter copies derived from our more vivid sense impressions. To check that an alleged concept really is a genuine concept and to ensure that the meaning of the concept is fixed clearly and unambiguously, we must seek the impression from which the concept is derived:

> *By what invention can we throw light upon these ideas, and render them altogether precise and determinate to our intellectual view? Produce the impressions or original sentiments, from which the ideas are copied. These impressions are all strong and sensible. They admit not of ambiguity. They are not only placed in a full light themselves, but may throw light on their correspondent ideas, which lie in obscurity.* (Hume 1975: 62)

However, when we apply this method to the analysis of cause and effect, we find that we are never able to find any impression of power or necessary connection, a *causal glue*, which binds one event to another. Hume illustrates the point with his now famous example of the billiard balls. One billiard ball, A, collides with another, B, which then moves off. We may repeat the experiment and the observation many times, but that is all that ever appears to the outward senses. One ball is seen to move and touch the other, which then moves away. In not a single instance do we observe anything between the two balls which suggests any kind of linkage between them. As Hume himself makes clear:

> We only find that the one does actually, in fact, follow the other. The impulse of one billiard ball is attended with a motion in the second. This is the whole that appears to the outward senses. The mind feels no sentiment or inward impression from this succession of objects: Consequently, there is not, in any single, particular instance of cause and effect, anything which can suggest the idea of power or necessary connection. (Hume 1975: 63)

In the *Treatise* Hume writes in a similar vein:

> It has been observ'd already, that in no single instance the ultimate connexion of any objects is discoverable, either by our senses or our reason, and that we can never penetrate so far into the essence and construction of bodies, as to perceive the principle, on which their mutual influence depends. 'Tis their constant union alone with which we are acquainted, and 'tis from the constant union the necessity arises. (Hume 1978: 64)

However, this passage appears to imply, as the passage from the *Enquiry* does not, that there is a hidden link between cause and effect but it is not discernible either by sense-experience or reason. From the human standpoint then (and what other standpoint is available to us?) the secret nexus between cause and effect, to adapt a remark of Wittgenstein's, whilst not a nothing is not a something either, because it is not discoverable within the limits of experience and nothing can be said about it – 'a something about which nothing can be said is as good as a nothing'.

No impression of necessary connection discernible to the outer senses

It would then appear that, lacking any sense impression of a necessary connection linking the motions of the billiard balls to each other, we have no corresponding concept of it either. Despite what our common sense way of thinking about the matter urges upon us, there is no necessary connection between the motions of the billiard balls. Experience supplies no grounds for belief in such a connection, and indeed, if Hume is right about the origins and applicability of concepts, the very idea of such a connection between events makes no sense. All events, including those that we customarily describe as causes and effects, would seem to be loose and separate and unlinked by any necessitating relation.

But even if we do not acquire the concept of necessary connection from what appears to the outward senses, the possibility still remains that we acquire it by reflection on the inner operations of our own mind and Hume duly considers this possibility. Perhaps, Hume says, it will be claimed that we are at every moment conscious of an internal power, the feeling that by the command of our will, we can move our limbs. However, although we know that we can move our limbs and certain parts of our body if we choose to, we have not the faintest inkling of how we actually do this. We know, from experience, that we have control over some parts of our bodies but not others: we can move our arms, for example, but not our hearts or livers. But as to why we have the ability to move some parts and not others, we are entirely in the dark: 'Were we empowered, by a secret wish, to remove mountains, or control the planets in their orbit; this extensive authority would not be more extraordinary, nor more beyond our comprehension' (Hume 1975: 65).

No impression of necessary connection discernible to the inner senses

We would not be embarrassed by the question of how it is we can move some parts of our bodies and not others were we conscious of a power in the former case and not in the latter. Clearly then, as we have no idea of how it is we can exercise control over some bodily parts and not others, we are not conscious of a power. This conclusion is supported by reflection upon what happens when a person is paralysed:

> *A man, suddenly struck with a palsy in the leg or arm, or who had newly lost those members, frequently endeavours, at first, to move them, and employ them in their usual offices. Here he is as much conscious of a power to command such limbs, as a man in perfect health is conscious of power to actuate any member which remains in its natural state and condition. But consciousness never deceives. Consequently, neither in the one case nor in the other, are we ever conscious of any power. We learn the influence of our will from experience alone. And experience only teaches us, how one event constantly follows another; without instructing us in the secret connection, which binds them together, and renders them inseparable.* (Hume 1975: 66)

But if we do not get the concept of necessary connection from inspection of events from the outward senses, nor from reflection of the operations of our own minds, where, then, does it come from? Hume considers briefly, only to dismiss, one other theory, namely the *occasionalism* invented by Nicholas Malebranche (1638–1715), although Hume does not mention him by name. According to this theory, God is present on all occasions (hence the name occasionalism) when one thing is apparently causing another thing to happen, but in reality it is God who is making the event we call the effect happen by an act of divine volition:

> *Instead of saying that one billiard-ball moves another by a force which it has derived from the author of nature, it is the Deity himself, they say, who, by a particular volition, moves the second ball, being determined to this operation by the impulse of the first ball; in consequence of those general laws which he has laid down to himself in the government of the universe.* (Hume 1975: 70)

Dismissal of occasionalism

But, Hume points out, this explanation explains nothing, for we are not only completely ignorant of how the divine mind is supposed to operate upon matter, but in making such claims, we have totally left the realm of experience within which alone we can make meaningful utterances:

> *We are got into fairy land, long ere we have reached the last steps of our theory; and there we have no reason to trust our common methods of argument, or to think that the usual analogies and probabilities have any authority. Our line is too short to fathom such immense abysses. And however we may flatter ourselves that we are guided, in every step we take, by a kind of verisimilitude and experience, we may be assured that this fancied experience has no authority when we apply it to subjects that lie entirely out of the sphere of experience.* (Hume 1975: 72)

Necessary connection is in the mind as a result of custom or habit

We are still left facing, then, the question of where the idea of necessary connection comes from. Hume's answer is that the very first time we observe one type of event to follow another type, we have no authority to pronounce that the first event is the cause of the second event. But after we have seen a succession of events similar to the first original event constantly followed by the event of the second type, then in future when we see the first kind of event, we form the expectation that the second type of event not only will, but must, occur:

> [T]here is nothing in a number of instances, different from every single instance, which is supposed to be exactly similar; except only, that after a repetition of similar instances, the mind is carried by habit, upon the appearance of one event, to expect its usual attendant, and to believe that it will exist. This connection, therefore, which we feel in the mind, this customary transition of the imagination from one object to its usual attendant, is the sentiment or impression from which we form the idea of power or necessary connection. Nothing farther is in the case.   (Hume 1975: 75)

In more precise detail, what is occurring is this, according to Hume. The senses provide us with an impression of the cause A, and as a result of custom or habit formed by repeated observation of the impression of the cause A being followed by the impression of B, we come to expect the idea of B that is derived from the impression of B as a faint copy. However, we do not merely acquire the idea of B when we have the impression of A, but rather come to believe that B will occur. How does this belief come about? Hume's answer, in line with his claim that belief is 'nothing but a more vivid and intense conception of an idea' (Hume 1978: 119–20), is that the impression of A not only gives rise to the fainter idea of B but transmits a share of its vivacity to the idea of B, transforming it in this way from a mere idea to an actual belief that B will occur. Here then are two further principles governing the operations of the mind which were not discussed by Hume in his chapter dealing with the association of ideas. (a) The experience of constant conjunction creates a union in the imagination of things of two types and, (b) the force and vivacity of a present impression is conveyed to the idea which, through custom, has become associated with it. Hume summarises this line of thought as follows:

> Again, when I consider the influence of this constant conjunction, I perceive, that such a relation cannot be an object of reasoning, and can never operate upon the mind, but by means of custom, which determines the imagination to make a transition from the idea of one object to that of its usual attendant, and from the impression of one to the more lively idea of the other.
>   (Hume 1978: 170)

review activity

1. What method does Hume recommend for becoming clearer about whether we posses a concept of a necessary connection between a cause and its effect?

2. How does Hume explain the formation of our belief that causes necessitate their effects?

We still need to consider the question of what ultimately the idea of necessary connection amounts to for Hume. It would seem that this idea is an exception to Hume's claim that all ideas are copied from impressions, for there is no impression of necessary connection – all we observe in any single instance, or collection of such instances, is that one type of event is followed by another type – and hence it would seem to follow that there can be no idea of necessary connection. Why, then, does Hume repeatedly speak as if there is?

The clue is to be found at the end of the passage quoted above: 'This connection, therefore, which we feel in the mind, this customary transition of the imagination from one object to its usual attendant, is the sentiment or impression from which we form the idea of power or necessary connection. Nothing farther is in the case' (Hume 1975: 75).

Customary transition from idea of cause to idea of effect is a mental operation, not a mental content

In speaking of sentiments or impressions, on the one hand, and ideas on the other, in this passage, Hume, in accordance with the terminology of impressions and ideas he outlined in Section II, would appear to be speaking of *mental contents*. However, it has been convincingly argued by R. P. Woolf (1960: 99–128) that when Hume speaks of the impression of necessary connection he is not speaking of a *content* but an *activity* of the mind. Having no category into which to put such mental operations, Hume resorted to lumping them in with impressions of reflection (see Chapter 2 p. 22). The human mind has a small number of innate propensities, which may be understood in turn as dispositions to form dispositions. When the mind is presented with constant conjunctions of certain sorts of events, the disposition to form a habit of association is activated, so that upon the appearance of the impression of the cause, the idea of the effect consequent upon it arises. Hume writes that the internal impression of necessary connection is the propensity, which custom produces, to pass from an object to the idea of its usual attendant. He also claims that 'the customary transition is the same with the power and necessity'. As Woolf makes clear, Hume is not saying that

> [T]he impression arises from the transition or is conjoined with the impression or is dependent upon the transition; he is saying that the impression is the transition. Now this is plainly an error in classification. 'Customary transitions' and 'propensities' are mental operations or powers, not contents of consciousness. If the idea of necessary connection is a copy of the transition from an impression to its usual attendant, then it is a copy of a mental activity. It is in fact the idea of the mind's disposition to produce related perceptions in the imagination.
> (Woolf 1960: 112)

review
activity

Hume acknowledges that neither the outward nor the inner senses reveal any impression of necessary connection between cause and effect, yet he still persists in talking of such an impression. Why does he do this and what error does he make in the process?

The following passage from the *Treatise* would appear to be in strong accord with Woolf's interpretation of what necessary connection amounts to for Hume:

Upon the whole, necessity is something, that exists in the mind, not in objects; nor is it possible for us ever to form the most distant idea of it, consider'd as a quality in bodies. Either we have no idea of necessity, or necessity is nothing but that determination of the thought to pass from causes to effects and from effects to causes, according to their experienc'd union.

(Hume 1978: 165–6, emphasis added)

In the *Treatise*, Hume provides what he calls the following two definitions of a cause:

T1) We may define a CAUSE to be: 'An object precedent and contiguous to another, and where all objects resembling the former are plac'd in like relations of precedency and contiguity to those objects, that resemble the latter.'

T2) 'A CAUSE is an object precedent and contiguous to another and so united with it, that the idea of the one determines the mind to form the idea of the other, and the impression of the one to form a more lively idea of the other.

(Hume 1978: 170)

In the *Enquiry*, the corresponding definitions become:

E1) [W]e may define a cause to be an object, followed by another, and where all objects similar to the first are followed by objects similar to the second. We say, for instance, that this vibration is followed by this sound, and that all similar vibrations have been followed by similar sounds.

E2) We may ... form another definition of a cause, and call it, an object followed by another, and whose appearance always conveys the thought to that other. '... this vibration is followed by this sound, and that upon the appearance of one the mind anticipates the senses, and forms immediately an idea of the other.'

(Hume 1975: 76–7)

These statements attempting to specify the nature of causation require some comment.

Precedence and contiguity

Contiguity not essential for causality

Whilst in both the *Treatise* and *Enquiry* definitions of the temporal precedence of the cause to the effect are retained (Hume does not consider cases where a cause and its effect coexist, as in a ball resting on a cushion and causing a depression in it), the requirement of contiguity is dropped in the *Enquiry*. This would appear to be the right move to make as it is not difficult to think of instances of cause and effect where the cause is not spatially contiguous to the effect – gravitational and magnetic attraction or repulsion suggest themselves as examples. Moreover, in the mental realm, the question of contiguity cannot arise. A sudden pain in the chest might cause me to think, for the moment, that I am having a heart attack. A pin, stuck in my leg, causes me to feel pain, but the pain is not an object contiguous to the point of the pin.

Objects and events

Hume, somewhat unusually, in both sets of definitions, speaks not of events following each other, but 'objects'. This can make it appear that he is speaking of things causing each other. However, from the example of causation in connection with its definition that he provides in the *Enquiry*, and from the general tenor of his writing about cause and effect, it seems clear that by objects he really intends events. To take the example Hume provides in the *Enquiry*, both vibrations and sounds are occurrences, not things. A guitar string, which is classifiable as an object or thing, is plucked and begins to vibrate; the plucking is an occurrence, and the event consisting of the vibration it gives rise to has a beginning, a duration and an end. Likewise, the sound, caused by the vibration, begins, persists for a time, and then fades away and dies.

Objects, or things, are continuants that persist throughout the changes to the features or properties they possess. So, for example, you and I are continuants: we have changed a lot as we were born, but we have persisted throughout the very considerable alterations in ourselves. An event, by contrast, is not a continuant, and does not persist, but consists instead of temporal stages that can be traced from the beginning of the event until it is over and done with. Consider the event of our birth: in each of our cases, it started presumably with contractions on our mother's part, continued with her going into labour, and eventuated in our gradual emergence into this world.

Events, not objects, the relata of the causal relation

Although Hume frequently uses the term 'object' in various other places he explicitly speaks of events rather than objects: 'It appears, then, that this idea of a necessary connexion among events arises from a number of similar instances which occur of the constant conjunction of these events' (Hume 1975: 75). Hume also, in effect, uses the terms object and event interchangeably in various places:

> *After he has observed several instances of this nature, he then pronounces them to be* connected. What alteration has happened to give rise to this new idea of connexion? *Nothing but that he* feels *these events to be connected in his imagination, and can readily foretell the existence of the one from the appearance of the other. When we say, therefore, that one object is connected with another, we mean only that they have acquired a connexion in our thought*
>
> (Hume 1975: 75–6, emphasis added)

The problem of similarity

Some philosophers, for example, Richard Taylor have found a weakness in Hume's definitions of cause in terms of similarity or resemblance: 'we may define a cause to be an object, followed by another, and where all objects similar to the first are followed by objects similar to the second' (Taylor 1967: 56–66).

Rejection of similarity as a component of an analysis of causality

What does similarity amount to here? If it means exact similarity, even down to spatial and temporal location, then the only events similar to the events in question are the events themselves. On the other hand, if it means a high degree of similarity, then a problem arises, as George Dicker (1998 p. 17) points out. The essence of the objection is this: take some event pair, E1 and E2 such that E1 causes E2, for example, the striking of a match causes it to burst into flame. Now 'E1 causes E2', on Hume's analysis, amounts to (a) E1 is followed by E2, and (b) all events similar to E1 are followed by events similar to E2. Now if these two statements taken together amount to an analysis of 'E1 causes E2', neither can be false 'if E1 causes E2' is true, because together (a) and (b) are supposed to constitute the meaning of 'E1 causes E2'. The problem, however, is that there can be cases where 'E1 causes E2' is true, but (b) is false. There can be cases where events similar to E1 – the striking of a damp match, say, – are *not* followed by events similar to E2, the bursting of the match into flame. The problem cannot be solved by saying that similar must mean similar in relevant respects because this is tantamount to saying 'causally relevant' and this spoils the original analysis of 'E1 causes E2' by importing circularity into it: we clearly cannot use the term 'cause' in trying to provide a definition of what causality is.

Causality obtains between types of event

The objection can be avoided if, rather than using the notion of similarity, we speak instead of one kind or type of event being followed by another type; and in fact we can find this usage in Hume himself, though he prefers to employ the term 'species' instead of 'type'.

> *It is only when two* species of objects are found to be constantly conjoined, that we can infer the one from the other; and were an effect presented, which was entirely singular, and could not be comprehended under any known species, *I do not see, that we could form any conjecture or inference at all concerning its cause.*   (Hume 1975: 148, emphasis added)

review
activity

What weakness affects the attempt to analyse the notion of cause and effect using the concept of similarity, and what is a better alternative analysis?

Evaluating Hume's two definitions of 'cause'

Two different and complementary views of causality

It seems unlikely that, despite his descriptions of them, Hume intended his characterisations of cause and effect as strict definitions, that is, as statements of necessary and sufficient conditions. In any case, in both the *Treatise* and the *Enquiry* the second descriptions T2 and E2 respectively, cannot be equivalent to the first descriptions T1 and E1, as in both cases a psychological element is brought in, describing the effect on the mind of observing repeated instances of similar objects being followed by similar objects. Elsewhere, Hume remarked that his aim was to provide two different views of the same subject. Clearly, the descriptions of causation that include a characterisation of the mental operations produced in us by the experience of regularities cannot be the whole story as it would imply that causality does not exist unless it were actually experienced by some mind or other, or, more weakly, that it was capable of being experienced. But in the natural realm, independently of human minds, contiguity, priority, and constant conjunction continue to operate regardless of whether anyone has experience of them. Indeed, it could be argued that what goes on in the world of nature is the more basic description of causation, as the mind's activity of anticipating the effect upon experience of the cause depends upon the experience of natural regularities and not the other way around. As Hume himself remarks:

Causality consists in universal regularities in nature

What! The efficacy of causes lies in the determination of the mind! As if causes did not operate entirely independent of the mind, and wou'd not continue their operation, even tho' there was no mind existent to contemplate them, or reason concerning them. Thought may well depend on causes for its operation, but not causes on thought. This is to reverse the order of nature, and make that secondary, which is really primary.

(Hume 1978: 167)

In this way, we arrive at a regularity theory of causation: considered in itself independently of its effects on human minds, causality amounts to universal regularities between specified types of event. As Barry Stroud points out:

The existence and precise nature of minds is irrelevant to the question whether members of one class of things are regularly followed by members of another class. But it is only because there are minds that any things at all fulfil the conditions of the second 'definition' [T2 and E2], and it is only because those minds are the way they are that things fulfil the conditions of the second 'definition' whenever they are observed to fulfil the conditions of the first.

(Stroud 1977: 90)

Stroud goes on to say that whilst it appears to be a fundamental principle of the human mind that prolonged exposure to constant conjunctions of different types of events leads a person to expect the second type of event upon experience of the first, it is conceivable that there could be minds that are differently constituted from ours such that the expectation that an event of type B *must* occur, given the occurrence of event of type A, is never formed. These minds will believe that when A occurs B *will* follow, but not that it *must*. Thus Hume's theory commits him to a subjectivist theory of causal necessity: the necessitating relation between cause and effect lies entirely within us, and our belief in its existence is contingent upon the fabric and operations of the mind peculiar to us as a species.

review
activity

Are causes merely natural regularities for Hume?

Hume's projectivism

Why, then, given that the necessary connection between cause and effect, the necessitating relation, lies entirely within us, do we believe that it exists objectively between events occurring independently of human minds? The answer is supplied by Hume's projectivism:

'Tis a common observation that the mind has a great propensity to spread itself upon external objects, and to conjoin with them any internal impressions, which they occasion, and which always make their appearance at the same time these objects discover themselves to the senses. Thus, as certain sounds and smells are always found to attend certain visible objects, we naturally imagine a conjunction, even in place, betwixt the objects and the qualities, tho' the qualities be of such a nature as to admit no such conjunction, and really exist nowhere ... Meanwhile, 'tis sufficient to observe that the same propensity is the reason, why we suppose necessity and power to lie in the objects we consider, not in our mind, notwithstanding it is not possible for us to form the most

distant idea of that quality, when it is not taken for the determination of the mind, to pass from the idea of an object to that of its usual attendant.

(Hume 1978: 167)

Here Hume identifies another principle or propensity of the human mind not mentioned or discussed in the section concerning the association of ideas. It is a principle he will invoke in other contexts, to explain, for example, why we believe the beauty of objects lies in them, rather than in us, or that the vice of a murder is a property of the murder itself, rather than a human reaction to it.

Assessing the regularity theory of causation

Does causation really amount, ultimately, to nothing more than universal regularities obtaining between different types of event, or does this analysis leave something out? Several thinkers have deemed that it does because it seems possible to provide examples of regularities where causality is not involved. An early example is due to Thomas Reid: night regularly follows day, but day is not the cause of night. Arnold Geulincx (1624–69), with his image of two synchronised clocks to illustrate Leibniz's doctrine of pre-established harmony, also called causality, construed as constant conjunction, into question.

Geulincx's objection to the regularity analysis of causality

We are to imagine two clocks, one of which is slightly slower than the other. These clocks run with perfect regularity forever. Spatial contiguity or proximity, a requirement of causality which Hume put in the *Treatise* but dropped in the *Enquiry*, can be provided for by having the clocks touching each other. Now clearly in this situation a particular time, say, one minute to three, on one clock, will always be accompanied by a particular time, say three o'clock, on the other. But neither the first nor second clock is causing the other to show the time it does: the correlation and constant conjunction between the two times is due merely to the near synchronicity of the two clocks.

A more modern example can be found in *Hume's Epistemology and Metaphysics: An Introduction* by George Dicker (1998: 120). We are to suppose that whenever school bells ring in Washington DC, students in New York City schools go to lunch. So when a school bell rings in Jefferson High in Washington, this is followed by students at Dewey High in New York going to lunch. This statement is an instance of the more general statement that all events of the kind school bells ringing in Washington DC are regularly followed by events of the kind students going to lunch in New York. This would seem to satisfy the regularity theorist's analysis of causation, and yet quite plainly it is grossly implausible to suppose that the first type of event gives rise to the second.

A defender of the regularity theory could object that the example of the ringing of the school bells is merely an accidental generalisation that is restricted to a limited range of places, times and individuals. This is what distinguishes it from a genuine causal regularity, a causal law, which employs terms that refer to types of event and is universally true. Causal laws cannot utilise terms that refer to named individuals, places, and times, because they would then lack the required degree of generality.

Genuine causal laws entail counterfactual conditionals

However, whilst this may be true, it does not bring out another very important difference between causal laws and accidental regularities which may be used to distinguish them from each other, namely that genuine causal laws sustain counterfactual conditionals, whereas accidental regularities do not. What this means is best understood by reference to an example. It would appear to be true that if organisms like human beings ingest 10 g of strychnine, then death is the inevitable result. Then we can say that, if human beings do *not* take strychnine, then, all else being equal, they will *not* die. Hume saw this implication of a genuine causal statement when he offered what he thought was an alternative formulation of his first definition of a cause. The first definition runs E1) 'we may define a cause to be an object, followed by another, and where all objects similar to the first are followed by objects similar to the second'; Hume then glosses this statement, 'Or in other words where, if the first object had not been, the second had never existed' (Hume 1975: 76).

Non-equivalence of the regularity theory with the counterfactual analysis

However, as commentators have been quick to point out, these are not merely 'other words'. The second statement is not equivalent to the first. The first type of statement expresses a brute fact of regularity theory: all being equal, whenever one A type of event occurs, a B type of event follows it. But the second statement states a subjunctive, contrary-to-fact conditional, namely that if A had not existed, then B would not have existed. This does appear to capture what is essential to causality and does help us to distinguish between genuine causal sequences and accidental generalisations. Is it true that if the school bells do *not* ring in Washington DC, then the students in New York City will *not* go to lunch? Plainly not, the students will still go to lunch, so we may conclude the ringing of the bells makes no difference and exerts no causal influence. Similarly, in the case of Geulincx's clocks, stopping or removing either one, will not result in any changes to the behaviour of the other. Thus in both these cases no true counterfactuals are sustained and hence causality is not involved.

It is not difficult to construct other cases where one type of occurrence is regularly followed by another type and yet there is no causal relation between them. Consider the true statistic that there is a correlation between the amount of damage done at a fire and the number of fire engines present; the more damage, the more fire engines are there. But although these types of events are constantly conjoined we may not conclude that the fire engines are causing the damage. The explanation of the correlation is or should be obvious: the bigger the fire, the more damage it causes, but then more fire engines are needed to put out a larger conflagration. The two occurrences, the damage and the presence of fire engines, are the collateral products of a single underlying cause, the presence and extent of the fire.

Illustration of the counterfactual analysis of causality

The same point can also be made clear with reference to the shadows on the wall of Plato's cave. A group of prisoners are chained up in such a way that they can only see the cave wall in front of them. Behind them is a low curtain wall and beyond that a fire. Between the fire and the wall there is a procession of people carrying a variety of objects on their heads, and these cast shadows on the wall. Suppose now that the same objects are carried in the same sequences again and again. This means that there will be regularities in the sequences of shadows appearing before the prisoners: a shadow of a vase, say, will always be regularly followed by a shadow of a drinking vessel. Here it might seem that the vase shadow was causing the drinking vessel shadow, as the former regularly precedes the latter. But it is obvious that the shadows are causally impotent to produce other shadows. The real causal work is being done by the fire and the objects that are interposed between it and the wall: this is what is causing the shadows to appear in just the sequences they do. Here then we have constant conjunction but no causality, and this claim can be put to the test by applying the contrary-to-fact conditional analysis of causality to it. Does it follow that if the vase shadow had not occurred, then neither would have the drinking vessel shadow? Clearly not: if the person carrying the vase on his or head had dropped out of the procession, causing the removal of the vase shadow, the drinking vessel shadow would still have been there. This instantly reveals the non-causal relationship between the shadows.

The counterfactual analysis captures the dependency of the effect upon its cause

The great strength of the contrary-to-fact conditional analysis is that it appears to capture something the regularity theory does not, namely the *dependency* of the effect for its occurrence on the cause. As effects can be produced by a multitude of different causes – think of all the possible causes of death, for example – the specification of the cause must take the form of a disjunction, a statement of alternative possible causes. Then we can say 'If it is *not* the case that either John is poisoned, or stabbed, or shot or suffers a heart attack, or ..., or ..., and so on, until all possible causes of death are listed, then he will not die.' In practice we convert this into the modal claim, not merely that he *will* not die, but that he *cannot* die, the possibility of his dying is ruled out, or in other words, it is necessary (though not logically necessary) in some sense that he cannot die. It is this dependency of one type of event on another, something that is objectively discoverable and holds independently of our feelings or thoughts about it, which supplies the necessitating link between cause and effect, and amounts, in effect, to a conception of natural necessity. This link could only be provided for by the regularity theory by locating it within us as an habitual association formed by the operation of custom upon the fabric of the human mind, thus making the necessity entirely subjective.

review
activity

1. Explain and illustrate an objection that can be brought against a regularity theory of causation.

2. What alternative account does Hume suggest?

It has to pointed out that some philosophers would eschew the contrary-to-fact analysis because it appears to rule out the possibility of overdetermination, the kind of case where two independent causes both bring about an effect, even though each one, operating independently of the other, is sufficient to bring about that effect. The standard example here is the firing squad. Let us suppose that there are two soldiers, one on the right whom we will label R, and one on the left, L. These soldiers simultaneously fire their bullets into a vital organ of the prisoner being executed. Intuitively, we want to say that both R and L were causally responsible for the prisoner's death, which is overdetermined by the shootings, even though R alone would have killed the prisoner if L had not fired, and L alone would have killed the prisoner if R had not fired. But the counterfactual analysis prevents this conclusion for the following reasons:

1. If R caused the prisoner's death, then it follows that if R had not fired, the prisoner would not have died. But this is not true, because the prisoner died owing to the actions of L. Hence the original claim that R caused the prisoner's death must be false.

However, equally:

2. If L caused the prisoner's death, then it follows that if L had not fired, the prisoner would not have died. But this is not true, because the prisoner died owing to the actions of R. Hence the original claim that L caused the prisoner's death must be false.

Problems for the counterfactual analysis

We have ended up with the strange conclusion that neither R nor L could have killed the prisoner; because of neither shooting is it true that if it hadn't occurred, the death would not have occurred. Here we are presented with a choice for easing the difficulty we find ourselves in: we can reject the possibility of overdetermination, but this is a highly counter intuitive move; or we can conclude that the counterfactual analysis, despite its obvious appeal as a neat way of distinguishing between genuine causal laws and non-causal regularities, is false. Unfortunately, however, there is no further room to pursue this issue here, but we hope that readers will want to take it forward for themselves. The whole issue of how causality is to be understood is still a vibrant and highly controversial area of philosophy, and, as we hope to have shown, the impetus and contribution Hume imparted to the debate remains one of his greatest achievements.

review
activity

What philosophical difficulty is faced by a counterfactual analysis of causation?

Section VIII: 'Of Liberty and Necessity' Part I

Introduction

This section contains what Hume has to say regarding the ancient and intractable problem of free will and responsibility versus determinism. Nature operates in a uniform and law like manner; certain sorts of events are constantly conjoined with others, such that if an event of type A occurs, then an event of type B follows, given that certain background conditions obtain. In the natural world, and arguably equally in the human realm, the realm of self-conscious active agents, universal causality reigns supreme. Every event that occurs is caused by some other event or combination of events which are sufficient to bring it about, such that were the causes of the event in question removed, it would not happen. This is the doctrine of *determinism*, which was given a striking formulation by the French physicist and mathematician, Pierre-Simon LaPlace:

Explanation of determinism

> *An intellect which at any given moment knew all the forces that animate Nature and the mutual positions of the beings that comprise it, if this intellect were vast enough to submit its data to analysis, could condense into a single formula the movement of the greatest bodies of the universe and that of the lightest atom: for such an intellect nothing could be uncertain; and the future just like the past would be present before its eyes.* (LaPlace 1951)

But if future events are fixed or determined in advance by past events, what becomes of our belief in free will, the belief that at least on some occasions we could have acted differently from the way we actually did act? A good reason for thinking that determinism and free will are *incompatible* is provided by the following argument:

1. All events are caused by other events which are sufficient to bring them about.
2. An event that is caused is necessitated, and no alternative could have occurred.
3. So all events are inevitable.
4. Human actions are events.
5. So human actions are inevitable.
6. Therefore, whatever anyone does had to occur, and no alternative action was possible, given the preceding circumstances.
7. Thus, belief in genuine choice and free will is an illusion.

Apparent incompatibility of determinism and free will

It is difficult to resist the force of this argument, but if we accept it we are placed in a difficult position. Can we really believe, and go around acting on this belief, that no one can ever really help what they do, that their actions, for at least some of the time, are genuinely up to them, and they may legitimately be held to account for them? Yet this is the conclusion to which the argument above appears unavoidably to lead. But what is Hume's response to the issue, and is he correct?

review activity

What do you understand by determinism? Explain in your own words why it is supposed to rule out free will.

Hume's approach to the free will issue

Hume's view: the free will problem is merely a verbal dispute

Hume begins by remarking that when a topic, such as the one at present, has been long discussed, without any settled agreement being reached on the matter, then the dispute is likely to have resulted from a lack of clarity regarding the terms in which it is framed. In other words, the dispute is merely a verbal one, and 'a few intelligible definitions would immediately have put an end to the whole controversy'. In fact, Hume avers, issuing what is in effect a challenge: 'we shall find that all mankind, both learned and ignorant, have always been of the same opinion with regard to this subject ... and that the whole controversy has hitherto turned merely upon words' (Hume 1975: 81).

Hume begins by acknowledging that causality reigns in the natural world: 'every natural effect is so precisely determined by the energy of its cause that no other effect, in such particular circumstances, could possibly have resulted from it' (Hume 1975: 82).

Hume's first and second analyses of causation

This would appear to be in substantial agreement with the thesis of determinism outlined in the introduction to Section VIII (p. 283): effects are necessitated by their causes in the sense that given the occurrence of those causes, the effects that flow from them are unavoidable. However, when Hume turns to a consideration of what necessity means in this context, we find he immediately reverts to his first analysis of causality as constant conjunction and the determination of the mind through habit to infer the effect whenever the cause is experienced. The second counterfactual analysis, according to which, with respect to past actions, (a) *if A had been the case, then B would have been the case*, and regarding future actions, (b) *if A were to be the case, then B would be the case* (see Section VII, p. 280) that Hume suggested, but did not develop, is ignored, and left to one side. We shall return to a consideration of this later. For the moment, let us see how Hume develops his argument in favour of the reality of freewill.

review activity

In what important way does Hume's second analysis of causality differ from his first analysis?

With causality construed as constant conjunction, and the regular, uniform operation of natural causes and effects as exemplified by the laws of nature firmly in mind, Hume extends his analysis to cover the voluntary actions of people and the operations of their minds. We will equally find regularity and uniformity in realm of human psychology and agency, and, given this understanding of what causal necessity really ultimately amounts to, we will find that 'all mankind have ever agreed in the doctrine of necessity, and that they have hitherto disputed merely for not understanding each other' (Hume 1975: 81).

Hume takes great pains in an endeavour to establish the truth of his claim that there is as great a regularity and uniformity in motives and conduct of people as in any part of nature, providing numerous and varied examples: the same motives have operated throughout history; if you want to understand the ancient Greeks, observe the modern French and you will discover that most of what you learn can be transferred, without much change, to the Greeks; if you leave your purse on the pavement at Charing Cross, an area notorious for thieves and prostitutes in Hume's time, you may as well believe it will fly away like a feather as that you will find it untouched an hour later; sellers carry goods to market in the expectation that people will buy them, and they are not disappointed; I can be quite certain that a close and intimate friend will not suddenly fall upon me in a frenzy in order to rob me of a cherished possession; dramas are judged as badly written if the characters do not behave in the ways we have come to expect from experience of common life.

Without the striking uniformity of motive and action, cooperation among people would be ruled out and society rendered impossible. Politics could not be a science, Hume observes, if there were not a uniform influence of laws and forms of government on societies, nor would morality be possible without the constant operation of certain emotions to produce particular sorts of actions. The same applies, we may add using our own example, to teaching: if we had no idea of what methods were likely to help students learn efficiently, or what sanctions and rewards to apply to produce appropriate conduct, educational institutions could not function, nor pedagogy be a discipline worthy of study and implementation.

In short:

Hume's first analysis of causation extended to cover human behaviour

> [T]his experimental influence and reasoning concerning the actions of others enters so much into human life that no man, while awake, is ever a moment without employing it. Have we not reason, therefore, to affirm that all mankind have always agreed in the doctrine of necessity according to the foregoing definition and explication of it.
>
> (Hume 1975: 89)

review
activity

Invent your own example of the uniformity of motive and action.

Apparent counter-examples to the uniformity of motive and action

Hume considers a counter example to his thesis: do we not find irregularities in the behaviour of people, when they do things unexpectedly and predictably? But there is a simple explanation for departures from normal patterns, namely the secret operation of hidden causes. This applies as much in the natural world as the human: a clock stops working, but do we do not conclude that the laws of nature have somehow been suspended and ceased to operate. Further investigation reveals that dust has got into the clock, and this is preventing its normal operation. Similarly, to use Hume's own example:

> The most irregular and unexpected resolutions of men may frequently be accounted for by those who know every particular circumstance of their character and situation. A person of an obliging disposition gives a peevish answer: But he has the toothache or has not dined. A stupid fellow discovers an uncommon alacrity in his carriage: But he has met with a sudden piece of good fortune. Or even when an action, as sometimes happens, cannot be particularly accounted for, either by the person himself or others; we know, in general, that the characters of men are, to a certain degree, inconstant and irregular. This is, in a manner, the constant character of human nature.
>
> (Hume 1975: 88)

review
activity

Why do irregularities in human behaviour *not* show that causality sometimes fails to operate?

Hume's compatibilism: determinism and freedom are compatible

Hume now proceeds to offer his own answer to the problem of free will. Although people behave pretty much predictably, and the same motives give rise to the same actions, the most we can say is that the same actions *follow* the same motives, but are never forced or necessitated by them. There is no necessity out there in the world; it lies entirely in us. From knowledge of a person's desires and beliefs, we can say what he or she *will* do, but not what he or she *must* do. A person wants to buy some cigarettes and believes the shop across the road sells them. He has sufficient money and no other desire, such as the desire to give up smoking, is in the background. Consequently he crosses the road, enters the shop, and purchases the cigarettes. He buys them freely: he is not necessitated to cross the road, or forced, say, at the point of a gun, to hand over his money in exchange for the cigarettes. His action is perfectly explicable in terms of his desires and beliefs, and as the person we are considering is an habitual smoker, and frequently goes past shops selling cigarettes when the craving comes upon him, he often goes into those shops and buys cigarettes. But all the time he performs these actions freely, at least according to Hume. Hume makes the same point in this way:

> *For what is meant by liberty, when applied to voluntary actions? We cannot surely mean that actions have so little connexion with motives, inclinations, and circumstances, that one does not follow with a certain degree of uniformity from the other, and that one affords no inference by which we can conclude the existence of the other. For these are plain and acknowledged matters of fact. By liberty, then, we can only mean a power of acting or not acting, according to the determinations of the will; that is, if we choose to remain at rest, we may; if we choose to move, we also may. Now this hypothetical liberty is universally allowed to belong to everyone who is not a prisoner or in chains. Here, then, is no subject of dispute.* (Hume 1975: 95)

review
activity

What does Hume claim is the true opposite of liberty (free will)? What difficulties does this claim raise?

Hume thus reveals himself to be what has become known as a *compatibilist*: the true opposite of acting freely is acting under constraint, not causation. In the eighteenth century this was known as the *liberty of spontaneity*: as long as you are not forced or constrained to behave in a certain way, and can act in accordance with your wishes and desires, you are free, and can legitimately be held responsible for what you do.

However, there was another conception of liberty current at the time, the so-called *liberty of indifference*, a notion that challenges the belief that the liberty of spontaneity is sufficient for genuine choice and free will. Whilst the liberty of spontaneity, Hume writes in the *Treatise*, 'is oppos'd to violence', (i.e. is the opposite of constraint), the liberty of indifference 'means a negation of necessity and causes' (Hume 1978: 407). In a contemporary formulation owing to Alvin Plantinga, (1932–) an action cannot be free and fully caused, so that only that particular action, in those particular circumstances, could have resulted. What is needed for genuine freedom, Plantinga maintains, is that, 'A person is free with respect to an action A at a time T only if no causal laws and antecedent conditions determine either that he performs A at T or that he refrains from so doing' (Plantinga 1974: 170–1).

The idea lying behind this is that if people were put back in exactly the same situation as the one in which they performed the original action, with all the causal factors exactly the same, they could nevertheless have acted differently from how, in fact, they did act.

The irreconcilability of Hume's second counterfactual analysis of causality with free will

It is difficult to see how this requirement could be reconciled with Hume's second counterfactual analysis of causality. What that analysis would seem to show is that any given type of event is dependent for its occurrence on certain earlier types of event. The recognition of the truth of this is exemplified in the precautions we take to prevent fires. We know that in a given situation there are only a finite number of possible and likely ways in which a fire can start. We therefore take precautions to ensure that the possible and likely causes of fires are eliminated in the hope of rendering the occurrence of a fire physically impossible. The occurrence of a fire is dependent upon conditions discoverable out there in the world: it is therefore an *objective* dependency, one which exists independently of us, and our habits of thinking; it is not merely a subjective feeling projected upon the world, contrary to what Hume's constant conjunction analysis of causality insists. This, I suggest, offers a reasonable account of what causal necessity amounts to, and for the reasons given it seems incompatible with genuine freedom of choice and responsibility.

Incidentally, there is some evidence that Hume was not totally happy with his account of freedom:

> I pretend not to have obviated or removed all objections to this theory, with regard to necessity and liberty. I can foresee other objections, derived from topics which have here not been treated of. It may be said, for instance, that, if voluntary actions be subjected to the same laws of necessity with the operations of matter, there is a continued chain of necessary causes, pre-ordained and pre-determined, reaching from the original cause of all to every single volition [act of will] of any human creature. No contingency anywhere in the universe; no indifference; no liberty. While we act, we are, at the same time, acted upon. The ultimate Author of all our volitions is the Creator of the world, who first bestowed motion upon this immense machine, and placed all beings in that particular position, whence every subsequent event, by an inevitable necessity, must result.
>
> (Hume 1975: 99)

However, to return to the main discussion, it is far from clear that the invocation of the liberty of indifference will supply what we are looking for. Plantinga's denial that a free action has causally sufficient conditions amounts to a statement of *indeterminism*, and there is good reason to think that, at least without the supplementation of a fuller explanation, indeterminism cannot deliver free will. Hume saw very clearly why when he wrote:

> Actions are, by their very nature, temporary and perishing; and where they proceed not from some cause in the character and disposition of the person who performed them, they can neither redound to his honour, if good; nor infamy, if evil. The actions themselves may be blameable; they may be contrary to all the rules of morality and religion: But if the person is not answerable for them; and

as they proceeded from nothing in him that is durable and constant, and leave nothing of that nature behind them, it is impossible he can, upon their account, become the object of punishment or vengeance. According to the principle, therefore which denies necessity, and consequently causes, a man is as pure and untainted, after having committed the most horrid crime, as at the first moment of his birth, nor is his character anywise concerned in his actions, since they are not derived from it, and the wickedness of the one can never be used as a proof of the depravity of the other. (Hume 1975: 98)

Indeterminism cannot guarantee free will

If our actions are not fully caused, there would appear to be an element of randomness in their occurrence. But then they ultimately lack a secure connection to us. Thus, it seems that simply invoking indeterminism to explain how freedom is possible will not work. Thus, attempts which appeal to indeterminism at the quantum level are also ruled out, quite apart from the fact that such indeterminacy does not translate through to the molecular level at which brain processes occur. What more positive account can be offered, however, is unfortunately beyond the scope of this book.

review activity

Why is indeterminism insufficient to account for free will and responsibility?

some questions to think about

1 What is the importance of Hume's remark for the nature of his philosophy that 'all our ideas or more feeble perceptions are copies of our impressions or more lively ones'?

2 'According to Hume, the mind is passive; merely gathering the information given through the senses.' To what extent is this a satisfactory account of Hume's position in the *Enquiry*?

3 Critically evaluate Hume's three principles of the association of ideas.

4 What is Hume's distinction between 'matters of fact' and 'relations of ideas', and what is its importance for his philosophy?

5 'Nothing, at first view, may seem more unbounded than the thought of man, which not only escapes all human power and authority, but is not even restrained within the limits of nature and reliability.' In what way does Hume believe it is possible to possess knowledge of matters of fact beyond the evidence of memory and the senses?

6 Does Hume's account of impressions and ideas show that there are restrictions on thought?

7 Assess Hume's reasons for denying the existence of the idea of necessary causal connection. How does he account for our belief in causal relations and how might that account be criticised?

8 In what way does Hume account for the common belief that the doctrine of necessity does not apply to human conduct? Critically evaluate Hume's view that liberty and necessity are compatible.

9 To what extent is Hume's analysis of the concept of cause acceptable?

10 In matters of human action and freedom, was Hume a determinist?

further reading

▶ Dicker 1998 is a very clear and comprehensive discussion of Hume, which students will find extremely valuable for getting to grips with his thought.

▶ Flew 1986 is an acknowledged expert on Hume, and this book provides valuable insights. However, there may be difficulty in finding it now as it is out of print.

▶ Noonan 1999 is a clear and rigorous book that contains excellent discussions on Hume's empiricism.

▶ Norton (ed.) 1993 is a useful collection of essays on Hume, pitched at a reasonably demanding level.

▶ Stroud 1977 is another very worthwhile book in its scope and treatment of Hume.

III

important terms

John Stuart Mill: *On Liberty*

Anarchy: a society without state rule or any form of coercive authority.

Calvinism: a form of Christian Puritanism, which forbade many activities otherwise regarded as harmless or pleasurable. In its extreme form, it was sometimes understood as holding that pleasure was, by definition, wrong.

Consequentialist: one who believes that the morality of actions is determined by their consequences.

Constitutional: lawful.

Democracy: government of the people, by the people, for the people; a political system where the government is appointed by majority vote of the electorate; in modern times, generally understood to imply that all adult citizens have political equality.

Deontologist: one who believes that moral action consists in doing one's duty.

Dialectic: a means of philosophical enquiry or debate in which a thesis is opposed by an antithesis. Discussion produces a synthesis, which becomes a new thesis for further debate.

Elitism: (belief in) government by the most fitted or able citizens.

Government: ruling or controlling political power.

Hedonist: one who pursues pleasure in the belief that it is the highest good.

Hedonistic (Felicific) calculus: Jeremy Bentham's suggested method of the measurement of happiness, involving such factors as the intensity and duration of the pleasure produced, and the likelihood of an action's long term

The origin and background to utilitarianism: Jeremy Bentham; James Mill; John Stuart Mill

In 1768 Joseph Priestly wrote 'An Essay on Government'. When Jeremy Bentham (1748–1832) read this essay shortly after its publication and found within it the phrase 'the greatest happiness for the greatest number' he realised that this was his own guiding principle in all aspects of morality. The other major factor in his political thought was his later conversion to belief in the virtues of democracy. This change of mind was caused by the Government's failure to fulfil its promise to build a model prison of his design, the Panopticon. In Bentham's view, this innovation would have had enormous benefits both for convicted criminals and law-abiding citizens. A Government that could refuse to implement a plan which was so obviously advantageous to society was not, he reasoned, a Government that had the interests of the people at heart. Therefore, only a Government that was truly representative of the population could ensure that the good of the people was its first priority. In this, of course, Bentham differed from Plato (c.428 BC–347 BC), who is generally regarded as the founder of Western philosophy. Plato held that democracy consisted of people voting for and getting what they want, rather than what they need. He argued that the needs of society, as opposed to its desires, could only be understood, let alone met, by those who possessed wisdom, those whom he called the philosopher-kings. Such people would be relatively few in number, and would require both natural aptitude and proper training for the role of government. Plato's position can be criticised as elitist, or applauded as hard-headed realism. In either case, it is certainly unfashionable and probably politically incorrect in twenty-first-century Western society. In 1808, Jeremy Bentham met James Mill (1773–1836), and under James' influence, Bentham began to take an increasingly active interest in social and political issues. Bentham became a close family friend of the Mills, and was also greatly involved with the education of the young John Stuart Mill (1806–73), who was just two years old at their first meeting.

Bentham's main concern in his writing was the desire to formulate and justify a legal code for society as a whole, rather than a moral code for the individual. He rejected natural moral law, as promulgated by St Thomas Aquinas and others, on the grounds that law and morality are distinct. A law, according to Bentham, is a command, enforced by sanctions such as fines, imprisonment or other punishment. Good laws promote happiness, bad laws do not. A law banning effects producing further pleasure or pain.

Jurisprudence: the science or philosophy of law.

Legislation: the making of laws.

Liberal Party: the party that emerged in the twentieth century as successor to the Whigs (and therefore, until the twentieth century, the major opposition party to the Conservatives).

Liberty: freedom.

Morality: virtue or ethics.

Natural moral law: the doctrine that morality can be deduced from the natural order of things.

Natural rights: rights that are allegedly possessed by all humans, simply because of the fact that they are human. These tend to include the right to life, to freedom, etc.

Policing: keeping in order, or within limits.

Politics: the art or science of government; the making of policy.

Practice: the application of principles in action.

Principle: a general rule that guides conduct, especially in moral and political matters.

Radical: relating or belonging to a political party that favours thorough but constitutional political and/or social reform.

The harm principle: the doctrine that the only legitimate reason to limit freedom is the prevention of harm to others.

The tyranny of the majority: the denial of freedom, whether through law or public opinion, to members of minorities by the majority.

Utilitarian: one who believes that the morality of an action is determined by its usefulness in producing the greatest happiness for the greatest number.

theft is a good law, as it tends to prevent unhappiness. A law requiring everyone to give up coffee, for example, would be a bad law as it would deprive many people of innocent pleasure. Laws may, therefore, be moral or immoral. Bentham did not doubt that laws were necessary, as anarchy, he said, does not promote happiness. A legislative code which was good rather than bad would contain only those laws that conformed to the principle of utility, in other words, those which promoted 'the greatest happiness for the greatest number'.

It is reasonable to observe here that the principle of utility is both unproved and unprovable. One cannot use it to prove itself – that would constitute a circular argument. However, to judge it by any other criterion would be to abandon the principle. Nonetheless, it does seem to be the case that many people and societies, knowingly or unknowingly, accept some version of the principle as a matter of practice.

John Stuart Mill's father, James Mill, was a political radical who attempted to make 'the human mind as plain as the road from Charing Cross to St Paul's' In his *Analysis of the Phenomena of the Human Mind* (1829) he asserted that all knowledge can be reduced to what he called feelings. These consist of sensations, ideas, pleasures and pains. To explain a thought is to analyse it into ideas that have become associated through frequently repeated experience. In this, he was consciously echoing Hume's concept of 'the association of ideas' (see *An Enquiry concerning Human Understanding*, 1777). James Mill firmly believed that education could, potentially, achieve virtually anything. He thought that through education, people's natural tendency to seek personal happiness could be transformed into a desire to achieve the common good. His entry under 'Education' in the 1820 edition of the *Encyclopaedia Britannica* includes an explanation and attempted justification of this view. Modern parlance would probably prefer to describe the process by which we come to consider and act upon the needs and desires of others as 'socialisation', as it appears to occur even in societies where no formal education takes place. In ethics, James Mill's contention was that right actions are those which promote the general happiness, and that approval or disapproval, punishment or reward, are social devices designed to encourage right actions or discourage socially harmful behaviour. He rejected the concept of natural rights. Again, in the 1820 *Encyclopaedia Britannica*, when writing under 'Government', he attempted to demonstrate that representative government is right on utilitarian grounds alone, a contention which was strongly attacked by Macaulay in the 1829 *Edinburgh Review*. Despite opposition, Mill never lost his confidence in the effectiveness of government by representative institutions elected by middle-class adult males. In his view, the only members of society with a sufficiency of education to be able to make informed choices were middle-class adult males. In fairness to James Mill, educated women and educated members of the working classes were virtually unheard of at that time. He also believed that there should be complete freedom of discussion in all moral, political and other contentious spheres.

All the above ideas are important not least because of their influence on John Stuart Mill. Whilst James Mill and Jeremy Bentham are both important British philosophers, John Stuart Mill's reputation and influence far outshine theirs.

John Stuart Mill (1806–73)

Pleasure – the ultimate desire

The preserved body of Jeremy Bentham, founder of utilitarianism. The corpse still attends dinner at the University of London whenever there would otherwise be 13 persons at the table

Nonetheless, without the background and education which they provided, he could not have produced the work which he did.

James Mill had his son educated at home for the first 18 years of the boy's life. John Stuart's lifelong philosophical interests and his dedication to political and other philosophical theorising were undoubtedly formed in childhood. During his twenties he came to disagree to some extent with the theories inculcated by his father, Bentham and the rest of their circle. He formed the opinion that strict utilitarianism, with its hedonistic calculus of pleasures and pains, was too narrow and inflexible. He also differed from Bentham in that, whilst Bentham's main concern was the wish to draw up a legal code for society, John Stuart Mill was more concerned to apply legal theory to private morality. His interest was more to do with the individual than with the masses. This led to the emphasis on personal freedom, which is a defining characteristic of his work. Freedom of opinion, speech and action form no part of Bentham's list of pleasures, and neither is their absence recognised as pain. With this newly added principle of personal liberty, John Stuart Mill significantly extended the scope of the principle of utility.

J.S. Mill seems to assert as a matter of empirical observation that people value pleasure as a good. 'The sole evidence that it is possible to produce that anything is desirable, is that people actually do desire it' (Utilitarianism). Whilst we cannot prove that health is a good, it is possible to demonstrate that people hold it to be so. Everything we desire is, ultimately, pleasurable. Pleasure, therefore, is an end, to which money, health, occupation and many other things are means. Whether or not this argument is accepted, John Stuart Mill's further contention, that the happiness required by the utilitarian standard is 'that of all concerned', is far more problematic. Whilst it might be a good moral precept that we should all care about the happiness of others, it is by no means clear that we do so in fact. Being concerned with the welfare of others seems to be a characteristic into which we are socialised, or educated. A newborn baby has no obvious recognition of the existence, let alone of the needs and desires, of others as individual beings. A baby instinctively seeks only to fulfil its own needs and to obtain comfort for itself. It can be argued that few, if any, people ever do achieve the empathy that J.S. Mill espouses. Indeed, according to current psychological thought, around one per cent of the population is sociopathic and, therefore, psychologically incapable of empathy, whilst often tending to be very successful in the business of making a living.

J.S. Mill's contributions to politics and philosophy began in the early 1830s, when he wrote a number of essays on economic issues, which were published in 1844. He also wrote on the philosophy of logic and it was the publication, in 1843, of A *System of Logic, Ratiocinative and Inductive* that made his name. *Political Economy* followed in 1845. *On Liberty*, described by J.S. Mill as 'a joint work' with his wife Harriet, was published in 1859, a year after her death.

J.S. Mill was a champion of the rights of women and of the working classes, and an activist for political reform. His election as Member of Parliament for Westminster in 1865 enabled him to add a proposal for votes for women as an amendment to Disraeli's Franchise Bill. By the time of his death at the age of 67, J.S. Mill was recognised as the leading English radical of his generation, and the major link between liberal thinking in England and other nations, notably France, where he maintained a second home for much of his life.

J.S. Mill's utilitarianism

Higher and lower pleasures

Mill's moral and political theories are based upon two fundamental principles:

1. Pleasure alone is good or desirable in itself.
2. Actions are right if they tend to promote the happiness of all concerned, wrong if they tend to cause unhappiness. Mill defines happiness as pleasure and the absence of pain.

He did not, in fact, hold that all pleasures are equally desirable (although he did describe himself as a hedonist). He distinguished between higher and lower pleasures, and urged that people should choose the higher. These include the pleasures of generosity and the intellect. He held that 'It is better to be a human being dissatisfied than a pig satisfied; better to be Socrates dissatisfied than a fool satisfied.' Socrates himself maintained that the pleasures of the intellect are to be preferred to the pleasures of the flesh, adding that all those who have experienced both would agree.

Whilst a number of students of philosophy and other subjects have vehemently disagreed during the last two or three thousand years, Socrates would have argued that they have had neither the maturity nor the experience to make a valid judgement until after the age of at least 30. An important question is whether, in fact, all people are capable of experiencing intellectual pleasure. J.S. Mill held that, with education, they could become so. Socrates would certainly have disagreed, on the grounds that only a minority of people are born with the necessary capacity to experience intellectual pleasure. This is an important argument in politics, and for society as a whole. J.S. Mill disapproved of state-provided education, but given that it exists, proper and appropriate educational policy would need to be very different depending upon whether Mill's or Socrates' view is correct.

Pleasure through intellectual attainment

If Socrates is right, and only some people have the inborn ability for intellectual activity and the pleasure that it can generate, then selection on the basis of ability and potential achievement, with separate schooling for those of differing levels of ability, is obviously the proper educational route. Indeed, the tripartite grammar, technical and secondary modern school system which existed in Britain from 1944 until the 1960s (and in some areas, to the present day) was formulated upon the basis that Plato's *Republic* depicted an accurate reflection of the academic and intellectual potential of the members of society. If, on the other hand, J.S. Mill is right in saying that everyone can achieve intellectual attainment and get pleasure therefrom, then everyone should, logically, advance through the same comprehensive system, although perhaps at different rates.

When he argued that people should act so as to promote 'the greatest happiness for the greatest number,' J.S. Mill asserted that 'the aggregate of all persons' regarded the general happiness as a good. This may or may not be true, but commentators have generally agreed that J.S. Mill's works do not contain its proof. Mill held that people do in fact possess social impulses and tend to consider the welfare and happiness of all concerned. This tendency, he maintained, can be strengthened by training and practice. In this, he seems to be thinking along similar lines to Aristotle, who, in *The Nicomachean Ethics*, wrote that one can become virtuous in character by practising the performance of virtuous acts. Mill was certainly at one with Jeremy Bentham, who stated that our decisions are made because of our characters and beliefs, and that it is possible, if one wishes to do so, to change one's character for the better and to amend and improve one's beliefs. If this is true, it must still be asked how and why it is possible for people to develop the desire to change.

J.S. Mill holds that education is the means whereby change is effected. Is it also the case that education can provide the motive for desiring to change? Or is it the case that social disapproval of some actions, or the unpleasant results that some actions may bring about, causes the desire for change, and that education then provides the means? It is by no means clear that social disapproval always exists, even where actions are causing unhappiness to others. Neither is it the case that all actions that damage others have unpleasant consequences for oneself. Mill's contention that social impulses exist in most people is certainly not proved.

There are many arguments against utilitarianism in general. The utilitarian maxim 'always act so as to promote the greatest happiness for the greatest number' can be attacked on two major grounds, both of which make the argument that consequentialism is simply not the correct way to make moral decisions.

Deontologists would argue that some things are always right and/or that other things are always wrong. They would claim, perhaps, that God prescribes proper behaviour, or that we owe our duty to some other code. If it is wrong to murder, for example, then it is possible to argue that euthanasia and abortion are both forbidden. The other ground of disagreement is the impossibility of knowing the consequences of one's actions. Mill seems to argue that, in general, we can know the probable outcomes of our actions, and that we should be guided by the normal rules in society which have been developed through experience. Only when two duties conflict do we have to calculate in order to find the best, most moral, course of action.

Liberty as a general principle

The exercise of liberty

The principle of utility, J.S. Mill held, requires the exercise of liberty. He wrote 'I regard utility as the ultimate appeal on all ethical questions ... utility in the largest sense, grounded on the permanent interests of man as a progressive being' (Mill, On Liberty: 1859). Therefore, he argued, we should all have freedom to pursue 'our own good in our own way, so long as we do not attempt to deprive others of theirs, or impede their efforts to obtain it'. Freedom, he argues, is necessary for 'mental well-being' and therefore conduces to happiness.

Here Mill is developing Bentham's utilitarianism. Bentham did not list freedom, or the lack of it, in his felicific calculus. In saying that good government and jurisprudence must uphold individual freedom, Mill is introducing a new criterion, but maintaining the primacy of the principle of utility.

Mill is very clear that the liberty that he supports is not free will (which he rejected as a concept) but 'civil, or social, liberty: the nature and limits of the power which can be legitimately exercised by society over the individual' (Mill, On Liberty: 1859).

In the past, he maintains, the rulers were likely to oppress the populace and rights had to be fought for or negotiated. As various forms of democracy gradually replaced tyranny, the belief tended to be that the people no longer needed protection from their Government, as democratic government is of the people. However, he states that there is a threat contained within democratic societies: 'the tyranny of the majority'. It is possible, he says, that 'the people ... may desire to oppress a part of their number' – and that legislation may be drawn up to enact this desire to oppress. In modern times, various groups including, for example, travellers and asylum seekers may believe themselves to have reason to agree with this analysis.

Further, says Mill, quite apart from oppression via the legal system, minorities may find themselves subject to 'social tyranny ... the tendency of society to impose ... its own ideas and practices as rules of conduct on those who dissent from them' (Mill, On Liberty: 1859).

It may well be the case that, at least in some sections of society, people whose race, religion, culture, lifestyle or opinion places them in a minority can find themselves socially excluded and harassed by the legal system. This, indeed, is one of the arguments of the Countryside Alliance in relation to hunting with hounds. They assert that a ban on hunting with hounds is the imposition of the values of an urban majority upon the rural minority. Those who live in towns have no knowledge or understanding of the lifestyle and needs of those who live in rural areas, yet ignorantly impose their prejudices upon country-dwellers.

Mill argues that agreement to differ has never, in practice, been granted. He holds that society as a whole expects every individual to conform to custom, and that every attempt is made to enforce this expectation. Only in matters of religious belief has tolerance been extended – and then only in theory or within limits.

In Mill's analysis, government interference in the nineteenth century was less onerous in England than in other democracies, although the weight of public opinion was greater. He predicted that when the public identifies more closely with politicians, 'individual liberty will probably be as much exposed to invasion from the government as it already is from private opinion' (Mill, On Liberty: 1859).

The 'nanny state' There are a number of contemporary issues that may illustrate J.S. Mill's thesis. It might be salutary to reflect upon whether, now that most MPs are from the ever-expanding middle and professional classes, 'nanny-statism' has indeed increased. Intolerance of smoking in public places, as well as the bill to ban fox-hunting mentioned above, and attempts to outlaw physical chastisement by parents of their children are all, arguably, constraints upon the liberty of the individual. Campaigns designed to regulate diet and other health issues, concerning which the Government is considering possible legislation, might be subject to the same criticism. If people choose to smoke and to eat unhealthily until they are claimed by an early grave, of what business, a libertarian might ask, is that to the Government? Those who die early, after all, save society a fortune in unpaid pensions, do not need long-term medical treatment and nursing care in frail old age, and, in the case of smokers, contribute huge amounts of tax revenue for the benefit of society.

Nor is it a valid argument to say that recent legislation and proposed legislation is in line with the principle, espoused by Mill, that all activities that are harmful to others are the proper concern of the law. Whether passive smoking does, in fact, kill, is still contested. Even if it does, the figure quoted by anti-smoking campaigners is usually around 46 untimely deaths per year. Most, if not all, of these could be avoided only if smoking was banned in the home, which is where non-smokers, including children, are most exposed to the fumes of smoking relatives. Even the Kingdom of Bhutan, which has recently outlawed the sale of tobacco products, has not gone to such an extreme. Individuals may still import cigarettes and cigars for their own personal consumption at home, albeit subject to 100 per cent taxation. The consumption of alcohol is related to far more human suffering inflicted upon others than is the use of tobacco. Quite apart from the death, injury and damage inflicted by drunken driving (which is, of course, a criminal offence), a large percentage of other crime and antisocial behaviour is carried out by those who have had too much to drink. This includes domestic violence, criminal damage, the abuse and neglect of children, brawls and arguments in public places and other generally unpleasant behaviour. Add to this the number of unwanted pregnancies, infections by sexually transmitted diseases and other personal and social problems suffered by those under the influence of alcohol, and there is probably a better case for outlawing the consumption of intoxicating liquor than there is for banning smoking. There is no question at all that the banning of private cars would save innumerable people from death and injury every day, as well as being a major factor in limiting damaging air pollution and the emission of greenhouse gases. When it comes to fox hunting, the only human beings damaged thereby are the riders who fall and kill or injure themselves. Mill would maintain that putting oneself into danger is a voluntary act, which is no business of the state's. Whilst it is true that some foxes are killed, it is also the case that we routinely exterminate other vermin such as rats, fleas, head lice, clothes moths, wasps and flies, among others. There are relatively few who object to this. Indeed, bacteria and viruses, both of which are unquestionably life forms, are eradicated at the public expense by the provision of medication on prescription. It is interesting, too, to note that coarse fishing and angling are not currently under threat of legal sanction. Practitioners with rod and line unquestionably enjoy their activity (as do hunters with hounds) and frequently do not eat, nor do they intend to eat, their catch. Where, if at all, is there any moral difference between the two pursuits? And where would a utilitarian draw the line between issues properly to be addressed by legislation and those that are matters of private morality?

Personal freedom and the harm principle

Mill's basic premise is that the only moral justification for interference with anyone's liberty is to prevent harm to others. He states categorically that it is wrong to visit any sanction, legal or social, upon one who is harming only himself or herself. Whilst he accepts that there are good reasons for arguing with, or trying to persuade, someone who intends self-harm, there are no good reasons to compel him to abandon his intended course of action. 'Over himself, over his own body and mind, the individual is sovereign.'

Not all societies are equal

Mill does recognise some exceptions to this doctrine. Those who are not yet adult need to be protected from themselves. Interestingly, Mill accepts that the age of adulthood is properly fixed by law. Given that the legal age of adulthood varies between different communities and can be anything from 12 to 21 years of age, there are obvious issues for discussion here. Mill also refers to 'backward states of society in which the race itself may be considered as in its nonage' (Mill, On Liberty: 1859). Politically incorrect as this may be thought today, in the nineteenth century it was uncontroversial to assert that some societies were more mature, both politically and morally, than others. It is certainly still true that democracy (and its underlying political assumptions) is non-existent in some parts of the world, and in its infancy in others. And indeed there are those today who argue that some cultures are underdeveloped with regard to political maturity. Quite how 'backward states of society' are to be treated is not clear. Should they be left alone until they 'mature'? Or should more 'enlightened' nations make paternalistic attempts to provide the necessary political education, that they be led to maturity? At the time of the British Empire, most people would have argued that we were right to 'shoulder the white man's burden' and show less enlightened nations the way forward. Some contemporary commentators have said the President George W. Bush believes that going to war with Iraq, the toppling of Saddam Hussein and the subsequent democratic elections have been the means of instituting political development in that country. Arguments put forward by both American and British politicians, that the war and its aftermath have prevented more harm than they caused, for example, 'More people would have died under Saddam' do sound as if they have a utilitarian basis. So too does the argument that the replacement of tyranny by democracy will bring about greater happiness. Others might argue that no individual has the right to interfere with another's actions save to prevent harm to others; by analogy, no state should interfere with the actions of another sovereign state save in defence of itself or a third party.

However, as J.S. Mill was in fact mostly concerned with Britain, it is most appropriate to consider his dicta in that context. A truly free society, says Mill, allows three basic freedoms: liberty of thought, which includes freedom to speak and to write one's opinions; liberty of tastes and pursuits, so that we can live as we choose so long as we harm no one else; and liberty of combination – the right to unite with others provided there is no intention to cause harm and provided those with whom we unite are adult, not forced and not deceived.

Liberty of thought and discussion

Freedom of expression

Mill supports liberty of thought and discussion of 'any doctrine, however immoral it may be considered'. To suppress an opinion, even if held by only one person, is to rob the human race, both now and in the future, of the chance to develop. If the opinion is right, we are robbed of the opportunity to correct our existing errors; if it is wrong, we are denied the capacity to more clearly appreciate the truth.

None of us is infallible; therefore, an opinion with which we disagree may nonetheless be true. Different cultures at different times have all been certain that the general opinion is right – but this is clearly not the case, given the huge differences in prevailing beliefs over time and throughout the world. We need to test the truth of, or recognise the error in, all beliefs, no matter how widely held. To censor alternative opinions because we believe them to be 'bad' is to stifle the opportunity to learn and progress. Mill argued that, at the time he wrote, certain beliefs were regarded as worthy of protection from challenge because of their usefulness to society. Mill maintains the overriding importance of truth. 'The truth of an opinion is part of its utility ... no belief which is contrary to truth can be really useful' (Mill, On Liberty: 1859). Here again we have an example of the fact that Mill believed in the capacity of all to recognise and understand the truth. Plato had no faith in the universality of this capacity. He argued that as most people would never achieve knowledge of the truth, it would be necessary for the philosopher-kings, who did, to promulgate a myth which the ordinary people would accept. In this way, society could be run by the knowledgeable for the benefit of all. Plato, therefore, would have claimed, had the word been current at the time, that untruth could be utilitarian!

Mill discusses the case of belief in God. There is no problem, in his view, with an individual so believing. The problem arises when anyone tries to impose this belief upon others, or to prevent them from hearing the opposing arguments. He points out that both Socrates and Jesus of Nazareth were condemned to death for their allegedly anti-religious statements – Socrates for impiety and immorality, Jesus for blasphemy.

Religious persecution

Yet both Socrates and Jesus are now recognised as, at the very least, great moral teachers. Marcus Aurelius, a great ethicist and humanitarian, persecuted Christianity in the sincere belief that it was socially harmful. Mill acknowledges that there is an argument for saying that truth will out: attempted repression of that which is true will ultimately fail. As Gamaliel put it in Acts 5 'if this work be of men, it will come to naught: but if it be of God, ye cannot overthrow it'. Mill is less complaisant: 'History teems with instances of truth put down by persecution, if not suppressed for ever, it may be thrown back for centuries.'

At the time he wrote, however, he accepted that actual persecution, in the sense of legal sanctions, had become rare. Almost more worrying, however, was the fact that everyone apparently felt obliged to pay lip service to received opinion, thus stifling intellectual debate in the interests of peace.

It may be salutary to consider whether this tendency has continued to grow in society today. It is certainly true that in many parts of the world religious observance is no longer expected, but political correctness has arguably rendered some opinions socially unacceptable. In particular, minority views about issues of sexual morality, such as fornication, divorce, single parenthood and homosexuality may go unvoiced for fear of ridicule or worse. Minority views about racial issues can rarely be voiced in polite conversation. Such timidity, argues Mill, may be denying the world previously unknown truths. It is the duty, he declares, of a thinker to follow his intellect. Even if he is led into error, Truth will ultimately gain as the error, if stated, can be recognised and corrected.

Even where the truth is known, unless it is open to challenge it becomes 'dead dogma'. People accept the received opinion without understanding the premises upon which it is based. Unless they have the opportunity for discussion, they will be unable to defend the truth if and when it is challenged. In any case, one should know the reasons for one's opinions, else truths become, effectively, mere superstition. This, Mill suggests, is what had already happened to Christianity in the nineteenth century. 'The doctrines have no hold on ordinary believers – are not a power in their minds. They have ... no feeling which spreads from the words to the things signified ...' (Mill, On Liberty: 1859).

It may be relevant here to consider how closely Mill's argument in favour of being able to support one's views reflects the suggested definition of knowledge as 'justified true belief' which was discussed in Plato's *Theaetetus*. It would seem that Mill does indeed hold that one should be able to give good reason for holding a belief; be able to refute opposing arguments; and where possible, demonstrate the truth, or likelihood, of one's belief.

Except in subjects such as mathematics, where there is absolute certainty, one should, says Mill, study both sides of the argument. This even applies in science, where different hypotheses compete, and is even truer in morality, religion, politics, law and similarly disputed areas.

Mill contrasts the state of religious belief, and the understanding of the underlying principles thereof in his own time, with that of the Early Church. Members of the Early Church had continually to defend their beliefs against well educated and intelligent opponents. In nineteenth-century Britain, the doctrines of the Church were more or less unthinkingly adopted by most members of society. As a result, few people could defend the teachings if challenged.

Today, the wheel may almost have been said to have come full circle. In the Western world, active believers are in a minority in many countries. Christians and other religious believers who are most articulate about their beliefs, or at least, most noticeably so, are those who feel most threatened by the norms of modern society. Opponents, for example, of legal abortion, the genetic engineering of embryos and other medical and scientific innovations, along with the proponents of biblical fundamentalism and, for example, the judicial death penalty, are well versed in their own arguments and in those of their adversaries. Similarly, adherents of minority political opinions tend to be more familiar with the various arguments from all parties than otherwise politically inactive voters for the more mainstream parties.

Truth or falsehood?

So, says Mill, we should listen to contrary opinions (a) because they might be true, and displace an accepted falsehood; (b) because if false, they ensure that we can understand and articulate the truths which we hold. More often, though, he says, the two 'conflicting doctrines … share the truth between them, and the nonconforming opinion is needed to supply the remainder of the truth' (Mill, On Liberty: 1859). Here we arguably have a species of dialectic, where thesis and antithesis are transmuted through discussion into synthesis. Most of the truths we know, says Mill, are partial, or mixed with falsehood. Unusual, or non-mainstream, opinions frequently contain the missing parts of the truth or corrections to the falsehoods. He adduces the necessity for both conservative and progressive political parties to exist 'until the one or the other shall have so enlarged its mental grasp as to be a party equally of order and of progress' (Mill, On Liberty: 1859). Interestingly, many commentators and voters say that they can see little difference between the two major parties in Britain now, though few, if any, individual members of society would argue that either party has achieved a full grasp of the truth. The smaller parties, however, are still usually identifiable as being of the right ('orderly') or left ('progressive') persuasions. Mill makes it clear that no views should be suppressed on the grounds that they are offensive. He is adamant that the giving of offence does not, of itself, constitute harm. Therefore, views should not be suppressed simply on the grounds that they cause offence. Those who employ unfair tactics in argument damage their own case, but the law should have no part in suppressing the free expression of opinion. In fact, there are laws in Britain against slander and libel (deliberate lies, spoken and published respectively) against living persons. As the truth or otherwise of statements about people's actions and characteristics can be argued in the courts, this may be fair enough, provided no one is prevented from pursuing a case on financial grounds. However, lies about the dead are not legally punishable, although they might lead to personal or academic criticism. Perhaps Mill's strictures are more relevant to blasphemy laws. Although little used in recent times, blasphemy against Christianity (although not against other faiths) is still a punishable offence. Are the feelings of Christians properly to be considered in this way? Or is Richard Dawkins right when he argues that he sees no reason to respect religious sensibilities as faith has no basis in logic or in reasoned argument?

Individuality: liberty to act upon one's opinions

Liberty and the harm principle

Mill accepts that actions cannot be as free as opinions. One is only entitled, when acting, to put oneself at risk. The harm principle forbids damaging or endangering others. Even opinions may not be freely expressed in circumstances where such expression could cause harm. Mill uses the example of telling an excited mob, gathered outside a corn dealer's house, that corn dealers starve the poor. This could be an incitement to violence. In more recent times, the declaration (often unfounded) that a member of the local community is a paedophile has led to criminal damage and assault. On one occasion, the unfortunate victim was in fact a paediatrician – a doctor specialising in the treatment of children! 'The liberty of the individual must be thus far limited; he must not make himself a nuisance to other people' (Mill, On Liberty: 1859). The facts (as Mill sees them) of human fallibility, that known 'truths' are only partial truths, and that diversity is a good, lead inescapably to the conclusion that actions which affect only oneself should be free. It is good that different modes of living should be empirically tested. Mill is concerned 'that individual spontaneity is hardly recognised by the common modes of thinking as having any intrinsic worth'. Indeed, he says, individuality of expression is seen as 'troublesome and rebellious'. Whilst generations of young people may enthusiastically have agreed with these propositions, one has to ask at what stage one should draw the line. Mill says that one may offend, but not harm. The distinction is not always clear – it is not always possible to foresee the results of ones actions. I may be irritated by the noise and disturbance of fireworks at any time, but if I have a migraine, I will suffer additional pain from the loud sounds and bright lights. I may be offended by the gang of teenagers demanding 'trick or treat' on my doorstep on a dark night, but the widowed little old lady with a weak heart who lives next door may be frightened and suffer physical harm as a result. Some lifestyle choices might in fact cause damage that only becomes obvious after the event. Single parenthood, studies seem to show, does in general have a deleterious effect upon the children, with consequent damage to society in terms of increased delinquency, lower employability and a greater susceptibility to health problems. Interestingly, surveys suggest that the children of widows and widowers do not seem to experience the same problems as do the children of divorced parents or those born to parents who never were married. Mill accepts that social customs are based upon experience 'and as such, have a claim to [the individuals] deference'. However, he argues, this experience may be too narrow or may have been misinterpreted. Even where the interpretation is correct, it may not apply to every individual, as some people's circumstances may be unusual. In addition, to blindly follow custom is not to develop the human qualities of 'perception, judgement, discriminative feeling, mental activity and even moral preference' (Mill, On Liberty: 1859). Those who allow custom to rule their lives have only one faculty: 'the ape-like one of imitation'. Those who consciously choose how they should act are making use of all their faculties. Mill asserts that self-discipline and conscience are needed. He accepts that in the past, law and religious discipline were necessary to deal with strong characters whose energies exceeded their self-control. He goes on, however, to state that the pendulum has swung too far and that people now act as they believe they should, rather than as they wish to do.

To conform or not? However that may have been in the nineteenth century, it should be considered whether this analysis is true of individuals today. Is it the case that individuals feel under pressure to conform? Do conformists, in fact, make a reasoned choice to be so? And, perhaps more tellingly, it should also be asked how can anyone be nonconformist if there is no socially accepted norm? One can only be different, nonconformist or eccentric if there is a usual standard from which to vary. Mill criticizes the Calvinistic view that everyone should obey a strict set of religious and moral laws, which, he claims, in a diluted form have spread to many others. He holds that it is more likely that a 'good Being' who created us would wish 'all human faculties [to] be created and unfolded'. This view is indeed in line with mainstream Christian thought today – although perhaps with the caveat that just as human beings should not be harmed, neither should God be mocked. In other words: 'Love the Lord thy God with all thy heart, soul, mind and strength, and love thy neighbour as thyself. This is the whole of the law: the rest is commentary' (Rabbi Hillel, endorsed by Jesus in his conversation with the lawyer, which preceded the parable of the Good Samaritan). It is interesting that this religious doctrine implies the need for self-love: in this too it differs from utilitarianism. However, Mill also goes on to argue 'in proportion to the development of his individuality, each person becomes more valuable to himself, and is therefore capable of being more valuable to others' (Mill, On Liberty: 1859). And indeed, to decide to act as an individual argues a belief in one's own self-worth. Mill goes on to argue that those who have originality of thought may lead others to learn. The world is not yet perfect; those who discover new truths (or who prove the existing beliefs to be wrong) are 'the salt of the earth, without them human life would become a stagnant pool'. Whilst Mill concedes that it is true that only a small number of individuals are persons of genius, 'in order to have them, it is necessary to preserve the soil in which they grow'. Here, Mill does seem to acknowledge that some people are more fitted to be leaders – at least in terms of academic and intellectual thought – than are others. He criticises a tendency towards mediocrity and a belief that original thought is either dangerous or useless. In this, he reflects Plato's comments about how Greek society in the fourth century BC regarded philosophers. Mill asserts that individuals have lost power:

> *In politics, it is almost a triviality to say that public opinion now rules the world. The only power deserving of the name is that of masses, and of governments whilst they make themselves the organ of the tendencies and instincts of masses ... in England, chiefly the middle class is probably ... a collective mediocrity ... Their thinking is done for them by men much like themselves, ... Speaking ... through their newspapers.* (Mill, On Liberty: 1859)

The reader may judge how true this criticism remains today; always allowing that TV may now be the most influential medium. The question also arises: do the media reflect, or give rise to, public opinion? Does a red-top newspaper campaign against asylum seekers, for example, report existing beliefs in society, or does it cause people to adopt the viewpoint urged? Is it really true that 'it was the *Sun* what won it' in the case of a general election?

Quite apart from the benefits of nonconformity for the gifted 'one of few' (a refection of Plato's philosopher-kings again?) Mill argues that, as conformity to the mediocre is so established, 'the mere refusal to bend the knee to custom is itself a service'. It shows others that one can dare to be different. 'That so few now dare to be eccentric marks the chief danger of the time.' In any case, says Mill, just as we all vary in the size of shoes or clothes that best fit us, so we vary in the lifestyle which gives each individual the maximum benefit. Mill further urges that nations are only progressive and influential as long as individuality flourishes. Once custom becomes the accepted arbiter, progress ceases. In this he may or may not be right – recent history, however, would argue that whilst some individuals have departed from social norms and had enormous impact, they have unfortunately rarely adhered to the harm principle in the process. Here there is a criticism not only of Mill but of radical/progressive theorists in general. Many political commentators have observed that there is a tendency for those on the left of politics to believe in the essential goodwill of all human beings. Historical examples of those such as Hitler or Stalin, who would seem to indicate otherwise, are seen by progressive thinkers as aberrant, or indeed insane. Right-leaning thinkers tend to have a more cynical view of human nature and are wary of the damage that charismatic individuals can do. It may well be that there is an ultimately true synthesis somewhere between these positions, but adherence to the harm principle only takes place where law and public opinion enforce it. If law and public opinion oppose it, are indifferent to it, or interpret it in a way which Mill would have abhorred, we end up with concentration camps and genocide, or at a less extreme level, with the forced repatriation of immigrants and their descendants as a declared political stratagem.

Homogenisation of experience

Mill worries that as European society becomes increasingly homogenous and lacking in 'variety of situations', stasis will set in. He was concerned that, in his day, people's experiences were becoming increasingly alike. Whether this has continued to be true is a matter for debate. It could be argued that cheap and rapid travel has led to many people experiencing other cultures and ways of living. Few people, other than the rich, had the time or money for extended travel in Mill's day. How much there is an appreciation of these differences in outlook and lifestyle may, however, be questionable. If it is the case, as some allege, that most travellers spend their time in the hotel and on the beach, and tend to seek out and eat similar foods to those which they enjoy at home, this would tend to support Mill's contention. In fact, holiday travel and the desire on the part of tourist centres to provide for their guests' preferences may be leading to more similarity between previously differing societies and cultures. This would further lessen the variety that Mill espouses.

Liberty of combination

Freedom to come together

In *On Liberty*, J.S. Mill does not devote a separate chapter to the freedom to associate with whom one pleases. It is nonetheless clear that he believed that people should have the right to come together for any purpose, provided all consented to any activity which was taking place, and that the harm principle was not violated. In general, this freedom is recognised in democratic societies, although there are exceptions. Elsewhere in the world, however, political and religious meetings of various descriptions are, and have been, banned. In Soviet Russia, for example, churches and synagogues were forcibly closed or forbidden to increase their membership. In some (but by no means all) Islamic societies, the congregation of adherents to other faiths is unlawful. Even closer to home, some political organisations, such as the IRA, are proscribed. Legal action can be taken to criminalise demonstrations or rallies of organisations of which the authorities disapprove. It is even possible to enact legislation to prevent the protests of individuals – such as the anti-Iraq war protester in Parliament Square, Westminster. It is already unlawful for consenting adults in private to indulge in a number of sexual activities, despite the fact that no one and nothing else is at risk. These have been adduced as real-life examples of the tyranny of the majority. Whilst religious codes may forbid group activities of various kinds, and whilst most people might be repelled by some chosen practices, it is clearly neither liberal nor utilitarian for the state to intervene except to protect the vulnerable or unwilling.

review
activity

1. With what kind of liberty is Mill concerned?
2. What conflicts may arise between the exercise of liberty and the functions of the state?
3. To what extent, in Mill's view, should the state have power?
4. What are the dangers of democracy?

The limits to the authority of society over the individual

The power of public opinion

Mill was not just a theorist. He genuinely wanted his ideas to affect the political system and, therefore, the entire population. He tried to consider how far liberty could in fact be implemented whilst repudiating any idea that everyone who receives the protection of society owes a return for the benefit and he was concerned that all individuals should treat other individuals appropriately. Therefore, no one should injure another, and each should, to the appropriate extent, defend society and its members where necessary. Society is entitled to enforce these duties. Public opinion may go further and express disapproval of hurtful behaviour. A modern example of the latter, based on ancient law, occurs in orthodox Jewish communities in Britain and elsewhere. Under Jewish law, a certificate of divorce can only be issued to the husband. A wife may be granted a divorce by the Beth Din (Jewish court) for good reason. In practice, 'good reason' usually includes any of the justifications for divorce in civil society. However, once the wife has received the judgement, the husband has to apply for the certificate. Husbands do not always do so, and if they will not, the woman cannot remarry in Jewish law. If the certificate is granted, religious remarriage is permitted in a synagogue. In cases where the husband is uncooperative, groups of women sometimes gather outside his home and/or place of work and courteously inform his friends and colleagues of his behaviour and their disapproval. A number of men have chosen to change their minds as a result. However, others have chosen to tolerate the protests. Similarly, according to J.S. Mill, we each have the right to disapprove of someone else's behaviour and to act accordingly. We may choose to avoid their company. We may tell them of our disapproval and try to persuade them to act differently. We may, provided we stick to the truth, inform other people of the behaviour and invite them to share our disapproval. It may be that these opinions and actions will lead to a change of mind – or it may not. In either case, we should respect the right of the individual to make the choice, whilst maintaining our own right to an opinion regarding that choice. J.S. Mill is adamant, however, that provided the person in question is 'of full age, and the ordinary amount of understanding' then self-regarding acts should not be the business of the law. Apart from the problem of 'full age', this begs the question of what constitutes the 'ordinary amount of understanding'. Ordinary in what circumstances? With regard to contemporary society? Or to the section of it in which one lives? If it is true that societies progress (as Mill believed) or that they may regress (as those who decry 'dumbing down' in education hold), then 'ordinary understanding' is a very fluid concept. Mill was almost certainly thinking that those with mental health problems were the ones who lacked 'ordinary understanding'. However, even this definition is not as clear as one would wish. What constitutes mental illness is subject to perpetual revision. In Britain today, suicidal thoughts are usually regarded as symptomatic of psychological illness, whereas at other times and in other cultures suicide has been seen as the logical response to various situations. In Britain and the USA, attention deficit hyperactivity disorder (ADHD) is diagnosed as a disease of the neurological system (and therefore a mental health disorder), whereas it is virtually unknown in continental Europe. Children with a number of genetic disorders, including Down syndrome, were previously regarded as unteachable. Many now attend mainstream schools and go on to earn their living. These are questions that need to be addressed if we are to decide which of us is vulnerable, and therefore in need of protection from our own self-regarding acts, and which of us has the capacity, and therefore the right, in Mill's view, to demand liberty from the attentions of government and the law when we are only endangering ourselves.

The consequences of
our actions

Mill does hold that we should encourage one another to 'help distinguish the better from the worse', but his own lauding of eccentricity and individuality might militate against the effectiveness of such exhortation. Mill goes so far as to say that 'notions of politeness' too often prevent us from warning people that they will be regarded as contemptible or foolish if they persist in a particular course of conduct, but insists that if, having been so warned, someone persists nonetheless, he or she should be allowed to do so, within the limits of the harm principle. The question begged here is important. Is any action truly self-regarding? John Donne famously held that 'No man is an island'. Every action has potential, albeit unforeseeable, consequences for others. The person who commits suicide today will not be at work or school tomorrow. His or her absence may affect the outcome of some event at one of those venues – and so on. A refusal to fully realise ones talents may deprive society of a great doctor or judge or tradesman or artist or scientist whose career would have had the potential to benefit many others. Or, as Ben Elton put it in *Blast from the Past*: 'Every moment we decide to stay alive we are making a moral choice, because our existence has repercussions, like a pebble in a very polluted pond.' Mill himself realises that these are serious objections. He recognises that some actions have always been regarded as damaging, and that any action may have consequences for others – not least, friends and family. He is quite clear, for example, that financial neglect of one's family is always wrong. This is true whether the money is spent in gambling or carefully invested. Someone without responsibilities, however, should be allowed to gamble if he or she so wishes. Mill is clear, however, that acts, and even dispositions, such as 'cruelty ... malice ... envy' and others, are properly the concern of society and, in extreme cases, the law. Whilst we may avoid, pity or dislike the person whose self-regarding actions we deprecate, we reserve punishment for those whose other-regarding actions have negative consequences.

J.S. Mill develops this theme by considering drunkenness. If a drunk harms no one, he or she is blameless, but a soldier or police officer who is drunk on duty deserves punishment. Definite damage or risk of damage is culpable; inconvenience should be borne 'for the sake of the greater good of human freedom'. It is still not clear, some would say, where the line can be drawn – are drunken insults, which may cause fear, examples of 'damage' or of 'inconvenience'? If the fear of drunken insult leads to elderly and other vulnerable people refusing to leave their homes, is that 'damage' or only 'inconvenience'?

Mill claims that society has sufficient influence over individuals during their childhood to 'make them capable of rational conduct in life'. He has great faith in education, and holds that if society cannot raise a generation 'as good as, and a little better than, itself ... society has itself to blame for the consequences' (Mill, On Liberty: 1859). This is a matter open to discussion! However, it could pertinently be asked whether 'society' is now (or was in Mill's day) an homogenous whole. It is possible to argue that the increasing toleration of individual lifestyles and attitudes, which Mill believed to be a good thing, has led to a lack of social consensus and cohesion between different groups within modern society. Census and other survey data recognise that there are enormous variations in attitude between different social groups. Indeed, it is commonplace for some of the media to refer to an 'underclass' in contradistinction to 'the expanding middle class'. Unlike the situation in the nineteenth century, free education is now supplied – indeed, is generally compulsory – to all in economically developed countries, but there are enormous differences in belief about its importance or usefulness. It seems from sociological research that the parental view of the usefulness of schooling is the major factor in how far state education and its values are effective in determining the lives and outlook of individual children.

The 'moral police'

Mill goes on to say that self-harming behaviour, when practised, has results which are likely to deter others. Observing the effects upon others of drunkenness, drug addiction, or other dangerous practices would, he believed, serve as an effective warning against doing likewise. Sadly, it could be argued today that the increasing levels of abuse of dangerous drugs (both legal and illegal) and the rising spread of sexually transmitted diseases and associated problems does not seem to support this contention. Mill maintains that 'A person's taste is as much his own peculiar concern as his opinion or his purse.' He holds that we are usually able to see, individually and as a society, which acts are self-regarding and which have the capacity to harm others. Yet, he says, humans as a group seem to want to extend the bounds of the 'moral police'. He gives examples from his own time. Pork is a forbidden food for Muslims, and they regard its consumption as disgusting. In many Islamic countries, the eating of pork is forbidden to all, not just Muslims. This, says Mill, is an example of 'the tyranny of the majority'. Similarly, it was at one time the case that in Spain, only Roman Catholic worship was lawful. Members of other denominations and faiths were not permitted to gather together for services and festivals. In New England, as in Britain under Cromwell, Puritans forbade all public and many private amusements, such as music, dancing, sports and the theatre. At the time Mill wrote, there were a number of influential people in Britain who had sympathy with these views. Mill prophesised that the ownership or spending of wealth might come to be condemned – prescient, perhaps, in view of the rise of socialism and Marxism in the early twentieth century and their political consequences in many parts of the world. Mill adduces further instances including the prohibition of alcohol in the USA (and attempts to introduce this in Britain). Mill quotes Lord Stanley, a prohibitionist politician, as claiming that 'traffic in strong drink ... invades my social rights ... [of] security ... equality ... free moral and intellectual development' (Mill, On Liberty: 1859). Mill responds that this concept of 'social rights' implies that 'it is the absolute social right of every individual, that every other individual shall act in every respect exactly as he ought' – and if he does not, that the law should do something about it. This, says Mill, is 'Monstrous. . . There is no violation of liberty which it would not justify.' Effectively, says Mill, Lord Stanley's attitude implies that we can all demand that everyone be perfect – according to our own definition of perfection. This is clearly unworkable.

Religion and morality   Mill adduces sabbatarianism as another example. Whilst allowing that a day of rest is a good thing, and accepting that the same day of rest for all has practical advantages, he holds that it should not be a matter for hard and fast legislation. It is interesting to note that when Sunday trading was legalised in the 1980s, it was a Conservative government that promulgated the new laws. The Labour opposition objected, partly on the grounds that employees, particularly those on low pay, would be forced to work on Sundays against their will. Religious principles, says Mill, should not inform laws, although religious believers may of course act upon their principles unhindered. He illustrates this by reference to the Mormons (Church of Jesus Christ of Latter Day Saints), which was a new movement in the USA at the time when he was writing. Mormons were persecuted mainly because at that time (although not now) they sanctioned polygamy, or the marriage of many wives to one husband. The reason why the state of Utah now belongs to, and is largely populated by, Mormons, is because they were effectively exiled into the US desert by this persecution. Perhaps ironically, today, Utah provides an example of the tyranny of the majority – alcohol is forbidden to Mormons, and may not be sold in the state, even to those of other faiths or none. Whilst disapproving of much Mormon teaching and practice, Mill was adamant that relationships undertaken voluntarily by adults do not warrant persecution – and after all, many other religions and cultures practised, and still practise, polygamy without incurring social condemnation. It may be that some would hold that many, if not all, of the instances that Mill criticised were based on, or inspired by, religious beliefs and teachings. In twenty-first-century Britain, we have rid ourselves of most, if not all, laws that have nothing but a religious foundation. Laws against murder and theft, whilst reflecting religious teaching, have obvious utilitarian applications quite apart from that. Certainly it is true that since the 1960s, adultery, homosexual activity, suicide and abortion have ceased to be illegal. Legal divorce is now widely available, licensing laws have been hugely relaxed, and shops do a busy trade each Sunday. It may seem, then, that Mill's argument has been won. However, it may be that whilst laws with a religious basis have been revoked, a new set of conventions is informing policing.

For example, whilst alcohol is legally on sale for longer hours, some local authorities are banning its consumption in many public places such as parks. Antisocial Behaviour Orders (ASBOs) are being issued to young people who may not have been found guilty of any criminal offence. Fast driving, even on an otherwise empty road, can lead to a fine and put one's driving licence at risk. The sale and use of fireworks is increasingly tightly controlled. The private ownership of firearms, even by Olympic champion medal winners, has been made all but impossible, yet gun crime, which almost always involves illegally held firearms, has increased. The use of recreational drugs (many of which were legal before the First World War) is still largely forbidden. In France, legislation has outlawed the wearing by Muslims of the *hijab*, (veil or headscarf), by Sikhs of the turban, and by Christians of 'ostentatious' crosses or crucifixes in schools and other places.

Perhaps Mill's contention, that there is a universal desire to police minority practices, is still true, the only difference being that of which groups of people form the minorities in any given time or place. Whether it is the case, as the examples above might suggest, the fact that the tyranny of the majority is exercised mainly against young people in Britain and mainly against religious believers in France, is an interesting socio-political question beyond the scope of this chapter.

review
activity

1. What roles do convention and public opinion play, according to Mill?
2. Define tyranny of the majority in your own words.

Applications of Mill's principles

Mill uses a number of examples to illustrate how his views would apply to real-life situations. He considers the issues of individual autonomy, self-regarding actions, personal accountability and other-regarding actions. He is careful, however, to stress that those situations which he adduces are only examples of practical applications, and that the harm principle should be used to determine correct behaviour in all situations.

Examples of Mill's views

There are occasions, he says, when causing pain or loss to others is legitimate: for instance, the achievement of professional or academic successes which can only be done by overcoming competition from others who will inevitably be disappointed. Provided the competition has been fair, however, it is in the utilitarian interest that such things should happen. Mill also supports the market economy as being in the utilitarian interest, subject to rules about hygiene, quality of goods and so on. Mill probably cannot be blamed for not having foreseen the problem, frequently discussed now, of the effective monopoly of the super- and hypermarkets. These, by controlling the vast majority of household spending, effectively determine the market. Their economies of scale drive smaller independent shops out of business, ultimately limiting consumer choice. He certainly did not foresee what has been called the problem of globalisation. Mill held that prohibition of the sale of some goods (for example, opium in China, and restrictions on the sale of poisons) are unwarrantable interference in the liberty of the buyer.

This, he acknowledges, raises the question of how far the function of policing (in the sense of government legislation and enforcement) is to prevent crime or accident, and how far the function of policing is punitive. He holds that the preventive function is far more open to abuse, and indeed could be extended to virtually every human activity (what is now referred to as 'the nanny state'). He also points out that it is legitimate to interfere if 'any one [is] evidently preparing to commit a crime'. Poisons may be bought for reasons other than murder, so a purchase of poison is not necessarily an indication of intention to murder, and their sale should not be prohibited. However, poisons should be appropriately labelled in order that people be aware of the risks of both deliberate and accidental misuse. It is also reasonable that the fact and time of sale, amount sold and to whom, with the declared intended use, should be recorded in front of a witness. In this way, should the purchased poison be used to carry out a crime, there would be a high chance of its detection. Today, the sale of most poisons is prohibited or subject to severe limitation. Arsenic, for example, is available only with a legal certificate for approved industrial use. Strychnine may, theoretically, be purchased provided a poisons book entry along the lines that J.S. Mill suggested is completed. However, it is almost unheard of for such a sale to take place. Heroin, methadone and other dangerous drugs require a special prescription and their dispensing must be recorded in a separate book. It may be argued that, when Mill was writing, substances toxic to humans were often required for innocent purposes, whilst today there are other chemicals available. In the nineteenth century, arsenic was one of the only effective remedies for infestation by rats and flies. However, modern science has devised safer alternatives (for humans, if not for rats and flies!). Were these to be used in an attempt to murder, their detection would also be more likely than was the case with arsenical deaths, which were often mistaken for accidental food poisoning. Therefore, no individual today has a legitimate need to buy arsenic for domestic use. Whilst this may be true, it does not address the issue of heroin and other potentially lethal drugs, which undoubtedly give pleasure, albeit at the price of personal harm to the user. Mill would have argued that provided such drug use harmed no one else, it should be permitted in a free society. There is also the well-documented problem that crimes may be carried out by addicts desperate to fund the next dose. This could be overcome if heroin and so on were on sale in the same way as cigarettes and alcohol are – to adults only, at a stated level of strength and purity, and from duly licensed premises. Provided those who bought the substances were aware of the dangers (as smokers are), this would be the utilitarian answer.

Education and information about the risks involved in activities are crucial. One can interfere in the liberty of others in order to try to prevent accidents. If someone was approaching a dangerous bridge and there was no time to warn him, it would be legitimate to grab hold of him to stop him. As the person wants to cross the river, rather than fall into it, his liberty has not been infringed. Otherwise, given that he is an adult in possession of his faculties, he should be warned and allowed to make his own decision.

Mill moves on to consider perhaps more commonplace problems. Drunkenness is a personal choice – but one who has been convicted of violence when drunk may be legally prevented from reaching that state again, as one who becomes violent when drunk damages others. Idleness is not of itself culpable, provided the idler does not expect the state to support him, and his inactivity is not a breach of contract; but the idler who fails to support his children can be forced to work as he is damaging the children by his refusal.

Mill also condemns public indecency, as it is a breach of good manners. This seems to be an exception to his rule that offence does not constitute harm. He seems to be drawing a distinction between intellectual offence, such as might be caused by an anti-war protester in argument with Tony Blair, and personal offence, such as might be caused by public swearing or nudity. He is clear that some actions that are acceptable in private should be eschewed in public for the sake of others' sensibilities. Once again, it is unclear where one should draw the line. What, precisely, constitutes 'indecency'?

In this context, cultural norms are enormously variable. It is forbidden in some countries for couples to hold hands, let alone be more physically intimate, in public. People visiting from other countries can unwittingly cause grave offence. Spitting on the ground is normal in many societies but regarded as disgusting in others. Acceptable dress and hairstyle vary tremendously between cultures. Men with long hair are regarded as indecent in some places, and women who bare their arms or legs are similarly viewed in others. These were lesser problems in times past when few travelled, but can cause problems for larger numbers of people now.

The expression of opinions and personal gain

Mill considers the problems involved in advising others about conduct that will only affect the participant. He concludes that it must be acceptable to express opinions and suggestions, provided the adviser has no personal benefit to gain. In other words, I may suggest that if someone hates her job, she should find alternative employment and then hand in her resignation, but it would be wrong to do this if I actually wanted her job for myself and was trying to create a vacancy. Mill is also concerned about those 'with an interest opposed to what is considered the public weal, [welfare] and whose mode of living is grounded on the counteraction of it' (Mill, On Liberty: 1859). Whilst fornication and gambling must, according to Mill's principles, be tolerated even if disapproved of, a question arises about whether pimps, brothel-keepers and the owners of casinos, who profit from the desires and work of others, are to be permitted to go about their business. Mill believes there are arguments on both sides here. He ends his ruminations on this subject by deciding that policing forces such activities into 'secrecy and mystery, so that no one knows anything about them but those who seek them'. This, he concludes, is probably the best outcome for which society can aim.

Here we have a sharp contradistinction with modern society. It is still not permitted to advertise sexual services for money, although it is legal for escort agencies and massage parlours to advertise. At the time of writing, the government is framing legislation to encourage casinos to proliferate, whilst the National Lottery has been legal for many years. Both freely advertise, and there are betting shops in every high street. There is little question that those involved in prostitution are far worse off in every way than those who work in betting shops and casinos. The earnings of prostitutes are mostly, if not entirely, handed over to those who control them. Those working in the legal betting trade, on the other hand, have the full protection of employment law. Many modern-day utilitarians argue that the answer to the problems in the sex trade is to be found in countries such as Holland, where prostitution is legal and the workers have enforceable rights. Mill, however, would certainly have thought the displays of near-nudity in Amsterdam's red light district to be indecent and an offence against good manners!

A further question arises, says Mill: should the state discourage, even though it should not forbid, damaging behaviour? Taxation of, for example, alcohol, he states, is different only in degree from prohibition, as it limits, though it does not prevent, a consumer's capacity to buy the product. The modern-day 'booze cruises' to mainland Europe enabling Britons to buy and import much cheaper alcohol and cigarettes might seem to endorse this proposition. They are also, arguably, an illustration of how punitive taxation can be counterproductive, as people are spending their money abroad rather than benefiting the local economy. However, Mill concludes that as taxation is inevitable, it should be on luxury rather than necessary goods.

Mill further acknowledges that the sale of, for example, alcohol should be controlled and perhaps limited to 'persons of ... respectability and conduct' and subject to licensing laws. He maintains that the working classes should not be treated as children unless and until all attempts at education fail and it is proved that they cannot be governed as 'freemen'. The presumption that their liberty needs to be rigorously controlled by law is, he says, absurd.

Mill holds that people should definitely be prevented from selling themselves into slavery, as they should not give up their liberty. Once enslaved, they can no longer change their minds and become free. No one should be 'free not to be free'. For the same reason, contracts which concern only the individuals involved should be revocable. Marriage, in particular, 'should require nothing more than the declared will of either partly to dissolve it'. This is, effectively, the position now, whereas in the nineteenth century an individual Act of Parliament was required for divorce in every case, and was only available in very limited circumstances and to those who could afford it. Mill accepts that there are moral responsibilities, especially towards the children of the marriage (if any), but deprecates that the question 'is usually discussed as if the interest of children was everything, and that of grown persons nothing'.

State education   In present times, it is sometimes asserted that the pendulum has, if anything, swung too far the other way. It is frequently asserted that too many parents assert their own right, as they see it, to the pursuit of happiness, to the detriment of their children's wellbeing.

Mill was opposed to the fact, as it was then, that men had legal authority over their wives and children. In particular, he criticised the fact that many fathers refused to allow the ongoing education of their children, insisting instead that their offspring should be earning money from the earliest possible age. On the face of it, these problems should have been solved by the Married Women's Property Act, Votes for Women, and universal compulsory education, freely available from the state. However, with regard to education, Mill's belief was that whilst the state should require parents to ensure the education of their offspring, the state should not provide it. He believed that whilst state funding should be made available for the schooling of the poor, the free market would provide the necessary schools and other institutions. This idea looks somewhat similar to the concept of education vouchers, frequently considered and as frequently rejected over the last few decades. A variation of this idea is still occasionally floated in conservative political circles. Mill regarded a state education system as inimical to liberty, 'a mere contrivance for moulding people to be exactly like one another'. The increasing centralisation today of decisions about the content of state education may or may not bear out Mill's contention. Certainly, with the National Curriculum now including citizenship and with central control over the content of all subjects, there are some grounds for agreement. On the other hand, City Academies, despite being largely funded by central government, have more freedom than other schools within the maintained sector.

Mill argues that there should be compulsory examinations to ensure that children have reached the appropriate educational standard. Fathers should be required to ensure that their children are appropriately educated in core subjects. This is somewhat reminiscent of key skills certificates, and begs the question: who should decide upon the core curriculum and its detailed content? If children failed the exams, fathers would be fined for dereliction of duty. Further examinations, in Mill's proposed system, would be voluntary. In disputed subjects such as religion and politics, the exams would be confined to ensuring that candidates were aware of the variety of opinions held and by whom. If parents wished their children to adopt particular beliefs, they could have them educated within the desired belief system, but 'A student of philosophy would be the better for being able to stand an examination in Locke and in Kant, whichever of the two he takes up with, or even if with neither' (Mill, On Liberty: 1859).

In other words, as Mill has previously argued, people should know not only their own views, but the different and sometimes opposing views of others. Interestingly, Mill does not see the liberty to reproduce as universal. He approves of European societies, in the nineteenth century, which had laws preventing marriage between those without the means to support a family. To produce a child whose life will be miserable is, he says, an offence against that child. Note that this is not an argument for abortion, but an argument against sexual activity leading to a pregnancy where the parents cannot ensure the wellbeing of a child once born. Modern contraception could, of course, solve this problem, provided it was compulsorily enforced upon those whose circumstances made child rearing impractical. It would, however, be impossible to enforce, for fairly obvious reasons. Compulsory sterilisation, as advocated by the eugenics movement in the interwar period, and as practised at that time in some parts of the USA, became discredited because of Hitler's belief in the cause, and could probably not be imposed in any democracy today. Compulsory abortion did take place in some parts of Eastern Europe during the Soviet era, and allegedly still occurs in modern China, but in most countries would be opposed on human rights or other grounds.

Social welfare

Finally, Mill considers what he declares to be a tangential issue: should the state actively encourage beneficial activity? Thus far, his arguments have been negative, in the sense of saying that government (and individuals) should not interfere with the liberty of others, within the limits of the harm principle.

Now he asks whether the Government tries to make peoples lives better. Firstly, he says, government should not try to do anything that individuals and groups can do more effectively. He discusses this only briefly, as he regards it as being more a matter for political economists. However, it is worth considering whether social welfare is better provided by Government officials, subject as they are to bureaucratic procedures, or by enlightened employers (such as Rowntree, Cadbury and others in Mill's day) and by the charitable individuals and organisations who still provide much assistance to the homeless, sick and other vulnerable people today. Mill goes on to argue that even if the Government is more efficient, it develops the 'mental education' of individuals to undertake such philanthropic functions themselves. Thus he justifies jury trial, parish councils and charitable works, among other social activities. He argues that such social involvement leads people 'out of the narrow circle of personal and family selfishness' and helps them to adopt a wider and more socially aware outlook. Secondly, says Mill, local activities tend to promote experiments and to use a variety of methods depending upon their suitability to particular conditions. This is in keeping with Mill's previously stated principles. Thirdly and most importantly, Mill argues, it is important to limit the power of government as far as possible. The more power the Government has, the more people become 'hangers on of government or of some party which aims at becoming the government'. The greater the number of people who depend upon the state for their employment and income, the less freedom there is in society.

Currently, the state sector employs a greater percentage of the workforce than at any time in history. In terms of voter turnout, fewer people are politically active than ever before. Whether or not these facts support Mill's condemnation of centralisation is a moot point.

The civil service and bureaucracy

At the time Mill was writing, it was being proposed that the civil service should introduce competitive examination with the aim of employing all the 'most intelligent and instructed persons procurable'. A system of competitive examination for the civil service is now in operation, although it is inevitably true that many people of high ability choose to pursue careers elsewhere. Mill was unhappy with this proposal, as it would, in his opinion, make the bureaucracy unchallengeable. He asserts that in (pre-Soviet) Russia, this had already taken place: 'The Czar himself is powerless against the bureaucratic body; he can send one of them to Siberia, but he cannot govern without them, or against their will' (Mill, On Liberty: 1859). The relationships between politicians and civil servants in *Yes Minister* and *Yes Prime Minister* may confirm that Mill's fears were not unfounded. Mill goes on to say that he disapproves of societies where the Government is expected to provide for everyone. He also rejects the view that government should instruct people as to what they should do. In such societies, he said, the population tends to abnegate personal responsibility and hold the state to blame for any evils which may befall. He admires countries (such as, in his time, France and America) where people are accustomed to taking personal and corporate responsibility and can function, if necessary, without organised government. It is essential, says Mill, that there are those outside the bureaucratic system who have equal ability to those within it. Only where this is the case can constructive criticism take place. Ideal government, Mill contends, consists of 'the greatest dissemination of power consistent with efficiency; but the greatest possible centralisation of information, and diffusion of it from the centre' (Mill, On Liberty: 1859). In practice, this seems to resolve itself into as much personal autonomy as is commensurate with the harm principle, and then legislation and government at as local a level as possible. The role of central government should be the collection and distribution of information, and the giving of advice and rules for guidance to local officers. All this is intended to lead to the flourishing of the individual – probably the most important level of liberalism, and the highest form of liberty.

review
activity

1. Outline the 'harm principle'.

2. What is negative freedom?

3. What is the value of liberty, according to Mill?

some questions
to think about

1 Is it possible to distinguish offence from harm in practice?

2 Is difference good for its own sake?

3 If freedom of thought, expression and action are generally to be approved, what exceptions should be made?

4 Are Mill's views on the education of children practical?

5 To what extent should the state be responsible for the welfare of its citizens?

6 Are all people capable of exercising freedom? If not, how can we decide who is or is not?

7 How important is truth, in relation to other values?

further
reading

▶ Ryan 1974 is a thorough and authoritative work.

▶ Ten 1980 wrote specifically of Mill on liberty.

Nietzsche: *Beyond Good and Evil*

important terms

Absolutism: the belief that there are absolute principles in philosophy, ethics, morals, etc.

Apollonian: orderly, rational and self-disciplined.

Ascetic: someone who exercises severe self-discipline and avoids physical pleasure.

Atomistic: in psychology, the theory that mental states consist of elementary particles.

Decadence: moral decay.

Deconstruction: the belief that language is unable adequately to represent reality, leading to the assertion that the written word cannot have a fixed or stable meaning.

Dionysian: wildly sensual and unrestrained.

Dogmatist: someone who insists upon the rightness of a belief or set of beliefs.

Dualism: the theory that there are two independent principles (such as form and content) underlying reality.

Monad: an ultimate unit of being which encompasses the physical and the spiritual aspects.

Nihilism: denial of the existence of objective truth.

Pessimism: the doctrine that the world is bad rather than good.

Protestant: a Christian who believes that individuals can approach God, understand The Scriptures, etc., without the need for a priest as mediator.

Prototype: the original object or working model.

Relativism: disbelief in the existence of absolute truths.

Sublimation: to divert primitive (e.g. sexual) energy into some higher activity.

Introduction

Friedrich Nietzsche (1844–1900) was born in what was then Rocken, Saxony, in central Europe. His father and two of his grandfathers were Lutheran (Protestant Christian) clergymen. He had no formal philosophical training, but was a gifted student of classics and of the science of languages, especially their historical development. He became Professor of Philology at Basel University when aged only 24. His interest in philosophy was aroused when, during his student days, he read the works of Schopenhauer. He became famous for his rejection of Christian and liberal values, his attacks upon the concept of democracy, and his creation and celebration of the concepts of the superman, the death of God, and the will to power. Having served as a medical orderly in 1870, during the Franco-Prussian war, he returned to the university with damaged health.

Nietzsche's first book, *The Birth of Tragedy*, was published in 1872. This was concerned with the contrast between Dionysian and Apollonian values. Nietzsche was in favour of the Dionysian. He was in agreement with Schopenhauer in believing that the world is godless and irrational, involving strife and suffering. However, he did not share Schopenhauer's ultimate pessimism. He tried to find a philosophy that could show that life, despite all its problems, is in fact nonetheless worth living. When he was young, Nietzsche all but idolised Wagner, the composer whose work was almost entirely pessimistic. He considered Wagner as a possible role model for the worthwhile life, and dedicated *The Birth of Tragedy* to him. Indeed, Nietzsche saw Wagner's *Siegfried* as the prototype of his superman. However, in 1876, he became disillusioned with Wagner, whom he came to believe was the embodiment of decadence. He particularly objected to Wagner's *Parsifal* on the grounds that the Christian convictions found in that work, and in that work alone of all Wagner's output, were dishonest, insincere and expressed for reasons of political expediency. Notwithstanding this disillusionment, Nietzsche continued to search for a way to overcome nihilism and affirm life. This quest continued throughout his active career. He retired from the academic life in 1879 because of increasing ill health. The extent of his medical problems at this time is not precisely known, but unquestionably he suffered, possibly among other complaints, from severe and frequent migraines, which partly explain his style of writing. His short sentences and paragraphs reflect the fact that reading and writing for any extended period of time brought on excruciating headaches and disturbances of vision. The consequent literary style can sometimes appear disjointed and does not always make for easy reading. From 1879

Work ethic: the belief that hard work is of high moral value.

Friedrich Nietzsche
(1844–1900)

until 1889 Nietzsche devoted himself to philosophical reading, meditation and writing. He lived in various resorts in France, Italy and Switzerland during this time. Nietzsche was never to be aware of his fame – he was little known until 1888 when Georg Brandes lectured on his work. In 1912, F.M. Cornford hailed *The Birth of Tragedy* as 'a work of profound imaginative insight'. Nietzsche, probably because he was in the final stages of syphilis (a sexually transmitted disease, incurable before the discovery of penicillin), became incurably insane in January 1889 and remained in that state until his death in 1900. He was first nursed by his mother, and then, until his death, by his sister Elizabeth at Weimar, in what is now Germany.

Between 1872 and 1889, Nietzsche produced a stream of unconventional works, often poetic and highly literary in form. He was not only an unusual and controversial philosopher, but was also influential upon psychoanalysis and literary existentialist thought and writing. The works of many other scholars are thought to have been affected by Nietzsche's writings, including those of Karl Jaspers, Martin Heidegger, Thomas Mann, W.B. Yeats, Karl Mannheim and Michel Foucault.

'You would not enjoy Nietzsche, sir – he is fundamentally unsound.' So said Jeeves to Bertie Wooster, (P.G. Wodehouse, *Jeeves Takes Charge*, 1919) and many readers since have agreed. Bertrand Russell was reportedly so disgusted with Nietzsche's work that he threw the book across the room and did not complete his reading. Nietzsche has also been unfairly accused of proto-Nazism. Reading of his work refutes this. Sadly, however, during his long final illness his sister Elizabeth, who was an active proto-Nazi, altered his auto-biography, *Ecce Homo* (*Behold the Man*). Nietzsche had completed this work in 1888, but his sister spent time making her amendments in order to try to make it appear that her brilliant brother supported her views. As a result, its publication was delayed until 1908.

The will to power

Nietzsche's early work considered the classical Greek outlook, with an unusual emphasis upon the Dionysian and tragic elements of the culture. He saw the festivals in honour of Dionysus, god of wine, as life-affirming. They involved the enjoyment of wine and of orgiastic sexual activities. The Apollonian outlook, by contrast, was life-denying. As time went on, he came to believe that the most important determining factors throughout human social and political history are fear, and the striving for power. Nietzsche then tried to see how far these two concepts, the striving for power, and fear, were explanatory of human behaviour not only in social and political movements but also in personal and public actions. (Simon Raven, in his novel *Doctors Wear Scarlet* (1950) gives one fictional account of how they might apply, to some extent at least, in the lives of a small social circle.) Eventually, Nietzsche concluded that 'the will to power' is the primary driving force in human nature. Indeed, according to *Thus Spake Zarathustra*, published 1882, this is true of every living being. This concept of the will to power has been widely misunderstood. The will to power is, in its finest and uncorrupted form, the will to have power over oneself – the desire to recreate and perfect oneself. In this, Nietzsche is, although he probably was not aware of the fact, echoing the Islamic doctrine that 'the most important struggle is the struggle to overcome the evil within oneself'. Only where this desire is frustrated (as, given human nature and the state of the world, often it must be) does one settle for physical power over others. Nietzsche maintained that his conception of human nature – his belief that humans were capable of being creators rather than creatures – was to show humans capable of better things and finer lives than his detractors would be prepared to acknowledge.

In order to fully comprehend what Nietzsche meant by the 'will to power' it is also necessary to understand the concept of sublimation. Briefly, sublimation involves the channelling of energy from the pursuit of a less desirable or worthy ambition into the attempt to achieve a better one. Nietzsche was the first to use this term in its modern psychological sense. Nietzsche attacks Christianity and many other moralities on the grounds that they demand 'not the control but the extirpation of the passions'. In other words, in his analysis, these belief systems try to eliminate or destroy strong feelings. Nietzsche would rather that the energies of those feelings should be controlled and channelled into creative activity. Moralities which advise the elimination of passion are herd moralities. In contrast to the cult of Dionysus, they are life-denying. They express the will to power of the weak, those who resent the strength of others and who try to bring everything down to their own level, rather than to rise above it. Unable to succeed in the terms of this world, they concentrate instead upon some imaginary other world where they will be powerful and others will be miserable. Instead of this, Nietzsche believes, what they should try to do is to better themselves, rather than resenting, and attempting to frustrate, those in more desirable circumstances.

Christians, and other religious believers, might well challenge this analysis of what religion actually demands. Certainly, celibates would argue that because their energies are not directed into sexual activity, personal relationships, family life and all the responsibilities involved therein, they are free to devote their time, and, crucially, all their energy, to the direct service of God. Arguably, religion, at its best, is not about eliminating the passions. Rather, it is concerned with directing them appropriately, according to the will of God.

review
activity

State the implications of the will to power in your own words.

Beyond Good and Evil

This book was first published in German as *Jenseits von Gut und Bose* in 1886. It was published in English translation in 1907. In this text, I have concentrated upon those sections that are examined at A2 level. The other sections are not necessarily easy reading, but they do throw further light upon some of Nietzsche's views.

'On The Prejudices of Philosophers'

The value of truth

Thoughts on truth

Nietzsche begins by questioning the value of truth itself. Why do philosophers want the truth? The obvious rejoinder, that if truth, untruth and ignorance are irrelevant, then there is little point in Nietzsche or anyone else joining in the debate, is tempting but glib. Nietzsche is making a rather more subtle point than at first appears: we tend to think in terms of opposites, or dualisms, such as truth/falsehood, altruism/selfishness, etc. This has generally led thinkers from Plato onwards to the belief that the physical world is one thing and the realm of truth, and all other pure abstractions, is another thing altogether. Perhaps, Nietzsche suggests, this is error. Perhaps we are receiving only a partial view of the way things are. Maybe these apparent opposites are in some causal relationship with one another. Indeed, it may even be the case that they are identical with each other. Perhaps, he suggests, we should pay more attention to 'appearance, the illusion, to egoism and desire' and pay less heed to some possibly fictitious other realm of absolute truths and values. He foresees a new breed of philosophers: 'philosophers of the dangerous Perhaps.'

Modern philosophy has certainly developed, to some extent, along the lines that Nietzsche foretold. Relativism is probably a more widely held stance now than is absolutism – at least in the fields of ethics and aesthetics. Deconstruction, whatever its merits or demerits, is fundamentally concerned to show that the preference for one out of two polar opposites is 'ultimately untenable' in the words of David Farrell Krell, as the preferred term is always 'parasitic upon or contaminated by the marginalised term' (*The purest of bastards*: 2000).

Philosophy as an expression of self-interest; truth and interpretation

Instinct and self-preservation

Nietzsche holds that most conscious thinking is, though unrecognised as such, guided by the instincts. Even logic has underlying value judgements designed to preserve a 'particular kind of life'. Here he may have hit upon another psychological truth: it can certainly be argued that people in general react to a situation and then look for reasoned justifications for those reactions, rather than reasoning first and drawing conclusions thereafter. He maintains that fundamentally we do not look for truth: we judge in favour of self-preservation and preservation of the species. Whilst Professor Richard Dawkins has not, so far as I am aware, specifically commented upon Nietzsche, this assertion would seem to be supported by the central tenet of *The Selfish Gene* (Dawkins 1976). Nietzsche maintains that as soon as we recognise the fact that our philosophy accepts some fictions because of their preserving properties, that philosophy 'has already placed itself beyond good and evil'. He argues that the problem with most philosophers is that they refuse to accept or admit that this is what they are, in fact, doing. Every philosophy, he asserts, is 'the personal confession of its author, a kind of unintended and unwitting memoir' and is motivated by the author's moral agenda. Other scholars, he states, may be motivated by the desire for knowledge in their work, but their real interests – their selves – will be occupied elsewhere. Philosophers, however, wholeheartedly desire to impose their own beliefs upon others and employ scholarly methods in their attempts to do so. Philosophy, then, is a working out of 'the most spiritual form of the will to power'. To put it another way, every philosopher, in Nietzsche's view, wants his or her ideas to shape and then to rule the thinking, and, by extension, the behaviour, of other people.

Some philosophers, he argues, want to return to previous modes of thinking. Whilst they are right, he says, to want to get away from the present, yet the real challenge is to go forward and to advance to the new. Reversion to the old ways is an error.

Nietzsche criticises Kant's work, especially his attempts to demonstrate the truth of synthetic *a priori* judgements. The truth of such judgements, says Nietzsche, is irrelevant – these judgements are necessary. That is entirely sufficient justification. (It may be worth noting here that mathematicians happily make use of the square root of minus one and other non-existent quantities in some equations and calculations! They do so because these entities are logically necessary.) Nietzsche pointed out that we have accepted that many things are not as they seem. The earth orbits the sun, despite appearances to the contrary. Matter is not solid, as the majority of each atom consists of space. We need similarly, he says, to rethink (but not necessarily to reject) the concept of soul. Soul as an invisible monad is unacceptable to Nietzsche, but he allows that other descriptions may be valid. The concept of soul has indeed undergone much discussion and, arguably, revision, since Nietzsche's time, and it may be that he would be happier with some of the more modern theological thinking today than he was with that of the churchmen of his own time.

Even physics, says Nietzsche, is a human interpretation of the world rather than an explanation of its reality. Concepts of immediate certainties, absolute knowledge and the thing in itself are, Nietzsche says, self-contradictory. On analysis, any statement such as 'I think' breaks down into a 'series of audacious assertions that would be difficult if not impossible to prove'. And in any case, 'why not insist on truth?'

Nietzsche develops his assertion that it is difficult to say anything definite about thinking. Even to say 'there is thinking' implies the existence of a thinker – which is unproved. Similarly, the concept of free will, though regularly discredited, survives in the popular mind. This, he says, is nothing but prejudice. Willing involves 'a multiplicity of feelings' – it is certainly not atomistic. Essentially, it resolves into a variety of emotions, and the preponderant emotion is that of superiority: 'I am free: "he" must obey'. Freedom of the will equates to commanding and expecting obedience despite resistance, and of succeeding in being obeyed. It is no different from a society where 'the ruling class identifies with the success of the community as a whole'.

The bewitchment of language

Ideas, thought and language

Nietzsche also asserts that philosophy develops along lines determined by language, and that this explains the differences in philosophic thought between different cultural groups. Locke's view of the origin ideas, says

Nietzsche, is superficial – ideas are shaped by the available words. In this, Nietzsche is almost echoing the thoughts of his contemporary, the novelist Anatole France, who contended that without language, there could be no abstract thinking.

Cause and effect in Nietzsche's view, are, similarly, fictitious concepts. They are man-made and explain nothing. Here we seem to have an echo of Hume's argument that we assume the reality of cause and effect, which is, ultimately, incapable of proof.

Nietzsche also holds that there are neither free nor unfree wills. In reality, he says, there are only 'strong and weak wills'. Philosophers who talk of coercion, pressure, and so on are simply revealing their own inadequacies. Both those who insist upon the reality of personal responsibility and those who talk of social or other determinism are equally deluded.

Rejection of God or any other master in favour of 'the law of nature' is equally delusory. This is just another interpretation. We need to travel, maintains Nietzsche, difficult though it is, beyond morality and, indeed, to crush the concept from our thinking. The way to find the reality about basic issues is through psychology.

review
activity

1. For what reasons does Nietzsche criticise previous philosophers?

2. What are the motives of philosophers, Nietzsche's estimation?

3. Distinguish between truth and interpretation.

'The Free Spirit'

The new philosopher and the notion of superiority

Superiority and solitude

Nietzsche declares that one of the defining characteristics of an exceptional person is the craving for solitude. Yet as they desire knowledge, these exceptional people also feel the need to interact with, and undertake the observation of, others. Exceptional people can be assisted in their quest by the cynics – those others who observe the faults of their fellow human beings objectively and without surprise or emotion. Cynical people tell the truth. In contrast, those who become indignant when faced with the reality of the deficiencies of human nature are those who tell lies about it.

Independence, asserts Nietzsche, is the prerogative of the strong. Anyone who tries to be independent when there is no need to do so is 'bold to the point of recklessness'. He deliberately places himself in solitude and in danger. This shows such a person to be exceptional, one who has the will to power over himself.

According to Nietzsche, philosophical insight is by definition incomprehensible to many. The true philosopher does not just observe from the outside (taking the exoteric view) but, metaphorically speaking, takes the view from above (the esoteric view). This assertion seems to be not dissimilar from the theme of Thomas Nagel's attempt to gain 'the view from nowhere'. Seen from above, says Nietzsche, tragedy ceases to be tragic and pity becomes inappropriate. That which is good for the masses is damaging to the superior person.

The stages of morality

The moral period Nietzsche asserts that in times past, and in undeveloped cultures, the moral worth of actions was judged by their consequences, rather than the principles upon which they were based. This attitude typified the pre-moral period. However, during the last few thousand years, in his analysis, the origin of the action has been the basis for moral judgement. The origin is the intention of the agent. In other words, the morality of the action is judged according to the reasons for which it was carried out. This stage can be called the moral period. Nietzsche calls now for the extra-moral period, when the value of an action is to be judged by the non-intentional or instinctive motivation. We should, he argues, overcome morality, by which he means traditional moral values, and embark upon what might now be styled a post-moral world. We need to question our beliefs in 'devotion, sacrifice for our neighbour ... self-renunciation'. Here he is saying that we should be wary of, and question our motives for, acting in accordance with moral codes based upon rational thought. These codes, and the principles to which they give rise, are seductive ideas, but the fact that we like them is not an argument in their favour. 'So let's be cautious!'

Philosophical questions

We also need to question whether our faith in 'immediate certainties' is justified. Perhaps, he says, we need to come to terms with 'degrees of apparency'. Things which appear to be the case may only reveal varying degrees of reality. For us humans, the only given reality, says Nietzsche, is instinct. Maybe the rest of the physical world is similar to us in this. Given that the human will is causal, one might hypothesize that 'all mechanical events, insofar as an energy is active in them, are really the energy of the will, the effect of the will ... "will to power" and that alone' (Nietzsche *Beyond Good and Evil*).

The new philosophers The new philosopher, says Nietzsche, needs to be without illusion, independent, essentially solitary and uncommitted to anything or anyone. New philosophers must be experimenters. Lovers of 'truth' they may be, but dogmatists they will not be. Their 'truths' will be individual; they will say 'My judgement is *my* judgement: no one else has the right to it so easily'. There will be few of these new philosophers, and each one of them will be extraordinary and individual.

Nietzsche's denial of the existence of absolute truths has become something of a commonplace today. Moral relativism, often summed up in the phrase 'It's true for me', is by no means an unusual attitude. In Nietzschean terms, the very popularity of the viewpoint means that it cannot be truly philosophical. True philosophy is, in his estimation, rare by definition. In Simon Raven's novel *Fielding Gray*, the eponymous main character makes a similar point. When urged to consider common sense, he replies to the effect that he prefers the uncommon kind, which was necessarily rarer and therefore more valuable. It is only fair to point out that Fielding Gray was, at this stage in the novel, an argumentative teenager at odds with his father, rather than a serious and considered attempt to make a philosophical point. Nietzsche also denies that there can be 'common goods', on the grounds that 'The term contradicts itself: anything that is common never has much value.' As a philologist, Nietzsche was fond of wordplay, but a pun, however apt, has no particular philosophical value. Nietzsche's contention that good, like truth, is relative to each individual, is still matter for argument rather deeper than this.

The new philosophers, whose existence Nietzsche envisages, will be truly free spirits. Nietzsche differentiates between the new philosophers and those regarded as the free spirits of his age. These latter, he states, are not new philosophers, but the 'loquacious scribbling slaves of the democratic taste'. Democracy is antipathetic to new philosophy, as democrats are levellers, bringing everyone down to the level of mediocrity or worse and therefore opposing those who wish to rise. Democrats, says Nietzsche, try to make life safe and happy for the herd, and blame human misery on previous forms of government. This, in his view, is the opposite of the truth. In fact, he holds that the idea that suffering must be eliminated is itself a great mistake. It is in facing and enduring all evil and suffering that the human spirit is made strong. To eliminate suffering, therefore, is to destroy opportunities for exceptional characters to experience psychological and spiritual development. In fact, those new philosophers who go beyond good and evil realise that comfort is counterproductive to creativity and achievement. Above all, says Nietzsche, solitude and individuality are the hallmarks of the free spirits and it is they who may perhaps become the new philosophers.

review
activity

1. What are the defining characteristics of the new philosopher?
2. Outline the three stages of morality.

'The Religious Disposition'

Self-denial and sacrifice

Differences between religious movements

Nietzsche is clear that the faith of the Early Church differed from that of many later Christians and Christian movements. For example, the interpretations of Christianity exemplified by the ascetic Protestantism of Luther and Cromwell were not those of the Early Church as described in the Acts and Epistles of the Christian New Testament. It must be remembered that Nietzsche was himself brought up in the Lutheran Church by those who were clergymen or ardent members of that denomination. He therefore knew much of that denomination through his own experience. The faith of the Early Church, he says, is akin to that of Pascal and involves 'an ongoing suicide of reason'. It demands 'sacrifice of freedom, pride, spiritual self-confidence'. He believed that this fact is not appreciated by modern Christians. The first believers were required to undertake a re-evaluation of all values. The sceptical tolerance of established religion which characterised the Roman Empire was anathema to the slave class – and most of the Early Church was made up of slaves. Slaves want the unconditional. They do not understand nuance – they are absolutist. 'Religious neurosis' always demands 'solitude, fasting and sexual abstinence'. These demands are symptomatic of self-denial, that is, denial of the will. How, asks Nietzsche, is this denial possible? In other words, how is it possible to behave in such a way that one becomes a saint? The phenomenon of saint-hood is interesting because it is apparently miraculous – a 'bad person' becomes his own opposite, a 'saint'. To be sure, the saint is exercising his will to power – but in perverse form. He achieves power over himself and wins respect thereby, but does not develop himself as Nietzsche would have him do. He uses his self-discipline, his power over himself, to make himself less than he could be. He diminishes himself, rather than expanding his horizons. Whilst admiring the exercise of the will to power, Nietzsche disapproves of the effects. Nietzsche contrasts the Old Testament, which he admires as showing 'what man used to be' with the New Testament which has 'much in it of the proper delicate dank odour of devotees and small souls' (Nietzsche *Beyond Good and Evil).*

Here, Nietzsche's biblical scholarship may be open to question. Whilst the Old Testament (Hebrew Scriptures) does indeed record tales of great heroism, other renowned characters therein do not necessarily exhibit such characteristics. Joseph, for example, appears to have accepted his many vicissitudes without complaint, even when he had every right to make them. (See Genesis 37–40.) On the other hand, Jesus overturning the tables in the temple (John 2: 13–17; Matthew 21: 12-13; Luke: 25–26) shows a very assertive spirit. It is always possible to selectively quote from the Bible, and it is at least arguable that Nietzsche saw what he wished to see, rather than the totality of what is actually there to be read. In fairness to Nietzsche, interpretation of the text is, and always has been, a matter for debate among both scholars and lay persons.

The ladder of sacrifice

Religion and the work ethic

Nietzsche outlines what has been described as his 'ladder of sacrifice'. At first, he says, religious devotees sacrificed other humans, 'perhaps even those whom they loved best'. Secondly, people came to sacrifice their strongest instincts, and from this comes asceticism. Finally, people sacrificed God himself – this is the current stage of religious development, Nietzsche avers, at the time in which he wrote.

Nietzsche puts forward the interesting theory that the work ethic is inimical to religious faith. The genuine religious life, he claims, depends upon having the leisure to enable self-examination, prayer and other religious activities. Those people who adopt the work ethic have not the time actually to practise religion. He has previously commented on the hold that Catholic Christianity has taken on southern European cultures, which, both traditionally and in the present day, place emphasis upon the importance of leisure. This contrasts with the weaker hold that any form of Christianity has taken in the northern part of the continent. It is obviously true that, since the Reformation, there has been a north/south divide between the Protestant and Catholic denominations of Christianity. Catholicism, which has been the major Christian denomination in southern Europe, is, in Nietzschean terms, far more life-affirming. It celebrates more festivals and is generally more colourful and visual in worship than is Protestantism. The Reformation led to most of northern Europe adopting Protestant forms of Christianity. These groups tended to emphasise the importance of hard work and to be more austere in their worship. Indeed, some Protestant denominations would appear to have regarded all pleasure as of questionable moral worth, if not actually sinful by definition. For example, Cromwell's Roundheads forbade the celebration of Christmas, in the sense that traditional foods such as mince pies were deemed illegal. Stained glass windows in churches were destroyed. It is true, too, that the work ethic is a far more northern (or Anglo/Germanic) mindset than it is Latinate. The fact that it is often referred to as 'the Protestant work ethic' is itself telling. The idea that, in order to please God, one should work hard and eschew frivolity is characteristic of northern, rather than southern, Europe. Whether or not the relationship between these facts is causal and, if so, in which direction, is open to debate. Hotter countries tend to take longer midday breaks, but this may be for the very sensible reason that no one wants to risk sunstroke. In more southern climes, too, there are longer hours of daylight, so staying up late, whether for work or pleasure, is more feasible. It is also interesting to reflect upon the implications of the fact that Catholicism seems to have retained more importance in southern Europe than Protestantism has done in the northern part of the continent. Whilst it is still true that more British people attend church than go to watch football matches, church attendance in northern Europe is declining. By contrast, in southern Europe, the decline is far less. In Africa and South America, Catholicism is growing rapidly. For all Nietzsche's admiration for 'tropical man', it seems that these are the very people who are embracing religion most fervently!

Loving others in order to please God is, according to Nietzsche, the noblest and most far-fetched idea yet. It presupposes, he says, that the philanthropic instinct is a brutish stupidity, rather than a natural instinct which is of value in itself. It may be worth asking whether the philanthropic instinct is, in fact, as universal as Nietzsche seems to imply. Love of those one is related to, by blood or intimacy, is one thing. As Professor Richard Dawkins has pointed out, there are good Darwinian biological reasons to wish that those who share, or are more likely to share, one's genes should survive to contribute to the next generation. However, it is valid to ask whether concern for strangers is actually a universal instinct. It may be that for some people, at least, some other motive is needed before they are willing to help others with whom they feel no intimacy. According to statistics, it certainly seems to be the case that religious believers, on average, contribute more to charitable causes than others do. It may well be that their motivation is the belief that God commands them to do so. In the cases of observant Jews and Muslims, who are required, according to religious law, to donate a percentage of their income (10 per cent and 2.5 per cent respectively), this is certainly true. Indeed, Judaism lays down that the highest form of charitable giving is that where the donor does not know the identity of the individuals who will benefit, and the receiver does not know who gave the assistance. In this way, the donor cannot even expect thanks or recognition for the deed. Nietzsche may well describe this as noble and far-fetched, but it is a matter for debate whether religious observance, including the alleviation of the suffering of others, is more or less valuable than Nietzsche's own ideas about how individuals should govern their lives.

Religion as a tool for social bonding

Nietzsche accepts that religion can be useful – and says that the new philosophers should make use of it. Religion can help to influence 'selecting and breeding'. It must be emphasised here that Nietzsche was not arguing for a superior race in ethnic terms. His concept of superman (*Übermensch*) is of an intellectual elite, dedicated to the enhancement of life, particularly in the fields of culture, art and the literary life. For the new philosophers, religion can be used as a tool for the increase and encouragement of social bonding. A few of the new philosophers may be inclined to the contemplative life, exercising their authority only over a small number of 'selected disciples'. For these people, religion provides a socially acceptable justification for such a choice. The discipline of religion, Nietzsche acknowledges, can purify the character of those who possess the capacity for leadership. For the rabble, the herd, religion provides solace. Karl Marx may well have been thinking along similar lines when he described it as the 'opiate of the people'. Provided they have a belief in the consolations of religion, the masses can bear the harshness and suffering of life. This means that they are less likely to cause trouble.

Nietzsche was in no doubt, however, that religion for its own sake is dangerous and counterproductive to new philosophers in particular. As a tool in the hands of new philosophers, it is useful, but religions by their very nature encourage the preservation of the weak. Religions hold society back by keeping in existence 'that which ought to perish'. This, he alleges, has been counterproductive to human progress. As a result, Europe has become degenerate. Nietzsche acknowledges the very real contributions of religion to some aspects of European culture, especially in art and literature. Nevertheless, he feels that these are outweighed by the fact that religion in general tends to uphold, and even to make heroes of, the weak, the members of the herd, and thus to impose herd morality as the norm for society. 'Christianity has been the most disastrous form of human presumption yet.' On Nietzsche's thesis, instead of shaping mankind so as to encourage noble individuals, Christianity has insisted upon 'equality in the eyes of God'. The result of this doctrine has been the degeneracy of Europeans into a sickly herd.

review activity

1. How does Nietzsche regard the religious demands for self-denial and sacrifice?
2. In what ways is religion useful?

'Epigrams and Interludes'

This section is not examined at A2 level. It consists mainly of single-sentence thoughts. It is worth reading, if only to get a flavour of Nietzsche's views, especially about women, intellectuals and humankind in general. However, it is not discussed in detail here, as it is even more disconnected in style than most of his work, and discussion of it would take up a lot of space. From the point of view of the A level scholar, this is more than its peripheral importance would justify.

'Towards a Natural History of Morals'

Nietzsche's critique of modern ideas about morality

Morality and moral sensibility

European moral sensibility was, in Nietzsche's opinion, considerably more mature than the 'crude' science of morality. In fact, to use the term 'science' when applied to morality, he says, is to claim too much. At the time he wrote, he believed, people had not yet passed the information-gathering stage. Many philosophers believed themselves to have explained morality – but all had assumed the existence of a real and existent morality. All had believed that there was an ultimate morality that was external to human experience and thought. Whilst they may have been aware of the morality of their own kind, they were nonetheless ignorant of the other moral codes which had been, and still were, in existence throughout history and across the world. Hence there had been no rigorous comparison and contrast of differing moral codes. Nor was there any recognition that the concept of morality was in itself problematic. The various moral assertions made by different philosophers (including Kant with his categorical imperative) may or may not be valuable in themselves. Unquestionably, however, these moral assertions tell us something about the persons who assert them. Their usefulness as guidance to life and behaviour is far more problematic. Nietzsche identifies a number of motives, albeit unknown to the philosophers who make them, for holding the views which they do.

A philosopher, says Nietzsche, may wish to justify himself, to soothe and content himself, to humiliate himself, to exact vengeance on his own behalf, to hide himself or to place himself on a higher level than others. Some philosophers wish to exert power. It may be, Nietzsche thinks, that Kant wished to show that his capacity to obey is honourable. He may also have wished to enforce the same type and level of obedience upon others. Whatever the motive, moral codes, according to Nietzsche, do no more than signify the emotions and desires of the writer. They cannot and do not articulate actual moral truths.

Nietzsche holds that the fact, as he sees it, that moral codes are tyrannical, and opposed to reason and nature, is not in itself objectionable. We cannot justify a moral code that opposes tyranny or irrationality any more than we can defend any other type of moral code.

The need for self-discipline

In fact, achievement in all worthwhile fields has, paradoxically, been made in opposition to moral codes, and, crucially, without those codes the opposition would never have arisen and the achievements would not have taken place.

People need discipline – the discipline of guidelines, rules and expectations. These may extinguish much creativity, but they act as a spur to those who have the capacity to go beyond them. Obedience is a necessary precondition for freedom. Only those who have achieved the necessary level of self-discipline can proceed to the stage of successful rebellion.

Those who are accustomed to the discipline of work find leisure difficult – hence the misery of the British on Sundays. Here, Nietzsche is referring to the traditional Protestant Victorian Sunday when all entertainment and frivolity was regarded as inappropriate and actively discouraged. Shops, theatres and other places were forbidden to open, and the hours during which other venues were accessible were severely restricted. It may be worth noting that Sunday trading was only fully legalised in England and Wales during the 1980s. Fasting, says Nietzsche, heightens the appetite. He says that this may explain why it was during Europe's most Christian period 'that the sexual drive was sublimated into love'. Once sex became transmuted into a facet of a lifelong committed relationship, and therefore abstinence outside marriage was the accepted norm, sex took on an importance that it had not previously possessed. It has to be said that anthropology does not seem to bear out this asseveration. It is also a matter for debate whether, since sexual mores relaxed during or after the 1960s, sex has become more or less important in most people's view.

Nietzsche says that Plato interpreted Socrates as saying that bad acts are involuntary as they harm the soul, and no one wishes to do himself harm. This, says Nietzsche, is the argument of the rabble, who equate 'good' with 'useful and pleasant'. All such utilitarian arguments are examples of herd morality. Socrates struggled with the problem of instinct versus reason (or faith versus knowledge). Whilst initially supporting reason, he came to the view that both instinct and reason have value – we use reason to justify our instinctive judgements. Moral judgements are, at bottom, irrational. Plato, however, wished to say that instinct and reason both point towards the Good, and theologians and philosophers ever since have regarded instinct or faith as the pointer to morality. For Nietzsche, instinct is simply the mentality of the herd. He singles out Descartes as the philosopher who alone held out for the pre-eminence of reason, but then, without argument or reason, dismisses him as superficial.

Morality and good conscience

Nietzsche's comments on the sources of morality are interesting. It can certainly be argued that we tend to react first when faced with any situation requiring moral judgement, and only later justify ourselves, if justification turns out to be necessary. Much religious teaching talks of conscience (which may as well be designated 'instinct') as the internal voice of God. Given the variety of conscientious reactions to the same situation, however, instincts would seem at least as much to be formed by nurture as they are by nature. People of good conscience may be pro-choice or anti-abortion, for or against euthanasia, capital punishment, compulsory military service and many other things. Members of some societies feel revulsion against burial, which leaves the soul trapped within a decomposing body. By contrast, in other societies cremation, which destroys the vessel that will take the soul to eternal life, is anathema. Whilst, therefore, we should not underestimate the importance of instinct in moral decision-making, Nietzsche's apparent belief that instinct equals universal human nature is questionable.

Nietzsche draws attention to the problems of perception. People do not observe closely or accurately – they see some salient facts or words and fill in the rest from their imaginations. This is unquestionably true. The huge differences between the accounts of eye witnesses and the evidence of CCTV cameras at crime scenes are testimony to that. At a more mundane level, philosophy students regularly misread 'causal' as 'casual'! However, Nietzsche goes on to say that the contents of our dreams and imaginations are as much a part of ourselves as objective reality – if there is such a thing. We are changed in outlook as much by our thoughts as by our experience. This begs the question of from whence our thoughts derive. If not from experience, then from what? Nietzsche has already stated that psychology is key to knowledge of human nature. Psychology tells us that all our ideas are derived from experience. This experience may be personal, or the reported experience, in conversation or literature, of others, but it comes from the physical world. If Nietzsche is saying that there is some other fount of ideas, he has not sufficiently made out his case. If there is an external source of ideas, then this begins to allow the possibility of a God, and that possibility would lead us in directions which Nietzsche does not wish to go.

The possessors and possessed

Nietzsche goes on to say that the desire to possess is intrinsic to human nature. Men, he says, desire to possess women. The ultimate expression of this desire is the wish that the woman should come to know the worst of his real nature, and still be prepared to make sacrifices for his sake. Parents, he says, regard their children as possessions, and philanthropists help others in the expectation of gratitude and subservience. All those with power, he maintains, see other people as potential possessions.

Nietzsche seems to see possessiveness as a one-way street. Those with power are possessive. Those without it are possessions. Yet the possessive woman was hardly unknown, even at the time he was writing – a time when women lacked effective power in law, politics and public life generally. Children, despite having much in the way of power, regularly try to impose standards of behaviour upon their parents. Comments to the effect that 'You can't wear that to the parents' evening! It's too short/too casual' (or whatever else may be uncool at the time in question) are regularly made. Whilst these examples may show the universality of the will to power, they do not support his contention that possessiveness is symptomatic of the exercise of it by those with power. Indeed, if possessiveness is universal, or at least widespread, it would tend to show that we all have the will to power at an individual level.

Nietzsche holds that the Jewish race is to blame for the beginning of 'the slave revolt in morals'. This he defines as the inversion of morality so that 'poor' came to mean 'saint' and 'friend'. This is, at best, an oversimplification. The Old Testament, which Nietzsche professes to admire, is clear that it is not wealth, but riches dishonestly acquired (through fraud, for example) which is condemned. Indeed, Judaism and the later Protestant work ethic hold that honest work may well be rewarded with financial wellbeing. Alongside this, however, run beliefs that charitable works are praiseworthy and pleasing to God, and that poverty is not of itself blameworthy.

Nietzsche postulates that European society has, under the influence of the herd morality of religion, degenerated into mediocrity. It is tropical man, he believes, who retains vigour and the capacity for greatness. Alternatively, the new philosophers must adopt the untrammelled approach of the tropical mindset. European morality now, says Nietzsche, is generalised (where it should be individual) and aimed at diluting, containing and moderating the passions. Failing this, it tries only to allow their free expression to those 'who can't do much harm any more'.

The herd morality

Throughout the ages, people have lived in herds. There have been few leaders, and many obedient followers. The average person, therefore, 'is born with a need to obey'. This is true, he says, to such an extent that the commanders can only justify their position if they believe themselves to be obeying some higher authority – be it custom, law, God, or some other. Leaders today claim to be possessed of herd values such as public spirit, benevolence, etc. What is needed, according to Nietzsche, is not herd animals leading the rest of the herd, but absolute commanders such as Napoleon. What Nietzsche might have thought of Hitler and Stalin, for example, had he lived to see them, is a matter of speculation.

His thoughts on leadership, however, are in some ways similar to Plato's vision of philosopher-kings. For Plato, true philosophers thought entirely differently from the hoi polloi, and would rule by virtue of persuading them to believe a fundamental myth, in rather the way Nietzsche promotes the exploitation of religion and religious teaching and ideas.

Fear and perceived immorality

Stable societies, says Nietzsche, try to stamp out the very qualities that enabled them to become established societies in the first place. 'Adventurousness, recklessness ... lust for power' were honoured in former days (they enabled the conquering and holding of land, apart from anything else) but are now perceived as dangerous to the preservation of community. Now, love of neighbour (which was in times past morally neutral) is favoured, but is actually activated by fear of neighbour. Indeed, 'fear is the mother of morality'. A strong individual threatens the self-esteem of society, and is therefore condemned as immoral, threatening and dangerous. That which is average is regarded as moral, because it does not evoke fear. When societies become really peaceful and orderly, any kind of sternness causes unease. 'There can come a point of such sickly morbidity and pampered indulgence in the history of a society that ... it even takes the side of the one who does it harm, the criminal' (Nietzsche *Beyond Good and Evil*). Whether current judicial and penal policy supports Nietzsche's contention that we now aim to render criminals harmless rather than to punish them in the way that, he would hold, they deserve, is an interesting topic for discussion. Current criminal procedure and practice can be argued either way. In Britain, we detain a greater percentage of population in prison than does any other European state. Anti Social Behaviour Orders (ASBOs) and electronic tagging of miscreants are recent innovations. Capital punishment for murder no longer exists on the statute books. At the same time, a number of householders who have inflicted injury upon those who have broken into their homes have found themselves charged with criminal assault. Increasing numbers of doctors, teachers, and other professionals are suspended from work and subject to disciplinary investigation on the basis of the otherwise unsupported word of a single individual. Arguably, we are currently somewhat schizophrenic, as a society, about whether we need to protect law-abiding citizens, or the criminals. Nietzsche's conclusion on this subject, namely that the mainspring of morality is the desire to eradicate reasons for fear, is equally problematic. However, if it is the case that behaviour which is generally frightening is caused by strong emotion, and that mediocrity, in emotion as in all else, is the aim of modern stable societies, then he might have a point.

Nietzsche anticipates that he will be criticised for describing humans as herd animals with herd instincts. However, he says, in having come to a consensus that we now know good and evil, we are simply following the judgement of the herd. Current European morality is only one of many moralities. Recognition of this fact is resisted by society in general. Aided by Christianity, herd morality has become institutionalised within European society, and hence 'the democratic movement is Christianity's heir'. The anarchists of Nietzsche's day who apparently opposed the current system were in fact just as much bound by it as was the rest of society. The contention of the anarchists is that the herd is not getting enough power fast enough. They wish to reject God and masters – in this they wish to render the herd more herdlike still. Their belief is in the community. They deny, or fail to recognise, the importance of individuality.

New philosophers reject democracy as decadent. 'They will teach humans that their future is their will.' They will bring about new forms of thinking and of living, and a 'revaluation of values'. The new philosopher will also be aware that the dreams of democracy, involving the 'diminution of man into a perfect herd animal' is only too possible, if other leaders do not arise, or if such potential leaders are deflected from their destiny. In this event, democracy will succeed in achieving the widespread acceptance, and therefore the domination, of herd morality.

review
activity

1. What is 'herd morality'?
2. Why does Nietzsche dislike 'modern ideas'?

'We Scholars'

Science versus philosophy

Nietzsche is concerned about academic trends. In particular, he perceives that science has a growing tendency to regard itself as superior to philosophy. Too many scientists, says Nietzsche, are ignorant of philosophy, yet dismiss the possibility that it is a valuable field of study. Sometimes it is held by utilitarians that academic philosophy is useless; others believe that philosophy verges on mysticism, whilst others again reject all philosophy because they disagree with particular philosophers. Too often, though, the latter's dismissal of philosophy, in Nietzsche's contention, stems from a previous reverence for a particular philosopher. Having been persuaded to dismiss the ideas of the others, they have then become disenchanted with their previous guru as well. These assertions can all be challenged. The last seems to be based upon anecdotal evidence at best. Whilst it is true that philosophers are regarded by some as useless mystics, this has always been the case. Indeed, Plato made the same point. Whilst science was in the ascendant when Nietzsche was writing, scientists are increasingly recognising the value of philosophy today. Nietzsche cannot be blamed for having failed to know what would happen a hundred years after his own death, but the course of events may be instructive for students now. Inevitably, Darwin's discoveries and theories brought biology into the spotlight. Freud and Jung, among others, popularised psychiatry and psychology. Sociology became a separate discipline during the twentieth century. The newer disciplines inevitably took hold of the public imagination. However, scholars are generally agreed that true knowledge is holistic. In other words, everything should be capable of explanation within one set of rules which is universal. As Dr Tim Mowlem once expressed it in conversation: 'Everyone's looking for GUTs and TOEs.' GUTs are Grand Unifying Theorems; TOEs are Theories Of Everything. At present, a number of scholars are thinking along the following lines: sociology and psychiatry are branches of psychology; psychology is a branch of biology; biology can be explained in terms of chemistry; chemistry reduces to physics; physics reduces to mathematics. As mathematics is abstract, it is arguably a branch of philosophy. Certainly Plato believed that mathematics was the next most true discipline to philosophy. Maybe Oxford and Cambridge were prescient when, in the past, they awarded philosophy students degrees in natural sciences.

Modern philosophy

Nietzsche says that recent philosophy has been 'human, all too human' and has certainly lacked the breadth of vision contained in the philosophy of the classical Greeks. Modern society, he believes, is inimical to philosophic development. There is now so much to learn that people may give up, or specialise before reaching their peak, or 'reach the top too late' to be effective. Moreover, modern philosophers take time and thought before reaching conclusions, aware as they are that their decisions are about life and values, rather than about simple matters of fact. The popular conception of the philosopher or wise man is the prudent hermit. According to Nietzsche, the true philosopher is almost certainly the opposite. He is unwise and imprudent, a risk-taker. The scholar, says Nietzsche, is respectable, but inexperienced and of limited value. The new philosophers will be characterised by genius rather than by scholarship.

Nietzsche has previously accepted that some of the new philosophers may prefer to choose a solitary life with a limited number of disciples. He has said that the acceptance of religious forms of life will give such people social respectability. Here he seems to say that these will be the exceptions – notwithstanding his previous emphasis upon the love of solitude that will characterise the new philosopher. Nietzsche has also emphasised the necessity for discipline in early life if the new philosopher is to develop. Scholarship is a discipline. Presumably Nietzsche believes that discipline, taken to excess, frustrates the development of the new philosopher, but he does not make it clear how much discipline is too much.

Nietzsche says that, from the point of view of the new philosophers, the objective scholar is a precious tool, but no more than a tool. He is focused upon knowledge and consequently loses sight of himself as a person. He thinks in generalities and for that reason fails to consider individuals and individualism. He becomes a cipher, having no effect upon the society from which he stands apart.

Unlike the scholars, the new philosophers are not sceptical, which lays them open to much suspicion. The new philosopher is active – he does not merely say 'no', or will 'no' – he acts accordingly. Active naysayers or yeasayers evoke fear. Scepticism, especially the scepticism of scholars, is a tranquilliser against this fear. 'Uncertainty has its charms.' Nietzsche blames the desire for a sceptical outlook, which leads to inactivity, on to a mixing of classes and therefore races. This mixture, he says, has produced a confused generation which is unsure of itself. The result, often, is a paralysis of the will which leads to the adoption or acceptance of intellectual fashion rather than the pursuit of disciplined philosophical insight.

Nietzsche has earlier made it clear that he is not opposed to interracial breeding. Whilst the results of such relationships are unpredictable, he says, they may nonetheless lead to greatness. However, it was the common view of his day, which he shared, that mental, intellectual and psychological traits were as heritable as physical characteristics. This level of faith in genetics would today be regarded as highly questionable, if not entirely discredited. Much twentieth-century research has led to a fairly widespread agreement that characteristics and intelligence are formed by complex interactions between genetic factors and environmental conditions. However, he may have a point in that some research indicates that being brought up in a multi-cultural family, or indeed society, might lead to confusion about values and identity. At the very least, it exposes children especially to a wider variety of choice of value systems. Social mobility between classes, races and cultures is much more common today than it was in the nineteenth century when Nietzsche was writing. It is arguable that in politics, philosophy and the arts there is a confusion, or at least a lack of consensus, partly arising from the large number of different moralities and cultural viewpoints which may be contained within any particular society. Liberal democracy, in the widest sense of that term, seems to be the preferred European response to this situation. Nietzsche would probably have interpreted this as the triumph of herd morality. It is certainly only fair to say here that it has become the case in respectable circles that anyone who expresses doubt, let alone disagreement, with the prevailing liberal consensus will at best be dubbed 'politically incorrect' and at worst denied political or other office. Whilst classical liberalism, as expounded by John Stuart Mill, states unequivocally that offence is not the same thing as harm, current thinking seems to disagree. Freedom of speech is not untrammelled. Those who give offence, as opposed to causing physical or financial harm, pay a penalty. A Harvard professor was recently censured for suggesting that the relative scarcity of female scientists might be due to innate differences in scientific ability between the genders. Whether or not he was right, the fact remains that he was condemned for expressing an opinion. Others in public life have had their careers hindered because they were known to have particular views about abortion or other moral issues.

Here it may be noted that in many instances today, those who oppose the herd, in the sense that they champion currently unfashionable views, do so on religious grounds. In Nietzsche's day, to practise religion was to be one of the majority. In most of the developed world today, the majority of the population is secular. Only a minority actively practise religion. It could be argued, therefore, that those who declare their beliefs in defiance of majority opinion are the nearest thing we have to the new philosophers! Nietzsche would, however, doubtless repudiate this thesis on the grounds that they are returning to past values rather than moving on to re-evaluated values.

Nietzsche's political prognostications for Europe were interesting and somewhat salutary. 'In Russia ... the energy to will has long been stored up in reserve; that is where the will ... waits ominously to be released,' and 'The time for petty politics is over; even by the next [i.e. the twentieth] century, we will be battling for mastery over the earth – forced into politics on a grand scale' (Nietzsche *Beyond Good and Evil*). The Russian revolution and two world wars do not seem to negate these prognostications.

Nietzsche considers whether the new warlike age, which he foresees, may lead to stronger scepticism. It is possible, he believes, that a 'manly' scepticism, such as developed in Germany – fatalistic, ironic and Mephistophelian – might arise. The new philosopher might need this type of scepticism as one aspect of his character, but only as an aspect. New philosophers will also be critics and experimenters. They will have a passion for knowledge that will lead them into danger where necessary. They will be independent, self-reliant and capable of harshness towards themselves and others. Disciplined and rigorous in spirit, they will reject naive enthusiasm and insist that they are more than just critics, indeed that the mere critics are their tools. Philosophical workers and, indeed, academics in general, are not true philosophers. The true philosopher may have to pass through those stages, but he travels beyond. It is for him to create values. Philosophical workers analyse and clarify the thinking of the past; 'true philosophers are commanders and lawgivers'. In other words, it is they who shape the future. They create. Because they are of the future, they necessarily conflict with the norms of the present. They analyse and expose the value and, also, therefore, the weaknesses of currently received wisdom. They see new truths and virtues, and expose the obsolescence of the old. Nietzsche pauses to ask whether greatness, the greatness required to be alone, to suffer in order to go beyond good and evil, is actually possible. Given the degenerate state, as he sees it, of contemporary society, he reaches the pessimistic conclusion that it is open to doubt.

Nietzsche believed that philosophers were born, not made. He believed that breeding counts – one must inherit not only the philosophical mind, but also characteristics such as the readiness for responsibility and the capacity for individuality, for separation from the herd ...

Nietzsche's ideas, whilst unfashionable in most of modern Europe, are not so different from the beliefs of, for example, English aristocrats of his time who believed that they, and their sons, were suitable rulers by virtue of their inherited characteristics. Whilst the appropriate upbringing and training was seen as important – that was what public schools were for – 'breeding' was believed to be the primary factor for fitness to command. In fact, most of the male aristocracy did rule, or at least govern, in various parts of the British Empire, in

Parliament and as officers in the armed forces. The degree of their success as rulers and commanders is still matter for debate, and rather depends upon a number of moral judgements. The appropriate definition of 'success' in this context is also an open question.

Leaving aside the eugenic arguments, Nietzsche's comments about those who do not wish, or flatly refuse, to follow the herd are worthy of consideration. It seems to be true that those who are different from the majority even in minor ways are often seen as shocking, or possibly threatening. To take just one commonplace example, someone who says she does not watch TV will inevitably provoke a surprised response. The most usual initial reaction is to accuse her of lying. Typically, the interlocutor will say: 'But you must do!' and follow this up with 'What, you mean you only watch the news and documentaries?' When assured that no, there is no TV in the house, the next response tends to be: 'Well what do you do then?' or, (most frequently) 'You're weird!' These latter two remarks are usually accompanied by looks of some apprehension. Unorthodox tastes, even in such unimportant matters, are viewed as suspicious, if not actually frightening.

Unorthodox views

The person who expresses unorthodox opinions is regarded with even greater suspicion. Boris Johnson, then a shadow minister for the Conservative Party in the House of Commons, and still, at the time of writing, editor of *The Spectator* magazine, was excoriated in the press and forced to apologise when he published a particular article. He did not write it himself, but was held responsible, as editor, for the offence which it caused. The article in question (which was published as an unsigned editorial) referred to the brutal murder, by terrorists, of Ken Bigley. Mr Bigley originally came from Liverpool, although he had not lived there for many years. When Mr Bigley died, having been held hostage for some time, there were public demonstrations of grief on the streets of Liverpool. The writer of the article suggested that such demonstrations, by people who had never met Mr Bigley, were excessively and self-indulgently sentimental. Outrage ensued.

Similarly, at the time of the death of Diana, Princess of Wales, an enormous public outpouring of emotion resulted. Anyone who suggested that it was inappropriate to behave in this way over the death of a total stranger was treated with suspicion and disdain.

In Britain, it has recently become a custom among some people to lay flowers at the scene of fatal road traffic accidents. Analysed logically, this means that people are driving to a place which is obviously hazardous, as someone has died there. Having done so, they park their cars, get out, lay flowers, and then drive away again. Such impromptu shrines have even been seen on the hard shoulder of a motorway! Anyone, including the police, who dares to point out that this behaviour is less than sensible is criticised for lack of sensitivity and failure to feel sympathy for the bereaved.

Similarities with Plato's views

Nietzsche may have had a point, therefore, when he suggests that the 'softer' emotions are now overestimated as virtues, and that the clearer thinkers are likely to be regarded with suspicion. Certainly many classical Greek philosophers would have sympathised with this assertion, as well as with some of his other views. Comment has already been made regarding the similarity, in some respects, of Nietzsche's new philosophers to Plato's philosopher-kings. Additionally, it is clear from Plato's work (especially the *Republic*) that a belief in good breeding is another common factor in their writings – always allowing that not all offspring will resemble their parents. Plato recommended a selective breeding programme, plus aptitude tests and training, to maximise the chances of producing, identifying and educating the philosopher-kings. Nietzsche and Plato also share a belief in the importance of education plus intuition and the make-up of the philosophic soul.

The similarities cannot be taken too far. Plato's world of ideal forms finds no comparator in Nietzsche's philosophy, and indeed Nietzsche specifically rejects such a concept. Similarly, the importance of religion and its effects which Nietzsche identifies is very different from the Greek point of view. Having said that, it is the case that Christianity and the other living faiths of the modern world are very different, both intellectually and psychologically, from that of classical Greece. For this reason, it would be more surprising if there was any similarity between their views on this subject.

The social implications of both systems, however, would have some parallels. Both Nietzsche and Plato specifically reject democracy as a desirable political system. This applies both to the direct democracy of Plato's day and to the representative democracy of later times. The reasoning in both cases is the same. The majority of people, they aver, do not know what is good for them. For both Nietzsche and Plato, ideally there would be a ruling – or commanding – class of philosophers whose thought processes would be alien to the rest of society. In Plato's *Republic*, there would be a class of administrators, craftsmen and other specialists and technicians who would be the 'tools' of the philosopher-kings. Nietzsche saw scholars as fulfilling a similar role for the new philosophers. Finally, there would be the hoi polloi, or the herd, who would be kept acquiescent by means of the noble lie, or the consolations of religion.

Before rejecting such social structures on the grounds of political correctness, it is necessary at the least to analyse the effectiveness of the way in which we currently organise ourselves. Do any of the current systems of democracy used throughout the world actually work well? Would a society be better off, materially or in terms of human happiness, if governed by an elite with the skills to undertake the task? It may be so. The obvious problem is the identification of such an elite, even if it exists. It is also the case that, by definition, most of us would not be part of it. This would almost certainly lead to alienation from, and resentment of, the elite on the part of the governed. Noble lies or religious observance would not necessarily ensure eternal quiescence. The consequences of a majority underclass of the disenfranchised disliking their rulers not infrequently include revolution of one degree of violence or another. The history of all too many nations, including France and Russia, testify to that. It may be that democracy, with all its manifold faults and failings, is the best we can do. Or, as Winston Churchill put it when he spoke in the House of Commons on 11 November 1947: 'No one pretends democracy is perfect or all-wise. Indeed, it has been said that democracy is the worst form of government except all those other forms that have been tried from time to time.'

activity

Distinguish between the sceptic and the critic.

'What is Noble?'

Sections 257–70 are discussed here. The rest of the text is not examined.

The development of value systems

Values and the class system

Nietzsche maintains that the evidence of history demonstrates that only aristocratic societies have succeeded in elevating 'the type "human being"'. In aristocratic societies, it is the fact that there are distances in value between different classes. The aristocrats are at the top. Below them come various inferior workers. At the very bottom there is some type of slave class. He maintains that without this fact of social distance between classes, the 'longing for ever greater distances within the soul itself ... in short, the elevation of the type "human being"' (Nietzsche *Beyond Good and Evil*), the continual 'self-overcoming of the human' could never come about. We should beware, he says, of 'humanitarian delusions' about the actual origins of these societies. In his analysis, 'every previous higher culture on earth' began at a stage in history when that race was made up of 'people who still had a nature that was natural [who were] ... barbarians ... predatory humans' (Nietzsche *Beyond Good and Evil*). These people exercised their will to power, which had not yet been stifled, upon weaker individuals or groups, and overcame them. Therefore, 'At the beginning, the noble caste was always the barbarian caste'. Those with the will to power became the aristocrats. The rest were the inferiors over whom the aristocrats ruled.

So far, this viewpoint may appear to be relatively uncontroversial. Where Nietzsche differs from many analysts, however, is that he asserts that 'the barbarian caste' came to dominance mainly by its spiritual, rather than its physical strength. It was their possession of the will to power which made them successful. In fact, if it is true, as Nietzsche would have it, that those who exercise the will to power are in the minority, it cannot have been that they succeeded through sheer weight of numbers. Were it to be suggested that superior intelligence might have been a factor, Nietzsche would almost certainly have responded with the view that superior intelligence tends to be a feature of the nobility, along with the will to power. He maintains that 'barbarians' are 'more complete human beings' (which at every level also means 'the more complete beasts').

Nietzsche says that aristocracies become corrupted when they cease to believe in the importance of their continued existence for its own sake. If they begin to see themselves as a function of something else, such as monarchy or the community, then the rot sets in. A 'good and healthy aristocracy' sees itself as the reason for which society should continue to exist. Society is the scaffolding upon, and up which, the aristocracy can grow. Non-aristocrats are there in order to be exploited, 'oppressed and diminished' so that the aristocracy might flourish.

Nietzsche goes on to say that the concept that all people are of equal value is a mistake. Given the state of the world, this cannot be a basic principle. People are not, in fact, of equal value. To 'refrain from injuring, abusing or exploiting one another' on principle is to be life-denying. Such a course of action can only lead to 'dissolution and decline'. The essence of life is the will to power. To refrain from trying to achieve greater heights is simply an integral part of being alive. The attempt to progress necessarily involves 'appropriating, injuring, overpowering those who are foreign and weaker'. Nietzsche declares that this fundamental nature of the will to power is 'the original fact of all history'. Despite this, it 'is what the common European conscience' refuses to learn. Such denial Nietzsche condemns as dishonesty. Nietzsche may have a point in that humans inevitably try to avoid unpalatable truths. Therefore, if what he says is actually true, it is likely that he will nonetheless be disbelieved. Where he can be challenged is in his assertion that the will to power is a noble characteristic. It is at least possible that the exploitation of others, certainly of one's competitors, is a necessary stage in the development of human societies. Whether it is noble to continue to feel free to do so, without any actual need, is another matter. It may be that it is a trait of nobility to do as much as is necessary to achieve the desired goal, and then to recognise when to stop.

Master and slave moralities

Nietzsche's studies of the moralities throughout history and in his own day led him to categorise them into two types. These he described as 'master moralities' and 'slave moralities'. In primitive cultures, these are distinct. In more developed cultures, particularly where class distinctions have become less rigid, they are less so. Some societies attempt to mediate between the two. Sometimes the two become confused, and sometimes they are found alongside one another, perhaps even within the same person. Unfortunately, Nietzsche gives no actual instances of these phenomena. Unsurprisingly, in view of his categorisation, Nietzsche holds that moral values for any given society or stratum within it may be determined either by the master caste or by the dependent/slave caste.

Master morality

Where the masters set the standards, then 'noble' equals 'good'. This sounds remarkably like the 'one of us/not one of us' or 'U and non-U' type of categorisation traditionally used by the English aristocracy. In Nietzsche's view, for the nobles, the opposite of 'good' or 'noble' is 'bad'. The concept of 'evil' is characteristic of slave moralities. Noble values include courage, large-mindedness, trust, a sense of self-worth and truthfulness. Noble moral codes flow from the actual characteristics of noble people. Because nobles believe that their judgement is necessarily right, anything they do is necessarily good. Nobles are creators of value. Nietzsche argues that moral historians have failed to appreciate the true origin of moral codes. When they ask why certain actions are praiseworthy, they are asking the wrong question. Moral codes reflect the instinctive (not reasoned) values of the nobility. Actions were praised to the extent that they were coherent with the aristocratic code, not for any value they have in themselves.

Another quality of nobles, according to Nietzsche, is generosity. They help the unfortunate, not out of pity (which is certainly not a noble value) but because of 'the urgency created by an excess of power'. This sounds remarkably like some Christian teaching about the reason for the creation of life, the universe and everything, namely that God did it 'from an outpouring of His overflowing love'. Nietzsche's nobles, possessing abundant power rather than abundant love, and having the will to use it, will do so to help others if they have no better use for it at the time.

Nobles – generosity and harshness

However, nobles value their capacity for harshness. This includes their ability to practise self-discipline, or harshness towards themselves. Nietzsche approves of the Viking reverence for harshness. Nobles also revere old age and their origins, which form the basis for all law, and prejudice towards ancestors rather than the next generation. In Darwinian terms this latter seems somewhat counterproductive. If biology dictates that our instinctive concern is for the survival of our own contribution to the gene pool, it would be expected that we should be biased towards our children rather than our forebears. This, however, does not fit with Nietzsche's thesis that a belief in progress and in the future is the hallmark of the ignoble mind. In saying this, he seems to be contradicting his invocation to the new philosophers to go forward rather than back. However, in the sense that he believes the noble values of the past are superior to the decadent morality of modern Europe, there is in fact some consistency. Those who go beyond good and evil will, like the nobles of old, act according to their own values. In fact, they will create value. In that sense, his envisaged new philosophers have more in common with the past than with the present or the immediate future in Europe. Modern minds reject noble values. In particular, the modern European mind is incapable of grasping that, according to Nietzsche, we only owe duties to our equals. Lesser beings we may treat as we please. Other characteristics of nobles which are currently unacceptable include 'a certain need for enemies'.

Slave morality

'Goodness' and 'badness'

As one would expect, slave morality is created by the value judgements of the oppressed. Those who are oppressed are, understandably, pessimistic, distrustful and sceptical. In particular, they are wary of all things that their oppressors regard as being good. They are appreciative of anything that relieves their misery, including such qualities as pity, kindness, patience and humility. They see values which are in opposition to these and similar qualities as evil. 'Evil' differs from 'bad' in that evil evokes fear. The nobles do not fear non-noble characteristics. They simply regard them as different, and therefore valueless or bad. Slaves, by contrast, fear nobility and everything associated with it. This inevitably includes the moral values of the nobles. The nobles see their own values as good, and accept that these are also values which give rise to fear in their inferiors. So far as they are concerned, there is no contradiction involved. Nobles define their values as good, regardless of their effect upon others. In fact, it is only natural, and therefore right, that inferior people should be afraid of their betters. Inferior people are bad, because they are not noble. However, they are not evil, because they do not constitute a threat. Whereas the nobles see themselves as good by definition and also as capable of harm, slave morality has a different viewpoint. For the slave, a good person is harmless – someone who will not damage them. In slave moralities, therefore, goodness may be associated with a certain lack of intelligence. Relatively stupid people are unlikely to successfully plot or act to one's detriment. Another aspect of slave morality is a valuing of, and desire for, freedom. Noble moralities, by contrast, value certain types of psychological enslavement: 'artistic, rapturous reverence and devotion . . . [and] passionate love'.

It is notable that in Nietzsche's analysis, master morality develops positively. The master, in effect, says 'This is how I am, therefore this is right'. He then defines anything other as bad. Slave morality, by contrast, has negative origins. The slave thinks 'This is my condition. It should be changed. The things which will improve it are good. The things which cause it are evil'. Nobles are proactive: they create. Slaves are reactive: they respond to the conditions which others have created.

Vanity

The valuation of self and the judgements of others

Nobles, says Nietzsche, find it difficult to understand vanity. The noble simply assumes that his own assessment of himself is true in fact. If others have a good opinion of him, that may be pleasant, but it is ultimately unimportant. The negative comments of others are equally meaningless. Slaves, on the other hand, define themselves by the opinions of others. They believe the valuation which their masters put upon them. They do not define themselves – they are the subjects of the definition of others. Nietzsche elaborates by giving instances from his own time. He claims that women, who are in his opinion generally inferior beings, accept the judgements of their priests. Christians, bound as they are to a slave morality, accept that their valuation in the eyes of the Church is correct. If he ever heard it, there is no doubt that Nietzsche would have evidenced the *Jesus Prayer*, which dates from the Early Church, as supportive of his theory. The *Jesus Prayer* is used as a sort of mantra, or aid to evoke the atmosphere required for a period of meditation, and runs: 'Lord Jesus Christ, Son of God, have mercy on me, a sinner.' For Nietzsche, this would have typified slave morality.

review activity

Describe the origins of noble and slave moralities.

The effects of social change in history

Nietzsche says that, through time, the interbreeding of masters and slaves led to a tendency towards democracy. Because of this interbreeding, the 'noble impulse . . . to ascribe one's own values and "think well" of oneself is more and more encouraged and widespread' (Nietzsche *Beyond Good and Evil*). So far, so good. But the inherited slave tendencies lead to vanity becoming widespread too. Vain people take pleasure in every good opinion expressed about themselves, regardless of whether these opinions are useful or accurate. The vain person also takes all criticism to heart, regardless of how far it may be justified, or of the reliability or otherwise of its source. In other words, the vain person submits to the views, and therefore to the values, of others. He does not create his own values. Vanity has overtaken individualism, hence the moral degeneracy of modern societies.

How and why societies decline

Survival of the fittest

Nietzsche considers the development of species and concludes that they come into being in response to unfavourable conditions. In situations of difficulty, only the strong, or the well adapted, survive long enough to breed. Thus far, his argument is common-sense Darwinism. Species develop according to their conditions and only the fittest survive. The same principle, says Nietzsche, applies to societies. Ancient societies were faced with difficulties at home and dangers abroad. They adapted and developed in the face of these threats. They organised themselves in such a way that they could maximise the chances of the society's long-term survival. Systems of education, marital customs and the punishment of the deviant (i.e. law and justice) were all arranged with a view to the preservation of the society. However, successful societies eventually reached a position of stability. Threats have been eliminated, or have faded away of their own accord. The good times arrive. At this point, the society relaxes and 'the coercing band of the old discipline is torn apart'. There is some historical evidence to support this theory. The decline and fall of the Roman Empire may be a case in point. On the other hand, Switzerland, which is both stable and disciplined, may be a counter-example. However, in general we may go so far with Nietzsche as to allow that increased personal freedom and decreasing emphasis upon tradition tend to be characteristic of long-established, stable and wealthy societies.

Nietzsche goes on to say that when species find themselves in more favourable conditions, deviant forms tend to flourish. In hard times, variants fail. This, he says, is also true of human societies. The easier conditions for survival lead to a relaxation of the moral code. This in turn releases the energy to allow individuals to please themselves. He allows that variant individuals may be better or worse than the norm. What is certain, however, is that all the various types will compete with one another. Nietzsche describes this phase in society as providing 'tropical' conditions. There is a sudden growth of all manner of types of life. In such conditions, some of the types perish, whilst others are the cause of their perishing. This leads to a new, threatening condition for society as a whole. Once again, danger, 'the mother of morality', is present. In such times, says Nietzsche, the moral philosophers, 'those keen observers and idlers,' will decide 'that things are quickly going downhill'. The only likely survivors, they will conclude, are the mediocre, the ordinary people, the herd. ' "Be like them! Become mediocre!" will henceforth be the only moral code that makes sense' (Nietzsche *Beyond Good and Evil*). However, says Nietzsche, they will not be so blunt as to use those words. Instead, they will express themselves in terms of 'proportion and dignity and duty and brotherly love'.

A problem with this analysis is that, in every generation throughout recorded history, leading figures have complained that society has gone downhill. The behaviour of 'young people today' was criticised in classical Athens.

Moreover, it seems that the mediocre, the norm, has varied considerably between generations. What is socially acceptable seems to have changed from year to year and from one generation to the next. Nietzsche may be over-stating his case, at least so far as the stasis of societies is concerned. However, it may be allowed that less harsh periods of history do seem to permit more individual self-expression than do times of hardship. Nonetheless, it is still difficult to prove the existence of a society that has shown no change in moral standards at all, whatever privations it may have suffered.

Reverence

Nietzsche maintains that nobles have an instinct to respect and revere that which is 'of the first rank'. Such things include anything notable, such as great jewels, and, perhaps surprisingly, holy books. He even goes so far as to say that the continuing reverence for the Bible is perhaps the best thing Christianity ever did for Europe. At least it enabled people to have the opportunity to experience and express reverence. It is indeed a great achievement, he says, when 'the great crowd (the shallow and diarrhoeal ...)' finally accepts the need to show respect. This, he says, 'is virtually its highest ascent to humanity'. In fact, the 'educated' of his day, the 'believers in "modern ideas"' show less nobility in this respect as they have lost the capacity for awe.

The heritability of character

Nietzsche reverts to his belief that characteristics are inherited. He states that 'all that the best upbringing or education can do is to deceive others' about the fact of inferior breeding. Even Plato, over 2000 years earlier, accepted that no selective breeding plan can be certain. For that reason, in Plato's *Republic*, even the children of slaves would be given the opportunity for a philosophical education if they showed that they had the necessary aptitude. The eleven-plus examination system, which prevailed in England and Wales until the 1970s, and which still exists in some areas today, was predicated upon the Platonic view that people from unpromising backgrounds might yet have the aptitude for academic study. Nietzsche appears to believe that the genotype is all. Nature, says Nietzsche, cannot be beaten.

Common and uncommon people

Outside the herd

Uncommon people, by definition, have less in common with the herd. Therefore, they are less likely to be accepted by it or in communication with it. They will tend to be left alone, which makes them more vulnerable. Being solitary, they are also less likely to form relationships with members of the opposite sex and to go on to procreate. As a result, the herd does most of the breeding and, therefore, herd characteristics tend to predominate in society. Once again, this is, so far, classical Darwinism. Within any society, over time, there tends to be a regression towards the norm. This is likely to be true even if two exceptional individuals breed. Biologists tell us that, on average, any heritable characteristics will be less marked in the offspring than in the parents. If two very tall parents have children together, those children will still tend to be tall, but will usually be closer to average height than their parents are. It has already been noted that Nietzsche's belief in the heritability of psychological characteristics is now widely discredited. Whilst being brought up by two eccentric parents might initially encourage unusual behaviour and attitudes, current thinking is that the social pressure exerted by school and the peer group would tend to modify this effect. Someone who nonetheless remained eccentric into adult life would, admittedly, have more difficulty than most in sustaining a long-term relationship. Of itself, however, in current social conditions, this would not necessarily prevent such a person from having children.

Psychological reflections

Nietzsche asserts that psychologists have discovered that 'it seems to be the rule that higher people come to ruin, that souls that are constituted differently are destroyed' (Nietzsche *Beyond Good and Evil*). When Nietzsche was writing, psychology and psychiatry were in their infancy as scientific disciplines. Whether psychologists today would report the same impression is a very open question. Nietzsche avers, in the light of such psychological knowledge as was available to him at the time, that the great men, the ones whom the crowds admire, are the most tormented. Women, being in his opinion blessed with greater intuition, may realise this, but they labour under the mistaken delusion that love can transform and redeem. In fact, says Nietzsche, love is destructive. It is even possible, in his view, that Jesus sought death because of his need for love. As human love could never satisfy him, it may be that he invented 'a God who was all love, all capacity for love ... One who knows about love like that – seeks death' (Nietzsche *Beyond Good and Evil*). There is no space here to grapple with the major theological issues raised by this thesis. Suffice it to say that Jesus' concept of God was the same as the traditional Jewish concept. As Jesus was himself an observant Jew, this is unsurprising. The book of Hosea, in the Old Testament, which Nietzsche professes to admire, is also an admirable, and psychologically convincing, exploration of human and divine love. At a later date, the poetry of, among others, John Donne (1573–1631), Dean of St Paul's Cathedral from 1621 to 1631, admirably covers the same ground.

It is more than possible that, in writing this passage, Nietzsche was actuated by personal experience and unable to be as objective as he believed himself to be. Nietzsche's home life does not appear to have been characterised by any great affection, although there is no doubt that an active sense of duty prevailed. Indeed, this was exemplified by the care which his mother and sister extended towards him during the last 12 years of his life, during which time he was incurably insane. This insanity was almost certainly the result of a sexually transmitted disease. Whilst the precise details of his emotional and personal life can never be definitely determined, it is widely believed that he contracted this complaint from a prostitute, and that this encounter was his only sexual relationship. This misfortune may also go some way towards explaining his attitude to women, which tends to be uncomplimentary. Nietzsche may be right in his belief that grand passion can be destructive – indeed, this is the theme of many classical and popular tragedies – but it is not inevitably the case that this is so. There are other 'higher characters' whom Nietzsche does not list, such as Einstein, who do not seem to have been sufferers.

The effect of suffering upon the character

Suffering and superficiality

Nietzsche observes that those who have suffered deeply develop a spiritual arrogance. They are certain that their experiences have given them more wisdom than is possessed by others. 'Deep suffering makes us noble; it separates.' As a result, he says, the one who has undergone deep suffering adopts a disguise. These people try, in one way or another, to appear more superficial than is in fact the case, and to persuade others that the human condition in general is superficial. It is, says Nietzsche, 'a sign of a more subtle humanity to revere "the mask" and not pursue psychology or curiosity in the wrong place'. In thus identifying that we all have a persona, an aspect of the personality that we show to others, whilst concealing other and more important characteristics, Nietzsche is undoubtedly correct. Indeed, Nietzsche's philosophy may be characterised as unsystematic, inevitably influenced by the ideas of his time (some of which are now known to be incorrect or questionable), eccentric and sometimes offensive. Having said all that, he showed insight and imagination in so many fields of scholarship, not least philosophy, that he repays critical study.

some questions
to think about

1 To what extent is Nietzsche justified in his criticisms of democracy?

2 Is it the case that some people are more valuable than others? If not, why not? If so, explain how the more valuable are to be identified.

3 In the present day, is practising religion a herd activity, or an expression of individuality?

4 How would Nietzsche's 'noble values' work out in today's society?

5 What are the 'correct' philosophical questions?

6 Is Nietzsche right to see the scholar as a tool, rather than someone of value for his or her own sake?

7 Are philosophers primarily interested in imposing their own views upon others?

further
reading

▶ Hayman's book in the Great Philosopher Series, 1997 is a short and readable introduction to Nietzsche's work in general.

▶ The same author also wrote a longer book: *Nietzsche: A Critical Life*, 1980.

▶ Also see *Nietzsche: the Last Antipolitical German*, Bergmann 1987.

V

important terms

A posteriori: known on the basis of experience. For example, causes can only be known through experience and not purely by reason.

A priori: known to be true independently of experience, for example the propositions of mathematics and geometry. They cannot be disconfirmed by observation and experiment.

Deduction/deductive argument: in an argument that is deductively valid, the conclusion is logically entailed by the premises, so that to assert the premises but deny the conclusion leads to a contradiction. This is because the information contained in the conclusion is already present implicitly in the premises.

Foundationalism: the theory that knowledge has foundations in the form of statements that are not inferred from any more basic statements. What these basic statements are, and how they are known to be true, is controversial. Russell thinks that it is statements that describe the immediate contents of experiences which possess primitive certainty, and on the foundation of which all our knowledge is built up.

Global scepticism: the attempt to call everything into question, and to maintain that there is nothing that we can know for certain.

Induction/inductive argument: an inductive argument is one where the premises do not logically entail the conclusion, because the conclusion contains information which goes beyond what is found in the premises. The typical form of an inductive argument is 'all the Xs observed so far have been Ys, therefore all the Xs there are, are Ys'. The problem of the justification remains a much-debated issue ever since Hume drew attention to it.

Russell: *The Problems of Philosophy*

Russell's life and works

Born in 1872 and dying in 1970, Bertrand Russell had a long and distinguished career. His grandfather was Lord John Russell, the famous Liberal statesman, who served Queen Victoria twice as Prime Minister, and was the author of the Great Reform Act of 1832, as well as the initiator of many other reforms. As a reward for his political services he was given Pembroke Lodge in Richmond Park in Surrey, where Russell was subsequently to grow up. Russell's father was Lord Amberley, and his mother was the daughter of another Liberal politician, Lord Stanley of Alderley. His godfather was the philosopher John Stuart Mill, a close friend of the Amberleys, and whom they much admired. Russell's parents died before he was four years old, and his grandfather when he was six. Subsequently, Russell was brought up by his grandmother, who went on to live many years.

Throughout his early adolescence and adult years, Russell was a prolific writer, producing over 60 books, as well as uncounted papers and articles. These cover a wide and varied field including philosophy, geometry, mathematics, the philosophy of science, epistemology, ethics, political theory, religion, and education. Russell took an early interest in the question of God's existence, and his notebooks reveal that by the time he was 15, he was effectively an atheist, a position from which he never wavered. Hume had written, 'Generally speaking the errors in religion are dangerous, those in philosophy merely ridiculous' and, like Hume, Russell was distrustful of institutionalised religious belief, because of the intolerance and fanaticism to which it can lead. Later he wrote the pamphlet *Why I am not a Christian* in which he attacks the Church for retarding progress. Besides philosophy, Russell's passion was for mathematics, and this was to culminate in the monumental *Principia Mathematica*, written in collaboration with Alfred North Whitehead, and published between 1910 and 1913. The aim of the book was to show how mathematics is derivable from logic, and if Russell had died immediately after its completion, he would have still gone down in history as a great thinker. As it turned out, he was to live another 57 years. It was an eventful and fruitful life in every respect.

In 1894, Russell completed his degree at Trinity College, Cambridge, and went on to become a Fellow, until 1916, when he was dismissed for his opposition to the First World War. In his autobiography he tells how he was moved by the

Idealism: the theory that everything that exists is purely mental in nature. Things are either immaterial minds or in minds as ideas.

Knowledge by acquaintance: knowledge of things by direct acquaintance with them through experience and which is logically independent of knowledge of truths. Knowledge of our own sense-data would qualify as this type of knowledge.

Knowledge by description: knowledge of things that have not been directly experienced but which have been inferred from knowledge by acquaintance. For Russell, all knowledge of the material world is knowledge by description because he thinks we cannot be directly acquainted with it, but only our sense-data. Thus knowledge by description of a tree would be 'the thing that gives rise to such and such sorts of sense-data'.

Logically proper names: Russell's idea of a logically proper name is a name whose meaning is the object to which it refers, unlike ordinary names in everyday life which are supposedly disguised descriptions. Examples of logically proper names are 'this' and 'that' where these refer to an immediate object of experience, such as a sense-datum.

Methodological scepticism: the attempt to arrive at knowledge by subjecting statements to the test of whether they can be doubted and only retaining those which are immune to question.

Pyrrhonian scepticism: the global or radical scepticism associated with Pyrrho of Elis (c.365–270 BC)

Sense-data (singular: sense-datum): sense-data are supposed to be the immediate givens or deliverances of the senses, existing in the mind and not the physical world. They are radically private to the individual percipient and exist, like sensations, only when the person is conscious of them.

inscription in the flyleaf of his grandmother's Bible: 'Never follow a multitude to do evil', and this was a precept he followed all his life, twice being arrested for following his conscience. On the first of these two occasions, in 1918, he was locked up for six months because he had written a pamphlet suggesting, satirically, that American soldiers would make good breakers of strikes undertaken in opposition to the war. He put his time in incarceration to good use, however, producing *An Introduction to Mathematical Philosophy*. Years later, after he had helped to found the Campaign for Nuclear Disarmament, he was arrested again, remarkably, at the age of 89, this time in Trafalgar Square, for taking part in a demonstration against the bomb, and refusing to move on when requested by the police. As a result he was given a sentence of four weeks, which time he spent in the prison hospital. It is impossible not to marvel at Russell's moral commitment and the fortitude that the two incidents reveal. In between writing, Russell found time to be married four times, and have several affairs along the way. He founded and owned a school at one time, an episode he later came to regret, and was briefly to stand, without success, as an MP for Labour. On the death of his elder brother, Frank, in 1931, he became the third Earl Russell, but he scarcely availed himself of the privilege of sitting in the upper chamber of the House. However, one of his three children, Conrad Russell, is currently a vigorous member of the Lords. Russell was awarded the Order of Merit in 1949 and the Nobel Prize for Literature in 1950. It is a mark of Russell's characteristic impish sense of humour, alluded to by T.S. Eliot in his indelible portrait of the philosopher, the poem entitled *Mr Apollinax*, that in one of Russell's books the last two pages are covered with the multitude of honorary degrees he had received, the very last entry of all, however, reading: 'Judged not fit to be a Fellow of Trinity College.'

A note on the text

The edition we are studying was first published in 1912 by the Home University Library, and reissued in 1967 by Oxford University Press. *The Problems of Philosophy* is arguably one of the best introductions to philosophy, even though it does not attempt a comprehensive or neutral survey of philosophical issues, but is unashamedly partisan in presenting Russell's own views. It affords a glimpse of the state of British philosophy in the early years of the twentieth century, and despite innovations such as the distinction between knowledge by acquaintance, and knowledge by description, together with the associated Theory of Descriptions, reveals the debt it owes to the work of Locke, Berkeley and Hume, the British empiricists, as well as the more remote influences of Descartes and Plato. Russell emphasises the importance of both experience and reason for the acquisition of knowledge, and calls into question any attempts to prove, merely by logical reasoning, what reality must be like. But he also stresses the power and beauty of logic and mathematics in contributing towards an understanding of our existence, provided these disciplines are confined within their proper spheres. Russell is not always as careful as he might be in avoiding ambiguity or inconsistency – parts of the book give the impression that it was written very rapidly in an extemporary fashion – but that is a small price to pay for the intellectual excitement evident in his thinking.

Chapter 1: 'Appearance and Reality'

Bertrand Russell (1872–1970)

Cartesian methodological scepticism

Russell begins by asking whether there is any knowledge in the world that is so certain that no reasonable person could doubt it. In asking this question Russell effectively reprises Descartes, who had resolved at the beginning of the *Meditations* to reject not only what was false, but also what could not be doubted. This is known as systematic doubt, and it illustrates what is known as methodological scepticism. The intention that informs this scepticism is entirely benign: it aims at discovering knowledge so certain that it cannot be doubted and hence can serve as the rock solid foundations of the edifice of knowledge. Russell shows his appreciation of Descartes regarding the use of methodological scepticism as a means of acquiring knowledge, when he comments that it 'may still be used with profit' (Russell 1967: 7), and 'By inventing the method of doubt, and by showing that subjective things are the most certain, Descartes performed a great service to philosophy, and one which makes him still useful to all students of the subject' (Russell 1967: 8). The second remark reveals that, like Descartes, Russell is an epistemological foundationalist. Knowledge is conceived of as consisting of a hierarchy, the tiers built one upon the other. The foundations of the building are indubitable truths: for Descartes, the *Cogito*, 'I think therefore I am'; and for Russell, statements about 'our particular thoughts and feelings that possess primitive certainty' (Russell 1967: 8).

Global or Pyrrhonian scepticism

However, as we shall see, the Cartesian method of doubt, despite its positive intentions, ultimately proves to be a poisoned chalice, leading inexorably to solipsism, and the impossibility of knowing anything beyond the closed circle of one's own consciousness. It leads, in other words, down into radical, or global scepticism – Pyrrhonian scepticism, as it was referred to by Hume – and to which he confessed he was incapable of providing a resolution.

The stages of doubt

How does the method of doubt proceed? Descartes imagines he is seated in his chair, in front of the fire, in his dressing gown, and holding a piece of paper in his hands. He then proceeds to call this claim into question. Perhaps he is only dreaming he is doing so, or more radically, perhaps an evil demon is deceiving him in this belief. So the confidence he reposes in his senses and the truth of his beliefs founded upon their deliverances, deserts him. Russell similarly thinks that such beliefs as that it seems to him that he is sitting in a chair, that he can see buildings and clouds and the sun out of the window, that he knows the sun is 93 million miles from earth and it will rise every morning, can all reasonably be doubted. His belief that another person can see the same tables and chairs as he does may also be called into question, as can equally his belief that the table he feels pressing against his arm is one and the same table which he can see.

Cartesian doubt contrasted with ordinary everyday doubt

It is important to realise that the doubt in which Descartes and Russell are engaging is not ordinary everyday doubt, such as the uncertainty which might legitimately arise when Russell looks out of the window and is not sure whether the leafless tree which he sees is a hornbeam, as opposed to a lime tree. Here, if there is any doubt about what type of tree Russell sees, the doubt could soon be settled by going and taking a closer look. If Russell's first judgement about what kind of tree he sees is wrong, closer inspection could settle the question. Further sense-experience and investigation could be used to correct the first faulty judgement and dispel any doubt about the matter. But it is plain that this will not satisfy Russell, because correcting one faulty perceptual judgement by an appeal to further sense-experience would be, for him, going in a circle: how can he trust *any* judgement founded upon sense-experience? This brings out the peculiarity of Cartesian scepticism as opposed to ordinary everyday doubt about particular things, namely that it is universal in its scope. This is bound to leave us with the frustrated feeling that philosophical doubt is unanswerable, because whatever we appeal to as certain knowledge will similarly be called into question, just like the original claim.

review
activity

1. Briefly outline the stages of systematic doubt and explain its purpose.

2. Explain in your own words how Cartesian doubt differs from ordinary non-philosophical doubt.

So what are Russell's, and by implication Descartes', grounds for doubt? It cannot be that because the senses have sometimes let us down, they might always do so. For a start, we only found out in the first place that the senses deceived us on the basis of further experience. Moreover, the supposition that we might always have been deceived, from the very inception, makes no more sense than the supposition that all the money there ever has been in the world, is currently, and will be, could be counterfeit, for without a contrast the word loses its meaning. To put it paradoxically, if all perceptual judgements are false, then none are. If it is insisted that all such judgements are false, then the distinction between the true and the false would simply re-emerge as the contrast between the false, and the false-false.

The bare conceivability of the falsity of empirical as a ground for doubt

The explanation for Russell's and Descartes' scepticism runs as follows. It is a characteristic of synthetic statements which figure in empirical judgements that they are capable of being false or true. Indeed, this is their defining characteristic, for if they were logically incapable of falsehood, they would be analytic rather than synthetic. As it is logically possible that synthetic statements could be false, it follows that it is possible to conceive or imagine that they are false. This is the philosophical point Descartes is making by means of his picturesque and memorable fantasy of an omnipotent deceiving evil demon. Regarding any particular statement, or any class of such statements, the possibility that they are false cannot be ruled out. But we might question whether the mere imaginability or conceivability that a statement or group of statements could be false is a genuine ground for doubting those statements.

Certainly, if we take it to be so, together with the claim that any ground for doubt instantly excludes knowledge, there is going to be little, if anything, we could be said to know. This will be true even of first-person, present-tense reports of sensations or perceptions of colour, despite Russell's conviction that such statements are incorrigible and immune from rejection, as the following remark reveals: 'Thus it is that our particular thoughts and feelings have primitive certainty' (Russell 1967: 8), However, as John Austin aptly remarks, in making a judgement about what is apparently a magenta-coloured sense-datum, for example, a supposedly purely subjective experience, there is more room for error than merely making a slip of the tongue:

> *I may say 'Magenta' wrongly either by a mere slip, having meant to say 'Vermilion'; or because I don't quite know what 'magenta' means, what shade of colour is called magenta; or again, because I was unable to, or perhaps just didn't, really notice or attend to or size up the colour before me. Thus, there is always the possibility, not only that I may be brought to admit that 'magenta' wasn't the right word to pick on for the colour before me, but also that I may be brought to see, or perhaps remember, that the colour before me just wasn't magenta. And this holds for the case in which I say, 'It seems, to me personally, here and now, as if I were seeing something magenta,' just as much for the case in which I say, 'This is magenta.' The first formula may be more cautious, but it isn't incorrigible.*
> (Austin 1962: 113)

No special class of incorrigible statements

Austin goes on to claim that there is no special class of statements as such, for example, sense-datum statements, which makes it unreasonable to doubt them. What is important is the circumstances in which they are made. The smell of a pig in the room, together with some pig hairs and droppings, make it reasonable to suppose a pig is in the offing. But for all that, there is some room for doubt, as the apparent evidence for the pig could have been planted, or the pig long gone. But if the pig comes and stands in front of us, in a good light, and we all agree we can see and hear it, the point will rapidly come when any expression of doubt is groundless, and the judgement that a pig is present will, for all practical purposes, be incorrigible.

Conceivability of the falsehood of a statement not a ground for doubt

To bring this discussion to a close, the correct response to Cartesian methodological scepticism should be this. Firstly, the mere conceivability of the falsehood of a statement as a ground for doubt should be rejected. Although it is conceivable that a proposition P is false and it is logically possible to suppose it is false, this does not supply a genuine reason for doubting P, much less for thinking it to be false. In comparison, it is conceivable that the sun will not rise tomorrow, but that is no reason for thinking it will not rise. It is logically possible, and, hence imaginable, that a man might survive having his head chopped off, but that is no reason for thinking that anyone to whom this misfortune befalls will go on living, or that there is serious room for doubt regarding the outcome of a beheading.

Infallibilism sets the standard for knowledge self-contradictorily high

Secondly, even where a genuine doubt regarding the truth of a belief is possible, and not merely the bare imaginability of the falsity of the belief, i.e. the theoretical possibility of its falsity, making indubitability a requirement for knowledge arguably has the effect of restricting knowledge to analytic truths, whose falsehood is not logically possible, and hence cannot be conceived to be false. For example, suppose I hear on the news that a derelict space craft is due to crash on Earth. I have some reason for thinking it just might demolish my house whilst I am out at work. Let us now suppose that I am now at work, having left my house safe and sound that morning, and I claim I have good reason for thinking it still to be standing intact. Suppose further that in fact my house is standing untouched. I have strong reasons, moreover, for thinking that it is safe, so my claim to know that my house is still standing is true and it is supported by strong justifications because of the very remote chance that the space craft will fall on that very spot. Nevertheless, it has to be admitted that there is room for a genuine doubt to enter in, because the probability the house will be destroyed, although extremely small, cannot be entirely excluded. Hence the faintest smidgeon of a doubt about the security of my house can enter in. Does this mean, because of the possibility of a genuine doubt, that I do not know my house is still standing when I am at work and I had good reason earlier in the day for claiming it was safe and sound? Again, the adoption of this position, infallibilism as it is known among philosophers, appears to set too high a standard for the possibility of knowledge, threatening to deprive the concept of any useful work to do. It amounts to a demand for empirical knowledge to be possible that is self-contradictorily high, for it effectively wants synthetic truths to be like analytic truths, whilst implicitly acknowledging that synthetic truths can never be equivalent to analytic truths. In fact, going further, it is not clear that the requirement for the impossibility of doubt regarding knowledge of analytic truths can be met even in their case, for however much one checks a logical demonstration, the possibility of going wrong through a lack of attention or thoroughness can never perhaps entirely be excluded. For this reason, a more relaxed position, fallibilism, which does not require that all doubt about the truth of a statement should be eliminated if that statement can be known, appears to be a more reasonable position to adopt.

review activity

How does Descartes' methodological scepticism lead to setting the standard for empirical knowledge to be possible self-contradictorily high?

As a postscript, it is worth remarking that it might be thought that the two reasons supplied for rejecting the Cartesian conception of knowledge really amount to the same thing. This, however, is not so. The first maintains that the bare logical possibility of falsehood constitutes a ground for doubt. The second, by contrast, maintains, in effect, that we can accept as knowledge beliefs that still may need to be reappraised in the light of further evidence that could come in.

Sense-data as the immediate objects of perception

Russell now turns from more general arguments for scepticism regarding the external world to arguments derived from the nature of perception. The primary aim of all these arguments is to persuade us that in perception we are not immediately aware of physical objects and phenomena, which can exist independently of our awareness of them, but mental images that are radically private to the observer. For Locke and Berkeley these images were known as *ideas*; Hume called them *impressions*; and since the beginning of the twentieth century, they have been known as *sense-data* (singular: *sense-datum*). Sense-data are dependent for their existence on being perceived, like sensations, such as pains and itches. They are thus like Berkeleyan ideas, whose essential feature is that they exist in some mind or other, God's at least, if not the minds of other human beings, or minded beings, of whatever variety. As Berkeley says, in the case of ideas, their '*esse is percipi*' ('to be', 'to exist') is to be perceived. Moreover, whereas physical objects can appear to have qualities they do not in fact possess, or do not appear to possess qualities they actually have, in the case of sense-data what you see is what you get. As Hume remarked, 'Since consciousness never deceives, they must appear in every particular what they are, and be what they appear'. Judgements regarding sense-data are thus allegedly indubitable and incorrigible, beyond the reach of correction and revision, comprising just the hallmarks of certainty and stability of the foundations of the epistemologies which Russell and Descartes are proposing.

There are basically three sorts of argument advanced by Russell in support of sense-datum theory, and these we shall need to examine critically in turn:

1. the argument from perceptual variability
2. the secondary qualities argument
3. the time lag argument.

1. The argument from perceptual variability

This argument begins with the familiar fact that a thing can look very different to the same person at different times, or to different people at the same time, depending on the surrounding conditions such as the lighting, where the observer is relative to the object seen, the angle at which the object is seen, and so forth. It trades on the fact that there can often be a disparity between how things look or appear to someone, and how they actually are: the content of the visual experience does not match the external reality. In Chapter 1 Russell puts forward two versions of this argument, one designed to show that, in themselves, objects, strictly speaking, do not possess colours, the colours instead being located in the mind of the perceiver as sense-data; and the other, directed at the shapes of things, which again are supposed to comprise private mind-dependent entities.

The argument from perceptual variability

In support of the first argument, Russell considers the example of a table. He notes that it does not look the same colour all over, some parts looking brighter than other parts, and, if he moves, the apparent distribution of the colours will change. Moreover, no two people will see the same distribution of colours, because no two people can see the table from exactly the same point of view as they cannot be in the same place at the same time. He concludes that there is no reason, therefore, for regarding some colours of the table as more really its colour than any of the others, moving to the conclusion, with breathtaking swiftness, that colour is not something inherent in the table, but something that depends upon the spectator, the nature of the table, and the way the light falls upon it.

Critical evaluation of the argument from perceptual variability

What has gone wrong here? Firstly we may note the invalid move of passing from the alleged difficulty of determining what the real colour of a thing is, to the conclusion that it isn't really coloured. But is there usually any difficulty in saying what the 'real' colour of an object is? Suppose I see a defunct pillar box that someone has appropriated as a garden ornament and painted green. I might say to someone from abroad who is not acquainted with pillar boxes, 'That's not its real colour, you know. It should be red.' It would be a strange misunderstanding to take me as claiming that the green colour of the pillar box is somehow unreal, a hallucination perhaps, or that the pillar box doesn't really have a colour. It plainly is green, though one would expect it to be red, like standard pillar boxes. Of course, a red pillar box need not always *look* red as it does in ordinary daylight. In a street lit by mercury vapour lamps the pillar box will look a dark shade of grey, but why should this lead to the conclusion that the pillar box isn't really red, or, even more alarmingly, that the pillar box has no colour at all? When I see the pillar box at night lit by the mercury vapour lamps, the correct answer to the question 'What do you see?' is not 'I see a dark grey pillar box' but 'I see a red pillar box which appears grey'. But from this we may not infer that I am not aware of the pillar box itself, because the pillar box is red, but what I see is grey. What I see is *not* grey; it is red, but only *appears* grey under the conditions described. To conclude that I see a grey thing, a grey mental image, and not a red pillar box, appearing grey to me, is to *reify* the way something appears, to turn it illegitimately into a thing. But the appearance of a thing is not itself an entity, something perhaps like a membrane which could somehow detach itself from the object and exist independently in its own right, being placed conveniently in the mind of the perceiver because there is apparently no other place for it to be located. No doubt, because the word 'appearance' is a noun, and we all learn at school that nouns acquire their meanings by naming things, we are tempted to think of appearances as things. But when I see a red pillar box that looks grey, there are not two things, a red pillar box and a grey appearance, i.e. a sense-datum, but only one thing, the red pillar box that looks grey. Only someone who had already adopted the theory of sense-data in advance could fail to be persuaded by the correctness of these observations.

Essentially the same criticism can be made of the argument concerning the variability of the apparent shapes of things. As we move around the room, Russell claims that the shape of the table constantly changes its appearance:

> But the 'real' shape is not what we see; it is something inferred from what we see. And what we see is constantly changing in shape as we move about the room; so here again the senses seem not to give us the truth about the table itself, but only about the appearance of the table. (Russell 1967: 3)

The reification of appearances

But, contrary to what Russell avers, what we see is *not* constantly changing its shape: tables are rigid objects whose shape does not change as we walk around and look at them. The appearance of the table, how it looks to us, changes as we walk around it. We can say that it *appears* to change its shape, but we cannot claim that it actually *does* change its shape. To make this claim illegitimately reifies the apparent shape of the table, the way it appears to us. So once again, we do not have two sorts of thing on our hands, the physical table and its appearances existing purely in the mind of the perceiver, but only one thing, the table, which appears to us in different ways. Thus Russell's claim that the 'senses seem not to give us the truth about the table itself, but only about the appearance of the table' (Russell 1967: 3) is blocked, and we are not forced to embrace his conclusion that we are irrevocably cut off from the material world which becomes unknowable.

review
activity

Explain how the error of reifying appearances renders the argument from perceptual variability invalid.

2. The secondary qualities argument

Primary and secondary qualities

The distinction between primary and secondary qualities goes back at least as far as Epicurus (341–270 BC) but came to prominence in the seventeenth century, notably in the works of Locke (1632–1704). Primary qualities were supposed to be really inherent in bodies and comprised qualities such as extension, shape, motion or rest, solidity, and number. Secondary qualities were colour, taste, sound, smell, and tactile qualities. These, as experienced phenomenally by us, were claimed not to be inherent in bodies, but produced in us by the action of streams of minute corpuscles whose only properties were the primary qualities mentioned above. In this way, primary qualities came to be viewed as explanatorily basic: we can explain why things look the colour they do, for example, by reference to the action of the corpuscles on our sensory apparatus.

Nowadays we would not speak of corpuscles but of wavelengths of light. Light of a certain wavelength is reflected into our eyes and stimulates our retinas in a certain manner – different wavelengths stimulate the retinal cells in different ways – and this physical chain of events is conveyed via the optic nerve to the occipital lobes of the brain, where the end result is our perception of colour. The perception of colour is the end result of this process, not the beginning, and as it appears to make no sense to claim that colours are conveyed along the nerves, it seems that colour is an entirely subjective phenomenon, by contrast with the objective physical processes that give rise to it. As Russell remarks:

> To begin with, it is plain that the colour we see depends only on the nature of the light-waves that strike the eye, and is therefore modified by the medium intervening between us and the object, as well as by the manner in which the light is reflected from the object in the direction of the eye. (Russell 1967: 17–18)

Secondary qualities as subjective and mind-dependent

This view has some support from Locke's observation, namely that if you take an almond and cut it, it will be sweet and white, but if you then pound it, it will smell and taste bitter, and go a dirty grey colour. Yet what has produced the changes in the secondary qualities but a change in the primary qualities? There thus appears to be a one-sided dependence of secondary qualities, as experienced by us, on the primary qualities of bodies: we change secondary qualities by altering primary qualities, and not the other way around. In other words, when accounting for secondary qualities, primary qualities are explanatorily basic. Should we then conclude, as Russell does, that secondary qualities are not part of the physical world? He writes: 'it is quite gratuitous to suppose that physical objects have colours, and therefore there is no justification for making such a supposition,' adding, 'Exactly similar arguments will apply to other sense-data' (Russell 1967: 18).

Now, there is no doubt about the powerful appeal this way of approaching the issue can exert upon us. But do we want to accept that colour is ultimately a kind of illusion and not really part of physical reality? There is no easy way of settling this vexed issue, and no agreement generally on how it should be resolved, with philosophers lining up on both sides of the debate. What we can say positively is that colours have a physical basis in that the light reflected from their surfaces is determined by the atomic structure of those surfaces, so redness, for example, is a property of the object in the sense that it has a disposition to appear red to normal people in standard circumstances. The fact that an object cannot be seen to have a colour in the dark does not disturb this point, for the claim is only that the object *would* appear red to observers *if* certain conditions were to be fulfilled.

Explanations of phenomena need not amount to explaining the phenomena away

It might also be pointed out that just because we can *explain* why things look the colour they do, this is no reason to think that this amounts to *explaining away* the colour. Within the human world, the world of familiar everyday experience, there is all the difference between things which possess colour and those which lack it, such as a colourless gas, for example, and no amount of scientific theorising, it could be argued, can make us deny this common fact of experience.

Perhaps a parallel example is constituted by the explanation of why things are solid in terms of the behaviour of atoms, this explanation containing the startling information that atoms are comprised mainly of empty space. How then, we wonder, can objects be solid and offer resistance to touch, if they are really more like nets, into whose holes we can easily poke our fingers? But clearly we cannot give up the common-sense belief that there are solid objects in the world, as we are all familiar with being able to touch objects, and we know about such things as car crashes, for example. As Calvin Pinchin goes on to point out in his discussion of this issue:

> [I]f we revised our conception of solidity so that anything which can have electrons passing through it is to be called 'non-solid', then we are going to have to say that just about everything is non-solid. The problem would then be to give a meaning to 'solid', and if we could not do this, then how could 'non-solid' have a meaning?
>
> (Pinchin 2005: 26–7)

It has to be acknowledged, however, before we leave this difficult issue, that it might be objected that the cases of colour and solidity are not really parallel, and that phenomenal colours, that is, colours as experienced by us, retain their subjectivity, and therefore their irreducibility, to the physical structures and processes that can account for them. But this is a problem to be commended to the reader for further exploration and discussion.

review activity

Is Russell correct to conclude that it is quite gratuitous to attribute colours to physical objects?

3. The time lag argument

This argument, which occurs in Chapter 3, need not detain us long. Briefly, it says that as the sun is 93 million miles away and it takes the light from the sun about 8 minutes to reach us, were the sun to cease to exist during that time, we would not know, and our experience of seeing the sun would continue uninterrupted, even though the sun no longer existed. The implication appears to be that we cannot possibly be aware of the sun, as it is no longer there to be seen, but as we are still aware of something rather than nothing, it must be a sensedatum of which we are conscious. This argument, were it to be acceptable, could be generalised to all cases of visual perception, as even with regard to physical objects very close to us, it still takes a finite time for light from the objects to reach our eyes, albeit an infinitesimal fraction of temporal duration.

The time lag argument fails to establish sense-datum theory

But the conclusion, as will be readily apparent, can easily be sidestepped, and we are not committed to embrace sense-data, as the immediate logically private objects of vision, rather than physical phenomena. We can always insist that we see the sun, but we see it how it was 8 minutes ago. In other words, we see into the past, just as we hear the report of distant guns some time after they have been fired.

The causal argument for sense-data

Incidentally, before we leave this topic it will be worth briefly describing a related argument, not explicitly canvassed by Russell in *The Problems of Philosophy*, but which repeatedly recurs in attempts to argue for sense-datum theory. This is the *causal argument*, and it goes something like this. An object affects our eyes, and triggers a long causal train of events, reaching from the periphery of our sense organs via the retina and the optic nerve, to the occipital lobes of the brain, which are known to deal with visual perception. These physical events somehow then give rise to a visual experience, and it is this of which we are immediately aware, rather than the physical object that triggered the causal chain in the first place. The visual experience, of course, is a sense-datum which is private to the individual, and exists only as long the person is aware of it.

Rejection of the causal argument

The problem with this story is not difficult to discern. Once again, as we saw earlier in this chapter, if all we are aware of is a sense-datum in the privacy of our minds, how can we possibly know there is a physical world corresponding to it and which is causally responsible for its existence? Going further, how can we know that eyes, retinas, optic nerves, brains, and the skulls to contain them exist, as these are all part of the physical world? Yet it is just these things the theory requires to get started. So the theory ends in self-contradiction by sawing off the branch it is sitting on.

Causal realism: objects cause us to see them

Does this mean we need to deny that perception has causes, including most importantly the object that is perceived? By no means. We merely need to re-arrange the causes not so that they form a linear chain, reaching from the outside world into the inner private recesses of the mind, but as the conditions that make seeing the object possible. The object causes us to see *it* itself, and not some proxy or substitute for it. But it is not causally sufficient alone to be able to do this: other things have to go on, such as light being present, the optic nerve functioning in the right way, the eyes being open and the head being correctly orientated, and so forth. In conclusion, a causal theory of perception need not be interpreted so that it inexorably (and paradoxically) leads us into acceptance of sense-datum theory.

review activity

What is the causal argument for sense-data and how does it contradict itself?

Chapter 2: 'The Existence of Matter'

Russell now turns his attention more explicitly to the question of whether we can know that the material world exists independently of our experience of it. If we cannot know this, then we cannot know of the existence of other people's bodies, and this in turn would preclude any knowledge of other minds, as it is only on the basis of what flesh-and-blood people say and do, that we have any evidence for the existence of minds other than our own.

Commitment to sense-datum theory makes knowledge of the existence of the external world problematic

Russell sees clearly that if each individual consciousness possesses, as its total perceptual resources, nothing but fleeting and logically private sense-data, there appears to be no prospect of knowing that an independently existing public world of material objects exists. If all we are acquainted with are our private sense-data, how can we possibly infer the existence of an external world?

The impossibility of inferring the existence of the external world from sense-data either deductively or inductively

Deductive inference is out of the question because the meaning of talk about sense-data concerns a realm of logically private sense-dependent objects, whereas the meaning of talk about objects concerns independently existing public things. It is plain that the first kind of discourse can logically entail nothing about the second, as the information contained in the conclusion of a deductive argument is already implicitly contained in the premises. Neither is inductive inference possible because we are acquainted with only one term of the inductive relation, namely our own private sense-data. Inductive inferences are ampliative, that is, their conclusions go beyond the information contained in their premises. Thus, it is only where a correlation has been established between two types of phenomena that induction is possible. For example, suppose a correlation has been established between it raining and students invariably being late for classes. On this basis, the next time it rains I confidently expect students will be late, and subsequently so they are, confirming my induction. But I cannot in principle establish a correlation between the presence of my sense-data, and a physical object of which they are supposedly signs, because I can only have one term of the relation available to me, as the physical object, if there is one, is hidden behind the veil of sense-data. Thus, we are forced to conclude that if sense-data are the immediate objects of perception, we cannot know the physical world exists.

Like Hume before him, Russell is prepared to accept that this despairing conclusion *could* be true, although he adds that he sees no reason for supposing that it actually *is* true. However, the fact remains, as Russell acknowledges, 'In one sense it must be admitted that we can never prove the existence of things other than ourselves and our experiences. No logical absurdity results from the hypothesis that the world consists of myself and my thoughts and feelings and sensations, and that everything else is mere fancy' (Russell 1967: 10).

However, the position is, if anything, rather worse than this. Firstly, how can Russell even *wonder* whether there is an external world, as this term will have no application to anything in his possible experience to which it could possibly answer? A concept which has no application to a possible experience is a concept in name only, and possesses no meaning. As Kant remarked in the *Critique of Pure Reason*, 'Concepts without intuitions [experiences of particular things] are empty, intuitions without concepts are blind [particular

sense-experiences could be as nothing to us, if not brought under concepts]'
(Kant 1963: 93).

Does commitment to belief in sense-data rule out knowledge of the existence of the external world?

Reservations regarding the existence of a single self

Russell now considers how Descartes' systematic doubt, the programme of methodological scepticism, led to the *Cogito*, 'I think therefore I am', so that at least this one thing was absolutely certain to him, providing him with a sure foundation on which to build the edifice of knowledge. Russell has reservations as to whether Descartes can show by means of this reasoning that there is a single subject of experience, a single self. It might be that the subject of experience exists only momentarily and changes from instant to instant. Russell will return to this issue later when he considers, but does not quite embrace at this stage of his philosophy, a Humean view of the self as a bundle of experiences.

The external world as the best hypothesis for explaining the nature and order of our experiences

The use of the *Cogito* as an epistemological first principle on the basis of which knowledge is to be reconstructed is thus ruled out for Russell, as indeed is also any appeal to God by means of which knowledge of the external world is to be secured. Descartes appealed to an all-powerful, non-deceiving God, as the solution; essentially God would not let me persist in the happy belief that there was an external world if there wasn't one. Russell, having eschewed belief in God at a very early stage of his philosophical life, could not avail himself of this strategy. Instead, as an alternative to Hume's naturalistic, psychological account of why we can't help believing in bodies in the absence of any possibility of a rational philosophical demonstration that solipsism is false, he awarded the status of a theory or hypothesis to the existence of the external world as the most simple and systematic explanation, of the coherence and regularity of the bulk of our experience. Russell, however, does share Hume's belief that our belief in the existence of an external reality is instinctive, and not the product of any process of reasoning of reflection. Hume had written:

> *It seems evident, that men are carried, by a natural instinct or prepossession, to repose faith in their senses; and that, without any reasoning, or even almost before the use of reason, we always suppose an external universe, which depends not on our perception, but would exist, though we and every sensible creature were absent or annihilated ... It seems also evident, that, when men follow this blind and powerful instinct of nature, they always suppose the very images, presented by the senses, to be the external objects, and never entertain any suspicion, that the ones are nothing but the representations of the other.*

> (Hume 1975: 151)

Rejection of scepticism regarding the existence of the external world

The operation of this instinct, according to Hume, leads to a mistake. Russell, by contrast, draws a more virtuous conclusion:

> *Of course it is not by argument that we come by our belief in an independent external world. We find this belief in ourselves as soon as we begin to reflect: it*

is what may be called an instinctive *belief. We should never have been led to question this belief but for the fact that, at any rate in the case of sight, it seems as if the sense-datum itself were instinctively believed to be the independent object, whereas argument shows that the object cannot be identical with the sense-datum. This discovery, however ... leaves undiminished our instinctive belief that there are* objects *corresponding to our sense-data. Since this belief does not lead to any difficulties, but on the contrary tends to simplify and systematise our account of our experiences, there seems no good reason for rejecting it. We may therefore admit – though with a slight doubt derived from dreams – that the external world does really exist, and is not wholly dependent for its existence upon our continuing to perceive it.* (Russell 1967: 11)

review activity

Is Russell right to conclude that the existence of the external world is not a fact, but merely a hypothesis?

Chapter 3: 'The Nature of Matter'

Natural phenomena should be reduced to wave motions

Having tentatively concluded that material things do exist, and that they are responsible for our sense-data, Russell now turns his attention to the question of the nature of matter. The answer supplied by science is that natural phenomena ought to be reduced to wave motions. Material bodies emit waves, which are responsible for our perception of heat, light and sound, and the bodies themselves are 'either "ether" or "gross matter"' (Russell 1967: 13). Russell wants to draw a sharp distinction between light waves, and light as experienced by us – what we can call *phenomenal* light. We could explain to a blind person what light waves are, but we cannot explain to him or her what phenomenal light is, because, according to Russell, this is not something to be found in the outer world. Rather, it is a sensation, and sensations of light, colour and sound, 'are absent from the scientific world of matter' (Russell 1967: 14). (Later, he remarks that 'it is quite gratuitous to suppose that physical objects have colours' (Russell 1967: 18).)

Public and private space

Both of these remarks confirm that Russell is indeed a sense-datum theorist, and regards secondary qualities, such as colours and sounds, as logically private to the percipient. Russell extends this claim to include space, or at least space as experienced by us. He grants that real space is public, but apparent space, the space of sight and the space of touch, is a private affair: 'The real space is public, the apparent space is private to the percipient' (Russell 1967: 14). We may reasonably infer from this remark that Russell thinks that apparent space, space as it appears to us, along with colours and sounds, is also in the mind of the percipient. The question then arises as to what the relation is between the public space of science, and 'the spaces we see and feel'. There must be a public space, Russell believes, because it is needed to contain objects, including our bodies, sense organs, nerves and brain. However, we must not forget that as a sense-datum theorist he cannot possibly know this, because all he has acquaintance with are the private contents of his mind, enclosed in his own consciousness.

Incomprehensibility of the notion of private space

On this basis, Russell goes on to make some extremely puzzling remarks; puzzling, because it is far from clear that they are intelligible. Russell maintains that there is some kind of correspondence between the public spatial relations that hold between objects in real, public space, and the private spatial relations that obtain between sense-data in our private spaces. But the idea of private spatial relations holding between mental contents appears to be incomprehensible.

To appreciate this point, contrast a case where the notion of correspondence of the kind Russell wants does make sense. Suppose I like building models of towns, and have one in my room. Clearly, there could be some kind of correspondence between the spatial relations holding between my scaled-down buildings, and the spatial relations between the buildings they represent. For example, if the real church is so many metres north of the town hall, my model could be so oriented that the model church is north of the model town hall, at a scaled-down distance that represents the real distance. It makes sense to suppose this correspondence obtains, because the buildings of both the real town and my model miniatures are physical objects in a common spatial framework. It would even be possible to draw lines of projection from my models connecting them to the real buildings they represent. But how could there be any kind of correspondence of this type between private sense-data and external reality, because sense-data have no genuine dimensions, and no occupancy of space: they merely *appear to.* When it seems to me, in a dream, that I can see mountains in the distance, we cannot ask whether these are literally north of where I am, or how far away, because dream mountains are not objects that can stand in spatial relations to each other. Really, there are no objects there at all to stand in relations to each other, because it is only a dream. To say these things exist in a dream world amounts only to the claim that one dreamt about them: a dream world is not another place that could contain scaled-down representations of external objects in the way my room can contain models of real buildings. So to ask whether there can be a correspondence between the spatial relations which genuinely hold between ordinary physical objects, and the private spatial relations that supposedly hold between sense-data, is to ask a meaningless question.

review
activity

Using your own analogy (or analogies), explain whether Russell's notion of private spaces makes sense.

Knowledge of the nature of space is possible

Because Russell believes that we are not acquainted with the physical world, he thinks we can know nothing of what physical space is like itself. We only have acquaintance with our own allegedly private space. This just seems to be a mistake. If we reject the sort of representative realist theory Russell adopts, then we can say that it is physical objects themselves that we see and touch. Moreover, we can move them from one location to another, and move around and between them, as well as measuring the distances between them. Hence we do have an understanding of what it means to say physical objects are in, and occupy, regions of space.

Objective measurement of time, contrasted with our subjective experience of duration

Having attempted to draw a distinction between public space and private space, Russell tries to do the same with time. There is a difference between genuine duration and our feeling of duration: we may judge that a certain interval of time has elapsed, and then find we have overestimated it, something that tends to happen when we are bored. Conversely, when we are interested in what we are doing, the time we spend doing it seems much shorter. But rather than talking about public time and private time, it would be better simply to draw the distinction between the objective measurement of time by a timepiece, and our *experience* of time. Talking about private time encourages the mistaken and confused view that there is some ghostly counterpart of duration existing in a hidden medium, no doubt the medium of the mind.

Naturally, we can draw a valid distinction between objective and subjective time relations, as Kant did in the *Critique* in the following way. Consider an array of objects. Now, all these objects can coexist at a given instant, or over a period of time. But our *experiences* of these objects may well be successive, as, say, we move along a row of them, looking at each one in turn. Moreover, phenomena which are simultaneous may be experienced by us successively: Russell gives the example of thunder and lightning, which occur together, but appear successive because it takes sound longer than light to reach our sense organs.

Impossible to determine whether sense-data resemble external objects

Russell begins to draw the chapter to a close by raising the question of whether our sense-data are like the physical objects that give rise to them. He concludes that they may be more or less alike. However, he is not entitled to help himself to this conclusion, as nothing on his view could count as having acquaintance with physical objects to make the comparison. He is also inconsistent on this point, because a paragraph earlier he maintains that physical objects 'remain unknown in their intrinsic natures' (Russell 1967: 17), meaning by this, presumably, not that we have acquaintance with physical objects but cannot work out what their intrinsic natures are, but that we have no contact with physical objects and phenomena in the first place.

Chapter 4: 'Idealism'

Berkeley's Idealism

In Chapter 4, Russell undertakes to refute Berkeley's Idealism. Berkeley wanted to construe the material world purely in terms of ideas, or sense-data, which exist in some mind or other, God's, if not anyone else's. The table is a collection of ideas in God's mind, what Berkeley calls an archetype, i.e. a blueprint of things, and he chooses to make copies of this archetype, or ectypes, available to individual minds or spirits. The table does not go out of existence when we leave the room, because God is always perceiving it, just as God was always perceiving rocks and flowers, and indeed the whole earth itself, before any minded creatures appeared on the planet. The sceptical problem of how we can know public persistent material objects exist on the basis of fleeting and subjective sense-data cannot arise for Berkeley, because there is no gap between sense-data and material objects to be bridged, and thus no inferences from the one to the other to be made. Material objects, according to Berkeley are just collections of sense-data, contrary to our common understanding of what material objects are. There are not sense-data *and* material objects, but only sense-data, which *are*, or perhaps, to put it more perspicuously, comprise material objects. In the language of logical positivism, material objects are logical constructions out of sense-data or ideas.

Avoidance of a Lockean unknown material substratum as a motivation for Idealism

One strong motivation for Berkeley's Idealism was his attack on the notion of a material substratum, unknown and unknowable, a 'something we know what' in the words of Locke, who posited the notion, in which the properties of bodies inhere. The idea of such a substratum runs directly contrary to empiricism, which insists all meaningful concepts must have an application to a possible experience. The search for such a substratum would be recursive, like chasing a will-o'-the-wisp, for whatever further investigation uncovered would merely count as yet another property, hitherto undiscerned, and the goal of our enquiry, the material substratum itself, would merely retreat before us. By turning material objects into collections of ideas or sense-data, existing in non-physical minds, the problem of the existence of a material substratum is solved at one stroke. But such a radical course of action is strictly unnecessary, because it is possible to dismiss the notion of an, in principle, unknowable support for properties of things whilst still retaining realism regarding physical objects.

review activity

Why does the rejection of the notion of an unknown material substratum as a support for properties of things not depend on accepting Idealism?

Russell's contention: Berkeley failed to distinguish the act of perceiving from the object of perception

We now come to the details of Russell's attack on Berkeley. Russell's contention is that Berkeley's key mistake is that he fails to draw the distinction between the act of perception, on the one hand, and what is perceived on the other, and, as a result comes to the erroneous conclusion that because the act of perception is in the mind, the object of perception must also be. Now, this distinction between the awareness of an object, and the object itself, is perfectly legitimate where the object is a material thing as ordinarily conceived by a realist, and Russell makes this point in Chapter 1, where he distinguishes between the sensation, that is, the awareness, and that which the awareness is of: 'The colour is that of which we are immediately aware, and the awareness is the sensation' (Russell 1967: 4). In conformity with this, he also writes, in Chapter 4 that,

> *Our previous arguments concerning the colour did not prove it to be mental; they only proved that its existence depends upon the relation of our sense-organs to the physical object – in our case, the table. That is to say, they proved that a certain colour will exist, in a certain light, if a normal eye is placed at a certain point relatively to the table. They did not prove that the colour is in the mind of the percipient.* (Russell 1967: 21–2)

Later on, Russell was to develop the notion of *sensibilia* or unsensed sense-data, locating them as physical events in the nervous systems of people affected by an external stimulus, such as a flash of red light (see Pears 1967: 34). However, it should be apparent that thinking of sense-data in this manner is inconsistent with what Russell generally says about sense-data in *The Problems of Philosophy*.

It is clear that, for the most part, he construes them as Berkeleyan ideas, or Humean impressions, whose *esse is percipi*. Indeed, if Russell were not thinking of sense-data in this fashion, the problem of the existence of the external world could not arise in the way he thinks it does.

Inapplicability of the act/object distinction in the case of sensations and sense-data

This means that Berkeley did not make the error of which Russell accuses him. As the opening of A *Treatise Concerning the Principles of Human Knowledge* makes abundantly clear, Berkeley uncritically accepted the Lockean doctrine that the immediate objects of perception are ideas, or as we would now call them, sense-data. Given that this is so, Berkeley could not be accused of failing to distinguish between the act and object of perception, because, according to the traditional conception of sense-data, this distinction cannot be made. To see why, recall that Berkeley frequently refers to ideas as sensations. For example, in the *Three Dialogues between Hylas and Philonous*, he debates whether sound, as perceived by us, is a sensation in the mind. But the act/object distinction has no application in the case of sensations. When I feel a pain, there is not my awareness *and* an object of which I am aware. There is not a relation between two distinct things, myself and my pain, a *dyadic* relation as philosophers call it, but the *condition* of a single thing, namely me, the person who is hurting or suffering the pain. Pains, and other sensations, it might be said, are *modes* of awareness, *ways* of being aware, hence the *act of perception/object of perception* distinction, is inadmissible. Russell's objection to Berkeley misses the point, for he attempts to foist upon him an error of which Berkeley simply was not guilty, and for which he could not, therefore, legitimately be taken to task.

review
activity

In what way does Russell convict Berkeley of an error he never made?

Berkeley's real mistake, which Russell overlooks, is to conflate *perception* with *sensation*. Consider the following two statements that bear a close resemblance to each other:

1. I feel a stone in my shoe.
2. I feel a pain in my toe.

Statement (1) represents a *perceptual* use of 'feel'. The stone is perceived because my foot is touching it – I feel the stone by touching it with my foot. Moreover, the stone could be shaken out of my shoe and exist independently of me on its own. Statement (2), by contrast, exemplifies a *sensation* use of 'feel'. It makes no sense to say that I feel the pain by touching it, neither can I shake the pain loose from my toe. The pain is plainly not a thing, a logical substance that can exist in its own right, but a condition, a property, if you like, of me, the experiencing subject. But now suppose usages (1) and (2) are conflated, and in the first instance (2) is understood on the model of (1). This would lead to the strange consequence of thinking that pains, like stones, could exist independently of being felt, so that Mrs Gradgrind's remark in Dicken's *Hard Times*, 'I think that there's a pain somewhere in the room, but I couldn't positively be sure that I have got it', instead of being an ironic joke, could quite literally be true.

Berkeley's real error: the conflation of perception with sensation

However, now suppose that (1) is understood on the model of (2). This delivers us instantly into the arms of Idealism. Just as pains and other sensations cannot exist unless someone is aware of them, so stones also cannot exist unless some mind or other is conscious of them. It would then really be true, in the case of material objects, that their *esse is percipi*, that their being consists in being perceived. The moral of all this is that the concepts of sensation and perception should be distinguished and kept apart, and then a spurious support for Idealism is lost. There may be other good reasons for embracing Idealism, but trading on the conflation of sensation and perception should not be one of them.

review
activity

How does the conflation of sensation and perception lead to Idealism?

In anticipation of the next chapter, Russell draws a preliminary distinction between what he calls knowledge by acquaintance and knowledge by description. He writes:

> *If I am acquainted with a thing which exists, my acquaintance gives me the knowledge that it exists. But it is not true that, conversely, whenever I can know that a thing of a certain sort exists, I or someone else must be acquainted with the thing. What happens, in cases where I have true judgement without acquaintance, is that the thing is known to me by description, and that, in virtue of some general principle, the existence of a thing answering to this description can be inferred from the existence of something with which I am acquainted.*
> (Russell 1967: 23–4)

All knowledge, then, for Russell, ultimately rests on knowledge by acquaintance, and this is something he emphasises several times. For Russell's further development and use of the distinction between knowledge by acquaintance and knowledge by description, we now proceed to Chapter 5.

Chapter 5: 'Knowledge by Acquaintance and Knowledge by Description'

Knowledge of things and knowledge of truths

Russell provides more details of his distinction between knowledge by acquaintance and knowledge by description, by distinguishing between two sorts of knowledge, knowledge of things and knowledge of truths. Knowledge of truths is what today we would call propositional knowledge, knowledge that something or other is the case, such as that the sun is 93 million miles from Earth, a synthetic truth, or that the square on the hypotenuse of a right-angled triangle is equal to the sum of the squares on the other two sides, an analytic truth.

Knowledge by acquaintance is immediate and non-inferential

Russell explains that his present concern is exclusively with knowledge of things, and immediately distinguishes between what he calls knowledge by acquaintance and knowledge by description. By acquaintance, Russell means anything of which we are directly aware, without any intermediate process of inference, or any knowledge of truths, being involved. So acquaintance with the sense-data occasioned by the table would be, as such, immediate non-inferential knowledge. Although such acquaintance may lead to knowledge of truths about the shape and colour of the table, Russell does not think this improves the direct acquaintance he has with the sense-data which comprise the appearance of the table:

> *The particular shade of colour that I am seeing may have many things said about it ... But such statements, though they make me know truths about the colour, do not make me know the colour any better than I did before: so far as concerns knowledge of the colour itself, as opposed to knowledge of truths about it, I know the colour perfectly and completely when I see it.* (Russell 1967: 25)

Knowledge of material things is knowledge by description, knowledge of truths

This does not amount to direct knowledge of the table, however, because the table is a material object, and Russell believes that the immediate objects of perception are sense-data. 'There is no state of mind in which we are directly aware of the table; all our knowledge of the table is really knowledge of truths, and the actual thing which is the table is not, strictly speaking, known to us at all' (Russell 1967: 26). Thus, where knowledge of the table is concerned, this amounts to knowledge by description, and 'in order to know anything about the table, we must know truths connecting it with things with which we have acquaintance: we must know that "*such and such sense-data are caused by a physical object*"' (Russell 1967: 26).

The existence of material things is a hypothesis, not a truth

As we observed earlier, it is difficult to see how we can know that sense-data are caused by physical objects, as the only objects of our acquaintance are sense-data, according to Russell. Their causes must remain necessarily unknown, as it is only on the basis of experience, as Hume showed, and not *a priori*, that we are enabled to judge what is the cause of what. If the supposed causes of sense-data lie beyond the veil of our sense-data, we can say nothing about them, as they lie beyond all conceivable experience. Thus, as we noted earlier, the existence of material things remains a postulate or a hypothesis, not something we can claim as a truth.

Universals as possible objects of acquaintance and as indispensable components of sentences

As well as acquaintance with sense-data, we are also acquainted with universals, which are the references of general terms like, 'whiteness', 'diversity', and 'brotherhood'. Russell will devote a chapter to universals later in the book. Without knowledge of universals that correspond to the predicates in subject-predicate statements, we could know nothing about the past, nor possess any knowledge by description, for that requires language, and statements cannot be comprised only of subject expressions. As Russell himself remarks, 'Every complete sentence must contain at least one word which stands for a universal, since all verbs have a meaning which is universal' (Russell 1967: 53). We are also supposed to have acquaintance with things through memory: Russell here seems to think that memory resurrects the very same sights and sounds that we experienced in the past, writing, 'It is obvious that we often remember what we have seen or heard or had otherwise present to our senses, and that in such cases we are still immediately aware of what we remember, in spite of the fact that it appears as past and not as present' (Russell 1967: 26). This seems to be a mistake. If I remember celebrating my birthday a year ago, it cannot literally be the birthday and the celebrations themselves that appear in my memory, but a memory trace caused by those past events.

Russell's search for the bare self, the possessor of experiences

We are also directly acquainted with the contents of our own minds by introspection, and Russell thinks that not only are we aware of things, but that we can also be aware of *being aware* of things. So I am not only aware of my thoughts or my sense-data, I am aware that I am aware of my thoughts and sense-data. Animals, by contrast, may be aware of sense-data, but they are not aware that they are aware of their sense-data. In other words, self-consciousness is not possible for animals, unlike for ourselves. Russell describes our awareness of our awareness rather quaintly when he says 'When I see the sun, I am often aware of my seeing the sun; thus *"my seeing the sun"* is an object with which I have acquaintance' (Russell 1967: 27). This makes it sound as if 'my seeing the sun' is a peculiar kind of object which I introspect and with which I have the same kind of direct acquaintance as I do with sense-data. And indeed this is essentially the way Russell thinks of it. 'My seeing the sun' has two components: there is the mental state of 'seeing the sun' and there is the subject of experience, the 'my' or 'I' which has the experience and which is not reducible to the experience. Russell is happy to grant consciousness of particular thoughts and feelings, but he is less certain about what the reference of 'my' or 'I' is. As Hume does, he introspects to see if he can find the reference of 'I', the bare self as he calls it, but he is not sure whether he can disentangle acquaintance with the 'I' from acquaintance with other things, for example, sense-data. He writes:

> [W]e know the truth 'I am acquainted with this sense-datum'. It is hard to understand how we could know this truth, or even understand what is meant by it, unless we were acquainted with something which we call 'I'. It does not seem necessary to suppose that we are acquainted with a more or less permanent person, the same today as yesterday, but it does seem as though we must be acquainted with that thing, whatever its nature, which sees the sun and has acquaintance with sense-data. Thus, in some sense it would seem we must be acquainted with our Selves as opposed to particular experiences.
>
> (Russell 1967: 28)

Russell's conclusion: only probable we have acquaintance with ourselves

However, doubtless with Hume's fruitless search for an inner bare self, the possessor of experiences, in mind, Russell tentatively concludes that it is only *probable* that we have acquaintance with ourselves. Later, he was to abandon this view and take the full Humean position, embracing the view that subjects of experience do not exist over and above experiences, but are constructed out of them, just as material objects are logical constructions out of sense-data. This doctrine ultimately became known as *neutral monism*, monism because there is only one kind of building block out of which to assemble minds and material things, namely experiences, and neutral because those building blocks considered in themselves were theoretically neither mind nor matter. It was only when the blocks were arranged in certain ways that they became minds and material objects. Thus, all the sense-data of a particular table in various minds comprised the table, and all the sense-data of different things in one mind comprised the mind in question.

review
activity

Why does Russell conclude that it is only probable that we have acquaintance with ourselves?

Rejection of the Cartesian assumption that the reference of 'I' must be to something 'inner' and private

After the work of Wittgenstein and neo-Kantian philosophers such as Sir Peter Strawson, the empiricist approach to the self and self-consciousness enshrined in the writings of Hume and Russell looks very antiquated. Russell never questioned the Cartesian assumption that the reference of 'I' must be to something private and inner, available only to the individual by introspection. He does not consider that 'I' acquires its meaning and use because it indicates the person out of whose mouth it comes, and that subjects of experience are the flesh-and-blood persons of everyday life who can mutually identify and re-identify each other. Conceiving of persons, *pace* Strawson, as those sorts of thing to which both material object predicates, M-predicates, can be ascribed, as well as person predicates, P-predicates, which attribute, or imply, the possession of consciousness, makes possible secure identifying references to subjects of experience. Conceiving of persons in this manner can also explain how we learn to ascribe experiences to ourselves, not, as Wittgenstein demonstrated in his argument against the possibility of a logically private language, through acquaintance with states of mind thought of as logically private inner objects, but in connection with publicly observable behaviour which supplies the criterion of correctness for the use of mental terms. Even in the case of self-ascription, which is criterionless, the link with third-person criterial ascription is not, in principle, lost.

Self-consciousness only possible for language users

The work of Kant and Wittgenstein makes possible an entirely different explanation of what self-consciousness amounts to, and makes plain why only language users, and not non-human animals, can possess it. To be self-conscious requires that a person be able to think of himself, over time, as the numerically identical continuing subject of constantly changing states of mind and experiences. However, to do this requires that self-reference be possible, as well as the possibility of the self-ascription of mental states. But these activities are inherently linguistic in nature; hence it should come as no surprise that animals are not capable of them, and therefore cannot be conceived of as self-conscious beings.

review
activity

Evaluate the claim that only language users have the capacity for self-consciousness.

Definite descriptions

We turn now to the details of Russell's account of knowledge by description. He distinguishes between definite descriptions which take the form 'the so-and-so' and ambiguous descriptions, which we can also call indefinite descriptions, of the form 'a so-and-so'. Russell concentrates on definite descriptions, for example, 'the man in the iron mask' and goes on to say that an object is known by description when we know that it is the so-and-so, that is, when we know that there is one object, and no more, having a certain property. If we are acquainted with the object which is the so-and-so, we know the so-and-so exists, but we can also know the so-and-so exists even when we are not acquainted with any object which we know to be the so-and-so.

We now need to explain what Russell means by a logically proper name. Ordinary everyday proper names, for Russell, are really descriptions in disguise, and he thinks that 'the thought in the mind of a person using the proper name correctly can generally only be expressed explicitly if we replace the proper name by a description' (Russell 1967: 29).

Logically proper names: the meaning of the name is the object denoted

Logically proper names, by contrast, refer to objects with which we are directly acquainted. Russell ignores Gottlob Frege's (1848–1925) distinction between the meaning and the reference of an expression. Indeed, reportedly he did not understand it. For Frege, the reference of the expression 'the morning star' is the planet Venus, and the meaning of the expression is given by the statement that it is the star which appears in the morning. For Russell, the reference of a logically proper name is the meaning of that name. So if the object denoted by the logically proper name is destroyed, the meaning of the name is destroyed. It also follows that if we assert an object exists using a logically proper name, we shall merely produce a tautology. And equally if we deny that an object exists using a logically proper name, we shall be guilty of a contradiction.

To illustrate what he means by a logically proper name, Russell gives the example of 'this' as it occurs in the sentence 'This is white', where the intention is to refer to a white dot, i.e. a white sense-datum, in the middle of one's visual field. A major problem with this claim is that firstly, a person's sense-datum never stays constant, so the meaning of 'this' must constantly be changing. In *The Philosophy of Logical Atomism*, Russell wrote:

> *You can keep 'this' going for about a minute or two. I made that dot and talked about it for some little time . . . . If you argue quickly, you can get some little way before it is finished. I think that things last for a finite time, a matter of some seconds or minutes or whatever it may happen to be.*

> (Russell 1956: 318)

Problems with logically proper names

Overlooking the point that Russell meant to be talking about a sense-datum of the dot rather than the dot itself, which is a material thing, the difficulty is that by the time a person reaches the end of his argument, he will be talking about something numerically different from what he started with, because his sense-data are in constant flux. So it would be impossible to construct an argument which featured 'this' in its premises, as the 'this' in the first premise is almost certainly bound to be different in meaning from the 'this' in a later premise, owing to the interval of time it takes to get from one premise to the other. Moreover, no two people could ever mean the same by 'this' because it would refer to different sense-data, different private objects, in different people's minds. Russell recognises this consequence, but somewhat perversely draws the conclusion that the ambiguity of language, the private meanings it has for each of us, makes communication by language possible. The converse, however, is surely true and communication between people would be rendered impossible, as no one, in principle, could ever find out if anyone else meant the same thing that they did.

activity

What is a logically proper name for Russell, and to what difficulties does it lead?

In actual fact, the situation is much worse than this, as Wittgenstein demonstrated in his attack on the notion of a logically private language, a language which, like Russell's sense-datum language, is supposed to secure its meanings purely by the acquaintance of an individual with the logically private states of mind its words denote.

Impossibility of a logically private language

The notion of a logically private language is enshrined in Cartesianism. Descartes never seems to have questioned his central belief that even if it should turn out that the only thing he could know was that he and his mental states existed, he would still be able to talk about the private contents of his mind, albeit any conversation he had about these contents would, perforce, have to be entirely with himself. Russell, as we have seen, also never calls this assumption into doubt. But if Wittgenstein is right, the notion of logically private language of this type, a language of which the meanings of the words it contains is determined by the radically private objects and the states of affairs to which those words refer, is a logical impossibility. The reason is that the meaning of a word is determined by a rule which dictates when a word is being applied correctly in accordance with a rule, and when it isn't. However, in the world of the private linguist there is no way of distinguishing between thinking mistakenly you are following a rule, and really following the rule. Wittgenstein remarks: 'One would like to say: whatever is going to seem to be right. And that only means that here we cannot talk about "right"' (Wittgenstein 1986: para. 258). Language can only acquire a genuine use in a public social context: a background of shared customs and practices is presupposed against which usage can be assessed as correct or incorrect. 'An inner process,' says Wittgenstein, 'stands in need of outward criteria' (Wittgenstein 1986: para. 580). So the real problem with the notion of a private language whose words are to get their meaning by reference to the private contents of sense-data is not merely that we cannot communicate with other people and understand what they are saying, as we don't have acquaintance with the private objects that determine the meanings of their words, nor they with ours, but that we cannot even engage in silent soliloquy. But if talk about mental states does not acquire its meaning in the way the private linguist maintains, how *does* it get its meaning? Wittgenstein's answer is that it is outward public behaviour which comprises the criterion against which the use of a mental vocabulary is to be assessed for the correctness of its application, even in those cases where, without observation or inference, I ascribe a mental state to myself.

review
activity

How does Wittgenstein argue against the possibility of a logically private language, and what difficulties does this pose for Russell's philosophy?

Ordinary proper names are disguised descriptions composed of elements with which we are acquainted

Let us now return to the theory of descriptions, which Russell applies to the case of Bismarck. Assuming there is acquaintance with oneself, Bismarck could use his name as a logically proper name to refer to himself. The meaning of 'Bismarck', for Bismarck, would be himself, his 'bare' self. The actual Bismarck could thus figure as a constituent of a proposition made by himself about himself. But this is not possible for anyone other than Bismarck, because the most they could be acquainted with are the sense-data allegedly caused by Bismarck's body. This has the consequence that the name 'Bismarck' as it is used by anyone other than Bismarck, is either meaningless, as it cannot function as a logically proper name and directly designate Bismarck himself, or else it acquires its meaning in some other way. As we saw earlier, Russell thinks that ordinary proper names are disguised descriptions, and the components of these descriptions are all known by acquaintance. The principle that underlies this claim is that 'every proposition which we can understand must be composed wholly of constituents with which we are acquainted' (Russell 1967: 32).

Definite descriptions are existential statements in disguise

The problem of how to account for the meaning of ordinary proper names which lack a reference had arisen some years earlier, and Russell's solution was outlined in a paper called 'On Denoting' published in *Mind*, 1905. Russell considered the statement: 'The present King of France is bald.' It could be said that this is true if the King of France is bald, and false if he is not. But what should we say, knowing that France is a republic, and that there is no King of France? How can either the claim that the King of France is bald, or the counter-claim that he is not bald, be true or false, if there is no King of France for the statements to be about? We cannot simply say that the original statement is false, for that implies there is a King of France (who is not bald). Russell's response was that the statement, contrary to appearances, is not a subject-predicate statement at all, and that its true logical form needs to be revealed by analysis. Russell contended that the statement was an existential statement in disguise and should be stated using the existential quantifier, 'There is at least one X such that X is ...' as well as the universal quantifier, 'For all X ...' to secure uniqueness of reference, as there is only one King of France at a given time. Russell suggested the following analysis: 'There is an X, such that X now is King of France, and for all Y, if Y now is King of France, Y is identical with X, and X is bald.' Simplifying, this becomes: 'There is one, and only one, thing such that that thing is King of France, and it is bald.'

If we apply this analysis to Bismarck, we will first need to replace the name with a definite description, say 'the first Chancellor of the German Empire'. It is also true of Bismarck that he is supposed to be the cause of certain types of sense-data. So to a contemporary of Bismarck who could have known him in the sense of experiencing sense-data occasioned by Bismarck's body, the analysis would run:

'There is an X, such that X is the first Chancellor of the German Empire, and for all Y, if Y is the first Chancellor of the German Empire, then Y is identical with X, and X is the cause of such-and-such sense-data.' This statement is composed of elements with which we are acquainted, either universals like 'Chancellor' or 'German' (many things could be Chancellor or German) or particular sense-data we are experiencing. Hence it meets Russell's stricture mentioned earlier, namely that 'every proposition which we can understand must be composed wholly of constituents with which we are acquainted' (Russell 1967: 32).

Ingenious though this analysis is, it unfortunately does not get round the problem posed by sense-data noted earlier. How can there be shared public descriptions and knowledge, if each of us is imprisoned in the logically private world of our own sense-data and, therefore, no two people can ever refer to the same particulars?

review activity

In your own words, outline Russell's Theory of Descriptions and the problem it is supposed to get round.

Chapter 6: 'On Induction'

Those who already know what Hume has to say about induction in the *First Enquiry* will discern many similarities in Russell's account. Hume raised the question of how it is possible to go beyond the evidence of memory and our senses, to knowledge of things we have never personally experienced, and, therefore, could also have no personal memories regarding. If the extension of our knowledge in this way were not possible, the sphere of our knowledge would be severely restricted. We would be limited essentially to the contents of our own individual experiences. There must be some general principle at work, Russell argues, that enables us to extend our knowledge beyond the merely personal, and he finds it in the fact that 'the existence of one sort of thing, A, is the sign of the existence of some other thing, B, either at the same time as A, or at some earlier or later time, as, for example, thunder is a sign of the earlier existence of lightning' (Russell 1967: 33).

The use of induction to go beyond the evidence of our memory and senses

Hume gave the similar example of finding footprints in wet sand on the seashore. We would immediately conclude that someone had walked that way, but we could only make this inference if we had experienced in the past a correlation between people walking on wet sand and a trail of footprints being left behind as a consequence. Similarly, Russell makes use of Hume's example of the sun rising everyday. We believe, indeed really can't help believing, that the sun will rise tomorrow. If asked why, we shall unhesitatingly reply 'Because it always has risen everyday in the past to the best of our knowledge'. We know that the sun will appear to rise because the earth is rotating on its axis, and the past gives us no reason to think that anything will interfere with this. Moreover, we believe that the laws of motion and gravity which govern the motion of the Earth will continue to hold today and tomorrow as they have always done. Russell points out that we have a greater body of evidence in favour of the continuation of the operation of the laws of motion than we do in favour of the continuation of the sunrise, because the latter constitutes just one particular example of the operation of those laws.

Can induction be rationally justified?

Now, there is no doubt that we do form expectations of future events, as well as extrapolate backwards in time to provide explanations of past phenomena, on the basis of repeated instances of past experience. This is our practice which, until we study philosophy, we take for granted. But what *rational* justification is there for such a practice? How can what has happened in the past provide *any* guide at all for what will happen in the future? Through repetition and habit, human beings, as well as animals, are caused to form expectations about the future, but the formation of expectations is a psychological process and does not amount to a rational justification of those expectations. Like Hume, Russell points out that the repeated occurrence of two types of event together in the past can offer no logical draft on the future. It does not logically follow from the fact that the sun has risen in the past that it will tomorrow, and no logical contradiction results from denying it will, even if that prediction, in the event, turns out to be mistaken. As Russell puts it, 'the fact that two things have often been found together and never apart does not, by itself, suffice to *prove* demonstratively that they will be found together in the next case we examine' (Russell 1967: 36). Russell had earlier cited the case of the chicken that had formed the expectation that whenever it saw the farmer coming it would be fed. In the event, the chicken was disappointed because came the day when the farmer wrung its neck.

Can belief in the uniformity of nature be rationally justified?

Of course, the regularity exemplified by the farmer coming and feeding the chicken is an accidental regularity because it is of severely restricted generality, and is always liable to exceptions. Had the chicken a wider knowledge of the behaviour of farmers, and human beings at large, it might have formed more refined views about what was likely to befall it. But what about a regularity which has achieved the status of a law of nature because, providing certain background circumstances are in place, no exceptions to the law have ever been found? Here we are speaking of the uniformity of nature. Described at a sufficiently general level, in terms of the most widely applicable basic laws which describe the occurrence of natural phenomena, we expect the course of nature to continue uninterrupted without exception. But again, how can this belief be justified?

Russell considers the argument

> that we have reason to know that the future will resemble the past, because what was the future has constantly become the past, and has always been found to resemble the past, so that really we have experience of the future, namely of times which were formerly future, which we may call past futures. But such an argument really begs the very question at issue. We have experience of past futures, but not of future futures, and the question is: Will future futures resemble past futures? This question is not to be answered by an argument which starts from past futures alone. We have therefore to seek for

some principle which shall enable us to know that the future will follow the same laws as the past. (Russell 1967: 36–7)

However, it seems that no such principle is to be found and the inductive principle cannot be proved by an appeal to experience: 'All arguments which, on the basis of experience, argue as to the future or the unexperienced parts of the past or present, assume the inductive principle; hence we can never use experience to prove the inductive principle without begging the question' (Russell 1967: 38).

The same point was made by Hume, when he wrote:

> *You say that one proposition is an inference from the other. But you must confess the inference is not intuitive; neither is it demonstrative: Of what nature is it, then? To say it is experimental, is begging the question. For all inferences from experience suppose, as their foundation, that the future will resemble the past, and that similar powers will be conjoined with similar sensible qualities. If there be any suspicion that the course of nature may change, and that the past may not be a rule for the future, all experience becomes useless, and can give rise to no inference or conclusion. It is impossible, therefore, that any arguments from experience can prove this resemblance of the past to the future; since all these arguments are founded upon the supposition of that resemblance.*
>
> (Hume 1975: 37–8)

Experience can neither confirm, nor disconfirm, belief in induction

Hume concluded that there is no rational foundation for accepting induction, and that it is the result of custom or habit. Russell, in a similar vein, views belief in induction as a belief which experience can neither confirm nor confute, finally noting that it 'appears to be as firmly rooted in us as any fact of experience' (Russell 1967: 38).

review activity

Explain in your own words why the inductive principle cannot be proved by experience.

Chapter 7: 'On our Knowledge of General Principles'

Russell begins by reminding us that although the principle of induction cannot be proved by experience, it is unhesitatingly believed by everyone, and this is a feature it shares with other principles that we employ in our thinking. We arrive at these principles, Russell claims, by recognising some particular application of a principle, and then generalise it by leaving out what is peculiar to the particular case, and therefore irrelevant. A concrete illustration is provided by two plus two equals four. This is learnt first of a particular pair of couples and then perhaps another pair, until we come to realisation that it is true of any pair of couples. The same is equally true of other logical principles. In trying to decide the date, if someone knows that today is the 15th, then tomorrow must be the 16th. And we may suppose the person does know today is the 15th because he put it in his diary, so he can conclude with certainty that tomorrow is the 16th.

This is how Russell explains that if all the premises of a deductive argument are true, and the argument is valid, that is to say, if the conclusion really does follow logically from the premises, then the conclusion must be true. Set out formally the argument would look like this:

Premise (1) If today is the 15th, then tomorrow must be the 16th. (True)
Premise (2) And today is the 15th. (True).
Conclusion: So tomorrow is the 16th. (True)

The conclusions of valid deductive arguments with true premises must be true

This principle is used in all logical reasoning and although it may appear trivial, its use is of the greatest consequence, as it can be employed in mathematics, logic, and geometry to arrive at knowledge which does not derive from sense-experience. Russell summarises this principle as the principle which states that 'whatever follows from a true proposition is true'. He regards it as self-evident and as merely one of a number of other principles which have to be accepted as true before any argument or proof is possible.

Russell lists three other principles which have traditionally been known as the 'Laws of Thought'.

1. The law of identity: 'Whatever is, is.'
2. The law of contradiction: 'Nothing can both be and not be.'
3. The law of the excluded middle: 'Everything must either be or not be.'

'Laws of Thought' logically, not psychologically, true

The term 'Laws of Thought' is misleading because it can make it look as if these principles are merely contingently true generalisations derived from the empirical investigation of how the mind works and how people think. But these laws are not merely contingently and psychologically true, but also necessarily and logically true. In other words, they are analytically true, and there is no possibility of their falsehood. To deny these laws leads to a formal contradiction.

review
activity

How do deductive arguments differ from inductive arguments?

Rationalism versus empiricism

Russell reminds us of two great schools of philosophy, the rationalists, Descartes, Spinoza, and Leibniz on the one hand, and the empiricists, Locke, Berkeley, and Hume, on the other. The empiricists maintained that all knowledge of what exists is derived from experience. By contrast, the rationalists thought that it was possible to arrive at irrefragable truths about reality purely on the basis of reason. For example, Descartes believed that he could prove that God existed using the ontological argument and the trademark argument. Kant and Hume demonstrated that these arguments cannot possibly succeed, and God's existence can only be known, if indeed it can be known at all, on the basis of empirical evidence, the apparent order exhibited by the universe, for example, which forms the starting point of the teleological argument. Generalising the point, Russell points out that the empiricists were in the right regarding the claim that nothing can be proved to exist, or not exist, *a priori* purely on the basis of logic. But the rationalists were correct in maintaining that the logical principles outlined earlier can be neither proved nor overturned by experience.

A priori *and* a posteriori *knowledge*

Knowledge that can be arrived at purely by logical reasoning and independently of experience is said to be *a priori*, whereas that known on the basis of experience is called *a posteriori*. The rationalists had a tendency to equate *a priori* with 'innate' knowledge, which is born in us, and Locke mounted a famous attack on this idea, arguing that at birth, the mind is *tabula rasa*, a blank slate, and it is only after experience has supplied us with the basic ingredients of knowledge in the form of concepts, that knowledge will become possible. As Russell remarks: 'It would certainly be absurd to suppose that there are innate principles in the sense that babies are born with a knowledge of everything which men know and which cannot be deduced from experience' (Russell 1967: 41). There is still a debate regarding whether there is innate knowledge; for example, Chomsky has argued that we must all have a wired-in knowledge of the principles of grammar, but be that as it may, nowadays the notion of what is innate is sharply distinguished from the notion of the *a priori*, a concept which belongs firmly in the realm of logic.

A priori *truths are true in all possible worlds*

Russell went on to point out that all knowledge which rests wholly or partly on experience is empirical knowledge, and knowledge of the existence of things is firmly in this camp, whereas '*a priori* knowledge concerning existence is hypothetical, giving connexions among things that exist or may exist, but not giving actual existence' (Russell 1967: 42). All knowledge of mathematics is *a priori* knowledge, contrary to what some empiricists wanted to maintain when they suggested that we come to know that two and two are four as a result of finding that repeated instances of the addition of couples equals four. We know that by virtue of the meanings of the terms comprising two and two are four that it must logically be true, and it would be pointless to search out particular cases in an attempt to establish this. The same is true of geometry. A demonstration of a truth about a flat-plane Euclidean triangle, such as that the exterior angle of the triangle is equal to the sum of the two opposite interior angles, must be true of all triangles in advance, and is not open to confirmation or disconfirmation by experience. Mathematics and geometry do not just happen to be true. If proofs have been carried out correctly, the conclusions deduced from the premises must be true. As Russell says, 'In any possible world ... we feel that two and two would be four: this is not mere fact, but a necessity to which everything actual and possible must conform' (Russell 1967: 43). To make the point completely clear Russell contrasts the empirical generalisation that 'All men are mortal' with 'two and two are four'. It is conceivable that the former could be false because we can think of a race of men such as Swift's Struldbrugs, who never die. But we cannot conceive of the possibility of two and two making five because this would be a logical contradiction.

review activity

How do *a priori* truths differ from *a posteriori* truths?

Russell concludes the chapter by observing that, with regard to *a priori* propositions, deduction is the right mode of argument, and with empirical generalisations, induction. There would be no point in using induction to arrive at a general principle, such as all men are mortal, and then use deduction to conclude that, as Socrates is a man, he too must be mortal. This is going round the houses, and it would be simpler and more direct to infer inductively from the fact that as all the men we have ever known have proved mortal, there is a very high probability that Socrates is also mortal.

Chapter 8: 'How *A Priori* Knowledge is Possible'

Knowledge of cause and effect is a posteriori, not a priori

Up until Kant (1724–1804), it was taken for granted that any knowledge known *a priori* must be analytic. Examples of analytic statements are 'A bald man is a man' and 'A plane figure is a figure'. In these cases it can be clearly seen that the predicate can be derived merely by analysing the subject as it is already contained in the subject. Hence, in these sorts of cases, to retain or assert the subject but remove or deny the predicate leads to a contradiction. This is clearly seen if we say that 'A bald man is not bald' or 'A bald man is not a man'. The rationalists had supposed that statements of cause and effect were of this type and that it was possible to logically deduce the cause from effect, merely by scrutiny of the effect alone. The trademark argument for God's existence, mentioned in the last chapter, relied on this belief, arguing that because I have an idea of God in my mind, this idea can only have come from God himself, on the basis that a finite being has not the resources to generate the idea of a perfect being greater than itself, and the idea of the infinite and perfect must therefore be derived from God himself. This claim relies on the causal adequacy principle, which says, effectively, that whatever is found in the effect must have already been present in the cause, and any features the effect has, it must have inherited them from the cause, as an heirloom is passed down the generations. Hume rejected this view of the matter, arguing that experience is the sole source of knowledge of cause and effect, and that for all we can tell prior to experience, anything could be the cause of anything. We can suppose, without logical contradiction that a falling pebble, for instance, might extinguish the sun, or a man, by a simple wish, might control the planets in their orbits. Statements of cause and effect are synthetic according to Hume, and are known to be true *a posteriori*, purely on the basis of experience. Mathematical statements are analytic and known to be true *a priori*, purely on the basis of reason. In theory, the categories of synthetic/analytic and *a posteriori/a priori* could be combined to yield four different types of statement as the following table shows:

Different types of statement	Known *a posteriori*	Known *a priori*
Synthetic	Synthetic *a posteriori*	Synthetic *a priori*
Analytic	Analytic *a posteriori*	Analytic *a priori*

Are synthetic a priori *statements possible?*

We have seen examples of synthetic *a posteriori* statements and analytic *a priori* statements. The category of the analytic *a posteriori* can be eliminated, as if a statement is analytic it is necessarily true by virtue of the meanings of the terms it contains, and thus is known independently of experience. That leaves the synthetic *a priori* as a possible type of statement. Such statements, if they were possible, could be known to be true independently of experience in the manner of analytic statements, and, like these statements, they would also possess an exceptionless necessity. However, unlike analytic statements, their predicates would not merely unfold what was already contained in their subjects, but provide genuinely new information.

Mathematical and geometrical truths are analytic, not synthetic

It was Kant who first raised the possibility of synthetic *a priori* truths. He maintained that $7 + 5 = 12$ is an example of such a truth, because 7 and 5 have to be put together to yield 12, and he claimed that the idea of 12 is not contained in them, nor even in the idea of adding them together. This claim is ambiguous. Certainly, someone might not realise that 7 and 5 equal 12, and when they do come to realise it, what they discover is *psychologically* new, in that it represents a piece of information which they now have but which they previously lacked. But *logically* the result of adding 7 and 5 to get 12 is not new, and $7 + 5$ is one way of unpacking the information already contained in 12. Nowadays philosophers would classify $7 + 5 = 12$ as an analytic truth, in common with all the other analytic truths comprising mathematics and geometry.

A priori conditions presupposed by the very possibility of experience

Where Kant made his most original and compelling contribution to philosophy was in his suggestion that experience must possess certain very general features for it to be possible. These features are not derived from experience, but presupposed by it, as a condition of its very possibility. They are thus *a priori*, not only in the sense that they do not arise from experience and are independent of it, but also in the sense that they are innate, part of the inner fabric of the mind. The details of Kant's proposal are intricate and difficult, but one way of approaching the issue, although not ultimately philosophically the best way, is to go on the path Russell himself selects in providing his exposition of Kant.

Structure of the human mind imposed upon all the contents of experience

We can distinguish in all experience two elements, one contributed by objects, and the other due to our own nature. The human mind has a certain structure, and this is imposed on it by all the elements that comprise the contents of experience. An analogy often used here to make the point clearer runs as follows. Imagine you are wearing a pair of blue-tinted spectacles, which you cannot take off. Everything you see will necessarily look blue, or at least have a bluish hue. The colour of the glasses will unavoidably be imposed on all the objects of vision. Kant divides the mind into two faculties: the senses, or sensibility as he calls it, and the understanding from which arise concepts. Experience is the product of the application of concepts to individual sense-experiences, or intuitions, as Kant calls them. The notion of raw, unconceptualised experiences Kant dismisses as a blind play of representations, less even than a dream. Intuitions need to be brought under concepts if they are to amount to anything we can recognise as experience. That is why Kant remarks, 'Intuitions without concepts are blind', adding, 'just as concepts without intuitions are empty'. In other words, a concept has to have a content if it is to amount to an experience.

Now, the sensibility has a certain formal structure, analogous to the blue of the spectacles. That structure is time and space, and this means that all experience will necessarily be temporal in character, and those portions of experience dealing with outward objects will necessarily be spatial in character. In a like manner, the understanding provides certain concepts, what Kant calls the 'categories', under which it brings the elements of raw experience. Chief among these are the categories of substance and causality. In other words, we necessarily apply the concept of individual independently existing and relatively permanent things, substances, to outward objects, as well as experiencing events connected to each other in regular patterns of cause and effect. A totally chaotic world, and a world in which we cannot form a conception of objects existing independently of us, is not a possible object of experience for us.

If the a priori *conditions of experience merely reflect the structure of human minds now, it is conceivable that these could change or vary from species to species*

This picture of the mind making nature, what has been called transcendental psychology, is perhaps of some value in providing an inkling of Kant's thinking. But it is of limited value because it represents a philosophical thesis masquerading as a psychological one, and this leaves it vulnerable to the following objection. Kant tried to identify and articulate the general features *any* experience must possess if it is to count as such. This implies the experience of *any* type of creature, *anywhere*, *anytime*. But if we think of experience more narrowly in terms of the contribution our human nature makes to it, it can instantly be objected that the fact that human minds are structured in a certain way is a mere contingent fact. So it becomes a mere contingency that our experience has the general character described above. Other creatures whose minds are structured differently could experience the world as possessing a totally different character, so that it is not of a world of more or less permanent objects, connected into causal regularities with each other, but of some entirely different character, impossible even to guess at. Moreover, if it is only contingently true that our nature has the character it does, what is to stop that nature changing, and thereby giving rise to a completely different order of experience? As Russell puts it: 'Our nature is as much a fact of the existing world as anything, and there can be no certainty that it will remain constant' (Russell 1967: 49). Thus it might happen, as not merely our experience is supposed to possess an *a priori* character, but the statements of mathematics as well, that tomorrow two and two become five. In other words, as Russell points out, thinking of the *a priori* in terms of the innate structure of the mind which it imposes on experience and mathematics alike, 'destroys the certainty and universality which he [Kant] is anxious to vindicate for arithmetical propositions' (Russell 1967: 49), and, we might add, it would also destroy the universality of a certain general character of any conceivable experience that Kant is keen to demonstrate.

The situation is by no means hopeless, however, for Kant argued for his conclusions *philosophically*, and did not merely use the deeply flawed apparatus of transcendental psychology. The details of that account are beyond the scope of this book, but besides the *Critique of Pure Reason*, the reader is encouraged to delve into *Kant*, by Roger Scruton, (1982) *Individuals* by P.F. Strawson, (1959) and *The Bounds of Sense*, (1966) by the same author.

review
activity

What objection can be brought against the claim that all concepts must derive from experience?

Chapter 9: 'The World of Universals'

At the end of the previous chapter, Russell rightly rejected the idea that our *a priori* knowledge concerns merely the constitution of our minds, maintaining instead that it 'is applicable to whatever the world may contain, both what is mental and what is non-mental' (Russell 1967: 50). He believes that all our *a priori* knowledge is concerned with entities that, strictly speaking, exist in neither a mental nor a non-mental realm. These entities consist in those things that are referred to by those parts of speech which do not name things, non-substantives as they are commonly known, by contrast with nouns. Non-substantives include *properties* of things, such as whiteness, but also *relations* between things. For example, if I am in my room, as opposed to outside of it, I stand in a certain relation to my room, the relation of being inside it. We can understand the relation denoted by 'in' and reflect on what it means, and it seems wrong to think of this relation is something produced by the mind, because if I am in my room, it still remains true that I am, quite independently of whether I, or anyone else for that matter, is aware of the fact. But what is the nature of relations like 'in', which could be true of many pairs of things, for example, coins in pockets, or canaries in cages, as well as properties, such as white, which can be shared by many things?

Universals name properties and relations which do not belong to either of the categories of mental or physical

Because relations and properties can be shared by many different things and situations, they are said to be universals, by contrast with particular things of which they can be true, and the question Russell confronts is what is the nature of universals, how should they be conceived, and what, in particular, is their ontology, their mode of being. Plato faced the same question more than 2500 years ago, and Russell acknowledges that the account he provides of universals, is essentially Plato's, 'with merely such modifications as time has shown to be necessary' (Russell 1967: 52). Plato raised the question 'What is justice?', but as an answer he did not merely want particular *examples* of justice, but an account of what justice *is*, what features of an act, or a policy, make it a just act or policy. In other words, he was searching for the essential features of justice, the indispensable features required to make an act or policy just.

Universals exist independently of sensible particulars in another realm

Like Plato, Russell concludes that justice itself cannot be identified with the particular things which partake of it, and as it is not a particular it must exist in a realm distinct from the domain of the senses. Particulars are short-lived, imperfect, and constantly changing, whereas universals are eternal, perfect and immutable. Plato calls universals, so conceived, the world of the Forms. The world of the Forms is the truly real world, and the world we see around us is a pale reflection of a greater reality. It will be appreciated that Plato is a fully-fledged realist about the existence of universals, and it is realism of a particularly strong kind, because it does not merely assert that universals exist, but that they can exist independently of all particulars. This doctrine was later to be challenged by Plato's pupil, Aristotle, as we shall see, but Russell says nothing about Aristotle's criticisms.

Language cannot function without general terms which refer to universals

Russell reminds us that language could not function without terms that name universals: even a simple sentence such as 'I like this' contains a general term that refers to a universal, because many different particular things could be liked. Proper names and pronouns stand for particulars, and Russell includes 'now' in the list as the name of the present moment. Adjectives, verbs (and presumably adverbs), and prepositions stand for universals. It is surprising, Russell reflects, that nearly all the words in the dictionary stand for universals, but it is rare to find anyone, with the exception of students of philosophy, who recognises the existence of universals. Even among philosophers there has been a tendency to concentrate on universals named by adjectives, which express qualities or properties of things, by contrast with verbs and prepositions, which express relations between things.

Empiricism: the denial of universals conceived of as abstractions

Russell is prepared to admit that it is difficult to prove the existence of universals, in the manner conceived by Plato, and that anyone who denies there are such entities cannot be shown to be definitely wrong. He cites the example of the British empiricists, Berkeley and Hume, who wanted to deny the existence of abstractions such as whiteness, or squareness, and who maintained instead that when we want to think about whiteness, we call up an image of a particular white thing, and reason about this, 'taking care not to deduce anything concerning it which we cannot see to be equally true of any other white thing' (Russell 1967: 55). The same thing is supposed to happen in geometry. If I want to engage in reasoning about triangles, I may draw a triangle on the board, and then attempt to demonstrate some particular theorem about it, say, the claim discussed earlier that the external angle of a triangle is equal to the sum of the two interior opposite angles. This will be true of all Euclidean triangles, irrespective of their size or form, i.e. whether they are scalene, equilateral, isosceles, etc. These features are disregarded and left out of account as having no relevance to the application of the theorem in question. However, to be able to say the theorem applies to other types of triangle, we have to be able to recognise these other things as *triangles*, rather than, say, as squares, and this seems to imply that these triangles share a common feature, triangularity, by virtue of which they are what they are. This feature, shared by all particular triangles, will then be a universal. So once again we are committed to a realist theory of universals, though not necessarily of the Platonic variety, as we shall see later.

review
activity

Briefly explain what is meant by the claim that Russell held a realist theory of universals.

Recurrence and resemblance theories of universals

At this point we stand on the threshold of the debate between what are known as *recurrence* theorists, and *resemblance* theorists concerning the existence of universals. Recurrence theorists maintain that unless particulars share common properties or relations we cannot explain how general terms are possible. For example, if snow is white, and a blank sheet of paper is white, this can only be that these things share a common property that recurs, or is instantiated, in two different particulars. Similarly, if Aberdeen and Glasgow are both north of London, they share the relation of 'being north of', which is repeated in the case of two different Scottish cities. Thus recurrence theorists are prepared to make an ontological commitment to the existence of properties and relations as universals.

Resemblance theorists wish to avoid this commitment, although it is far from clear that they can. The proposal is that the application of general terms is to be based on resemblance. A particular is selected to serve as a standard, and then other things are judged to resemble each other by virtue of their resemblance to the standard particular. In this way, a reference to a common quality is avoided, and with it a commitment to the existence of a universal.

Resemblance is itself a universal, so the existence of other universals should be admitted

However, there are two problems with this proposal. Firstly, things do not merely resemble each other; they must resemble each other in certain *respects*. A square piece of white paper and a circular piece of white paper resemble each other, but not by virtue of their shape, but by their colour, white. So it is hard to see how we can avoid positing something – the whiteness – they both share. But there is perhaps an even more serious difficulty pointed out by Russell. If things resemble each other, as with the two pieces of paper, then resemblance itself must be a universal, for it is supposed to obtain between many pairs of white things. Russell comments:

> It will be useless to say that there is a different resemblance for each pair, for then we shall have to say that these resemblances resemble each other, and thus at last we shall be forced to admit resemblance as a universal. But once we have admitted the existence of this universal, there seems little point in trying to show that universals like whiteness and triangularity do not exist.

(Russell 1967: 55)

Universals are not mental entities but exist objectively

Russell is at pains to point out that universals should not be thought of as mental entities, but exist objectively. For example, the relation of 'being north of' as applied, say, to Edinburgh in relation to London, holds independently of our knowledge of it, or thoughts about it. There is another reason why Russell is right to reject the conception of universals as mental entities as the following example shows. Suppose I imagine a white patch, and try to think of this as the universal *white*. It is clear that this suggestion cannot work, for all I will have succeeded in doing is producing a particular instance of white, albeit a mental instance. In addition, although the awareness of whiteness is undoubtedly mental, it does not follow that the whiteness itself is. Russell goes on to argue that if whiteness were one and the same as the thought of whiteness, then no two different people could think of it, nor one and the same person at different times, for one person's act of thought is necessarily different from another person's, but the whiteness is the common object of all their thoughts.

review
activity

1. Explain the difference between recurrence and resemblance theories of universals.

2. Which theory does Russell opt for, and how convincing is his choice?

*Universals:
unchanging, perfect,
eternal. Particulars:
constantly changing,
imperfect, fleeting*

This leaves us with a puzzle, however, about what the existence of whiteness consists in. Where, and when, precisely, does the universal whiteness exist? Russell's answer is effectively Plato's: 'It is neither in space nor in time, neither material nor mental; yet it is something' (Russell 1967: 56). Russell amplifies this remark in characteristically Platonic terms: 'The world of universals . . . [is] the world of being. The world of being is unchangeable, rigid, exact, delightful to mathematicians (like Russell!), the logician, the builder of metaphysical systems, and all who love perfection rather than life' (Russell 1967: 57). By contrast, 'The world of existence is fleeting, vague, without sharp boundaries, without any clear plan or arrangement, but it contains all our thoughts and feelings, all the data of sense, and all physical objects, everything that can do good or harm, everything that makes any difference to the value of life and the world' (Russell 1967: 57).

*Plato's Third Man
argument*

However, having committed himself, like Plato, to this two worlds theory, the world of the Forms and the world of imperfect sensible particulars, Russell recognises it will then be necessary to consider their relation to each other. It was just this question to which Plato devoted himself in his later dialogue, the *Parmenides*, with the disturbing result that he ended up demolishing his own theory. The principal instrument, by means of which he achieved this, was the Third Man argument, which goes like this. Suppose we construe the relation between the universal and the Forms as one of resemblance. Then we can ask why a group of particulars, men, say, should be classed together. The answer Plato would give is that all these men resemble each other, because each of them resembles the Form of the Man, the universal. But if we explain the resemblance the men have to each other by reference to the Form 1 of the Man, then the question arises as to by virtue of what do all the individual men and the Form of the Man resemble each other. It seems that we can only answer this question by postulating a further Form of the Man, Form of the Man 2, which the original Form of the Man, together with all the particular men, resemble. But then how do we explain this resemblance? It seems yet another Form of the Man, Form of the Man 3, needs to be postulated. This pattern of argument can be repeated over and over, leading to the unacceptable conclusion that there must be vicious infinite regress of Forms of Forms of Form . . . Somewhat surprisingly, Russell makes no reference to this paralysing objection by Plato to the latter's own realist theory of universals, nor does he consider an alternative realist theory put forward by Aristotle. Aristotle thought that universals do exist, but that they cannot exist in splendid isolation from the particulars which exemplify them. This is a bold claim, which instantly runs into the objection that we can all think of universals that do not have, and never will have, any exemplifications, such as centaurs and snarks. Unfortunately, however, there is not the room here to say any more about this issue, and the nature of universals generally. There is an extensive literature available on the subject, and readers are invited to make their own explorations.

review
activity

Explain in your own words Plato's Third Man argument to his own theory of the relation between universals and particulars.

Russell concludes the chapter by a brief survey of the sources of knowledge.

Knowledge of things/
knowledge of truths

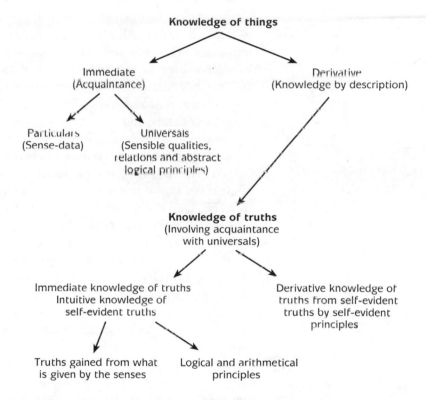

We can see, as Russell points out, that all knowledge of truths depends upon our intuitive knowledge, that is, truths given immediately by the senses, and the truths of logic and arithmetic, which involve direct acquaintance with universals in the case of the latter, and both particulars and universals with regard to the former.

Chapter 10: 'On our Knowledge of Universals'

Russell now turns his attention from the nature of universals to the nature of our knowledge of them. Among the universals we are acquainted with, Russell lists the following:

1. Sensible properties exemplified by sense-data, such as colours, tastes, sounds, solidity, and so forth
2. Relations, such as spatial relations, e.g. to the left or right of, to the north of, being inside or outside something
3. Before and after in time, and simultaneity
4. Resemblance or similarity

Just as there can be relations between particulars, so there can equally be relations between universals, such as the relation of 'greater than ', as in the case where we perceive the resemblance between two shades of green is greater than the resemblance between a shade of green and a shade of red. Our perception of the relations between universals, Russell thinks, is as immediate and indubitable as our perception of the qualities of sense-data. The fact that there can be relations between universals helps us to understand the nature of *a priori* propositions better. All *a priori* knowledge deals with the relations between universals. This was anticipated by Hume in the distinction he made between matters of fact and relations of ideas. Matters of fact are synthetic statements which are contingently true or false depending on how the world they attempt to describe happens to be. Relations of ideas describe relations between concepts, and are necessarily true or false by virtue of the meanings of the concepts. An example would be 'all green things are coloured'. This must be true and can never be false, because green is a colour among many others. The contents of the concepts correspond to universals. Hume pointed out that it is not necessary for there to be any triangles in order for us to be able to demonstrate analytic truths, known *a priori*, regarding them, and Russell makes the same point when he remarks that in order to know that two and two make four, it is not necessary to know that there are particular couples of which this is true. 'Two plus two is four' neither states nor implies there is any particular couple, or group of couples. In fact, towards the end of the chapter, Russell shows how it is possible for us to know the truth of an *a priori* proposition, not only if do not know any instances of it, but even if, in principle, we *cannot* know any instances of it. Russell gives the example of 'All products of two integers, which have never been and never will be thought of by any human being, are over 100' (Russell 1967: 62), where the class of integers is not to include those that have actually been multiplied together and found to be 100 or less, but all those infinitely many integers which have never been thought of by human beings, and never will, and whose products when multiplied together are greater than 100. Clearly, we cannot give an instance of these pairs of integers, as they are excluded by the very terms of the question.

The difference between genuine *a priori* judgements and empirical generalisations can now be seen clearly. We can understand the generalisation 'all men are mortal', but we cannot tell merely by inspection of it whether it is true or false. For that we need evidence in the form of innumerable instances of men dying, together with what we know about the functioning of the human body and physiology generally. But we do not know it is true because we directly perceive a connection between the universal *man*, and the universal *mortal*, unlike the case where we perceive that something which is a Euclidean triangle will entail that it has internal angles equal to 180°.

We might arrive at a true *a priori* judgement on the basis of induction, and only afterwards be able to provide a mathematical demonstration of it. An actual historical example is provided by Kepler's laws describing planetary motion. Kepler arrived at these laws using the data on planetary positions provided by the astronomer Tycho Brahe. Brahe devised the laws which would best fit the behaviour of the planets, knowledge of which was arrived at empirically, hence the formulas he produced are known as semi-empirical laws. But he did not know why the laws applied and took the form that they did, for he had no theory of universal gravitation and the laws of motion which comprise an integral part of it. It was left to Newton subsequently to derive Kepler's laws mathematically and thus *a priori*, from the more general laws of motion which describe the movements of both terrestrial and extraterrestrial bodies.

review
activity

How does Russell explain the difference between *a priori* judgements and empirical generalisations?

Chapter 14: 'The Limits of Philosophical Knowledge'

Russell begins by dismissing grand metaphysical attempts to prove religious dogmas, the rationality of the universe, the illusoriness of matter, and the unreality of evil. Philosophical reasoning cannot prove, *a priori*, what does or does not exist, a reiteration of a point we witnessed earlier when Russell, like Hume before him, dismissed the ontological argument for God's existence.

An example of an all-inclusive metaphysical scheme, of the kind Russell wishes to dismiss, is provided by Hegel. Everything short of the Whole is fragmentary, and cannot survive except in relation to the rest of the world. It should be theoretically possible to reconstruct the whole world from one small fragment of it, as an anatomist, presented with one bone from an animal, can infer what the rest of the animal must have been like. The various bits of reality are supposed to hook on to each other to comprise a unity. A possible metaphor that can used to express what Hegel appears to be arguing for is a jigsaw piece. Any individual piece owes its identity and its function to its relation to all the other pieces that collectively make up the total picture comprised by the jigsaw. The nature of the jigsaw piece cannot be understood except in relation to the whole jigsaw. Bereft of its context, it becomes merely a strangely shaped piece of card with some colours on it, and in this way is incomplete.

Hegel extends this notion to the world of thought, claiming, according to Russell, that 'if we take any idea which is abstract or incomplete, we find, on examination, that if we forget its incompleteness, we become involved in contradictions' (Russell 1967: 83).

A thesis, to use Hegel's terms, gives rise to an antithesis, its opposite, and to discover a less incomplete idea we have to find a combination of the two contradictory terms, a synthesis. But this synthesis in turn will still not be wholly complete, and will give rise to another antithesis, which will then be completed into a new synthesis. This process – the dialectic – will continue until the Absolute Idea is reached, which, being complete, has no antithesis, and the dialectical progression will cease. It is to be expected that the reader will find it very far from clear precisely what Hegel is claiming here, but it has been alleged by Sir Karl Popper that it represents an apologetic for the Prussian state, which is supposed to be the incarnation of the Absolute Idea on Earth, the apotheosis of the dialectic, complete and perfect in itself, with no room or need for further change (Popper 1945: 49). Students of Marx will recognise the application he made of this idea, standing Hegel on his head, by turning the stages of the dialectic from immaterial, spiritual processes, into material ones. Thesis and antithesis find their embodiment for Marx in class struggle, which, according to him, has typified all of human history so far. This discord will only stop when the proletariat overthrow the bourgeoisie and appropriate the means of production and private capital, so that it may be dedicated for the use of all, abolishing classes in the process, and bringing about the ideal communist state on Earth, a harmonious unity, no longer subject to the conflict of the dialectic.

Russell attacks Hegel by rejecting the idea that the elements out of which a system is built up must be incomplete and not truly self-subsistent, so that the nature of a thing requires some ineliminable reference to the things outside itself. Russell interprets the notion of the nature of a thing, as understood by Hegel, to mean 'all the truths about the thing' (Russell 1967: 83). If we accept this way of looking at the matter, then we can never know a thing's nature until we know its relations to everything else, and this consequence Russell firmly wants to reject. '(1) Acquaintance with a thing does not logically involve a knowledge of its relations, and (2) a knowledge of some of its relations does not involve a knowledge of all its relations nor a knowledge of its "nature" in the above sense' (Russell 1967: 84). A person can have a complete acquaintance with, and knowledge of, his toothache, without knowing about its cause, for example. The fact that a thing has relations to something else does not mean it must have relations to other things.

Hence, Russell concludes, we cannot show by the method of reasoning Hegel recommends that the universe forms a single harmonious system, and nor, therefore, can we show the truth of the further consequences Hegel believes this conception of the universe entails, namely the unreality of space and time, together with the non-existence of matter and evil. There is thus no substitute for the patient piecemeal investigation of the world, which science and inductive method exemplify.

review activity

How does Russell dismiss Hegel's claim that metaphysics can show that the universe is a single harmonious whole, and that space, time and evil are unreal?

Russell reminds us again that really nothing can be proved from *a priori* considerations of what must exist, and provides the following example. It seems that space and time must be infinitely divisible, because any given spatial or temporal interval can be halved, but some philosophers have argued there cannot be infinite collections of things, and Kant, who emphasised the problem, drew the conclusion that space and time must ultimately comprise merely subjective phenomena. However, the mathematician George Cantor showed belief in the impossibility of infinite collections to be a mistake, so Kant was left without a ground for his conclusion. The matter cannot be pursued here, but it is arguable that ultimately Kant was not committed to the subjectivity of space and time, that thesis merely being a part of the apparatus of transcendental psychology whose legitimacy we questioned earlier. The necessity for the temporal character of all experience, and the spatial character of the greater part of it, for experience to be possible, can be made to rest on a more secure independent philosophical foundation.

Russell goes on to refer implicitly to the discovery of non-Euclidean geometries, by mathematicians such as Lobachevsky and Riemann. It was believed, by Kant among others, that the geometry of free space was Euclidean in nature, but now it appears that this is mistaken, and that space is curved. The angles of triangles subtended by beams of light, a physical interpretation of straight lines in space, do not obey the Euclidean theorem that the angles of a triangle equal 180° or the axiom of parallels, namely that parallel lines cannot meet. What this shows is that, considered purely in itself, it is possible to know all the truths of a geometrical system *a priori*. But this does not entail that the system amounts to a correct description of reality. This, like all knowledge of matters of fact, as Russell frequently reminds us, can only be known on the basis of experience.

The role of logic, now, is not to prescribe, by *a priori* principles, what the universe must be like, but instead to awaken the mind to possible worlds not open to unreflective, common sense experience, and then decide which of these possibilities is actual. In this way, knowledge of what exists is limited to what we can learn from experience. This does not mean that we can have experience of everything – there are things known purely by description which in principle we cannot experience directly, such as physical objects. But, Russell avers, these can be inferred from the sense-data with which we have direct unmediated acquaintance, by 'connexion of universals', the principle that 'sense-data are signs of physical objects' exemplifying just such a connection. However, as we saw earlier, Russell has to face a real difficulty here: if sense-data comprise his entire resources, and sense-data are logically private and evanescent, Russell can move neither inductively, nor deductively, to knowledge of public, persistent, physical things. A principle, such as the law of gravitation, is known by a combination of experience, through observation, and the application of the inductive principle which Russell counts as *a priori*, as it is neither confirmable, nor disconfirmable, by experience. All our intuitive knowledge ultimately resolves into pure *a priori* knowledge – mathematics, geometry, and logic – and pure empirical knowledge, supplied by the sciences and related disciplines.

review activity

Which two broad classes of knowledge does Russell recognise?

Russell claims that ultimately philosophical knowledge does not differ essentially from scientific knowledge, the main difference between the two consisting in criticism. This overlooks, firstly, a major difference between a philosophical theory and a scientific theory, familiar to us now from the work of Karl Popper, namely that scientific theories, in principle, are open to falsification empirically, whereas philosophical theories are not. Philosophical theories in need of overthrow require a philosophical refutation and that cannot be supplied by throwing science at them. Secondly, scientists are equally critical of their methods of working and resultant theories, as are philosophers in their domains, but the modes of criticism will often differ, given that physics, say, is empirical by its very nature, and philosophy is not. This finds its reflection in the different kinds of questions posed by scientists and philosophers. For example, a scientist will look for the causes of things, whereas a philosopher will ask what it *means* to say that one thing is the cause of another. Or again, we now appreciate that Thales' question, 'What is the world made of?' is a scientific question, to be answered by empirical investigation, and not by philosophical reflection; whereas 'How may properties be distinguished from things, and what are things and their properties anyway?' is a question of no interest to the pure scientist, but demands a philosophical treatment, as we have partially seen illustrated in the work of Plato.

Russell concludes that the adoption of global or Pyrrhonian scepticism is not a possible basis on which to proceed in the search for knowledge, for there must be some piece of knowledge, or at least something accepted as such, which disputants share. Against the absolute sceptic no arguments can be advanced, by contrast with the methodological scepticism of Descartes, which, like the academic or mitigated scepticism Hume refers to in the *Enquiry*, proceeds slowly and carefully, testing each conclusion and subjecting the arguments for it to critical scrutiny, hopefully eventually arriving in this more modest and restrained manner at the truth. The critical role of philosophy is not to indulge in absolute scepticism, for that is fruitless, but rather to consider 'each piece of apparent knowledge on its merits, and retains what still appears to be knowledge when this consideration is completed' (Russell 1967: 88).

review
activity

Explain in your own words Russell's positive characterisation of philosophy.

some questions
to think about

1 Critically assess Russell's claim that the real table is an inference from what is immediately known. (AQA Examinations Board 2002)

2 Critically assess Russell's attempt to distinguish knowledge by acquaintance and knowledge by description. (AQA Examinations Board 2003)

3 Critically assess Russell's rejection of Idealism. (AQA Examinations Board 2004)

4 Discuss Russell's distinction between private space and physical space (the space of science) and assess his view of how they are connected. (AEB Examinations Board 1996)

5 Give a critical account of Russell's treatment of the inductive principle. (AEB Examinations Board 1995)

6 Describe what Russell understands by an *a priori* principle, giving appropriate examples. Discuss his reasons for holding that there must be such principles. (AEB Examinations Board 1988)

7 How does Russell refute the view that we cannot know that anything exists with which we are not acquainted? (AEB Examinations Board 1990)

8 On what grounds does Russell reject Kant's account of the *a priori* and what alternative account does he offer?

9 What are Russell's reasons for stating that the real table is not immediately known to us and does he justify his later conclusion that there is a real table? (AEB Examinations Board 1994)

10 Discuss Russell's attempt to substantiate his claim that knowledge of the universe as a whole is not to be obtained by metaphysics. (AEB Examinations Board 1993)

11 Outline and briefly illustrate what Russell means by the Laws of Thought. (AQA Examinations Board 2004)

12 Explain why Russell thinks that we are probably acquainted with ourselves, and give a critical evaluation of his position on the self. (AQA Examinations Board 2002)

13 Is Russell a rationalist or an empiricist?

14 Outline Russell's solution to the problem of *a priori* knowledge. (AQA Examinations Board 2002)

15 Critically evaluate Russell's account of universals.

further reading

▶ Ayer 1972 is a much tougher book than the two that follow, but it does provide a comprehensive and sophisticated treatment of Russell's philosophy.

▶ Baggini 2002, apart from the section on Russell in Pinchin 2005 (see below), is the only commentary of which I know that is directed specifically at *The Problems of Philosophy*. It is lucid and uncluttered and thus provides a very useful guide for students encountering Russell for the first time.

▶ Although Odell 2000 is not directed specifically at *The Problems of Philosophy*, this is another useful guide to Russell for beginners because of its brevity and straightforwardness.

▶ Pinchin 2005 contains a helpful exposition and critique of *The Problems of Philosophy* and would be an ideal starting point for those reading the book for the first time.

▶ Russell 1956 is very useful for providing a background to, and deeper details of, Russell's thought, especially on the topic of logically proper names, but it is considerably harder than the three texts above.

▶ Urmson 1956 is a useful introduction to the sort of philosophical analysis that Russell's work provoked, but it may be difficult to find.

VI

A priori: used to denote knowledge that is claimed on the basis of reason or logic, but prior to, and therefore independent of, experience.

A posteriori: used to denote knowledge that is based on experience.

Cognitive/non-cognitive: used of statements that do/do not convey factual information.

Deduction: an argument from premises to conclusions based on logic rather than on empirical evidence.

Empiricism: the view that all knowledge starts with sense-data.

Induction: an argument based on the assessment of empirical evidence.

Metaphysics: the study of the fundamental structures of reality, going beyond empirical evidence.

Naturalistic fallacy: the error in ethical argument (pointed out by David Hume and G.E. Moore) of trying to derive an 'ought' from an 'is'.

Phenomenalism: the view that statements about objects are equivalent to (or may be reduced to) statements about sense-data.

Reductionism: the view that complex wholes may be reduced to, and explained in terms of, the elements of which they are composed.

A.J. Ayer: *Language, Truth and Logic*

In context

In many ways, it was every young philosopher's dream; to get a first from Oxford, spend a few months in Vienna attending meetings of some of the most radical thinkers of the day, and then to return to the conservative philosophy department in Oxford University to publish – at the age of only 25 – a book that was to shake the English-speaking philosophical world.

Language Truth and Logic, as we shall see as we analyse the text and set it in context, was more a manifesto than a balanced survey of philosophy. It was a challenge to the establishment, a radical criticism of the theory of knowledge, but even more of morality and religion. It proclaimed much that had been regarded as the bedrock of philosophy and theology as 'senseless'. The provocative nature of its claims and the force of its arguments might have suggested that it was the work of someone who was about to storm out of the world of philosophy in disgust at its follies.

Instead, for all its limitations, which Ayer himself was later to acknowledge, it was the book that established him as a dangerous new thinker; a book whose arguments, succinctly and entertainingly presented, remain a challenge to any unthinking acceptance of traditional beliefs.

It is also a book written with a touch of arrogance. The young Ayer, who had only started to study philosophy six years earlier, claimed to refute long-established philosophical tradition, to expose much of what he had studied at Oxford as metaphysics and therefore meaningless. Opinionated but brilliantly argued, it is a book to provoke thought and to challenge assumptions. Hence, although it may now seem rather dated and very much a book of its time (for reasons that we shall examine later), it remains a classic example of clear thinking and argument, and of the kind of enthusiasm for ideas that motivates the very best philosophy.

Probably the best way to start a study of this book, and to get a feel for the young Ayer's campaigning zeal, is to read with care the preface to the first edition. In just a couple of pages, he sets out his agenda. Notice the following:

- He traces the philosophical impetus behind his approach back to the empiricism of Berkeley and Hume.

A. J. Ayer (1910–89)

- From Hume he sets out the division between matters of fact, known through experience (*a posteriori*) and those statements that are known to be true by virtue of the meaning of the terms used (*a priori*).

He then sets the context for, and agenda of, the book by saying that, 'in giving an account of the method of their validation I claim also to have explained the nature of truth.'

- He describes *a priori* statements as tautologies; they cannot give us information about the world, but only of the way in which words are used.
- Therefore, all claims to give us factual information are to be tested by his verification principle, which requires that they be verifiable through sense-experience.
- Whatever cannot be so verified is described as metaphysics. As such it is neither true nor false, but literally senseless.
- He immediately and controversially dismisses the idea that people have immortal souls, or that there exists a transcendent God.
- He therefore claims that there is no need to maintain the conflicting schools of philosophy, and he makes the following, amazing claim: 'And I attempt to substantiate this by providing a definitive solution to the problems which have been the chief sources of controversy between philosophers in the past' (Ayer 2001: 10).
- He maintains that the task of philosophy is analysis, claims that G.E. Moore (a hugely important figure at that time) did not go far enough, and acknowledges his debt to the Vienna School of Philosophy.

By the end of those two pages, he has placed his argument in the context of the prevailing philosophies of his day, and also set out his task as dismissing metaphysics and setting aside problems that had bedevilled the philosophical world for two millennia. In short, he claims to have explained the nature of truth. And all this at the age of 25! The book could not help but be hugely provocative and controversial.

But whatever view you take of the conclusions to which Ayer came, *Language, Truth and Logic* is worth studying for the clarity of the arguments it puts forward. It sets a standard for clear thinking and careful argument.

Ayer's life and works

As *Language, Truth and Logic* was written at the beginning of his academic career, it can best be understood in terms of the thinkers that had influenced Ayer up to that point, rather than in the development of his own thought.

It is also important, in studying a text, to appreciate the argument as it is presented and not confuse it with the argument that the author might, with hindsight, have wanted to present. Ayer tended to be both honest and generous in dealing with criticism. He frequently agreed with critics and admitted shortcomings in his own work, refining his views as time went on. Hence, by the end of his life, he had gone beyond most of the specific arguments used in *Language, Truth and Logic*, although he still agreed with the central thrust and purpose of that book. So care should be taken, if looking at later comments by Ayer, to make sure that they are understood in terms of his response to criticism, or later clarification of his thought. As such they are relevant to an *evaluation* of the text, rather than to understanding the text as we have it before us.

Note: A.J. Ayer wrote two volumes of autobiography: *Part of My Life* (1977) and *More of My Life* (1985). However, for the purposes of understanding the background to *Language, Truth and Logic*, students may find that 'My Mental Development', an autobiographical essay written in 1986, is quite sufficient (in Hahn (ed.) 1992).

Born in 1910, he was sent to a boarding school in Eastbourne at the age of eight, and at 13 gained a scholarship to Eton (almost by accident, he claims, as he went along to keep another boy company and to get practice at sitting examinations). By the age of 18, he had read and 'swallowed whole' G.E. Moore's famous *Principia Ethica*, and had bought and read Bertrand Russell's *Sceptical Essays*. In his biographical essay, Ayer quotes the following from the opening of that book: 'I wish to propose for the reader's favourable consideration a doctrine which may, I fear, appear wildly paradoxical and subversive. The doctrine in question is this: that it is undesirable to believe a proposition when there is no ground whatever for supposing it true.' He comments that this quote, 'has served me as a motto throughout my philosophical career'. It also serves as an introduction to the key theme in *Language, Truth and Logic*, namely the elimination of metaphysics and the attempt to set down clear criteria for judging whether a factual statement is meaningful.

At Oxford he studied Classics and then Greats (ancient history and philosophy). Whilst there he presented a paper to the Philosophical Society on Wittgenstein's *Tractatus Logico-Philosophicus*, of which at that time hardly any notice had been taken at Oxford, but by which he had been 'captivated' and which was to be hugely influential in his own philosophical development.

At the end of his undergraduate career, although he had originally intended to become a barrister, his increasing interest in philosophy led him to apply for a research lectureship at Christ College. Having given him the post, the college found that it had no need of his services for two terms, and he was therefore given the opportunity to continue with his studies elsewhere. Rather than going to Cambridge, where Wittgenstein was teaching, his tutor (Gilbert Ryle) suggested that he should go to Vienna. Ayer had just married and thought Vienna a very suitable venue for a honeymoon! There he met Moritz Schlick and was invited to attend meetings of the Vienna Circle – the experience that led him to write *Language, Truth and Logic* on his return to Oxford.

During the remainder of the 1930s he held a research studentship, became involved in politics, and worked on his *The Foundations of Empirical Knowledge*, which was published in 1940. After the war period, during which he worked in military intelligence, he became a tutor and Dean of Wadham College, but then moved to become Professor of the Philosophy of Mind and Logic at University College, London. There, as well as his teaching, he edited a major series of books for Penguin, and wrote *The Problem of Knowledge*, which was published in 1956. In 1959 he introduced and edited *Logical Positivism*, a book that reviewed the impact of his own early work. Increasingly well known through his writing and broadcasting, and often being invited to give lectures abroad, he returned to Oxford as the Wykeham Professor of Logic that same year, and settled in to New College. His other major publications include *The Central Questions of Philosophy* (1973) and *Philosophy in the 20th Century* (1981).

His list of publications – both books and articles in academic journals – is impressive, and he wrote and broadcast widely, but to the end of his life (he died in 1989) *Language, Truth and Logic* remained his best-known work.

Background

Scientific certainty

In 'modern' philosophy, there are two very clear but opposite starting points for the quest for certainty, represented by Descartes and by the Empiricists, particularly Hume. For Descartes, certainty lies with the fact of one's own thought ('I think, therefore I am') in the face of a radical dismissal of all that could possibly be doubted. For Hume, by contrast, knowledge starts with sense-experience, and all claims to truth are to be judged accordingly. (Recognising the force of the argument for both these positions, Kant concluded that the mind imposes categories that regulate and order the uncertain range of experienced phenomena.)

The a priori/a posteriori distinction

You therefore have the basic division, as outlined by Ayer in the very first paragraph of his preface (following Hume) between *a priori* knowledge (which takes the form of analytic statements, and is exemplified by mathematics and logic) and *a posteriori* knowledge (synthetic statements, based on sense-experience). Of these two positions, Ayer recognises that science is based on the latter; that it is based on, and developed as a result of, the examination of evidence.

The success of scientific method

By the end of the nineteenth century, there was a sense that science had triumphed, and that there was probably little left to discover – the radical ideas of the twentieth century, including relativity and quantum theory, had not yet disturbed the sense that Newtonian physics, along with the relatively recent acceptance of Darwinian evolution, had mapped out most of what there was to know. The accepted scientific method, characterised by 'induction' (see the chapter on the 'philosophy of science' for an outline of this), had yielded demonstrably sound results. All around was the technology to show the triumph of building knowledge on the foundation of experience, and the empirical data of observations and experiments. Science seemed progressive and sound in its approach to truth.

By contrast, philosophy was for ever returning to old questions and re-examining them. It was divided into different factions and had no overall strategy or agreed set of criteria for getting at the truth. It was lack of such criteria for truth that Ayer felt had led to the existence of the different philosophical schools.

Science applied to philosophy

Ayer was therefore concerned to show that, by using scientific criteria for examining the claims made in philosophy, he would be able to show the nature of truth. He was not the first to attempt this. Hume, for example, in assessing the possibility of miracles, emphasised that the wise man always proportioned his belief to the evidence, exactly as a scientist might assess the results of an experiment. Russell's logical atomism, and Wittgenstein's argument in *Tractatus*, paved the way for Ayer's argument. But most directly, he found that the ideas being discussed in the Vienna Circle, a gathering of philosophers and others with a particular interest in science and mathematics, brought to philosophy the systematic rigour of those other disciplines.

Creeping metaphysics

Metaphysical ideas can creep into statements that sound factual. For example, the words 'space' or 'time' are used to describe and analyse experience; we could not do without them, and know what they mean. However, these same words sound like names – so it is possible to consider 'space' or 'time' to be metaphysical realities, which might be described in themselves. Many old quips illustrate this problem via a metaphysical interpretation of the word 'nothing'. You could say, 'Nothing looks better than my new suit', but does that mean that you would look better if you wore nothing? Positivists wanted to avoid all such problems.

Truth conditions

Ayer was also interested in establishing the 'truth conditions' of statements: in other words, those things that will indicate whether the statement is true or false. In science, the issue is determined by setting up experiments to test out a hypothesis. Take the famous example by which Descartes challenged reliance upon sense-experience. He argued that one might be asleep and dreaming one's experience. Indeed, there is no way of being able to prove that one is now awake, as the experience of dreaming this would be equally convincing. No evidence from within an experience can guarantee to you that the experience is real and not part of a dream. In other words, there are no facts that can decide the matter; no 'truth conditions' to decide whether a statement about the experience is true or false. In the eyes of Ayer and the logical positivists, such debate becomes nonsense.

And beneath all this is the basic idea that permeates all science, that is, that every claim needs to be validated with reference to sense-experience. And that implies that every scientific claim must, in the end, be backed by a set of truth conditions (i.e. facts that can show it to be true or false) that are empirical.

Points to consider:

1. Does this approach imply that *only* scientific statements count as valid knowledge? (Such a view is generally termed 'scientism'.) As you study the text, you may want to consider whether Ayer's position leads to scientism.

2. Is a scientific 'truth' ever certain, or must it remain a hypothesis open to revision if new evidence is found to contradict it? (You may want to refer to the chapter on the 'philosophy of science' for background information on this.) If it remains open to revision, is it a good model for assessing meaningfulness and truth in philosophical discussions?

Hume

Later in his life, Ayer himself was to refer to *Language, Truth and Logic* as 'Hume in modern dress' (Gower 1987: 24). Clearly, he felt that he was continuing a philosophical tradition established by Hume, and for good reason. The following features of Hume are relevant to our study of Ayer:

1. Empiricism: Hume argued that all knowledge came through sense-experience, and that a wise person weighs evidence and comes to a conclusion on that basis. Similarly, Ayer takes a definite empiricist line on epistemology (theory of knowledge), insisting that factual claims are only meaningful if backed up by some relevant sense-data.

2. Analytic/synthetic distinctions: Hume made a clear division between analytic statements, which are known to be true by definition and are a matter of logic, and synthetic statements, which are based on experience and judged by evidence. This distinction became important for many thinkers (e.g. Kant), but it is also central to Ayer and logical positivists in general, as they applied verification to synthetic rather than analytic statements, regarding the latter as tautologies.

3. Is-ought in ethics: from Hume, and later from G.E. Moore, there came the fundamental argument that it was impossible to derive an 'ought' from an 'is'. In other words, facts themselves cannot provide a basis for moral judgements – the attempt to do which was called a 'naturalistic fallacy'. In his verificationalist attack on ethics, and his development of an 'emotive' approach to understanding ethical statements, Ayer follows this fundamental principle of Hume's.

4. The attack on metaphysics: Hume was notorious for wishing to dismiss what he called 'sophistry', in other words, metaphysics. Things were, for him, either known to be true by logic or by evidence. Claims that were based on neither were to be 'committed to the flames'. In Hume's words:

If we take in our hand any volume: of divinity or school metaphysics, for instance; let us ask, Does it contain any abstract reasoning concerning quantity or number? No. Does it contain any experimental reasoning concerning matter of fact and existence? No. Commit it then to the flames: for it can contain nothing but sophistry and illusion. (Ayer 2001: 40)

And Ayer comments:

What is this but a rhetorical version of our own thesis that a sentence which does not express either formally true propositions or an empirical hypothesis is devoid of literal significance? (Ayer 2001: 40)

This was exactly the sentiment that gave *Language, Truth and Logic* its appeal and its notoriety.

Russell

Logical atomism

In his introduction to *Principia Mathematica* (1910), Bertrand Russell introduced the theory known as logical atomism. Just as it is possible to take any complex physical object and analyse it down into the atoms of which it is comprised, so Russell argued that the same process could be applied to statements, analysing them into logical, rather than physical atoms. Just as science examines 'atomic facts' in the physical world, so the concern of the philosopher should be to analyse the 'atomic propositions' that refer to them.

This theory was also taken up by Wittgenstein, and is found in his *Tractatus*, but there are differences between the two of them. Russell thought of an 'atomic proposition' as comprising a proper name and a predicate, which would generally denote a universal. (In fact, most statements take this form. 'Henry is a cat' simply identifies an individual object 'Henry' with a general class 'cat', thereby explaining what Henry is.) Wittgenstein, however, analysed statements into their simple logical components which he considered to be just 'names', which stood for 'objects' in the physical world.

The details of logical atomism are beyond what is required for understanding Ayer's book. The key thing to appreciate, however, is that Ayer took from Russell the basic idea that the task of philosophy is *analysis*; breaking down complex statements into more basic ones, which can then be verified with reference to facts in the world. However, Russell and Wittgenstein were not alone in seeking to do this; another important philosopher of that time, G.E. Moore, also saw the task of philosophy as one of analysis. From Moore, Ayer also appreciated what he termed the 'common-sense' view of the world, which most people would see as self evident, namely that the world comprises material objects and acts of consciousness, along with a basic framework of space and time.

For a detailed survey of the ideas from Russell and Wittgenstein that influenced Ayer, see 'Logical Atomism' by Peter Simons in *The Cambridge History of Philosophy 1970–1945* (p. 383)

Wittgenstein

There were three separate and distinct phases to the work of Wittgenstein:

1. The first found expression in his book *Tractatus*, published in 1921. In it he sees words as pointing to, and corresponding to, empirical reality and he therefore sets out the limits of what can and cannot be said.

2. In the second phase, which he developed at the very time when the logical positivists were discussing and publicising his first phase, Wittgenstein suggested that the meaning of language was to be found in its use, thereby expanding the range of what language could do. Pointing to reality was only one such use.

3. In the third phase, which he was developing at the time of his death, he was concerned with the problem of finding a foundation which could be used as the criterion for determining which among the whole variety of meanings of language could be deemed true.

It was the first of these phases – the one summed up in his *Tractatus* – which influenced Ayer prior to writing *Language, Truth and Logic*. Wittgenstein famously opened his book with the statement 'The world is all that is the case' and ended it with 'Whereof we cannot speak, thereof we must remain silent.' In between those two statements he set out a series of numbered claims, which define the meaning for language in terms of a direct correspondence between words and that to which they point – physical reality.

Wittgenstein (like Ayer, later) considered that by setting out clearly what language could and could not do, he would expose and end all philosophical problems.

Wittgenstein's logical atomism

Wittgenstein's view of language was that all complex statements could be broken down into simpler ones, and that eventually they could all be reduced to statements that were elementary, each of which corresponded to a description of an observable event. In the end, therefore, language corresponds to the observable world, and statements are true or false depending on whether they do so accurately. So Wittgenstein's aim was to 'translate out' all statements into sense-data. In doing this, Wittgenstein offered a clear but narrow definition of meaning, and this appealed to both mathematicians and scientists, and in particular the philosophers from those backgrounds who were to form the Vienna Circle.

Ayer's interpretation of Wittgenstein's *Tractatus* (which may not necessarily have been the way Wittgenstein himself would have presented it) was that he identified 'atomic facts' with 'the data of sense-experience'. This was to play a key role in *Language, Truth and Logic*.

The Vienna Circle

Headed by Moritz Schlick, the Vienna Circle was an informal gathering of intellectuals who combined thinking in philosophy, logic, mathematics and science. It was influential within the European philosophy, but initially was little known within the English-speaking philosophical world.

Ayer arrived in Vienna at the end of 1932, spent four months there, and was invited by Schlick to attend meetings of the Circle. This was a remarkable privilege for someone of only 22 and newly graduated. Without sufficient German to contribute to the debates, he nevertheless understood enough to listen to and absorb what was being discussed. There was at the same time the only other foreigner to be allowed in, a 24-year-old American, later to be world-famous for his philosophy: Willard Quine.

The Vienna Circle of thinkers were developing what they termed 'logical positivism', and Ayer found it a refreshing approach when compared with the very traditional approach taken by the faculty in Oxford. In fact, the original title for what was later called *Language Truth and Logic* was just that – *Logical Positivism* – and his book was seen as a manifesto for that approach, aiming to make it more widely known and studied in the English-speaking world. The work is therefore one of interpretation. However, it would be wrong to characterise it as no more than that, for Ayer was also keen to explore the implications of logical positivism for ethics and for religious language, which went beyond the work of the Vienna Circle, and which gave his book its particularly controversial bite.

Ayer described his relationship with the Vienna Circle in the introduction in the book he edited in 1959, entitled *Logical Positivism*. Moritz Schlick, who had set up the group soon after arriving in Vienna, was Professor of Philosophy at the University there, but he had originally trained as a physicist and was mainly interested in the philosophy of science. Also influential was Rudolph Carnap, who had studied under the famous logician and mathematician Frege. Otto Neurath was particularly interested in Marxist political philosophy and the Circle included logicians and mathematicians, such as Kurt Godel and Hans Hahn. In general, their approach was radical and scientific. Major influences on the Vienna Circle included Ernst Mach, the mathematician and philosopher, and Einstein.

Here is Ayer, later in his life, commenting on the Vienna Circle:

> *It wasn't so much that they used science in their philosophy as that they thought the whole field of knowledge was taken up by science. Science describes the world, the only world there is, this world, the world of things around us; and there isn't any other domain for philosophy to occupy itself with. So what can it do? All it can do is analyse and criticise the theories, the concepts, of science. This is how science came in. And logic came in as supplying them with a tool.*

(Magee 1978: 120)

By the time he joined the group, it was coming towards the end of its time, and it was meeting strong criticism. When, in 1936, Schlick was murdered by a demented student, the academic obituaries were highly critical of his work.

Issues for the Vienna Circle

Within the philosophy of science, there are debates about scientific theories that go beyond what can be verified through experiments, particularly concerning the ambiguity about how to validate them, and how to judge between rival theories. This has led some to hold an *instrumentalist* view (i.e. that a theory is judged according to its usefulness, rather than by any absolute judgement about its being true or false). However, *positivism* was the general tendency to overcome such problems by concentrating on evidence, and seeing theories primarily as ways of anticipating further evidence. Positivists generally did not examine the causes of what was experienced, nor did they refer to any reality over and above the evidence on which scientific theories were based.

Evidence and the new physics

The Vienna Circle, very aware of mathematics and physics, was particularly engaged in questions about foundationalism – about what, if anything, could be taken as a basic starting point for knowledge. This was made more complicated by developments in physics. With his theory of general relativity, Einstein saw the idea that time was the same everywhere as meaningless. Quantum theory saw the idea that one could know both the momentum and the location of a particle as meaningless. And this was because there would always be a conflict in the evidence – either one thing could be known, or the other, but not both at once. Science was therefore suggesting that some questions might be meaningless, simply because there was no possibility of getting suitable evidence upon which an answer could be based.

Questions of evidence and meaninglessness were therefore very relevant to developments in physics. Ayer's philosophy was therefore picking up on a feature of the science of his day. This was yet another reason for the appeal and relevance of his book; it seemed to champion modern science against the errors of metaphysics and religion.

For a useful guide to the background of *Language, Truth and Logic* in the philosophy of science, see Hesse in Gower (ed.), *Logical Positivism in Perspective*, 1986.

Logical positivism

Ayer himself describes the positivism he encountered in Vienna as 'uncompromising', characterised by, 'its blanket rejection of metaphysics, its respect for scientific methodology, its assumption that in so far as philosophical problems are genuine at all they can be definitively solved by logical analysis'.

But he was never of the opinion that logical positivism was something new. He saw it as rooted in the empiricism of Hume. Indeed, he quotes with approval Hume's famous saying (quoted above) that whatever is not a statement of logic or of matters of fact is 'sophistry and illusion' and that it should be 'committed to the flames', describing it as 'an excellent statement of the positivist position'.

Positivism and metaphysics

However, he recognised that the positivist criticism of metaphysics was quite specific:

> *The Viennese positivists did not go so far as to say that all metaphysical works deserved to be committed to the flames: they allowed, somewhat perfunctorily, that such writings might have poetic merit or even that it might express an exciting or interesting attitude to life. Their point was that even so it did not state anything that was either true or false and consequently that it could contribute nothing to the increase of knowledge.* (Ayer 1959: 10)

In other words – and this is crucial for appreciating the central thrust of *Language, Truth and Logic* – he appreciated that the positivists thought that metaphysics was to be condemned for *pretending to be cognitive*. Metaphysical statements may have their value, but are not to be mistaken for statements of fact.

Central to logical positivism was the verification principle, the definition of which was given by Schlick, but may have originated with Wittgenstein, with whom he was regularly in touch: 'The meaning of a statement is the method of its verification.' They hoped, by using this principle, to eliminate all metaphysics, by showing it to be senseless, and also, more positively, to give philosophy the task of assisting all other areas of study (and particularly the sciences) to clarify the statements they made.

Wittgenstein and the Vienna Circle

According to Oswald Hanfling, in the introduction to his *Essential Readings in Logical Positivism*, Wittgenstein discussed his ideas with Waismann, who wrote them down in systematic form with a view to publication and also introduced them into discussions at the Circle. Hence Wittgenstein had a greater influence on the Vienna Circle than might otherwise be assumed, although he was never a member of that group. In any case the Circle acknowledged its debt to Wittgenstein's *Tractatus*, which informed much logical positivist thinking.

Positivism and realism

To get a very clear picture of how Schlick saw positivism, it is worth considering a paper he wrote in 1932–3 – at exactly the time that Ayer was in Vienna. His paper (reproduced in Hanfling 1981: 83) was entitled 'Positivism and Realism'. He starts by considering what is meant by positivism (a term that was coined by Auguste Comte). It is generally taken to be a rejection of metaphysics. But how is that defined? He points out that if metaphysics refers to 'reality in itself' (or some similar term), then it generally stands in contrast to the world of appearances (as, for example, in Plato's analogy of the cave, where what is experienced by the prisoners through their senses is merely a set of shadows, not reality itself).

But here there is a problem. If positivism simply eliminates everything that transcends ordinary experience, it amounts to saying that there is no metaphysics and, therefore, that *only* what is given in experience is real. But this is as much a metaphysical position as saying that what is given is unreal! (How could you decide between those positions?) Schlick recognises this and points out that it is as metaphysical to declare that only the given is real as it is to argue for a transcendent level of reality. Indeed, the problem with that position is that it leads to a form of *solipsism* (the view that one cannot know anything other than the contents of one's own mind), or, by taking shared experience into account, to something like Berkeley's *idealism*. He therefore concludes that all such debate about the nature of reality and its relation to experience is a pseudo-problem.

Rather than try to resolve this impossible dilemma, Schlick wants to take a very different approach, and argues that *the task of philosophy is to clarify the meaning of claims and questions*. In other words, one must ask what must be the case in order for this or that claim to be true. His key point is this: that if I have no idea of how I might go about verifying that a proposition is true, then clearly I have no idea of what it is saying. Thus: 'To state the circumstances under which a proposition is true is the same as stating its meaning, and nothing else' (Hanfling 1981: 89). And the circumstances are, of course, to be found in 'the given', the actual reality of life as we experience it. And here is the nub of the logical positivist test of meaning: 'A proposition for which the world looks exactly the same when it is true as it does when it is false, in fact says nothing whatever about the world; it is empty, it conveys nothing, I can specify no meaning for it' (Hanfling 1981: 89). He then goes on to say that we cannot be in a position to verify every statement, the key thing is that a statement should be such that *we know what it would take to verify it*. Verification simply needs to be 'thinkable' and therefore 'logically possible'.

A scientific example   The example Schlick gives is a scientific one. Suppose one were to claim that there was a nucleus within every electron, but that it produced absolutely no effect outside, so that its existence was not discernible. Such a claim would be meaningless, for there would be no way of ever knowing if it was correct. He therefore regards his principle of verification as far from new – it is, and has always been, self-evident in science. He also acknowledged (again from a scientific perspective) that nothing is ever conclusively verified. Every claim remains a hypothesis; it must always be open to challenge on the basis of new experienced data.

Of what cannot be said   Schlick then makes a point that follows the end of Wittgenstein's *Tractatus*: that if anyone claims that a proposition has a meaning that goes beyond any form of verification, then he or she is claiming something that goes entirely beyond language, beyond what we can say. Of all claims that go beyond this limit, Schlick does not say that they are false (that would be the conclusion to be reached from a failure of verification) but that they are meaningless.

He argues that science deals with empirical reality. Even things that are invisible, such as fields of force, are nevertheless part of the empirical world. They do not exist 'in themselves' separate from what we perceive them to be. The *realist* view is that the external world lies behind the experienced data – but that is a metaphysical assumption, we cannot show it to be the case. The *positivist* position, however, is to regard the external world as what we know in the experienced data – that *is* the empirical world. He makes the point that the non-metaphysician lives in the same world as everyone else. It is just that he or she does not add meaningless statements to his or her description of it.

Therefore, Schlick does *not* claim that only the given is real, nor does positivism deny the existence of the external world. Logical positivism and realism are not opposed to one another in such a straightforward way. Logical positivism does not say that those who believe in transcendent reality are wrong; it just says that they do not understand what they are talking about!

The debate Ayer probably witnessed

The debate between Schlick and Neurath (at the time Ayer was attending the Circle), was whether the observable terms by which statements could be verified were sensory (and therefore related to perception) or physical (having objective existence). Ayer tended to agree with Schlick, who held the former view. (In other words, for Ayer, it is the act of perceiving that provides the data against which meaningful statements are checked.) The basic position held by Schlick was that to define something, you had to end up by pointing to that to which it referred – in other words, there had to be a straight correlation between meaning and sense-data. I may well start to define one thing in terms of another, but at some point, unless there is to be an infinite regress of explanations, I have to stop and point!

review
activity

1. Read through the preface of *Language, Truth and Logic* at least twice. Make sure you understand the general point that Ayer is making in every sentence, and look up any terms he uses and thinkers to whom he refers. (For this you may need to refer back to work done in epistemology from your AS level course.)

2. Logical positivism was influenced by science. Do you think that scientific criteria are adequate for dealing with the range of issues with which philosophy deals?

Language, Truth and Logic – key arguments

Start your study of *Language, Truth and Logic* by looking carefully at the preface to the first edition; its claims are astounding. Ayer gives a summary of what he hopes to achieve in the book, and sets out clearly the fundamental distinction between 'relations of ideas' (analytic statements) and 'matters of fact' (synthetic statements) and, for the latter, he explains that he is to offer his modified principle of verification. Ayer declares that the task of philosophy is to clarify the propositions of science, rather than to indulge in speculative truths, and that he intends to provide definitive solutions to the problems that have divided philosophers in the past. Whatever the limitations of the arguments that are to follow, this stands as his manifesto.

The verification principle

Ayer's first chapter is boldly entitled 'The Elimination of Metaphysics', and in it he sets about promoting an empirical approach to verifying the truth or falsity of factual statements: 'We may begin by criticising the metaphysical thesis that philosophy affords us knowledge of a reality transcending the world of science and common sense' (Ayer 2001: 13).

He makes it clear that his starting point for knowledge is sense-experience, and, like Kant, he cannot accept that any statement that purports to give information about that which transcends such sense-experience can have 'any literal significance'. This final point is important, for language may have emotional significance, may express personal insights and the like. Ayer is not concerned with that (he will return to it with his consideration of ethics and religious language); rather, he is concerned with literal meaning – the conveying of information about the world.

The limits of possible knowledge

But is it possible that we can have knowledge that goes beyond that conveyed by our senses, for example, of objects as they are in themselves, rather than as we perceive them to be? He quotes Wittgenstein (2001: 15) as saying that in order to draw a limit to thinking, you have to see both sides of that limit. We cannot know that something lies beyond the limits of what we can know!

The criterion of factual significance

The verification principle is key to his argument. He expresses it thus:

> *The criterion which we use to test the genuineness of apparent statements of fact is the criterion of verifiability. We say that a sentence is factually significant to any given person, if, and only if, he knows how to verify the proposition which it purports to express – that is, if he knows what observations would lead him, under certain conditions, to accept the proposition as being true, or reject it as being false.*
>
> (Ayer 2001: 16)

Ayer then clarifies that one cannot always have positive proof for or against a statement, simply that one must be able to say what might count for or against it. But notice how he defines the sort of statements to which the verification principle applies. He intends to show that 'all propositions which have factual content are empirical hypotheses; and that the function of an empirical hypothesis is to provide a rule for the anticipation of experience' (Ayer 2001: 23). In other words, people want to make statements about general events (e.g. that water will boil at a certain temperature) because such statements are valuable for anticipating future events (e.g. that in future, if the statement is true, I can anticipate when my water will boil). He therefore makes the important point that 'every empirical hypothesis must be relevant to some actual, or possible, experience, so that a statement which is not relevant to any experience is not an empirical hypothesis, and accordingly has no factual content. But this is precisely what the principle of verifiability asserts' (Ayer 2001: 24).

Science and sense-experience

This point is crucial to an appreciation of Ayer's argument. He is not saying that statements that are not empirical hypotheses are nonsense, he is simply saying that such statements would have no 'factual content'. And, of course, he considers factual content to be a reference to the empirical world – the world that can be examined by science.

In other words, he is saying that science deals with the world of facts, and it does so on the basis of empirical evidence. Hence if any statement is to claim to be factually significant, it too must conform to that scientific principle, and be verifiable, at least in theory, with reference to the data of sense-experience.

One may make a joke, recite poetry, use words in a free-floating, stream-of-consciousness way. None of this is invalidated by Ayer's verification principle. What is invalidated is the attempt to pass off as a factually significant statement one that contains metaphysics; in other words, one that goes beyond what is empirically verifiable. And this, of course, is exactly what Ayer considered traditional ethics and religious language to be doing. He saw them making claims (such as the existence of God) for which there appeared to be no evidence that could count for or against their truth, and which he therefore did not consider to be factually significant – 'senseless', to use his provocative term.

Difficult areas for verification

The past　There is a problem with the past, in that we cannot observe it directly. What does it mean to make a statement about an event in history? Ayer's view at the time of writing *Language, Truth and Logic*, was that its meaning was given by the evidence; so the meaning of saying that something happened was given in terms of how you would research it in the present through books, archaeology, recordings, and so on. By the end of his life, he described this view as 'desperately implausible' (in an interview with Bryan Magee, 1978).

Other people　If you tell me that you are feeling sad, the only method I have of verifying that statement is to observe your face and behaviour. Yet clearly, the feeling of sadness gives rise to those physical things, and not the other way round. This too, Ayer admitted, soon came to be challenged and doubted.

Dispositional properties　Some statements refer to facts that could be observed in the future but not at the moment when the statement is made. Consider the 'dispositional properties' of an object. I can say that a glass is fragile, a piece of metal brittle, or a person liable to fly into a rage. We all know what such things mean; that if you drop the glass, bash the metal or irritate the person, they may be expected to exhibit a certain experienced pattern – shattering or shouting. So far, to Ayer, dispositional properties are most naturally described in terms of their method of verification. But what of the claim that the object is 'fragile'? It is clearly a quality of that thing, but not a quality that can be observed in the way that its other physical properties can be observed. If dispositional properties are meaningful, it suggests that we should adopt (as Ayer did) a 'weak' form of the verification principle (see p. 405). In other words, to allow that the statement is meaningful if there exists the potential of verification, even if it cannot be verified at this very moment. The question remains, however, whether a dispositional property actually inheres in the object to which it is applied. Is, 'it is fragile' the same kind of statement as 'it is red', if their methods of verification are so different?

Criticisms and Ayer's responses

A frequently cited criticism of the verification principle is that it is neither simply a definition of words, nor a statement that can be checked with reference to sense-experience. Therefore, it cannot itself be verified, and so, on its own terms, it becomes senseless.

At first sight this seems plausible enough, but it fails to take into account the limitation that Ayer placed on the verification principle, namely that it was concerned with statements that claimed to be factual. Now the verification principle is not a factual statement; it is a policy for the way in which statements should be evaluated. Within the Vienna Circle it was agreed that the verification principle was 'a convention' or discipline; it was a suggested use of language. *So the verification principle cannot be condemned for failing to be something that it never claimed to be!*

Strong and weak verification

The '*strong form*' of the verification principle: all statements are either of logic/ mathematics, in which case they are tautologies, or they are empirical statements of fact. The *meaning* of a factual statement is its method of verification. The '*weak form*' of the verification principle: empirical statements are said to be meaningful if empirical evidence is relevant to their being true or false.

The strong form of the verification principle, which Ayer encountered in Vienna, did not last very long. It made the claim that the meaning, and thus the content, of a statement was identical to its method of verification. That became increasingly implausible. It was replaced by the weak form, which is the form in which Ayer introduced it in *Language, Truth and Logic*. It simply claims that, for a statement to be meaningful, some evidence must in principle be relevant to deciding whether it is true or false. This does not claim that it is necessary to claim to have evidence in order to ascribe meaning; merely that evidence is relevant. And that, of course, means that the *content* of the statement is no longer identified with the evidence, merely that the content can only be considered meaningful if evidence is relevant to its truth.

Ayer clarified this in the same year that *Language, Truth and Logic* was published. Professor W.T. Stace had objected to the verification theory (in *Mind*, October 1935), pointing out the problems (mentioned above) about verification for claims about the past and about other minds. Ayer responded to it in *Mind*:

> *The first point that I must make clear is that I do not hold that a sentence can be factually significant only if it expresses what is conclusively verifiable; for I maintain that no empirical propositions are conclusively verifiable. All that I require of a putative statement of fact is that it should be verifiable in what I have called the 'weak' sense of the term; that some possible observations should be relevant to the determination of its truth or falsehood.* (Hanfling 1981)

This clarifies that it is the weak form that Ayer was presenting from the start, as opposed to the earlier strong form that had been discussed by Schlick in Vienna.

Notice that the strong version of the verification principle is a theory of meaning, and it refers to the *content* of a statement. The weak version is simply a test for *meaningfulness*. If something cannot be verified, even in theory, then it is meaningless. However, that is *not* the same as saying that the content of what is said, and the way in which it may be verified, are identical. Ayer's version is that 'A statement is meaningful if and only if it is verifiable', which is weaker than the original devised by Wittgenstein and Schlick.

The probability of verification

It is also clear (as explained, for example, in Foster 1985) that the weak form used by Ayer is essentially *probabilistic*. In other words, it does not try to claim that there can ever be *complete* verification, merely that there is sense-data relevant to the truth or falsehood of a claim. And this, of course brings it into line with scientific hypotheses, which are never certain, but always open to challenge. The strong version implies that when we speak about objects, we are actually speaking about the sense-data that constitute them (as it is sense-data that form the method of verification).

Ayer's retreat from a complete reduction

In a lecture reviewing the significance of *Language, Truth and Logic* 50 years after its publication (Gower 1987: 29), Ayer made the important point that the verification principle served two purposes, which he did not originally distinguish:

1. It established a criterion for claiming that a proposition was literally meaningful.
2. It implied that the content of a significant proposition, when fully analysed, was identical to the sense-data upon which it was based.

It is this second view that he subsequently thought was wrong. He recognised that it was impossible to carry through a complete reduction of physical statements (i.e. about the world) to sensory statements (i.e. about the data of sensation). He went on to examine these matters in his *Foundations of Empirical Knowledge* (1940) and in *Philosophical Essays* (1954).

The above issue is discussed in detail in the article by Michael Dummett entitled 'The Metaphysics of Verification' in Hahn (1992). The key point he makes is that the strong form of the verification principle implies a *phenomenalist* conception of physical reality. A phenomenalist holds that sense-data form the substance of the universe; they *are* the world, and knowledge of the world is verified through them.

On the fiftieth anniversary of publication of *Language, Truth and Logic*, Ayer gave an example to make this issue clear. The fact that I have blood on my coat may be evidence in favour of the truth of the proposition that I committed the murder. But having blood on one's coat is not part of the *meaning* of having committed a murder. So the verification does not require that the *content* of the statement being verified is identified with every statement that verifies it.

Hence to develop Ayer's example, if there is no evidence at all relevant to the claim that I have committed a murder (i.e. no body, murder weapon or blood), then the statement that I have committed a murder becomes meaningless, in the sense that it gives us no knowledge about the world. However – and this is a criticism of the strong form of the verification principle – that is not to say that 'he committed murder' is the same as 'he has blood on his coat' or 'there is a body with a knife in it'. They are both relevant to the truth or falsity of the statement, and may therefore be considered to be its 'truth conditions' (which is what every detective has to collect), but to not define its content.

It is far from clear that Ayer is always consistent in this. For a further examination of this point see Foster (1985: p. 26).

review activity

1. What exactly counts as 'knowledge', according to Ayer?

2. Give examples of statements to which the application of the verification principle is relevant (whether you agree with it or not), and of those to which it is not.

The function of philosophy

By eliminating metaphysics, Ayer considered that much of what people had assumed to be the appropriate sphere of philosophy was now invalid. In particular he was critical of attempts to base knowledge of a set of *a priori* truths, for he considered them to be tautologies, and from tautologies you can only deduce further tautologies! He also criticised the idea that philosophy is the study of reality 'as a whole'.

He restates his fundamental view that 'there is no field of experience which cannot, in principle, be brought under some form of scientific law' (Ayer 2001: 32). Hence there is no scope for philosophy to offer some alternative route to science for gaining knowledge of the world.

Philosophy as analysis   Ayer argued that the responsibility of the philosopher was to examine what was said, and to analyse the significance of each factual and other claim. Unlike the sciences, which were able to contribute to new knowledge through finding new empirical facts, philosophy had no such special area of knowledge, but was essentially a tool of analysis, ensuring that all other language was clear about what it was saying, and how its claims could be justified.

One way of describing the function of philosophy, according to Ayer, is to say that it is an 'activity' rather than a 'doctrine'. In other words, there is nothing distinctive for philosophy to be about, no content that is not already either an empirical statement of fact (and therefore within the remit of the sciences) or a statement of logic or mathematics. Analysis is the activity, and it can be applied to all areas of discourse – philosophy 'of' something then refers to an analytic approach to the statements made within that something; it does not imply that there is some metaphysical, esoteric information to which philosophy has access but to which science does not.

Earlier philosophers   Whilst admitting that much philosophy in the past had been metaphysics, Ayer did not thereby discredit all earlier thinkers. He suggests that John Locke's *Essay Concerning Human Understanding* was essentially analytic in its approach. Nor does he believe that Berkeley was a metaphysician, and – naturally enough, as he is a principle source of Ayer's inspiration – he sees David Hume as one who would have nothing to do with speculative metaphysics, and considers much of his work to be analytic. Plato, Aristotle, Kant, Hobbes, Bentham and Mill are also cited as forerunners of what he sees as analytic philosophy. Ayer mentions them in order to emphasise that his new analytic approach is genuinely in line with what was previously termed simply 'philosophy', and that all he seeks to do is prune out the 'metaphysics' with which it was associated.

He summarises a key feature of the analytic approach thus:

> [T]*he philosopher, as an analyst, is not directly concerned with the physical properties of things. He is concerned only with the way in which we speak about them. In other words, the propositions of philosophy are not factual, but linguistic in character – that is, they do not describe the behaviour of physical, or even mental, subjects; they express definitions, or the formal consequences of definitions. Accordingly, we may say that philosophy is a department of logic.*
>
> (Ayer 2001: 44)

Fifty years later, reviewing the position he took in *Language, Truth and Logic* on the role of philosophy, Ayer said:

> [P]*hilosophy was not a natural science nor did it provide an alternative account of reality; its function, apart from exposing metaphysics, was that of analysis and elucidation; that in the last resort all empirical facts were atomic, identifiable with items of sensory experience; and that the principal task of philosophical analysis was to exhibit not only the propositions of common sense but also the constituents of scientific theories as logical constructions out of descriptions of these sensory items.*
>
> (Gower 1987: 25)

Thus, even if philosophy appears to be about objects in the physical world, or the sense-data by which we are aware of them, it is really about the logical implications of our descriptions of them. He ends the second chapter by making this point absolutely clear:

> *We may speak loosely of him [the philosopher] as analysing notions, or facts, or even things. But we must make it clear that these are simply ways of saying that he is concerned with the definition of the corresponding words.*
>
> (Ayer 2001: 44)

review activity

1. If everything in the world can (in theory) be known through science, is there any point in philosophy? Use this question as the basis for explaining how Ayer sees the function of philosophy.

2. Do you think the earlier philosophers mentioned by Ayer would have thought of themselves as dealing mainly with the meaning of words? Answer with reference to any one of them that you have studied earlier in your course.

Definitions and analysis

In-use definitions

At the beginning of Chapter 3, Ayer makes the important distinction between *explicit* and *in-use* definitions:

*   An 'explicit' definition, as found in dictionaries, gives synonyms for the word being defined. To use Ayer's own example, an 'oculist' is defined as an 'eye-doctor'; if you know the meaning of 'eye' and 'doctor', the definition enables you to grasp the meaning of 'oculist'.

*   An 'in-use' definition takes a sentence in which the term to be defined is being used, and translates it into equivalent sentences which do not use that term or any of its synonyms. In other words, it provides alternative

ways of saying what would normally be said by the word or phrase that is being defined.

Consider Ayer's example of the sentence 'The round square cannot exist.' Notice that you cannot give an explicit definition of a 'round square' in order to see whether or not it exists. But it is possible to mistakenly assume that there may be something called 'a round square' out there – some metaphysical entity which may or may not exist. Ayer translates the sentence into 'No one thing can be both square and round.' This makes it clear that there cannot be a round square, without attempting to give an explicit definition of something that cannot possibly exist.

The sort of problem that Ayer is attempting to avoid here may also be illustrated by the following lines of dialogue:

'Nothing works quicker than this tablet in bringing about recovery.'
'Fine; I'll take nothing and recover more quickly!'

The joke, of course, is that in the second line of dialogue 'nothing' is taken to be some entity, whereas in the first it is a word that establishes the relationship between the tablet and recovery. An 'in-use' definition of 'nothing' in the first line would have avoided that misunderstanding (see also 'Creeping metaphysics' p. 395).

By carrying out this process of giving an 'in-use' definition of descriptive phrases, Ayer hopes that people will not fall into the 'naive assumption' that such phrases are demonstrative symbols, in other words, that they refer to some entity that exists. To do that would be to lapse into metaphysics; to assume that there is a level of reality beyond that which we encounter through the senses. And, of course, the avoidance of such metaphysics is the purpose of his book.

To take the example given above, it is as though, having decided to recover more quickly by taking 'nothing', the patient then sets about a philosophical examination of that mysterious thing called 'nothing', as though it were a reality somehow out there in the world. That is metaphysics; and Ayer has no time for it. Although, of course, there were other philosophers at that time who certainly did think it was a valid activity to explore the nature of nothingness, among them Heidegger and Sartre.

Thus, his definition 'in-use' confirms Ayer's approach to philosophy as analysis. It examines the meaning that is implied by the way in which terms are used; it confirms that philosophers should not be speculating about whether descriptive phrases refer to entities in the world, but analysing the meanings they have and the way in which those meanings are expressed through the evidence of the senses.

He therefore sums up the purpose of a philosophical definition thus:

In general, we may say that it is the purpose of a philosophical definition to dispel those confusions which arise from our imperfect understanding of certain types of sentence in our language, where the need cannot be met by the provision of a synonym for any symbol, either because there is no synonym, or else because the available synonyms are unclear in the same fashion as the symbol to which the confusion is due.   (Ayer 2001: 51)

review
activity

1. Explain in your own words the difference between an explicit and an 'in-use' definition, and say how it relates to Ayer's idea of philosophy as analysis and avoids metaphysics.

2. Give an 'in-use' definition of 'nothing' in the proposition 'nothing works quicker than this tablet in bringing about recovery'. In other words, provide an alternative sentence or sentences which convey exactly the same meaning, without using the term 'nothing' or any synonym for it.

Linguistic phenomenalism

How do we know that objects exist? Generally because of sense-data that we receive when we encounter them. Hence I can describe the book in front of me in terms of its size, weight, colour, the colour of its cover, and so on. These sensations are what I know of the book, and the sequence of them (first I see it, then I touch it, and the one set of sensations corresponds to the other) confirms in my mind that there exists an object that is the cause of them. But how do I know that? Might I be dreaming? If all we know are sensations, then how do I know that there is something *beyond* those sensations which is the cause of them? (Those who have studied Kant will recognise the distinction between noumena and phenomena: things as they are in themselves, and things as we perceive them to be.)

'Phenomenalism' is the view that to say that objects exist is equivalent to describing sensations; to say that something exists is to say what it is perceived to be. Ayer is concerned with language, but it is language that is related very directly to the sense-data. The strong form of the verification principle claimed that the meaning of a statement was its method of verification, and even the weak form insisted that some empirical evidence was needed if a claim was to be meaningful. Hence Ayer's linguistic analysis relates very directly to phenomenalism.

Avoiding reductionism? It is possible to define any object (Ayer's example is the desk at which he sits) in terms of the sense-data that make up that object. This gives the impression that the symbol 'desk' is reduced to symbols for the various sense-data – colour, hardness, and so on – that make up the experience of the desk. This would be a *reductionist* account of the desk; in effect, that the desk is 'nothing but' those sense-data. But that is to confuse 'explicit' and 'in-use' definitions. The reductionist account would amount to an explicit definition of 'table', whereas what Ayer wants to offer is an 'in-use' definition, by which it is shown that sentences referring to the table can be translated into equivalent sentences which do not use that word. Ayer points out that the problem of the reduction of objects to sense contents is a major part of the traditional philosophical problem of perception. It is always going to be difficult to describe the way in which a person's subjective experience relates to the external object which gives rise to it.

This issue of perception highlights again the nature and purpose of linguistic analysis. Ayer is arguing that the function of philosophy is not to speculate about what exists, nor to 'reduce' physical objects to sense-experience, but *to analyse language*. And this can be done by taking a sentence and showing how it can translate out into other sentences, thereby defining its terms 'in-use'. A table is not reduced to sense-experiences (of being brown, hard and cold to the touch, and so on), but these experiences are what lead us to give the name 'table' to that experience. Just as a scientist might analyse an object into its physical components, right down to the atoms of which it is comprised, so the philosopher, performing logical analysis, takes apart the sentence in which I might claim to be sitting at a table, and translates it out into the elements, confirmed by sense-experience, of which it is comprised.

And here we may return to the verification principle: for my claim to be sitting at a table is only factually significant if there is empirical evidence that can count for or against it, in other words, if 'I am sitting at a table' can be translated out into a sentence that expresses the empirical evidence for sitting at a table.

review
activity

1. Is philosophy about words or about things? How might Ayer answer that question? Would you agree with him?

2. Define in your own words 'phenomenalism' and 'reductionism'. Then say whether you consider Ayer's argument requires him to accept either or both of these.

Induction and the *a priori*

Ayer describes his philosophy as 'a form of empiricism', as he considers it to be characteristic of empiricism to hold that 'every factual proposition must refer to sense-experience'.

Hence he needs to deal with a central problem of empiricism, namely that evidence cannot lead to logical certainty; evidence, at best, gives degrees of probability. The method of argument which starts from evidence and uses it to make a general statement is known as *induction*. (As opposed to deduction, which starts from general principles and deduces facts from them.) The problem with induction is that, even if you have a hundred examples that confirm your general principle, there is always the chance that the next one will go against it, and you will have to think again. A classic example of this would be the logical assumption on the part of zoo-free, untravelled Europeans that all swans are white. As Ayer puts it, 'this means that no general proposition referring to a matter of fact can ever be shown to be necessarily and universally true. It can at best be a probable hypothesis' (Ayer 2001: 64). The alternative to this is rationalism, which holds that there are truths that we can know independently of experience. This, of course, Ayer cannot accept, as it would be 'incompatible with our fundamental contention that a sentence says nothing unless it is empirically verifiable' (Ayer 2001: 64). It is therefore vital for Ayer that he find an empirical basis for propositions of logic and mathematics, which appear to be both certain, but which do not obviously seem to be the result of an inductive argument from experience. How then can their truth be validated?

Mathematics and logic as analytic propositions

Ayer holds that the principles of logic and mathematics are universally true simply because they are *analytic propositions*, and, therefore, for him, tautologies. He refers back to Kant, who made the distinction between analytic and synthetic judgements: in the former, the predicate is contained within the subject (and thus they are universally true); in the latter, the predicate adds something to what is known of the subject, and therefore depends on experience. 'A cat is an animal with four legs and a tail' would be considered analytic; 'My cat is outside the door' is synthetic; the first is a matter of definition, the second known only through observation.

Ayer's criticism of Kant

For Kant, an analytic statement unpacks and clarifies the meaning of its subject, it does not add to our knowledge of it; a synthetic statement adds information. However, Ayer criticises Kant for not giving a sufficiently clear criterion for distinguishing between the two. He argues, for example, that, for Kant, when someone says $5 + 7 = 12$, the intention in the mind of the speaker when he or she says '$5 + 7$' is not the same as the intention '12'. Information has been added, and therefore the statement is synthetic. This Ayer sees as a psychological criterion, rather than a logical one. He also points out that the statement '$5 + 7 = 12$' cannot be denied without self-contradiction. And it is this logical argument that Ayer sees as conclusive, not the psychological one.

Analytic statements, Ayer argues, cannot be contradicted by experience, but he does not consider them to be nonsense (as he does metaphysics). Rather, he holds that analytic propositions give information about 'linguistic usage'. He therefore concludes Chapter 4 by stating that, 'To say that a proposition is true *a priori* is to say that it is a tautology. And tautologies, although they may guide us in our empirical search for knowledge, do not in themselves contain any information about any matter of fact' (Ayer 2001: 83).

Background to Ayer's view

Gottlob Frege (1848–1925), a mathematician whose work was very influential in the early years of the twentieth century, had argued that the laws of logic were actually non-empirical, necessary truths about reality. The opposite view was taken by Wittgenstein, who argued that all analytic statements are simply tautologies; they are about language, not about reality.

All necessary truths, according to Wittgenstein followed by the logical positivists, are therefore truths about the meanings of words; they do not describe any external reality. For such information, one must always turn to evidence and statements that derive from it: synthetic statements. Hence an analytic statement is merely a *linguistic convention*; it conveys no content. What is more, as analytic statements are merely conventions about our use of language, there is no reason why we cannot change them. So an analytic statement cannot claim to be true in any absolute sense.

Carnap, a key thinker in the Vienna Circle, argued for a 'principle of tolerance'. He held that there was no right or wrong in terms of linguistic conventions; we simply decide what rules we wish to adopt. Hence it is possible that an analytic statement that is 'true' according to one set of linguistic conventions may be 'false' under another. Hence he considered that analytic statements can have no inherent truth.

Challenges to the analytic/synthetic distinction

A criticism of logical positivism in general, related to the distinction between analytic and synthetic statements, is made by Stephen F. Barker in *The Legacy of Logical Positivism*. He shows that in many cases sentences can be regarded as analytic if interpreted one way, and synthetic in another:

> *For example, when its terms are taken in their standard senses, does the sentence 'A person knows something only when his belief is based on evidence' express something analytic or something synthetic? It is doubtful that there is any definitely correct answer here, for our standard sense of the word 'know' seems open and indefinite with respect to this.*   (Barker 1969: 231)

His point is that the logical positivists assumed that sentences would be either inherently analytic or inherently synthetic, whereas he argues for language that has an 'open texture'.

This echoes the best-known challenge to the analytic/synthetic distinction, which was made in 1951 by Willard Quine (who, of course, attended the Vienna Circle alongside Ayer) in a famous article entitled 'The Two Dogmas of Empiricism'. In this Quine challenged:

1. the basic division between analytic and synthetic statements
2. the assumption that all meaningful statements can be reduced to the data of immediate experience.

Quine suggested that the positivists had considered each statement and its verification in isolation from all others. And this, of course, was fair comment, as the positivists had been influenced by, for example, the logical atomism of Russell, whose whole intention was to break down complex wholes into their logical atomic components. But Quine argued that in order to understand one sentence one had to understand a whole language. Significance is not found in a single impression or observational statement, but in the whole system of beliefs that gives rise to them.

The issues here take us beyond what is required for a study of *Language, Truth and Logic*, but you should at least be aware that Ayer's view of *a priori*, analytic statements as tautologies was later open to serious challenge.

review activity

1. Why can induction never yield certainty?
2. Explain, with examples, the distinction between analytic and synthetic statements. Show how these relate to the idea of knowledge being either *a priori* or *a posteriori*

.

Mathematics

In Chapter 4, as part of his consideration of analytic propositions, Ayer considers the status of mathematics. It is a topic about which he later came to the conclusion that what he had written in *Language, Truth and Logic* was inadequate. As with the issue of analytic and synthetic statements, much of what he presented in this book is found in the work of those who influenced him.

413

A.N. Whitehead and Bertrand Russell, in their influential *Principia Mathematica* (1910–13), had argued that mathematics is able to be reduced to basic principles of logic. A study of mathematics could not be a matter of experience. Mathematics did not provide synthetic statements, the truth or falsity of which could be checked against evidence. Hence mathematics was seen as analytic and formal, and, as such, it did not convey any factual information. If you set out a mathematical equation, you know it is true, because that truth is included in the meaning of the symbols you have used. Once you know the meaning of '2', '4', '+' and '=', you cannot deny that '2 + 2 = 4'.

Earlier, Kant had held that mathematical statements were examples of *synthetic a priori* knowledge: '2+2 = 4' says something about the real world, but it is also known to be true – true by definition. By contrast, Ayer follows Russell in seeing mathematics and logic as analytic, not synthetic. In other words, they are not based on experience, nor do they express factual content; rather, they are about our use of words.

Conventions? Anthony O'Hear in 'Ayer on Logic and Mathematics' makes the following criticism:

> [M]ost of mathematics and logic are analytic on Ayer's view only given that analytic truths are true by virtue of initial definition and their logical consequences, and it is just the notion of logical consequences that the conventionalist of LTL [Language, Truth and Logic] does not (cannot?) explain.
> (Gower 1987: 117)

In other words, it is one thing to claim that logic and mathematics are conventions, but quite another to say *why* those conventions should apply.

There is a further problem here, for Ayer claimed that any denial of the principles of mathematics or logic involved self-contradiction, but self-contradiction is itself a logical principle. We therefore appear to be going in circles; his mathematical and logical conventions depend upon a logical principle, which is itself a convention!

Invention and discovery in mathematics If logic and mathematics offer propositions that are certain because they are no more than tautologies, it should follow that we should never be surprised by them, as a tautology simply unpacks or explains what is already known.

Ayer quotes Poincaré (1854–1912; a mathematician, physicist and philosopher) as finding it incredible that all mathematics should 'serve no other purpose than to say in a roundabout fashion "A = A"'. Poincaré's answer to this was to accept a synthetic element (thus making mathematics not entirely a matter of definition, but related to the nature of reality), but Ayer will not accept that, and wants to keep mathematics entirely a matter of convention. Ayer's answer is therefore that mathematics and logic can surprise us simply because we are limited in our reasoning, and do not appreciate all the mathematical and logical possibilities to which the definitions upon which they are based can give rise.

His example for this is long multiplication. We calculate the result and know it to be true, but we do not immediately see that result when we see the two things to be multiplied together. We might make a mistake in our calculations, and, if the mathematical formula is complex, we may misunderstand how to calculate the result. That gives an element of surprise, although the result is already fixed in the meaning of the numbers and the terms with which we start.

He also claims that framing definitions is a creative thing, and can lead us to see logical implications that might not otherwise have occurred to us. But none of this requires him to go beyond his basic view that all such propositions in mathematics and logic are analytic and *a priori* – they are all a matter of conventional definitions and the propositions to which they give rise are tautologies.

review activity

1. If mathematics is a matter of conventional definitions, can it ever tell you something new?

2. If mathematics were not conventional, but synthetic and based on evidence, might we find one day an example where 2 + 2 = 5? If not, why not?

Although not part of the required reading for the A2 examination, Chapter 5 of *Language, Truth and Logic* examines issues of truth and probability. In particular, Ayer is concerned to show that 'truth' is not some quality, it is simply the assertion of that which is called 'true'. To say 'X is true' is equivalent to saying 'X'; to say it is false is to assert 'not X'. Clearly, this follows from his elimination of metaphysics, and for his assertion that the proper function of philosophy is analysis.

The emotive theory of ethics

Chapter 6 deals with the implications of Ayer's approach for ethics. Having established the clear distinction between fact and value, it is clear that he cannot accept the claim that something is good or right as a statement of fact. If it tries to be cognitive, it fails to satisfy the verification principle.

Against making moral pronouncements

Ayer starts by examining different forms of ethical language. Naturally enough, he accepts that the definition of ethical terms is a valid activity for philosophy. He also accepts what is generally termed 'descriptive' (as opposed to 'normative') ethics, namely the description of the lifestyle and moral norms of any given society, but he insists that such description of ethical behaviour is either psychology or sociology. Nor does he see moral commands as a valid part of philosophy, for they are not propositional (i.e. they do not say what is or is not the case), but simply exhort people to take a particular action. But this leads him to make the amazing claim that 'A strictly philosophical treatise on ethics should therefore make no ethical pronouncements' (Ayer 2001: 105).

His concern, therefore, is to examine the nature and use of ethical terms, not to make moral claims as such. But in examining ethics, his agenda is very clear: 'What we are interested in is the possibility of reducing the whole sphere of ethical terms to non-ethical terms' (Ayer 2001: 106). So we may reasonably assume that this will be a criterion by which he is to assess other ethical theories.

Rejection of other ethical theories

- *Subjectivists* relate ethical judgements to the 'feelings of approval' of those who make them. He rejects this on the basis that it is not self-contradictory to say that something is wrong, even if it is generally approved of.
- *Utilitarians* relate ethical judgements to benefit, happiness or satisfaction. But again Ayer cannot accept this, as it would not be self-contradictory to say that something is wrong, even if a majority would gain happiness through it.

Notice that Ayer uses *self-contradiction* as his criterion for assessing these. In ordinary ethical language, by his argument, we seem to apply the terms 'good' or 'right' to an action without necessarily relating that either to its results or to the approval of people. Hence it is clear that we assume there to be some other absolute standard which we have in mind when we call something 'good'.

But notice the implication of this. Ayer's criticism only works because he uses an independent definition of 'good'. A utilitarian might well argue that it *is* self-contradictory to say that something is not good, even if it gives the greatest happiness to the greatest number, because that is what the utilitarian understands by 'good'.

Here, Ayer makes a crucial point. He is not saying that it is impossible to do just as I have suggested above, and define 'good' in utilitarian terms. Rather, he argues that such a definition does not work as an analysis of *what people actually mean* when they speak of right or wrong. When they say that something is 'wrong' they do not mean that they have calculated the consequences and have decided that it does not offer the greatest happiness to the greatest number. They mean something rather more absolute than that. But how do they know what is 'wrong'? Intuition provides Ayer with no answer to this, for two people may equally have intuitions about what is wrong, but disagree with one another, and there can be no empirical way of deciding between the two.

Ethical pseudo-concepts

His conclusion was that ethical concepts cannot be analysed because they are pseudo-concepts. 'The presence of an ethical symbol in a proposition adds nothing to its factual content' (Ayer 2001: 110). Hence, to use his example 'Stealing money is wrong', he says that it 'has no factual meaning, that is, expresses no proposition which can be either true or false. It is as if I had written "Stealing money!!" – where the shape and thickness of the exclamation marks show, by a suitable convention, that a special sort of moral disapproval is the feeling which is being expressed'(Ayer 2001: 110). Thus, Ayer insists that all he is doing, in making a moral assertion, is asserting his moral sentiments. He is not making any factual claim, and therefore he is not making a statement that can be either right or wrong.

As a background note, ethics was not a topic that Ayer inherited from the Vienna Circle. Indeed, Schlick took a utilitarian view of the subject – it was a matter of seeing what people wanted and how their desires could best be fulfilled. Ayer's 'emotive' theory was not entirely new, however, as he admitted in 1986 (Gower 1987: 26), having been introduced by C.K. Ogden and I.A. Richards in *The Meaning of Meaning*, published in 1923, and of which he was aware. Nevertheless, Ayer's development of the theory was very much his own.

As he took the view that ethical statements simply expressed the emotions or wishes of the person who made them, Ayer's approach is generally termed 'emotivism'. A moral statement (e.g. you should not commit murder) is therefore asserting two things:

1. the fact (murder has taken place)
2. the emotion with which that is asserted (disapproval).

He is also prepared to say that moral injunctions take the form of commands. In saying that something is right, I am telling you that it is something you should do. Commenting on his ethics in 1959, Ayer pointed out that 'normative statements are not derivable from descriptive statements' (Ayer 1959: 20). This amounts to a restatement of Hume's principle (and Moore's) that one cannot derive an 'ought' from an 'is' – once again showing that Ayer's thinking is in many ways a development of Hume's.

Ayer held (in his 1946 introduction to the second edition) that his emotive analysis of moral language was capable of standing up to scrutiny on its own account, quite apart from the validity of any challenges to his work as a whole, but it is clear that his approach to ethics broadly follows from his more general elimination of metaphysics. If there is no cognitive content to the claim that something is right or wrong, the only meaning that those two words can have (and they *do* have meaning, because they are widely used and understood) is one that looks at the context of the statement in which they are placed. Is it a disguised command? Does it aim to express an emotion?

Expressing, not describing

There is a common misunderstanding of Ayer on this point. Expressing an emotion is not the same as describing it. Of course, those who say that an action is wrong are referring outside themselves to that action, not attempting to analyse their own emotions. Indeed, even if Ayer is right and the moral claim is no more than an expression of the emotion of the speaker, that speaker may remain entirely unaware of it. It is the tone and nature of the moral claim that demonstrates the emotion of approval or disapproval that lies behind it.

Responding to Moore

Ayer was responding to G.E. Moore's non-naturalist position on ethics, namely that there was a quality (good) that inhered in actions and which could be known through intellectual intuition, but which could not be described in terms of simpler qualities, any more than the colour yellow could be described in terms of other things – you just point to it. Ayer's criticism of Moore is based on the fact that Moore's non-naturalistic judgements cannot be verified, nor are they simply a matter of logic. Ayer argues that, if judgements are made on intuition, there seems no way of deciding between conflicting intuitions. Moore had argued that you could not derive an 'ought' from an 'is' (the naturalistic fallacy) and therefore that you could *not* reduce moral statements to empirical statements. But for the logical positivists and Ayer, unless you could do such a reduction, moral statements would remain meaningless.

Make sure you understand the difference between cognitive and non-cognitive approaches to ethics. Be aware that a non-cognitive approach is not going to yield a conclusion that an action is right or wrong in any absolute sense.

Non-cognitive relativism

Naturally this (and any other) *non-cognitive approach* is going to be criticised by those who seek some objective measure of goodness, and see any such alternative as subjective and relativist. If all moral claims simply express approval or disapproval, then there can be no objectively agreed right or wrong; I approve, you disapprove and we agree to differ.

Some problems with Ayer's view

What do people mean?

In assessing utilitarian and subjectivist theories, Ayer was very willing to say that they did not take into account what people *actually meant* when they said an action was right or wrong (e.g. by 'right' they did not mean 'offering the greatest happiness to the greatest number'). But surely, if one person says 'stealing money' (in whatever tone of voice) and another says 'stealing money is wrong', the latter means something more than the former. After all, 'you stole the money!' could be said in surprised and delighted amazement, in which case, it would certainly not be the equivalent of 'stealing money is wrong'.

Ethical debates?

The key problem with an emotivist approach to ethics is that it makes ethical debate impossible. If I say that something is right and you say that it is wrong, we are simply expressing our own approval or disapproval of that thing. We are not making any claims that can be assessed objectively. But, in fact, people engage in ethical debates, and think that, in doing so, they are talking about real and important issues. They would argue that they are not simply comparing feelings with one another.

It is interesting to note that Ayer criticised the non-naturalistic position of G.E. Moore on the grounds that, if 'good' were only known by intuition, there would be no way to judge between conflicting intuitions. However, his own theory has exactly the same weakness. The difference, however, is that Moore thought he was actually describing a non-natural quality, whereas Ayer only claims that ethical statements express the sentiments of the person who makes them.

Ayer himself accepted the criticism that, if ethical statements cannot be either right or wrong, it becomes impossible to explain ethical debates. Actually, he ascribes this point to G.E. Moore, who used it against subjectivist arguments in general. Ayer's response was to suggest that debates about moral issues are only possible on the basis of *shared fundamental values*. Where these differ, there is no common ground, and therefore no basis upon which to agree or differ about ethical issues.

Words, meanings and society

A.J. M. Milne makes a number of related criticisms of Ayer's approach (Gower 1987: 89). He points out that Ayer considers that, because ethical statements are not descriptive, they cannot be validated by evidence, the exception being ethical statements that give the ethical status of an action with a society. For example, to say 'in society X you are allowed to marry more than one person' you are describing an ethical issue, but doing it in a factual way that can be confirmed by normal evidence. However, to go one step further and say 'marrying more than one person is wrong' one is making an evaluative judgement, and, therefore, according to Ayer, it does not express an empirical proposition at all.

Milne points out that, even if a statement is merely descriptive (e.g. 'you stole the money'), it actually employs words that are themselves evaluative – in this case the word 'stole'. So the statements 'you took the money' and 'you stole the money', although they describe the same action, are in fact different, *because the values are embedded in the choice of words.*

Milne uses the example of calling something 'unfair'. It may well be that in making that judgement I am expressing an emotion (anger? disgust?). But the meaning of 'unfair' is not a description of the emotion, it is of something that provokes in me that reaction and emotion. Hence moral language is trying to express something of objective quality, going beyond our emotional responses to it. He also examines the key idea of 'obligations' and sees them as 'unconditional imperatives'. He sees the idea of obligation as universal. Societies have different moral principles, but all alike have the sense that there are principles to which everyone should relate for a guide to action. Suppose we consider the word 'untrustworthy'. To call someone untrustworthy is to comment on his or her behaviour, as defined by actions in which an agreed or implied trust is broken. It is not really about the emotions we have concerning that person; it is more objective in that it is a moral judgement based on the evidence of behaviour. His general point is summed up as, 'Every morality reflects some understanding of the world and of the human situation within it, and this understanding can be subjected to critical examination' (Gower 1987: 107). It is this critical examination that Ayer's emotive theory precludes, by making morality no more than an expression of the emotions involved.

review
activity

1. Explain why an emotive theory of ethics may be described as non-cognitive and as relativist.

2. Do you consider that Ayer's view does justice to what is happening when people make moral assertions and engage in moral debates? If not, what more is needed?

Religious language

Having dealt with metaphysics and ethical language, Ayer turns to religious language, and particularly to the question of the existence of God. He is concerned to consider the God of traditional theism, and starts by making the point that if the existence of God is to be demonstratively proved, then the premise on which his existence is to be deduced must be certain. Ayer's argument is very straightforward:

*   No empirical proposition can ever be more than probable; it cannot be certain. So a proof for the existence of God cannot be based on an empirical proposition.
*   A *priori* propositions are certain, but, as they are tautologies, nothing but other tautologies can be deduced from them.
*   Hence the existence of a God cannot be demonstrated.

But Ayer wants to take a further step and show that the existence of a god is not even probable. He argues that, if the existence of a god were probable, the proposition that he existed would be an empirical hypothesis. From that, other propositions might be deduced, for example, that there is a certain regularity in nature (the design argument). But to assert that there is a god is not the same as asserting that nature has regularity; the theist will want to say that God is transcendent. But if God is transcendent, the claim that he exists is a metaphysical claim (in that it is not a proposition concerning either matters of fact, or the meaning of terms), and Ayer concludes:

> [I]f 'god' is a metaphysical term, then it cannot be even probable that a god exists. For to say that 'God exists' is to make a metaphysical utterance which cannot be either true of false. And by the same criterion, no sentence which purports to describe the nature of a transcendent god can possess any literal significance.
> (Ayer 2001: 120)

This does *not* mean that Ayer agrees with an atheist or an agnostic position (as he points out on p. 121) to deny the existence of God is equally meaningless.

Science and religion

Ayer's view, and that of logical positivism generally, was one of great respect for science. He is concerned to make it clear that there cannot be any genuine conflict between science and religion. If religious claims are not factual propositions, they cannot conflict with science. On the other hand, science, by giving people more control over their own destiny, takes away a motive for being religious.

Mystical intuition

If religious knowledge is a matter of faith or intuition, and if it therefore goes beyond what is ordinarily intelligible (e.g. mystical experience), this implies that the attempt to describe it (as it is beyond description) will end in nonsense. Hence Ayer argues that the mystical intuition cannot be genuinely cognitive. Hence, although he accepts that people may have religious experiences, he will not accept that any such experiences can validly be used to prove the existence of a transcendent 'god'. Theological statements say something about a person's feelings about life, but Ayer argues that they are not cognitive – in other words, they do not give us information about the world.

He concludes with his challenge to both the moralist and the theist: 'The theist, like the moralist, may believe that his experiences are cognitive experiences, but unless he can formulate his "knowledge" in propositions that are empirically verifiable, we may be sure that he is deceiving himself' (Ayer 2001: 126).

The gardener

Ayer's point may be illustrated by the 'gardener' story, used by Anthony Flew in 1955 (but originally devised by John Wisdom). In it, two explorers come across a clearing that contains a mixture of flowers and weeds and debate whether there is a gardener. All tests for a gardener prove negative, but the one who believes in the gardener will not allow the lack of positive evidence to count against his belief; he simply refines what he means by 'the gardener' (and therefore 'God'). Flew's conclusion is that the gardener dies 'the death of a thousand qualifications'. Similarly, Ayer will not accept that you could claim that a statement is literally meaningful (i.e. giving information about the world) unless you are prepared to accept that there must be some state of affairs that can count for or against that being true.

Explanatory hypothesis

In 1973, in his Gifford lectures, Ayer was rather more open to the claims of theology than he had been in 1936. He was prepared to accept that theism might act as an 'explanatory hypothesis', just as science posits unobservable entities in order to make sense of what one is examining. However, he still concluded that, as an explanatory hypothesis, theism was vacuous.

In any case, given the shift in the understanding of religious language that has taken place since 1936, it is doubtful whether many theologians today would be happy to consider theism as no more than an explanatory hypothesis, vacuous or not!

review
activity

1. Is 'God exists' a factual proposition? If so, can it be verified?

2. Consider the view that Ayer's argument gives no more comfort to the atheist than to the theist, and least comfort at all to the agnostic.

General criticisms

The most relevant and severe critic of *Language, Truth and Logic* was its own author. The introduction he wrote to the 1946 edition of the book, which you may now find reprinted as an appendix to the text, revealed the extent to which, in the first 10 years after its publication, Ayer had developed in his thinking on many of the topics it covered. Typically sharp in his comments, when asked in 1978 about the book's limitations, he replied, 'Well, I suppose the most important of the defects was that nearly all of it was false' (Magee 1978: 131).

He felt that the verification principle was never properly formulated. We have already noted (see p. 405) the difference between the 'strong' and 'weak' forms of verification; Ayer started promoting the 'strong' form as he inherited it from Schlick, but then developed the 'weak' form, having recognised the limitations of the former. He also recognised that it was actually impossible to reduce all statements to those about sense-data. This was an important development, which he shared with the other visitor to the Vienna Circle, Quine, who was later to challenge the fundamental distinction between analytic and synthetic statements, a distinction that we have seen is absolutely crucial to the verificationist position. He also felt that his approach to ethics was not at that time sufficiently developed, although it had been 'along the right lines'.

Overall, he felt that the book had been liberating for many people, and radical in the way that it challenged the existing traditions in philosophy. And that, in many ways, reflects the consensus – namely that, brilliant though it was, *Language, Truth and Logic* was very much a work of its time. It shattered many people's assumptions about the subject matter and role of philosophy.

Whether it provided a solid basis for the further development of philosophy is more debatable. By the time it became famous, shortly after the Second World War and on through the 1950s, its ideas had already been overtaken by the later work of Wittgenstein, and the agenda for both philosophy and ethics was shifting away from the issues as Ayer had seen them in 1936.

Foster's criticisms   John Foster (1985) makes the point that Ayer seems to take the view that a statement has factual significance only if its content is purely observational. Hence he is concerned to verify only statements with observational content. Foster calls this the 'content-principle', which Ayer himself did not examine, but which lies beneath the work. That Ayer was concerned with the 'unobservability' of things is shown in his preface to the 1946 edition. The issue in that edition appears to be whether legitimate statements *entail* statements about sense-data, or whether they can be *translated into* statements about sense-data.

John Foster's criticism of the verification principle is that Ayer actually goes beyond the 'weak' form of verification that he outlines (i.e. that there should be sense-data relevant to the truth or falsity of a statement) to something rather stronger, in which the content of any factually significant statement is able to be reduced to a complex of sentences in an observational language. And of this he says, 'Thus any attempt to translate statements about the physical world into statements about sense-contents, or statements about other minds into statements about behaviour, seems to involve a radical distortion of what the original statements mean' (Gower 1987: 27). By contrast, he says that, if Ayer were to simply stick to an evidence-principle (in other words, that evidence is relevant to meaningfulness, but does not determine the content of what is claimed), he would not need to be reductionist, and, of course, it is the reductionist interpretation of Ayer that appears to be most implausible.

The issue here is that Ayer is, in actual fact, not consistent in his claims. He does sometimes seem to be arguing for just such a 'content-principle' and reductionist approach, but at others – especially where he contrasts his 'weak' form of the verification principle with the original 'strong' form that he encountered in the Vienna Circle – he seems to be backing away from such reductionism. Whatever was the case at the time of writing *Language, Truth and Logic*, and 10 years later when adding the revised introduction, with the benefit of hindsight he himself moved away from the strong, narrow and reductionist interpretation. In his own way, therefore, Ayer confirmed the limitation that Foster was later to point out.

Moving on. . .

Although *Language, Truth and Logic* was hugely influential, the world of philosophy has moved on significantly since it was written, sometimes prompted to do so by the challenge posed by Ayer and logical positivism.

Language

There is an assumption in Ayer of the 'correspondence' theory of truth, i.e. that language corresponds (if its statement are true) with the physical state of the world. To know if a statement is true, one must check it against the facts to which it refers; his concern was with the *literal* use of language. We saw that this emphasis grew out Russell's logical atomism, Wittgenstein's early work, and the sense that language should be considered along scientific lines. Ayer always admitted that there were other uses for language, but pointed out that they were not factually significant, in other words, they were not making claims about the world.

Wittgenstein moved on, and with him much of the philosophical world. He recognised that the meaning of a statement was given by its use, rather than by reference to evidence. The varied and subtle use of language became of interest in philosophy, and the narrower, literal use was put into that broader perspective. Even the basic division between synthetic and analytic statements was challenged by Quine (see p. 413), suggesting that the basis upon which Ayer and others had been working was itself inadequate.

The logical positivists considered language from very much a scientific and mathematical point of view. Later philosophy saw that making claims about the world was only a small part of what language was actually about, and set about examining its other functions.

Science In the philosophy of science there has been a general move (seen in the work of Kuhn and Feyerabend, for example pp. 166 and 180) towards a more relativist approach to scientific theories. There is no single definition of what is scientific and what is not, but theories have value and compete with one another in giving an adequate explanation of things.

Such tendencies in language and science – the very areas that *Language, Truth and Logic* tried to span – indicate that Ayer's simple test of meaningfulness and the hope of achieving scientific precision in language, was inadequate for its intended purpose. It may be valid within a limited sphere (which, of course, is true of almost all replaced theories), but once you get beyond literal statements of the content of sense-experience and start to embark on a range of uses of language, such basic factual testing itself becomes meaningless.

Ethics Other philosophers developed Ayer's 'emotivist' approach to ethics. C.L. Stevenson (*Ethics and Language*, 1944) had a similar form of emotivist argument to that of Ayer, but was already considering the meaning of ethical statements to be related to their *use*. In particular, he pointed out that moral statements are intended to *do* something, not just observe something. What they tried to do was to *persuade* someone, and to say that something is good or right is a 'persuasive definition'. A further development, 'prescriptivism', is associated particularly with the work of R.M. Hare (in *The Language of Morals*, 1952 and *Freedom and Reason*, 1963). Ayer himself, in reviewing the development of logical positivism, acknowledges these two developments.

An outline of both of these ethical theories may be found in *Understanding Philosophy for AS Level*, as they are part of the discussion of 'metaethics' (see pp. 160–70) and will therefore not be repeated here.

These approaches see moral language as *functional* – to be judged by what they do. And this, of course, is seen also in the general shift in Wittgenstein's thought (for his later philosophy is concerned with observing the way in which language is used – he was concerned with 'speech acts') whereas his earlier work (which influenced the Vienna Circle) took the narrower descriptive use to be the norm.

Religious language Ayer was concerned with literal language and with the elimination of metaphysics. Clearly, traditional religious language fell foul of the verification principle. Ayer, like Wittgenstein in *Tractatus*, recognised the limited scope of what they were trying to do. But whereof they could not speak, thereof they should have remained silent (to paraphrase the end of *Tractatus*). Ayer delighted in not doing this, and for him the attack on traditional religious claims was part of his more general challenge to the philosophical, moral and religious establishment.

But from 'the god of the gaps' argument, which – with the advance of science – saw the danger of 'god' retreating into the ever-diminishing gaps in our knowledge, about the retreat of religious explanations in the face of the advance of science, to Flew's parable of the gardener and the meaningfulness of religious claims, the philosophy of religion has taken into account the serious challenge of logical positivism, and has widely accepted the symbolic, metaphorical and functionalist nature of religious language.

review activity

For four subjects with which philosophy is concerned – science, language, ethics and religion – summarise the contribution and the limitations of *Language, Truth and Logic*.

some questions to think about

1 Is it possible to take a 'scientific' approach to language? What limitations might science impose on what you could meaningfully say?

2 How convincing do you find Ayer's 'emotive' view of ethics? Are you conscious of expressing your own emotional evaluation of situations through the moral statements you make about them? Are there aspects of moral language that Ayer's view cannot explain?

3 Following Ayer's argument, God can never be a feature in a literal understanding of the world. Do you agree with that view? What might be the implications of this for religion?

4 How would you account for the huge popularity of *Language, Truth and Logic*?

further reading

▶ Ayer 1959 includes Ayer's own summary of his position.

▶ Gower 1987 includes Ayer's reflections on *Language, Truth and Logic* 50 years after it was written.

▶ Foster 1985, the first part of which is concerned with *Language, Truth and Logic*.

▶ Baldwin 2003 (ed.) includes valuable sections giving background to the study of this text.

bibliography

Achinstein, P. and Barker, S. F. (eds) (1969), *The Legacy of Logical Positivism* (Baltimore: Johns Hopkins Press).

Ackrill, J.L. (1980), 'Aristotle on *Eudaimonia*' in Rorty (ed.) (1980), pp. 15–33.

Annas, J. (1992), 'Ancient Ethics and Modern Morality' in Tomberlin (ed.) (1992), pp. 119–36.

Austin, J.L. (1962), *Sense and Sensibilia* (Oxford: Clarendon Press).

Ayer, A.J. (1958 [1940]), *The Foundations of Empirical Knowledge* (London: Macmillan).

Ayer, A. J. (ed.) (1959), *Logical Positivism* (London: Allen & Unwin).

Ayer, A.J. (1963), *The Concept of a Person* (London: Macmillan).

Ayer, A.J. (1971), *Russell and Moore: The Analytical Heritage* (London: Macmillan).

Ayer, A.J. (1972), *Bertrand Russell, Modern Masters* (New York: The Viking Press), ed. Frank Kermode.

Ayer, A.J. (1978), *Hume* (Oxford: Oxford University Press).

Ayer, A.J. (2001 [1936]), *Language, Truth and Logic* (London: Penguin).

Bacon, F. (1605), *The Proficience and Advancement of Learning* (available at www.luminarium.org/sevenlit/bacon/baconbib.htm).

Bacon, F. (1620), *New Organon or True Directions Concerning the Interpretation of Nature* (available at www.luminarium.org/sevenlit/bacon/baconbib.htm).

Bacon, R. (1268), *On Experimental Science* in Thatcher (ed.) (1901), pp. 369–76.

Baggini, J. (2002), *Philosophy: Key Texts* (Basingstoke: Palgrave Macmillan).

Baldwin, T. (ed.) (2003), *The Cambridge History of Philosophy 1870–1945* (Cambridge: Cambridge University Press).

Barnes, J. (1982), *Aristotle* (Oxford: Oxford University Press).

Barnes, J. (2000), *Aristotle: A Very Short Introduction* (Oxford: Oxford University Press).

Bedford, S. (1958), *The Best We Can Do: Account of the Trial of John Bodkin Adams* (London: Penguin).

Bennett, J. (1971), *Locke, Berkeley and Hume: Central Themes* (Oxford: Oxford University Press).

Bergmann, P. (1987), *Nietzsche: The Last Antipolitical German* (Indiana: Indiana University Press).

Berkeley, G. (1910), *A Treatise concerning the Principles of Human Knowledge* in Lindsay (ed.) 1910, pp. 87–195.

Butts, R. E. (ed.) (1989), *William Whewell: Theory of Scientific Method* (Cambridge IN: Hackett Publishing Company).

Carruthers, P. (1986), *Introducing Persons* (London: Croom Helm).

Chalmers, D. (1996), *The Conscious Mind* (Oxford: Oxford University Press).

Churchland, P. (1988), *Matter and Consciousness* (London: MIT Press).

Cottingham, J. (1986), *Descartes* (Oxford: Blackwell).

Cottingham, J. (1993), *A Descartes Dictionary* (Oxford: Blackwell).

Crane, T. (1995), *The Mechanical Mind* (London: Penguin).

Crane, T. (2001), *Elements of Mind* (Oxford: Oxford University Press).

Crane, T. (2003), 'Mental Substances' in O'Hear (ed.) (2003), pp. 229–50.

Curd, M. and Cover, J.A. (1998), *Philosophy of Science: the Central Issues* (New York: W.W. Norton & Co.).

Davidson, D. (1970), 'Mental Events' pp. 207–27 in Davidson (ed.) (1980), *Essays on Actions and Events* (Oxford: Oxford University Press).

Dawkins, R. (1976), *The Selfish Gene* (Oxford: Oxford University Press).

Descartes, R. (1968 [1637 and 1644]), *Discourse on Method and Meditations* (London: Penguin) tr. F.E. Sutcliffe.

Descartes, R. (1986), *The Principles of Philosophy* (London: Everyman Classics).

Dicker, G.D. (1998), *Hume's Epistemology and Metaphysics: An Introduction* (London: Routledge).

Edwards, J. (1701), *A Free Discourse Concerning Truth and Error.*

Feyerabend, P. (1975), *Against Method* (London and New York: Verso).

Feyerabend, P. (1987), Farewell to Reason (London and New York: Verso).

Flew, A.G.N. (ed.) (1964), *Body, Mind and Death* (London: Macmillan).

Flew, A.G.N. (1986), *David Hume, Philosopher of Moral Science* (Oxford: Blackwell).

Flew, A.G.N. and Vesey, G. (1987), *Agency and Necessity* (Oxford: Blackwell).

Fodor, J. (1987), *Psychosemantics* (Cambridge MA: MIT Press).

Foster, J. (1985), *Ayer* (London: Routledge).

Foster, J. (1991), *The Immaterial Self* (London and New York: Routledge).

Frankena, W. (1973), *Ethics*, 2nd edn (New Jersey: Prentice Hall).

Garrett, B. (1998), *Personal Identity and Consciousness* (London and New York: Routledge).

Geach, P. and Anscombe, G.E.M. (eds) (1970), *Descartes: Philosophical Writings* (London: Nelson University Paperbacks for The Open University).

Gosling, J.C.B. and Taylor, C.C.W. (1982), *The Greeks on Pleasure* (London: Clarendon Press).

Gower, B. (ed.) (1987), *Logical Positivism in Perspective* (London: Croom Helm).

Graham, G. (1993), *Philosophy of Mind: an Introduction* (Oxford: Blackwell).

Guttenplan, S. (ed.) (1984), *A Companion to the Philosophy of Mind* (Oxford: Blackwell).

Hacker, P. (1972), *Insight and Illusion: Wittgenstein on Philosophy and the Metaphysics of Experience* (Oxford: Clarendon Press).

Hacker, P. (1997), *Wittgenstein* (London: Phoenix Press).

Hahn, L.E. (ed.) (1992), *The Philosophy of A.J. Ayer* (La Salle IL: Open Court).

Hanfling, O. (ed.) (1981), *Essential Readings in Logical Positivism* (Oxford: Blackwell).

Hayman, R. (1997), *Nietzsche*, in The Great Philosophy Series, (London: Phoenix Press).

Hayman, R. (1980), *Nietzsche: A Critical Life* (Oxford: Oxford University Press).

Heil, J. (1998), *Philosophy of Mind: A Contemporary Introduction* (London: Routledge).

Heil, J. and Mele, A. (eds) (1995), *Mental Causation* (Oxford: Clarendon Press).

Heydebrand, W. (ed.) (1994), *Max Weber: Sociological Writings* (London and New York: Continuum).

Hughes, G.J. (2001), *Aristotle on Ethics* (London: Routledge).

Hume, D. (1975 [1777]), *An Enquiry concerning Human Understanding* (Oxford: Clarendon Press), ed. L.A. Selby-Bigge 3rd edn, with text revised and notes by P.H. Nidditch.

Hume, D. (1978), *A Treatise of Human Nature* (Oxford: Clarendon Press), ed. L.A. Selby-Bigge 2nd edn, with text revised and notes by P.H. Nidditch.

Jones, R. A. (1986), *Emile Durkheim: An Introduction to Four Major Works* (Beverly Hills, CA: Sage Publications Inc.).

Kant, I. (1963 [2nd edn 1787]), *Critique of Pure Reason* (London: Macmillan).

Kenny, A. (1968), *Descartes* (New York: Random House).

Kenny, A. (1973), *Wittgenstein* (London: Penguin).

Kenny, A. (1978), *The Aristotelian Ethics* (Oxford: Clarendon Press).

Kim, J. (1993), *Supervenience and the Mind* (Cambridge: Cambridge University Press).

Kim, J. (1996), *Philosophy of Mind* (Boulder CO and Oxford: Westview Press).

Kim, J. (1998), *Mind in a Physical World* (Cambridge MA: MIT Press).

Klibansky, R. and Mossner, E.C. (eds) (1969), *The Letters of David Hume* (2 Vols.), Vol. 1 (Oxford: Oxford University Press).

Kraut, R. (1989), *Aristotle on the Human Good* (Princeton NJ: Princeton University Press).

Kuhn, T. (1962), *The Structure of Scientific Revolutions* (Chicago: University of Chicago Press).

Lakatos, I. (1970), *Criticism and the Growth of Knowledge* (Cambridge: Cambridge University Press).

LaPlace, P. (1951 [1820]), *A Philosophical Essay on Probabilities* (New York: Dover), trs E.W. Truscott and F.L. Emery.

Leibniz, G.W. (1982), *New Essays concerning Human Understanding* (Cambridge: Cambridge University Press), eds P. Remnant and J. Bennett.

Locke, J. (1961), *An Enquiry concerning Human Understanding* (London: Everyman).

Locke, J. (1966), *Second Treatise of Government* (Oxford: Blackwell).

Lovejoy, A.O. (1962), 'The Meaning of "Emergence" and Its Modes' in Dicker (ed.) (1962).

Lowe, E.J. (2000), *An Introduction to the Philosophy of Mind* (Cambridge: Cambridge University Press).

Lycan, W. (1990), *Mind and Cognition* (Oxford: Blackwell).

MacDonald, C. (1989), *Mind/Brain Identity Theories* (London: Routledge).

MacIntyre, A. (1981), *After Virtue, A Study in Moral Theory* (London: Duckworth).

MacKay, A.J. (1989), 'David Hume' in Gilmour (ed.) (1989), pp. 63–73.

Mackie, J.L. (1976), *Problems from Locke* (Oxford: Clarendon Press).

Madell, G. (1988), *Mind and Materialism* (Edinburgh: Edinburgh University Press).

Magee, B. (1978), *Men of Ideas* (London: BBC Publications).

McCulloch, G. (1995), *The Mind and Its World* (London and New York: Routledge).

McGinn, C. (1982), *The Character of Mind* (Oxford: Oxford University Press).

McGinn, C. (1984), *Wittgenstein on Meaning* (Oxford: Blackwell).

McGinn, M. (1997), *Wittgenstein* (London: Routledge).

Mill, J.S. (1843), *Systems of Logic* (Introduction available on www.marxists.org/reference/subject/philosophy/works/en/mill.htm).

Mill, J.S. (1988 [1859]), *On Liberty* (Oxford: Oxford World Classics, OUP).

Mill, J.S. (1889), *An Examination of Sir William Hamilton's Philosophy* (New York: Longmans Green and Co., Inc.).

Moore, G.E. (1903), *Principia Ethica* (Cambridge: Cambridge University Press).

Moravcsik, J.M.E. (ed.) (1967), *Aristotle: A Collection of Critical Essays* (London: Macmillan).

Moya, C.J. (1990), *The Philosophy of Action: An Introduction* (Cambridge: Polity Press).

Nagel, T. (1970), 'Physicalism' in Borst (ed.) 1970, pp. 214–30.

Nagel, T. (1974), 'What is it Like to be a Bat?' *Philosophical Review* 80, 435–50.

Nagel, T. (1989), *The View From Nowhere* (Oxford: Oxford University Press).

Newton-Smith, W.H. (2000), *A Companion to the Philosophy of Science* (Oxford: Blackwell).

Nietzsche, F. (2003), *Beyond Good and Evil* (Penguin Classics: Penguin).

Noonan, H. (1999), *Hume on Knowledge* (London: Routledge).

Norman, R. (1998), *The Moral Philosophers: An Introduction to Ethics* (Oxford: Oxford University Press).

Norton, D.F. (ed.) (1993), *The Cambridge Companion to Hume* (Cambridge: Cambridge University Press).

Odell, S. (2000), *On Russell* (Belmont CA: Wadsworth).

O'Hear, A. (2003), *Minds and Persons*, (Cambridge: Cambridge University Press).

Papineau, D. (ed.) (1996), *The Philosophy of Science* (Oxford: Oxford University Press).

Papineau, D. (2002), *Thinking about Consciousness* (Oxford: Clarendon Press).

Parfit, D. (1984), *Reasons and Persons* (Oxford: Clarendon Press).

Passmore, J. (1952), *Hume's Intentions* (Cambridge: Cambridge University Press).

Pears, D. (1967), *Bertrand Russell and the British Tradition in Philosophy* (London: Collins).

Penelhum, T. (1993), 'Hume's Moral Psychology' in Norton (ed.) (1993), pp. 117–47.

Pinchin, C. (1999), *Issues in Philosophy* (London: Macmillan).

Pinchin, C. (2005), *Issues in Philosophy*, 2nd edn (Basingstoke: Palgrave Macmillan).

Plantinga, A. (1974), *God, Freedom, and Evil* (London: Allen & Unwin).

Poincaré, J.H. (1902), *La Science et l'hypothèse* (Paris: Dover Publications).

Pojman, L.B. (2001), *Ethics: Discovering Right and Wrong*, 4th edn (Belmont CA: Wadsworth).

Polyani, M. (1969), *Knowing and Being* (London: Routledge).

Popper, K. (1934), *The Logic of Scientific Discovery* (London: Routledge).

Popper, K. (1945), *The Open Society and its Enemies, Vol. 2, Hegel and Marx* (London: Routledge & Kegan Paul).

Popper, K. (1969), *Conjectures and Refutations* (London: Routledge).

Priest, S. (1991), *Theories of the Mind* (London: Penguin).

Putnam, H. (1975), *Mind, Language and Reality: Philosophical Papers Vol. II* (Cambridge: Cambridge University Press).

Rawls, J. (1999), *A Theory of Justice* (Oxford: Oxford University Press).

Rorty, A. O. (ed.) (1980), *Essays on Aristotle's Ethics* (Berkeley CA: University of California Press).

Rosenthal, D. (ed.) (1991), *The Nature of Mind* (Oxford: Oxford University Press).

Ross, D. (1964), *Aristotle* (London: Methuen).

Rousseau, J. (1999), *The Social Contract* (Oxford: Oxford World Classics, OUP).

Russell, B. (1956), 'The Philosophy of Logical Atomism' in Marsh (ed.) (1956) pp. 175–281.

Russell, B. (1967 [1912]), *The Problems of Philosophy* (Oxford: Oxford University Press).

Russell, B. (1963), *The Practice and Theory of Bolshevism* (London: HarperCollins).

Ryan, A. (1974), *J.S. Mill* (London: Routledge).

Ryle, G. (1973 [1949]), *The Concept of Mind* (London: Penguin).

Sabine, G. (1980), *A History of Political Theory* (Thompson learning).

Sainsbury, R.M. (1979), *Russell* (London: Routledge & Kegan Paul).

Sartre, J. (1992 [1946]), *Existentialism and Humanism* (London: Methuen), tr. P. Mairet.

Savile, A. (2000), *Leibniz and the Monadology* (London: Routledge).

Scruton, R. (1982), *Kant* (Oxford: Oxford University Press).

Searle, J. (1983), *Intentionality* (Cambridge: Cambridge University Press).

Searle, J. (1989), *Minds, Brain and Science* (London: Penguin).

Searle, J. (1991), *Searle and His Critics* (Oxford: Blackwell) eds E. Lepore and R. van Gulick.

Searle, J. (1992), *The Rediscovery of the Mind* (Cambridge MA: MIT Press).

Searle, J. (1997), *The Mystery of Consciousness* (London: Granta Books).

Searle, J. (2004), *Mind: A Very Brief Introduction* (Oxford: Oxford University Press).

Shoemaker, S. (1963), *Self-Knowledge and Self-Identity* (Ithaca NYS: Cornell University Press).

Shoemaker, S. and Swinburne, R. (1984), *Personal Identity* (Oxford: Blackwell).

Smart, J.J.C. 'Sensations and Brain Processes' *Philosophical Review Vol. LXVIII*, pp. 141–56.

Smith, P. and Jones, O.R. (1986), *The Philosophy of Mind* (Cambridge: Cambridge University Press).

Staniland, H. (1972), *Universals* (London: Macmillan).

Strawson, P.F. (1952), *An Introduction to Logical Theory* (London: Methuen).

Strawson, P.F. (1959), *Individuals: an Essay in Descriptive Metaphysics* (London: Methuen).

Strawson, P.F. (1966), *The Bounds of Sense* (London: Methuen).

Stroud, B. (1977), *Hume: The Arguments of the Philosophers* (London: Routledge), ed. T. Honderich.

Swinburne, R. (1986), *The Evolution of the Soul* (Oxford: Oxford University Press).

Swinburne, R. (1996), *Is there a God?* (Oxford: Oxford University Press).

Taylor, R. (1967), 'Causation' in Edwards (ed.) (1967) pp. 56–66.

Ten, C.L. (1980), *Mill on Liberty* (Oxford: Oxford University Press).

Thatcher, O. J. (ed.) (1901), *The Library of Original Sources* (Milwaukee WI: University Research Extension Co.).

Thompson, M. (2003), *Teach Yourself: Philosophy of Science* (London: Hodder & Stoughton).

Tomberlin, J. E. (1992), *Philosophical Perspectives 6 (Ethics)* (Ridgeview Publishing Co).

Unger, P. (1990), *Identity, Consciousness and Value* (Oxford: Oxford University Press).

Urmson, J.O. (1956), *Philosophical Analysis: Its Development Between the Two World Wars* (Oxford: Clarendon Press).

Warnock, G. (1971), *The Object of Morality* (London: Methuen).

Williams, B. (1973), *Problems of the Self* (Cambridge: Cambridge University Press).

Winch, P. (1970), *The Idea of a Social Science and its Relation to Philosophy* (London: Routledge & Kegan Paul).

Wittgenstein, L. (1986), *Philosophical Investigations* (Oxford: Blackwell), tr. G.E.M. Anscombe.

Woolf, R.P. (1960), 'Hume's Theory of Mental Activity' *Philosophical Review* Vol. LXIX, reprinted in Chappell (ed.) (1966), pp. 99–128.

Index

a posteriori 248
  defining 132, 346, 391
a posteriori knowledge 375, 394
a priori 248
  causes 269
  defining 132, 346, 391
  induction 411–13
a priori knowledge 375–9, 394
absolutism, defining 316
abstract functionalism 39–40
abstract ideas 256–7
acting, ignorance 220
action/behaviour, social sciences 195–6
actions
  consequences 305–6
  intentionality 30–1
Against Method 180–6
analogy, other minds 60–1
analytical behaviourism 28–38
  defining 28
anarchism 107, 127
anarchists 97–8
anarchy, defining 290
anomie 189
  defining 187
anti-realism, defining 158
Appearance of Reality 348–56
appollonian, defining 316
arete, defining 202
Aristotle 135–40
  causality 268
  life 202–3
  works 202–3
  see also Nicomachean Ethics
ascetic, defining 316
(Of the) Association of Ideas
  Hume, David 253–63
  problems 244–5
atomism 134
atomistic, defining 316
authority 124–7
  democracy 125–6
  individuals 304–8
  legitimacy 124–5
  obedience to the state 125–6
  power 124–5
  resistance 127
  societies 304–8
autonomy 90
  defining 86
Ayer, A.J. 391–424

criticisms 404–7, 421–2
definitions and analysis 408–10
emotive theory of ethics 415–19
function of philosophy 407–8
induction 411–13
key arguments 402–21
language 422–3
Language, Truth and Logic 391–424
life 392–4
linguistic phenomenalism 410–11
logical positivism 400–2
mathematics 413–15
religious language 419–21, 423–4
verification principle 403–7
Vienna Circle 398–9
works 392–4

Bacon, Francis 143–6
Bacon, Roger 140–2
bat, being a 21–2
behaviour
  mental states 59–60
  micro-/macro- 49–50
behaviour/action, social sciences 195–6
behaviourism 28–38
  analytical 28–38
  disembodied existence 38
  'hard' 29–33
  Hempel's 'hard' behaviourism 30–3
  mental states 37
  pain behaviour, mental terms 64–5
  pretence 37–8
  Ryle's 'soft' behaviourism 33–8
  'soft' 29–30, 33–8
beliefs
  dispositionality 265–6
  governing principles 265
  ideas 264–5
  as maps 265
  nature of 264–5
  probability 266
  vividness 264–5
Bentham, Jeremy 290–3
Berkeley's Idealism 242, 361–4
beyond current sense-experience and
  memory, knowledge 258–9
Beyond Good and Evil 316–45
biological naturalism 49–50
  defining 48
blame 222–3
blue, missing shade of 248–9

body, numerical identity of 71–2
brain, numerical identity of 72–4
brain-state transfer device, personal
  identity 78
branch-line cases, personal identity 78–9
Broca's area 18
Butler's approach, personal identity 77–8

Calvinism, defining 290
Cartesianism 61–4
  defining 28
causal adequacy principle, Descartes 268
causal argument 356
causal closure of the physical world 56–7
causality
  Aristotle 268
  contiguity 275
  events 275–6
  Hume, David 284–5
  logical deduction 269
  objects 275–6
  precedence 275
  similarity 276–7
causation, regularity theory 279–82
cause and effect 259–63
  customary transition 274–5
  necessary connection 269–71
cause, defining 275, 277–9
causes, *a priori* 269
character
  heritability 342
  suffering effect 344
Chinese room argument, functionalism
  44–5
choice 220–1
circularity
  'hard' behaviourism 31–3
  'soft' behaviourism 35
civil service 313–14
class systems 337–8
co-variation, supervenience 51
cognitive/non-cognitive, defining 391
colligation 151–2
combination, liberty of 303
common/uncommon people 342–3
communitarianism, defining 128
compatibilism 286–7
  defining 236
completeness of physics 56–7
compulsion 219–20
computational functionalism 42–3

Index

concept possession 251–3
conflicting interests, freedom 112
conformity, individuality 301–3
connection, Of the Idea of Necessary Connection 237, 267–82
consciousness
  functionalism 45–7
  problem 52–3
consequences, actions 305–6
consequentialism, defining 86
consequentialist, defining 290
conservatism 101–3
constant conjunction, defining 132
constitutional, defining 290
contemplation 136–9
  as divine 233–4
  Nicomachean Ethics 233–5
contiguity, causality 275
contingent things 223
Copernicus 174
copy principle 247
crime prevention, law 121–3
criterial approach, other minds 65–8
'crown of creation' 168
custom, habit 263
customary transition, cause and effect 274–5

de facto, defining 124
de jure, defining 124
deconstruction, defining 316
dedadence, defining 316
deduction
  defining 132, 346, 391
  science 139–40
deductive argument 374
  defining 346
deductive-nomological method
  defining 132
  science 156–7
definitions and analysis, Ayer, A.J. 408–10
deliberation 136–9, 221
democracy 88–9, 98–9
  authority 125–6
  defining 86, 290
deontologist, defining 290
deontology, defining 124
dependence, supervenience 52
Descartes
  arguments, substance-dualism 6–10
  causal adequacy principle 268
  God's existence 268
  rationalism 243
determinism 283
  defining 236
  free will 283, 286–7
deterrence, law 120
dialectic, defining 290
dionysian, defining 316
disembodied existence 6
  behaviourism 38
dismissal of occasionalism 272
disposition 34–5
  defining 28

dispositional properties 404
dispositionality, beliefs 265–6
doctrine of the mean 217–19
dogmatist, defining 316
doubt 348–51
doubt argument, substance-dualism 7–9
dualism 3–15
  defining 3, 316
  mind/body relation 11–12
  problems 10–15
  property-dualism 3–5
  substance-dualism 3–10
duty, reason 227–8

education, state 311–12
effect, cause and effect 259–63, 269–71, 274–5
eliminative induction 149
elitism, defining 290
emotions, reason 226–9
emotive theory of ethics 415–19
emotivism 226–7
empiricism 239–44
  defining 236, 391
  Principle of Empiricism 247–53
  vs rationalism 374–5
Epigrams and Interludes 326–7
epiphenomenalism
  defining 48
  supervenience 55
ergon
  defining 202
  Nicomachean Ethics 209–14
erosion, science 158–60
ethical pseudo-concepts 416–17
ethics
  emotive theory of ethics 415–19
  limitations 205–6
eudaimon 90
  defining 86
eudaimonia
  defining 202, 207–9
  Nicomachean Ethics 206–9, 233–5
Eudoxus 230–1
events, causality 275–6
Existence of Matter 357–9
experience
  homogenisation of 303
  Hume, David 242
  sense-experience 258–9, 403–4
experimentation, social sciences 190–1
expression, freedom of 298

falsehood/truth 300
falsificationism 158–65
  criticisms 162–3
  defining 158
  sophisticated 172–7
Farewell to Reason 180–6
fascism, defining 128
fear, morality 330–1
feelings, reason 217
Feyerabend, Paul 180–6
Form of the Good, Plato 207
foundationalism, defining 346

The Free Spirit 321–3
free will 283–8, 286–8
  determinism 283, 286–7
freedom 107–12
  conflicting interests 112
  of expression 298
  harm principle 297–304
  personal 297–304
  religious persecution 298–9
  rights 110–12
  types 108–10
fulfilment *see* eudaimonia
function argument *see* ergon
function of philosophy 407–8
function, reason as 209–10
functional prerequisites, social sciences 195
functionalism 39–47
  abstract 39–40
  Chinese room argument 44–5
  computational 42–3
  consciousness 45–7
  defining 39
  metaphysical 40
  personal identity 79
  problems 44
  psycho- 41
  qualia 47
  strengths 44
  subjectivity 45–7
  Turing machine 42–3

global scepticism, defining 346
God's existence, Descartes' reasoning 268
golden mountain 247
Good, study of 207–9
  Nicomachean Ethics 204–6
  Plato 207
goodness, hedone 229–33
government 91–7
  classical period 88–9
  defining 290
  development 92
  overview 91–2
Greek terms 204
Greek thinkers, early 133–5

habit
  custom 263
  defining 236
  necessary connection 273–4
  Nicomachean Ethics 214–17
  role 214–17
  virtue 216–17
happiness
  defining 207–9
  examination 206–9
'hard' behaviourism 29–33
  circularity 31–3
harm principle
  defining 291
  freedom 297–304
  liberty 300–1
hedone
  defining 202
  goodness 229–33

Nicomachean Ethics 229–33
hedonist, defining 290
hedonistic (felicific) calculus, defining 290
Hempel's 'hard' behaviourism 30–3
herd morality 330
heritability, character 342
heuristic, defining 158
heuristics, negative/positive 173–4
Hobbes, social contract 93–4
homogenisation of experience 303
Hume, David 236–82, 395–6
    (Of the) Association of Ideas 253–63
    Berkeley's Idealism 242
    causality 284–5
    critical evaluation 251–3
    empiricism 239–44, 247–53
    experience 242
    free will 283–8
    on human nature 237–9
    Hume's problem, induction 146–8
    (Of the) Idea of Necessary Connection 237, 267–82
    ideas 244–63
    is-ought fallacy 210–12
    (Of) Liberty and Necessity 282–8
    (Of the) Origin of Ideas 244–53
    Principle of Empiricism 247–53
    (Of) Probability 266–7
    Sceptical Solution of these Doubts 263–6
hypothetico-deductive method
    defining 132
    science 151–3

(Of the) Idea of Necessary Connection 237, 267–82
ideal types
    defining 187
    social sciences 195–6
idealism 170–1, 242, 361–4
    defining 347
ideas
    abstract 256–7
    (Of the) Association of Ideas 253–63
    beliefs 264–5
    defining 236
    general 256–7
    Hume, David 244–63
    impressions 245–8
    innate 239–40
    (Of the) Origin of Ideas 244–53
    relations of ideas 237, 257–8
    vividness 264–5
identity, numerical *see* numerical identity
identity, personal *see* personal identity
identity, qualitative 69–70
identity theory
    mind/brain 16–27
    problems 20–7
    reductionism 16–17
    spatiality objection 20–1
    strengths 19–20
    token-token 18–19, 50–2
    type-type 17–18, 50–1
ideology, defining 86

ignorance, acting 220
imaginability argument, substance-dualism 6–7
impressions
    defining 236
    ideas 245–8
incommensurability 166–7
    defining 158
indeterminism, defining 236
individual liberty 90
individuality
    conformity 301–3
    liberty 300–3
individuals, authority of society 304–8
induction
    defining 132, 236, 391
    eliminative 149
    Hume's problem 146–8
    (On) Induction 371–3
    inferences 148
    justifying 262–4
    Mill's approach 148–53
    a priori 411–13
    probability 266–7
    science 139–50
induction/inductive argument, defining 346
inferences 258–9
    induction 148
innate ideas 239–40
inner senses, necessary connection 272
instrumentalism
    defining 158
    vs realism 178–80
    science 177–80
intellectual virtues, *Nicomachean Ethics* 223–9
intentional mental states
    identity theory 22–5
    naturalism 23–4
intentionality 22–7
    defining 16
irrationalism 172
irreducibility, supervenience 51
is-ought fallacy 210–12

jurisprudence, defining 291
just/unjust law 117–19
justice, law 114–16

Kepler 174–5
knowledge
    beyond current sense-experience and memory 258–9
    kinds of 206
    standard 348–51
knowledge by acquaintance 364–71
    defining 347
knowledge by description 364–71
    defining 347
(On our) Knowledge of General Principles 373–6
Knowledge of Universals 383–5
Kuhn, Thomas 165–72

Lakatos 172–7

language
    Ayer, A.J. 422–3
    bewitchment of 320–1
    linguistic phenomenalism 410–11
    religious language 423–4
language and science, social sciences 197–8
Language, Truth and Logic 391–424
law 113–23
    crime prevention 121–3
    deterrence 120
    functions 113–14
    just/unjust 117–19
    justice 114–16
    morality 114–16
    protection of society 121
    punishment 119–20
    reform 121
    rehabilitation 121
    resistance 116
    retribution 120
legislation, defining 291
legitimacy, authority 124–5
Leibniz's Law 3, 8–9
    identity test 20–2
Leibniz's rationalism 244
Liberal Party, defining 291
liberalism 103–5
liberals 97–8
liberty
    of combination 303
    defining 236, 291
    exercising 294–5
    harm principle 300–1
    individual 90
    individuality 300–3
    Mill, John Stuart 294–6
    'nanny state' 295–6
(Of) Liberty and Necessity 282–8
limitations, ethics/politics 205–6
Limits of Philosophical Knowledge 385–8
linguistic phenomenalism 410–11
Locke, social contract 94–6
Lockean approach, personal identity 75
logic, end of 170
logical atomism 396–7
logical deduction, causality 269
logical positivism 400–2
logically proper names 368–70
    defining 347

maps, beliefs as 265
master morality 338–9
materialism
    defining 39, 132
    social sciences 196–7
mathematics, Ayer, A.J. 413–15
matters of fact
    defining 236–7
    relations of ideas 257–8
mean, doctrine of the 217–19
means
    objective 217
    relative 217
measurement, social sciences 192
mental states

Index

behaviour 59–60
behaviourism 37
  intentional 22–5
  multiple realisability 19
  physical states 21–2
mental terms
  meanings 64
  natural pain behaviour 64–5
meritocracy, defining 86
metaphysical functionalism 40
metaphysics 395
  defining 39, 391
  positivism 400
methodological objections, social sciences
    190–3
methodological scepticism 348
  defining 347
micro-/macro-behaviour 49–50
Milgram experiments 191
Mill, James 290–3
Mill, John Stuart 290–315
  On Liberty 290–315
  Mill's approach, induction 148–53
  pleasure 293–4
  principles, application 308–14
  utilitarianism 293–4
mind/body relation, dualism 11–12
mind/brain identity theory 16–27
mind, contents of 244–6
minds, other *see* other minds
missing shade of blue 248–9
monad, defining 316
monism, defining 16
'moral police' 306–7
moral responsibility, *Nicomachean Ethics*
    219–23
moral virtues 229
  Nicomachean Ethics 214–19
morality
  defining 291
  fear 330–1
  good conscience 328–9
  herd 330
  law 114–16
  master 338–9
  moral sensibility 327
  religion 307–8
  slave 339–40
  stages 322
  Towards a Natural History of Morals
      327–31
multiple realisability, mental states 19

'nanny state' 295–6
natural law, defining 86
natural moral law, defining 291
natural pain behaviour, mental terms 64–5
natural rights, defining 291
naturalism 238
  biological 48
  defining 16, 237
  intentional mental states 23–4
naturalistic fallacy, defining 391
Nature of Matter 359–61
necessary connection

cause and effect 269–71
  defining 237
  habit 273–4
  inner senses 272
  outer senses 271–2
Necessary Connection, Of the Idea of
    267–82
necessary things 223
necessity, Of Liberty and Necessity 282–8
negative/positive heuristics 173–4
Newton, Isaac 155, 174–5
Nicomachean Ethics 202–35
  context 203–4
  doctrine of the mean 217–19
  ergon 209–14
  eudaimonia 206–9
  Good, study of 204–6
  habit 214–17
  hedone 229–33
  intellectual virtues 223–9
  moral responsibility 219–23
  moral virtues 214–19
  political science 204–6
Nietzsche, Friedrich
  Beyond Good and Evil 316–45
  Epigrams and Interludes 326–7
  The Free Spirit 321–3
  Plato 335–6
  On The Prejudices of Philosophers
      319–21
  The Religious Disposition 323–6
  Towards a Natural History of Morals
      327–31
  We Scholars 331–7
  What is Noble? 337–44
nihilism, defining 316
numerical identity 69–74
  of body 71–2
  of brain 72–4
  personal identity 70–4
  cf. qualitative identity 69–70
  of soul 70–1

obedience to the state, authority 125–6
obeying orders, social sciences 191
objective means 217
objects, causality 275–6
observation, social sciences 190
occasionalism, dismissal of 272
oligarchy, defining 86
On Liberty 290–315
ontological objections, social sciences
    193–8
ontological reduction, defining 16–17
opinions, expressing 310–11
orders, obeying 191
(Of the) Origin of Ideas 244–53
other minds 59–68
  analogy 60–1
  criterial approach 65–8
  private ostensive definition 61–3
  private rule-following 63–4
  problem 59–60
  Strawson's approach 66–8
  Wittgenstein's approach 60–4

outer senses, necessary connection 271–2

pain behaviour, mental terms 64–5
pain, pleasure 230
paradigms 166–7
  defining 158
Parfit's approach, personal identity 76–7
participant observation, defining 187
paternalism 102–3
perception
  public language of 164–5
  qualities 244–5
perception argument, substance-dualism
    9–10
perceptual variability 352–3
personal freedom 297–304
personal identity 69–83
  brain-state transfer device 78
  branch-line cases 78–9
  Butler's approach 77–8
  functionalism 79
  Lockean approach 75
  numerical identity 70–4
  Parfit's approach 76–7
  physical continuity 78–80
  psychological continuity 74–6
  reductionism 80–1
  Reid's approach 75–6
pessimism, defining 316
phenomenalism
  defining 391
  linguistic phenomenalism 410–11
philosopher-kings 89–90
philosophical questions, Nietzsche,
    Friedrich 322–3
philosophy, vs science 331–2
phronesis 225–6, 234–5
  defining 202
physical continuity, personal identity 78–80
physical states, mental states 21–2
physicalism, defining 39
physics, *completeness of physics* 56–7
Plato 87–90, 135–6, 230–1
  Form of the Good 207
  Nietzsche, Friedrich 335–6
  Third Man argument 382–3
pleasure
  Mill, John Stuart 293–4
  Nicomachean Ethics 229–33
  pain 230
Poincaré's contribution, science 153–6
policing, defining 291
political ideologies 86–107
political science, *Nicomachean Ethics*
    204–6
politics
  defining 291
  limitations 205–6
Popper, Karl 159–62
positive/negative heuristics 173–4
positivism 188–9
  defining 187
  logical positivism 400–2
  metaphysics 400
  realism 400–1

possession 329–30
power
    authority 124–5
    state, the 128–9
    will to power 317–18
practical wisdom 225–6, 234–5
practice, defining 291
pragmatism 178
praise 222–3
precedence, causality 275
(On The) Prejudices of Philosophers
    319–21
pretence, behaviourism 37–8
principle, defining 291
Principle of Contradiction 243
Principle of Empiricism 247–53
Principle of Sufficient Reason 244
private ostensive definition, other minds
    61–3
private rule-following, other minds 63–4
private space 359–60
(On) Probability 266–7
probability
    beliefs 266
    defining 237
    induction 266–7
properties 3–5
property-dualism 3–5, 48–58
    difficulties 57–8
    problems 53
protection of society, law 121
Protestant, defining 316
prototype, defining 316
psycho-functionalism 41
psychological continuity, personal identity
    74–6
psychological reflections 343
public opinion 304–5
public space 359–60
punishment, law 119–20
pyrrhonian scepticism 348
    defining 347

qualia
    defining 17
    functionalism 47
qualitative identity, cf. numerical identity
    69–70

radical, defining 291
rationalism
    defining 237
    Descartes' 243
    vs empiricism 374–5
    Leibniz's 244
    rejection 243–4
    Spinoza's 243
Raven paradox 152–3
Rawls, social contract 96–7
realism
    defining 158
    vs instrumentalism 178–80
    positivism 400–1
    science 177–80
reason

duty 227–8
emotions 226–9
feelings 217
    as function 209–10
reductionism 134–5
    defining 132, 391
    identity theory 16–17
    linguistic phenomenalism 410–11
    personal identity 80–1
reform, law 121
regularity theory, causation 279–82
rehabilitation, law 121
Reid's approach, personal identity 75–6
relations of ideas
    defining 237
    matters of fact 257–8
relative means 217
relativism 171
    defining 132, 316
reliable indication, identity theory 25–7
religion
    morality 307–8
    social bonding 326
The Religious Disposition 323–6
religious language, Ayer, A.J. 419–21,
    423–4
religious persecution 298–9
replicability
    defining 187
    social sciences 192
research programmes, science 176–7
resistance
    authority 127
    law 116
retribution, law 120
reverence 342
rights, freedom 110–12
risk, science 161–2
Rousseau, social contract 96
Russell, Bertrand 346–90, 396–7
    Appearance of Reality 348–56
    Existence of Matter 357–9
    Idealism 361–4
    On Induction 371–3
    (On our) Knowledge of General
        Principles 373–6
    Knowledge of Universals 383–5
    Limits of Philosophical Knowledge
        385–8
    Nature of Matter 359–61
    a priori knowledge 375–9
    Universals 379–85
    World of Universals 379–83
Ryle's 'soft' behaviourism 33–8

sacrifice 323–6
scatter graph 154
Sceptical Solution of these Doubts, Hume,
    David 263–6
schools systems 191
science
    deduction 139–40
    deductive-nomological method 156–7
    erosion 158–60
    falsification 153

falsificationism 158–65, 172–7
foundations 132–57
hypothetico-deductive method 151–3
incommensurability 158, 166–7
induction 139–50
instrumentalism 177–80
language and 197–8
paradigms 158, 166–7
vs philosophy 331–2
Poincaré's contribution 153–6
progress 158–86
Raven paradox 152–3
realism 177–80
research programmes 176–7
risk 161–2
scientific method 139–40
theory-laden observations 163–5
see also social sciences
scientific certainty 394–5
Searle's biological naturalism 49–50
secondary qualities argument 354–5
secularism 113–14
    defining 113
self-consciousness 367–8
self-denial 323–4
self-discipline 327–8
self-preservation 319–20
semantics, defining 39
sense-data 355–6, 361, 363
    defining 347
sense-experience 403–4
    beyond current sense-experience and
        memory 258–9
similarity, causality 276–7
situation ethics 217–19
slave morality 339–40
social bonding, religion 326
social change, effects 340–1
social contract 92
    defining 86
    Hobbes 93–4
    Locke 94–6
    Rawls 96–7
    Rousseau 96
    theories 93–7
social facts 189
social sciences 168–9, 187–200
    action/behaviour 195–6
    behaviour/action 195–6
    experimentation 190–1
    functional prerequisites 195
    ideal types 195–6
    language and science 197–8
    materialism 196–7
    measurement 192
    methodological objections 190–3
    obeying orders 191
    objections 189–98
    observation 190
    ontological objections 193–8
    replicability 192
    schools systems 191
    'social structure' 194–5
    'society' 194–5
    testing 192

value freedom 192–3
'social structure', social sciences 194–5
social welfare 312–13
socialism 105–7
societies
    authority 304–8
    decline 341–2
    equality 297
'society', social sciences 194–5
sociology, origins 188
'soft' behaviourism 33–8
sophia, defining 202
sophisticated falsificationism 172–7
soul 3–5, 11–12
    counting 13–15
    elements 223–4
    faculties 224–5
    Nicomachean Ethics 212–14
    numerical identity of 70–1
spatiality objection, identity theory 20–1
Spinoza's rationalism 243
state education 311–12
state, the 128–30
    'nanny state' 295–6
    obedience to 125–6
    power 128–9
    role 128–9
Strawson's approach, other minds 66–8
subjectivity, functionalism 45–7
sublimation, defining 316
substance 250–1
    defining 3
substance-dualism 3–10
    Descartes' arguments 6–10
    doubt argument 7–9
    imaginability argument 6–7
    perception argument 9–10
superiority 321–2
supervenience
    co-variation 51

defining 48
dependence 52
epiphenomenalism 55
irreducibility 51
relation 53–5
token-token identity theory 50–2
survival of the fittest 341–2
syntax, defining 39

techne, defining 202
teleological explanations, defining 187
telos, defining 202
terms, Greek 204
testing, social sciences 192
theocracy 90–1
    defining 86
theoria, *Nicomachean Ethics* 233–5
theory, characteristics of good 169
theory-laden observations 163–5
Third Man argument, Plato 382–3
timarchy 88
    defining 86
time lag argument 355–6
token-token identity theory 18–19
    supervenience 50–2
Towards a Natural History of Morals
    327–31
truth conditions 395
truth/falsehood 300
truth, value 319–20
Turing machine functionalism 42–3
Turing test 35–6
type-type identity theory 17–18, 50–1
tyranny 89
    defining 86
tyranny of the majority, defining 291

uniformity of motive and action 284–5
Universals 379–85
unorthodox views 335

utilitarian, defining 291
utilitarianism 100–1
    background 290–6
    defining 108
    Mill, John Stuart 293–4
    origins 290–6

value freedom
    defining 187
    social sciences 192–3
value systems 337–8
vanity 340
verification principle 403–7
verificationism 30–1
    defining 28
Vienna Circle 398–9
virtue
    acquisition 215–16
    defining 216–17
    habit 216–17
    intellectual 223–9
    moral 214–19, 229
    Nicomachean Ethics 212–14, 215–16,
        223–9
    theory 228–9
vividness
    beliefs 264–5
    ideas 264–5

We Scholars 331–7
welfare, social 313–14
What is Noble? 337–44
Whewell, William 151–2
will to power 317–18
wisdom, practical 225–6, 234–5
wish 221–2
Wittgenstein 397–8
Wittgenstein's approach, other minds
    60–4
World of Universals 379–83